Applied Exercise Psychology

Applied Exercise Psychology emphasizes the application of evidence-based knowledge drawn from the fields of exercise psychology, health psychology, clinical and counseling psychology, and exercise physiology for physical activity behavior change. The book provides readers with

- theoretical bases for understanding and promoting physical activity behavior;
- interventions to use for facilitating physical activity behavior change and the tools for measuring the effectiveness of these interventions;
- cross-cultural considerations for practitioners to ensure multicultural competency;
- considerations to guide best practices with special populations (e.g., persons with medical conditions and persons with mental health conditions); and
- overall applied implications and future directions.

The collection builds a bridge between up-to-date research findings, relevant field experiences, and applied implications. This is the first book to cover such breadth of topics in applied exercise psychology, with chapters bringing often overlooked issues to the attention of practitioners to promote not only evidence-based practice but also responsible ethics and referral.

Selen Razon is an assistant professor in the Department of Kinesiology, College of Health Science, at West Chester University.

Michael L. Sachs is a professor in the Department of Kinesiology, College of Public Health, at Temple University.

"Applied Exercise Psychology is an exceptional contribution to the field. Razon and Sachs focus on the immense challenges associated with increasing exercise participation rates. This thought-provoking compendium includes a diverse array of 32 chapters that focus on theoretical foundations and applied suggestions for exercise adoption and adherence by respected researchers in the field."

– Bonnie G. Berger, Bowling Green State University, USA

"Razon and Sachs, along with nearly 60 international scholars, seek to narrow the gap between people's good intentions toward living healthy, active lifestyles and their achievement of these goals. Their book uniquely links theory, research, and practice together in relatable, relevant, and nuanced ways – ways that can truly make a difference!"

– Bradley J. Cardinal, Oregon State University, USA

"This text provides a timely and important integration of research and application and will be essential reading for anyone interested in the field of applied exercise psychology. It breaks new ground regarding best practice, compiling contributions from world-leading scholars and highlighting important cross-cultural and demographic considerations. I can recommend it to students, researchers, and practitioners alike."

– Chris Wagstaff, University of Portsmouth, UK

Applied Exercise Psychology

The Challenging Journey from
Motivation to Adherence

Edited by
**Selen Razon and
Michael L. Sachs**

Routledge
Taylor & Francis Group

NEW YORK AND LONDON

First published 2018
by Routledge
711 Third Avenue, New York, NY 10017

and by Routledge
2 Park Square, Milton Park, Abingdon, Oxon, OX14 4RN

Routledge is an imprint of the Taylor & Francis Group, an informa business

Library of Congress Cataloging-in-Publication Data
Names: Razon, Selen, editor. | Sachs, Michael L., editor.
Title: Applied exercise psychology : the challenging journey from
    motivation to adherence / edited by Selen Razon and Michael L. Sachs.
Description: New York, NY : Routledge, 2018. | Includes bibliographical
    references and index.
Identifiers: LCCN 2017016017 | ISBN 9780415702720 (hb : alk. paper) |
    ISBN 9780415702737 (pb : alk. paper) | ISBN 9780203795422 (eb)
Subjects: LCSH: Sports—Psychological aspects. | Exercise—Psychological
    aspects. | Psychology, Applied.
Classification: LCC GV706.4 .A65 2018 | DDC 613.71—dc23
LC record available at https://lccn.loc.gov/2017016017

ISBN: 978-0-415-70272-0 (hbk)
ISBN: 978-0-415-70273-7 (pbk)
ISBN: 978-0-203-79542-2 (ebk)

Typeset in Gaillard
by Apex CoVantage, LLC
Printed and bound by CPI Group (UK) Ltd, Croydon, CR0 4YY

Contents

About the Editors

Selen Razon is an assistant professor in the Department of Kinesiology, College of Health Sciences, at West Chester University. Dr. Razon has received her master's degree in Counseling Psychology (University of Miami) and her Ph.D. in Sport and Exercise Psychology (Florida State University). Her research interests focus on exercise promotion in underserved populations and the effects of exercise on cognitions and affects.

Michael L. Sachs is a professor in the Department of Kinesiology, College of Public Health, at Temple University. Dr. Sachs has received master's degrees in general-experimental psychology (Hollins College) and Counseling Psychology (Loyola University) and his Ph.D. in Movement Science and Physical Education (Florida State University). His research interests focus on motivation and adherence for exercise, exercise addiction, and excusercise.

About the Contributors

Edmund O. Acevedo, Virginia Commonwealth University, USA

Allison Daniel Anders, University of South Carolina, USA

Mark H. Anshel, Middle Tennessee State University, USA

Amy Baltzell, Boston University, USA

Monna Arvinen-Barrow, University of Wisconsin–Milwaukee, USA

Itay Basevitch, Anglia Ruskin University, UK

Maurizio Bertollo, University "G. D'Annunzio" of Chieti–Pescara, Italy

Lindsey C. Blom, Ball State University, USA

Leeja Carter, Long Island University–Brooklyn, USA

Jeff Cherubini, Manhattan College, USA

Jennifer B. Ciaccio, Temple University, USA

Damien Clement, West Virginia University, USA

Ashley Anderson Corn, G.U.T.S Coaching, Colorado, USA

Trevor Cote, Boston University, USA

J. Gualberto Cremades, Barry University, USA

James M. DeVita, University of North Carolina, USA

Selenia di Fronso, University "G. D'Annunzio" of Chieti–Pescara, Italy

Urska Dobersek, Florida State University, USA

Zoe Durand, University of Hawaii, USA

Panteleimon Ekkekakis, Iowa State University, USA

Robert C. Eklund, Florida State University, USA, and University of Stirling, UK

Edson Filho, University of Central Lancashire, UK

Leslee A. Fisher, University of Tennessee, USA

Kisha D. Grady, Temple University, USA

Stephanie J. Hanrahan, The University of Queensland, Australia

Brook Harmon, University of Hawaii, USA

Brandonn S. Harris, Georgia Southern University, USA

Kate F. Hays, The Performing Edge, Ontario, Canada

Jasmin Hutchinson, Springfield College, USA

Heather Leach, Colorado State University, USA

Rebecca E. Lee, Arizona State University, USA

Scherezade K. Mama, The Pennsylvania State University, USA

Kerry R. McGannon, Laurentian University, Canada

Claudio R. Nigg, University of Hawaii, USA

Kate L. Nolt, Creighton University, USA

David Pargman, Florida State University, USA

Gloria H. M. Park, Perform Positive Consulting, Virginia, USA

Nathan H. Parker, University of Houston, USA

Amanda M. Perkins, Missouri State University, USA

Claudio Robazza, University "G. D'Annunzio" of Chieti–Pescara, Italy

Emily A. Roper, Sam Houston State University, USA

Mikihiro Sato, James Madison University, USA

Robert J. Schinke, Laurentian University, Canada

Christine L. B. Selby, Husson College, USA

Vanessa R. Shannon, West Virginia University, USA

Jardana Silburn, Long Island University–Brooklyn, USA

Duncan Simpson, IMG Academy, USA

Erica G. Soltero, Arizona State University, USA

Lauren S. Tashman, Barry University, USA

Gershon Tenenbaum, Florida State University, USA

Amanda J. Visek, The George Washington University, USA

Heather E. Webb, Texas A&M University, USA

Robert Weinberg, Miami University, USA

Kira M. Werstein, Iowa State University, USA

Zachary Zenko, Iowa State University, USA

Sam J. Zizzi, West Virginia University, USA

1 Introduction and Book Objectives

Selen Razon

Applied exercise psychology is an area within the broader scope of Sport, Exercise, and Performance Psychology, to use the title of the society within the American Psychological Association (Division 47) (www.apa.org). Although sport and performance psychology may make the headlines and newspapers more regularly, exercise psychology really affects every individual and, as such, has the broadest scope of all. If we want every individual to engage in exercise/physical activity on a regular basis, then we have a remarkable challenge ahead of us. Fortunately, we are prepared for this challenge, and this book will further help in continuing our efforts to do so.

There is ample evidence that demonstrates a link between physical inactivity and increased risk for all causes of mortality, some types of cancers, and cardiovascular diseases. In fact, the benefits of physical activity and physically active lifestyles have been known since the 1950s and were included in recommendations in the 1996 Surgeon General's Report on Physical Activity and Health, the 2008 Physical Activity Guidelines for Americans, the Surgeon General's Call for Action to Promote Walking and Walkable Communities (2015), and the National Physical Activity Plan in 2016 (Kohl et al., 2012; National Coalition for Promoting Physical Activity, 2016; United States Department of Health and Human Services, 1996, 2013, 2015).

Nevertheless, physical inactivity is ever present. An estimated 31% of the world's population do not meet recommended levels of physical activity (Kohl et al., 2012). In the United States alone, 51% of adults do not meet physical activity guidelines based on self-reported data, nor do nearly 96.5% of adults ages 20 to 59 years based on objective data (i.e., accelerometry) (Centers for Disease Control and Prevention, 2016; Troiano et al., 2008). Thus, physical inactivity remains the most prevalent public health issue of the 21st century (Blair, 2009).

To help individuals adopt and maintain active lifestyles, recent accounts have emphasized the importance of behavioral approaches (Shuval et al., 2017). The main purpose of this book is to give a theoretical background followed by practical recommendations and guidelines to facilitate the understanding and promotion of physical activity behavior in people. Consequently, although this book is primarily intended for practitioners in the field of exercise psychology, all practitioner audiences who aim to modify physical activity behaviors in their clients/patients will find its content useful. The main objective of this book is to provide graduate students and/or practitioners with the information needed to design effective behavioral interventions to promote physical activity in others by developing a greater understanding of individuals' journeys from exercise adoption to maintenance. This book differs from others because it centers around an evidence-based applied focus to promote activity and is not a compilation of mere theories and relevant empirical evidence in exercise and sport psychology. The ultimate goal of this book is to help the reader critically evaluate the use and benefits of varied approaches to promote behavior change in a diverse and unique society.

This book includes five sections. The first section serves as an introduction to the psychology of exercise behavior as well as an overview of physical inactivity behavior and models of health behavior change. The present chapter serves as a preface and outlines our goals and objectives. Chapter 2, by Nigg and Harmon, describes in details the epidemic of sedentariness and the relative importance of the demographic factors that contribute to the problem. Chapter 3, by Ciaccio and Sachs, is unique in that it reviews the language practitioners use with clients to express the importance of promoting physical activity behavior and provides insights to overcome the reasons why current physical activity promotion strategies often fail. Chapter 4 by Webb and Acevedo addresses questions about what happens to the body and brain in response to exercise. Chapter 5 by Weinberg focuses on the most commonly used theories of health behavior change, among which are the health belief model, the theory of planned behavior, the social determination theory, the transtheoretical model, and social ecological approaches. Chapter 6 by Cherubini and Anshel focuses on alternative models, such as the disconnected values model, with the purpose to provide inactive, unfit individuals with renewed incentives to initiate and maintain exercise behavior. The final chapter of this section, Chapter 7 by Sato, illustrates how personal resources, such as exercise behaviors and attitudes toward exercise, combined with environmental resources, including available recreational facilities and participatory sport events, can contribute to one's general sense of well-being.

The second section of this book reviews the use and effectiveness of conventional and innovative intervention modalities to increase physical activity behavior. Chapter 8 by Tashman, Simpson, and Cremades describes the use of psychological skill training (PST), including goal setting, arousal control, imagery, attention and concentration, self-talk, and mindfulness, to promote exercise adoption and adherence. Chapter 9 by Razon, Hutchinson, and Basevitch sheds light on the use of alternative approaches, including imagery, music, and odorants, for decreasing perception of effort and increasing positive affective responses to exercise. Chapter 10 by Filho and Tenenbaum examines how advanced technological tools including electromyography (EMG), electrocardiography (ECG), electroencephalography (EEG), global positioning systems (GPS), accelerometers, kinematics analysis, and more recently video game technology and smartphones may inform new approaches to exercise adoption and adherence within applied settings. Subsequently, Chapter 11 by Filho, di Fronso, Robazza, and Bertollo reviews the phenomenon of exergaming and provides an overview of the target population, principles, types, benefits, and applied potentials of exergaming for promoting exercise behavior. Chapter 12 by Nigg and Durand outlines the goals of physical activity–related measurements and illustrates the reasons why researchers and practitioners should consider measurements beyond sole physical activity behavior when determining the impact of their physical activity interventions or programs. The final chapter of this section, Chapter 13 by Lee, Mama, Leach, Soltero, and Parker, lays out the policies that shape and increase physical activity behavior. Based primarily on the tenets of the Ecological Model of Physical Activity (EMPA), the chapter highlights how impactful policies can be in guiding individuals' health behavior choices, including the adoption of physical activity behavior.

The third section of this book provides a foundation on several cross-cultural and demographic considerations that practitioners need to note within a diverse and multicultural society. Chapter 14 by McGannon and Shinke reviews the principles of cultural awareness and cultural competence as basic components of quality physical activity interventions and of effective practice to best address the needs of diverse individuals. Chapter 15 by Roper examines the concepts of gender and gender socialization within the context of exercise. The chapter describes feminist perspectives on exercise and explores exercise as a gendered activity. Chapter 16 by Carter, Grady, and Silburn focuses on exercise adherence, as well as culture-specific barriers and intervention strategies for African American, Hispanic, Native American, and Asian American women. Chapter 17 by Perkins weighs the importance of socioeconomic status (SES) in regard to health disparities and exercise behavior adherence. The chapter explores the relationship between sedentary behaviors and major components of SES, including education, income, and occupation, and extends recommendations and strategies to promote activity within low-SES populations. Chapter 18 by Fisher, Anders, and DeVita analyzes sexual orientation and gender expression in physical activity. The chapter emphasizes the importance of everyday awareness of the ways in which sex assignment at birth, gender identity, gender expression, and sexual orientation are embodied within individuals and may in return affect physical activity behaviors. Chapter 19 by Hanrahan reviews considerations when working with people with disabilities. The chapter explores psychosocial issues and factors affecting exercise behavior in amputees, blind and visually impaired individuals, the deaf, wheelchair participants, and individuals with cerebral palsy and intellectual disabilities. Using Welk's Youth Physical Activity Promotion Model (YPAP) as the guide, Chapter 20 by Blom, Visek, and Harris provides information regarding children's and adolescents' physical activity patterns, extends explanations for these, and overviews intervention methods for promoting physical activity in children and adolescents. Chapter 21 by Pargman and Dobersek provides an overview of research findings that bear upon aging in relation to exercise—with special emphasis on psychological considerations for improving exercise in the elderly. The chapter illustrates the mechanisms underlying the psychological correlates of health and wellness, and the mediating role of psychological factors within the exercise, health, and wellness link.

The fourth section of this book provides a comprehensive account of physical inactivity and sedentary behaviors in special populations and reviews strategies to address common issues to promote activity. Chapter 22 by Nolt examines the issues of overweight and obesity, diabetes, arthritis, coronary heart disease, stress, depression, low self-esteem, social incompetence, anxiety, heightened stress response, and a general lack of motivation, all of which may preclude one from engaging in regular physical activity. Chapter 23 by Ekkekakis, Zenko, and Weirstein documents the often-underestimated problem of low physical inactivity and avoidance of activity all together among individuals who are obese. The chapter introduces the hedonic framework as the basis for empirical evidence and practical recommendations, and reviews research demonstrating how specific components of the exercise stimulus and the social environment in which it is embedded may generate negative affective and emotional experiences for obese participants. Chapter 24 by Hays reviews the relationship between mental health conditions and physical activity. The chapter examines a number of mental and emotional conditions including dysthymia, depression, anxiety, substance abuse and addictions, post-traumatic stress disorder (PTSD), and persistent mental illness as well as co-morbid disorders, and presents empirical evidence of the effects of exercise on each of them. Chapter 25 by Sachs explores the darker sides of exercise and defines exercise addiction. The chapter provides an overview of the signs and symptoms associated with the condition. The chapter also reviews an ensemble of measurement tools for determining the presence of the condition and select relevant counseling strategies for aiding its recovery. Chapter 26 by Arvinen-Barrow and Clement describes the role of injury and injury recovery within the journey from exercise adoption to adherence. The chapter places a special emphasis on individuals' reactions to injury and rehabilitation and reviews strategies to motivate individuals through rehabilitation to facilitate a safe return to activity post-injury and rehabilitation. Chapter 27 by Dobersek and Eklund examines relatively understudied conditions, including social physique anxiety (SPA) and muscle dysmorphia (MD). The chapter offers an account of the mechanisms that contribute to the development of SPA and MD among physically active individuals. The final chapter of this section, Chapter 28 by Selby, defines eating disorders and identifies their risk factors. The chapter focuses on the misuse of exercise in the context of eating disorders to subsequently address how exercise can be used in the successful treatment of eating disorders.

The fifth and final section of this book, entitled "Applied Exercise Psychology," offers a review of traditional and recent tools to aid practitioners' applied work. Within this section, Chapter 29 by Baltzell and Cote focuses on mindfulness. The chapter defines mindfulness, outlines the effect of regular mindfulness practices on one's experience, and offers empirical evidence and practical implications of mindfulness for increased exercise adoption and adherence. Chapter 30 by Park and Corn presents the basic tenets of positive psychology and explores how positive psychology–based interventions may also help exercise adoption and adherence. Chapter 31 by Nolt details the methods to help productive and person-centered communication and rapport building with clients. The chapter places a special emphasis on clients' cultural backgrounds to understand their habits and health behaviors. The final chapter of this section and of the book, Chapter 32 by Shannon and Zizzi, focuses on the training of exercise psychology practitioners as well as the common ethical issues related to content knowledge, training, and practical experiences in the field. The chapter advances a framework for practitioners who seek professional training and aspire to ethically sound practice in the field of applied exercise psychology.

We hope that you find the information contained in these chapters useful for your work in applied exercise psychology. With physical inactivity being one of the primary public health issues of the 21st century, this is an exciting time for applied exercise psychology, and many great possibilities await us. Enjoy the journey . . .

REFERENCES

Blair, S. N. (2009). Physical inactivity: The biggest public health problem of the 21st century. *British Journal of Sports Medicine, 43*, 1–2.

Centers for Disease Control and Prevention. (2016). *Exercise or physical activity*. Retrieved from cdc. gov/nchs/fastats/exercise.htm.

Kohl, H. W., Craig, C. L., Lambert, E. V., Inoue, S., Alkandari, J. R., Leetongin, G., . . . Lancet Physical Activity Series Working Group. (2012). The pandemic of physical inactivity: Global action for public health. *The Lancet, 380*, 294–305.

National Coalition for Promoting Physical Activity. (2016). *National physical activity plan*. Retrieved from ncppa.org/national-physical-activity-pla

Shuval, K., Leonard, T., Drope, J., Katz, D. L., Patel, A. V., Maitin-Shepard, M., . . . Grinstein, A. (2017). Physical activity counseling in primary care: Insights from public health and behavioral economics. *CA: A Cancer Journal for Clinicians, 67*, 171–253

Troiano, R. P., Berrigan, D., Dodd, K. W., Mâsse, L. C., Tilert, T., & McDowell, M. (2008). Physical activity in the United States measured by accelerometer. *Medicine and Science in Sports and Exercise, 40*, 181–188.

United States Department of Health and Human Services. (1996). *Physical activity and health: A report of the surgeon general*. Atlanta, GA: Author.

United States Department of Health and Human Services. (2013). *Nutrition, physical activity and obesity: Data, trends and maps*. Retrieved from https://nccd.cdc.gov/NPAO_DTM/

United States Department of Health and Human Services. (2015). *Step it up! The surgeon general's call to action to promote walking and walkable communities*. Retrieved from surgeongeneral.gov/library/calls/walking-and-walkable-communities/

2 The Sedentariness Epidemic—Demographic Considerations

Claudio R. Nigg and Brook Harmon

DEFINING SEDENTARY BEHAVIOR

Past conceptualizations of sedentary behavior have equated it with the lowest end of the physical activity continuum or a lack of physical activity. However, accumulating evidence indicates sedentary behavior is unique and independent from a lack of moderate-to-vigorous physical activity (MVPA) in both adults and youth (Brodersen, Steptoe, Williamson, & Wardle, 2005; Tremblay, Colley, Saunders, Healy, & Owen, 2010; Vaeth, Amato, & Nigg, 2012). The "active couch potato" and like terms have emerged to distinguish individuals who meet physical activity guidelines yet also engage in prolonged, unbroken periods of sedentary time (Owen, Healy, Matthews, & Dunstan, 2010). Therefore, sedentary behavior is defined as extended periods of time in which energy expenditure is close to the resting metabolic rate, or the equivalent of 1.5 METS or less, and which have important independent effects on health (Heinonen et al., 2013; Pate, O'Neill, & Lobelo, 2008; Tremblay et al., 2010). Emerging research on sedentary behavior points to implications for chronic disease prevention, considerations necessary when defining, measuring, and intervening on sedentary behavior. Furthermore, demographic differences exist in the prevalence and trajectory of sedentary behavior in the population, which has implications for allocating resources and providing intervention.

The purpose of this chapter is to provide an understanding of sedentary behavior and considerations for population subgroups. We present our current understanding of the relationship between sedentary behavior and health, describe different types of sedentary behaviors, and present demographic factors to consider when conducting interventions/programs to address sedentary behaviors.

SEDENTARY BEHAVIOR AND HEALTH

In the past two decades evidence has emerged that sedentary behavior is linked to several adverse health outcomes. Adult women who sit for 10 or more hours per day have an increased risk of cardiovascular disease (CVD) compared with women who sit 5 hours or less when adjusting for physical activity (Chomistek et al., 2013). This association was stronger in overweight and older women. Women who sit for 10 hours or more and were inactive had the highest CVD risk (Chomistek et al., 2013). Matthews et al. (2012) also reported the relationship between sedentary behavior and CVD in older adults of both sexes using another definition (seven hours or more versus one hour or less of television [TV] time per day, adjusted for MVPA) and extended this to all-cause mortality and cancer mortality. Even with over seven hours of MVPA per day, high TV time (seven or more hours per day) was associated with all-cause and CVD mortality, and overall sitting was associated with all-cause mortality

(Matthews et al., 2012). Studies on the relationship of sedentary behavior with cancer were reviewed (Lynch, 2010) and concluded that sedentary behavior is associated with increased risk of colorectal, endometrial, ovarian, and prostate cancer, cancer mortality in women, and weight gain in colorectal cancer survivors.

Several studies have reported on the association of sedentary behaviors with obesity and related indicators. Sisson et al. (2009) reported that sedentary behavior in 2- to 15-year-old children increased with weight (for normal weight children, 44.6% had two or greater sedentary behavior hours; overweight children, 50.8%; and obese children, 58.5%). Kronenberg et al. (2000) found that TV watching was negatively associated with body mass index (BMI), waist circumference, waist-hip ratio, and skinfolds; positively associated with triglycerides; and slight negatively associated with HDL (in men). However, no association was found with carotid artery intima-media wall thickness. Similarly, sedentary behavior (independent of physical activity) was associated with increases in waist circumference, C-reactive protein, triglycerides, HOMA-%B, HOMA-%S, and insulin and with slight decreases in HDL, using accelerometer data (Healy, Matthews, Dunstan, Winkler, & Owen, 2011). In two separate studies, increases in TV time was associated with obesity and weight gain as well as with type 2 diabetes (independent of exercise and diet) (Hu, 2003; Hu, Li, Colditz, Willett, & Manson, 2003). Over 40 hours/week of TV was associated with a threefold increase in risk for

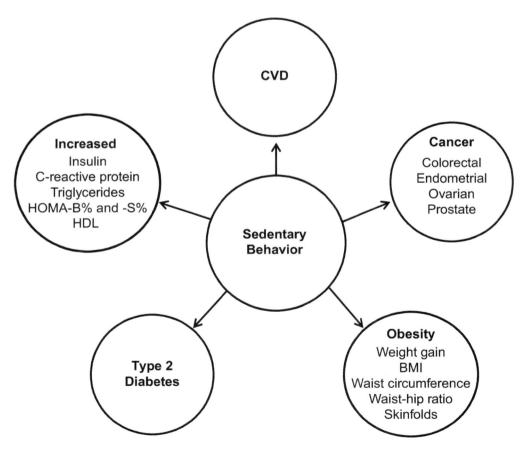

Figure 2.1 Adverse Outcomes

type 2 diabetes compared to less than 1 hour/week (Hu, 2003). Hu et al. (2003) estimated that 30% of new cases of obesity and 43% of new type 2 diabetes cases could be prevented by limiting TV to less than 10 hours/week and adding 30 minutes or more of brisk walking. These findings about TV viewing were also reported in Finish young adults by Heinonen et al. (2013), who found that TV viewing (versus other sedentary behavior types) is most consistently related to increased BMI and waist circumference in women and men. Findings from China reported that for any physical activity level, increased sedentary time was associated with greater prevalence of increased BMI (Du et al., 2013). Findings from a longitudinal study of adults in Hawai'i, found that sedentary behavior, as measured by TV/video viewing, was not associated with self-reported quality of life (Chai et al., 2010). However, participants with "high" TV viewing only viewed approximately four hours per day, much lower than some other studies of TV viewing. Additional studies on the association between sedentary behavior and quality of life are needed.

Figure 2.1 provides an overview of the health outcomes research has shown to be adversely affected by increases in sedentary behaviors.

TYPES OF SEDENTARY BEHAVIOR

An important component of sedentary behavior research is the ability to measure it in such a way as to make comparisons across studies and populations; however, sedentary behavior comes in many forms, and conceptualizations for assessment are varied. Tremblay et al. (2010) suggested using parameters similar to those used to measure physical activity (frequency, intensity, time/duration, type), except instead of intensity of physical activity, interruptions in sedentary behavior would be measured. Most sedentary behavior research to date use a proxy measure for sedentary behavior versus an exhaustive list and focuses on the parameters of duration and type, or the number of hours spent in a particular behavior.

TV watching is the second-most-frequently reported leisure-time sedentary behavior among adults, only behind eating and drinking, according to data from the American Time Use Survey (Tudor-Locke, Johnson, & Katzmarzyk, 2010). Thirty-three percent of youth ages 8–16 report watching TV or videos more than the recommended two hours per day (Sisson, Broyles, Baker, & Katzmarzyk, 2010). Given the large percentage of hours per day spent watching TV, it is a commonly used measure of sedentary behavior, especially leisure-time sedentary behavior, in both adults and youth (Hu, 2003; Hu et al., 2003; Kronenberg et al., 2000; Maniccia, Davison, Marshall, Manganello, & Dennison, 2011). Other studies, especially studies of children and adolescents, have expanded this concept to assess "screen time," which includes TV watching, computer time, and time spent in video games (Ramirez et al., 2011; Tremblay et al., 2010). Efforts have been made by some researchers to distinguish between "screen time" related to studying and "screen time" spent in leisure activities (Buckworth & Nigg, 2004). More recently the use of cell phones has been examined as a potential contributor to increased screen time and sedentary activities. In a cohort of US college students, high-frequency cell phone users were found to engage in a greater number of sedentary activities than low-frequency users, suggesting that cell phone use may be another viable marker for sedentary behavior (Lepp, Barkley, Sanders, Rebold, & Gates, 2013).

Among adults, there is also concern about society's change to more sedentary jobs and the increase in workplace sitting (Owen et al., 2010). Also included in some measurements of sedentary behaviors is time spent in sedentary community (Owen et al., 2010). The built environment strongly influences time spent in sedentary travel, with less-walkable neighborhoods, in the growth of suburbs or more rural areas, and limited transit options all contributing to more sedentary travel (Kozo et al., 2012; Owen et al., 2011).

Future directions for research into the various types of sedentary behaviors include research into the reliability and validity of measures of various types of behaviors beyond TV watching (Clark et al., 2009), as well as intervention work that specifically targets the reduction of sedentary behavior (Crespo, Sallis, Conway, Saelens, & Frank, 2011; Maniccia et al., 2011). While intervention work on reducing sedentary behavior has begun, calls have been made to ensure that such work is theoretically based and that efforts are made to tease out the benefits of reducing sedentary behavior from interventions that often also include efforts to increase physical activity and improve diet (Garber & Nigg, 2012; Nigg & Paxton, 2008). Work validating the construct of stages of change from the Transtheoretical Model indicates the need to develop stages of change related to a global or type-specific definition of sedentary behavior in order to establish readiness of children to decrease sedentary behavior (Haas & Nigg, 2009). In addition, interventions should look at long-term assessments of sedentary behavior, the influence of sedentary behavior on health, and the trajectory of sedentary behavior over time (Nigg & Paxton, 2008).

SEDENTARY BEHAVIOR AND DEMOGRAPHIC DIFFERENCES

The sedentariness epidemic is not distributed equally and appears to differ by gender, age, ethnicity, urban and rural areas, and socioeconomic status. Figure 2.2 provides an overview of demographic variables associated with more time spent in sedentary behaviors. Upward arrows indicate increases or higher amounts while question marks indicate more research is needed.

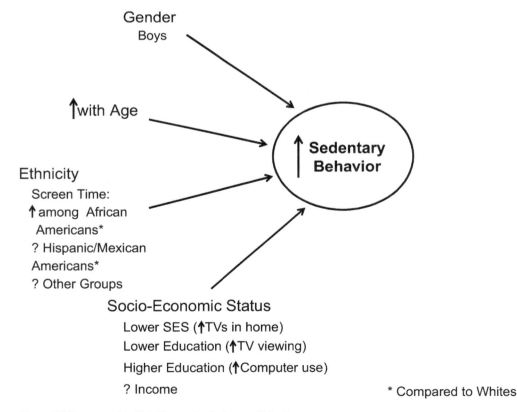

Figure 2.2 Demographic Risk Factors for Sedentary Behavior

Gender

The physical activity literature has shown us that boys tend to be more physically active than girls, especially in older age groups (Nader, Bradley, Houts, McRitchie, & O'Brien, 2008; Van Der Horst, Paw, Twisk, & Van Mechelen, 2007). It also appears that boys may spend more time than girls in sedentary pursuits as well. A study of the US National Health and Nutrition Examination Survey (NHANES) from 2001–2006 showed a higher percentage of boys spent two or more hours per day watching TV/videos ($34.1 \pm 1.3\%$ versus $31.7 \pm 1.4\%$, boys and girls respectively), using the computer ($8.1 \pm 0.6\%$ versus $5.2 \pm 0.6\%$, boys and girls respectively), and in total screen time ($49.4 \pm 1.2\%$ versus $45.0 \pm 1.6\%$, boys and girls respectively) compared to girls (Sisson et al., 2009). Data from the Youth Risk Behavior Surveillance System (YRBSS) 2011 found similar trends for high school boys (9th–12th grades) compared to high school girls (Eaton et al., 2012). Approximately 35% of boys reported spending three or more hours a day playing video games or using the computer recreationally, compared to 27% of girls (Eaton et al., 2012). The percentages for watching three or more hours of TV were still higher for boys than girls, but the gap was much smaller (27% versus 24%, respectively) (Eaton et al., 2012).

A recent review of studies assessing sedentary behavior in adults around the world indicates that men may spend more time in sedentary behaviors such as computer and video game use as well as total screen time (Rhodes, Mark, & Temmel, 2012). Analysis of accelerometer data from the 2003–2004 NHANES found that women were more sedentary than men from youth into adulthood, with the relationship reversing after 60 years of age (Matthews et al., 2008). However, the interaction between gender and age was only significant among Whites and not among Mexican Americans or African Americans (Matthews et al., 2008). A study of primarily White college students found that male students self-reported more sedentary behavior in the form of TV/video watching and computer use than their female counterparts (Buckworth & Nigg, 2004).

Age

Analysis of NHANES data has shown that time spent in sedentary behaviors appears to increase during childhood, with a peak occurring during late adolescence (Matthews et al., 2008; Sisson et al., 2009). However, a study of school children ages 11–12 in the United Kingdom found that age was only a significant predictor of sedentary behavior, measured using weekend screen time, for boys and not for girls (Brodersen et al., 2005). A longitudinal study of youth in Sweden and Estonia who participated in the European Youth Heart Study found similar gender differences in the influence of age on sedentary behavior (Ortega et al., 2013). Using accelerometer data, with sedentary behavior defined as less than or equal to 100 counts/minute. the study followed a cohort of 9 year olds and a cohort of 15 year olds. Time spent in sedentary behavior and MVPA were monitored at baseline and again 6 to 10 years later, depending on the country. Researchers found sedentary behavior increased from childhood to adolescence, but not from adolescence to young adulthood, and this increase was greater for boys than for girls (Ortega et al., 2013). YRBSS 2011 data found 9th graders reported more recreational computer use and TV watching than 12th graders did, with the decrease beginning in 11th grade for boys and 10th grade for girls (Eaton et al., 2012). Among adults, sedentary behavior appears to remain between seven and eight hours/day until after 60 years of age, when it increases to over eight hours/day (Matthews et al., 2008). However, the type of sedentary behavior may determine whether an increase or decrease is seen with age during adulthood. TV viewing may increase with age, while computer use may be higher during young and middle adulthood (Rhodes et al., 2012).

Ethnicity

Some studies have found ethnic differences when assessing time spent in sedentary behaviors; however, the results have been mixed and dependent on the type of sedentary behavior being assessed. Assessments of screen time among youth and adults indicates that ethnic minorities may spend more time watching TV, using the computer, or playing video games, but overall they may not spend more time being sedentary than other ethnic groups. An assessment of screen time among youth (2–15 years old) from NHANES 2001–2006 found a higher proportion of African Americans who had screen time totals of two or more hours (66.1 ± 1.1%) compared to Mexican Americans (46.1 ± 1.2%) and Whites (42.5 ± 1.5%) (Sisson et al., 2009). The only ethnic difference found in the analysis of 2003–2004 NHANES accelerometer data was a lower amount of time spent in sedentary behavior among Mexican Americans starting in late adolescence (16–19 years old) and continuing into adulthood (Matthews et al., 2008). YRBSS 2011 data indicates a higher percentage of African American high school students spend three or more hours a day playing video games or using the computer recreationally (38%) compared to Hispanic (32%) or White (28%) students (Eaton et al., 2012). Similar percentages were seen for watching three or more hours of TV a day (African Americans—55%, Hispanics—38%, Whites—26%) (Eaton et al., 2012).

In a study of low-income African American and White adults living in the Southeastern US, African Americans reported more time spent in TV watching, especially African American women compared to White women (3.94 ± 2.99 hours/day versus 3.32 ± 2.69 hours/day, respectively) (Cohen et al., 2013). However, when overall time spent in sedentary behaviors was assessed, there was little difference by ethnicity (Cohen et al., 2013). Understanding ethnic differences and the interaction with sedentary behavior type is important both for future surveillance and for intervention studies.

Location

The influence of sedentary behavior on adverse health outcomes seems to be true across the globe (see sedentary behavior and health section). However, no studies were identified that compared sedentary behavior in rural versus urban environments. YRBSS data indicate sedentary behavior, as defined by recreational computer and video game use and TV watching, may be higher in urban settings than in rural areas (Eaton et al., 2012). The YRBSS 2011 data showed that nationwide 31% of students reported using computers and video games for three or more hours a day, compared to 35% for students in large urban schools. Similar percentages were seen with watching three or more hours of TV (Nationwide—32%, Urban Schools—41%) (Eaton et al., 2012). This is an area that should be explored further and may have implications for resource allocation.

Socioeconomic Status

Assessments of sedentary behavior among differing socioeconomic groups have used a variety of measures to understand the relationship between socioeconomic status and time spent in sedentary behavior. Since socioeconomic status can encompass education as well as income and can influence the neighborhood and home in which one lives, these variables have been included in various studies. Analysis of NHANES data from 2001–2006 found lower percentages of youth participating in two or more hours of screen time a day as income increased, especially as household income exceeded $45,000 per year (less than $25,000 51.4 ± 1.6%,

$25,000–45,000 51.2 ± 1.6%, over $45,000 42.6 ± 1.5%) (Sisson et al., 2009). Analysis of data from the Neighborhood Impact on Kids (NIK) study found no differences in time spent in sedentary behavior (parent's report of child's screen time) by socioeconomic status (Tandon et al., 2012). However, the environments in lower socioeconomic status homes were more conducive to sedentary behaviors (more TVs in rooms, less-portable play equipment) (Tandon et al., 2012). In a review of adult sedentary behavior studies, the type of sedentary behavior was associated with level of education. Studies found that computer time was associated with higher education, TV watching was associated with lower education, and no association was seen with overall sitting time (Rhodes et al., 2012). This corresponds with findings from a study of neighborhood walkability and sedentary behavior (Kozo et al., 2012). The study found that neighborhood walkability and income were not related to total sitting time; however, lower walkability was associated with increased drive time and more self-reported TV time (Kozo et al., 2012). In addition, participants in higher-income neighborhoods reported more time spent reading and using the computer, as well as more objectively measured sedentary time (Kozo et al., 2012).

SUMMARY OF CHAPTER AND PRACTICAL IMPLICATIONS

In this chapter we provided those intervening with individuals and groups the tools necessary to understand sedentary behavior, its unique influence on health, and the factors that should be taken into consideration when working with particular populations. As we move forward, additional research is needed on types of sedentary behaviors beyond TV watching and screen time (i.e., sedentary travel, worksite sedentary behaviors), as well as on differences that may be present in urban versus rural settings. Interventions aimed at reducing sedentary behavior have begun to be developed; however, they should be theoretically based, and efforts should be made to understand what components of multiple-behavior change interventions are aiding in the reduction of time spent in sedentary activities. Moving forward, research and practice-based programs should also aim to evaluate interventions for their long-term impact on reducing sedentary behaviors and improving health outcomes.

Practical Recommendations

Strategies for decreasing sedentary time can be divided into focusing on leisure time and focusing on work time. While the strategies provided can be applied with all demographic subgroups, an evaluation of the population of interest and targeting of the intervention or program will be needed as different groups may engage in some sedentary behaviors more frequently than others. Leisure-time strategies to reduce sedentary behaviors include the following:

- Engage in an activity during TV commercials (e.g., walk around the living room, lift small weights, play with your child or pet)
- Engage in a family activity (e.g., a walk) after dinner
- Take the stairs instead of escalators or elevators. If taking escalators, walk them.
- Walk along the sidelines when watching a child's sporting or other event
- Pace while talking on the phone/cell phone
- Walk through the store before starting to shop
- Choose an active hobby (i.e., bowling, gardening)

- Dance while listening to music
- Check out audiobooks from the library and listen to them while on the treadmill or walking around the neighborhood
- Play with your children or pets
- Move around the house, clean up, or iron/fold clothes while watching a TV show
- Make chores active (i.e., dance while dusting, fold laundry standing up)
- Keep a record of the time you spend watching TV, playing video games, or are in front of a screen. Use these logs to set goals and incorporate strategies to reduce screen time.
- Limit smartphone or web surfing to one hour/day and limit TV watching to another one hour/day

Strategies for the workplace to reduce sedentary behaviors include the following:

- Ride a bicycle or walk to work
- Walk during your coffee break
- Stand in meetings or incorporate activity breaks
- Pace or walk around while on phone calls or conference calls
- Park farther away and walk to work
- Visit your co-worker rather than emailing
- Take the stairs whenever possible
- Have a walking meeting
- Use half of your lunch break for physical activity
- Sit on an exercise ball
- Use a standing desk
- Use pedals at your desk

These leisure-time and work-time strategies are presented as suggestions and need to be tried to see what best fits into an individual's lifestyle. Every sedentary behavior that is cut short or interrupted by physical activity will help in fighting the obesity epidemic.

ACKNOWLEDGMENT

The authors would like to acknowledge the contributions of Marci Chock.

REFERENCES

Brodersen, N. H., Steptoe, A., Williamson, S., & Wardle, J. (2005). Sociodemographic, developmental, environmental, and psychological correlates of physical activity and sedentary behavior at age 11 to 12. *Annals of Behavioral Medicine, 29*(1), 2–11.

Buckworth, J., & Nigg, C. (2004). Physical activity, exercise, and sedentary behavior in college students. *Journal of American College Health, 53*(1), 28–34. doi: 10.3200/JACH.53.1.28-34

Chai, W., Nigg, C. R., Pagano, I. S., Motl, R. W., Horwath, C., & Dishman, R. K. (2010). Associations of quality of life with physical activity, fruit and vegetable consumption, and physical inactivity in a free living, multiethnic population in Hawaii: A longitudinal study. *International Journal of Behavioral Nutrition and Physical Activity, 7*, 83. doi: 10.1186/14795-8687-83

Chomistek, A. K., Manson, J. E., Stefanick, M. L., Lu, B., Sands-Lincoln, M., Going, S. B., . . . Eaton, C. B. (2013). Relationship of sedentary behavior and physical activity to incident cardiovascular disease: Results from the Women's Health Initiative. *Journal of the American College of Cardiology, 61*(23), 2346–2354. doi: 10.1016/j.jacc.2013.03.031

Clark, B. K., Sugiyama, T., Healy, G. N., Salmon, J., Dunstan, D. W., & Owen, N. (2009). Validity and reliability of measures of television viewing time and other non-occupational sedentary behaviour of adults: A review. *Obesity Reviews*, *10*(1), 7–16. doi: 10.1111/j.1467-789X.2008.00508.x

Cohen, S. S., Matthews, C. E., Signorello, L. B., Schlundt, D. G., Blot, W. J., & Buchowski, M. S. (2013). Sedentary and physically active behavior patterns among low-income African-American and white adults living in the southeastern United States. *PLoS One*, *8*(4), e59975. doi: 10.1371/journal.pone.0059975

Crespo, N. C., Sallis, J. F., Conway, T. L., Saelens, B. E., & Frank, L. D. (2011). Worksite physical activity policies and environments in relation to employee physical activity. *American Journal of Health Promotion*, *25*(4), 264–271. doi: 10.4278/ajhp.081112-QUAN-280

Du, H., Bennett, D., Li, L., Whitlock, G., Guo, Y., Collins, R., . . . Chen, Z. (2013). Physical activity and sedentary leisure time and their associations with BMI, waist circumference, and percentage body fat in 0.5 million adults: The China Kadoorie Biobank study. *American Journal of Clinical Nutrition*, *97*(3), 487–496. doi: 10.3945/ajcn.112.046854

Eaton, D. K., Kann, L., Kinchen, S., Shanklin, S., Flint, K. H., Hawkins, J., . . . Wechsler, H. (2012). Youth risk behavior surveillance—United States, 2011. *Morbidity and Mortality Weekly Report Surveillance Summaries*, *61*, 1–162.

Garber, C., & Nigg, C. R. (2012). Perspectives on intervening on physical inactivity and diet: A commentary. *Health Education & Behavior*, *39*, 123–126.

Haas, S., & Nigg, C. R. (2009). Construct validation of the stages of change with strenuous, moderate, and mild physical activity and sedentary behaviour among children. *Journal of Science and Medicine in Sport*, *12*(5), 586–591. doi: 10.1016/j.jsams.2008.11.001

Healy, G. N., Matthews, C. E., Dunstan, D. W., Winkler, E. A., & Owen, N. (2011). Sedentary time and cardio-metabolic biomarkers in US adults: NHANES 2003–06. *European Heart Journal*, *32*(5), 590–597. doi: 10.1093/eurheartj/ehq451

Heinonen, I., Helajärvi, H., Pahkala, K., Heinonen, O. J., Hirvensalo, M., Pälve, K., . . . Raitakari, O. T. (2013). Sedentary behaviours and obesity in adults: The cardiovascular risk in Young Finns Study. *BMJ Open*, *3*(e002901). doi: 10.1136/bmjopen-2013-002901

Hu, F. B. (2003). Sedentary lifestyle and risk of obesity and type 2 diabetes. *Lipids*, *38*(2), 103–108.

Hu, F. B., Li, T. Y., Colditz, G. A., Willett, W. C., & Manson, J. E. (2003). Television watching and other sedentary behaviors in relation to risk of obesity and type 2 diabetes mellitus in women. *Journal of American Medical Association*, *289*(14), 1785–1791. doi: 10.1001/jama.289.14.1785

Kozo, J., Sallis, J. F., Conway, T. L., Kerr, J., Cain, K., Saelens, B. E., . . . Owen, N. (2012). Sedentary behaviors of adults in relation to neighborhood walkability and income. *Health Psychology*, *31*(6), 704–713. doi: 10.1037/a0027874

Kronenberg, F., Pereira, M. A., Schmitz, M. K., Arnett, D. K., Evenson, K. R., Crapo, R. O., . . . Hunt, S. C. (2000). Influence of leisure time physical activity and television watching on atherosclerosis risk factors in the NHLBI Family Heart Study. *Atherosclerosis*, *153*(2), 433–443.

Lepp, A., Barkley, J. E., Sanders, G. J., Rebold, M., & Gates, P. (2013). The relationship between cell phone use, physical and sedentary activity, and cardiorespiratory fitness in a sample of U.S. college students. *International Journal of Behavioral Nutrition and Physical Activity*, *10*, 79. doi: 10.1186/14795-8681-07-9

Lynch, B. M. (2010). Sedentary behavior and cancer: A systematic review of the literature and proposed biological mechanisms. [Research Support, Non-U.S. Gov't Review]. *Cancer Epidemiology Biomarkers & Prevention*, *19*(11), 2691–2709. doi: 10.1158/1055-9965.EPI-10-0815

Maniccia, D. M., Davison, K. K., Marshall, S. J., Manganello, J. A., & Dennison, B. A. (2011). A meta-analysis of interventions that target children's screen time for reduction. *Pediatrics*, *128*(1), e193–210. doi: 10.1542/peds.2010-2353

Matthews, C. E., Chen, K. Y., Freedson, P. S., Buchowski, M. S., Beech, B. M., Pate, R. R., & Troiano, R. P. (2008). Amount of time spent in sedentary behaviors in the United States, 2003–2004. *American Journal of Epidemiology*, *167*(7), 875–881. doi: 10.1093/aje/kwm390

Matthews, C. E., George, S. M., Moore, S. C., Bowles, H. R., Blair, A., Park, Y., . . . Schatzkin, A. (2012). Amount of time spent in sedentary behaviors and cause-specific mortality in US adults. *American Journal of Clinical Nutrition*, *95*(2), 437–445. doi: 10.3945/ajcn.111.019620

Nader, P. R., Bradley, R. H., Houts, R. M., McRitchie, S. L., & O'Brien, M. (2008). Moderate-to-vigorous physical activity from ages 9 to 15 years. *Journal of American Medical Association*, *300*(3), 295–305. doi: 10.1001/jama.300.3.295

Nigg, C. R., & Paxton, R. (2008). Conceptual perspectives used to understand youth physical activity and inactivity. In A. L. Smith & S. J. H. Biddle (Eds.), *Youth physical activity and inactivity: Challenges and solutions* (pp. 79–113). Champaign, IL: Human Kinetics

Ortega, F. B., Konstabel, K., Pasquali, E., Ruiz, J. R., Hurtig-Wennlö, A., Mäestu, J., . . . Sjöström, M. (2013). Objectively measured physical activity and sedentary time during childhood, adolescence and young adulthood: A cohort study. *PLoS ONE*, *8*(4). doi: 10.1371/journal.pone.0060871

Owen, N., Healy, G. N., Matthews, C. E., & Dunstan, D. W. (2010). Too much sitting: The population health science of sedentary behavior. *Exercise and Sport Sciences Reviews*, *38*(3), 105–113.

Owen, N., Sugiyama, T., Eakin, E. E., Gardiner, P. A., Tremblay, M. S., & Sallis, J. F. (2011). Adults' sedentary behavior determinants and interventions. *American Journal of Preventive Medicine*, *41*(2), 189–196. doi: 10.1016/j.amepre.2011.05.013

Pate, R. R., O'Neill, J. R., & Lobelo, F. (2008). The evolving definition of " 'sedentary". *Exercise and Sport Sciences Reviews*, *36*(4), 173–178.

Ramirez, E. R., Norman, G. J., Rosenberg, D. E., Kerr, J., Saelens, B. E., Durant, N., & Sallis, J. F. (2011). Adolescent screen time and rules to limit screen time in the home. *Journal of Adolescent Health*, *48*(4), 379–385. doi: 10.1016/j.jadohealth.2010.07.013

Rhodes, R. E., Mark, R. S., & Temmel, C. P. (2012). Adult sedentary behavior: A systematic review. *American Journal of Preventive Medicine*, *42*(3), e3–28. doi: 10.1016/j.amepre.2011.10.020

Sisson, S. B., Broyles, S. T., Baker, B. L., & Katzmarzyk, P. T. (2010). Screen time, physical activity, and overweight in U.S. youth: National survey of children's health 2003. *Journal of Adolescent Health*, *47*(3), 309–311. doi: 10.1016/j.jadohealth.2010.02.016

Sisson, S. B., Church, T. S., Martin, C. K., Tudor-Locke, C., Smith, S. R., Bouchard, C., . . . Katzmarzyk, P. T. (2009). Profiles of sedentary behavior in children and adolescents: The US National Health and Nutrition Examination Survey, 2001–2006. *International Journal of Pediatric Obesity*, *4*(4), 353–359. doi: 10.3109/17477160902934777

Tandon, P. S., Zhou, C., Sallis, J. F., Cain, K. L., Frank, L. D., & Saelens, B. E. (2012). Home environment relationships with children's physical activity, sedentary time, and screen time by socioeconomic status. *International Journal of Behavioral Nutrition and Physical Activity*, *9*, 88. doi: 10.1186/14795-8689-88

Tremblay, M. S., Colley, R. C., Saunders, T. J., Healy, G. N., & Owen, N. (2010). Physiological and health implications of a sedentary lifestyle. *Applied Physiology, Nutrition, and Metabolism 35*, 725–740. doi: 10.1139/H10-079

Tudor-Locke, C., Johnson, W. D., & Katzmarzyk, P. T. (2010). Frequently reported activities by intensity for U.S. adults: The American Time Use Survey. *American Journal of Preventive Medicine*, *39*(4), e13–20. doi: 10.1016/j.amepre.2010.05.017

Vaeth, J., Amato, K., & Nigg, C. R. (2012). Physical activity, inactivity, and nutrition behavior among children: Investigating compensation and transfer effects. In J. E. Maddock (Ed.), *Public health—social and behavioral health* (pp. 153–164). Rijeka, Croatia: Intech.

Van Der Horst, K., Paw, M. J., Twisk, J. W., & Van Mechelen, W. (2007). A brief review on correlates of physical activity and sedentariness in youth. *Medicine & Science in Sports & Exercise*, *39*(8), 1241–1250. doi: 10.1249/mss.0b013e318059bf35

3   A Rose by Any Other Name . . .

Jennifer B. Ciaccio and Michael L. Sachs

"A rose by any other name would smell as sweet" (Shakespeare, trans. 2008, 2.2.1–2). Or would it? This quotation from William Shakespeare's *Romeo and Juliet*, written more than 400 years ago, epitomizes the challenge we sometimes face in selecting the best word to use with our clients in encouraging them to engage in regular exercise/physical activity (E/PA). Chapter 2 has already outlined the issues inherent in our current obesity and sedentariness epidemic. This chapter will note the language we use with clients to express the importance of promoting E/PA on a regular basis to overcome these issues as well as the reasons why current strategies often fail.

It is true that words have power, and the term *applied exercise psychology* utilized throughout this book clearly includes the word *exercise*. Why then is use of the word *exercise* sometimes an issue? Some of our clients report that they don't like to exercise. Running 10 miles, participating in a challenging CrossFit class, doing plyometrics, or even going to a gym simply scares them (Carroll, 2016). This is particularly true for those who have been sedentary for many years. The term *exercise* has been associated by these individuals with high levels of activity, vigorously pursued, that requires much training and effort, with inevitable discomfort. For many, exercise implies a lack of enjoyment (Nesti, 2016). These negative associations may be due to previous or recent unpleasant experiences in physical education or fitness classes; regardless of the origin, participating in exercise is not perceived as something of interest or as potentially enjoyable (Downs, Nigg, Hausenblas, & Rauff, 2014; Nesti, 2016). Exercise is typically considered work. Indeed, we often call an exercise session "working out." Work, as opposed to play, has negative connotations, hence the resistance to doing something that is not perceived as enjoyable can be a barrier to exercise (Ruby, Dunn, Perrino, Gillis, & Viel, 2011; Salmon, Crawford, Owen, Bauman, & Sallis, 2003).

There are many definitions of exercise. Acevedo (2012) defines exercise as "a form of structured physical activity with the specific objective of improving or maintaining physical fitness or health" (p. 4). Another definition is "any activity involving generation of force by activated muscles, including activities of daily living, work, recreation, and competitive sport" (Knuttgen, 2003, p. 31). A quick online search yields countless definitions that lean more toward the idea that exercise is intense physical activity that requires significant effort and is done solely for health and fitness—in short, physical activity that is not fun. These definitions are relatively innocuous sets of words, but the images they convey for many are unappealing. Additionally, the definitions of exercise are not solely connected with recreation and sport, but also with activities of daily living and work. These diverse areas of human endeavor may all involve physical activity, but the concept of E/PA gets too messy when considering all of these meanings together.

There are numerous guidelines for the FITT of exercise—frequency (how many times per week), intensity (how vigorous), time (how long), and type (what type of activity). The American College of Sports Medicine (ACSM, 2011) recommends 150 minutes of moderate to vigorous physical activity per week for cardiorespiratory exercise (Garber et al., 2011). The Centers for Disease Control (CDC) guidelines are identical (US Department of Health and Human Services [USDHHS], 2008).

Physical activity as exercise can also include participating in sport activities (e.g., tennis, basketball, soccer) on a regular basis because most sport activities involve levels of structured activity with subsequent health benefits (Khan et al., 2012). Although this may at times lead to other issues, such as exercise addiction (see Chapter 25), the practice of applied exercise psychology primarily focuses on individuals who resist calls to engage in E/PA and are at the precontemplation or contemplation stage of the Transtheoretical Model of behavior change (TTM) (Prochaska & DiClemente, 1992; Prochaska, Redding, & Evers, 2002) (see Chapter 5), for those practitioners who use the model for PA adoption and maintenance (Cardinal, 1997).

Acevedo (2012), in *The Oxford Handbook of Exercise Psychology*, notes that "in parallel with the literature, 'physical activity' and 'exercise' are often used interchangeably" (pp. 4–5). PA is most commonly defined as any physical movement that works muscles and requires more energy than being at rest (National Institutes of Health [NIH], 2016). Examples of PA include walking, dancing, playing, yoga, or even gardening, and PA is typically considered to be a less-structured activity than exercise (NIH, 2016). Most people engage in some degree of PA just by virtue of living "normal" lives, with the occasional exception of the person who works from home and almost never leaves the house, but that is rare. The key question then is how much PA does a person really get during a typical day? Of importance to practitioners, there are a number of ways of getting PA that are not commonly thought of as exercise. Some of these include cleaning the house, walking the dog, travelling, doing yard work, running after children, and so on (NIH, 2016; World Health Organization [WHO], 2016). Regardless of whether the terms *exercise* and *physical activity* are used interchangeably or distinctively, it is important to note that the goal of applied practice is typically to help clients reach and maintain optimal PA levels that include enjoyable, preferably vigorous, extensive, physical movement on a regular basis (Association for Applied Sport Psychology [AASP], 2017).

To that end, as part of the initial intake, practitioners need to find out how much E/PA their clients are already engaging in. There are numerous intake recommendations used within exercise and sport psychology, including Taylor and Schneider's (1992) pioneering sport-clinical intake protocol. In their recommendations, Taylor and Schneider outlined the need to ascertain the problem the client is experiencing, the athletic history of the client, the social support network the client has in place, any recent significant life events, overall health, and any changes that occurred before the problem was present (Taylor & Schneider, 1992). This could be easily adapted to include concepts of PA and exercise, and although the practice of clinical and counseling psychology emphasizes clinical issues, practitioners in applied exercise psychology could still benefit from these resources and modify them as appropriate when trying to set an E/PA baseline for clients.

The next question is whether practitioners can rest easy if they find through initial intake that their clients are engaged in E/PA. The simple answer is no. As practitioners, we want to make sure that individuals engage in E/PA to derive the maximum benefits of those activities as related to physical and mental health. This may entail a discussion with clients about the role and meaning of E/PA in their lives, noting the language they choose to refer to it. It would be important to learn at this point whether E/PA appears to be playing a "therapeutic" role (e.g., stress management/relief) or is a potential source of stress (e.g., addiction to exercise, overly competitive) in the client's life. In cases when the client is regularly active and assigns activity a therapeutic role, one can feel optimistic that the E/PA will continue. All other cases of inactivity, irregular activity, and/or assigning activity a negative connotation (e.g., work, stress) may be worth addressing to move clients to adopt a more therapeutic perspective.

Consequently, if we find that our clients do not engage in E/PA, then the challenge lies in convincing them to do so. To do this, we must first find out if they are receptive to the possibility of discussing the adoption of E/PA. As discussed in other chapters in this book, part of the applied work within health realms encompasses reviewing activities that will affect and potentially maximize or optimize physical and mental health, including diet, substance use/abuse (alcohol, drugs), and E/PA. As noted above, part of one's intake process should address current and past E/PA levels. This is because there is a big difference in working with someone who had been regularly active and has simply lapsed into sedentariness for a short period of time versus someone who has been sedentary with no consideration of activity for many years. Encouraging clients to return to E/PA can be much easier for those who have lapsed or relapsed recently (see Chapter 5 on TTM) than working with clients for whom sedentariness has become an ingrained habit over many years.

An important tool for the practitioner is motivational interviewing (MI). MI can present benefits for encouraging exercise in our day-to-day interactions with clients (see Chapter 31; Breckon, 2015; Clifford & Curtis, 2016). Other approaches include the use of exercise within psychotherapy (see Chapter 24; Hays, 1999; Hays, 2002). The idea here is not that therapists will prescribe exercise per se—that's the role of professionals with backgrounds in exercise physiology (generally personal trainers with appropriate certifications, from organizations such as the American College of Sports Medicine (ACSM) or the National Strength and Conditioning Association (NSCA) (2017). Rather, the focus is on identifying the interests of clients in engaging in E/PA and discussing it in terms that best capture their interests (Clifford & Curtis, 2016). To that end, developing a sense of exercise identity, similar to the concept of athletic identity, would be ideal. Individuals would perceive exercise as an important part of who they are and engage in exercise on a regular basis. But even if a sense of exercise identity is not established, identity as an individual who engages in PA on a regular basis is still critical.

Although the terms *physical activity* and *exercise* are commonly used interchangeably, we suggest the use of the term *exercise* within consulting settings. It is preferable for clients to engage in a regular program of structured PA, preferably aerobic in nature (accounting for individual differences). The inconsistency inherent in some forms of PA suggests exercise as a preferable movement orientation, as opposed to an orientation focused on PA. Some recent PA recommendations even encourage getting a dog to meet PA needs (Epping, 2011). While walking one's dog is a daily (even twice a day or more) physical activity, other activities are seasonal (yard work) or episodic (house cleaning) and hence rather inconsistent. Exercise, on the other hand, is viewed as a consistent, regular, volitional activity. We, as exercise psychology professionals, want individuals to exercise regularly, perhaps not seven days a week, but three to six days a week, with some rest periods in between.

Nevertheless, as we have discussed, if clients hold negative perceptions of the term *exercise* and prefer the idea of engaging in PA (which could include "alternative" activities, such as ice skating, ballroom dancing, frisbee, bowling, Quidditch, etc.), then adopting the term *physical activity* is acceptable. Consultants should therefore endeavor to convince clients that E/PA is something that should be engaged in on a regular basis. It may be a challenge for individuals to participate on a regular basis, but it is worth trying to convince them to do so. Whether it is for health promotion or treating important health concerns such as obesity (Heymsfield & Wadden, 2017), the term *physical activity* is still appropriate and at times may prove more productive in the course of our interactions with clients.

The initial mission of the consultant is to have a conversation with clients to help them identify how they relate to the term *exercise*. If the term *exercise* appears to possess a negative connotation for them, one then needs to decide whether changing the perception of the term is worth the effort or whether moving instead to PA recommendations is preferable. In a nutshell, and all semantics aside, this is the notion that PA is something we all have to do to survive, while exercise is optional but preferred.

In the final analysis, whether we use the term *exercise* or *physical activity*, we want our clients moving on a regular basis to maximize their likelihood of experiencing optimal physical and mental health for the long run. The semantics that relate to how to refer to that activity are secondary. In the meantime, perhaps one of you will come up with different or better terminology, a new species of rose, as it were. Until then, enjoy your exercise/physical activity/ sport adventures and encourage your clients to do the same.

REFERENCES

Acevedo, E. (2012). Exercise psychology: Understanding the mental health benefits of physical activity and the public health challenges of inactivity. In E. O. Acevedo (Ed.), *The Oxford handbook of exercise psychology* (pp. 3–8). New York, NY: Oxford University Press.

American College of Sports Medicine. (2011). *ACSM issues new recommendations on quantity and quality of exercise*. Retrieved from www.acsm.org www.acsm.org/about- acsm/media-room/news-releases/2011/08/01/acsm-issues-new-recommendations-on- quantity-and-quality-of-exercise

Association for Applied Sport Psychology. (2017). *About applied sport & exercise psychology*. Association for Applied Sport Psychology. Retrieved from www.appliedsportpsych.org/about/about-applied-sport-and-exercise-psychology/

Breckon, J. (2015). Motivational interviewing, exercise, and nutrition counseling. In M. B. Andersen & S. J. Hanrahan (Eds.), *Doing exercise psychology* (pp. 75–100). Champaign, IL: Human Kinetics.

Cardinal, B. J. (1997). Predicting exercise behavior using components of the transtheoretical model of behavior change. *Journal of Sport Behavior, 20*(3), 272–283. Retrieved from https://search-proquest-com.libproxy.temple.edu/docview/18864350?accountid=14270

Carroll, A. E. (2016, June 20). Closest thing to a wonder drug? Try exercise. *The New York Times.*

Clifford, D., & Curtis, L. (2016). *Motivational interviewing in nutrition and fitness*. New York, NY: The Guildford Press.

Downs, D. S., Nigg, C. R., Hausenblas, H. A., & Rauff, E. L. (2014). Why do people change physical activity behavior? In C. R. Nigg (Ed.), *ACSM's behavioral aspects of physical activity and exercise* (pp. 1–38). Philadelphia, PA: Lippincott Williams & Williams.

Epping, J. N. (2011). Dog ownership and dog walking to promote physical activity and health in patients. *Current Sports Medicine Reports, 10*(4), 224–227. doi: 10.1249/JSR.0b013e318223ee41

Garber, C. E., Blissmer, B., Deschenes, M. R., Franklin, B. A., Lamonte, M. J., Lee, I., . . . Swain, D. P. (2011). Quantity and quality of exercise for developing and maintaining cardiorespiratory, musculoskeletal, and neuromotor fitness in apparently healthy adults: Guidance for prescribing exercise. *Medicine & Science in Sports & Exercise, 43*(7), 1334–1359. doi: 10.1249/MSS.0b013e318213fefb

Hays, K. F. (1999). *Working it out: Using exercise in psychotherapy*. Washington, DC: American Psychological Association.

Hays, K. F. (2002). *Move your body, tone your mood*. Washington, DC: American Psychological Association.

Heymsfield, S. B., & Wadden, T. A. (2017). Mechanisms, pathophysiology, and management of obesity. *The New England Journal of Medicine, 376*(3), 254–266. doi: 10.1056/NEJMra1514009

Khan, K. M., Thompson, A. M., Blair, S. N., Sallis, J. F., Powell, K. E., Bull, F. C., & Bauman, A. E. (2012). Sport and exercise as contributors to the health of nations. *The Lancet, 380*(9836), 59–64.

Knuttgen, H. G. (2003). What is exercise? A primer for practitioners. *The Physician and Sport Medicine, 31*(3), 31–49. doi: 10.1080/00913847.2003.11440567

National Institutes of Health. National Heart, Lung, and Blood Institute. (2016). *What is physical activity?* Retrieved from www.nhlbi.nih.gov/health/health-topics/topics/phys

National Strength and Conditioning Association. (2017). *Certification*. Retrieved from www.nsca.com/certification/

Nesti, M. S. (2016). Exercise for health: Serious fun for the whole person? *Journal of Sport and Health Science, 5*, 135–138. doi: 10.1016/j.jshs.2016.03.003

Prochaska, J. O., & DiClemente, C. C. (1992). Stages of change in the modification of problem behaviors. In M. Hersen, R. M. Eisler & P. M. Miller (Eds.), *Progress on behavior modification* (pp. 184–214). New York, NY: Academic Press.

Prochaska, J. O., Redding, C. A., & Evers, K. (2002). The transtheoretical model and stages of change. In K. Glanz, B. K. Rimer & F. M. Lewis (Eds.), *Health behavior and health education: Theory, research, and practice* (3rd ed., pp. 97–122). San Francisco, CA: Jossey-Bass, Inc.

Ruby, M. B., Dunn, E. W., Perrino, A., Gillis, R., & Viel, S. (2011). The invisible benefits of exercise. *Health Psychology, 30*(1), 67–74. doi: 10.1037/a0021859

Salmon, J., Crawford, D., Owen, N., Bauman, A., & Sallis, J. F. (2003). Physical activity and sedentary behavior: A population-based study of barriers, enjoyment, and preference. *Health Psychology, 22*(2), 178–188. doi: 10.1037/0278-6133.22.2.178

Shakespeare, W. (2008). Romeo and Juliet. In S. Greenblatt, W. Cohen, J. E. Howard, & K. E. Maus (Eds.) *The Norton Shakespeare, based on the Oxford edition* (pp. 2.2.1–2). New York, NY: W.W. Norton.

Taylor, J., & Schneider, B. A. (1992). The sport-clinical intake protocol: A comprehensive interviewing instrument for applied sport psychology. *Professional Psychology: Research and Practice, 23*(4), 318.

United States Department of Health and Human Services. (2008). *2008 physical activity guidelines for Americans.* Retrieved from www.health.gov/paguidelines

World Health Organization. (2016). *Physical activity.* Retrieved from www.who.int/mediacentre/factsheets/fs385/en/

4 It's All Psychophysiological!— Effects of Exercise on Your Body and Psyche

Heather E. Webb and Edmund O. Acevedo

THE PSYCHOBIOLOGY OF STRESS: THE IMPACT OF PHYSICAL ACTIVITY

For a prolonged period, Western medicine and society have considered the mind and the body to be individual entities, acting separate from each other in influencing the psychological and physiological functions of the body. Even though William James (James, 1890) advocated in his text *The Principles of Psychology* that the scientific study of psychology should be grounded in an understanding of biology, this concept has been slowly embraced by researchers. While there is the realization that biological and psychological functioning are intertwined when considering their influence on health, the actual practice of investigating both the mental and physical components of health, beyond cursory variables, is still limited in scope.

A contemporary of James, Claude Bernard, put forward the concept of *milieu intérieur*, which suggests that the internal environment must maintain its uniformity for conditions of life to be sustained (Bernard, 1974; Sterling, 2012). This concept was later renamed *homeostasis* by Walter Cannon and was further described as a system that maintains equilibrium by a process of automatic adjustment to keep internal disturbances, which are caused by changes in external environment, within narrow limits (Cannon, 1929). Cannon's work also suggested that the sympathoadrenal (SA) axis was influenced by psychological factors, but at that time there was no evidence that any other neuroendocrine systems were activated by psychological stressors (Mason, 1971).

To date, investigations addressing topics of a psychobiological nature are often addressed from a unidirectional perspective, with the physiological or psychological aspects of responses often addressed singularly. Hence, researchers have tended to selectively ignore pertinent findings in the divergent areas. The reasons behind this disconnect between the psyche and the body is a paradox. Even with the suggestions of James and Bernard that biology should not be investigated without considering the mind, both psychologists and biologists tend to ignore this recommendation. Or when considering the mind-body connection, researchers investigate from their own unique perspective, which tends to focus on concepts and ideas with which one is most familiar (psychological or physiological facets, depending on one's training). This has inherent strength in its focused approach, and inherent weakness in its likelihood of inadvertent errors of omission.

Theories and Models

One of the earliest suggestions for the integration of body and mind into a medical model was called for by Engel (1960). The biopsychosocial model postulates that biological, psychological, and social factors all integrate into human functioning in the context of health,

20

disease, or illness (Engel, 1960; 1977; 2012). Engel recognized that an individual's responses to situations could influence physiological outcomes and advocated for this new perspective in the training of medical students (Engel, 1976; 1977; 1982; 1983).

While Engel postulated the interactions between the psychological, social, and physical components, he left much of the experimental research on this topic for others to perform, as he only published a limited number of articles in this area (Adang, Kootstra, Baeten, & Engel, 1997; Adler, MacRitchie, & Engel, 1971; Engel, 1952; 1961; 1978; Engel, Frader, Barry, & Morrow, 1984). However, it is important to note that Engel's biopsychosocial model does not provide a forthright or easily examined model for explaining the interactions or causations for each of the components (biological, psychological, or social). Instead, the model provides a general framework to guide theoretical and empirical explorations. Thus, this model has been used to support the scientific rationale for a great deal of research since Engel's early articles (Armitage & Conner, 2000) and has led to the formulation of multiple other models and theories, including the health belief model, the theory of reasoned action, the theory of planned behavior, and the transtheoretical model, among others (Armitage & Conner, 2000; Carels et al., 2005; Carels, Douglass, Cacciapaglia, & O'Brien, 2004; Garcia & Mann, 2003; Schwarzer, 1992).

While each of the models identified above is based on the biopsychosocial model, the actual research component of each of them often does not specifically measure the direct influence of physiology on behavior. Rather, physiological measures are often included as outcome measures, essentially a measure of "effect" based on behavioral changes ("cause"). Regardless of these issues, researchers in the area of psychobiology have identified specific areas of research that do lend themselves more easily to looking at biological and psychological factors.

One area of investigation that intrinsically incorporates a combination of psychological and physiological perspective is the concept of stress. When Hans Selye first proposed the notion of stress, he focused on the chemical (physiological) descriptors (Selye, 1936; 1950) of the body's response to noxious stimuli. It was not until his later writings that Selye began to include psychological factors into his consideration of stress (Cooper, 1983; Goldberger & Breznitz, 1982; Selye, 1974; 1976; 1978; 1980). However, his earlier work did inspire others to investigate the broad concept of stress.

Lazarus (1966) proposed that an individual's assessment or "appraisal" of a situation is a critical component in the stress response and resulting emotional outcomes. Lazarus recognized that the stress response is idiosyncratic and conditional to a specific situation, and that a situation considered as either threatening or as challenging by one individual may be perceived differently by another individual or even by the same individual under different circumstances. Hence, Lazarus proposed that an individual is constantly involved in evaluating the environment and assessing possible threats, with the ultimate goal of self-preservation. These observations suggest that psychological factors could affect physiological responses and be a mediating factor in the stress response.

Advancing these propositions, Mason (1971) suggested that psychological stimuli were directly involved in the secretion of cortisol and other adrenocortical hormones and that separating a physical stimulus from its emotive connection was not possible. Mason's research has formed the basis for contemporary investigations into the psychoneuroendocrinology of stress.

Stress has been a topic of numerous investigations, and many investigators have included both physical and psychological perspectives. However, there are numerous areas of investigation that fall under the umbrella of psychobiology. Psychological factors have also been shown to affect physical performance and efficiency, and many successful athletes have been shown to have greater self-confidence, suffer from less anxiety, and have a greater ability to focus and concentrate than their less successful competitors (Mahoney & Avener, 1977; Highlen &

Bennett, 1979). It has been suggested that psychological variables have assisted these competitors in achieving better performance due to the strategies employed. And it has been often cited by those in the field that the difference between the winner of a race and second place is not physiology, but psychology.

Morgan and Pollock (1977) classified competitive (elite) marathoners' cognitive activities as primarily associative (paying attention or responding to physiological cues), while Acevedo and colleagues (1992) found that ultra-marathoners' thoughts were predominantly dissociative (skewing one's attention away from the activity one is engaged in). Both associative and dissociative attentional foci provide methods for competitors to achieve success; however, it must be recognized that success is open to the individual's interpretation. As an example, a player's team may win a championship, but if the player does not believe that they performed well in the game, their personal view of the team's success may be somewhat clouded. In a similar manner, an individual may not win a race, but if they set a personal best, they may feel very successful, regardless of their official finishing place. This implied connection between attentional focus and human performance has received significant attention in the literature, although plausible physiological mechanisms have not been explored.

Differences in physiological status (strength, cardiorespiratory endurance, etc.) at elite levels may be very small, and psychological differences may account for differences in performance. For sub-elite competitors, however, the variation in both physiological and psychological factors can be greater. This may alter the influence of psychological and physiological variables on performance. In these sub-elite or lower levels of competition, we may often see "lesser" physiologically "gifted" individuals out-perform those who are more gifted, for reasons that we cannot always determine. The performance of the "underdog" in these situations may be the result of adaptations they have made that allow them to be more competitive against an opponent who is more physically gifted.

Psychobiological Adaptations to Physical Stress

Dienstbier (1989; 1991) investigated the relationship between psychological provocation (arousal) and physiological responses (toughness). While the physiological reactions to stress have been investigated quite frequently, Dienstbier (1991) also observed that an individual's responses would adapt over time to repeated exposure to physiological stress. This interaction between an organism and stimulus was in response to an individual's interpretation of the stressor as either challenging (effective response) or negative stress (ineffective response). Dienstbier examined the work carried out in the area of reactions to stressors and determined that a "toughened response" was elicited following intermittent exposure to a stressor in animal models.

Dienstbier (1991) posited that the conceptualization of physiological toughness is the appraisal of stress as a challenge, creating a resistance to the detrimental physiological effects of exposure to stress. Based on these observations, Dienstbier proposed that there are four toughening manipulations that influence the physiological mediators, which in turn are the cause of the performance and temperament characteristics. These characteristics included (1) early experiences, including the ways in which children have faced stress in their early life; (2) passive toughening, in which repeated exposure increases stress tolerance (although this could also be depression or learned helplessness); (3) active toughening, which is the suggestion that exposure to one physiological stress, such as aerobic exercise, results in a toughening response to other stressors; and (4) aging, in which it was proposed that the effects of aging are generally opposite to the three other manipulations, as aging was hypothesized to increase (enhance) the negative responses to stress

Each of Dientsbier's characteristics presents difficulties in evaluating their attributes in humans due to inherent ethical and methodological issues. Of the four characteristics, active toughening presents the least difficulty in examining its potential benefits. However, gaining an understanding of active toughening has proven to be difficult, primarily due to the use of different research methodologies, including measurement techniques, and differences in participant characteristics.

Extending Dienstbier's (1989, 1991) physiological model of toughness, Acevedo and Ekkekakis (2001), proposed the transactional psychobiological model, which suggests that cognitive appraisals can interact with and cause alterations in peripheral physiological responses. This model suggests that during exercise, an individual's perception of the demands imposed by psychological and physical stressors is related to an individual's perceived ability to meet these demands. This model proposes that the appraisal (perception) of stress can determine the emotional response and thereby influence the amount of effort put forth by an individual to either cope with or adapt to the stress, whether it be a challenge or a threat. Their conceptual representation of this model is presented in Figure 4.1.

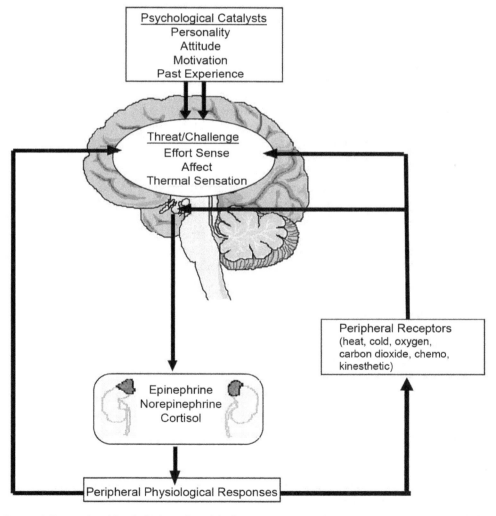

Figure 4.1 Transactional Psychobiological Model of Cognitive Appraisal During Exercise (Acevedo & Ekkekakis, 2001)

This model represents a unique view of the concept of psychobiological theory, in that it recognizes the complex and multidimensional nature of human responses to stress, with hormonal, environmental, and psychological mediators affecting behavior and behavioral factors affecting psychological and hormonal responses. Various factors (psychological mediators and peripheral receptors) are outlined in the model as affecting perception and the resulting responses from within the brain. While the factors that affect the peripheral receptors (heat, cold, oxygen, carbon dioxide, chemicals, and kinesthetic) are difficult to regulate in the field setting, they are much simpler to maintain at a controlled level in a laboratory. Therefore, in the laboratory situation, it is typically the psychological mediators that are manipulated, but even these can be difficult to quantify.

Each of the psychological factors included in the transactional psychobiological model can be measured through various psychometric tests, but even factors that seem as simple to measure as past experience are subject to individual interpretation. For example, experience may be a relatively simple variable to measure, but the relationship between experience and physiological outcomes is more difficult to predict (Moran, 1998).

Familiarity with a stressful event is shown to reduce the effects of the stressor (Ersland, Weisaeth, & Sund, 1989; Fenz & Epstein, 1967). Furthermore, less-experienced or novice individuals will often report higher levels of state of anxiety, arousal, and fear than more-experienced persons when exposed to the same task. Researchers have documented this concept among pilots (Drinkwater, Cleland, & Flint, 1968; Mefferd, Hale, Shanno, Prigmore, & Ellis 1971) and individuals participating in parachute maneuvers (Fenz & Epstein, 1967). Moreover, experienced individuals consistently report lower perceptions of stress following a disaster than less-experienced or novice workers (Ersland et al., 1989; Norris & Murrell, 1988). However, few studies have included differentiations between fitness levels, and this lack of distinction has made it difficult to determine whether the differences observed were linked to psychological or physiological adaptations.

In addition, in contrast to the models of Dienstbier (1991) and Acevedo and Ekkekakis (2001), Moran (1998) suggests that experience may need to be specifically related to the task. The exposure to a specific stressful situation provides a filter through which the individual appraises their surroundings when faced with acute stress. The process of continuous appraisal through the ever-increasing foundation of past experiences may allow an individual to develop the coping skills necessary to respond to a situation in a manner that elicits a physiological response that is less detrimental to an individual's physiology.

As stipulated by Acevedo and Ekkekakis (2001), the individual's perception of a situation as a threat or challenge can determine that individual's response to an event. Hence, the ability to quantify the influence of factors such as experience can be difficult to determine, as each individual presents differently in terms of the type of, exposure to, and situational issues surrounding each stress experience. In physiological terms, the hormonal shifts that occur are not singularly related to physical responses to stressors, such as intensity and duration, but are also related to emotion. It is apparent that the neuroendocrine system is not just a system that responds to physiological mechanisms, but also one that responds to psychosocial influences (Henry & Grim, 1990; Mason, 1975).

It has been shown that brief periods of mental or physical challenge will elicit the release of hormones such as epinephrine and norepinephrine from the sympathoadrenal (SA) axis and cortisol from the hypothalamic-pituitary-adrenocortical (HPA) axis (Besedovsky & Del Rey, 2000). This hormonal response, initiated from central nervous system activation, prepares the body to react to the situation at hand, otherwise known as the "fight or flight" response (Chrousos, 1998). The subsequent cardiovascular, metabolic, and immune system adaptations are changes that initially activate the physiological systems necessary for addressing the challenge, then subsequently counter-regulate these responses.

In utilizing a psychobiological approach, acute psychological stress can be induced in laboratory settings through the use of mental challenges such as the Stroop color and word task (SCW; [Stroop, 1935]), modified SCW tasks (Acevedo et al., 2006; Gerra et al., 2001; Webb et al., 2008), the Trier Social Stress Test (Kirschbaum, Pirke, & Hellhammer, 1993), and mental arithmetic (MA; [Acevedo et al., 2006; Webb et al., 2008]) tasks. Each of these tasks has been repeatedly shown to cause elevations in catecholamines and cortisol while participants were in a physiological resting state and are considered to be classic techniques when trying to invoke a stress response.

In humans and most animals, the stress response is coordinated in the central nervous system (CNS) and periphery (Chrousos & Gold, 1992). Behaviorally, the sympathetic response to a stressor includes increased arousal and vigilance, improved cognition, and focused attention (Chrousos, 1998; Erickson, Drevets, & Schulkin, 2003; Melis & van Boxtel, 2001). Physiologically, the stress response includes enhanced energy conservation and redirection of resources (blood, oxygen, and nutrients) to sites where they are needed most (Cannon, 1914; Cannon & De La Paz, 1911; Frankenhaeuser, 1991; Gerra et al., 2001; Schoder et al., 2000).

Investigators have documented that elevations in epinephrine and norepinephrine from the SA axis (Gerra et al., 2001; Schoder et al., 2000) and cortisol from the HPA axis (Gerra et al., 2001) occur in response to each of these types of mental stressors (Birkett, 2011; Hellhammer & Schubert, 2012). The acute psychological stress that activates the SA axis results in increases in the circulating catecholamines (epinephrine, norepinephrine), heart rate, and systolic blood pressure (SBP; [Allen, Stoney, Owens, & Matthews, 1993; Boone, 1991; McAdoo, Weinberger, Miller, Fineberg, & Grim, 1990]). Concomitantly, activation of the HPA axis stimulates release of adrenocorticotrophic hormone (ACTH) from the anterior pituitary, which stimulates cortisol release from the adrenal gland.

In a similar manner, hormonal responses to exercise (acute physiological stress) include a curvilinear NE increase as workload increases, and increases in EPI at workloads over 60% VO_{2max} (Frankenhaeuser, 1991). Further, an HPA axis response to a physical challenge yields significant increases in cortisol at moderately high aerobic exercise intensity levels ($\geq$ 80% VO_{2max}) (Hill et al., 2008; Wittert et al., 1991) or longer durations (> 60 min) at moderate intensities (70% VO_{2max}) (Inder, Hellemans, Swanney, Prickett, & Donald, 1998).

The release of these stress hormones are similar, but different, in that while a psychological stress only needs to be considered in order to invoke a physiological response, a physical stress requires a higher intensity or longer duration to invoke the same hormonal responses. These differences suggest that different neurological pathways may be responsible for the varying patterns of release (Dayas, Buller, Crane, Xu, & Day, 2001; Dayas, Xu, Buller, & Day, 2000).

One other notable inclusion of the transactional psychobiological model (Acevedo & Ekkekakis, 2001) is the consideration of how a combination of both physical and psychological challenges may affect an individual's responses. Whereas the previous models addressed physiological responses to a psychological provocation, or psychological perceptions to a physical experience, the psychobiological model has provided an integrative model for looking at the combination of these challenges. While this may seem trivial to consider, many professions are subjected to a combination of physiological and psychological stressors as part of their occupational duties (emergency services, military personnel, athletes, etc.) and often people will utilize exercise as a psychological stress-reduction activity.

Exercise as an Anxiolytic

The use of exercise as a stress-reduction technique is touted by many in the medical and allied health professions. Exercise is believed to have an attenuating effect on an individual's stress reactivity level, and research has shown this to generally be true (Porges, 1995; Schuler & O'Brien, 1997; Sothmann et al., 1996), with individuals of higher fitness levels exhibiting a lesser heart rate response to psychological stress (Boutcher & Nugent, 1993; Claytor, 1991; Spalding, Jeffers, Porges, & Hatfield, 2000), as well as an attenuated EPI and NE response (Boutcher & Nugent, 1993). Parasympathetic tone has also been shown to increase after training, and this adaptation may assist in blunting heart rate and blood pressure increases (Dishman & Jackson, 2000; Porges, 1995).

Psychological states have been shown to influence cardiovascular and metabolic efficiency during exercise (Crews & Landers, 1987; Petruzzello, Landers, Hatfield, Kubitz, & Salazar, 1991). Exercise has also been associated with decreased anxiety, tension, depression, anger, fatigue, and confusion (Dishman & Jackson, 2000; Morgan & Goldston, 1987; Sachs & Buffone, 1997; Sacks & Sachs, 1981). Furthermore, exercise training has been shown to attenuate the stress response and facilitate coping with chronic stress (Petruzzello et al., 1991). Investigators have shown that psychological stress may be attenuated by a number of factors including physical activity (Acevedo, Dzewaltowski, Kubitz, & Kraemer, 1999; Chatzitheodorou, Kabitsis, Malliou, & Mougios, 2007; Crews & Landers, 1987; de Geus, van Doornen, de Visser, & Orlebeke, 1990; Schuler & O'Brien, 1997; Sloan et al., 2011; van Doornen & de Geus, 1989; van Doornen, de Geus, & Orlebeke, 1988). Additionally, exercise has been shown to have immediate psychological benefits compared to those of other traditional therapeutic modalities (Hamer, 2006; Hamer, Taylor, & Steptoe, 2006; Petruzzello et al., 1991). One possible explanation for these benefits is that exercise may act as a distracter, focusing an individual's attention away from the stressful situation (Bahrke & Morgan, 1978; Rejeski, Gregg, Thompson, & Berry, 1991). It is quite possible that these same benefits could also be accomplished through other techniques, such as quiet rest, meditation, and relaxation. However, it has been shown that exercise is a more effective anxiolytic agent than cognitive therapies (Hamer et al., 2006; Petruzzello et al., 1991).

Studies involving acute exercise have tended to focus on the psychological benefits while omitting the possible physiological mechanisms that underlie any potential psychobiological benefits. Furthermore, many studies focusing on the topic of psychological stress and acute exercise have often compared individuals of high fitness to those of low fitness, thereby directly or indirectly examining chronic exercise and its effect on stress reactivity.

Other factors, such as personality (Johansson & Frankenhaeuser, 1973), characteristics of the stressor (Marianne Frankenhaeuser & Gardell, 1976; Johansson & Aronsson, 1991), total load of the stressor (Aronsson & Rissler, 1998), and additional stressors, may inhibit the ability to relax (Frankenhaeuser et al., 1989) and may influence the rate of stress attenuation. While these factors may have an impact on attenuation of chronic stress, these same factors could also contribute to the attenuation of an acute stressor.

The use of exercise as a moderating factor for psychological stress is well founded. However, there have been suggestions that there may not always be a beneficial physiological response to exercise, as it has been shown that there can be exacerbated release of cortisol when psychological stress precedes low-intensity physical exercise (Webb et al., 2011), and higher intensities of exercise may actually be detrimental to effect (Acevedo, Kraemer, Haltom, & Tryniecki, 2003; Acevedo et al., 2007). Additionally, it has been shown that two similar bouts of exercise, separated by a rest period, will cause significant increases in epinephrine, norepinephrine, ACTH, and cortisol after the second bout of exercise compared to the first (Ronsen, Haug, Pedersen, & Bahr, 2001). These increases in stress hormones suggest that the SA and HPA axes seem to be prepared for activation after a stressful event, and this preparation can result in a greater response than the initial stressor alone, suggesting a priming effect. These investigations, however, have not addressed the possibility for a delayed effect on the enhanced clearance of the stress hormones, another possible mechanism for the anxiolytic benefits of physical activity.

It has been shown that post-exercise anxiety levels can be influenced by pre-exercise levels of anxiety (O'Connor, Petruzzello, Kubitz, & Robinson, 1995; Rejeski, Gauvin, Hobson, & Norris, 1995). It is possible that when a situation with resultant increases in state anxiety concludes, a rebound effect occurs that causes a reduction in anxiety as a result of the removal of the anxiety-increasing stimulus (mental stress). Studies specifically addressing this supposition have not been conducted. Previous investigations have examined the impact of intervention programs involving different types of exercise (Focht & Koltyn, 1999; Focht, Koltyn, & Bouchard, 2000; Oda, Matsumoto, Nakagawa, & Moriya, 1999), exercise intensity levels (Focht & Koltyn, 1999; Focht et al., 2000; Kennedy & Newton, 1997; Pronk, Crouse, & Rohack, 1995), and the effect of fitness level (Claytor, 1991; de Geus et al., 1990; Rimmele et al., 2009; Rimmele et al., 2007; Sothmann, Hart, & Horn, 1991) on anxiety, cardiovascular measures, and HPA axis hormones in reaction to psychological stressors. These intervention studies have consistently found reductions in levels of anxiety, and typically the reductions are greater among individuals in the treatment groups when compared to the control group (Claytor, 1991; Sothmann et al., 1991). Interestingly, these studies also provide evidence that reductions occur in the control group, although the explanations for these reductions are generally not discussed.

The effect of fitness on cardiovascular responses to psychological challenges has been an area of research controversy. Numerous studies have been conducted to assess the impact of aerobic fitness on physiological responses to psychosocial stress, and in an effort to consolidate the findings, three separate meta-analyses have been conducted. The initial review by Crews and Landers (1987) essentially found that regardless of the type of stressor, individuals who are more aerobically fit had an attenuated response as compared with less-fit individuals. Subsequent investigations have demonstrated conflicting results (Forcier et al., 2006; Crews and Landers (1987). More specifically, more-fit individuals had lower heart rate and blood pressure responses to psychological stress and also had a faster heart rate recovery following the stress. However, Jackson and Dishman (2006) reported in their analysis of the data that there was no support for higher fitness demonstrating reduced physiological responses to stress, although they did report that fitness revealed a small effect for faster recovery times. The differences in these three analyses have been discussed by Hamer and colleagues (2006), who suggest that various inconsistencies in the research design (methodology, sample size, and demographics) are the culprit for the lack of consistent results among studies.

One issue of contention with these analyses (Crews & Landers, 1987; Dishman & Jackson, 2000; Forcier et al., 2006) has been the fact that they are based primarily on cardiovascular responses (heart rate and blood pressure), and only a few studies included neuroendocrine factors, such as epinephrine and norepinephrine, in the analysis (Hamer et al., 2006; Seraganian, 1993). However, analyses of these hormones are problematic when you consider that the resting values of the catecholamines are not affected by fitness level. In addition, although the epinephrine and norepinephrine responses to maximal exercise are enhanced with aerobic training, this adaptation may not occur at lower intensities of activity (Buckworth & Dishman, 2002).

Combined Mental and Physical Stress

While many of the studies in the preceding section have investigated the physiological responses to various psychological stressors, they have not investigated the combined effects of psychological and physical stress. The interplay between the SA and HPA axis is thought to be central in the development of stress-related disorders and an essential component to understanding the mechanisms in psychobiological outcomes.

As was previously mentioned, the SA axis is activated in response to both physical activity and psychological stress. Stimuli such as psychological and physical stress induce the release of epinephrine and norepinephrine from the adrenal medulla and cardiac nerve terminals (Dimsdale & Moss, 1980). Previous literature has documented elevations in catecholamine levels in response to exercise (Greiwe, Hickner, Shah, Cryer, & Holloszy, 1999; Kjaer, 1998; Mazzeo, 1991) and psychological stress (Cacioppo et al., 2000; Gerra et al., 2001; Henry, 1992; Pollard, 1997), independently, in order to supply the body with the necessary oxygen and nutrients for an increased metabolic demand. Additionally, when cortisol is released in response to a stress, it stimulates metabolism and serves as an anti-inflammatory agent (Chrousos, 1998), which is beneficial as a part of the acute stress response. However, chronic increases in cortisol are also associated with adverse health consequences, including depression, suppression of the immune system, and elevation of pro-inflammatory proteins (Chrousos, 2009; Ho, Neo, Chua, Cheak, & Mak, 2010; Kyrou, Chrousos, & Tsigos, 2006).

Examination of multiple, simultaneous challenges have recently received attention. In recognition of the limits of laboratory investigations, applied field-based examinations have fostered appreciation for the mind-body interaction that occurs in the "real world." Early investigations into combined stress used regression equations to predict additional cardiovascular adjustments (Carroll, Turner, & Rogers, 1987; Delistraty, Greene, Carlberg, & Raver, 1991; 1992; Turner & Carroll, 1985; Turner, Carroll, Hanson, & Sims, 1988). The resulting findings from these studies suggested that additional heart rate increases ranging from 10 to 14 beats per minute may be the result of cardiovascular hyper-reactivity.

These predictive studies later led to investigations incorporating a mental challenge while participating in aerobic exercise (Acevedo et al., 2006; Roth, Bachtler, & Fillingim, 1990; Rousselle, Blascovich, & Kelsey, 1995; Szabo, Péronnet, Gauvin, & Furedy, 1994; Webb et al., 2010; Webb et al., 2013; Webb et al., 2008), and each of these studies demonstrated a clear increase in cardiovascular adjustment to the combination of stressors. Additionally, many of these studies demonstrated alterations in perceptions of anxiety, exertion, and workload (Acevedo et al., 2006; Roth et al., 1990; Rousselle et al., 1995; Szabo et al., 1994; Webb et al., 2011; Webb et al., 2010; Webb et al., 2013; Webb et al., 2008) in response to the combination of stressors.

The literature is sparse regarding the hormonal responses to the combination of psychological and physical stress, although current research suggests that there is an additive or exacerbated effect on the stress hormones in response to mental challenges when added to exercise stress (Huang, Webb, Evans, et al., 2010; Huang, Webb, Garten, Kamimori, & Acevedo, 2010; Huang, Webb, Garten, Kamimori, Evans, et al., 2010; Webb, Garten, et al., 2011; Webb et al., 2013; Webb et al., 2008). Again, these same studies showed alterations in anxiety and perceived workload in response to dual challenges. These exacerbated responses may be due to distinct neural pathways that are stimulated during activation from mental and physical stimuli or to the inability of the hypothalamus to appropriately respond to the increased signaling that occurs during the activation of multiple pathways. Interestingly, the primary area for reception and integration of signals projecting from neurosensory (cortical, limbic, visual, auditory, olfactory, gustatory, somatosensory, nociceptive, and visceral) regions, as well as signals produced or conveyed in the blood (hormones, cytokines, peptides) are located in the hypothalamus and brainstem and initiate the stress response through distinct pathways (Buller, Dayas, & Day, 2003; Buller, Xu, Dayas, & Day, 2001; Chrousos, 1998; 2009; Dayas, Buller, Crane, et al., 2001; Dayas, Buller, & Day, 1999; 2001; 2004). Future investigations may be able to identify distinct pathways for physical versus mental activation.

Individuals in such professions as law enforcement and fire suppression have been shown to have a greater morbidity and mortality rate than cohort populations. Firefighters and law enforcement officers have higher rates of all-cause mortality and also have greater mortality rates related to cardiovascular disease and cerebrovascular accidents than others matched for age and sex (Hessl, 2001; Kales, Soteriades, Christophi, & Christiani, 2007; Vena & Fiedler, 1987; Vena, Violanti, Marshall, & Fiedler, 1986; Violanti, Vena, & Marshall, 1996). These individuals are regularly subjected to a combination of mental and physical stress during their occupational routines. These occupations have inherent physical dangers, psychological stress, and physiological exertion (Beaton, Murphy, Johnson, Pike, & Corneil, 1998; 1999; Vena & Fiedler, 1987; Vena et al., 1986), and stress has been implicated as a possible cause for the elevated risk of arteriosclerotic heart disease (Ely & Mostardi, 1986; Eysenck, Grossarth-Maticek, & Everitt, 1991; Henry, 1986; Violanti, Vena, & Petralia, 1998).

Given the demands of many emergency responders and military personnel, as well as athletes and others who are exposed to both mental and physical demands while performing their work-related activities, it is critical that possible mitigating factors be examined. One study by Throne and colleagues (Throne, Bartholomew, Craig, & Farrar, 2000) demonstrated that firefighters who engaged in 16 weeks of rowing exercises reacted with a significantly lower pulse and mean arterial pressure to a fire department strategy and tactics drill than their counterparts in the control condition who continued their normal exercise routine. The intervention group also reported significantly less stress-related state anxiety and negative affect. Similar findings were also seen by Rimmele and colleagues when comparing elite endurance athletes, amateur endurance athletes, and untrained men in their responses to a stressor (Rimmele et al., 2009; Rimmele et al., 2007). These findings demonstrate that aerobic training does seem to have a moderating effect on the cardiovascular stress response.

Webb and colleagues (2013) compared the neuroendocrine responses of eight individuals who had above-average fitness levels with eight individuals who had below-average fitness levels to a dual-stress condition (mental and physical challenge combined) and an exercise-alone condition. The results of this study revealed exacerbations in cortisol levels in the dual-challenge condition compared to the exercise-alone condition, and these exacerbations were even greater among the below-average fitness level individuals, especially during the psychological stress portion of the dual-challenge protocol. This study demonstrated differences in cortisol responses to concurrent mental and physical challenge between aerobically high-fit and low-fit individuals, and it suggests that increased cardiorespiratory fitness levels may be a viable intervention strategy for the detrimental effects of combined stress.

Concluding Thoughts

Although mind-body interaction must be considered to gain greater understanding of the human experience including the stress response and associated health outcomes, both investigative efforts and application of these principles are in their infancy. Much of the research conducted has demonstrated that there is interplay between body and mind—that each can influence the other. This information has come from both psychology and physiology labs, and these labs have often used a stressor or combined stressors to examine relationships and infer explanations for these relationships.

While there have been many discoveries made in terms of how the body and mind interact to influence each other, there is still a wide range of questions left to be answered. Researchers are only now beginning to understand how the relationship between psychological and physiological factors can contribute to both psychopathologies and physiological illness and disease. It is through these investigations that we may be able to enhance human performance and determine effective interventions and strategies to help individuals reduce their risk of illness.

REFERENCES

Acevedo, E. O., Dzewaltowski, D. A., Gill, D. L., & Noble, J. M. (1992). Cognitive orientations of ultramarathoners. *The Sport Psychologist*, *6*(3), 242–252.

Acevedo, E. O., Dzewaltowski, D. A., Kubitz, K. A., & Kraemer, R. R. (1999). Effects of a proposed challenge on effort sense and cardiorespiratory responses during exercise. *Medicine and Science in Sports and Exercise*, *31*(10), 1460–1465.

Acevedo, E. O., & Ekkekakis, P. (2001). The transactional psychobiological nature of cognitive appraisal during exercise in environmentally stressful conditions. *Psychology of Sport and Exercise*, *2*(1), 47–67.

Acevedo, E. O., Kraemer, R. R., Haltom, R. W., & Tryniecki, J. L. (2003). Perceptual responses proximal to the onset of blood lactate accumulation. *Journal of Sports Medicine and Physical Fitness*, *43*(3), 267–273.

Acevedo, E. O., Kraemer, R. R., Kamimori, G. H., Durand, R. J., Johnson, L. G., & Castracane, V. D. (2007). Stress hormones, effort sense, and perceptions of stress during incremental exercise: An exploratory investigation. *Journal of Strength and Conditioning Research*, *21*(1), 283–288.

Acevedo, E. O., Webb, H. E., Weldy, M. L., Fabianke, E. C., Orndorff, G. R., & Starks, M. A. (2006). Cardiorespiratory responses of Hi Fit and Low Fit subjects to mental challenge during exercise. *International Journal of Sports Medicine*, *27*(12), 1013–1022.

Adang, E. M., Kootstra, G., Baeten, C. G., & Engel, G. L. (1997). Quality-of-life ratings in patients with chronic illnesses. *JAMA- Journal of the American Medical Association*, *277*(13), 1038.

Adler, R., MacRitchie, K., & Engel, G. L. (1971). Psychologic processes and ischemic stroke (occlusive cerebrovascular disease). I. Observations on 32 men with 35 strokes. *Psychosomatic Medicine*, *33*(1), 1–29.

Allen, M. T., Stoney, C. M., Owens, J. M., & Matthews, K. A. (1993). Hemodynamic adjustments to laboratory stress: The influence of gender and personality. *Psychosomatic Medicine*, *55*(6), 505–517.

Armitage, C. J., & Conner, M. (2000). Social cognition models and health behaviour: A structured review. *Psychology & Health*, *15*(2), 173–189.

Aronsson, G., & Rissler, A. (1998). Psychophysiological stress reactions in female and male urban bus drivers. *Journal of Occupational Health Psychology*, *3*(2), 122–129.

Bahrke, M. S., & Morgan, W. P. (1978). Anxiety reduction following exercise and meditation. *Cognitive Therapy and Research*, *2*(4), 323–333.

Beaton, R., Murphy, S., Johnson, C., Pike, K., & Corneil, W. (1998). Exposure to duty-related incident stressors in urban firefighters and paramedics. *Journal of Traumatic Stress*, *11*(4), 821–828.

Beaton, R., Murphy, S., Johnson, C., Pike, K., & Corneil, W. (1999). Coping responses and posttraumatic stress symptomatology in urban fire service personnel. *Journal of Traumatic Stress*, *12*(2), 293–308.

Bernard, C. (1974). *Lectures on the phenomena of life common to animals and plants*. Springfield, IL: Thomas.

Besedovsky, H. O., & Del Rey, A. (2000). The cytokine-HPA axis feed-back circuit. *Zeitschrift für Rheumatologie*, *59*(8), II26–II30

Birkett, M. A. (2011). The Trier Social Stress Test protocol for inducing psychological stress. *Journal of Visualised Experiments*, 56, e3238, doi: 10.3791/3238 (2011)

Boone, J. L. (1991). Stress and hypertension. *Primary Care*, *18*(3), 623–649.

Boutcher, S. H., & Nugent, F. W. (1993). Cardiac response of trained and untrained males to a repeated psychological stressor. *Behavioral Medicine*, *19*(1), 21–27.

Buckworth, J., & Dishman, R. K. (2002). *Exercise psychology*. Champaign, IL: Human Kinetics.

Buller, K. M., Dayas, C. V., & Day, T. A. (2003). Descending pathways from the paraventricular nucleus contribute to the recruitment of brainstem nuclei following a systemic immune challenge. *Neuroscience*, *118*(1), 189–203.

Buller, K. M., Xu, Y., Dayas, C., & Day, T. (2001). Dorsal and ventral medullary catecholamine cell groups contribute differentially to systemic interleukin-1beta-induced hypothalamic pituitary adrenal axis responses. *Neuroendocrinology*, *73*(2), 129–138.

Cacioppo, J. T., Burleson, M. H., Poehlmann, K. M., Malarkey, W. B., Kiecolt-Glaser, J. K., Berntson, G. G., Uchino, B. N., & Glaser, R. (2000). Autonomic and neuroendocrine responses to mild psychological stressors: Effects of chronic stress on older women. *Annals of Behavioral Medicine*, *22*(2), 140–148.

Cannon, W. B. (1914). The emergency function of the adrenal medulla in pain and the major emotions. *American Journal of Psychiatry, 33*(2), 356–372.

Cannon, W. B. (1929). Organization for physiological homeostasis. *Physiological Reviews, 9*(3), 399–431.

Cannon, W. B., & De La Paz, D. (1911). Emotional stimulation of adrenal secretion. *Journal of the American Medical Association, 28*(1), 64–70.

Carels, R. A., Darby, L. A., Rydin, S., Douglass, O. M., Cacciapaglia, H. M., & O'Brien, W. H. (2005). The relationship between self-monitoring, outcome expectancies, difficulties with eating and exercise, and physical activity and weight loss treatment outcomes. *Annals of Behavioral Medicine, 30*(3), 182–190.

Carels, R. A., Douglass, O. M., Cacciapaglia, H. M., & O'Brien, W. H. (2004). An ecological momentary assessment of relapse crises in dieting. *Journal of Consulting Clinical Psychology, 72*(2), 341–348.

Carroll, D., Turner, J. R., & Rogers, S. (1987). Heart rate and oxygen consumption during mental arithmetic, a video game, and graded static exercise. *Psychophysiology, 24*(1), 112–118.

Chatzitheodorou, D., Kabitsis, C., Malliou, P., & Mougios, V. (2007). A pilot study of the effects of high-intensity aerobic exercise versus passive interventions on pain, disability, psychological strain, and serum cortisol concentrations in people with chronic low back pain. *Physiological Therapy, 87*(3), 304–312.

Chrousos, G. P. (1998). Stressors, stress, and neuroendocrine integration of the adaptive response. The 1997 Hans Selye Memorial Lecture. *Annals of the New York Academy of Sciences, 851,* 311–335.

Chrousos, G. P. (2009). Stress and disorders of the stress system. *Endocrinology, 5*(7), 374–381.

Chrousos, G. P., & Gold, P. W. (1992). The concepts of stress and stress system disorders. Overview of physical and behavioral homeostasis. *Journal of the American Medical Association, 267*(9), 1244–1252.

Claytor, R. P. (1991). Stress reactivity: Hemodynamic adjustments in trained and untrained humans. *Medicine and Science in Sports and Exercise, 23*(7), 873–881.

Cooper, C. L. (1983). *Stress research: Issues for the eighties.* Chichester, UK: New York, Wiley.

Crews, D. J., & Landers, D. M. (1987). A meta-analytic review of aerobic fitness and reactivity to psychosocial stressors. *Medicine and Science in Sports and Exercise, 19*(5 Suppl), S114–120.

Dayas, C. V., Buller, K. M., Crane, J. W., Xu, Y., & Day, T. A. (2001). Stressor categorization: Acute physical and psychological stressors elicit distinctive recruitment patterns in the amygdala and in medullary noradrenergic cell groups. *European Journal of Neuroscience, 14*(7), 1143–1152.

Dayas, C. V., Buller, K. M., & Day, T. A. (1999). Neuroendocrine responses to an emotional stressor: Evidence for involvement of the medial but not the central amygdala. *European Journal of Neuroscience, 11*(7), 2312–2322.

Dayas, C. V., Buller, K. M., & Day, T. A. (2001). Medullary neurones regulate hypothalamic corticotropin-releasing factor cell responses to an emotional stressor. *Neuroscience, 105*(3), 707–719.

Dayas, C. V., Buller, K. M., & Day, T. A. (2004). Hypothalamic paraventricular nucleus neurons regulate medullary catecholamine cell responses to restraint stress. *Journal of Comparative Neurology, 478*(1), 22–34.

Dayas, C. V., Xu, Y., Buller, K. M., & Day, T. A. (2000). Effects of chronic oestrogen replacement on stress-induced activation of hypothalamic-pituitary-adrenal axis control pathways. *Journal of Neuroendocrinology, 12*(8), 784–794.

de Geus, E. J., van Doornen, L. J., de Visser, D. C., & Orlebeke, J. F. (1990) Existing and training induced differences in aerobic fitness: Their relationship to physiological response patterns during different types of stress. *Psychophysiology, 27*(4), 457–478.

Delistraty, D. A., Greene, W. A., Carlberg, K. A., & Raver, K. K. (1991). Use of graded exercise to evaluate physiological hyperreactivity to mental stress. *Medicine and Science in Sports and Exercise, 23*(4), 476–481.

Delistraty, D. A., Greene, W. A., Carlberg, K. A., & Raver, K. K. (1992). Cardiovascular reactivity in Type A and B males to mental arithmetic and aerobic exercise at an equivalent oxygen uptake. *Psychophysiology, 29*(3), 264–271.

Dienstbier, R. A. (1989). Arousal and physiological toughness: Implications for mental and physical health. *Psychological Review, 96*(1), 84–100.

Dienstbier, R. A. (1991). Behavioral correlates of sympathoadrenal reactivity: The toughness model. *Medicine and Science in Sports and Exercise, 23*(7), 846–852.

Dimsdale, J. E., & Moss, J. (1980). Short-term catecholamine response to psychological stress. *Psychosomatic Medicine, 42*(5), 493–497.

Dishman, R. K., & Jackson, E. M. (2000). Exercise, fitness, and stress. *International Journal of Sport Psychology, 31*(2), 175–203.

Drinkwater, B. L., Cleland, T., & Flint, M. M. (1968). Pilot performance during periods of anticipatory physical threat stress. *Aerospace Medicine, 39*(9), 9949–99

Ely, D. L., & Mostardi, R. A. (1986). The effect of recent life events stress, life assets, and temperament pattern on cardiovascular risk factors for Akron City police officers. *Journal of Human Stress, 12*(2), 77–91.

Engel, G. L. (1952). Psychologic aspects of the management of patients with ulcerative colitis. *New York State Journal of Medicine, 52*(18), 2255–2261.

Engel, G. L. (1960). A unified concept of health and disease. *Perspectives in Biological Medicine, 3,* 459–485.

Engel, G. L. (1961). Biologic and psychologic features of the ulcerative colitis patient. *Gastroenterology, 40,* 313–322.

Engel, G. L. (1976). Editorial: Psychologic factors in instantaneous cardiac death. *New England Journal of Medicine, 294*(12), 664–665.

Engel, G. L. (1977). The need for a new medical model: A challenge for biomedicine. *Science, 196*(4286), 129–136.

Engel, G. L. (1978). Psychologic stress, vasodepressor (vasovagal) syncope, and sudden death. *Annals of International Medicine, 89*(3), 403–412.

Engel, G. L. (1982). Sounding board: The biopsychosocial model and medical education. Who are to be the teachers? *New England Journal of Medicine, 306*(13), 802–805.

Engel, G. L. (1983). The biopsychosocial model and family medicine. *Journal of Family Practice, 16*(2), 409, 412–413.

Engel, G. L. (2012). The need for a new medical model: A challenge for biomedicine. *Psychodynamic Psychiatry, 40*(3), 377–396.

Engel, G. L., Frader, M., Barry, C., & Morrow, G. (1984). Sadness evoked by a film on grief: An experimental study. *International Journal of Psychiatry Medicine, 14*(1), 1–30.

Erickson, K., Drevets, W., & Schulkin, J. (2003). Glucocorticoid regulation of diverse cognitive functions in normal and pathological emotional states. *Neuroscience Biobehavioral Review, 27*(3), 233–246.

Ersland, S., Weisæth, L., & Sund, A. (1989). The stress upon rescuers involved in an oil rig disaster. "Alexander L. Kielland" 1980. *Acta Psychiatrica Scandinavica, 80*(s355), 384–389.

Eysenck, H. J., Grossarth-Maticek, R., & Everitt, B. (1991). Personality, stress, smoking, and genetic predisposition as synergistic risk factors for cancer and coronary heart disease. *Integrated Physiological Behavioral Science, 26*(4), 309–322.

Fenz, W. D., & Epstein, S. (1967). Gradients of physiological arousal in parachutists as a function of an approaching jump. *Psychosomatic Medicine, 29*(1), 33–51.

Focht, B. C., & Koltyn, K. F. (1999). Influence of resistance exercise of different intensities on state anxiety and blood pressure. *Medicine and Science in Sports and Exercise, 31*(3), 456–463.

Focht, B. C., Koltyn, K. F., & Bouchard, L. J. (2000). State anxiety and blood pressure responses following different resistance exercise sessions. *International Journal of Sport Psychology, 31*(3), 376–390.

Forcier, K., Stroud, L. R., Papandonatos, G. D., Hitsman, B., Reiches, M., Krishnamoorthy, J., & Niaura, R. (2006). Links between physical fitness and cardiovascular reactivity and recovery to psychological stressors: A meta-analysis. *Health Psychology, 25*(6), 723–739.

Frankenhaeuser, M. (1991). The psychophysiology of workload, stress, and health: Comparison between the sexes. *Annals of Behavioral Medicine, 13*(4), 197–204.

Frankenhaeuser, M., & Gardell, B. (1976). Underload and overload in working life: Outline of a multi-disciplinary approach. *Journal of Human Stress, 2*(3), 35–46.

Frankenhaeuser, M., Lundberg, U., Fredrikson, M., Melin, B., Tuomisto, M., Myrsten, A. L., Hedman, M., Bergman-Losman, B., & Wallin, L. (1989). Stress on and off the job as related to sex and occupational status in white-collar workers. *Journal of Organizational Behavior, 10*(4), 321–346.

Garcia, K., & Mann, T. (2003). From "I Wish" to "I Will": Social-cognitive predictors of behavioral intentions. *Journal of Health and Psychology, 8*(3), 347–360.

Gerra, G., Zaimovic, A., Mascetti, G. G., Gardini, S., Zambelli, U., Timpano, M., Raggi, M. A., & Brambilla, F. (2001). Neuroendocrine responses to experimentally-induced psychological stress in healthy humans. *Psychoneuroendocrinology, 26*(1), 91–107.

Goldberger, L., & Breznitz, S. (1982). *Handbook of stress: Theoretical and clinical aspects.* New York, NY: Collier Macmillan.

Greiwe, J. S., Hickner, R. C., Shah, S. D., Cryer. P. E., & Holloszy, J. O. (1999). Norepinephrine response to exercise at the same relative intensity before and after endurance exercise training. *Journal of Applied Physiology, 86*(2), 531–535.

Hamer, M. (2006). Exercise and psychobiological processes: Implications for the primary prevention of coronary heart disease. *Sports Medicine, 36*(10), 829–838.

Hamer, M., Taylor, A., & Steptoe, A. (2006). The effect of acute aerobic exercise on stress related blood pressure responses: A systematic review and meta-analysis. *Biological Psychology, 71*(2), 183–190.

Hellhammer, J., & Schubert, M. (2012). The physiological response to Trier Social Stress Test relates to subjective measures of stress during but not before or after the test. *Psychoneuroendocrinology, 37*(1), 119–124.

Henry, J. (1986). Mechanisms by which stress can lead to coronary heart disease. *Postgraduate Medical Journal, 62*(729), 687–693.

Henry, J. P. (1992). Biological basis of the stress response. *Integrated Physiological Behavior Science, 27*(1), 66–83.

Henry, J. P., & Grim, C. E. (1990). Psychosocial mechanisms of primary hypertension. *Journal of Hypertension, 8*(9): 783–793.

Hessl, S. (2001). Police and corrections. *Occupational Medicine, 16*(1), 39–49.

Highlen, P. S., & Bennett, B. B. (1979). Psychological characteristics of successful and nonsuccessful elite wrestlers: An exploratory study. *Journal of Sport Psychology, 1*(2), 1231–37

Hill, E. E., Zack, E., Battaglini, C., Viru, M., Viru, A., & Hackney, A. C. (2008). Exercise and circulating cortisol levels: The intensity threshold effect. *Journal of Endocrinol Investment, 31*(7), 587–591.

Ho, R. C., Neo, L. F., Chua, A. N., Cheak, A. A., & Mak, A. (2010). Research on psychoneuroimmunology: Does stress influence immunity and cause coronary artery disease? *Annals of Acadademic Medicine Singapore, 39*(3), 191–196.

Huang, C. J., Webb, H. E., Evans, R. K., McCleod, K. A., Tangsilsat, S. E., Kamimori, G. H., & Acevedo, E. O. (2010). Psychological stress during exercise: Immunoendocrine and oxidative responses. *Experimental Biology and Medicine, 235*(12), 1498–1504.

Huang, C. J., Webb, H. E., Garten, R. S., Kamimori, G. H., & Acevedo, E. O. (2010). Psychological stress during exercise: Lymphocyte subset redistribution in firefighters. *Physiology and Behavior, 101*(3), 320–326.

Huang, C. J., Webb, H. E., Garten, R. S., Kamimori, G. H., Evans, R. K., & Acevedo, E. O. (2010). Stress hormones and immunological responses to a dual challenge in professional firefighters. *International Journal of Psychophysiology, 75*(3), 312–318.

Inder, W. J., Hellemans, J., Swanney, M. P., Prickett, T. C., & Donald, R. A. (1998). Prolonged exercise increases peripheral plasma ACTH, CRH, and AVP in male athletes. *Journal of Applied Physiology, 85*(3), 835–841.

Jackson, E. M., & Dishman, R. K. (2006). Cardiorespiratory fitness and laboratory stress: A metaregression analysis. *Psychophysiology, 43*(1), 57–72.

James, W. (1890). *The principles of psychology.* New York, NY: H. Holt and Company.

Johansson, G., & Aronsson, G. (1991). Psychosocial factors in the workplace. In G. M. Green & F. Baker (Eds.), *Work, health, and productivity* (pp. 179–197). New York, NY: Oxford University Press.

Johansson, G., & Frankenhaeuser, M. (1973). Temporal factors in sympatho-adrenomedullary activity following acute behavioral activation. *Biological Psychology, 1*(1), 63–73.

Kales, S. N., Soteriades, E. S., Christophi, C. A., & Christiani, D. C. (2007). Emergency duties and deaths from heart disease among firefighters in the United States. *New England Journal of Medicine, 356*(12), 1207–1215.

Kennedy, M. M., & Newton, M. (1997). Effect of exercise intensity on mood in step aerobics. *Journal of Sports Medicine and Physical Fitness, 37*(3), 200–204.

Kirschbaum, C., Pirke, K. M., & Hellhammer, D. H. (1993). The 'Trier Social Stress Test'—a tool for investigating psychobiological stress responses in a laboratory setting. *Neuropsychobiology, 28*(1–2), 76–81.

Kjaer, M. (1998). Adrenal medulla and exercise training. *European Journal of Applied Physiology and Occupational Physiology, 77*(3), 195–199.

Kyrou, I., Chrousos, G. P., & Tsigos, C. (2006). Stress, visceral obesity, and metabolic complications. *Annals of the New York Academy of Sciences, 1083*, 77–110.

Lazarus, R. S. (1966). *Psychological stress and the coping process.* Mishawaka, IN: Better World Book.

Mahoney, M. J., & Avener, M. (1977). Psychology of the elite athlete: An exploratory study. *Cognitive Therapy and Research, 1*(2), 135–141.

Mason, J. W. (1971). A re-evaluation of the concept of 'non-specificity' in stress theory. *Journal of Psychiatric Research, 8*(3–4), 323–333.

Mason, J. W. (1975). A historical view of the stress field. *Journal of Human Stress 1*(1), 6–12.

Mazzeo, R. S. (1991). Catecholamine responses to acute and chronic exercise. *Medicine and Science in Sports and Exercise, 23*(7), 839–845.

McAdoo, W. G., Weinberger, M. H., Miller, J. Z., Fineberg, N. S., & Grim, C. E. (1990). Race and gender influence hemodynamic responses to psychological and physical stimuli. *Journal of Hypertension, 8*(10), 961–967.

Mefferd Jr., R. B., Hale, H. B., Shannon, I. L., Prigmore, J. R., & Ellis Jr., J. P. (1971). Stress responses as criteria for personnel selection: baseline study. *Aerospace Medicine, 42*(1), 42.

Melis, C., & van Boxtel, A. (2001). Differences in autonomic physiological responses between good and poor inductive reasoners. *Biological Psychology, 58*(2), 121–146.

Moran, C. C. (1998). Stress and emergency work experience: A non-linear relationship. *Disaster Prevention and Management, 7*, 38–46.

Morgan, W. P., & Goldston, S. E. (1987). *Exercise and mental health.* Washington, DC: Hemisphere Publishing Corporation.

Morgan, W. P., & Pollock, M. L. (1977). Psychologic characterization of the elite distance runner. *Annals of the New York Academy of Science, 301*, 382–403.

Norris, F. H., & Murrell, S. A. (1988). Prior experience as a moderator of disaster impact on anxiety symptoms in older adults. *American Journal of Community Psychology, 16*(5), 665–683.

O'Connor, P. J., Petruzzello, S. J., Kubitz, K. A., & Robinson, T. L. (1995). Anxiety responses to maximal exercise testing. *British Journal of Sports Medicine, 29*(2), 97–102.

Oda, S., Matsumoto, T., Nakagawa, K., & Moriya, K. (1999). Relaxation effects in humans of underwater exercise of moderate intensity. *European Journal of Applied Physiology and Occupational Physiology, 80*(4), 253–259.

Petruzzello, S. J., Landers, D. M., Hatfield, B. D., Kubitz, K. A., & Salazar, W. (1991). A meta-analysis on the anxiety-reducing effects of acute and chronic exercise. Outcomes and mechanisms. *Sports Medicine, 11*(3), 143–182.

Pollard, T. M. (1997). Physiological consequences of everyday psychosocial stress. *Collegium Antropologicum, 21*(1), 17–28.

Porges, S. W. (1995). Cardiac vagal tone: A physiological index of stress. *Neuroscience and Biobehavior Review, 19*(2), 225–233.

Pronk, N. P., Crouse, S. F., & Rohack, J. J. (1995). Maximal exercise and acute mood response in women. *Physiology & Behavior, 57*(1), 1–4.

Rejeski, W. J., Gauvin, L., Hobson, M. L., & Norris, J. L. (1995). Effects of baseline responses, in-task feelings, and duration of activity on exercise-induced feeling states in women. *Health and Psychology, 14*(4), 350–359.

Rejeski, W. J., Gregg, E., Thompson, A., & Berry, M. (1991). The effects of varying doses of acute aerobic exercise on psychophysiological stress responses in highly trained cyclists. *Journal of Sport & Exercise Psychology, 13*(2), 188–199.

Rimmele, U., Seiler, R., Marti, B., Wirtz, P. H., Ehlert, U., & Heinrichs, M. (2009). The level of physical activity affects adrenal and cardiovascular reactivity to psychosocial stress. *Psychoneuroendocrinology, 34*(2), 190–198.

Rimmele, U., Zellweger, B. C., Marti, B., Seiler, R., Mohiyeddini, C., Ehlert, U., & Heinrichs, M. (2007). Trained men show lower cortisol, heart rate and psychological responses to psychosocial stress compared with untrained men. *Psychoneuroendocrinology, 32*(6), 627–635.

Ronsen, O., Haug, E., Pedersen, B. K., & Bahr, R. (2001). Increased neuroendocrine response to a repeated bout of endurance exercise. *Medicine and Science in Sports and Exercise, 33*(4), 568–575.

Roth, D. L., Bachtler, S. D., & Fillingim, R. B. (1990). Acute Emotional and cardiovascular effects of stressful mental work during aerobic exercise. *Psychophysiology, 27*(6), 694–701.

Rousselle, J. G., Blascovich, J., & Kelsey, R. M. (1995). Cardiorespiratory response under combined psychological and exercise stress. *International Journal of Psychophysiology, 20*(1), 49–58.

Sachs, M. L., & Buffone, G. W. (1997). *Running as therapy: An integrated approach.* Northvale, NJ: Jason Aronson.

Sacks, M. H., & Sachs, M. L. (1981). *Psychology of running.* Champaign, IL: Human Kinetics Publishers.

Schoder, H., Silverman, D. H., Campisi, R., Karpman, H., Phelps, M. E., Schelbert, H. R., & Czernin, J. (2000). Effect of mental stress on myocardial blood flow and vasomotion in patients with coronary artery disease. *Journal of Nuclear Medicine, 41*(1), 11–16.

Schuler, J. L., & O'Brien, W. H. (1997). Cardiovascular recovery from stress and hypertension risk factors: A meta-analytic review. *Psychophysiology, 34*(6), 649–659.

Schwarzer, R. (1992). *Self-efficacy: Thought control of action.* Washington, DC: Hemisphere Pubishing Corporation.

Selye, H. (1936). A syndrome produced by diverse nocuous agents. *Nature, 138*(3479), 32.

Selye, H. (1950). Stress and the general adaptation syndrome. *British Medical Journal, 1*(4467), 1383–1392.

Selye, H. (1974). *Stress without distress.* Philadelphia, PA: Lippincott.

Selye, H. (1976). *Stress in health and disease.* Boston, MA: Butterworths.

Selye, H. (1978). *The stress of life.* New York, NY: McGraw-Hill.

Selye, H. (1980). *Selye's guide to stress research.* New York, NY: Van Nostrand Reinhold.

Seraganian, P. (1993). *Exercise psychology: The influence of physical exercise on psychological processes.* New York, NY: J. Wiley.

Sloan, R. P., Shapiro, P. A., DeMeersman, R. E., Bagiella, E., Brondolo, E. N., McKinley, P. S., Crowley, O., Zhao, Y., Schwartz, J. E., & Myers, M. M. (2011). Impact of aerobic training on cardiovascular reactivity to and recovery from challenge. *Psychosomatic Medicine, 73*(2), 134–141.

Sothmann, M. S., Buckworth, J., Claytor, R. P., Cox, R. H., White-Welkley, J. E., & Dishman, R. K. (1996). Exercise training and the cross-stressor adaptation hypothesis. *Exercise in Sport Scientific Review, 24*, 267–287.

Sothmann, M. S., Hart, B. A., & Horn, T. S. (1991). Plasma catecholamine response to acute psychological stress in humans: Relation to aerobic fitness and exercise training. *Medicine and Science in Sports and Exercise, 23*(7), 860–867.

Spalding, T. W., Jeffers, L. S., Porges, S. W., & Hatfield, B. D. (2000). Vagal and cardiac reactivity to psychological stressors in trained and untrained men. *Medicine and Science in Sports and Exercise, 32*(3), 581–591.

Sterling, P. (2012). Allostasis: A model of predictive regulation. *Physiology & Behavior, 106*(1), 5–15.

Stroop, J. R. (1935). Studies of interference in serial verbal reactions. *Journal of Experimental Psychology, 18(6)*, 643.

Szabo, A., Péronnet, F., Gauvin, L., & Furedy, J. J. (1994). Mental challenge elicits "additional" increases in heart rate during low and moderate intensity cycling. *International Journal of Psychophysiology, 17*(3), 197–204.

Throne, L., Bartholomew, J., Craig, J., & Farrar, R. (2000). Stress Reactivity in fire fighters: An exercise intervention. *International Journal of Stress Management, 7*(4), 235–246.

Turner, J. R., & Carroll, D. (1985). Heart rate and oxygen consumption during mental arithmetic, a video game, and graded exercise: Further evidence of metabolically-exaggerated cardiac adjustments? *Psychophysiology, 22*(3), 261–267.

Turner, J. R., Carroll, D., Hanson, J., & Sims, J. (1988). A comparison of additional heart rates during active psychological challenge calculated from upper body and lower body dynamic exercise. *Psychophysiology, 25*(2), 209–216.

van Doornen, L. J., & de Geus, E. J. (1989). Aerobic fitness and the cardiovascular response to stress. *Psychophysiology, 26*(1), 17–28.

van Doornen, L. J., de Geus, E. J., & Orlebeke, J. F. (1988). Aerobic fitness and the physiological stress response: A critical evaluation. *Social Science and Medicine, 26*(3), 303–307.

Vena, J. E., & Fiedler, R. C. (1987). Mortality of a municipal-worker cohort: IV. Fire fighters. *American Journal of Industrial Medicine, 11*, 671–684.

Vena, J. E., Violanti, J. M., Marshall, J., & Fiedler, R. C. (1986). Mortality of a municipal worker cohort: III. Police officers. *American Journal of Industrial Medicine, 10*(4), 383–397.

Violanti, J., Vena, J., & Marshall, J. (1996). Suicides, homicides, and accidental death: A comparative risk assessment of police officers and municipal workers. *American Journal of Industrial Medicine, 30*(1), 99–104.

Violanti, J., Vena, J., & Petralia, S. (1998). Mortality of a police cohort: 1950–1990. *American Journal of Industrial Medicine, 33*(4), 366–373.

Webb, H. E., Fabianke-Kadue, E. C., Kraemer, R. R., Kamimori, G. H., Castracane, V. D., & Acevedo, E. O. (2011). Stress reactivity to repeated low-level challenges: A pilot study. *Applied Psychophysiology and Biofeedback, 36*(4), 243–250.

Webb, H. E., McMinn, D. R., Garten, R. S., Beckman, J. L., Kamimori, G. H., & Acevedo, E. O. (2010). Cardiorespiratory responses of firefighters to a computerized fire strategies and tactics drill during physical activity. *Applied Ergonomics, 41*(3), 376–381.

Webb, H. E., Rosalky, D. S., Tangsilsat, S. E., McLeod, K. A., Acevedo, E. O., & Wax, B. (2013). Aerobic fitness affects cortisol responses to concurrent challenges. *Medicine and Science in Sports and Exercise, 45*(2), 379–386.

Webb, H. E., Weldy, M. L., Fabianke-Kadue, E. C., Orndorff, G. R., Kamimori, G. H., & Acevedo, E. O. (2008). Psychological stress during exercise: Cardiorespiratory and hormonal responses. *European Journal of Applied Physiology, 104*(6), 973–981.

Wittert, G., De, S., Graves, S., Ellis, M., Evans, M., Wells, J., Donald, R., & Espiner, E. (1991). Plasma corticotrophin releasing factor and vasopressin responses to exercise in normal man. *Clinical Endocrinology, 35*(4), 311–317.

5 Theories and Models of Behavior Change Applied to Exercise

Research and Practice

Robert Weinberg

Despite the fact that there appears to be an increase in the importance of fitness and physical activity in our society, most Americans do not regularly participate in physical activity (Centers for Disease Control and Prevention, 2010). This is underscored by some telling statistics on the rise in obesity rates. Specifically, in 2013, two-thirds of all U.S. adults were overweight and one-third was obese. In 1990, no state had an obesity rate of greater than 19%, but by 2010, no state had an obesity rate of less than 20% (Centers for Disease Control and Prevention, 2010). Of course, obesity is not just the result of sedentary living, but statistics do show our decrease in physical activity levels. For example, approximately 50% of adults did not engage in a minimum of 20 minutes of vigorous physical activity for at least three days per week (little change from 2000) or moderate physical activity for at least 30 minutes at least five days per week (Centers for Disease Control and Prevention, 2011)

EXERCISE ADHERENCE

Many sedentary people do not exercise at all. But once sedentary people have overcome inertia and started exercising, the next barrier they face has to do with continuing their exercising program. Evidently many people find it easier to start an exercise program than to stick with it, as about 50% of participants drop out of exercise programs within the first six months. (Buckworth & Dishman, 2007). Certainly, most people intend to change a habit (not exercising) that negatively affects their health and well-being. In fact, fitness clubs traditionally have their highest new enrollments in January and February, when sedentary individuals feel charged by New Year's resolutions to turn over a new leaf and get in shape. So, why is it that some people never even start an exercise program? For people who start an exercise program, why do they fail to stick with it, whereas others continue to make it part of their lifestyle? To answer these questions, the current chapter will review the theories and models of exercise behavior and then demonstrate how these models can help inform our practice to enhance the initiation and maintenance of exercise.

THEORIES AND MODELS OF EXERCISE BEHAVIOR

One way to understand the reasons for adopting and eventually maintaining an exercise program is through the development of theoretical models (Culos-Reed, Gyurcsik, & Brawley, 2001). Of course no one model can explain all types of exercise behavior, and probably some combination of variables across models would be most efficient in predicting physical activity. However, reviewing the different models and theories will help us better understand how to intervene to increase exercise initiation and adherence.

Health Belief Model

The health belief model (HBM) is one of the most widely recognized enduring theoretical models associated with preventive health behaviors (Berger, Pargman, & Weinberg, 2007). The model states that the likelihood of an individual's engaging in preventive health behaviors (such as exercise) depends on the person's perception of the severity of the potential illness as well as his appraisal of the costs and benefits of taking action (Becker & Maiman, 1975). An individual who believes that the potential illness is serious, that she is at risk, and that the pros of taking action outweigh the cons is likely to adopt the target health behavior. Although there has been some success in using the health belief model to predict exercise behavior, the results have been inconsistent because the model was originally developed to focus on disease, not exercise. However, the HBM has provided the field with some important variables (variables used in other models), and by testing this theory, researchers and practitioners have learned a great deal about exercise behavior.

Theory of Planned Behavior

The theory of planned behavior (TPB; Ajzen & Madden, 1986) is an extension of the theory of reasoned action (TRA; Ajzen & Fishbein, 1980). The theory of reasoned action states that intentions are the best predictors of actual behavior. Specifically, intentions are the product of an individual's attitude toward a particular behavior and what is normative regarding the behavior (subjective norm). This subjective norm is the product of beliefs about others' opinions and the individual's motivation to comply with others' opinions. For example, if the individual is a non-exerciser and believes that other significant people in their life (e.g., spouse, children, friends) think they should exercise, they are more likely to actually exercise.

The theory of planned behavior extends the theory of reasoned action by arguing that intentions alone are not the only predictors of behavior, especially in situations in which people might lack some control over the behavior or there is a long time interval between intention and behavior. In addition to the notions of subjective norms and attitudes, TPB states that perceived behavioral control—that is, people's perceptions of their *ability* to perform the behavior—will also affect behavioral outcomes. The effectiveness of the different constructs within TPB to predict exercise behavior was supported in a meta-analysis review (Hagger, Chatzisarantis, & Biddle, 2002).

It is important to understand that behavioral intentions to increase exercise behavior have been distinguished from intentions to maintain exercise (Milne, Rodgers, Hall, & Wilson, 2008). Thus, when developing exercise interventions, the notion that exercise might unfold in phases (see transtheoretical model later in this chapter) needs to be considered. For example, in a study using TPB, e-mail messages were more effective in increasing both intentions to exercise and actual exercise behavior compared to a control condition (Parrott, Tennant, Olejnik, & Poudevigne, 2008). Finally, Dimmock and Banting (2009) argue that intentions alone, as the theory predicts, do not necessarily influence behavior; rather, the quality and strength of intentions are important.

The prominence of perceived behavioral control is also seen in a study directly testing TPB and TRA. Results revealed that TPB predicted exercise behavior significantly better than TRA, with the main difference attributed to perceived behavioral control (Hunt & Gross, 2009). Furthermore, studies focused on predicting exercise behaviors and adherence have revealed that an individual may need to meet a certain threshold regarding perceived behavioral control and subjective norms (Rhodes & Courneya, 2005).

From a practical point of view, practitioners need to help their clients by encouraging the clients' significant others to promote exercise (or, even better, exercise themselves) as this should enhance the clients' attitudes about exercise and then their intention to actually exercise. To help potential exercisers move from the intention to the actual exercise phase, researchers recommend "implementation intentions," which are specific goals that are easily followed. This helps ensure that the individual's intentions are converted into actions.

Social Cognitive Theory

Social cognitive theory (SCT; Bandura, 1977, 1986, 1997, 2005) originated with Bandura's early work on social learning theory, which he developed as a clinical psychologist. Specifically, SCT proposes that personal, behavioral, and environmental factors operate as reciprocally interacting determinants of each other. In essence, not only does the environment affect behaviors, but behaviors also affect the environment. All three factors together influence how we think, act, and feel. Such personal factors as cognitions or thoughts, emotions, and physiology are also important. Despite this interaction among different factors, probably the most critical piece to this approach is an individual's belief that he can successfully perform a behavior (self-efficacy).

Self-efficacy refers to efficacy beliefs and expectations, or, in simple terms, the "Can I?" question. Self-efficacy is very influential in many behaviors, especially those that challenge us, such as being more physically active or maintaining an exercise program for many years. If someone believes she can adopt and maintain the behavior in question, she is more likely to do so. Self-efficacy has been shown to be a good predictor of behavior in a variety of health situations, such as smoking cessation, weight management, and recovery from heart attacks (Bandura, 2005). In relation to exercise, self-efficacy theory has produced some of the most consistent findings, revealing an increase in exercise participation as self-efficacy increases (e.g., Buckworth & Dishman, 2007; Maddison & Prapavessis, 2004), as well as increases in self-efficacy as exercise participation increases (McAuley & Blissmer, 2002).

This important role of self-efficacy is especially evident when exercise is most challenging, such as in the initial stages of adoption or for persons with chronic diseases. For example, self-efficacy theory has predicted exercise behavior for individuals with Type 1 and Type 2 diabetes, as well as for those with cardiovascular disease (Luszczynska & Trybury, 2008; Plotnikoff et al., 2008). In addition, when individuals relapse in their exercise behavior, the best predictor of whether they will resume exercise was recovery self-efficacy (Luszczynska et al., 2007). In summary, research has consistently supported social cognitive theory and the role that self-efficacy plays in enhancing exercise behavior (Biddle et al., 2007).

Since social cognitive theory argues for reciprocal determinism, not only would self-efficacy predict behavior (in this case, exercise), but exercise would influence feelings of self-efficacy. More specifically, exercise can act as a source or catalyst for feelings of efficacy, in both chronic (fitness class program) and acute (graded exercise tests) forms. Support for these ideas have included a variety of exercise behaviors, such as walking, strength training, volleyball, aerobic dance, and exercise as part of a cardiac rehabilitation program (see Bandura, 1997; 2005)

Therefore, practitioners should try to implement programs in which changes in self-efficacy are a central component to changes in exercise behavior. For example, an intervention targeting increasing self-efficacy levels was attempted in a high-school physical education program over a 10-week period. Results indicated a strong relationship between participation in the program and enhanced self-efficacy levels, especially for females (Lubans & Sylva, 2009). Along these lines, Ashford, Edmunds, and French (2010) conducted a meta-analysis to determine the most effective intervention strategies for enhancing self-efficacy toward physical activity. They found 27 unique strategies to enhance self-efficacy. Those that included providing feedback based on prior performance as well as vicarious experiences (modeling) proved to be the most effective in generating changes in self-efficacy toward physical activity.

In summary, research has shown practitioners that there are several excellent ways to enhance self-efficacy toward physical activity; this in turn helps to facilitate actual increases in physical activity levels.

Self-Determination Theory

Although not a new theory, self-determination theory (SDT; Deci & Ryan, 1985) is a relative newcomer to the exercise psychology literature. However, studies using SDT have quickly generated an impressive literature in helping to explain exercise behavior. Self-determination theory focuses on three basic psychological needs: competence, relatedness, and autonomy. In addition, SDT also focuses on self-determined behavior on a continuum from external to internal motivation. More specifically, autonomous regulations are representative of self-determined behavior, which makes the behavior intrinsically motivating, while those behaviors that are not self-determined are controlled by some type of external rewards or pressures.

Regarding the three different psychological needs, Deci and Ryan (1994) argued that "people are inherently motivated to feel connected to others within a social milieu (relatedness), to function effectively in that milieu (competence) and to feel a sense of personal initiative in doing so (autonomy)" (p. 7). Hagger and Chatzisarantis (2007, 2008) have summarized the research using SDT to predict exercise behavior. The studies generally indicate that participants who display autonomy in their exercise behavior and have strong social support systems exhibit stronger motivation and enhanced exercise adherence. For example, Edmunds, Ntoumanis, and Duda (2006; 2007) conducted two studies investigating self-determination theory and its relationship to predicting exercise behavior. One study focused on obese individuals, and results revealed that after a three-month exercise intervention, obese individuals who had an increase in relatedness need satisfaction over time exhibited the greatest exercise adherence. Self-determination theory was also applied to current exercisers to help predict exercise adherence. Results showed that when the three psychological needs of relatedness, autonomy, and competence were met, adherence rates increased, as did levels of intrinsic motivation.

Along with studying the three basic human needs discussed earlier, SDT also proposes that intrinsic and extrinsic motivation occur on a continuum, starting from no motivation at all, to extrinsic motivation, moving through different types of extrinsic and intrinsic motivation, and eventually reaching intrinsic motivation (see Deci & Ryan, 1994 for an in-depth discussion). In essence, individuals feel a greater sense of autonomy and control as they move toward intrinsically motivated behavior since they are not dependent on an external source for their motivation. The three types of intrinsic motivation (knowledge, accomplishment, stimulation) represent what one wants to do as opposed to what one ought to do, and therefore they have been shown to be positively related to affective, cognitive, and behavioral outcomes (Vallerand & Rousseau, 2001).

The relationship between self-determination theory and intrinsic motivation in physical activity received further support by the finding that participants were able to make the distinction between intrinsic and extrinsic goals in a physical activity context (McLachlan & Hagger, 2011). Additionally, two studies (Duncan, Hall, Wilson, & Jenny, 2010; Lewis & Sutton, 2011) found that exercise that was regulated by more autonomous regulations produced higher levels of adherence than those regulated by controlled regulations.

So what does self-determination theory tell us from an applied perspective? One obvious application would be that people who were more intrinsically motivated (e.g., exercise for the fun and enjoyment they get) would more likely adhere to an exercise program than individuals extrinsically motivated (e.g., to improve appearance to the opposite sex). The challenge for practitioners remains how to create an autonomous-supportive climate in which self-determined forms of motivation dominate the physical activity context, but still allow for some external and less self-directed extrinsic motivation (e.g., social support, rewards). Specifically, whenever exercise leaders can make individuals in their classes feel more competent and autonomous, this should result in higher levels of adherence. In addition, providing an environment that is mutually supportive with the potential for positive social interactions should help satisfy the need for relatedness, thereby further increasing the likelihood for long-term adherence.

One possibility for structuring the environment to meet these needs would be to let different individuals be in charge of selecting the exercise regimen (or at least a couple of specific exercisers) on different days. This should in turn promote a sense of autonomy and responsibility. Another way would be designing a program in which individuals can feel a sense of mastery over different types of exercises (e.g., strength, endurance, flexibility) to enhance feelings of competence. For example, beginning exercisers often drop out because the exercise program is too difficult or taxing on their physical abilities (Buckworth & Dishman, 2007). Making sure exercises for new or beginning individuals are initially low intensity and short duration can help promote a sense of mastery, accomplishment, and satisfaction in these individuals. Finally, opportunities should be provided for social interaction and making friends as this can promote feelings of relatedness. To that end, having exercisers work in small groups from time to time would facilitate interactions and allow individuals to get to know each other.

Transtheoretical Model

Over the years, theories, models, and programs to alter behavior have focused predominantly on the elimination or control of negative behaviors, such as drinking, smoking, substance abuse, and overeating, rather than on increasing positive behaviors, such as exercise. In essence, the models and theories noted above (i.e., health belief model, theory of planned behavior, social cognitive theory, self-determination theory) as well as other models and approaches, such as classical conditioning, modeling, and stimulus-response relationships, have been used to prevent or reduce a variety of negative behaviors (Institute of Medicine, 2001). Majority of these studies concluded that it was extremely difficult to change behaviors that had become habitual over a long period. Although behavior change, such as quitting drugs, smoking, drinking, or overeating, was often seen as an acute event, repeated observations have shown that behavior change is a process that occurs over time. From these observations came the development of the transtheoretical model of behavior change (Prochaska, DiClemente, & Norcross, 1992).

Although the previous models are useful in attempting to understand why people do or do not exercise, they tend to focus on a given moment in time. However, the transtheoretical model proposes that individuals progress through stages of change and that movement through the stages is cyclic rather than linear, because many people do not succeed in their efforts of establishing and maintaining the desired lifestyle changes. The transtheoretical model would argue that different interventions and information need to be tailored to match the particular stage an individual is in at the time. In addition, based on the model, change is seen as a lengthy process involving stages with different cognitions and behaviors. Regarding physical activity, intervention research testing the tenets of transtheoretical model by focusing on matching stages of change to specific individual needs is extensive (albeit correlational) in demonstrating the linkage between stages of change and physical activity levels (Marshall & Biddle, 2001)

Along these lines, a one-size-fits-all approach does not work, as noted by top researchers in this area (Marcus et al., 2000). This notion of rejecting the one-size-fits-all approach was affirmed by a second study (Lippe, Ziegelmann, & Schwarzer, 2005) that used a stage-specific model that distinguished among non-intenders, intenders, and actors in terms of physical activity. In fact, earlier, Prochaska, Norcross, and DiClemente (1994) found that understanding the different stages that individuals are in (and then matching interventions to stages) helped predict the intended and actual exercise behavior.

Along these lines, it is important to note that the concept of stages falls somewhere between those of personality traits and states (see Chaplin, John, & Goldberg, 1988). Specifically, traits are typically viewed as stable and not open to change. States, on the other hand, are readily changed and typically lack stability. The stages in the transtheoretical model are both dynamic and stable. That is, although stages can last for a considerable period of time, they are susceptible to change. For example, a sedentary woman may think about exercising but enjoys watching her favorite programs on TV and thus stays sedentary for months. Then someone buys her a pair of walking shoes and volunteers to walk with her. After a year of walking, she gets an injury, stops walking entirely and does not pick it back up even after the injury is healed.

The following are the six stages in the transtheoretical model:

1. *Precontemplation stage.* In this stage, individuals are not active and do not intend to start exercising in the next six months. For practitioners, it is important to find out why the individual is not exercising. Do they not think it is important? Are they demoralized about their ability to change? Are friends and family also not exercisers?

2. *Contemplation stage.* In this stage, individuals seriously intend to exercise within the next six months but are not currently exercising. Despite their intentions, individuals may remain in this second stage for up to two years (Marcus et al., 1992)

3. *Preparation stage.* Individuals in this stage are exercising some, perhaps less than three times a week, but not regularly enough to produce major benefits. In the preparation stage, individuals typically have a plan of action and have indeed taken action (in the past year or so) to make behavioral changes, such as exercising a little.

4. *Action stage.* Individuals in this stage exercise regularly (three or more times a week for 20 minutes or longer) but have been doing so for fewer than six months. This is the least stable stage, as it tends to correspond with the highest risk for relapse. It is also the busiest stage, in which the most processes for change are being used. In essence, because relapse occurs most often in this stage, many different behavioral (e.g., reinforcement, counterconditioning) and cognitive (e.g., self-re-evaluation, environmental re-evaluation) processes are used to prevent relapse.

5. *Maintenance stage.* Individuals in this stage have been exercising regularly for more than six months. Although they are likely to maintain regular exercise throughout the life span, except for time-outs because of injury or other health-related problems, boredom and loss of focus can become a problem. The vigilance initially required to establish a new habit can be tiring and difficult to maintain. Although most studies testing the transtheoretical model have focused on the earlier stages, results from research investigating its later stages (Fallon, Hausenblas, & Nigg, 2005) revealed that increasing self-efficacy to overcome barriers to exercise was critical for both males and females to maintain behavior change (see Marcus et al., 1992, for a more detailed discussion)

6. *Termination stage.* Termination is the stage in which individuals have no temptation to engage in the previous behavior. Once an exerciser has remained in this stage for five years, the individual is likely to exercise for life. In fact, it appears that these potential lifelong exercisers not only acquire a strong belief in their ability to remain physically

active but are also resistant to relapse despite common barriers to exercise, including lack of time, energy, and motivation; depression; and bad weather (Spencer, Adams, Malone, Roy, & Yost, 2006). Due to the ongoing nature of barriers and temptations, for practitioners who may be attempting to promote exercise adherence, it might be a reasonable goal to aim for a lifetime of maintenance rather than a definitive termination in individuals.

Matching the Exercise Intervention to the Individual

A central theme in the transtheoretical model is that different intervention techniques would be more effective for people in different stages of change. For example, if an individual is in the contemplation stage but the intervention focuses on maintenance strategies (e.g., refining different types of exercise behavior) instead of motivational strategies, dropouts will increase. This notion was first tested by Marcus and colleagues (1992), who developed stage-matched self-help materials and other resources based on the exercise adherence literature. In addition, the self-help materials were informed by the transtheoretical model. As such, they developed the following research manuals for participants in different stages:

- "What's in It for You," for participants in the contemplation stage, focused on the benefits and barriers of intended physical activity.
- "Ready for Action," developed for participants in the preparation stage, focused on getting people to exercise three times a week by using such strategies as setting short-term goals, developing time management skills, and rewarding oneself for activity.
- "Keeping It Going," for participants in the action stage who exercise only occasionally and are at great risk of relapsing into the preparation stage, focused on troublesome situations that may lead to a relapse (e.g., injury, vacations, work situations) and provided suggestions for dealing with these potential situations (e.g., gaining social support).

Results from this early research (Marcus et al., 1992) revealed that between 30% and 60% of participants progressed to either the preparation or action stage, and only 4% in preparation and 9% in action regressed. These findings demonstrate that a low-cost, relatively low-intensity intervention can produce significant improvements in stage of exercise adoption. This matching approach has been successful in a nationwide sample of over 1,200 participants exercising to lose weight.

Furthermore, at times there may be things outside one's control that influence the maintenance of exercise. For example, a study showed that individuals who had more major life events occurring during maintenance exercised significantly less than those who had fewer major life events (Oman & King, 2000). Therefore, being prepared for "high-risk" situations that can lead to missed exercise sessions or to program attrition remains important. In addition, it appears that in a worksite setting (i.e., a setting where physical activity and fitness machines/equipment are on the same site as the company itself to make it easier for employees to exercise), a diversified intervention can increase energy expenditure of participants as well as move them from a lower (less active) stage of change to a higher (more active) stage of change (Titze et al., 2001). Research (Jo et al., 2010) has also supported the stages of change model in a walking program in Korea, although it was noted that it is still difficult to get people in the pre-contemplation and contemplation stages to undertake consistent physical activity. Furthermore, a thorough review of literature assessing the impact of the transtheoretical model on exercise behavior found that in 25 of 31 studies, a stage-matched intervention demonstrated success in motivating participants toward higher stages and amounts of exercise (Spencer et al., 2006) Finally, the stages of change model has been successfully applied to children, grades 4–6, to increase moderate-to-vigorous physical activity (Haas & Nigg, 2009).

Ecological Models

One class of models that has recently gained support in the study of exercise behavior comprises ecological models. The term *ecological* refers to models, frameworks, or perspectives rather than a specific set of variables (Dishman et al., 2004). Ecological models acknowledge that behavior can be influenced by social environment, physical environment, and public policy variables. The primary focus of these models is to explain how environments and behaviors affect each other, bringing into consideration intrapersonal (e.g., biological), interpersonal (e.g., family), institutional (e.g., schools), and political (e.g., laws at all levels) influences. Initially, Sallis and Owen (1999) applied this model to physical activity and defined the "behavioral setting" to describe social and physical (construed and natural) environmental factors that can facilitate or enable the behavior and the decisions to be more active. Results from their study revealed that changes in the physical environment produced the most changes in exercise behavior. For example, in a review of 129 studies from 1979–2003, the strongest evidence for influencing physical activity included prompts to increase stair use, access to places and opportunities for physical activity, school-based physical education programs, and comprehensive worksite approaches (Matson-Koffman et al., 2005).

Although all of the environments are important, Sallis and Owen (1999) have argued that physical environments are the hallmark of these ecological models. Their most provocative claim is that ecological models can have a direct impact on exercise above that provided by social cognitive models. Along these lines a recent study used an ecological perspective to help promote physical activity in middle school students (Zhang et al., 2012). Social environmental (support from parents, friends, and physical education teachers) and physical environmental (equipment accessibility, neighborhood safety) variables, along with barrier self-efficacy (belief you can overcome barriers to exercise), were found to predict physical activity. However, the environmental variables (social and physical) predicted physical activity beyond individual factors such as barrier self-efficacy. In essence, it appears that environmental variables add the most variance to the prediction of physical activity. For a balanced presentation, however, it should be noted that in one earlier study individual and social variables were more salient than environmental variables in explaining exercise behavior (Giles-Corti & Donovan, 2002).

The built environment (e.g., metropolitan land-use patterns, urban transportation, bike/walking paths, lighting,) is important in level of physical activity because it can be related to the choices individuals have for being physically active as part of their daily lives. A number of potential environmental influences on exercise behavior were assessed, mainly by self-report, in the 1990s. This can be problematic as self-reports can provide different results than objective measures (e.g., distance from facilities). For example, when measured by self-report, perceived access has not been related to adoption and maintenance of exercise behaviors. However, when access to facilities has been measured by actual distance, then there was a relationship between access and physical activity (Buckworth & Dishman, 2007).

That said, the clearest findings regarding the relationship between the built environment and physical activity have been in the use of parks and walking trails (Duncan & Mummery, 2005). These environmental improvements are also related to safety factors since many individuals report safety as a barrier to exercise. Thus, when builders are developing new communities and when individuals and families are considering where to live, access and safety issues related to parks, multi-use trails, par courses, and so on can have an important impact on the level of physical activity of the residents.

USING THEORY TO HELP INFORM PRACTICE

Much of this chapter has targeted understanding some of the major theories and models that have been developed to help explain and predict exercise behavior. From a practical point of view, let us take a look at how understanding these theories might help us in developing an exercise program and predicting the exercise behavior of an individual. Of course, each theory/model has its own specific components that are seen as central and most predictive of exercise behavior, as explained in detail throughout the chapter. The following vignette will focus on integrating different parts from the aforementioned theories to help the practitioner make more informed decisions for promoting exercise behavior.

Allison (age 27) has not exercised for several years. She is already overweight (and heading toward being obese), and her blood pressure and cholesterol are already high. Besides changing her diet (with the help of a registered dietician), you feel that a program of regular exercise would be beneficial. Being an exercise science major in college and starting to do some personal training, you are familiar with the theories of exercise behavior and plan to use this information to help Allison start and continue to exercise.

Using the transtheoretical model, you first ask Allison about her exercise habits and behaviors so you can find out what stage she is in and then devise an appropriate program to match her stage. You find out that she is in the contemplation stage and that she is seriously thinking about exercising due to her condition, but she has not done anything proactive thus far. Based on this, you inform her of the benefits of regular physical activity and review some of the typical barriers that she will need to overcome (as well as strategies for overcoming these barriers, such as time management and goal-setting skills).

According to the tenets of the health beliefs model, a person's likelihood of engaging in preventive health behaviors such as exercise depends on the person's perception of the severity of the potential illness as well as her appraisal of the costs and benefits of taking action. Therefore, you would attempt to convince Allison of the severity of her potential problems (e.g., obesity and high blood pressure can lead to such things as heart attacks and strokes) as well as all the psychological and physiological benefits of exercise (e.g., greater self-esteem, reduced risk of cardiovascular disease, weight control, and reduction of stress and depression). In addition, because the health beliefs model also argues that "cues to action" are important variables predicting exercise behavior, you may provide Allison with a new pair of running shoes, a video that points out the positive effects of exercise, or perhaps a one-month free membership at her local fitness club.

Based on the theories of reasoned action and planned behavior, subjective norms and perceived behavioral control are critical determinants of Allison's intention to exercise, which in turn should influence her actual exercise behavior. Along these lines, because subjective norms refer to the person's beliefs about others' opinions about the importance of exercise, you can try to convince Allison that exercising is positive and that all the important people in her life believe that exercise is a good thing. You may enlist her significant others in this effort. This positive social pressure to exercise should cause Allison to want to exercise, in part because the significant people in her life believe that exercise will produce positive benefits for her. In addition, it is important that Allison feels that changing her exercise behavior is under her control (perceived behavioral control). In this regard, changing a person's beliefs about her ability to exercise can directly affect behavior without influencing intentions and thus is a very powerful variable in predicting exercise behavior. Therefore, helping Allison build up her belief of control and convincing her that she does have the opportunity to exercise are important ways that you can influence her exercise behavior.

Based on the ecological model, the physical environment one lives in is also related to her physical activity. If plausible, you might encourage Allison to move to a community that has a more supportive environment than the one she lives in now, which has no exercise facilities and where safety is an issue. If a move is not possible, then possibly finding a buddy to exercise with or purchasing some exercise equipment for her apartment might also prompt some increase in exercise.

Finally, from self-efficacy theory you know that a key determinant in exercise behavior is a person's belief that she can execute the necessary behaviors to produce a desired response. Up to this point, Allison has not really believed in herself, and she is not sure that she has the ability or motivation to exercise on a consistent basis. Considering that the strongest source of self-efficacy is performance accomplishments, you can try to convince Allison that she can exercise on a regular basis. One of the best ways to do this is for Allison to actually start exercising so that she will believe that she can, in fact, exercise regularly. You agree to work with Allison and set a specific time to meet to exercise three to four days per week for 30 minutes each time. You also have Allison's family and friends encourage and support her exercise behavior and do whatever is necessary to allow her to exercise. Once Allison starts to exercise, exercise will likely positively affect her self-efficacy (see McAuley & Blissmer, 2002), and her self-belief should grow with each exercise bout.

In essence, knowing the explanations each theory proposes regarding exercise behavior helps inform practitioners about the factors to focus on in trying to have people start or continue an exercise program. It has been said that nothing is more practical than a good theory (Vansteenkiste & Sheldon, 2006), and this example illustrates that knowing the theories of exercise behaviors can help inform practice to enhance the likelihood of engaging in exercise behavior and adhering to an exercise program over time.

REFERENCES

Ajzen, I., & Fishbein, M. (1980). *Understanding attitudes and predicting social behavior.* Englewood Cliffs, NJ: Prentice Hall.

Ajzen, I., & Madden, T. J. (1986). Prediction of goal-directed behavior: Attitudes intentions, and perceived behavioral control. *Journal of Experimental Social Psychology, 22,* 453–474.

Ashford, S., Edmunds, J., & French, D. P. (2010). What is the best way to change self-efficacy to promote lifestyle and recreational physical activity? A systematic review with meta-analysis. *British Journal of Health Psychology, 15*(2), 2652–88

Bandura, A. (1977). Self-efficacy: Toward a unifying theory of behavioral change. *Psychological Review, 84,* 191–215.

Bandura, A. (1986). *Social foundations of thought and actions: A social cognitive theory.* Englewood Cliffs, NJ: Prentice Hall.

Bandura, A. (1997). *Self-efficacy: The exercise of control.* New York, NY: Freeman.

Bandura, A. (2005). Health promotion by social cognitive means. *Health Education and Behavior, 32,* 143–162.

Becker, M. H., & Maiman, L. A. (1975). Sociobehavioral determinants of compliance with health care and medical care recommendations. *Medical Care, 13,* 10–24.

Berger, B., Pargman, D., & Weinberg, R. (2007). *Foundations of exercise psychology* (2nd ed.). Morgantown, WV: Fitness Information Technology.

Biddle, S., Hagger, M., Chatzisarantis, N., & Lippke, S. (2007). Theoretical frameworks in exercise psychology. In G. Tenenbaum & R. Eklund (Eds.), *Handbook of sport psychology* (3rd ed., pp. 537–559). New York, NY: Wiley.

Buckworth, J., & Dishman, R. (2007). Exercise adherence. In G. Tenenbaum & R. Eklund (Eds.), *Handbook of sport psychology* (3rd ed., pp. 509–536). New York, NY: Wiley.

Centers for Disease Control and Prevention. (2010). *Behavioral risk factor surveillance system survey data.* Atlanta, GA: U. S. Department of Health and Human Services, Centers for Disease Control and Prevention.

Centers for Disease Control and Prevention. (2011). *Summary health statistics for U. S. adults: National health interview survey, 2011.* Atlanta, GA: U. S. Department of Health and Human Services, Centers for Disease Control and Prevention.

Chaplin, W. F., John, O. P., & Goldberg, L. R. (1988). Conceptions of states and traits: Dimensional attributes with ideals as prototypes. *Journal of Personality and Social Psychology, 54*(4), 541–557.

Culos-Reed, S. N., Gyurcsik, C., & Brawley, L. R. (2001). Using theories of motivated behavior to understand physical activity. In R. Singer, H. Hausenblas, & C. Janelle (Eds.), *Handbook of sport psychology* (2nd ed., pp. 695–717). New York, NY: Wiley.

Deci, E. L., & Ryan, R. M. (1985). *Intrinsic motivation and self-determination in human behavior*. New York, NY: Plenum Press.

Deci, E. L., & Ryan, R. M. (1994). Promoting self-determined education. *Scandinavian Journal of Educational Research, 38*, 3–41.

Dimmock, J., & Banting, L. (2009). The influence of implicit cognitive processes on physical activity: How the theory of planned behavior and self-determination theory can provide a platform for understanding. *International Review of Sport and Exercise Psychology, 2*, 3–22.

Dishman, R. K., Washburn, R. A., & Heath, G. W. (2004). *Physical activity epidemiology*. Champaign, IL: Human Kinetics.

Duncan, L., Hall, C., Wilson, P., & Jenny, O. (2010) Exercise motivation: A cross-sectional analysis examining its relationships with frequency, intensity, and duration of exercise. *International Journal of Behavioral Nutrition and Physical Activity, 7*, 1–10.

Duncan, M., & Mummery, K. (2005). Psychosocial and environmental actors associated with physical activity in regional Queensland. *Preventive Medicine, 40*, 363–372.

Edmunds, J., Ntoumanis, N., & Duda, J. (2006). A test of self-determination theory in the exercise domain. *Journal of Applied Social Psychology, 36* (9), 2240–2265.

Edmunds, J., Ntoumanis, N., & Duda, J. (2007). Adherence and well-being in overweight and obese patients referred to an exercise on prescription scheme: A self-determination theory perspective. *Psychology of Sport and Exercise, 8*, 722–740.

Fallon, E., Hausenblas, H., & Nigg, C. (2005). The transtheoretical model and exercise adherence: Examining construct associations in later stages of change. *Sport and Exercise Psychology Journal, 6*, 629–641.

Giles-Corti, B., & Donovan, R. (2002). The relative influence of individual, social, and physical environment determinants of physical activity. *Social Science and Medicine, 54*, 1793–1812.

Haas, S., & Nigg, C. (2009). Construct validation of the stages of change with strenuous, moderate, and mild physical activity and sedentary behavior among children. *Journal of Science and Medicine in Sport, 12*, 586–591.

Hagger, M., & Chatzisarantis, N. (2007). Editorial: Advances in self-determination theory research in sport and exercise. *Psychology of Sport and Exercise, 8*, 597–599.

Hagger, M., & Chatzisarantis, N. (2008). Self-determination theory and the psychology of exercise. *International Review of Sport and Exercise Psychology, 1*, 79–103.

Hagger, M., Chatzisarantis, N., & Biddle, S. (2002). A meta-analytic review of the theories of reasoned action and planned behavior in physical activity: Predictive validity and the contribution of additional variables. *Journal of Sport & Exercise Psychology, 24*, 3–32.

Hunt, H., & Gross, A. (2009). Prediction of exercise in patients across various stages of bariatric surgery: A comparison of the merits of the Theory of Reasoned Action versus the Theory of Planned Behavior. *Behavior Modification, 33*, 795–817.

Institute of Medicine. (2001). Health and behavior: The interplay of biological, behavioral and societal influences. Institute of Medicine (US), Committee on Health and Behavior: Research, Practice and Policy. Washington, DC: National Academies Press.

Jo, H., Song, Y., Yoo, S., & Lee, H. (2010). Effectiveness of a province-wide walking campaign in Korea on the stages of change for physical activity. *International Journal of Sport and Exercise Psychology, 8*, 433–445.

Lewis, M., & Sutton, A. (2011). Understanding exercise behavior: Examining the interaction of exercise motivation and personality in predicting exercise frequency. *Journal of Sport Behavior, 34*, 82–98.

Lippke, S., Ziegelmann, J., & Schwarzer, R. (2005). Stage-specific adoption and maintenance of physical activity: Testing a three-stage model. *Psychology of Sport and Exercise, 6*, 585–603.

Lubans, D., & Sylva, K. (2009). Mediators of change following a senior school physical activity intervention. *Journal of Science in Medicine and Sport, 12*, 134–140.

Luszczynska, A., Mazurkiewicz, M., Zieglemann, R. J., & Schwrzer, R. (2007). Recovery self-efficacy and intention as predictors of running or jogging behavior: A cross-lagged panel analysis over a two-year period. *Psychology of Sport and Exercise, 8,* 247–269.

Luszczynska, A., & Trybury, M. (2008). Effects of self-efficacy intervention on exercise: The moderating role of diabetes and cardiovascular disease. *Applied Psychology: An International Review, 57,* 644–659.

Maddison, R., & Prapavessis, H. (2004). Using self-efficacy and intention to predict exercise compliance among patients with ischemic heart disease. *Journal of Sport and Exercise Psychology, 26*(4), 511–524.

Marcus, B. H., Dubbert, P. M., Forsyth, L. H., McKenzie, T. L., Stone, E. J., Dunn, A. L., & Blair, S. N. (2000). Physical activity behavior change: Issues in adoption and maintenance. *Health Psychology, 19,* 42–56.

Marcus, B. H., Rossi, J. S., Selby, V. C., Niaura, R. S., & Abrams, D. B. (1992). The stages and processes of exercise adoption and maintenance in a worksite sample. *Health Psychology, 11,* 386–395.

Marshall, S., & Biddle, S. (2001). The Transtheoretical Model of behavior change: A metaanalysis of applications to physical activity and exercise. *Annals of Behavioral Medicine, 25,* 229–246.

Matson-Koffman, D., Brownstein, J., Neiner, J., & Greaney, M. (2005). A site-specific literature review of policy and environmental interventions that promote physical activity and nutrition for cardiovascular health: What works. *American Journal of Health Promotion, 19,* 167–183.

McAuley, E., & Blissmer, G. (2002). Self-efficacy and attributional processes in physical activity. In T. Horn (Ed.), *Advances in sport psychology* (2nd ed., pp. 185–206). Champaign, IL: Human Kinetics.

McLachlan, S., & Hagger, M. (2011). Do people differentiate between intrinsic and extrinsic goals for physical activity? *Journal of Sport and Exercise Psychology, 33,* 273–288.

Milne, M., Rodgers, W., Hall, C., & Wilson, P. (2008). Starting up or starting over: The role of intentions to increase and maintain the behavior of exercise initiates. *Journal of Sport and Exercise Psychology, 30,* 286–301.

Oman, R. F., & King, A. C. (2000). The effect of life events and exercise program format on the adoption and maintenance of exercise behavior. *Health Psychology, 19,* 605–612.

Parrott, M., Tennant, K., Olejnik, S., & Poudevigne, M. (2008). Theory of planned behavior: Implications for an e-mail based physical activity intervention. *Psychology of Sport and Exercise, 9,* 511–526.

Plotnikoff, R., Jippke, S., Courneya, K., Birkett, N., & Sigal, T. R. (2008). Physical activity and social cognitive theory: A test in a population sample of adults with Type 1 or Type 2 diabetes. *Applied Psychology: An International Review, 57,* 628–643.

Prochaska, J. O., DiClemente, C. C., & Norcross, J. C. (1992). In search of how people change. *American Psychologist, 47,* 1102–1114.

Prochaska, J. O., Norcross, J. C., & DiClemente, C. C. (1994). *Changes for good.* New York, NY: Avon.

Rhodes, R., & Courneya, K. (2005). Assessment of attitude, subjective norm, and perceived behavioral control for predicting exercise intention and behavior. *Psychology of Sport and Exercise, 6,* 349–361.

Sallis, J. F., & Owen, N. (1999). *Physical activity and behavioral medicine.* Thousand Oaks, CA: Sage.

Spencer, L., Adams, T., Malone, S., Roy, L., & Yost, E. (2006). Applying the transtheoretical model to exercise: A systematic and comprehensive review of the literature. *Health Promotion Practice, 7,* 428–443.

Titze, S., Martin, B., Seiler, R., Stronegger, W., & Marti, B. (2001). Effects of a lifestyle physical activity intervention on stages of change and energy expenditure in sedentary employees. *Psychology of Sport and Exercise, 2,* 103–116.

Vallerand, R. J., & Rousseau, F. L. (2001). Intrinsic and extrinsic motivation in sport and exercise: A review using the hierarchical model of intrinsic and extrinsic motivation. In R. Singer, H. Hausenblas, & C. Janelle (Eds.), *Handbook of sport psychology* (2nd ed., pp. 389–416). New York, NY: Wiley.

Vansteenkiste, M., & Sheldon, K. M. (2006). There's nothing more practical than a good theory: Integrating motivational interviewing and self-determination theory. *British Journal of Clinical Psychology, 45,* 63–82.

Zhang, T., Solomon, M., Gao, Z., & Kosma, M. (2012). Promoting school students' physical activity: A social ecological perspective. *Journal of Applied Sport Psychology, 24,* 92–105.

6 Alternative Models of Health Behavior Change

Jeff Cherubini and Mark H. Anshel

THE CALL FOR ALTERNATIVE MODELS

National and global objectives have called for developing innovative scientist–practitioner interventions that promote a person's decision to start and maintain an exercise program and other forms of physical activity (National Physical Activity Plan Alliance, 2014; U.S. Department of Health and Human Services, 2006, 2008). In an annual report to the U.S. Congress, the Task Force for Community Preventive Services (2011) recognized the importance of promoting and increasing everyday physical activity as a "highest-priority" topic. Noted strategies to increase physical activity throughout the country included enhanced school-based physical education, individually adapted health behavior change programs, and social support interventions in community settings.

Determining the best ways to help exercisers adhere to their respective fitness programs has challenged applied exercise science researchers and practitioners for many years (Anshel, 2014). Though typically guided by major theoretical models, the results of published psychobehavioral intervention studies have yielded only mixed results (De Bourdeaudhuij & Sallis, 2002). Critical analyses of exercise promotion interventions often point to conceptual and methodological limitations, including a lack of intervention follow-up (Dishman & Buckworth, 1997). Recently, Buckworth and Dishman (2013) further lamented on the absence of a theoretical framework or model to examine the efficacy of interventions intended to promote exercise participation and adherence. As Nestle and Jacobson (2000) previously contended, it is one thing to know the causes of obesity (i.e., poor eating habits, lack of physical activity), but quite another to motivate individuals to change the unhealthy habits that led to the excessive weight gain.

Further alluding to the methodological flaws inherent in extant research, Prochaska, Spring, and Nigg (2008) asserted that the majority of early exercise intervention research has relied on one-dimensional techniques and small sample sizes of highly selected participants (e.g., clinical populations, individuals already engaged in a specific program), and has tested the effectiveness of specific strategies (e.g., goal setting, listening to music, social support, positive self-talk) rather than a coherent intervention program. In their review of health behavior change research, Glasgow, Klesges, Dzewaltowski, Bull, and Estabrooks (2004) concluded, "it is well documented that the results of most behavioral and health promotion studies have not been translated into practice" (p. 3). Lox, Martin, and Petruzzello (2010) further concluded that "research is needed to determine the long-term effectiveness of [exercise] interventions and their utility in real-world settings" (p. 170). Thus, it appears that practical guides to behavior change with a focus on long-term exercise adherence are still needed.

Whereas prominent theories and models of health behavior change have been shown to be effective in changing behavior (see Chapter 5), maintaining an exercise habit in real-world settings continues to pose a challenge for both exercise professionals and participants. Therefore, the purpose of this chapter is to provide an overview of two alternate applied models of health behavior change with a focus on exercise behavior and adherence: the disconnected values model (DVM; Anshel, 2008) and the intentional development model (IDM; Cherubini, 2009a). From individual psychosocial variables to changes at the social and structural levels, the models integrate comprehensive theories inherent in behavioral psychology, exercise psychology, health psychology, and positive psychology, with practical applications for exercise researchers, practitioners, and participants.

THE DISCONNECTED VALUES MODEL (DVM)

The purpose of the disconnected values model (Anshel, 2008) is to provide inactive, unfit individuals with renewed incentive to begin and *permanently* maintain an exercise habit. DVM consists of the following stages performed in this order: (1) determining one's negative habits; (2) examining the benefits, costs, and long-term consequences of each unhealthy habit, with a particular reference to the lack of exercise and other forms of physical activity; (3) identifying the person's deepest values and core beliefs about what they consider most important in life; (4) detecting any inconsistencies, or disconnects, between the person's negative habits (e.g., lack of exercise) and her values; (5) identifying at least one disconnect between one's negative habits and values that the person feels is unacceptable; and finally, (6) generating and conducting each phase of an action plan that consists of performing new routines that will replace the former unhealthy habits.

Values are core beliefs that guide behavior and provide guidelines for assessing behavior (Rokeach, 1973). For example, a person who values health is more likely to carry out rituals leading to long-term habits that enhance physical and mental health. To Hogan and Mookherjee (1981), values form "one of the most distinguishing characteristics motivating human beings; the likely effects of values on human behavior, beliefs, and attitudes are indisputable" (p. 29). Thus, values are more central determinants of behavior than interests and attitudes, the latter of which are more situational and derived from a core set of values (Super, 1995). A plethora of interests and attitudes are derived from a relatively reduced number of values. It can be surmised that individuals who place a high value on health, family, faith, and knowledge, among others, are more likely to be concerned about their health and well-being than individuals who do not consider these values as among their most important (Anshel, 2008, 2014). Sometimes this is not true, however. For instance, persons whose values include good health and love for their family but who regularly smoke and acknowledge they "should" quit, or obese individuals who confess they "should" more closely watch their food intake and lose weight are demonstrating an inconsistency, or disconnect, between their values (i.e., health and family) and their actions (i.e., smoking and overeating). Overcoming these inconsistencies is a central feature of the DVM.

BRIEF OVERVIEW OF CONCEPTUAL FOUNDATIONS OF THE DVM

The DVM is anchored by concepts and theories related to other cognitive-behavioral frameworks that have successfully demonstrated health behavior change. These include cognitive dissonance theory (CDT; Festinger, 1957), motivational interviewing (MI; Rollnick, Miller, & Butler, 2008), and acceptance and commitment therapy (ACT; Ossman, Wilson, Storaasli, & McNeill, 2006). Briefly, Festinger's CDT posited that individuals naturally seek consistency among their cognitions. An inconsistency between the person's attitudes (i.e., cognitions) and behaviors results in a state of dissonance and is followed by an attempt to change the attitude in order to accommodate the actions. Dissonance may be minimized or eliminated by one of three strategies: (a) reducing the importance of the conflicting beliefs, (b) acquiring new beliefs that change the balance, or (c) removing the conflicting attitude or behavior.

As applied to health behavior change, the focus of MI is to increase a person's intrinsic motivation (i.e., one's sense of satisfaction, perceived competence, and self-determination) for adopting a healthier lifestyle (Rollnick et al., 2008). As such, the primary goal of MI is to increase the person's motivation to initiate short-term and long-term behavior change by resolving issues that create ambivalence and resistance (Resnicow et al., 2002).

This is accomplished by collaborating with the client to explore reasons in favor of and against changes in current unhealthy behaviors and to help the client take responsibility for initiating and maintaining behavior change. The client, in collaboration with a coach or mental health professional, determines how and when the change will occur. MI focuses on the person's concerns and perspectives by addressing specific changes in behavior that are most desirable and realistic, while at the same time addressing possible barriers to change.

ACT addresses a person's normal tendency to promote and distort unpleasant emotions that lead to engaging in inappropriate behaviors to avoid or reduce those unpleasant emotions (Ossman et al., 2006). The goal of ACT is not to change or control undesirable personal and private thoughts or emotions, but rather to develop effective behaviors of "proper" daily living. ACT helps clients acknowledge "the truth" about their negative (undesirable) habits by revealing their costs and long-term consequences. From an ACT perspective, the clients' goal is to commit to an action plan that leads to experiencing more desirable habits and developing new routines that are consistent with their values.

Initiating exercise behavior is a particular challenge to practitioners and researchers, usually because past experiences with exercise are accompanied by negative feelings and attitudes about exercise that reflect previous unpleasant experiences. Some of these could include the physical education teacher who used exercise as a form of discipline, burnout from too much physical training as a former athlete, injury, or failure to meet goals from previous exercise attempts. Furthermore, vigorous exercise requires exertion and, consequently, some degree of physical discomfort in order to obtain its benefits. Creating additional challenges to increasing physical activity is the financial costs associated with buying exercise clothing, particularly proper footwear, as well as memberships in fitness clubs or other facilities that promote various forms of physical activity (e.g., recreation centers, Boys or Girls Clubs). That said, none of these exercise barriers takes into account the most common reason for not exercising—lack of time. The DVM consists of an intervention that overcomes these barriers and ostensibly improves exercise participation and, potentially, long-term exercise adherence in developing a permanent lifestyle change. Furthermore, the DVM may be used by professionals with varying types of credentials and not exclusively by licensed psychologists or certified personal trainers. The DVM is illustrated in Figure 6.1.

The DVM is based on the interaction between a "personal coach" or sport/exercise psychology consultant and the client. The interaction reflects receiving information (e.g., facing the truth about who you are and how you live), self-reflection (e.g., acknowledging the costs and long-term consequences of current unhealthy habits, such as lack of exercise or poor nutrition), determining personal goals (e.g., feeling better, improved appearance), and identifying strategies needed to reach those goals (e.g., plan and carry out an exercise schedule, join a fitness club, hire a personal trainer).

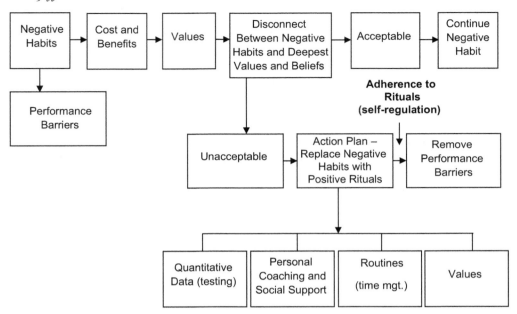

Figure 6.1 The Disconnected Values Model

Unhealthy/Negative Habits

Each of us possesses habits that we exhibit every day that can be categorized as unhealthy, negative, or undesirable. These negative habits are operationally defined as thoughts, emotions, or behaviors that we acknowledge as not being in our best interests, yet we continue to do them. Not exercising, poor nutrition, lack of proper rest or sleep, and poor work/life balance are among negative habits that individuals should improve to boost their quality of life.

Why do humans engage in self-destructive behaviors? Why do we maintain habits that we know are bad for our physical and, sometimes, mental health? Researchers and theorists contend that one reason is because the "benefits" of our negative habits are greater than the short-term costs and long-term consequences (Hall & Fong, 2007). Hall and Fong, in their temporal self-regulation theory, claimed that human behavior is driven by greater responsivity to immediate contingencies. That is, we are more consumed and driven by meeting short-term rather than long-term needs. In addition, our actions reflect competing motives between short-term benefits versus long-term costs. The benefits of exercise, for instance, are perceived as irrelevant in the short-term as compared to the perceived short-term benefits of *not* exercising. Hall and Fong contend that unhealthy habits do not exist without benefits. Cultures that prioritize immediate gratification as opposed to delayed gratification nurture the decision to engage in meeting short-term needs. Segar, Eccles, and Richardson (2011) also suggested that "because immediate payoffs motivate behavior better than distant goals, a more effective 'hook' for promoting sustainable participation might be to rebrand exercise as a primary way individuals can enhance the quality of their daily lives" (p. 94).

Performance Barriers

Performance barriers are persistent thoughts, emotions, or actions that compromise high-quality performance (Anshel, 2013). Whether these barriers can be objective and observable (e.g., injury, anger) or perceived (e.g., time restraints, anxiety), they are controllable and, thus, changeable. For instance, overweight, older persons who are uncomfortable and self-conscious about exercising among younger, fitter, thinner individuals at a fitness facility can focus on the specific exercises of their program while ignoring the presence of others. Another example is a person who has time restraints to exercise but can develop time management strategies to allow for exercise time. The root cause of performance barriers is negative habits.

The negative physical habit of poor work/life balance, for instance, results in poor relationships with family members and friends. One purpose of the DVM is to help clients detect their negative habits and identify how these habits lead to undesirable performance in various aspects of their life, not only health. After negative habits (e.g., lack of exercise) have been associated with limitations to physical performance, the person begins to self-examine the reasons for maintaining negative habits.

Perceived "Benefits" of Unhealthy Habits

There are perceived benefits to each of our unhealthy habits or else the unhealthy habits would not persist. It is important to recognize the term "perceived" in this context because persons who repeatedly and habitually engage in unhealthy, self-destructive behavior patterns are able to justify their actions, either rationally (e.g., satisfying hunger, too busy to exercise) or irrationally (e.g., "I am obese, but my doctor tells me I am healthy and my test scores are fine"). Perception, then, reflects the individual's reality and does not necessarily represent the actual reality, such as interpreting medical test data or the opinion of the person's medical practitioner. The "benefits" of not exercising, for example, include more time to do other things, not experiencing the discomfort of physical exertion, avoiding risk of injury, or not incurring expenses related to purchasing fitness club memberships and exercise clothing.

Costs and Long-Term Consequences of Unhealthy Habits

There are short-term *costs* and long-term *consequences* of our unhealthy habits (Hall & Fong, 2007). Costs of not engaging in exercise or other forms of regular physical activity include poor cardiovascular and strength fitness, weight gain, higher stress and anxiety, reduced physical energy, lower mental (cognitive) functioning, and less satisfactory sleep. The long-term consequences of inactivity, particularly among the elderly, include poorer physical and mental health; depression; greater likelihood of diseases such as diabetes, certain types of cancer, and cardiovascular disease; reduced quality of life; and shorter lifespan (Long & van Stavel, 1995; Stathopoulou, Powers, Berry, Smits, & Otto, 2006).

At this stage of the consulting process, when the coach/therapist addresses the cost-benefit trade-offs (i.e., long-term consequences) of maintaining unhealthy habits, the client is asked a very important question that requires a sincere reflective answer: "Are these costs and long-term consequences acceptable to you?" If the client concludes that maintaining a specific unhealthy habit is acceptable (e.g., not exercising, maintaining a sedentary lifestyle, overeating, maintaining a stressful lifestyle, poor sleep), the habit will likely continue. If, however, these costs and consequences are greater than the "benefits" of maintaining the unhealthy habit, and the person concludes that these costs are unacceptable, then a change in the unhealthy habit is far more likely. According to the DVM, however, the process of behavior change is not yet complete. Clients must acknowledge their deepest values and beliefs about what is really important in their life, and then identify a *disconnect* between their negative habit(s) and their most important values. This acknowledgement, along with the conclusion that at least one disconnect is unacceptable (ostensibly due to the dire costs and consequences of maintaining the unhealthy habit), forms the DVM's "ignition point" for health behavior change.

Identifying Important Values

Values are core beliefs that motivate and guide behavior, and provide standards against which we evaluate behavior (Rokeach, 1973). Values *should* (but do not always) predict behavior. For instance, a person who values health will have a favorable attitude toward developing daily rituals and long-term habits that enhance health and general well-being. However, humans are not always predictable; people may embrace a particular value, yet not exhibit a behavior pattern consistent with that value. Nevertheless, as Hogan and Mookherjee (1981) contend, values are "one of the most distinguishing characteristics motivating human beings; the likely effects of values on human behavior, beliefs, and attitudes are indisputable" (p. 29). Generally speaking, values are intended to guide behavior. Along these lines, sharing values with others enhances a person's commitment to sacrifice personal, self-serving needs for the benefit of others, particularly members of the same team or unit (Anshel, 2008). One important implication of the DVM in an exercise setting is that a person's values may or may not be compatible with the values of family members, friends, models, or employers.

Although there exists a long list of values, some of which are culturally defined and determined, most individuals possess similar, fundamental values (see Loehr & Schwartz, 2003, for a suggested list of values). When asked to rank their values, most people in Western culture and in certain geographical locations would include among their most important values health, family, character, integrity, honesty, faith, happiness, knowledge, performance excellence, commitment, genuineness, freedom, and concern for others. Thus, behavior change is more likely to be permanent when clients conclude that life satisfaction is linked to behaving in a way that is consistent with one's deepest values.

Establishing a Disconnect

Identifying a disconnect between one's values and acknowledged unhealthy habits requires asking clients to identify not more than five of their most important values and to list up to five of their most unhealthy habits (see Box 1). Clients are then asked to determine the inconsistency between their values and actual behavior patterns. The following set of questions might initiate this process:

To what extent are your values consistent with your actions?
If you value your health, do you have habits that are not good for you, and therefore, inconsistent with your values?
What about family? Do you value your spouse, children, or parents?
If you lead a sedentary lifestyle and are not involved in a program of exercise, yet one of your deepest values is to maintain good health, to what extent is your value inconsistent with your behavior?
Can you detect a "disconnect" between your beliefs about good health and your unhealthy behavioral patterns?

Accepting the Disconnect

If clients acknowledge that not engaging in exercise is, in fact, unhealthy, undesirable, and inconsistent with their deepest values and beliefs, the follow-up question must help ascertain if this disconnect is acceptable (e.g., "Is the lack of consistency between a lack of exercise or other forms of physical activity and the values of health, family, and faith you have stated acceptable to you—especially after knowing the costs and long-term consequences of this negative habit?"). If the disconnect *is* acceptable—and for many individuals who feel that

Box 1 Common Barriers that Compromise Health, Energy, & Performance

Circle **5** of the most important/destructive barriers that affect your life

1. Lack of assertiveness and self-direction
2. Poor team player (thinks "me" not "we")
3. Constant conflict with boss or coworker
4. Poor fitness
5. Poor organization and time management
6. Low motivation and passion at work
7. Fear and insecurity on the job
8. Poor communication skills
9. Low stress tolerance
10. Rigid and inflexible
11. Poor sleep habits
12. Low energy and fatigue
13. Poor work/life balance
14. Poor nutrition and hydration
15. Lack of trust in others
16. Lack of discipline and follow through
17. Lack of empathy and compassion
18. Negative and pessimistic thinker
19. Impatience, frustration, and anger
20. Failure to connect work to deepest values and beliefs
21. Poor relationships in personal life
22. Low control over own actions
23. Short attention span
24. Insert your own: _____

Values Checklist: **Check 3 of your most important values**

Balance	☐	Happiness	☐
Beauty	☐	Harmony	☐
Concern for others	☐	Health	☐
Character	☐	Humor	☐
Commitment	☐	Humility	☐
Compassion	☐	Integrity	☐
Courage	☐	Kindness	☐
Creativity	☐	Knowledge	☐
Excellence	☐	Loyalty	☐
Faith	☐	Perseverance	☐
Fairness	☐	Respect for others	☐
Family	☐	Responsibility	☐
Freedom	☐	Security	☐
Generosity	☐	Serenity	☐
Genuineness	☐	Service to others	☐
Wealth	☐	Independence	☐

Find at least *one* disconnect between your barriers and values, then ask, "Is this disconnect acceptable?"

changing the unhealthy habit is either undesirable or beyond their control—then no change in the unhealthy behavior pattern (i.e., exercise) will likely occur. It is necessary, therefore, to identify another area of inconsistency between the person's unhealthy habits and their values. Only when a particular disconnect is identified and is perceived as unacceptable to the individual will there be a commitment to behavior change.

Developing a Self-Regulation Action Plan

The person's decision to initiate an exercise program or, for that matter, change some other undesirable behavior, is followed by developing a detailed self-regulation action plan. As Lox and colleagues (2010) explained, action planning "entails forming concrete plans that specify when, where, and how a person will translate exercise intentions into action" (p. 153). Such a plan identifies the details of starting and maintaining a regular exercise program, including the type of exercise, exercise location(s), days of the week and times of day exercise will occur, strategies to obtain fitness data or the results of other types of tests (such as blood lipids, percent body fat, body mass index, or waist circumference) to establish a baseline of fitness and health indicators, and availability of social support (such as a workout partner or personal trainer). As Loehr and Schwartz (2003) contend, specificity of timing and precision of behavior dramatically increases the probability of successfully carrying out a self-controlled action plan. The self-regulation action plan serves the primary purpose of creating a more immediate payoff and providing clients with a sense of achievement and other immediate payoffs that have higher motivation value than using more distant goals (Segar et al., 2011).

INTENTIONAL DEVELOPMENT MODEL (IDM)

The Intentional Development Model (Cherubini, 2009a) encompasses the details needed for purposeful change and includes all the mechanisms and processes by which change occurs. The model uses an eco-developmental approach, focusing on both ecological and personal change over time. A basic assumption of the model is that the interaction of the individual and his environment over time will either enhance or detract from health-related behavior change (i.e., physical activity; Cherubini, 2009a). Within the model, motivation and adherence to physical activity are influenced through individual, social, and environmental factors dynamically interacting with developmental elements of attitude, attention, action, and adherence (see Figure 6.2). Researchers, practitioners, and participants can thoughtfully examine and

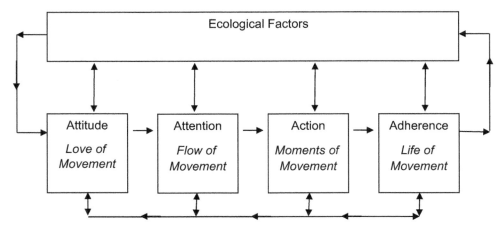

Figure 6.2 The Intentional Development Model

develop key areas that need focus for initiating, increasing, and maintaining physical activity once all the variables influencing physical activity have been broken down.

Complex issues relating to changing health-related behaviors are best presented in a way that clients can understand. As with the DVM (Anshel, 2008), the IDM is designed for practical use by both professionals (psychologists, personal trainers, physical educators, physical therapists) and non-professionals (community members, fitness clients, students, rehabilitation patients). With this in mind, the language used to communicate the model elements was purposely written in "layman's terms" to make it easier for all to understand and implement (Cherubini, 2009a). Whereas psychologists may spend hours discussing the scientific nature of *attitude*, the layperson simply interprets attitude as how she feels about something (good, bad, or indifferent). Similarly, the words *intentional* (used to highlight deliberate, planned, and purposeful behavior) and *development* (used to emphasize progress, growth, and positive change) summarize well the model's objectives for both professionals and participants.

AN ECOLOGICAL APPROACH

On the battlefield of health, there is often a clash of opinions over who, or what, is truly responsible for society's ills (especially when it comes to obesity and inactivity). On the one hand, a judgmental finger points directly at the individual with an accusatory "take responsibility" tone. On the other hand, the finger wiggles around looking for anything (and often everything) to hold accountable—releasing individuals from any and all responsibility. The truth is, as human beings, we are both products of our environment and individuals with the capacity to choose. Holding someone solely responsible (*choices*), without accounting for a variety of individual, social, and environmental concerns (the *chances* allocated) ultimately limits the effectiveness of our interventions (Becker, 1986; Cherubini, 2008, 2009a; Grzywacz & Marks, 2001).

While some give priority to chance (e.g., proposals limiting the sale of sugary drinks), others give priority to personal choice (e.g., consumers' right to choose to purchase the drinks), often noting concerns with equality and autonomy (Barnhill & King, 2013). Regardless, the reality is that both the chances we are granted and the choices we make affect our health (Cherubini, 2009a; Cockerham, Rutten, & Abel, 1997). Taken together, one of the most effective ways to view health behavior change is through an ecological lens—looking both upstream (at the factors influencing behaviors) and downstream (at the choices individuals make) (Cherubini, 2009a, 2008; McElroy, 2002; Sallis, Owen, & Fischer, 2008).

Individual Influences

Cross-cultural and demographic factors interact with other social and physical environmental influences that affect physical activity participation (Cherubini, 2008, 2009a). An understanding of the influence of age, gender, ethnicity, culture, socioeconomic status, sexual orientation, current level of health (including abilities and disabilities), core values, beliefs, knowledge, emotions, stage of change, and self-regulatory skills are all critical to a practitioner's understanding of physical activity behavior change (Anshel & Kang, 2007; Berger, 1998, Cherubini, 2008, 2009a, 2009b; Gill, 1999; King, 2001; Kumanyika, 2002; McElroy, 2002). Accounting for chance and choice, the IDM acknowledges these individual characteristics as being both ascribed and achieved (Cherubini, 2009a). In essence, we are born with certain characteristics and we earn, or achieve, others. Together and alone, these characteristics influence our health and health behavior change.

Acknowledging a variety of cross-cultural and demographic considerations is clearly significant to the success of exercise professionals and participants. Qualitative research associated with the IDM (Cherubini, 2008) highlighted personal identity, childhood activity, an innate love for movement, perceptions of health, and personal perspectives of exercise as individual influences that affect physical activity involvement. Programming must acknowledge and plan for the interacting influence (both facilitating and debilitating) of all potential ascribed and achievement factors on initiating and maintaining physical activity (Cherubini, 2008).

Social Environmental Influences

Social structure has long been acknowledged as a basic cause of sedentary living (McElroy, 2002). Kumanyika (2002) noted that even the most motivated individuals can succumb to social constraints. Home, work, daily routine, surroundings, transportation, health care, discretionary income, support, exposure to social stressors (plus accompanying stress), and gender (including demands for attention and cultural considerations) all have been found to have an influence (both facilitating and debilitating) on physical activity involvement (Brownson, Baker, Houseman, Brennan, & Bacak, 2001; Cherubini, 2008; Gill, 1999; Kumanyika, 2002; Martens, Mobley, & Zizzi, 2000).

The IDM highlights the interacting nature of the social environment on physical activity through the roles we play, the support we get, the culture in which we live, the impact of media and marketing, and the health and fitness genre as a whole (Cherubini, 2008, 2009a). Physical activity and exercise interventions directed toward children, women, and men, individually and together, need to be delivered in a culturally appropriate context. Programming delivered by socially appropriate role models, integrated with cultural traditions, will only enhance the quality and effectiveness of these exercise interventions (Cherubini, 2008; Pittman, 2001). Within the context of social networks (both in person and digital), constructive goals of human behavior, including involvement, encouragement, improvement, and accomplishment, can be established to help guide future health behavior change (Cherubini, 2009b; Lemire, 2007).

Physical Environmental Influences

The physical environment plays a prominent role in supporting health behavior change. Likeability, location, cost, safety, convenience, personal facilities (i.e., bathrooms), staff, square footage, equipment, music, time of year, and weather all influence activity levels (Cherubini, 2008, 2009a). But even with unlimited physical resources, there is still something rather attractive about sedentary living. For others, a true lack of healthy options leads to out of sight, out of mind forgetfulness (Cherubini, 2008).

Through increased awareness of both social and environmental influences, exercise professionals and participants can plan for and engage in more meaningful change. Ecological momentary assessment, experience sampling method, ecological task analysis, direct systematic observation, upstream analysis, and qualitative interviewing are all practical tools that professionals can employ to determine the impact of social and environmental influences on physical activity (Cherubini, 2008, 2009b; Foster & Lloyd, 2007; Kanning & Schlicht, 2010; Malloy & Rossow-Kimball, 2007; McKenzie, 2010; Ogilvie et al., 2011). Based on an accurate analysis of the environment, professionals can advocate for social and policy changes, with an emphasis on physical accessibility for all.

DEVELOPMENTAL ELEMENTS

The IDM accounts for the effect of all possible ecological factors influencing values, beliefs, thoughts, actions, and exercise involvement. Participants interacting within the environments in which they live, work, and play have an influence on their development within the following elements: attitude, attention, action, and adherence. These ecological and developmental elements interact with each other in a dynamic and continuous process that over time will either enhance or detract from health-related behavior change (Cherubini, 2008, 2009a).

Attitude—Love of Movement

Humans are inherently physically active, curious, and challenge-seeking creatures (Cherubini, 2009b; Heinrich, 2002; Millman, 1994). Blending physiology, psychology, anthropology, animal biology, and his love for ultra-distance running, Bernd Heinrich (2002) reflected that physical activity is at the core of our human nature with evolutionary processes contributing to a unique human capacity for, and interest in, both mental and physical endurance. Within the IDM, this human potential is actualized only under certain conditions, shaped by the environments in which we live, work, and play. Whitaker (2005) described this psychophysical potential through the Italian notions of *sfogarsi* (psychological release), *stare bene* (a sense of overall well-being), and *reintegrare* (to make whole again). Exercise professionals can help clients tap into these inherent characteristics through choosing activities that connect to values and are perceived to be captivating, enjoyable, and exciting (Anshel, 2008; Cherubini, 2009a, 2009b; Hunter & Csikszentmihalyi, 2003).

This innate *love of movement* is most robust when we live under conditions that foster self-determination, barrier self-efficacy, and human flourishing (Cherubini, 2009b; Millman, 1994; Ryan & Deci, 2007). Human agency, significant to action development, is an individual's belief in his or her abilities/skills to control choices, actions, and consequent results (Bandura, 1997, 2001; Cherubini, 2009a). Exercise professionals can nurture this agency through facilitating self-determined behavior (further satisfying innate needs for autonomy, competence, and relatedness) in which exercise participants feel in control, competent, and connected to their physical activity (Cherubini, 2009b; Kilpatrick, Hebert, & Jacobsen, 2002; Ryan & Deci, 2007).

When a person feels confident that she will be able to take action, regardless of potential barriers blocking progress, she is said to have a high barrier self-efficacy. This barrier self-efficacy has proven to be a strong correlate of physical activity and is certainly applicable for exercise practitioners and participants (Baruth et al., 2010; Zhang, Solmon, Gao, & Kosma, 2012). Barriers (real and perceived) such as health problems, lack of time, bad weather, anxiety, and frustration are all too common inhibitors of action. Practitioners can implement the following strategies to help clients develop barrier self-efficacy: (a) be supportive and allow sufficient time to practice needed skills, (b) identify strategies to overcome specific barriers that have worked in the past, (c) offer positive verbal persuasion, (d) offer resources that show others overcoming similar barriers, and (e) help clients interpret and control arousal that they may experience (Zhang et al., 2012).

Practically, our attitudes are better when we are living and participating in an environment with greater positive affect (love, joy, interest, hope) than negative affect (hurt, fear, boredom, frustration) (Cherubini, 2009b; Foster & Lloyd, 2007). Positive relationships motivate and negative relationships demotivate—and this is certainly true in physical activity and exercise environments. Exercise professionals and participants alike can *reflect* upon their own values and love of physical activity, *review* individual strengths and environmental challenges (connect and disconnect), and *revise*, as needed, influences affecting personal attitude toward physical activity and exercise.

Attention—Flow of Movement

When it comes to physical activity, and in particular exercise, contemporary societies appear fixated on the idea that happiness and fulfillment come solely from attaining some desired outcome (Cherubini, 2009b; Maddux, 1997). From this perspective, individuals (and groups) often view structured exercise as a chore, or job to do, and consequently either do not participate or miss out on opportunities to enjoy the time in which they are participating. With a focus on the process (i.e., the activity) as opposed to the product (i.e., weight loss), exercise researchers and practitioners can help participants acknowledge physical activity as a mindful practice rather than a mindless habit (Cherubini, 2009b; Maddux, 1997; McKenzie, 2007; Prusak & Vincent, 2005). The experience sampling method (ESM; Foster & Lloyd, 2007) is one tool that can be adapted to help identify levels of mindfulness during physical activities (Cherubini, 2009b). Feedback based on the ESM can be used to structure programming to increase overall engagement and intrinsic motivation for physical activity.

Whereas attitude (based on values) has a strong influence on behavior, too often the best placed intentions are pointed in the wrong direction. From a developmental perspective, initiating and maintaining appropriate levels of physical activity is best accomplished using a task-oriented approach (Boyd, Weinmann, & Yin, 2002; Cherubini, 2008, 2009a; Zizzi, Keeler, & Watson, 2006). However, distractions abound in our digital, fast-paced, and sedentary society. The key is to help clients stay on task and focused in the present while being aware of and controlling (to the best extent possible) everyday distractions and stressors (Cherubini, 2009a; Martin, Thompson, & McKnight, 1998). The awareness to predict distractions (both internal and external), control physical and mental arousal when distracted, and shift attention back to the task (attention control training) are all imperative to diminishing the debilitating influence of distractions on physical activity levels (Cherubini, 2009a; Nideffer, 1989).

Action—Moments of Movement

Within the IDM, developmental elements of attitude and attention influence physical activity in a variety of positive ways. Yet even with the best intentions and focus, we still need to actually take action in order to have success (Cherubini, 2009a); in essence, we need to have physical *moments of movement*. Hence, a focus on self-regulatory behavior, including action planning, must be at the center of effective behavior change programming. The following self-regulatory attributes and processes (adapted from Zimmerman, 2002), are critical to action development with the IDM and should be applied by both the practitioner and participant: (a) being self-motivated (using goal setting and barrier self-efficacy); (b) having a plan or routine (using task strategies and self-directed learning); (c) being timely and efficient (using time management); (d) being self-aware of task performance (using self-monitoring, self-evaluation, self-revision); (e) being socially sensitive and resourceful (seeking help when needed); and (f) being environmentally sensitive and resourceful (altering the physical environment).

In facilitating action, it is important for exercise practitioners to think through and match the demands of the exercise task with demographic characteristics (current health, fitness, perceived skill) and all other ecological resources and challenges (Cherubini, 2009a, 2009b). Using a task/skill balance within a mastery or process goal environment (focused on learning and self-improvement), practitioners can create *comfortably challenging* physical activity opportunities that contribute to both mindfulness and sustained activity (Cherubini, 2009a, 2009b; Mandigo & Holt, 2006). The development of process goals, consistent with core beliefs and values and employed within a performance and outcome hierarchy, is advantageous to action and effective behavior change (Anshel, 2008; Anshel & Kang, 2007; Cherubini, 2009a).

When initiating and maintaining physical activity, psychosocial mediators and processes of change are essential to a successful action plan (Baruth et al., 2010; Napolitano et al., 2008; Papandonatos et al., 2012). Practitioners can help facilitate action development by putting into practice the following mediators and processes of change: (a) cognitive processes of change (increasing knowledge, comprehending benefits), (b) decisional balance (weighing pros and cons of activity), (c) behavioral processes of change (enlisting support, substituting alternatives), (d) barrier self-efficacy (building confidence), (e) social support (utilizing social motivators specific to activity), (f) exercise-induced feelings (focusing on revitalization, positive engagement, physical exhaustion), (g) physical activity enjoyment (focusing on autonomy, choice, and relatedness), and (h) outcome expectancies (empowering clients to connect to valued outcomes).

Adherence—Life of Movement

The IDM applies an eco-developmental perspective, with physical activity motivation and adherence being a lifelong process. Within the IDM, facilitating ecological factors and positive developmental elements dynamically interact to enhance adherence. Contrarily, debilitating ecological factors with stability or regression will deter physical activity adherence. Researchers, practitioners, and participants are encouraged to examine motivation and adherence through this eco-developmental lens and implement the following behavior change strategies: (a) focus on values, intrinsic motivation, and self-regulated behavior; (b) select moderate-to-vigorous physical activities (MVPA) that are perceived to be interesting, challenging, and providing feelings of pleasure; (c) focus on a task-oriented approach emphasizing personal choice and mastery; (d) use process goals and activities that are perceived as comfortably challenging; (e) emphasize and promote constructive goals, supportive relationships, mentoring, and reinforcement of MVPA; (f) emphasize and promote MVPA as a positive social influence on the actions of others; and (g) empower individuals/groups with voluntary, structured behavior-change programs.

The key to a *life of movement* is the quality of the everyday physical activity experience (Cherubini, 2009b; Seligman & Csikszentmihalyi, 2000). Practitioners can enhance daily physical activity and exercise experiences through enabling (or disabling) impactful ecological factors while cultivating the development of a *love of movement* (connected to values, interests, choice, excitement, and achievement), the *flow of movement* (mindful, engaged, and focused on the task), and physical *moments of movement* (self-regulated, motivated, and supported).

CONCLUDING THOUGHTS

Considering the surplus of influences on our health behavior, we cannot safely assume everyone wants to, or is ready to, change their behavior, or whether their lifestyle and personal environment are even conducive to change. As Ockene (2001) correctly concludes, "change is a process, not a one-time event, and we cannot expect people to make changes at a level for which they are not ready. Our interventions need to be directed to where the individual is" (p. 45). In order to be successful in learning to change health behavior (using either the DVM or IDM), exercise practitioners and participants must assess the task at hand; evaluate current values, knowledge, and skills; initiate action; monitor progress; and adjust strategies as needed to ensure long-term adherence (Anshel, 2008; Cherubini, 2009a). With opportunities to analyze current health-related behavior, plan for change, execute change, and evaluate and reevaluate actions, both the DVM and the IDM serve as practical alternative models for successful health behavior change.

Perhaps it is human to engage in self-destructive behaviors, to do something every day that we *know* is unhealthy and not good for us. It is also human to blame our circumstances and barriers (from a variety of individual, social, and physical environmental sources) that prevent us from "doing the right thing" when it comes to maintaining good health. But as the British philosopher, George Bernard Shaw (1856–1950), once said, "People are always blaming their circumstance for what they are. I do not believe in circumstances. The people who get on in this world are the people who get up and look for the circumstances they want, and if they cannot find them, make them" (Cook, 1993, p. 439). Consistent with Shaw's statement, this chapter attempted to provide strategies to create the personal energy and situational conditions that will promote a healthy lifestyle and the motivation to change the way we live.

Successfully changing lifestyle habits that contribute to physical inactivity is primarily a psychological process, as shown by the models explained in this chapter. Our daily health-related self-talk often consists of "everything is fine," "my doctor says I'm healthy," "everyone in my family is overweight," and "I've always been this way." Long-term consequences of these soothing messages are usually ignored because, according to Loehr and Schwartz (2003), most of us have an infinite capacity for self-deception. The starting point for making changes in our life requires clearing away the "smoke and mirrors" and taking an open and honest look at ourselves. We need to analyze our perceptions from an eco-developmental perspective and seek the truth about the short-term costs and long-term consequences of habits that are unhealthy, dysfunctional, and self-destructive. This involves identifying all possible factors influencing our values, beliefs, thoughts, actions, and exercise involvement and setting forth an action plan based on this analysis.

Life's journey is a marathon, not a sprint, and requires energy and a sense of purpose to "go the distance" in making proper lifestyle changes. These changes must be driven by our values and persistence and mental toughness, including the understanding that failure (to change our behavior) is not an option. Lifestyle change is mental. In the words of former heavy-weight champion Mohammad Ali, "Champions aren't made in the gyms. Champions are made from something they have deep inside them—a desire, a dream, a vision."

REFERENCES

Anshel, M. H. (2008). The Disconnected Values Model: Intervention strategies for health behavior change. *Journal of Clinical Sport Psychology, 2*, 357–380.

Anshel, M. H. (2013). A cognitive-behavioral approach for promoting exercise behavior: The Disconnected Values Model. *Journal of Sport Behavior, 36*, 107–129.

Anshel, M. H. (2014). *Applied health fitness psychology*. Champaign, IL: Human Kinetics.

Anshel, M. H., & Kang, M. (2007). An outcome-based action study on changes in fitness, blood lipids, and exercise adherence based on the Disconnected Values Model. *Behavioral Medicine, 33*, 85–98.

Bandura, A. (1997). *Self-efficacy: The exercise of control*. New York, NY: Freeman.

Bandura, A. (2001). Social cognitive theory: An agentic perspective. *Annual Review of Psychology, 52*, 1–26.

Barnhill, A., & King, K. F. (2013). Ethical agreement and disagreement about obesity prevention policy in the United States. *International Journal of Health Policy and Management, 1*(2), 117–120.

Baruth, M., Wilcox, S., Dunn, A. L., King, A. C., Marcus, B. H., Rejeski, W. J., . . . Blair, S. N. (2010). Psychosocial mediators of physical activity and fitness changes in the activity counseling trial. *Annals of Behavioral Medicine, 39*(3), 274–289.

Becker, M. H. (1986). The tyranny of health promotion. *Public Health Reviews, 14*, 15–25.

Berger, J. T. (1998). Culture and ethnicity in clinical care. *Archives of Internal Medicine, 158*, 2085–2090.

Boyd, M. P., Weinmann, C., & Yin, Z. (2002). The relationship of physical self perceptions and goal orientations to intrinsic motivation for exercise. *Journal of Sport Behavior, 25*, 1–18.

Brownson, R. C., Baker, E. A., Houseman, R. A., Brennan, L. K., & Bacak, S. J. (2001). Environmental and policy determinants of physical activity in the United States. *American Journal of Public Health, 91*, 1995–2003.

Buckworth, J., & Dishman, R. K. (2013). *Exercise psychology* (2nd ed.). Champaign, IL: Human Kinetics.

Cherubini, J. (2008). Adult African American women's perspective on influences that affect their physical activity involvement. *International Council for Health, Physical Education, Recreation, Sport, and Dance (ICHPER·SD), Journal of Research, 3,* 84–96.

Cherubini, J. (2009a). Intentional development: A model to guide lifelong physical activity. *The Physical Educator, 66*(4), 197–208.

Cherubini, J. (2009b). Positive psychology and quality physical education. *Journal of Physical Education, Recreation & Dance, 80*(7), 42–47, 51.

Cockerham, W. C., Rutten, A., & Abel, T. (1997). Conceptualizing contemporary health lifestyles: Moving beyond Weber. *The Sociological Quarterly, 38,* 321–342.

Cook, J. (1993). *The book of positive quotations.* Minneapolis: Fairview Press.

De Bourdeaudhuij, I. D., & Sallis, J. (2002). Relative contribution of psychosocial variables to the explanation of physical activity in three population-based adults samples. *Preventive Medicine, 34,* 279–288.

Dishman, R. K., & Buckworth, J. (1997). Adherence to physical activity. In W. P. Morgan (Ed.), *Physical activity & mental health* (pp. 63–80). Washington, DC: Taylor & Francis.

Festinger, L. (1957). *A theory of cognitive dissonance.* Stanford, CA: Stanford University Press.

Foster, S. L., & Lloyd, P. J. (2007). Positive Psychology principles applied to consulting psychology at the individual and group level. *Consulting Psychology Journal: Practice and Research, 59,* 30–40.

Gill, D. L. (1999). Gender issues: Making a difference in the real world of sport psychology. In G. G. Brannigan (Ed.), *The sport scientists: Research adventures* (pp. 133–147). New York, NY: Addison Wesley Longman.

Glasgow, R. E., Klesges, L. M., Dzewaltowski, D. A., Bull, S. S., & Estabrooks, P. (2004). The future of health behavior change research: What is needed to improve translation of research into health promotion practice. *Annals of Behavioral Medicine, 27,* 3–12.

Grzywacz, J. G., & Marks, N. F. (2001). Social inequalities and exercise during adulthood: Toward an ecological perspective. *Journal of Health and Social Behavior, 42,* 202–220.

Hall, P. A., & Fong, G. T. (2007). Temporal self-regulation theory: A model for individual health behavior. *Health Psychology Review, 1,* 6–52.

Heinrich, B. (2002). *Why we run.* New York, NY: HarperCollins Publishers Inc.

Hogan, H. W., & Mookherjee, H. N. (1981). Values and selected antecedents. *Journal of Social Psychology, 113,* 29–35.

Hunter, J. P., & Csikszentmihalyi, M. (2003). The positive psychology of interested adolescents. *Journal of Youth and Adolescence, 32*(1), 27–35.

Kanning, M., & Schlicht, W. (2010). Be active and become happy: An ecological momentary assessment of physical activity and mood. *Journal of Sport & Exercise Psychology, 32,* 253–261.

Kilpatrick, M., Hebert, E., & Jacobsen, D. (2002). Physical activity motivation: A practitioner's guide to Self-Determination Theory. *Journal of Physical Education, Recreation, & Dance, 73*(4), 36–41.

King, A. C. (2001). Interventions to promote physical activity by older adults. *The Journals of Gerontology, 56,* 36–46.

Kumanyika, S. K. (2002). Obesity treatment in minorities. In T. A. Wadden & A. J. Stunkard (Eds.), *Handbook of obesity treatment* (pp. 416–446). New York, NY: The Guilford Press.

Lemire, D. (2007). Positive psychology and the constructive goals of human behavior. *The Journal of Individual Psychology, 63*(1), 59–66.

Loehr, J., & Schwartz, T. (2003). *The power of full engagement: Managing energy, not time, is the key to high performance and personal renewal.* New York, NY: Free Press.

Long, B. C., & van Stavel, R. (1995). Effects of exercise training on anxiety: A meta-analysis. *Journal of Applied Sport Psychology, 7,* 167–189.

Lox, C. L., Martin, K. A., & Petruzzello, S. J. (2010). *The psychology of exercise: Integrating theory and practice* (3rd ed.). Scottsdale, AZ: Holcomb Hathaway.

Maddux, J. E. (1997). Habit, health, and happiness. *Journal of Sport & Exercise Psychology, 19,* 331–346.

Malloy, D. C., & Rossow-Kimball, B. (2007). The philosopher-as-therapist: The noble coach and self-awareness. *Quest, 59,* 311–322.

Mandigo, J. L., & Holt, N. L. (2006). Elementary students' accounts of optimal challenge in physical education. *The Physical Educator, 63*(4), 170–183.

Martens, M. P., Mobley, M., & Zizzi, S. J. (2000). Multicultural training in applied sport psychology. *The Sport Psychologist, 14*, 81–97.

Martin, S. B., Thompson, C. L., & McKnight, J. (1998). An integrative psychoeducational approach to sport psychology consulting. *International Journal of Sport Psychology, 29*, 170–186.

McElroy, M. (2002). *Resistance to exercise.* Champaign, IL: Human Kinetics.

McKenzie, T. L. (2007). The preparation of physical educators: A public health perspective. *Quest, 59*, 346–357.

McKenzie, T. L. (2010). 2009 C. H. McCloy lecture: Seeing is believing: Observing physical activity and its contexts. *Research Quarterly for Exercise and Sport, 81*(2), 113–122.

Millman, D. (1994). *The inner athlete: Realizing your fullest potential.* Walpole, NH: Stillpoint Publishing.

Napolitano, M. A., Papandonatos, G. D., Lewis, B. A., Whiteley, J. A., Williams, D. M., King, A. C., . . . Marcus, B. H. (2008). Mediators of physical activity behavior change: A multivariate approach. *Healthy Psychology, 27*(4), 409–418.

National Physical Activity Plan Alliance. (2014). *2014 United States report card on physical activity for children and youth.* Retrieved from http://youthtoday.org/2014/04/2014-u-s-report-card-on-physical-activity-for-children-and-youth/

Nestle, M., & Jacobson, M. F. (2000, January/February). Halting the obesity epidemic: A public health policy approach. *Public Health Reports, 115*, 12–24.

Nideffer, R. (1989). *Attention control training for sport.* Los Gatos, CA: Enhanced Performance Services.

Ockene, I. S. (2001). Provider approaches to improve compliance. In L. E. Burke & I. S. Ockene (Eds.), *Compliance in healthcare and research* (pp. 73–80). Armonk, NY: Futura

Ogilvie, D., Bull, F., Powell, J., Cooper, A. R., Brand, C., Mutrie, N., . . . Rutter, H. (2011). An applied ecological framework for evaluating infrastructure to promote walking and cycling: The iConnect study. *American Journal of Public Health, 101*, 473–481.

Ossman, W. A., Wilson, K. G., Storaasli, R. D., & McNeill, J. W. (2006). A preliminary investigation of the use of Acceptance and Commitment Therapy in group treatment for social phobia. *International Journal of Psychology and Psychological Therapy, 6*, 397–416.

Papandonatos, G. D., Williams, D. M., Jennings, E. G., Napolitano, M. A., Bock, B. C., Dunsiger, S., & Marcus, B. H. (2012). Mediators of physical activity behavior change: Findings from a 12 month randomized controlled trial. *Health Psychology, 31*(4), 512–520.

Pittman, B. (2001). *Afrocentric kinesiology: Innovators and early adopters in a diffusion of innovations model.* Unpublished dissertation, Temple University, Philadelphia, PA.

Prochaska, J. J., Spring, B., & Nigg, C. R. (2008). Multiple health behavior change research: An introduction and overview. *Preventive Medicine, 46*, 181–188.

Prusak, K. A., & Vincent, S. D. (2005). Is your class about something? Guiding principles for physical education teachers. *Journal of Physical Education, Recreation, & Dance, 76*(6), 25–28, 35.

Resnicow, K., Dilorio, C., Soet, J. E., Borrelli, B., Hecht, J., & Ernst, D. (2002). Motivational interviewing in health promotion: It sounds like something is changing. *Health Psychology, 21*, 444–451.

Rokeach, M. (1973). *The nature of human values.* New York, NY: Free Press.

Rollnick, S., Miller, W. R., & Butler, C. C. (2008). *Motivational interviewing in health care: Helping patients change behavior.* New York, NY: Guilford.

Ryan, R. M., & Deci, E. L. (2007). Active human nature: Self-determination theory and the promotion and maintenance of sport, exercise, and health. In M. S. Hagger & N. L. D. Chatzisarantis (Eds.), *Intrinsic motivation and self-determination in exercise and sport* (pp. 1–19). Champaign, IL: Human Kinetics.

Sallis, J. F., Owen, N., & Fischer, E. B. (2008). Ecological models of health behavior. In K. Glanz, B. K. Rimer, & K. Viswanath (Eds.), *Health behavior and health education: Theory, research and practice* (4th ed., pp. 465–485). San Francisco: Jossey-Bass.

Segar, M. L., Eccles, J. S., & Richardson, C. R. (2011). Rebranding exercise: Closing the gap between values and behavior. *International Journal of Behavioral Nutrition and Physical Activity, 8*, 94–108.

Seligman, M., & Csikszentmihalyi, M. (2000). Positive psychology: An introduction. *American Psychologist, 55*(1), 5–14.

Stathopoulou, G., Powers, M. B., Berry, A. C., Smits, J. A., & Otto, M. W. (2006). Exercise interventions for mental health: A Quantitative and qualitative review. *Clinical Psychology: Science and Practice, 13*, 179–193.

Super, D. E. (1995). Values: Their nature, assessment, and practical use. In D. E. Super & B. Sverko (Eds.), *Life roles, values, and careers: International findings of the work importance study* (pp. 54–61). San Francisco: Jossey-Bass.

Task Force on Community Preventive Services. (2011). *Community preventive services task force first annual report to congress and to agencies related to the work of the task force*. Washington, DC: Centers for Disease Control.

U.S. Department of Health and Human Services. (2006). *Healthy people 2010 midcourse review*. Washington, DC: U.S. Government Printing Office.

U.S. Department of Health and Human Service. (2008). *2008 Physical Activity Guidelines for Americans*. Washington, DC: U.S. Government Printing Office.

Whitaker, E. D. (2005). The bicycle makes the eyes smile: Exercise, aging, and psychophysical well-being in older Italian cyclists. *Medical Anthropology, 24*, 1–43.

Zhang, T., Solmon, M. A., Gao, Z., & Kosma, M. (2012). Promoting school students' physical activity: A social ecological perspective. *Journal of Applied Sport Psychology, 24*, 92–105.

Zimmerman, B. J. (2002). Becoming a self-regulated learner: An overview. *Theory into Practice, 41*(2), 64–70.

Zizzi, S. J., Keeler, L. A., & Watson II, J. C. (2006). The interaction of goal orientation and stage of change on exercise behavior in college students. *Journal of Sport Behavior, 29*(1), 96–110.

7   Exercise and Well-Being

Mikihiro Sato

INTRODUCTION

In 2011, the Organization for Economic Cooperation and Development (OECD) launched the Better Life Index, which consists of 11 dimensions essential to well-being (health and education, local environment, life satisfaction, etc.; OECD, 2013). The national well-being index was also released in Canada in 2011 and in Great Britain in 2012. In the United States, several cities and states have launched community well-being initiatives, and the U.S. government has explored developing a federal happiness index (Rao, 2013; Walt, 2012). Recent well-being studies have sought to address the concern that standard economic indicators, such as GDP, do not account for all factors that contribute to the quality of life (OECD, 2013; Walt, 2012). Traditionally, most government policies and interventions have focused on economic benefits because economic growth is assumed to increase people's quality of life. Yet economic indicators omit much of what the society values (e.g., increasing life satisfaction, reducing distress), and noneconomic indicators, such as well-being, are critical to assess the effects of government interventions (Diener & Seligman, 2004). Assessing people's well-being has become even more important as economies and societies around the world have been stricken by the global financial crisis (OECD, 2013). It is important for policy makers to understand how they can develop successful government policies and programs that promote people's well-being.

Researchers have identified that, among various correlates of well-being, exercise plays an integral role (Caddick & Smith, 2014; Maher, Doerksen, Elavsky, & Conroy, 2014; Maher et al., 2013; Rejeski & Mihalko, 2001; Standage, Gillison, Ntoumanis, & Treasure, 2012; Strachan, Brawley, Spink, & Glazebrook, 2010). Exercise can contribute to people's life by enhancing their ability to perform daily activities, promoting enjoyment, or providing meaning in life (Berger & Tobar, 2011). In exploring the contribution of exercise to well-being, it is imperative to define the term *exercise* and to differentiate it from associated terms, such as *physical activity* and *sports*. Physical activity represents all types of human movement, including gardening and playing music instruments, whereas sports refers to organized competitive physical activity that focuses on winning and elite-level performance (Berger & Tobar, 2011). In contrast, exercise refers to structured and planned physical activities and often relates to activities that have a health, wellness, and recreational focus (Berger & Tobar, 2011). I follow Beaton and Funk (2008) in defining exercise as an activity that inherently requires moderately intense physical exertion and that is perceived by the individual as being relatively freely chosen as well as beneficial, enjoyable, or both.

The purpose of this chapter is to explore how personal resources related to exercise (e.g., exercise behaviors, attitudes toward exercise) and environmental resources related to exercise (e.g., parks, recreational facilities, participatory sport events) can contribute to well-being. The chapter first reviews subjective well-being, a key construct in well-being research. Building on previous social-ecological models, the chapter develops a theoretical framework for understanding the role of exercise in well-being. Research findings on environmental resources related to exercise are then provided. The constructs of behavioral involvement and psychological involvement, which represent measures of personal resources related to exercise, are offered and followed by the constructs' potential contribution to well-being. The chapter concludes with practical recommendations and future directions for exercise and well-being research.

SUBJECTIVE WELL-BEING

Although no single perspective can capture the diverse experiences of people's quality of life, one definition of a quality of life could be when a person thinks that her life is desirable regardless of how others see it. This phenomenon has been called *subjective well-being*, and scholars have used it as a key variable for over 50 years for analyzing quality of life (Andrews & McKennell, 1980; Andrews & Withey, 1976; Campbell, Converse, & Rodgers, 1976; Diener, 1984, 2000; Diener, Suh, Lucas, & Smith, 1999; Newman, Tay, & Diener, 2014; Sirgy et al., 2006; Wilson, 1967). People's quality of life depends on objective (e.g., economic or health indicators) and subjective (e.g., self-reported happiness or life satisfaction) assessments of their life (Dissart & Deller, 2000). In line with literature that examines the benefits of exercise (Caddick & Smith, 2014; Maher et al., 2014; Rejeski & Mihalko, 2001; Standage et al., 2012; Strachan et al., 2010), this chapter focuses on subjective well-being, a subjective assessment of people's quality of life.

Components of Subjective Well-Being

The concept of subjective well-being is usually divided into two components: affective well-being and cognitive well-being (Lucas, Diener, & Suh, 1996; Luhmann, Hofmann, Eid, & Lucas, 2012; see Figure 7.1). Affective well-being refers to the presence of positive

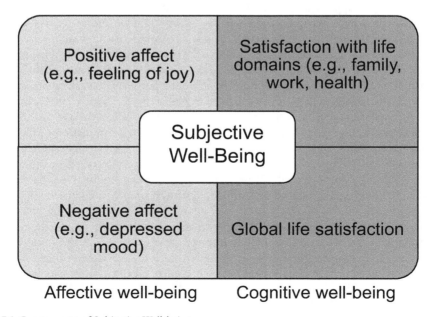

Figure 7.1 Components of Subjective Well-being

affect (e.g., feelings of happiness) and the absence of negative affect (e.g., depressed mood). To that end, the concepts of positive and negative affect were developed by Bradburn (1969), along with his Affect Balance Scale, which helps measure positive affect and negative affect. At any given moment, positive affect and negative affect could be highly and inversely correlated. This said, positive and negative affect often increasingly diverge as the mood of an individual is evaluated across an expanded timeframe (Sirgy et al., 2006). Although researchers can combine positive and negative affect into an affect balance or global happiness score, it would be desirable to assess positive affect and negative affect separately to capture the dynamics and unique variance of the two types of affective well-being (Diener, 2000; Sirgy et al., 2006).

Cognitive well-being consists of global life satisfaction and life domain satisfaction. Global life satisfaction is viewed as an attitude that arises from the cognitive evaluation of one's overall satisfaction with his life (Diener, 2000; Heller, Watson, & Ilies, 2004). In contrast, life domain satisfaction refers to satisfaction with key areas in life, such as family, work, and health. In the 1970s, national quality of life surveys in the United States asked respondents to formulate judgments about levels of satisfaction with life as a whole or with some specific domains of life (Andrews & Withey, 1976; Campbell, 1981). Recent research initiatives have also used the life-satisfaction measure to assess people's perceived quality for their daily life. For instance, *Healthy People 2020*, which guides the 10-year national health agenda in the United States, uses global life satisfaction as an indicator of well-being (U.S. Department of Health and Human Services, 2010). General social surveys in Australia (Australian Bureau of Statistics, 2011), New Zealand (Statistics New Zealand, 2013), and Great Britain (Office for National Statistics, 2015), as well as the Better Life Index by the OECD (OECD, 2013), also used global life satisfaction as an indicator of well-being.

Bottom-Up and Top-Down Approaches

To better understand what contributes to subjective well-being, scholars have adopted either top-down or bottom-up approaches (Diener et al., 1999; Heller et al., 2004; Maher et al., 2013). A top-down approach assumes a dispositional perspective that emphasizes the role of individuals' time-invariant factors, such as personality traits, in subjective well-being. For instance, the Big Five personality traits (i.e., openness to experience, conscientiousness, extraversion, agreeableness, and neuroticism) predict 18% of the variance in global life satisfaction (Steel, Schmidt, & Shultz, 2008). Moreover, given the relative consistency of the global life satisfaction measure across time, the top-down approach purports that global life satisfaction is rather associated with stable personality characteristics (Eid & Diener, 2004). In contrast, a bottom-up approach focuses on the role of events and situational factors in global life satisfaction and assumes that global life satisfaction is derived from a summation of pleasant and unpleasant experiences (Diener et al., 1999; Heller et al., 2004). Specifically, engaging in exercise could fulfill one's psychological needs, such as meaning, mastery, detachment, autonomy, and affiliation (Newman et al., 2014). Meeting such needs influences satisfaction with various life domains (e.g., family, health), which, in turn, promotes life satisfaction (Newman et al., 2014).

Given the theoretical relevance of the top-down and bottom-up approaches, the challenge is to understand how top-down internal factors (e.g., personality) and bottom-up situational factors (e.g., experiences from exercise) interact. Some top-down processes are likely involved, as people react to events subjectively, whereas the bottom-up approach is useful, as certain events should be pleasurable to most people (Heller et al., 2004). Indeed, personality has been suggested to influence exercise behaviors (Rhodes & Pfaeffli, 2012; Wilson & Dishman, 2015), attitudes toward exercise (Hoyt, Rhodes, Hausenblas, & Giacobbi, 2009), and life satisfaction (Diener et al., 1999; Steel et al., 2008). Consequently, the role of exercise in life domain satisfaction and global life satisfaction should be investigated after accounting for top-down factors, such as personality traits.

A FRAMEWORK FOR UNDERSTANDING ROLES OF EXERCISE IN WELL-BEING

The bottom-up approach provides a theoretical explanation of how the experience of exercise can contribute to people's subjective well-being. Besides individual factors, environmental factors can also be important correlates of exercise behaviors and well-being (Stokols, 1992, 1996). To explore the joint contribution of individual and environmental factors to subjective well-being, this section proposes a theoretical framework, as shown in Figure 7.2. The basis of the proposed framework is attributed to previous social-ecological models of exercise and health promotion (Sallis et al., 2006; Stokols, 1992, 1996).

Figure 7.2 illustrates that various personal and environmental resources can contribute to well-being. These resources consist of multiple levels of influence, including individual, interpersonal (family, friends), organizational (schools, workplaces), community, and policy. Although the focus of previous social-ecological models has been on the role of personal and environmental determinants of health-related behaviors, such as exercise promotion (Biddle, 2011; Sallis et al., 2006), a few studies have used a social-ecological model to explain how individual and environmental determinants contribute to people's well-being (Stokols, 1992, 1996; Stokols, Grzywacz, McMahan, & Phillips, 2003). The framework shown in Figure 7.2 illustrates that personal and environmental resources, as well as the interactions between these resources, contribute to various measures of well-being, such as subjective well-being. The sections below discuss key resources related to exercise and measures for well-being.

Resources Affecting Well-Being

Personal Resources

In Figure 7.2, personal resources are shown in the oval on the left side. Personal resources include demographic and genetic factors (e.g., personality), as well as behaviors, attitudes, knowledge, and skills related to exercise. Behaviors, attitudes, knowledge, and skills are distinguished from demographic and genetic factors because the latter are less likely to be influenced by environmental resources within a short period of time. Personal resources related to exercise are highlighted in light gray in the figure to differentiate them from demographic and genetic factors.

Environmental Resources

Social-ecological models support the argument that environmental resources, in combination with demographic and genetic factors, influence attitudes, behaviors, knowledge, and skills related to exercise. Exercise settings provide opportunities for individuals to develop their behaviors, attitudes, knowledge, and skills related to exercise. Exercise settings will be evaluated by their characteristics and access to settings (Sallis et al., 2006). Environmental resources, such as the recreational environment (e.g., participatory sport events, recreational facilities), the neighborhood and home environments (e.g., parks, home exercise equipment), the workplace environment (e.g., facilities and programs that support employees' exercise), and the school environment (e.g., facilities, physical education programs) are considered exercise settings.

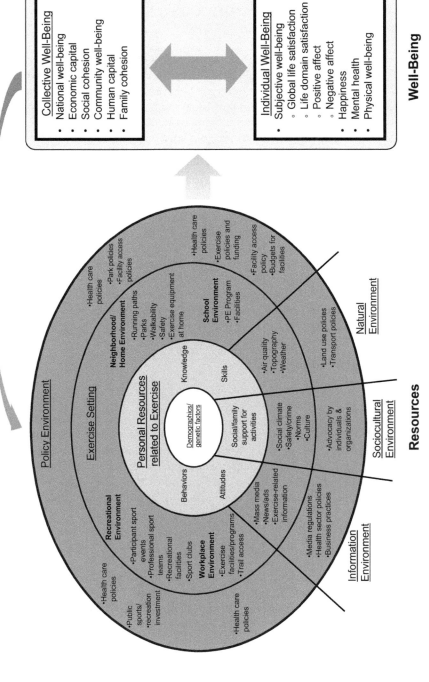

Figure 7.2 A Framework for Understanding the Role of Exercise in Well-being (adapted from Sallis et al., 2006)

The policy environment influences exercise settings. Specifically, policy impacts are exerted through various mechanisms, such as built environments, programs, and incentives (Sallis et al., 2006). Some policies, such as health care policies, are relevant to recreation, workplace, neighborhood, and school environments. In contrast, other policies, such as public sports and recreation investment, are more relevant to the recreational environment.

Consistent with Sallis et al.'s (2006) model, sociocultural environment variables are illustrated as cutting across other levels. Family structure can be seen as a demographic variable; social and family support for activities are considered personal resources related to exercise; social climate, safety, norms, and culture vary by exercise settings; and advocacy by individuals and organizations can shape policy environment.

The natural environment includes weather, air quality, and topography, all of which can be characteristics of exercise settings. Land-use policies can influence availability of public open space, and transport policies can influence air quality (Sallis et al., 2006). The information environment includes exercise-related information to promote active participation, news and advertising, and programming through mass media. Information sources can be televisions and the internet at home, printed and electronic notices in the workplace, and promotional materials at fitness centers. Environmental resources related to exercise are highlighted in darker gray in Figure 7.2 to differentiate from personal resources related to exercise.

Well-Being

Well-being (the rounded rectangle on the right side in Figure 7.2) consists of individual well-being and collective well-being (Sirgy, 2011). Measures of individual well-being include subjective well-being, happiness, mental health, and physical well-being. In contrast, collective well-being is measured at the interpersonal (e.g., family cohesion), organizational (e.g., human capital at a workplace), community (e.g., community well-being), and country (e.g., national well-being) levels. Individual and collective well-being are related to each other. For instance, the global life satisfaction of individuals can contribute their community's aggregate well-being (Stokols et al., 2003). Similarly, community well-being, such as social cohesion and economic capital, provides the basis for enriching individuals' satisfaction with their community life, a key life domain among individuals (Stokols et al., 2003). However, measures of individual well-being cannot directly assess collective well-being, as collective well-being can be more or less than the sum of the individuals' well-being making up their parts such as families, organizations, and communities (Oishi, 2012; Sirgy, 2011). Although well-being research has focused on identifying factors that affect individual well-being, it is critical to identify the collective power that promotes community and national well-being (Oishi, 2012; Glover & Stewart, 2013).

The better a person's well-being, the more likely he or she is to exercise and experience positive attitudes toward exercise. These positive attitudes can further enhance their individual well-being. More positive collective well-being can also contribute to the development of environmental resources related to exercise; for example, greater economic capital in a community leads to investing more in parks or recreational facilities in that community. These increased environmental resources can contribute to personal resources and then enhance individual and collective well-being.

In sum, the framework shown in Figure 7.2 proposes that personal and environmental resources individually and jointly contribute to well-being. The remainder of this chapter presents an example to elucidate the proposed framework. The example shows how environmental resources related to exercise can strengthen the personal resources gained through exercise and how these resources can contribute to global life satisfaction (see Figure 7.3).

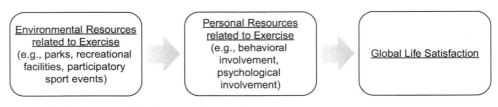

Figure 7.3 An Application of the Proposed Framework

THEORETICAL EXAMPLE

Role of Environmental Resources in Exercise

Various environmental resources are associated with exercise. Findings from meta-analyses have identified five environmental resources as potential correlates of exercise: accessibility of facilities (e.g., park, running path), opportunities for activity, aesthetics (e.g., the attractiveness and pleasantness of the neighborhood environment), weather, and safety (Humpel, Owen, Leslie, 2002; Owen, Humpel, Leslie, Bauman, & Sallis, 2004). Kaczynski and Henderson (2007) demonstrated the relationship between parks and recreation settings and exercise behavior. Among 50 articles published between 1998 and 2005, trails and paths were studied most frequently ($n = 17$) as environmental correlates of exercise behavior, followed by parks, open space, and recreation centers (Kaczynski & Henderson, 2007). Based on a review of 52 articles specific to trails and exercise behavior, Starnes, Troped, Klenosky, and Doehring (2011) found mixed effects of trails on the level of exercise, with, surprisingly, negative effects in some cases. In contrast, positive associations between the proximity of neighborhood parks and the level of exercise have been consistently supported (Cohen et al., 2010; Veitch, Ball, Crawford, Abbott, & Salmon, 2012). In addition to the proximity to parks, park size was a significant predictor of exercise behavior (Cohen et al., 2010; Sugiyama, Francis, Middleton, Owen, & Giles-Corti, 2010).

Although research has provided evidence on the degree to which recreational and neighborhood environments contribute to exercise behavior, results concerning the types of recreation settings and exercise are unclear (Ferdinand, Sen, Rahurkar, Engler, & Menachemi, 2012; Kaczynski & Henderson, 2007; Starnes et al., 2011). These inconsistent findings could be due to interactions between personal resources and environmental resources (Giles-Corti & Donovan, 2002). For instance, Huston, Evenson, Bors, and Gizlice (2003) found that, although trails and access to places for exercise might be associated with exercise levels, perceived neighborhood environments and access to places for exercise were strongly associated with demographic factors, such as race, education, and income. Additionally, McNeill, Wyrwich, Brownson, Clark, and Kreuter (2006) suggested that environmental resources not only have direct effects on the level of exercise but also have indirect effects through individual-level psychological variables, such as self-efficacy and motivation. Findings from these studies indicate that the roles of environmental resources in exercise behavior and its subsequent contributions to global life satisfaction should be assessed through personal resources, such as sociodemographic and psychological variables.

Personal Resources Related to Exercise

Personal resources represent individual characteristics that can influence well-being. A review of literature related to exercise and well-being indicates that various constructs can be considered personal resources related to exercise. These constructs include actual physical functioning and perceived physical functioning (Rejeski & Mihalko, 2001), athletic identity (Anderson, 2004; Brewer, Cornelius, Stephan, & Van Raalte, 2010), behavioral involvement and psychological involvement (Sato, Jordan, & Funk, 2014), commitment to goals (Diener et al., 1999), exercise identity (Anderson & Cychosz, 1994), meaning (Iwasaki, 2007), psychological needs (Rodríguez, Látková, & Sun, 2008), self-efficacy (Konopack & McAuley, 2012), and self-esteem (Maher et al., 2013). This chapter uses behavioral involvement and psychological involvement as measures of personal resources related to exercise. The next section reviews the role of exercise in global life satisfaction, followed by a review of psychological involvement and its influence on global life satisfaction.

Role of Exercise in Global Life Satisfaction

The relationship between exercise and global life satisfaction has been examined in numerous studies (Elavsky et al., 2005; Maher et al., 2013, 2014; Rodríguez et al., 2008; Strachan et al., 2010). McAuley et al. (2000) found that individuals who exercised more often during the intervention program showed a greater increase in global life satisfaction over the six-month program. Maher et al. (2013) also found that people reported greater global life satisfaction on days when they were more active. The relationship between exercise and global life satisfaction, however, is complicated by the diversity within exercise (e.g., aerobic vs. anaerobic, competitive vs. noncompetitive), characteristics of exercise (e.g., duration, intensity, frequency of activities), and characteristics of participants (e.g., age, gender, previous sports experience; Berger & Tobar, 2011). McAuley et al. (2000) investigated the effect of two different types of exercises, aerobic (i.e., brisk walking) and toning (i.e., stretching, limbering, mild strengthening), on people's global life satisfaction. They found that both aerobic and toning influence people's global life satisfaction in a similar way, suggesting that vigorous exercise is unnecessary for enhancing life satisfaction. In fact, excessive exercise behavior, as reflected by high frequency and long duration, can negatively affect people's attitude toward life (Berger & Tobar, 2011). Individuals who are addicted to exercise will continue to exercise despite social, medical, or vocational information to the contrary (Berger, Pargman, & Weinberg, 2007). Consequently, a compulsion to participate in exercise is likely to lower their global life satisfaction.

The direct impact of exercise on global life satisfaction has also been questioned. In a study of 633 middle-age, affluent individuals living in the United States, Rodríguez et al. (2008) found that although the frequency of running and walking had a significant effect on people's global life satisfaction, this activity accounted for only 1% of the unique variance of global life satisfaction. The evidence on indirect effects is clearer: both cross-sectional and longitudinal studies have indicated that the level of exercise indirectly contributes to global life satisfaction through its influence on physical self-worth, self-efficacy, affect, and mental and physical health status (Elavsky et al., 2005; McAuley et al., 2008). These findings imply that frequency of participation in exercise is necessary but might have limited direct benefits in people's global life satisfaction.

Furthermore, when examining people's involvement with exercise, both behavioral involvement and psychological involvement should be explored. Behavioral involvement refers to the frequency and duration of effort expended in pursuing exercise (Sato et al., 2014). Psychological involvement is defined as a multifaceted construct that comprises hedonic value, centrality, and symbolic value (Beaton, Funk, Ridinger, & Jordan, 2011). Hedonic value reflects the enjoyment derived from an activity. Centrality represents how central the activity is to the individual's lifestyle. Symbolic value demonstrates the self-expression value or level of symbolism of the activity (Beaton et al., 2011). Assessing psychological involvement extends the field's understanding of behavioral involvement by considering the meaning of exercise to an individual's life, which may positively contribute to people's global life satisfaction (Iwasaki,

2007). Although the relationship between behavioral involvement and global life satisfaction has been discussed, the connection between psychological involvement and global life satisfaction has been rarely examined (Havitz & Mannell, 2005). To fully assess the influence of exercise on an individual's global life satisfaction, I next review the conceptualization of psychological involvement, followed by its potential contribution to global life satisfaction.

Psychological Involvement

Over the past 30 years, scholars have used psychological involvement to understand people's psychological connection to a recreational activity (Beaton et al., 2011; Havitz & Dimanche, 1997; McIntyre, 1989; Sato et al., 2014). The construct of psychological involvement was initially introduced from work on social judgment theory (Sherif & Hovland, 1961). During the 1980s, Sherif and his colleagues' work was extended to consumer behavior research to understand purchase behavior of consumer goods (Laurent & Kapferer, 1985), and this understanding has since been applied to leisure contexts. In line with Rothschild's (1984) conceptualization, psychological involvement in a recreational activity has been defined as an unobservable state of motivation, arousal, or interest toward recreational activities or associated products that are evoked by a particular stimulus or situation and that have drive properties (Havitz & Dimanche, 1997).

Efforts to measure the involvement construct evolved primarily from Laurent and Kapferer (1985) and their multidimensional consumer involvement profile (CIP). McIntyre (1989) was the first to apply facets of the CIP to a recreational setting, which revealed a three-factor solution composed of hedonic value, centrality, and symbolic value in assessing psychological involvement in the activity. Within the focus of exercise behavior, psychological involvement is defined as an individual's attitudinal orientation toward an exercise activity (e.g., running, walking) formed by hedonic, central, and symbolic aspects of the activity. The multidimensional measure of psychological involvement is distinguishable from relevant constructs such as exercise identity (Anderson & Cychosz, 1994), which refers to a self-reflective, conscious evaluation of how individuals view themselves as exercisers, and has been measured by a unidimensional scale.

Role of Psychological Involvement in Global Life Satisfaction

A potential consequence of change to psychological involvement in an activity would be a corresponding change in global life satisfaction (Sato, Jordan, & Funk, 2015). Specifically, intrinsically motivated goals toward exercise provide a sense of meaning in life and maintain an individual's affect system, both of which likely contribute to people's life evaluation (Cantor & Sanderson, 1999; Diener et al., 1999). A higher level of psychological involvement in an activity is also likely to promote higher levels of flow, a state of optimal psychological experience (Havitz & Mannell, 2005). Experiencing flow then encourages habitual participation in the activity and promotes global life satisfaction by fostering the growth of skills and knowledge associated with the activity (Peterson, Park, & Seligman, 2005). Furthermore, psychological involvement is associated with an individual's participation in activities that convey the overall meaning of that activity in an individual's life, leading to positive life evaluations (Iwasaki, 2007). Finally, recent studies revealed that the more people were connected to running as an exercise, the more they would positively evaluate their life (Sato et al., 2014, 2015).

The notion of positive psychology also supports the argument that psychological involvement may serve as a potential contributor to global life satisfaction. Seligman (2002) proposed that the most satisfied people are those who orient their pursuits toward the three components of pleasure (the pleasant life), engagement (the engaged life), and meaning (the meaningful life). Pleasure is concerned with pursuing a life that maximizes positive emotions, whereas engagement refers to the psychological state that accompanies highly engaging activities in the person's life (Peterson et al., 2005). Meaning includes coherence in one's life or pursuit of purposeful life goals (Emmons, 2003). The three components of pleasure, engagement, and meaning in life are likely to promote an individual's global life satisfaction (Peterson et al., 2005; Schueller & Seligman, 2010). Seligman's conceptualization in positive psychology is similar to the conceptualization of psychological involvement that consists of three facets: hedonic value, centrality, and symbolic value (Beaton et al., 2011). As illustrated in Figure 7.4, the three facets of psychological involvement may contribute to the Seligman's three pathways that enhance life satisfaction (Sato et al., 2015). Specifically, hedonic value in exercise could contribute to a pleasant life, centrality in exercise could be equated to the pursuit of an engaged life, and symbolic value in exercise could be associated with a meaningful life. Given that various psychological interventions can influence people's happiness levels (Fredrickson, Cohn, Coffey, Pek, & Finkel, 2008; Seligman, Steen, Park, & Peterson, 2005), environmental resources related to exercise could promote individuals' hedonic value, centrality, and symbolic value regarding exercise, and these valuations, in turn, can help them develop a positive self-evaluation of life and contribute to global life satisfaction.

Although positive associations between behavioral involvement and global life satisfaction have been found (Maher et al., 2013; Rodríguez et al., 2008), measurements of behavioral involvement do not include the relative meaning of the activity, a factor that could influence respondents' reports of global life satisfaction (Sato et al., 2014). As such, behavioral involvement might not sufficiently explain people's global life satisfaction. Given that behavioral involvement and psychological involvement have moderate correlations (Sato et al., 2014), some level of behavioral involvement is necessary in predicting participants' global life satisfaction. Nevertheless, the benefits of exercise in people's global life satisfaction may be

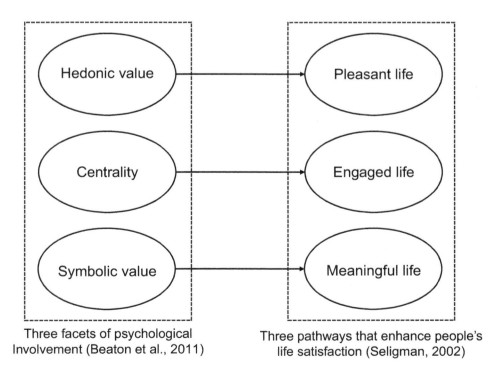

Three facets of psychological Involvement (Beaton et al., 2011)

Three pathways that enhance people's life satisfaction (Seligman, 2002)

Figure 7.4 Psychological Involvement and the Three Pathways that Enhance People's Life Satisfaction

achieved by stimulating a stable attitudinal orientation toward the activity, namely psychological involvement (Sato et al., 2015).

SUMMARY AND FUTURE DIRECTIONS

Given the growing concern with global well-being initiatives, investigation of how exercise contributes to well-being will likely remain a popular area of study among researchers and practitioners. Using the social-ecological model, this chapter developed a theoretical framework that suggests that personal and environmental resources related to exercise, as well as the interactions between them, contribute to well-being. The sections above described how the framework can be applied to exercise and well-being research (the relationship between environmental resources, behavioral and psychological involvement, and global life satisfaction). Based on the proposed framework as shown in Figure 7.2, more directions for future work are offered below.

Investigation of Multiple Levels of Environmental Resources

A recent investigation suggests that a distance-running event can serve as an environmental resource to promote people's psychological involvement in running as an exercise, which in turn promotes global life satisfaction (Sato et al., 2015). As the proposed framework indicates, however, other environmental resources related to exercise, such as neighborhood environment (e.g., park and training facilities) and sociocultural environment (e.g., social support from friends and family), may also contribute to people's global life satisfaction. Before concluding that an environmental resource plays a causal role, researchers must go beyond examining environmental resources individually and conduct multilevel research that includes the influence of individual, interpersonal, organizational, community, and policy circumstances (McLeroy, Bibeau, Steckler, & Glanz, 1988; Owen et al., 2004). Future research would do well to explore how multiple levels of environmental resources related to exercise, including training partners (interpersonal), fitness and sport clubs (organizational), and access to training facilities and running and waking paths (community and policy circumstances), collectively influence people's well-being.

Investigation of the Role of Personality Traits

The proposed framework indicates that environmental resources can promote behaviors and attitudes toward exercise, and exercise then contributes to global life satisfaction. However, given that personality traits have been a consistent predictor of people's exercise behaviors (Rhodes & Pfaeffli, 2012; Wilson & Dishman, 2015) and global life satisfaction (Steel et al., 2008), it is unclear how much an environmental resource such as a distance-running event (a) contributes to people's behavioral and psychological involvement in exercise and (b) subsequently promotes global life satisfaction. Future research could investigate how personal resources related to exercise (e.g., behavioral and psychological involvement) mediate the relationship between personality traits and well-being. Findings from such research would provide evidence on how engaging in exercise can contribute to well-being beyond the personality traits.

Investigation of the Relationship Between Behavioral Involvement and Psychological Involvement

Although neither the frequency nor the duration of exercise seems to have a direct association with global life satisfaction (Elavsky et al., 2005; McAuley et al., 2008; Sato et al., 2014), the benefits of behavioral involvement can be assessed by different well-being measures, such as mental health (reduced anxiety or depression) or physical well-being (e.g., muscle strength; Atlantis, Chow, Kirby, & Singh, 2006). Maher and colleagues (2013, 2014) also argued that exercise can contribute to global life satisfaction at the within-person level but not at the between-person level. Furthermore, behavioral involvement might provide an opportunity for individuals to stimulate attitudinal connection to the activity, which, in turn, contributes to global life satisfaction (Elavsky et al., 2005; Rejeski & Mihalko, 2001). For instance, increased attitudes resulting from exercise, such as self-efficacy, can be important mediators in the relationship between exercise behaviors and global life satisfaction (Elavsky et al., 2005; Rejeski & Mihalko, 2001). Future research should investigate how behavioral involvement influences attitudinal orientation toward exercise (e.g., psychological involvement), and, consequently, how that orientation contributes to various measures of individual well-being. These investigations may help shed light on the debate surrounding the direct impact of exercise behaviors on people's lives (Rodríguez et al., 2008) and broaden the theoretical understanding of how exercise contributes to people's well-being.

Investigation of Other Personal Resources Related to Exercise

This chapter used behavioral and psychological involvement as indicators of personal resources. However, other constructs can be considered to be personal resources gained through exercise, including actual and perceived physical functioning (Rejeski & Mihalko, 2001), athletic identity (Anderson, 2004; Brewer et al., 2010), commitment to goals (Diener et al., 1999), exercise identity (Anderson & Cychosz, 1994), meaning (Iwasaki, 2007), psychological needs (Rodríguez et al., 2008), self-efficacy (Konopack & McAuley, 2012), and self-esteem (Maher et al., 2013). To fully assess the role of exercise in well-being, future research should explore the relationship between these personal resources gained through exercise and well-being.

Investigation of Other Well-Being Measures

This chapter examined the contribution of exercise to global life satisfaction, a subjective measure of well-being. To understand this contribution, it is important to explore how personal and environmental resources related to exercise are associated with other measures of individual well-being, such as positive affect, negative affect, and happiness. As the proposed framework indicates, some environmental resources can also contribute to collective well-being (e.g., social cohesion, sense of community; Stokols, 1996; Stokols et al., 2003). Although an individual's well-being can contribute to improved community well-being (Stokols et al., 2003), research focusing on individual-level well-being cannot directly explain macro-level well-being (Sirgy, 2011). Given that enhancing collective well-being is becoming an important research area (Glover & Steward, 2013; Oishi, 2012), future research might investigate how environmental resources related to exercise can help build environmental resources in a community that, in turn, influence collective well-being, such as social cohesion and social capital in a community (Sirgy, 2011; Stokols et al., 2003).

REFERENCES

Anderson, C. B. (2004). Athletic identity and its relation to exercise behavior: Scale development and initial validation. *Journal of Sport & Exercise Psychology, 26,* 39–56.

Anderson, D. F., & Cychosz, C. M. (1994). Development of an exercise identity scale. *Perceptual and Motor Skills, 78,* 747–751.

Andrews, F. M., & McKennell, A. C. (1980). Measures of self-reported well-being: Their affective, cognitive, and other components. *Social Indicators Research, 8,* 127–155.

Andrews, F. M., & Withey, S. B. (1976). *Social indicators of well-being: Americans' perceptions of life quality.* New York, NY: Plenum Press.

Atlantis, E., Chow, C. M., Kirby, A., & Singh, M. A. F. (2006). Worksite intervention effects on sleep quality: A randomized controlled trial. *Journal of Occupational Health Psychology, 11*, 291–304.

Australian Bureau of Statistics. (2011). *2010 General social survey: Summary results.* Retrieved from www.ausstats.abs.gov.au/ausstats/subscriber.nsf/0/D0B6CB77DE0BF677CA25791A00824C41/$-File/41590_2010.pdf

Beaton, A. A., & Funk, D. C. (2008). An evaluation of theoretical frameworks for studying physically active leisure. *Leisure Sciences, 30*, 53–70.

Beaton, A. A., Funk, D. C., Ridinger, L., & Jordan, J. S. (2011). Sport involvement: A conceptual and empirical analysis. *Sport Management Review, 14*, 126–140.

Berger, B. G., Pargman, D., & Weinberg, R. S. (2007). *Foundations of exercise psychology.* (2nd ed.). Morgantown, WV: Fitness Information Technology.

Berger, B. G., & Tobar, D. A. (2011). Exercise and quality of life. In T. Morris & P. C. Terry (Eds.), *The new sport and exercise psychology companion* (pp. 483–505). Morgantown, WV: Fitness Information Technology.

Biddle, S. J. (2011). Overview of exercise psychology. In T. Morris & P. Terry (Eds.), *The new sport and exercise psychology companion* (pp. 443–460). Morgantown, WV: Fitness Information Technology.

Bradburn, N. M. (1969). *The structure of psychological well-being* (Vol. xvi). Oxford, UK: Aldine.

Brewer, B. W., Cornelius, A. E., Stephan, Y., & Van Raalte, J. (2010). Self-protective changes in athletic identity following anterior cruciate ligament reconstruction. *Psychology of Sport and Exercise, 11*, 1–5.

Caddick, N., & Smith, B. (2014). The impact of sport and physical activity on the well-being of combat veterans: A systematic review. *Psychology of Sport and Exercise, 15*, 9–18.

Campbell, A. (1981). *The sense of well-being in America: Recent patterns and trends.* New York, NY: McGraw-Hill.

Campbell, A., Converse, P. E., & Rodgers, W. L. (1976). *The quality of American life: Perceptions, evaluations, and satisfactions.* New York, NY: Russell Sage Foundation.

Cantor, N., & Sanderson, C. A. (1999). Life task participation and well-being: The importance of taking part in daily life. In D. Kahneman, E. Diener, & N. Schwartz (Eds.), *Well-being: The foundations of hedonic psychology* (pp. 434–450). New York, NY: Russell Sage Foundation.

Cohen, D. A., Marsh, T., Williamson, S., Derose, K. P., Martinez, H., Setodji, C., & McKenzie, T. L. (2010). Parks and physical activity: Why are some parks used more than others? *Preventive Medicine, 50*(Supplement), S9–S12.

Diener, E. (1984). Subjective well-being. *Psychological Bulletin, 95*, 542–575.

Diener, E. (2000). Subjective well-being: The science of happiness and a proposal for a national index. *American Psychologist, 55*, 34–43.

Diener, E., & Seligman, M. E. P. (2004). Beyond money: Toward an economy of well-being. *Psychological Science in the Public Interest, 5*, 1–31.

Diener, E., Suh, E. M., Lucas, R. E., & Smith, H. L. (1999). Subjective well-being: Three decades of progress. *Psychological Bulletin, 125*, 276–302.

Dissart, J. C., & Deller, S. C. (2000). Quality of life in the planning literature. *Journal of Planning Literature, 15*, 135–161.

Eid, M., & Diener, E. (2004). Global judgments of subjective well-being: Situational variability and long-term stability. *Social Indicators Research, 65*, 245–277.

Elavsky, S., McAuley, E., Motl, R. W., Marquez, D. X., Hu, L., Jerome, G. J., & Diener, E. (2005). Physical activity enhances long-term quality of life in older adults: Efficacy, esteem, and affective influences. *Annals of Behavioral Medicine, 30*, 138–145.

Emmons, R. A. (2003). Personal goals, life meaning, and virtue: Wellsprings of a positive life. In C. L. M. Keyes & J. Haidt (Eds.), *Flourishing: Positive psychology and the life well-lived* (pp. 105–128). Washington, DC: American Psychological Association.

Ferdinand, A., Sen, B., Rahurkar, S., Engler, S., & Menachemi, N. (2012). The relationship between built environments and physical activity: A systematic review. *American Journal of Public Health, 102*(10), e7–e13.

Fredrickson, B. L., Cohn, M. A., Coffey, K. A., Pek, J., & Finkel, S. M. (2008). Open hearts build lives: Positive emotions, induced through loving-kindness meditation, build consequential personal resources. *Journal of Personality and Social Psychology, 95*, 1045–1062.

Giles-Corti, B., & Donovan, R. J. (2002). The relative influence of individual, social and physical environment determinants of physical activity. *Social Science & Medicine, 54*, 1793–1812.

Glover, T. D., & Stewart, W. P. (2013). Advancing healthy communities policy through tourism, leisure, and events research. *Journal of Policy Research in Tourism, Leisure and Events, 5*, 109–122.

Havitz, M. E., & Dimanche, F. (1997). Leisure involvement revisited: Conceptual conundrums and measurement advances. *Journal of Leisure Research, 29*, 245–278.

Havitz, M. E., & Mannell, R. C. (2005). Enduring involvement, situational involvement, and flow in leisure and non-leisure activities. *Journal of Leisure Research, 37*, 152–177.

Heller, D., Watson, D., & Ilies, R. (2004). The role of person versus situation in life satisfaction: A critical examination. *Psychological Bulletin, 130*, 574–600.

Hoyt, A. L., Rhodes, R. E., Hausenblas, H. A., & Giacobbi Jr., P. R. (2009). Integrating five-factor model facet-level traits with the theory of planned behavior and exercise. *Psychology of Sport and Exercise, 10*, 565–572.

Humpel, N., Owen, N., & Leslie, E. (2002). Environmental factors associated with adults' participation in physical activity: A review. *American Journal of Preventive Medicine, 22*, 188–199.

Huston, S. L., Evenson, K. R., Bors, P., & Gizlice, Z. (2003). Neighborhood environment, access to places for activity, and leisure-time physical activity in a diverse North Carolina population. *American Journal of Health Promotion, 18*, 58–69.

Iwasaki, Y. (2007). Leisure and quality of life in an international and multicultural context: What are major pathways linking leisure to quality of life? *Social Indicators Research, 82*, 233–264.

Kaczynski, A. T., & Henderson, K. A. (2007). Environmental correlates of physical activity: A review of evidence about parks and recreation. *Leisure Sciences, 29*, 315–354.

Konopack, J. F., & McAuley, E. (2012). Efficacy-mediated effects of spirituality and physical activity on quality of life: A path analysis. *Health and Quality of Life Outcomes, 10*, 57.

Laurent, G., & Kapferer, J.-N. (1985). Measuring consumer involvement profiles. *Journal of Marketing Research, 22*, 41–53.

Lucas, R. E., Diener, E., & Suh, E. (1996). Discriminant validity of well-being measures. *Journal of Personality and Social Psychology, 71*, 616–628.

Luhmann, M., Hofmann, W., Eid, M., & Lucas, R. E. (2012). Subjective well-being and adaptation to life events: A meta-analysis. *Journal of Personality & Social Psychology, 102*, 592–615.

Maher, J. P., Doerksen, S. E., Elavsky, S., & Conroy, D. E. (2014). Daily satisfaction with life is regulated by both physical activity and sedentary behavior. *Journal of Sport & Exercise Psychology, 36*, 166–178.

Maher, J. P., Doerksen, S. E., Elavsky, S., Hyde, A. L., Pincus, A. L., Ram, N., & Conroy, D. E. (2013). A daily analysis of physical activity and satisfaction with life in emerging adults. *Health Psychology, 32*, 647–656.

McAuley, E., Blissmer, B., Marquez, D. X., Jerome, G. J., Kramer, A. F., & Katula, J. (2000). Social relations, physical activity, and well-being in older adults. *Preventive Medicine, 31*, 608–617.

McAuley, E., Doerksen, S. E., Morris, K. S., Motl, R. W., Hu, L., Wójcicki, T. R., . . . Rosengren, K. R. (2008). Pathways from physical activity to quality of life in older women. *Annals of Behavioral Medicine, 36*, 13–20.

McIntyre, N. (1989). The personal meaning of participation: Enduring involvement. *Journal of Leisure Research, 21*, 167–179.

McLeroy, K. R., Bibeau, D., Steckler, A., & Glanz, K. (1988). An ecological perspective on health promotion programs. *Health Education & Behavior, 15*, 351–377.

McNeill, L. H., Wyrwich, K. W., Brownson, R. C., Clark, E. M., & Kreuter, M. W. (2006). Individual, social environmental, and physical environmental influences on physical activity among black and white adults: A structural equation analysis. *Annals of Behavioral Medicine, 31*, 36–44.

Newman, D. B., Tay, L., & Diener, E. (2014). Leisure and subjective well-being: A model of psychological mechanisms as mediating factors. *Journal of Happiness Studies, 15*, 555–578.

Office for National Statistics. (2015). *Measuring national well-being: Personal well-being in the* UK, *2014 to 2015*. Retrieved from www.ons.gov.uk/peoplepopulationandcommunity/wellbeing/bulletins/measuringnationalwellbeing/20150-92-3#measuring-personal-well-being-in-the-uk

Oishi, S. (2012). *The psychological wealth of nations: Do happy people make a happy society*. Hoboken, NJ: John Wiley & Sons.

Organization for Economic Cooperation and Development (OECD). (2013). *How's life? 2013: Measuring well-being*. Paris: OECD Publishing. Retrieved from http://dx.doi.org/10.1787/9789264201392-en

Owen, N., Humpel, N., Leslie, E., Bauman, A., & Sallis, J. F. (2004). Understanding environmental influences on walking: Review and research agenda. *American Journal of Preventive Medicine, 27*, 67–76.

Peterson, C., Park, N., & Seligman, M. E. P. (2005). Orientations to happiness and life satisfaction: The full life versus the empty life. *Journal of Happiness Studies, 6*, 25–41.

Rao, M. (2013, April 23). *The "Wellbeing Index": Santa Monica joins U.S. cities tracking happiness*. Retrieved April 30, 2013, from www.huffingtonpost.com/2013/04/23/wellbeing-index-santa-monica_n_3118641.html

Rejeski, W. J., & Mihalko, S. L. (2001). Physical activity and quality of life in older adults. *The Journals of Gerontology Series A: Biological Sciences and Medical Sciences, 56*, 23–35.

Rhodes, R. E., & Pfaeffli, L. A. (2012). Personality and physical activity. In E. O. Acevedo (Ed.), *The Oxford handbook of exercise psychology* (pp. 195–223). Oxford, UK: Oxford University Press.

Rodríguez, A., Látková, P., & Sun, Y.-Y. (2008). The relationship between leisure and life satisfaction: Application of activity and need theory. *Social Indicators Research, 86*, 163–175.

Rothschild, M. L. (1984). Perspectives on involvement: Current problems and future directions. *Advances in Consumer Research, 11*, 216–217.

Sallis, J. F., Cervero, R. B., Ascher, W., Henderson, K. A., Kraft, M. K., & Kerr, J. (2006). An ecological approach to creating active living communities. *Annual Review of Public Health, 27*, 297–322.

Sato, M., Jordan, J. S., & Funk, D. C. (2014). The role of physically active leisure for enhancing quality of life. *Leisure Sciences, 36*, 293–313.

Sato, M., Jordan, J. S., & Funk, D. C. (2015). Distance running events and life satisfaction: A longitudinal study. *Journal of Sport Management, 29*, 347–361.

Schueller, S. M., & Seligman, M. E. P. (2010). Pursuit of pleasure, engagement, and meaning: Relationships to subjective and objective measures of well-being. *The Journal of Positive Psychology, 5*, 253–263.

Seligman, M. E. P. (2002). *Authentic happiness: Using the new positive psychology to realize your potential for lasting fulfillment*. New York, NY: Free Press.

Seligman, M. E. P., Steen, T. A., Park, N., & Peterson, C. (2005). Positive psychology progress: Empirical validation of interventions. *American Psychologist, 60*, 410–421.

Sherif, M., & Hovland, C. I. (1961). *Social judgment: Assimilation and contrast effects in communication and attitude change* (Vol. xii). Oxford, UK: Yale University Press.

Sirgy, M. (2011). Societal QOL is more than the sum of QOL of individuals: The whole is greater than the sum of the parts. *Applied Research in Quality of Life, 6*, 329–334.

Sirgy, M. J., Michalos, A. C., Ferriss, A. L., Easterlin, R. A., Patrick, D., & Pavot, W. (2006). The quality-of-life (QOL) research movement: Past, present, and future. *Social Indicators Research, 76*, 343–466.

Standage, M., Gillison, F. B., Ntoumanis, N., & Treasure, D. C. (2012). Predicting students' physical activity and health-related well-being: A prospective cross-domain investigation of motivation across school physical education and exercise settings. *Journal of Sport & Exercise Psychology, 34*, 37–60.

Starnes, H. A., Troped, P. J., Klenosky, D. B., & Doehring, A. M. (2011). Trails and physical activity: A review. *Journal of Physical Activity and Health, 8*, 1160–1174.

Statistics New Zealand. (2013). *New Zealand general social survey: 2012*. Retrieved from www.stats.govt.nz/~/media/Statistics/Browse%20for%20stats/nzgss/HOTP2012/nzgss2012HOTP.pdf

Steel, P., Schmidt, J., & Shultz, J. (2008). Refining the relationship between personality and subjective well-being. *Psychological Bulletin, 134*, 138–161.

Stokols, D. (1992). Establishing and maintaining healthy environments: Toward a social ecology of health promotion. *American Psychologist, 47*, 6–22.

Stokols, D. (1996). Translating social ecological theory into guidelines for community health promotion. *American Journal of Health Promotion, 10*, 282–298.

Stokols, D., Grzywacz, J. G., McMahan, S., & Phillips, K. (2003). Increasing the health promotive capacity of human environments. *American Journal of Health Promotion, 18*, 4–13.

Strachan, S. M., Brawley, L. R., Spink, K., & Glazebrook, K. (2010). Older adults' physically-active identity: Relationships between social cognitions, physical activity and satisfaction with life. *Psychology of Sport and Exercise, 11*, 114–121.

Sugiyama, T., Francis, J., Middleton, N. J., Owen, N., & Giles-Corti, B. (2010). Associations between recreational walking and attractiveness, size, and proximity of neighborhood open spaces. *American Journal of Public Health, 100*, 1752–1757.

U.S. Department of Health and Human Services. (2010). *Healthy People 2020.* Retrieved from www.healthypeople.gov/

Veitch, J., Ball, K., Crawford, D., Abbott, G. R., & Salmon, J. (2012). Park improvements and park activity: A natural experiment. *American Journal of Preventive Medicine, 42*, 616–619.

Walt, V. (2012, May 30). Why everyone's trying to measure well-being. *Time.* Retrieved from http://business.time.com/2012/05/30/why-everyones-trying-to-measure-well-being/

Wilson, K. E., & Dishman, R. K. (2015). Personality and physical activity: A systematic review and meta-analysis. *Personality and Individual Differences, 72*, 230–242.

Wilson, W. (1967). Correlates of avowed happiness. *Psychological Bulletin, 67*, 294–306.

8 Psychological Skills Training for Adopting and Adhering to Exercise

Lauren S. Tashman, Duncan Simpson, and J. Gualberto Cremades

INTRODUCTION TO PSYCHOLOGICAL SKILLS TRAINING

Psychological skills training (PST) can be defined as the "systematic and consistent practice of mental or physical skills for the purpose of enhancing performance, increasing enjoyment, or achieving greater sport and physical activity self-satisfaction" (Weinberg & Gould, 2015, p. 248). This approach stems from cognitive behavioral therapy in which the focus is on modifying ineffective and/or maladaptive cognitive processes (Hill, 2001). The interaction of thoughts, feelings, and behaviors within the framework of PST are explored in this chapter for the purposes of increasing adaptive behaviors and decreasing maladaptive behaviors.

In an attempt to determine adaptive behaviors, Vealey (1988, 2007) identified multiple psychological skills that influence one's potential for success and overall well-being. She organized them into four basic categories of skills: foundation, performance, personal development, and team (see Table 8.1). *Foundation* skills, including achievement drive, self-awareness, productive thinking, and self-confidence, are fundamental interpersonal processes that not only affect other psychological skills but also directly affect behavior. *Performance* skills, including perceptual-cognitive skill, attentional focus, and energy management, are critical for successful execution and coordination of physical skills during performance. The *personal development* skills of identity achievement and interpersonal competence correspond to deep-seated psychological functioning and needs that are fundamental aspects of the human condition. These skills represent one's self-awareness regarding identity and feelings of self-worth as well as one's ability to effectively interact with others. Finally, *team* skills, including leadership, communication, cohesion, and team confidence, are important for ensuring effective teamwork and an environment conducive to team success.

In fact, the premise of PST is that teaching clients these strategies for optimizing psychological skills will help them self-regulate their own thoughts, feelings, and behaviors. Thus, PST provides a means for clients to (a) identify patterns and problems in their thoughts, feelings, and behaviors; (b) commit to making the changes necessary to optimize their performance; (c) execute the processes to facilitate these changes; (d) manage any environmental factors or barriers that affect their performance; and (e) generalize this skill set to other similar situations and areas of their performance (Kirschenbaum, 1984).

Research indicates that PST can be used to improve psychological skills in a large variety of performance contexts (Vealey, 2007). While such research is not without methodological limitations (see Beauchamp, Harvey, & Beauchamp, 2012), findings generally indicate that PST results in positive outcomes for both sport and non-sport performers (Meyers, Whelan, & Murphy, 1996). As such, the focus on the application of PST has mainly been on improving sport (Weinberg & Gould, 2015) and, more recently, non-sport (e.g., military, business, music) performance (Hays, 2012). However, less has been written and researched on the

Table 8.1 Vealey's (1988, 2007) Categorization of Psychological Skills

Category	Psychological Skill	Exercise Example
Foundation Skills	Achievement Drive	Desire to put forth effort toward achieving one's exercise goals and persist when encountering challenges, such as slow goal achievement
	Self-Awareness	Openness to honestly self-reflect on the impact of one's thoughts, feelings, and behaviors when not meeting exercise goals
	Productive Thinking	Ability to have and effectively utilize positive, motivational thoughts when doing a challenging workout
	Self-Confidence	Belief in one's ability to successfully achieve exercise goals
Performance Skills	Perceptual-Cognitive Skill	Utilization of mental images to complete exercises with correct physical form
	Attentional Focus	Ability to maintain focus and disregard distractions while exercising
	Energy Management	Regulation of feelings states as well as mental and physical energy levels to optimally complete workouts
Personal Development Skills	Identity Achievement	Clarity of one's identity as an exerciser and understanding of the impact on one's self-worth
	Interpersonal Competence	Ability to effectively interact with other exercisers and fitness professionals involved in one's exercise participation and goals
Team Skills	Leadership	Ability of a fitness professional to effectively influence one's exercise clients
	Communication	Fitness professionals' verbal and nonverbal communication with exercise clients
	Cohesion	Effectiveness of the working alliance between fitness professional and exercise client
	Team Confidence	Fitness professional's and exerciser's belief in their work together and exercise program being implemented

application of PST in physical activity and exercise settings. While physical activity refers to any bodily movement resulting in physical exertion (e.g., gardening), exercise represents a structured form of physical activity (e.g., weight lifting) that has a particular objective (e.g., reducing stress; Lox, Martin Ginis, & Petruzello, 2010). Exercise is the term more frequently used in the fitness industry and sport psychology field (i.e., exercise psychology). Therefore, the focus of this chapter will center on relating PST to exercise, although the concepts and strategies discussed can certainly be related to other forms of physical activity.

Given the global increase in physical inactivity and its associated risks (e.g., obesity, ischaemic heart disease, breast and colon cancers, etc.; World Health Organization, 2013), PST may have a vital role to play in the adoption of and adherence to exercise. While further research evaluating the efficacy of PST in exercise settings is needed, the primary purpose of this chapter is to provide recommendations for practitioners to use evidence-based PST strategies to increase their clients' adoption of and adherence to exercise. Practitioners who aim to implement PST for exercise behavior change should first consider the broader context of behavior change theories. These theories outline important variables that pertain to exercise adoption and adherence and thereby facilitate effective design and implementation of PST for exercise behavior. Consequently, there are two parts to the present chapter. The first part, Theories of Behavior Change, provides connections between behavior change theories and PST. Several relevant psychological and behavior change theories will be reviewed, along with a discussion about the implications of these theories for encouraging more effective adoption of and adherence to exercise. The second part, Psychological Skills, extends an in-depth explanation of select psychological skills that may hold potential for targeting and influencing exercise behavior change.

THEORIES OF BEHAVIOR CHANGE

Transtheoretical Model

The transtheoretical model (TTM; Prochaska, DiClemente, & Norcross, 1992) can help practitioners understand their clients' readiness for behavior change. The model posits that people progress through five stages in order to change any given behavior. In the first stage, *precontemplation*, clients are unaware that any change is needed, even if others are indicating that their behaviors are not suitable. In the next two stages, *contemplation* and *preparation*, clients are cognitively processing the need for a change and determining potential means for achieving needed changes. In the final stages, *action* and *maintenance*, behavior change plans have been implemented, and the emphasis is on sustaining the changed behaviors. In exercise settings, the model can be used to identify and design appropriate interventions for a client during a particular stage.

Drawing from the model, researchers have suggested the use of both cognitive and behavioral strategies to facilitate adoption of and adherence to exercise (Dalle Grave, Calugi, Centis, El Ghoch, & Marchesini, 2011; Dishman, 1994). In the earlier stages (i.e., precontemplation, contemplation, and preparation), for instance, efforts should focus on making clients more self-aware of the need to make a change, helping them figure out how to make that change, and determining whether they are capable of that change. For example, in these earlier stages, a practitioner can engage in a discussion with the individual about the benefits of exercise, encourage him to seek out information regarding potential opportunities for engaging in exercise, and facilitate self-evaluation about his ability to begin exercising and the potential barriers for implementing such changes. Therefore, in these initial phases, PST should focus on helping clients cognitively restructure thought processes regarding attitudes toward exercise, analyze and reframe negative self-talk, increase self-confidence, understand and define personal motivation, and set achievable goals. In the latter stages (i.e., action and maintenance), the efforts should focus on helping clients to engage in and maintain their behavioral changes. To these ends, PST should aim to replicate existing successful behaviors through the use of goal setting and self-monitoring, attention control techniques, cue words, affirmations, and feedback, as well as self-reward strategies. As individuals progress through the stages, they perceive increased benefits and decreased barriers for making behavioral changes that will lead to exercise adoption and maintenance (Marshall & Biddle, 2001). Consistent with this notion, researchers (Zizzi & Gilchrist, 2014) have suggested that "movement into the action and maintenance stages of readiness is associated with an increase in self-efficacy or 'perceived capability,' a shift in the pros and cons of change, and the belief there is a potential for change" (p. 105).

That said, *relapse* (i.e., regression to a previous stage) is a common occurrence within behavior change (Prochaska & Bess, 2004) and can happen at any point during the five stages of the model. Therefore, it is important to integrate coping skills into PST programs so that clients do not relapse to prior stages of change or are able to overcome a relapse and return to exercise. To best avoid relapse, clients may engage in both emotion- and problem-focused coping by recognizing thoughts, feelings, and behaviors that might put them at risk of relapse. A useful coping strategy can include contingency planning of what the clients would do if these thoughts, feelings, and behaviors occur so that desired behaviors are maintained despite challenges. Additionally, clients can be taught PST strategies to cope with unforeseen circumstances or situations that may trigger a relapse (e.g., injury, family death, or traveling). For example, having self-talk statements ready for potential relapse situations, using imagery to visualize themselves sticking with their exercise routine, and identifying appropriate social support can be effective strategies for avoiding relapse. Furthermore, encouraging and building flexibility into realistic goal setting can also ensure that when minor relapses occur, clients can quickly advance through the stages in order to re-adhere to exercise.

Self-Efficacy Theory

Self-efficacy theory (Bandura, 1977) indicates that an individual's belief in her ability to successfully perform a desired behavior is one of the most critical predictors in whether or not she will perform that behavior and what she will think about the performance of that behavior. Research has provided support for the impact of self-efficacy on behavior (McAuley & Blissmer, 2000). Therefore, it is important to develop PST strategies and interventions that target a client's self-efficacy.

According to self-efficacy theory, there are six sources of information (i.e., past performance accomplishments, vicarious experiences, imagery, verbal persuasion, physiological states, and emotional experiences) that are used to develop beliefs and perceptions about one's confidence (Short & Ross-Stewart, 2009). These sources of self-efficacy can be used to develop effective PST interventions to target self-efficacy beliefs. *Past performance accomplishments* have the strongest effect on efficacy expectations (Buckworth, Dishman, O'Connor, & Tomporowski, 2013). Thus, a client's previous successes can be used to boost their self-efficacy. For example, having a client write, through personal reflection, a "success list" about exercise behaviors that have been accomplished or improvements that have been made (e.g., lifting a certain weight, running a certain distance, exercising on a particular day despite lack of motivation) can elicit feelings of self-efficacy. Similarly, helping the exerciser to identify his strengths can help build confidence (Beaumont, Maynard, & Butt, 2015) by focusing on the positive, controllable aspects of one's exercise behavior. In the absence of perceived successes, practitioners may need to consider alternative methods to increase self-efficacy. For example, exercise practitioners can implement the use of *vicarious experiences* by having clients identify role models and use their stories of success (e.g., weight loss) to enhance their own beliefs. Furthermore, practitioners can use *verbal persuasion*, such as feedback, praise, and constructive criticism, to help boost the self-efficacy in their clients to increase exercise behavior.

Assisting exercisers in effectively interpreting their *physiological states* can also be useful for increasing beliefs of self-efficacy. For example, teaching a client to perceive the increased heart rate she experiences prior to a new workout routine as an indication of readiness rather than anxiety can help increase perceptions of competence. Similarly, developing emotional intelligence[1] and the ability to effectively channel one's emotions into adaptive behaviors can help increase self-confidence and self-efficacy. Finally, teaching clients to *imagine* themselves being successful at making the desired changes (e.g., losing weight) may prove useful for building self-efficacy. It is important to note, however, that for the imagery to be most effective, the image must be vivid (i.e., include as many senses as possible), and the client should be able to control the image (i.e., direct such aspects as what is imagined, how the imagery progresses, timing of the images, etc.) (Isaac & Marks, 1995).

Developing self-confidence in clients through the use of these different sources of self-efficacy may be one of the most important determinants in the adoption of and adherence to exercise (McAuley & Blissmer, 2000). However, helping clients to identify their own sources of self-confidence may also be a useful strategy. For example, Hays, Thomas, Maynard, and Bawden (2009) developed and evaluated a confidence profiling strategy in order to aid individuals in identifying and evaluating their types and sources of confidence to encourage more focus on controllable rather than uncontrollable sources of confidence. Furthermore, practitioners cannot discount the benefits of simply helping individuals to become more educated about self-efficacy as well as enhancing their self-awareness about their own beliefs and confidence (Beaumont et al., 2015).

Theory of Planned Behavior

Perceptions of self-confidence affect not only behaviors, but also thoughts and emotional reactions (Short & Ross-Stewart, 2009). Therefore, examining and working on thoughts and emotions could be a key feature of utilizing PST for optimizing exercise behaviors. One of the theories that may help explain an individual's thoughts and emotions regarding exercise is the theory of planned behavior (Ajzen & Madden, 1986). The theory proposes that *intention* is the strongest predictor of whether someone will or will not actually perform a behavior. Intention is the product of one's *attitude* toward the behavior (i.e., what one thinks and feels about that behavior), the perceived *subjective norms* associated with that behavior (i.e., perceptions of important others' attitudes toward the behavior), and the individual's perceived *behavioral control* (i.e., autonomy over a given behavior). Therefore, in order to increase engagement in exercise, practitioners should account for clients' attitudes, subjective norms, and perceived behavioral control.

Specifically, practitioners can help change negative attitudes by educating clients about the benefits (consequences) and importance (evaluation of consequences) of engaging in certain activities. For example, frequently emphasizing the relationship between exercise and health can facilitate increased intention, more positive attitudes, and ultimately behavior changes (Digelidis, Papaioannou, Laparidis, & Christodoulidis, 2003; Ferguson, Yesalis, Pomrehn, & Kirkpatrick, 1989). It has also been suggested that highlighting both the pros and cons of engaging in exercise are important for encouraging effective behavior change (Marshall & Biddle, 2001). In addition, practitioners can enhance feelings of control and autonomy by providing clients with choices regarding their exercise behaviors. For example, the type, intensity, mode, and duration of the activities can be jointly decided by the exerciser and the practitioner in order to allow more autonomous, self-determined motivation. Lastly, practitioners may work with clients to evaluate and reframe negative and unrealistic subjective norms. For example, if an exerciser perceives that his significant other does not value the adoption of consistent exercise behavior, his intention to exercise may fade. Therefore, working with the exerciser to increase awareness of the effects of these subjective norms as well to adjust his perspective on those norms may help boost intention and enhance exercise behavior adoption and maintenance.

Motivational Theories

Several motivation theories are important to take into consideration when designing and implementing PST for exercise. According to achievement goal theory (Elliot & Dweck, 1988; Nicholls, 1984), it is important to understand the purpose (i.e., motivation) underlying someone's attempt to achieve a goal as well as how an individual defines success and failure. Furthermore, Dweck (2006) proposed the categorization of two mindsets (i.e., fixed versus growth) that determine how one will approach and respond to success and failure, thereby affecting one's motivation. On the one hand, a *fixed mindset* (e.g., I can't do push ups) stems from the belief that capability is inherited and stable, thus prompting an avoidance of challenge, a tendency to give up in the face of adversity, a belief that effort has no consequence, a perception that criticism is negative feedback about one's capability, and a threatened reaction to others' success. On the other hand, a *growth mindset* (e.g., I can't do push ups yet) is grounded in the belief that capability is developed, thus promoting one to embrace challenges, persist despite adversity and obstacles, view effort as the requisite condition for improvement and mastery, take the perspective that one can learn from criticism, and use others' success for inspiration.

In the context of exercise, it is essential to understand individuals' underlying motivations to change their behaviors, their inherent mindsets, and the specific goals that they are trying to achieve. Specifically, it is important to know whether a person is more driven to achieve a particular *outcome* (e.g., lose 10 pounds; beat exercise partner in a 5k run), *improve* oneself and/or *master* a new skill (e.g., improve strength and endurance; learn how to perform a maneuver in jiu-jitsu), or some combination of both. According to achievement goal theory, being driven to improve oneself or master a particular skill will result in stronger, more intense, more persistent long-term motivation.

In support of this notion, competence motivation theory (Weiss & Chaumeton, 1992) proposes that one's motivational orientation will affect the strength of one's perceptions of self-confidence and control, which will determine one's affect and subsequently one's motivation. According to the theory, the drive to feel competent leads to more positive affect and increased motivation; thus, the adoption of a *mastery/improvement* motivational orientation will be more beneficial in the end. For example, an exerciser who feels competent in his ability to perform a particular type of exercise or reach a specific exercise goal is more likely to enjoy what he is doing and be more motivated to continue to adhere to an exercise program.

It is critical to understand that motivation is not just about the *direction* of one's effort (i.e., whether one is motivated or not); it also involves understanding and improving the *intensity* and *duration* of one's effort (Weinberg & Gould, 2015). Therefore, it is important to determine what component(s) of motivation the individual may need to work on (i.e., direction, intensity, or duration). Based on self-determination theory (Deci & Ryan, 1985), for instance, the driving force underlying one's motivation lies on a continuum from amotivation to intrinsic motivation. Along the continuum, several forms of extrinsic motivation evolve from those with more controlled purposes for engaging in behaviors to those with more autonomous purposes for engaging in behaviors (Deci & Ryan, 1985). From a self-determination perspective, clients will have no motivation to engage in exercise when *amotivated*; thus, working on the direction of the individual's motivation toward exercise should be a key feature of PST. When *extrinsically motivated*, individuals may engage in exercise for a variety of external reasons. To that end, a client may exercise in an attempt to earn a reward or avoid punishment (e.g., receiving a prize for attending more training sessions; *external regulation*), satisfy a sense of obligation to be physically active (e.g., feeling guilty when missing an exercise workout; *introjected*), do it because the activity is valued (e.g., knowing that exercise is important; *identified*), or do it because it's part of their identity (e.g., I am a runner; *integrated*). As there are different types of motivation, it is important that practitioners discuss and understand their clients' motivations for exercising.

Practitioners can motivate their clients through extrinsic forms of motivation in the short term to increase adoption and adherence to exercise (e.g., implementing rewards for completing workout goals). However, in the long term, efforts should be aimed at increasing the clients' *intrinsic motivation* to exercise (e.g., completing workouts for the sense of accomplishment and enjoyment of the activity). In general, intrinsic motivation is experienced when one wants to gain the satisfaction of mastering a new skill and/or participates in an activity for the sheer pleasure or enjoyment of doing so. Thus, based on self-determination theory (Deci & Ryan,

1985), it is important to keep in mind the perceived value or importance of the desired behavior and outcome when designing and implementing PST that addresses motivation. Inherent in this consideration is the understanding that self-determined behavior is a result of one's attempts at meeting basic psychological needs for feeling autonomous, competent, and/or related to others. Therefore, exercisers will adopt more intrinsically derived motivation if they are encouraged to feel a sense of control and ownership over their goals and behaviors, have the opportunity to increase perceptions of their exercise competence, and feel like they belong to a community of exercisers, whether in the more local or general sense (Zizzi & Gilchrist, 2014).

Attribution Theory

Attribution theory (Weiner, 1985) focuses on one's perception of the causes of events and behaviors (i.e., the individual's explanation of what happened, why they succeeded, and why they failed). Thus, in order to understand one's motivation, practitioners need to examine attributions for their *stability*, *locus of causality*, and *locus of control* (Weiner, 1985). For example, after losing five pounds a client may say it happened because he was lucky (unstable) or has good genes (stable), put forth a lot of effort (internal) or had a good personal trainer (external), and stuck with their goal plan (controllable) or had easy access to workout facilities (uncontrollable). Typically, attributions that are internal (e.g., being persistent, putting effort toward accomplishing a task) and perceived as within one's control (e.g., setting goals and developing strategies to achieve them) will result in the best effects on motivation. Therefore, practitioners need to be aware of how clients define successes and failures and help them change any maladaptive attributions.

Social-Ecological Models

Social-ecological models suggest that not only *personal factors* but also *environmental variables* (e.g., physical spaces, community, society, government, etc.) need to be considered when designing and implementing interventions to increase physical activity (Sallis, Owen, & Fisher, 2000). For example, factors related to the individual exerciser, such as gender, age, and health, as well as various levels of environmental factors, such as family, peers, characteristics of the fitness facility, nature of the fitness industry, governmental policies, and culture, will affect physical activity behaviors and thus should be used to effectively design and implement PST interventions. At a more individual or microsystem level, intervention could consist of using PST to increase social support for individual exercisers and enhance group cohesion for a workout facility or group exercise class/program. On a broader level, this could entail designing and implementing PST on more large-scale levels for organizations or communities, or for the purposes of influencing public policy regarding health, physical activity, wellness, and well-being.

Consistent with social-ecological models, *social support* is an important consideration when designing and implementing PST interventions. Social support has been defined as "an exchange of resources between at least two individuals perceived by the provider or the recipient to be intended to enhance the well-being of the recipient" (Shumaker & Brownell, 1984, p. 13). Social support comes in many forms: instrumental, emotional, informational, companionship, and validation (Wills & Shinar, 2000). Exercise practitioners working with clients can help provide all types of social support themselves or can help clients identify others who may serve an important role for the support needed. For example, *instrumental* support involving the provision of tangible and practical assistance could include having a spotter at the gym; *emotional* support could involve verbally encouraging clients during difficult workouts; *informational* support may come in the form of designing workout plans; *companionship* support might entail encouraging the exerciser to work out with a friend or relative; and *validation* could be provided within exercise groups. Others have also conceptualized six types of social support into two categories (Taylor & Taylor, 1997). Of those, the *emotional* category encompasses four types of support, including (1) *listening* (i.e., having someone actively listen without advice or judgment to one's thoughts and feelings), (2) *emotional support* (i.e., getting support during emotionally challenging situations), (3) *emotional challenge* (i.e., having others who push and motivate one to achieve set goals and persist despite obstacles), and (4) *shared social reality* (i.e., having the support of others who have had or currently have similar values, goals, perspectives, or experiences). The *technical* category includes the last two types of support: (5) *technical appreciation* (i.e., receiving acknowledgment for the effort put forth or goals accomplished) and (6) *technical challenge* (i.e., receiving encouragement for pushing oneself farther, stretching oneself outside one's comfort zone, and setting further, more challenging goals). Taylor and Taylor (1997) proposed that anyone can provide emotional support; however, only someone who has perceived technical expertise can effectively provide technical support. Overall, it is important that practitioners assess the size of clients' social networks, identify the types of social support clients receive, and help them to determine their needs and preferences for different types of support.

Finally, with regard to exercise groups, practitioners need to consider *group cohesion*. There are two distinct types of group cohesion: social and task (Carron, Colman, Wheeler, & Stevens, 2002; Zaccaro, 1991). *Social cohesion* refers to the ability of the group members to get along interpersonally and socially, support and respect each other, and have a sense of pride in group membership (Carron, Hausenblas, & Eys, 2005). PST interventions aimed at improving social cohesion could include having "get togethers" or social events outside of the exercise context, incorporating mutual sharing activities and discussions among the group members, identifying similarities among the group members, developing and encouraging group identity, and having members create mission statements and mottos for the group. *Task cohesion* refers to the ability of the group members to coordinate their actions and interact effectively to achieve common goals (Carron et al., 2005). PST interventions aimed at improving task cohesion could include setting group goals, encouraging discussions about sacrifices and contributions to group goals, working on the nonverbal and verbal communication skills of the group members, and engaging in group imagery sessions.

PSYCHOLOGICAL SKILLS

Self-Talk

Both personal (e.g., beliefs, preferences, personality) and situational (e.g., task difficulty, leader behaviors, situational circumstances, environmental settings) factors affect one's self-talk. Furthermore, the nature of one's self-talk results in various consequences, such as influences on one's attention, motivation, self-confidence, behaviors, performance, affect, arousal, and anxiety (Hardy, Oliver, & Tod, 2009). The consequences associated with one's self-talk are likely to affect exercise adoption and adherence. Thus, in order for self-talk to have positive consequences, PST needs to consider both personal and situational factors that affect what one says to oneself as well as focus on the nature/content of self-talk. For example, attempts to change an exerciser's negative self-talk about her ability to perform a particular activity (e.g., "I hate running") will not be effective if she tends to be highly anxious and pessimistic and the specific situation she is in is not taken into consideration (e.g., beginning a new activity or exercise routine). In addition, practitioners need to consider the different types of self-talk: positive/motivational (e.g., "I can complete this set of squats"), negative (e.g., "I hate squats . . . I don't know if I can finish this set"), and instructional (e.g., "remember to breathe and keep my knees in line with my toes"; Weinberg & Gould, 2015). In fact, instructional self-talk can be aimed either at specific skills or be more general and strategic, while motivational self-talk can be focused on arousal, mastery, or drive (Walker & Hudson, 2013). Consequently, a client's self-talk needs to be examined for its frequency and effectiveness, as well as its particular content. Furthermore, practitioners must keep in mind the intended outcome or function of the client's self-talk (Walker & Hudson, 2013). Maximizing the effectiveness of one's self-talk will depend on whether the aim is to increase self-confidence, adhere to a new behavior, or enhance enjoyment/ motivation.

In order for practitioners to help clients change and optimize their self-talk, thought patterns should be investigated through self-awareness exercises. For example, practitioners can have clients write down the things they say to themselves during exercise. Activities encouraging individuals to write down coping strategies such as self-talk are effective because they decrease recall bias and selectivity. This results in the activities providing a potentially more accurate account of one's internal processes (Bolger, Davis, & Rafaeli, 2003) and facilitates a more useful reflection on the impact of one's thoughts, feelings, and behaviors (Tennen, Affleck, Armeli, & Carney, 2000).

Additionally, self-talk interventions can aim to stop and replace negative self-talk in order to make it more positive/motivational or instructional. This can be done by having clients write down negative self-talk statements and then re-write each statement in a positive/motivational or instructional way, according to the intended function of the self-talk. Particular attention should be paid to becoming aware of and challenging one's negative automatic thoughts (Kay & Shipman, 2014). However, Walker and Hudson (2013) warn against faultily assuming that all negative self-talk has negative consequences. They caution that the function and interpretation of one's self-talk are more important considerations than the content of the self-talk. Consistent with this notion, Taylor and Taylor (1997) suggest that negative self-talk can be categorized into "give up" versus "fire up" thoughts and self-statements, where the former results in negative consequences and the latter in motivational ones.

Alternatively, practitioners can use a different strategy of asking clients to state or record three positive things about each workout. This should encourage more positive perspectives of and emotional reactions to the client's experiences (Achor, 2010). In addition, the technique of reframing can be used to manage one's thoughts and optimize self-talk (Walker & Hudson, 2013). Using this strategy entails changing one's appraisal of their experiences by first becoming aware of one's self-talk and its effects and then reframing one's perspective of those experiences to encourage more facilitative internal processes. For example, an exerciser who quits before completing a challenging workout might utilize negative self-talk that decreases his motivation. Thus, reframing would involve highlighting the relationship between the self-talk and consequences. The client would then foster a change in perspective, such as looking at the situation as an opportunity to challenge oneself in the next workout.

A final aspect to keep in mind is the importance of believing in one's self-talk (Hardy et al., 2009). In other words, helping a client to change her negative self-talk to positive self-talk will not be effective if she does not believe the newly formulated statements. According to self-determination theory (Deci & Ryan, 1985), perceptions of autonomy, competence, and relatedness are influential in promoting intrinsically motivated behavior. Thus, belief in what one is saying to oneself reinforces basic psychological needs, in particular autonomy and competence. Moreover, according to cognitive evaluation theory (see Ryan, 1982), self-determined behavior is the result of a decreased perception of being controlled and an increased perception of positive information related to competence. Therefore, devising one's own self-talk statements, rather than being assigned statements, may also lead to more positive outcomes (Walker & Hudson, 2013). Thus, exercisers should be encouraged to create their own appropriate self-talk statements and reinforce their belief in self-talk by accomplishing small tasks first (e.g., walking for 15 minutes) while using appropriate self-talk.

Arousal Regulation and Attention

Efforts to regulate arousal and the stress/anxiety response are important components of PST. When implementing PST, practitioners need to understand that the two most common sources affecting one's stress response are the perceived importance and uncertainty of a situation or event (Horn, 2002). Furthermore, the more important a situation is believed to be and the greater the uncertainty associated with it, the more detrimental the stress response. For example, exercisers who believe that losing weight is extremely important to their health but at the same time are unsure of their ability to achieve that goal will likely experience higher levels of stress in their pursuit of losing weight. Thus, targeting perceptions (i.e., thoughts) about importance and uncertainty (i.e., working on self-confidence as mentioned above) is key to regulating the stress response.

PST interventions that include arousal regulation and/or coping responses will also help a client to deal with stress reactions as well as to reach an optimal state of arousal and well-being. That said, optimal levels of arousal are dependent on the person and the task (Hanin, 1978). Thus, some clients will need to be on the low end of the arousal continuum, some in the middle, and some at the high end. For example, a client who prefers to be more relaxed and calm may prefer to engage in activities such as yoga or hiking or alternative ways of lowering his arousal level. However, a client who prefers to be more aroused and energetic may prefer to engage in activities such as spinning, CrossFit, or alternative activities that raise one's arousal level. A related issue is the examination of somatic (e.g., increased heart rate and breathing) and cognitive (e.g., racing thoughts) reactions to stress. PST interventions should be targeted at producing the desired arousal level and take into consideration whether somatic, cognitive, or combinations of both methods need to be included. For example, breathing exercises, relaxation imagery, and progressive muscle relaxation can be used for reducing arousal or stress/anxiety responses, while self-talk interventions, implementing the use of high energy music, and motivational imagery can be used to increase arousal levels. Furthermore, an important consideration is to ensure that arousal regulation techniques match the type of anxiety experienced (Weinberg & Gould, 2015). For example, deep-breathing exercises may be effective for somatic anxiety, whereas cognitive anxiety would be more effectively dealt with by using cognitive restructuring. Also, an understanding of coping and the incorporation of different types of coping strategies (i.e., problem-focused, emotion-focused, and reappraisal-focused) can be useful (Nicholls & Polman, 2007). For example, problem-focused coping strategies (i.e., attempts to alter or manage the situation that is causing stress or inappropriate arousal) can be used when the client has control over the situation (e.g., better time management, information seeking), emotion-focused coping (i.e., regulating one's emotional responses) can be used when a client does not have control over the situation and the emotional response is maladaptive (e.g., acceptance, meditation), and reappraisal-focused coping strategies (i.e., changing the interpretation and meaning of a stressor) can be used when a client needs a change in perspective (e.g., cognitive restructuring).

Related to the regulation of stress and arousal are the effects that these responses have on attention. Lower levels of arousal and stress may result in broad attention that encompasses relevant attentional cues as well as susceptibility to distractions, whereas higher levels of arousal and stress may result in narrowing of attention in which the person may be unable to pay attention even to the relevant cues (Janelle, 2002). Thus, attention control strategies may be an important component to include in PST interventions to enhance exercise adoption and adherence. For example, examinations of typical and/or problematic distractions

Table 8.2 An Overview of Activities and Approaches for Implementing PST with Exercise Clients

Psychological Skills and Tools	Examples of PST Activities and Approaches	Using PST Activities and Approaches
Self-Awareness	Reflection activities (e.g., journaling; analyzing what was done well, what could be done better, and what was learned; interpersonal process recall) Performance profiling SWOT analysis Assessing readiness for change through interviewing/observation	Develop and implement early in exercise program Explore exerciser's intensity of motivation Evaluate exerciser's self-confidence for exercise and behavior change
Motivation	Assessing intrinsic/extrinsic motivation Defining one's purpose/intention Assessing goal orientation (mastery vs. outcome) Examining direction, intensity, and duration of one's motivation Examining rewards/reinforcement Imagery	Explore when adopting exercise and when hitting a plateau Combine with goal setting Explore motivation before and during bouts of exercise
Confidence	Evaluating trait and state confidence levels and patterns Reviewing past accomplishments Confidence profiling Imagery Examining nature and impact of self-talk Implementing positive self-talk and affirmations	Explore relationship between self-talk and confidence Evaluate and develop confidence at beginning and throughout exercise program Explore and develop confidence during bouts of exercise
Goal Setting	Defining success and failure Examining attributions SMART goal setting Outlining outcome, performance, and process goals Outlining outcome vs. action goals GOTE goal setting Monitoring and evaluating goals Contingency planning for potential barriers to goals and potential relapses Performance planning	Define goals at beginning of exercise program Monitor and evaluate goals throughout PST and exercise program Determine effectiveness of exerciser's goals and expectations Use range goals rather than definitive outcomes

Category	Techniques	Objectives
Thought Control	Examining nature/content of self-talk Examining thought patterns Examining intentions and attitudes toward exercise Examining thoughts related to perceived control over behavior Examining antecedents (personal and situational) of self-talk Cognitive restructuring/reframing	Explore thoughts before, during, and after bouts of exercise Explore relationship between thoughts and motivation Explore relationship between thoughts and self-confidence
Attention Control	Identifying distractions Mindfulness exercises Examining usefulness of association vs. dissociation Identifying appropriate attentional cues Self-talk cues Biofeedback training Imagery	Use PST strategies for increasing attention control during bouts of exercise Examine relationship between attention and motivation during bouts of exercise
Arousal Regulation	Identifying individual zone of optimal functioning (IZOF) Examining individual's stress response Examination of somatic and cognitive arousal reactions Implementing arousal regulation (relaxation and/or energization) techniques Examining coping strategies Biofeedback training	Evaluate arousal/stress/anxiety reactions and responses prior to and during exercise Examine effectiveness of coping strategies for relapses in exercise behavior Explore relationship between arousal/stress reactions and motivation
Interpersonal Skills	Examining impact of environmental factors Optimizing social support Improving group cohesion (task and social) Developing communication skills	Improve group cohesion for exercise groups Evaluate social factors affecting an exerciser's motivation, self-talk, and confidence Evaluate social support available to exerciser within and outside of exercise program

for exercise (e.g., relationship conflicts, poor job performance, other individuals exercising at the same time) can be useful for improving attention. Additionally, examining the benefits and effectiveness of association (i.e., paying attention to the task at hand) versus dissociation (i.e., distracting oneself from the task at hand) may also be useful. To this end, dissociation is thought to result in longer persistence during an activity and make exercise more enjoyable as it reduces anxiety, discomfort, and boredom (Masters & Lambert, 1989). Thus, this approach may be more beneficial for a new exerciser. For example, exercisers who are just starting to run may need to use music or imagery to distract themselves from running. However, it has been found that more experienced exercisers, specifically marathon runners, prefer to associate, particularly during their training runs (Masters & Lambert, 1989). To that end, a marathon runner may prefer to focus on pace and race plans/goals during a training run. Thus, a practitioner should take into consideration a client's attentional profile as well his level of experience with an activity when working on attention skills training.

Additionally, practitioners may want to explore mindfulness and its possible applications to exercise. Being mindful during an experience involves employing nonjudgmental awareness in the present moment (Kabat-Zinn, 1994). Practitioners can teach clients to become more aware of their internal states (e.g., physiological sensations, thoughts) and environmental factors (e.g., location, sounds) without applying any judgment to these areas of focus. Thus, through mindfulness training, clients can learn to better control attention and focus on the key aspects of the present moment.

Goal Setting

Self-awareness exercises such as performance profiling (e.g., self-assessment of strengths and weaknesses; Butler & Hardy, 1992) or SWOT analyses (i.e., examining strengths, weaknesses, opportunities, and threats; Valentin, 2001) may be useful prior to beginning the goal-setting process with a client. Traditional goal-setting practices such as the SMART framework and outlining outcome, performance, and process goals are useful to include in PST interventions for exercise (Weinberg & Gould, 2015). However, when creating realistic goals, it is important to keep in mind that there is a difference between outcome goals (i.e., what one wants to achieve) and action or process goals (i.e., what one is going to do to reach those achievements). Most people tend to focus on outcomes and do not understand that identifying an action plan for reaching those intended outcomes is just as, if not more, important. For example, an exerciser who sets the goal of losing weight may be challenged in determining what behaviors to implement to reach that goal, such as exercising three to five times per week for 30–45 minutes, using imagery prior to a workout to reach the optimal arousal level, and monitoring self-talk during workouts. Action or process goals are important because they are under the control of the individual, whereas outcome goals may not always be entirely controllable. Another useful framework for goal setting borrowed from acting is the GOTE strategy (Cohen, 2007). Goals (i.e., outcomes), obstacles (i.e., barriers, distractions, etc.), tactics (i.e., action goals), and expectations (i.e., when-then statements about goals) are outlined and explored to give an individual a plan for achievement. Lastly, the WDEP (i.e., want, do, evaluate, plan) system can also be used to help an exerciser identify her wants (W), analyze what she is currently doing (D), evaluate (E) the consistency between what she is doing and what she wants, and develop a plan (P) for achieving her goals (Zizzi & Glichrist, 2014).

Monitoring and evaluating goals are key components of effective goal setting. Furthermore, social cognitive theory (Bandura, 1986) places cognition and control at the center of understanding behavior. Thus, the ability to self-reflect and self-regulate become key to controlling and changing behavior (Buckworth et al., 2013). A useful framework for self-reflection involves analyzing "what, so what, and now what" (Rolfe, Freshwater, & Jasper, 2001). For example, when an exerciser misses a workout, a practitioner can help him to reflect on what happened, what this means about his motivation, and what he is going to do in order to stay on track with his exercise goals. Another reflective framework that can be used includes assessing what was done well, what could have been done better or different, and what was learned (e.g., Mugford, Hesse, & Morgan, 2014). For example, an exerciser might engage in the following assessment of her work toward exercise goals the previous week: "I kept my self-talk positive during workouts all week. I could do a better job of motivating myself prior to workouts, and I learned that if I focus on what I enjoy about a workout, I feel better about myself and am more motivated to work out again." Finally, a similar framework, start-stop-continue (e.g., Ryan, 2012), focusing more on action-based reflection, can be utilized. For example, at the end of the week, an exerciser might reflect on the following: "I need to start using more positive self-talk toward the end of a workout, stop letting my work schedule make me perceive that I have no time to exercise, and continue keeping track of my weekly exercise goals."

SUMMARY

PST interventions have largely targeted sport and non-sport performance clients in a wide range of settings (e.g., military, medical, performing arts, and various sports). However, these interventions may also be beneficial and effective for increasing adoption and adherence rates for exercise. As discussed above, a number of factors need to be considered in the effective application of PST for exercise. For example, exploration of barriers that potentially thwart or challenge exercise goal achievement, personal factors such as personality and motivation, as well as environmental/social factors, such as subjective norms, the availability of exercise resources, and geographical location, may help optimize PST interventions. These factors may in turn facilitate a more effective means of fostering positive exercise behavior change. This chapter has discussed considerations for implementing PST, such as targeting readiness for change, self-confidence, intentions, attributions, environment, thoughts and feelings, arousal regulation, attention, motivation, expectations and habits, social support, and group cohesion. Table 8.2 provides an overview of potential approaches, interventions, and uses of PST strategies for developing psychological skills in individuals in order to improve adoption and adherence to exercise. Last but not least, practitioners should note that a theory-based approach to designing and implementing PST interventions aids in the understanding of what, when, why, and how to include various PST strategies and techniques for sustainable exercise behavior change.

NOTE

1 "The ability to perceive and express emotion, assimilate emotion in thought, understand and reason with emotion, and regulate emotion in the self and others" (Mayer, Salovey, & Caruso, 2000, p. 396).

REFERENCES

Achor, S. (2010). *The happiness advantage*. New York, NY: Crown Publishing Group.
Ajzen, I., & Madden, T. J. (1986). Prediction of goal-directed behavior: Attitudes, intentions, and perceived behavioral control. *Journal of Experimental Social Psychology, 22*, 453–474.
Bandura, A. (1977). Self-efficacy: Toward a unifying theory of behavior change. *Psychological Review, 84*, 191–215.

Bandura, A. (1986). *Social foundations of thought and actions: A social cognitive theory.* Englewood Cliffs, NJ: Prentice Hall.

Beauchamp, M. K., Harvey, R. H., & Beauchamp, P. H. (2012). An integrated biofeedback and psychological skills training program for Canada's Olympic short-track speedskating team. *Journal of Clinical Sport Psychology, 6*, 67–84.

Beaumont, C., Maynard, I. W., & Butt, J. (2015). Effective ways to develop and maintain robust sport-confidence: Strategies advocated by sport psychology consultants. *Journal of Applied Sport Psychology, 27*, 301–318. doi. 10.1080/10413200.2014.996302

Bolger, N., Davis, A., & Rafaeli, E. (2003). Diary methods: Capturing life as it is lived. *Annual Review of Psychology, 54*, 579–616. doi. 10.1146/annurev.psych.54.1-16-1.145030

Buckworth, J., Dishman, R. K., O'Connor, P. J., & Tomporowski, P. D. (2013). *Exercise psychology* (2nd ed.). Champaign, IL: Human Kinetics.

Butler, R. J., & Hardy, L. (1992). The performance profile: Theory and application. *The Sport Psychologist, 6*, 253–264.

Carron, A. V., Colman, M. M., Wheeler, J., & Stevens, D. (2002). Cohesion and performance in sport: A meta analysis. *Journal of Sport & Exercise Psychology, 24*, 168–188.

Carron, A. V., Hausenblas, H. A., & Eys, M. A. (2005). *Group dynamics in sport.* Morgantown, VA: Fitness Information Technology.

Cohen, R. (2007). *Acting one* (5th ed.). New York, NY: McGraw-Hill.

Dalle Grave, R., Calugi, S., Centis, E., El Ghoch, M., & Marchesini, G. (2011). Cognitive-behavioral strategies to increase the adherence to exercise in the management of obesity. *Journal of Obesity, 2011*, 1–11.

Deci, E. L., & Ryan, R. M. (1985). *Intrinsic motivation and self-determination in human behavior.* New York, NY: Plenum Press.

Digelidis, N., Papaioannou, A., Laparidis, K., & Christodoulidis, T. (2003). A one-year intervention in 7th grade physical education classes aiming to change motivational climate and attitudes towards exercise. *Psychology of Sport and Exercise, 4*, 195–210.

Dishman, R. K. (1994). *Advances in exercise adherence.* Champaign, IL: Human Kinetics Publishers.

Dweck, C. S. (2006). *Mindset: The new psychology of success.* New York, NY: Ballantine Books.

Elliot, E. S., & Dweck, C. S. (1988). Goals: An approach to motivation and achievement. *Journal of Personality and Social Psychology, 54*, 5–12.

Ferguson, K. J., Yesalis, C. E., Pomrehn, P. R., & Kirkpatrick, M. B. (1989). Attitudes, knowledge, and beliefs as predictors of exercise intent and behaviour change in schoolchildren. *Journal of School Health, 59*, 112–115.

Hanin, Y. L. (1978). A study of anxiety in sports. In W. F. Straub (Ed.), *Sport psychology: An analysis of athlete behavior* (pp. 236–256). Ithaca, NY: Mouvement Publications.

Hardy, J., Oliver, E., & Tod, D. (2009). A framework for the study and application of self-talk within sport. In S. D. Mellalieu & S. Hanton (Eds.), *Advances in applied sport psychology: A review* (pp. 37–74). New York, NY: Routledge.

Hays, K. F. (2012). The psychology of performance in sport and other domains. In S. M. Murphy (Ed.), *The Oxford handbook of sport and performance psychology* (pp. 24–45). New York, NY: Oxford University Press.

Hays, K., Thomas, O., Maynard, I., & Bawden, M. (2009). The role of confidence in world-class sport performance. *Journal of Sports Sciences, 27*, 1185–1199.

Hill, K. L. (2001). *Frameworks for sport psychologists.* Champaign, IL: Human Kinetics.

Horn, T. (2002). *Advances in sport psychology* (2nd ed.). Champaign, IL: Human Kinetics.

Isaac, A. R., & Marks, D. F. (1995). Individual differences in mental imagery experience: Developmental changes and specialization. *British Journal of Psychology, 85*, 479–500.

Janelle, C. M. (2002). Anxiety, arousal, and visual attention: A mechanistic account of performance variability. *Journal of Sport Sciences, 20*(3), 237–251. doi. 10.1080/026404102317284790

Kabat-Zinn, J. (1994). *Wherever you go, there are you: Mindfulness meditation in everyday life.* New York, NY: Hyperion.

Kay, K., & Shipman, C. (2014). *The confidence code.* New York, NY: Harper Collins.

Kirschenbaum, D. S. (1984). Self-regulation and sport psychology: Nurturing and emerging symbiosis. *Journal of Sport Psychology, 6*, 159–183.

Lox, C. L., Martin Ginis, K. A., & Petruzello, S. J. (2010). *The psychology of exercise* (3rd ed.). Scottsdale, AZ: Holcomb Hathaway Pub.

Marshall, S. J., & Biddle, S. J. H. (2001). The transtheoretical model of behavioral change: A meta-analysis of applications to physical activity and exercise. *Annals of Behavioral Medicine, 23,* 229–246.

Masters, K. S., & Lambert, M. J. (1989). The relations between cognitive coping strategies, reasons for running, injury, and performance of marathon runners. *Journal of Sport & Exercise Psychology, 11,* 161–170.

Mayer, J. D., Salovey, P., & Caruso, D. R. (2000). Models of emotional intelligence. In R. J. Sternberg (Ed.), *Handbook of human intelligence* (2nd ed., pp. 396–420). New York, NY: Cambridge University Press.

McAuley, E., & Blissmer, B. (2000). Self-efficacy determinants and consequences of physical activity. *Exercise and Sport Science Reviews, 28,* 85–88.

Meyers, A., Whelan, J. P., & Murphy, S. M. (1996). Cognitive behavioral strategies in athletic performance enhancement. In M. Hersen, R. M. Eisler, & P. Miller (Eds.), *Progress in behavior modification* (Vol 30, pp. 137–164). Pacific Grove, CA: Brooks/Cole.

Mugford, A., Hesse, D., & Morgan, T. (2014). Developing the "total" consultant: Nurturing the art and science. In J. G. Cremades & L. S. Tashman (Eds.), *Becoming a sport, exercise, and performance psychology professional: A global perspective* (pp. 268–275). New York, NY: Psychology Press.

Nicholls, A. R., & Polman, R. C. J. (2007). Coping in sport: A systematic review. *Journal of Sport Sciences, 25*(1), 11–31. doi. 10.1080/02640410600630654

Nicholls, J. (1984). Achievement motivation: Conceptions of ability subjective experience, task choice, and performance. *Psychological Review, 91,* 328–346.

Prochaska, J. O., & Bess, M. H. (2004). The transtheoretical model: Applications to exercise. In R. K. Dishman (Ed.), *Advances in exercise adherence* (pp. 161–180). Champaign, IL: Human Kinetics.

Prochaska, J. O., DiClemente, C. C., & Norcross, J. C. (1992). In search of how people change. *American Psychologist, 47,* 1102–1114.

Rolfe, G., Freshwater, D., & Jasper, M. (2001). *Critical reflection in nursing and the helping professions: A user's guide.* Basingstoke, UK: Palgrave Macmillan.

Ryan, R. M. (1982). Control and information in the intrapersonal sphere: An extension of cognitive evaluation theory. *Journal of Personality and Social Psychology, 43,* 450–461.

Ryan, T. G. (2012). The facilitation of reflection within an online course. *Reflective Practice, 13,* 709–718.

Sallis, J. F., Owen, N., & Fisher, E. B. (2000). Ecological models of health behavior. In K. Glanz, B. K. Rimer, & K. Viswanath (Eds.), *Health behavior and health education: Theory, research, and practice* (4th ed., pp. 465–486). San Francisco: Jossey-Bass.

Short, S., & Ross-Stewart, L. (2009). A review of self-efficacy based interventions. In S. D. Mellalieu & S. Hanton (Eds.), *Advances in applied sport psychology: A review* (pp. 221–280). New York, NY: Routledge.

Shumaker, S. A., & Brownell, A. (1984). Toward a theory of social support: Closing conceptual gaps. *Journal of Social Issues, 40,* 11–36.

Taylor, J., & Taylor, S. (1997). *Psychological approaches to sport injury rehabilitation.* Philadelphia, PA: Lippincott Williams & Wilkins.

Tennen, H., Affleck, G., Armeli, S., & Carney, M. A. (2000). A daily process approach to coping: Linking theory, research, and practice. *American Psychologist, 55,* 626–636. doi. 10.1037/0003-006X.55.6.626

Valentin, E. K. (2001). SWOT analysis from a resource-based view. *Journal of Marketing Theory & Practice, 9,* 54–69.

Vealey, R. S. (1988). Future directions in psychological skills training. *The Sport Psychologist, 2,* 318–336.

Vealey, R. S. (2007). Mental skills training in sport. In G. Tenenbaum & R. Eklund (Eds.), *Handbook of sport psychology* (3rd ed., pp. 287–309). Hoboken, NJ: Wiley & Sons.

Walker, N., & Hudson, J. (2013). Self-talk in sport injury rehabilitation. In M. Arvinen-Barrow & N. Walker (Eds.), *The psychology of sport injury and rehabilitation* (pp. 103–116). New York, NY: Routledge.

Weinberg, R. S., & Gould, D. (2015). *Foundations of sport and exercise psychology* (6th ed.). Champaign, IL: Human Kinetics.

Weiner, B. (1985). An attribution theory of achievement motivation and emotion. *Psychological Review*, *92*, 548–573.

Weiss, M. R., & Chaumeton, N. (1992). Motivational orientations and sport behavior. In T. Horn (Ed.), *Advances in sport psychology* (pp. 101–184). Champaign, IL: Human Kinetics.

Wills, T. A., & Shinar, O. (2000). Measuring perceived and received social support. In S. Cohen, L. G. Underwood, & B. H. Gottlieb (Eds.), *Social support measurement and intervention: A guide for health and social scientists* (pp. 86–135). New York, NY: Oxford University Press.

World Health Organization (2013). *10 facts on physical activity*. Retrieved from: www.who.int/features/factfiles/physical_activity/facts/en/index.html

Zaccaro, S. J. (1991). Nonequivalent associations between forms of cohesiveness and group related outcomes: Evidence for multidimensionality. *Journal of Social Psychology*, *131*, 387–399.

Zizzi, S. J., & Gilchrist, L. (2014). A theory-based model for health performance consultation. In J. G. Cremades & L. S. Tashman (Eds.), *Becoming a sport, exercise, and performance psychology professional: A global perspective* (pp. 102–110). New York, NY: Psychology Press.

9 Use of Sensory Modalities

Selen Razon, Jasmin Hutchinson, and Itay Basevitch

Despite empirical evidence indicating ample benefits associated with a physically active life-style (Miles, 2007), physical inactivity remains a major public health concern (Blair, 2009) and a pandemic of the 21st century (Khan, 2013). Several theoretical perspectives may help conceptualize the key determinants of physical inactivity behavior. Of these applied to exercise behavior, the effort-related model (Tenenbaum, 2001) emphasizes the notion of increased perception of effort and aversive sensations during exercise. The model purports that as the intensity and time spent exercising increase, exercisers divert to an internal (associative) focus of attention to cope with perception of effort. Closely aligned with the effort-related model, the dual-mode model (Ekkekakis, 2003) stresses the notion of negative affective responses to exercise as a function of workload. The dual-mode model suggests that at or above anaerobic threshold, exercisers' perception is dominated by the physiological symptoms of fatigue, which in turn causes aversive affective responses to exercise.

The suggestion that increased perception of effort and/or negative affective responses may significantly contribute to subsequent physical inactivity behavior makes further sense in light of two major principles in psychology: (1) the hedonic principle of pleasure (Freud, 1950), and (2) remembering-self (Kahneman & Riis, 2005). Based on the pleasure principle, individuals approach pleasure and avoid pain. Drawing on the "remembering-self" concept, individuals evaluate the worth of an experience with distinct attention paid to its beginning, peak, and ending. Therefore, a critical assumption is the following: to the extent that exercise experience may end with high perceptions of effort and negative affective responses, individuals may evaluate the activity as not worthwhile, hence the subsequent inactivity behavior. Consequently, one can argue that individuals would likely adopt exercise behavior so long as the perception of effort associated with exercise is not too intense and the exercise experience leads to positive affective responses (i.e., pleasure).

In the last decade, a number of studies have focused on lowering the perception of effort and increasing positive affective responses to exercise by means of diverting attention to external stimuli. This chapter reviews the use of imagery and select sensory modalities for facilitating decreased perception of effort and increased positive affective responses to exercise. Specifically, innovative intervention strategies, including the use of mental imagery and olfactory, visual, and auditory stimuli, are reviewed, and empirical evidence pertaining to their effectiveness for facilitating perception of effort and optimizing affective responses to exercise are discussed. Subsequently, potential use of relatively unexplored sensory modalities (e.g., gustative and tactile channels) is outlined. Finally, gaps in the literature are identified and recommendations for researchers are provided. To conclude, practical implications and guidelines for best using these to promote long-term physical activity behavior in individuals are defined.

IMAGERY

Definition and Concepts

Briefly defined, mental imagery is the simulation or re-creation of a perceptual experience (Pearson, 2007). The practice of imagery in sport is not new in that imagery has been long used for enhancing athletic performance in competitive events (Stanley, Cumming, Standage, & Duda, 2012). As for its use in exercise, in the mid 1990s Hall (1995) suggested that imagery scenes depicting participating in preferred exercise activities and achieving exercise goals may benefit exercisers. Subsequently, drawing on Paivio's (1985) hallmark perspective, Martin, Moritz, and Hall (1999) conceptualized imagery's functions in five aspects: (1) *Cognitive-Specific* (mental practice of particular skills), (2) *Cognitive-General* (mental practice of tactics, routines, and game plans), (3) *Motivation-Specific* (mental practice of particular outcome goals), (4) *Motivation General-Arousal* (mental practice for affect regulation and anxiety reduction), and (5) *Motivation General-Mastery* (mental practice to increase confidence and maintain focus). Further emphasizing the *Motivation General-Mastery* function, Gammage, Hall, and Rodgers (2000) proposed that imagery may serve as a motivational tool for exercisers. Later evidence has also characterized imagery as an effective tool for optimizing self-regulation and self-efficacy in exercise settings (Giacobbi, Hausenblas, & Penfield, 2005).

Based on the tenets of the *functional equivalence theory* (Kosslyn, Ganis, & Thompson, 2001), imagery is thought to work by projecting on neural networks that are equivalent to actual perceptions and motor control. In short, the concept of *functional equivalence* implies that common brain mechanisms are at work during imagery, motor preparation, and motor performance (Callow, Roberts, & Fawkes, 2006).

Closely aligned with the concept of *functional equivalence*, PETTLEP (Physical, Environment, Task, Timing, Learning, Emotion, Perspective) principles of imagery further underline that motor imagery use is beneficial to the extent that the imagery content and the subsequent performance are consistent, that is, share *functional equivalence* on *physical*, *environmental*, *task*, *timing*, *learning*, *emotion*, and *perspective*-related aspects (see Callow et al., 2006; Holmes & Collins, 2001 for a review). Additional considerations for optimal use of imagery include its *vividness* and *meaningfulness*. To that end, clear and vivid imagery contents maximize motivational gains associated with imagery (Duncan, Hall, Wilson, & Rodgers, 2012). Likewise, participant-generated content translates to greater imagery ability (Wilson, Smith, Burden, & Holmes, 2010). Finally, it is important to note that imagery is an acquired skill and requires consistent practice (Short, Ross-Stewart, & Monsma, 2006; Weinberg, 2008). Because imagery demands repeated practice for optimal results, within the exercise and sport psychology literature, mental imagery is commonly called "mental practice" (Malouin & Richards, 2010).

Research Findings

Research into the effectiveness of imagery for reducing perception of effort in exercise has focused on the change in effort perception, dominant attention focus, and time on task while using imagery during exercise (Razon et al., 2010, 2011; Razon, Mandler, Arsal, Tokac, & Tenenbaum, 2014). Two types of imagery have been tested: associative and dissociative imagery. Associative imagery was defined as an imagery with task-relevant content, that is, with a focus on the physical task and associated somatic sensations. Consequently, associative content primed an internal (associative) focus of attention. For generating associative imagery content during cycling and handgrip squeezing protocols, participants were, for instance, instructed to visualize their legs and squeezing their hand getting bigger and stronger.

Dissociative imagery on the other hand was defined as an imagery with task-irrelevant content, that is, with a focus away from the physical task and associated somatic sensations. Consequently, dissociative content primed an external (dissociative) focus of attention. For generating dissociative imagery content during cycling and handgrip squeezing protocols, participants were, for instance, instructed to visualize solving a long-standing problem and achieving high grades in courses.

Major findings from this line of research indicated the benefits of dissociative imagery for decreasing effort perception and associative imagery for increasing time on task. In a recent study, comparing both types of imagery to no imagery use, either imagery seemed to help participants remain on task longer and accumulate increased levels of blood lactate during exercise (Razon et al., 2014).

Evidence-Based Applications

In exercise settings, imagery has long been used for its motivational properties (see Hausenblas, Hall, Rodgers, & Munroe, 1999). To the extent that more active individuals use particular imagery content (Kim & Giacobbi, 2009), it is important to highlight some of the most frequently used imagery scripts in exercise settings.

Empirical evidence on the frequency of imagery use reveals that exercisers up to 35 years of age draw greatest motivation from dissociative (i.e., task-unrelated) mental images of leaner and healthier physiques (Milne, Burke, Hall, Nederhof, & Gammage, 2005). Male exercisers, however, may at times report a preference for more associative content, such as improved technique and successful execution of moves in exercise (Gammage et al., 2000). Consistent with these findings, female exercisers of 35–65 years of age report drawing the greatest motivation from mental pictures of improved appearance, this tendency being particularly salient in younger female exercisers of this group (Giacobbi, Hausenblas, & Fallon, 2003; Kim & Giacobbi, 2009). Male exercisers of 35–65 years of age, on the other hand seem to be more decisively drawn to mental pictures of improved technique and/or execution of successful moves in exercise, which reportedly provides greatest exercise motivation to this group (Gammage et al., 2000; Kim & Giacobbi, 2009).

It is important to note that motivational content, whether dissociative or associative, may come in many shapes. For instance, departing from the "fit self" script, content depicting an out-of-shape self or even a feared self may be beneficial for exercise motivation (Murru & Ginis, 2010). Consequently, asking individuals to imagine their unhealthy and inactive or healthy and active self in 10 years can help increase motivation for long-term exercise adherence (Murru & Ginis, 2010). Additional promising content for motivation may be imagery of successfully overcoming barriers to exercising (i.e., scheduling, planning issues, etc.; Duncan, Rodgers, Hall, & Wilson, 2011). Finally, some more promising task-related content may aim at "enjoyment" and require exercisers to picture themselves as having fun during exercise (Stanley et al., 2012).

Future Directions

In line with the limitations and recommendations drawn from current research, additional empirical evidence is needed to determine the optimal use of imagery for further developing and maintaining exercise behaviors in individuals. As such, testing the effectiveness of hybrid imagery content that includes both dissociative and associative properties may prove beneficial. Specifically, hybrid imagery content may facilitate distraction and lower levels of perceived effort in exercisers, while simultaneously prolonging time spent exercising. Looking into the potential of additional imagery scripts is continually identified as an area that warrants further investigation (Callow et al., 2006; Watt, Morris, & Koehn, 2010). Future research is also called for investigating long-term effects of select imagery content. To that end, longitudinal studies may look into the adoption and maintenance of exercise behaviors in individuals as a result of consistent use of diverse imagery contents. From an evidence-based perspective, practitioners using imagery should be cognizant of the following: First, optimal effects of imagery are likely to occur with the use of participant-generated content (Holmes & Collins, 2001; Wilson et al., 2010). Thus, while practitioners may provide examples of suitable imagery contents, they should encourage individually meaningful and relevant mental pictures for their clients. Second, gender differences in imagery experience must be considered (Isaac & Marks, 1994). To that end, practitioners should be aware that female exercisers may be somewhat more responsive to depictions of improved appearance as a result of exercise, whereas male exercisers may be more responsive to depictions of finer execution of moves in exercise (Kim & Giacobbi, 2009). Finally, as powerful a tool as imagery is for motivation in exercise (Trethewey, 2013), it takes consistent practice to produce its desirable effects (see Weinberg, 2008, 2010). To optimize the effects of imagery, practitioners should initially provide their clients with an overview of imagery and then later monitor and determine its appropriate use.

MUSIC

Music use is ubiquitous in exercise settings. In a gym setting, background music is interlaced with the steady hum of treadmills and the clanging of weights, while sweaty bodies move in unison to pulsating beats in group exercise classes. Exercisers also like to move to a personal beat, and technological advances have facilitated this marriage between music and movement. Over the last 20 years, there has been a dramatic increase in empirical research on the physical and psychological effects of music in sport and exercise settings, which has led to the development of a conceptual framework and evidence-based applications for exercise practitioners.

Definition and Concepts

In the exercise domain, music can be used in both synchronous or asynchronous manners. The *synchronous* use of music involves repetitive movements performed in time with rhythmical elements, such as beat or tempo, whereas the *asynchronous* use of music involves no conscious synchronization between movement and music rhythm (Karageorghis & Priest, 2012a). In asynchronous use, music is simply played as an adjunct to a physical task, as in background music. Another important distinction, highlighted by Karageorghis and colleagues, pertains to the motivational qualities of a musical piece. *Motivational* music is defined in terms of its characteristics and potential benefits. It has a fast tempo (>120 bpm) and a strong rhythm, enhances energy, and promotes bodily movement (Karageorghis, Terry, & Lane, 1999). Music that is neither motivating nor demotivating is termed *oudeterous* (from the Greek word meaning neutral).

Terry and Karageorghis (2006) put forth a conceptual framework detailing the antecedents, intermediaries, and potential benefits of music in sport and exercise contexts. Music's influence is "contingent upon the listening context and the experiences and preferences of the listener" (Karageorghis & Priest, 2012a, p.48); thus the conceptual framework includes antecedents relating to the exerciser (personal factors) and the context (situational factors). *Personal factors* include age, gender, cultural background, athletic experience, and attentional style, while *situational factors* account for the exercise environment and the nature of the task. Four factors are thought to contribute to the potential impact of a musical piece. *Rhythm response* refers to the effects of musical rhythm, particularly the tempo (speed) of the musical stimulus. *Musicality* refers to the pitch-related elements of music, such as melody and harmony. *Cultural impact* concerns the pervasiveness of the music within a society or subcultural group. Finally, *association* refers to the extra-musical associations that may be evoked while listening to a particular musical piece (Karageorghis & Priest, 2012a). A classic example of association would be Survivor's "Eye of the Tiger," from the Rocky movie series. These four factors are arranged in a hierarchy, such that rhythm response is the most important element and association is the least important.

Research Findings

The benefits of listening to music while engaging in a sport or exercise setting are numerous and have received strong empirical support. Music can be used as either a sedative or a stimulant to engender the optimal arousal state prior to and during physical performance. Empirical research has broadly supported the assumption that stimulative music increases psychomotor arousal, while soft or sedative music decreases arousal and facilitates relaxation (e.g., Yamamoto et al., 2003). Gfeller (1988) suggests that music may also influence arousal if it evokes an extra-musical association that either inspires physical activity or promotes relaxation.

Mood responses and feeling states tend to be more positive under music versus no-music conditions (Edworthy & Waring, 2006; Hutchinson et al., 2011), with motivational music delivering a superior effect to oudeterous music (Hutchinson & Karageorghis, 2013; Karageorghis et al., 2009; Terry, Karageorghis, Mecozzi Saha, and D'Auria, 2012).

While listening to music, a performer's attention is narrowed, which can divert attention away from sensations of fatigue during a physical activity. This process is akin to the cognitive strategy of dissociation. This attentional shift appears, in turn, to lower perceptions of exertion in the order of approximately 10% (Karageorghis & Priest, 2012a). It is important to note that this particular effect appears to hold for low to moderate exercise intensities only. At high exercise intensities (i.e., those that exceed the ventilatory threshold), attentional processes are dominated by afferent feedback, which demands attention; thus perceptions of fatigue override the distractional capabilities of music (see Hutchinson & Tenenbaum, 2007).

Finally, music has an ergogenic (work-enhancing) effect, wherein the presence of music improves exercise performance by either delaying fatigue or increasing work capacity (Karageorghis & Priest, 2012a). This ergogenic effect has been observed across a range of exercise intensities and modalities (e.g., Karageorghis et al., 2009, 2013; Hutchinson et al., 2011; Razon, Basevitch, Land, Thompson, & Tenenbaum, 2009; Terry et al., 2012). The effect appears to be strongest when the motivational qualities of the music are high and music is applied synchronously, as opposed to asynchronously; however, music of any kind appears superior to none.

Significant research attention has been devoted to the optimal tempo for musical accompaniment to exercise. Tempo is considered the most significant factor in determining an individual's response to a piece of music and, from an applied standpoint, is among the easiest aspects of music to manipulate. Early theories presumed the relationship between preferred tempo and exercise intensity to be linear (Iwanaga, 1995), based on the relationship with psychomotor arousal. That is, when arousal is high, listeners prefer faster or more stimulating music (Berlyne, 1971). Moreover, in circumstances where high arousal is likely to facilitate performance, it is likely that a faster tempo will be preferred (cf. Karageorghis et al., 2011). Despite the intuitive logic of this theory, research has shown the exercise intensity–music tempo preference relationship to be more complex, demonstrating a cubic trend. Karageorghis and colleagues (2011) undertook an extensive examination of the relationship between exercise heart rate (HR) and preferred music tempo. They reported that at lower exercise intensities (40–60% maximal HR reserve [HRR]) the tempo–HR relationship was positive and linear, followed by a leveling out at moderate to high exercise intensities (60–80% HRR), with a slight dip at very high exercise intensity (80–90% HRR). Notably the preferred tempo band across the range of exercise intensities was relatively narrow, 125–140 bpm. This tempo range has become known anecdotally as "the sweet spot" (Reddy, 2013).

Evidence-Based Applications

Prior to selecting music for use in an exercise setting, personal and contextual factors should be taken into consideration. An exerciser should begin with a selection of familiar tracks that reflect their musical taste and preferences. Ideally, these tracks should have strong rhythmical elements and some personal meaning, which may be drawn from past experiences and accomplishments or from extra-musical associations to sport and exercise. Motivational and affirming lyrics can also provide meaning, as well as a powerful source of inspiration (e.g., "Stronger" by Kelly Clarkson). A good starting point for selecting songs is to consider what you want the music to do (Karageorghis & Priest, 2008). For example, are you using the music to relax and put the stresses of a hard day behind you, or to energize you during a warm up? Are you hoping the music will distract you from feelings of monotony or fatigue during a workout, or do you want the music to inspire you to perform at a higher level?

Next, the nature of the exercise activity should be considered. Activities that are repetitive in nature, such as jogging, stationary cycling, or circuit training, lend themselves particularly well to musical accompaniment (although clearly safety should not be compromised, and music use while running or cycling on roads is contraindicated). Exercisers should also consider such factors as desired intensity and duration of the exercise bout. Typically warm-up tracks will be slower (80–100 bpm), and the music program will gradually build in tempo with increasing workload to the ideal range of 125–140 bpm. When it comes to a prolonged exercise bout, such as distance running, it is advisable to choose songs that have a steady beat and similar tempos to help maintain a comfortable, steady pace. It is also beneficial for the rhythm of the music to approximate the motor patterns entailed where possible (Crust, 2008). This approach may serve to promote neuromuscular relaxation and cardiovascular efficiency (see Terry et al., 2012). Faster tempo tracks lend themselves to more intense workouts, although a ceiling effect exists at around 140 bpm. Tracks that greatly exceed this tempo tend not to be preferred and may result in negative affective experiences, such as boredom or irritation (Karageorghis, Jones & Low, 2006).

On occasion, particular tracks or segments of a musical piece can be tailored to various components of an exercise bout, for example, to distinguish work time and recovery time during interval training. Priest and Karageorghis (2008) reported that exercise participants experience a strong sense of expectancy regarding segments of a musical piece that they find especially motivational, such as the introduction or the chorus. Exercisers can tap into this phenomenon, known as *segmentation*, to coordinate bursts of effort or to plan a sprint finish.

Future Directions

Over the past 20 years empirical investigation of the effects of music in a physical activity setting has flourished, leading to the development of a theoretical framework (Karageorghis et al., 1999; Terry & Karageorghis, 2006), a psychometric instrument for assessing the motivational properties of music (Karageorghis et al., 1999, 2006), and specific recommendations for athletes, exercisers, and practitioners (e.g., Karageorghis & Priest, 2008). Nevertheless, several aspects of the music–exercise relationship remain critically understudied. Personal factors, including the role of age, gender, personality, and preferred attentional style on musical reactivity, need to be explored. Also, research endeavors ought to branch out to include other exercise modalities and populations.

Presently, there is an absence of work examining the ways in which music and video either oppose or interact with each other in an exercise setting. This is despite the fact that this type of delivery is becoming increasingly prevalent in health and fitness facilities. Future research should seek to understand the ways in which exercisers respond to music and video across a range of exercise intensities and modalities.

The potential recuperative role of post-task (cool down) music has received scant attention to date, and this is a fruitful area for future investigation, particularly in reference to the "remembering-self" concept (Kahneman & Riis, 2005), wherein exercise bouts that end with positive emotions are more likely to be repeated. It would be wise in such investigations to include psychobiological measures, such as salivary cortisol, to examine the mechanisms that underlie the potential benefits of post-task music (Karageorghis & Priest, 2012b).

OLFACTORY STIMULI

Definitions and Concepts

As with the previous sections of this chapter, the rationale for introducing olfactory stimuli during exercise bouts is to increase time spent exercising and enjoyment during exercise. Thus, similar to other sensory modalities (e.g., auditory) and imagery interventions, olfactory stimuli can be used to (a) decrease perception of effort, (b) increase external (dissociative) attention focus, and (c) optimize affect during effortful tasks (Hutchinson et al., 2011; Razon et al., 2011). Nonetheless, the majority of research examining the effectiveness of sensory modalities has focused on the visual, auditory, and tactile sensory systems, perhaps because these are considered central to human perception and cognition (Stockhorst & Pietrowsky, 2004). The olfactory system, despite being relatively well researched within animal studies (Shepherd, 2006), and regardless of its distinct biological and neural characteristics (e.g., complexity, amount of receptor cells, direct neural pathway), has been somewhat overlooked in human studies.

The olfactory system is unique in that it includes numerous receptor cells, is directly linked to the brain, and allows humans to detect and differentiate among artificial and natural scents (Kiecolt-Glaser, Graham, Malarkey, Porter, Lemeshow & Glaser, 2008). In addition, the odors within the system are subjectively processed, hence the large range of effects (e.g., relaxing/stimulating, pleasant/repulsive) associated with diverse olfactory stimuli.

Scarce research from the general and cognitive psychology domains has investigated the effect of olfactory stimuli on human behavior and performance during perceptual and physical tasks. These studies have primarily used pleasant synthetic scents (e.g., peppermint-stimulating, lavender-relaxing) (Barker, Grayhem, Koon, Perkins, Whalen & Raudenbush, 2003; Moss, Hewitt, Moss, & Wesnes, 2008). Findings from these works have suggested that olfactory stimuli affect emotional states, neural activation, information processing, and performance outcome, among other variables.

As for the effects of natural odors on behavior, the focus has been predominantly on animal samples. However, a natural odor that has been recently examined in humans is bodily odor, often referred to as pheromones (Wyatt, 2010). Although the mere existence and sensitivity to pheromones in humans is still debated and controversial (Doty, 2010), current evidence suggests that humans are able to detect natural bodily odors, which trigger physiological, endocrionoligcal, and psychological responses. Furthermore, research findings indicate that presentation of bodily odors activates the amygdala region in the brain and leads to increased neuron activation in regions associated with sexual behavior (Dulac & Kimchi, 2007). Female ovulation cues have been found to increase testosterone levels in males, subsequently increasing risk taking and aggressive and seductive behaviors. The effect of bodily odors on human behavior and performance is further salient within physical activity settings in that these settings are rife with bodily odors of male and female exercisers working out together.

Research Findings

Despite research findings indicating the importance of environmental settings and sensory stimuli (i.e., visual, tactile, and auditory) in sport and exercise activities, researchers have only recently started to examine the role of olfactory stimuli in exercise. Raudenbush (2000); Raudenbush, Corley, and Eppich (2001); and Simpson and colleagues (2001) conducted a series of studies examining the effects of lavender and peppermint odors on performance of a set of physical tasks (e.g., running, pushups, exercise bout). Findings from these studies revealed improvements on outcome performance variables as a result of odor exposure. That said, the effects were only observed on a number of selected tasks (e.g., running speed, handgrip strength). Furthermore, only a single cognitive variable (i.e., RPE) was assessed during the tasks, and differences among the groups were not observed. These non-conclusive results may suggest that perhaps only specific tasks are susceptible to olfactory simulation. Consequently, further investigation is warranted to expand the knowledge in the field.

Building on these earlier studies, a relatively recent study tested the effects of lavender and peppermint odorants on select performance variables (i.e., RPE, attention focus, time spent on task) during a handgrip squeezing task (Basevitch et al., 2011). Although exposure to olfactory stimuli was not shown to effect time on task, participants exposed to lavender odorant reported significantly greater focus off the effort as compared to their counterparts exposed to peppermint and placebo (i.e., water) odorants. More recent research using a similar paradigm has also tested the effects of female bodily odors (i.e., ovulation cues) on males' performance during an exertive task (Basevitch et al., 2013). Findings have indicated that exposure to female bodily odors did not result in significant changes in heart rate, skin conductance, time spent on task, and attention focus in male participants. That said, somewhat increased heart rates and more frequent external (dissociative) attention focus were noted in the experimental (i.e., exposure pheromone) condition throughout the task performance.

In light of these findings and assertions, the olfactory system seems to play a role in human behavior. Of specific interest here, the introduction of synthetic and natural odors can influence behavioral and performance variables within physical activity settings. As such, use of differential olfactory stimuli may prove useful for increasing motivation and adherence to exercise.

Evidence-Based Applications

Currently, there is no applied evidence that olfactory stimuli can improve motivation and promote exercise adherence. That said, exercisers and athletes make frequent use of alternative sensory simulation strategies during physical activity bouts and training sessions (e.g., use of MP3 players, video screens, and optimally designed clothes). In fact, somewhat mirroring the lack of empirical research, applied avenues for use of sensory modalities have been geared toward the three dominant sensory systems (i.e., visual, auditory, tactile), at the oversight of the olfactory one.

Nonetheless, there exist anecdotal accounts of exercisers and athletes making use of odorants to improve performance (e.g., baseball, long-distance running). As with music, when using odors during exercise it is important to have control over odor characteristics (e.g., intensity, type) and temporal use (e.g., pre-performance, onset of fatigue). The ability to select a preferred odor and subsequently adjust its intensity and/or type during different phases of the exercise regimen can enhance the benefits associated with the use of the olfactory stimuli.

Particular olfactory stimulation-based products that are commercially available include a peppermint nasal inhaler (www.sportsinhaler.com/) and (b) smelling salts, similar to those used extensively in boxing in the 20th century and by NFL players presently (Monkovic, 2011). However, additional research on these (and related) products is needed to provide empirical evidence for their effectiveness and to assure no harmful side effects are associated with their continued use.

Finally, olfactory stimuli have also been used sparingly in domains other than sport and exercise. These include marketing and advertising (e.g., perfumes in print media), as well as sport management (e.g., tropical scents to increase fan affiliation with Tropicana Field of the Tampa Bay Rays baseball team). Arguably, these alternative uses of olfactory stimuli may further attest to its potential for behavior change and attitude formation.

Future Directions

It is important to note that research into the possible effects of olfactory stimuli is still in its infancy, and findings associated with it are equivocal at best. Some of the questions that remain to be explored include what odor characteristics (e.g., type, intensity), presentation methods (e.g., nasal strips, air freshener), and temporal administration points (e.g., pre, during, specific moments) are most facilitative for optimal performance. How do the odors affect performance on tasks with different characteristics and requirements (e.g., aerobic vs. anaerobic tasks)? It is evident that additional research is needed to further understand the role of olfactory stimuli in exercise motivation and in human behavior at large.

The promotion and broad use of alternative sensory simulation products by exercisers suggest that it is only a matter of time before similar products targeting the olfactory system will be developed. Thus, it is our expectation that within the next two decades novel technologies and designs that may include "iSmell" devices, air-condition-scented gyms, fragrant sport attire, and comparable innovative olfactory products will be made available to consumers and used extensively in the exercise environment.

REFERENCES

Barker, S., Grayhem, P., Koon, J., Perkins, J., Whalen, A., & Raudenbush, B. (2003). Improved performance on clerical tasks associated with administration of peppermint odor. *Perceptual and Motor Skills, 97,* 1007–1010.

Basevitch, I., Razon, S., Boiangin, N., Gutierrez, O., Braun, R., Arsal, G., & Tenenbaum, G. (2013). The effect of olfactory ovulation cues on males' attention allocation and perception of exertion. *Journal of Multidisciplinary Research, 5*(2), 5–21.

Basevitch, I., Thompson, B., Braun, R., Razon, S., Arsal, G., Tokac, U., & Tenenbaum, G. (2011). Olfactory effects on attention allocation and perception of exertion. *The Sport Psychologist, 25*(2), 144–158.

Berlyne, D. E. (1971). *Aesthetics and psychobiology.* New York, NY: Appleton-Century-Crofts.

Blair, S. N. (2009). Physical inactivity: The biggest public health problem of the 21st century. *British Journal of Sports Medicine, 43,* 1–2.

Callow, N., Roberts, R., & Fawkes, J. Z. (2006). Effects of Dynamic and Static Imagery on Vividness of Imagery, Skiing Performance, and Confidence. *Journal of Imagery, Research in Sport and Physical Activity, 1,* 1–13.

Crust, L. (2008). The perceived importance of components of asynchronous music in circuit training exercise. *Journal of Sports Sciences, 23*, 1–9.

Doty, R. L. (2010). *The great pheromone myth.* Baltimore, MD: Johns Hopkins University Press. Retrieved from http://search.proquest.com/docview/622272724?accountid=4840

Dulac, C., & Kimchi, T. (2007). Neural mechanisms underlying sex-specific behaviors in vertebrates. *Current Opinion in Neurobiology, 17*(6), 675–683. doi: http://dx.doi.org/10.1016/j.conb.2008.01.009

Duncan, L. R., Hall, C. R., Wilson, P. M., & Rodgers, W. M. (2012). The use of a mental imagery intervention to enhance integrated regulation for exercise among women commencing an exercise program. *Motivation and Emotion, 36*, 452–464.

Duncan, L. R., Rodgers, W. M., Hall, C. R., & Wilson, P. M. (2011). Using imagery to enhance three types of exercise self efficacy among sedentary women. *Applied Psychology: Health and Well Being, 3*, 107–126.

Edworthy, J., & Waring, H. (2006). The effects of music tempo and loudness level on treadmill exercise. *Ergonomics, 49*, 1597–1610.

Ekkekakis, P. (2003). Pleasure and displeasure from the body: Perspectives from exercise. *Cognition & Emotion, 17*, 213–239.

Freud, S. (1950). *Beyond the pleasure principle.* New York, NY: Liveright. (Original work published 1920)

Gammage, K. L., Hall, C. R., & Rodgers, W. M. (2000). More about exercise imagery. *The Sport Psychologist, 14*, 348–359.

Gfeller, K. (1988). Musical components and styles preferred by young adults for aerobic fitness activities. *Journal of Music Therapy, 25*, 28–43.

Giacobbi, P. R., Hausenblas, H. A., & Fallon, E. A. (2003). Even more about exercise imagery: A grounded theory of exercise imagery. *Journal of Applied Sport Psychology, 15*, 160–175.

Giacobbi, P. R., Hausenblas, H. A., & Penfield, R. D. (2005). Further refinements in the measurement of exercise imagery: The exercise imagery inventory. *Measurement in Physical Education and Exercise Sciences, 4*, 251–266.

Hall, C. R. (1995). The motivation function of mental imagery for participation in sport and exercise. In J. Annett, B. Cripps, & H. Steinberg (Eds.), *Exercise addiction: Motivation for participation in sport and exercise* (pp. 15–21). Leicester, UK: British Psychological Society.

Hausenblas, H. A., Hall, C. R., Rodgers, W. M., & Munroe, K. J. (1999). Exercise imagery: Its nature and measurement. *Journal of Applied Sport Psychology, 11*, 171–180.

Holmes, P. S., & Collins, D. J. (2001). The PETTLEP approach to motor imagery: A functional equivalence model for sport psychologists. *Journal of Applied Sport Psychology, 13*, 60–83.

Hutchinson, J. C., & Karageorghis, C. I. (2013) Moderating influence of attentional style and exercise intensity on responses to asynchronous music. *Journal of Sport and Exercise Psychology, 35*(6), 625–643.

Hutchinson, J. C., Sherman, T., Davis, L., Cawthon, D., Reeder, N. B., & Tenenbaum, G. (2011). The influence of asynchronous motivational music on a supramaximal exercise bout. *International Journal of Sport Psychology, 42*(2), 135–148.

Hutchinson, J. C., & Tenenbaum, G. (2007). Attention focus during physical effort: The mediating role of task intensity. *Psychology of Sport and Exercise, 8*, 233–245.

Isaac, A. R., & Marks, D. F. (1994). Individual differences in mental imagery experience: Developmental changes and specialization. *British Journal of Psychology, 85*, 479–500.

Iwanaga, I. (1995). Relationship between heart rate and preference for tempo of music. *Perceptual and Motor Skills, 81*, 435–440.

Kahneman, D., & Riis, J. (2005). Living, and thinking about it: Two perspectives on life. In F. A. Huppert, N. Baylis & B. Keverne (Eds.), *The science of well-being* (pp. 285–304). Oxford: Oxford University Press.

Karageorghis, C. I., Hutchinson, J. C., Jones, L., Farmer, H. L., Ayhan, M. S., Wilson, R. C., & Bailey, S. G. (2013). Psychological, psychophysical, and ergogenic effects of music in swimming. *Psychology of Sport and Exercise, 14*, 560–568.

Karageorghis, C. I., Jones, L., & Low, D. C. (2006). Relationship between exercise heart rate and music tempo preference. *Research Quarterly for Exercise and Sport, 26*, 240–250.

Karageorghis, C. I., Jones, L., Priest, D. L., Akers, R. I., Clarke, A., Perry, J. M., . . . Lim, H. B. (2011). Revisiting the relationship between exercise heart rate and music tempo preference. *Research Quarterly for Exercise and Sport, 82*(2), 274–284.

Karageorghis, C. I., Mouzourides, D. A., Priest, D. L., Sasso, T., Morrish, D., & Walley, C. (2009). Psychophysical and ergogenic effects of synchronous music during treadmill walking. *Journal of Sport & Exercise Psychology, 31*, 18–36.

Karageorghis, C., & Priest, D. L. (2008). Music in Sport and Exercise: An Update on Research and Application. *Sport Journal, 11*(3).

Karageorghis, C. I., & Priest, D. L. (2012a). Music in the exercise domain: A review and synthesis (Part I). *International Review of Sport and Exercise Psychology, 5*, 44–66.

Karageorghis, C. I., & Priest, D. L. (2012b). Music in the exercise domain: A review and synthesis (Part II). *International Review of Sport and Exercise Psychology, 5*, 67–84.

Karageorghis, C. I., Terry, P. C., & Lane, A. M. (1999). Development and initial validation of an instrument to assess the motivational qualities of music in exercise and sport: The Brunel Music Rating Inventory. *Journal of Sports Sciences, 17*, 713–724.

Khan, K. M. (2013). Ode to Joy: Call to action for doctors to play their role in curing the global pandemic of physical inactivity: Drilling into one of the "7 investments"-simple solutions for the pandemic. *British Journal of Sports Medicine, 47*, 3–4.

Kiecolt-Glaser, J., Graham, J., Malarkey, W., Porter, K., Lemeshow, S., & Glaser, R. (2008). Olfactory influences on mood and autonomic, endocrine, and immune function. *Psychoneuroendocrinology, 33*, 328–339.

Kim, B. H., & Giacobbi, P. R. (2009). The use of exercise-related mental imagery by middle-aged adults. *Journal of Imagery Research in Sport and Physical Activity, 4*, Article 1.

Kosslyn, S. M., Ganis, G. G., & Thompson, W. L. (2001). Neural foundations of imagery. *Nature Reviews Neuroscience, 2*, 635–664.

Malouin, F., & Richards, C. L. (2010). Mental practice for relearning locomotor skills. *Physical Therapy, 90*, 240–251.

Martin, K. A., Moritz, S. E., & Hall, C. R. (1999). Imagery use in sport: A literature review and applied model. *The Sport Psychologist, 13*, 245–268.

Miles, L. (2007). Physical activity and health. *Nutrition Bulletin, 3*, 314–363.

Milne, M. I., Burke, S. M., Hall, C., Nederhof, E., & Gammage, K. L. (2005). Comparing the imagery use of older and younger adult exercisers. *Imagination, Cognition and Personality, 25*, 59–67.

Monkovic, T. (2011, January 18). Tom Brady says He was Sniffing Ammonia. *The New York Times.* Retrieved from http://www.nytimes.com

Moss, M., Hewitt, S., Moss, L., & Wesnes, K. (2008). Modulation of cognitive performance and mood by aromas of peppermint and ylang-ylang. *International Journal of Neuroscience, 118*, 59–77.

Murru, E. C., & Ginis, K. M. (2010). Imagining the possibilities: The effects of a possible selves intervention on self-regulatory efficacy and exercise behavior. *Journal of Sport & Exercise Psychology, 32*, 537–554.

Paivio, A. (1985). Cognitive and motivational functions of imagery in human performance. *Canadian Journal of Applied Sciences, 10*, 22–28.

Pearson, D. G. (2007). Mental imagery and creative thought. *Proceedings of the British Academy, 147*, 187–212.

Priest, D., & Karageorghis, C. I. (2008). A qualitative investigation into the characteristics and effects of music accompanying exercise. *European Physical Education Review, 14*, 347–366.

Raudenbush, B. (2000). The effects of odors on objective and subjective measures of physical performance. *Aroma Chronology Review, 9*(1), 1–5.

Raudenbush, B., Corley, N., & Eppich, W. (2001). Enhancing athletic performance through the administration of peppermint odor. *Journal of Sport & Exercise Psychology, 23*, 156–160.

Razon, S., Arsal, G., Nascimento, T., Simonavice, E., Loney, B., Gershgoren, L., Panton, L. B., & Tenenbaum, G. (2011). Imagery's effects on attention strategies and coping mechanisms in women with Fibromyalgia syndrome. *Journal of Multidisciplinary Research, 2*, 5–24.

Razon, S., Basevitch, I., Filho, E., Land, W., Thompson, B. Biermann, M., & Tenenbaum, G. (2010). Associative and Dissociative Imagery Effects on Perceived Exertion, and Task Duration. *Journal of Imagery Research in Sport and Physical Activity, 5*, 1–27.

Razon, S., Basevitch, I., Land, W., Thompson, B., & Tenenbaum, G. (2009). Perception of exertion and attention allocation as a function of visual and auditory conditions. *Psychology of Sport and Exercise*, *10*, 636–643.

Razon, S., Mandler, K., Arsal, G., Tokac, U., & Tenenbaum, G. (2014). Effects of imagery on effort perception and cycling endurance. *Journal of Imagery Research in Sport and Physical Activity*, *9*(1), 23–38.

Reddy, S. (2013, April 1). Optimal music for the gym. *The Wall Street Journal*. Retrieved from http://online.wsj.com

Shepherd, G. (2006). Smell images and the flavour system in the human brain. *Insight*, *444*, 316–321.

Short, S. E., Ross-Stewart, L., & Monsma, E. V. (2006). Onwards with the evolution of imagery research in sport psychology. *Athletic Insight*, *8*. Retrieved December 1, 2012, from www.athleticin sight.com/Vol8Iss3/ImageryResearch.htm

Simpson, W. F., Coady, R. C., Osowski, E. E, & Bode, D. S. (2001). The effect of aromatherapy on exercise performance. *Perceptual Motor Skills*, *88*, 756–758.

Stanley, D. M., Cumming, J., Standage, M., & Duda, J. L. (2012). Images of exercising: Exploring the links between exercise imagery use, autonomous and controlled motivation to exercise, and exercise intention and behavior. *Psychology of Sport and Exercise*, *13*, 133–141.

Stockhorst, U., & Pietrowsky, R. (2004). Olfactory perception, communication, and the nose-to-brain pathway. *Physiology & Behavior*, *83*, 3–11.

Tenenbaum, G. (2001). A social-cognitive perspective of perceived exertion and exertion tolerance. In R. N. Singer, H. A. Hausenblas, & C. Janelle (Eds.), *Handbook of sport psychology* (pp. 810–822), New York, NY: Wiley.

Terry, P. C., & Karageorghis, C. I. (2006). Psychophysical effects of music in sport and exercise: An update on theory, research and application. In M. Katsikitis (Ed.), *Psychology bridging the Tasman: Science, culture and practice—Proceedings of the 2006 Joint Conference of the Australian Psychological Society and the New Zealand Psychological Society* (pp. 415–419). Melbourne, VIC: Australian Psychological Society.

Terry, P. C., Karageorghis, C. I., Mecozzi Saha, A., & D'Auria, S. (2012). Effects of synchronous music on treadmill running among elite triathletes. *Journal of Science and Medicine in Sport*, *15*, 52–57.

Trethewey, N. (2013). The effects of mental imagery on implementation intentions: Specifically in regards to exercise goal achievement. *The Plymouth Student Scientist*, *6*, 272–288.

Watt, A. P., Morris, T., & Koehn, S. (2010). Developing scripts for imagery training in motor learning. In K. Thompson, & A. P. Watt (Eds.), *Connecting paradigms of motor behaviour to sport and physical education* (pp. 159–175), Estonia: Tallinn University Press.

Weinberg, R. S. (2008). Does imagery work? Effects on performance and mental skills. *Journal of Imagery Research in Sport and Physical Activity*, *3*, 1–21.

Weinberg, R. S. (2010). Integrating and implementing a psychological skills training program. In J. M. Williams (Ed.), *Applied sport psychology: Personal growth to peak performance* (6th ed., pp. 359–391). McGraw-Hill: New York.

Wilson, C., Smith, D., Burden, A., & Holmes, P. (2010). Participant-generated imagery scripts produce greater EMG activity and imagery ability. *European Journal of Sport Science*, *10*, 417–425.

Wyatt, T. D. (2010). Pheromones and behavior. In *Chemical communication in crustaceans* (pp. 23–38). New York, NY: Springer.

Yamamoto, T., Ohkuwa, T., Itoh, H., Kitoh, M., Terasawa, J., Tsuda, T., & Sato, Y. (2003). Effects of pre-exercise listening to slow and fast rhythm music on supramaximal cycle performance and selected metabolic variables. *Archives of Physiology and Biochemistry*, *111*, 211–214.

10 Advanced Technological Trends in Exercise Psychology

Edson Filho and Gershon Tenenbaum

The use of exercise-related technology has increased over the past decade (Chadwick, 2006). A recent survey by Motorola in the United States indicated that 85% of exercisers and recreational athletes use some sort of technology when exercising or playing sports (Hautanen, 2007). Additional accounts have also noted that exercisers of all ages use an array of technologies, including smartphones, music devices, and heart rate monitors (Grassi, Preziosa, Villani, & Riva, 2007), and are involved with a variety of video games to keep active (Russell & Newton, 2008). Athletes and exercisers are known to use advanced global positioning systems (GPS) to evaluate their physical workload (Aughey, 2011), signal processing technology to monitor their physiological reactions (e.g., electrocardiogram and electroencephalogram; see Reinecke et al., 2011), aerodynamic swimming suits to serve as radial accelerometers (Stamm, James, & Thiel, 2013), and sports wheelchairs (Burton, Fuss, & Subic, 2011). Consistent with these developments, DNA testing, along with a genetic-based training profile, has become increasingly popular in exercise practice (Wagner & Royal, 2012).

Our purpose in this chapter is to describe how advanced technological modalities may inform new approaches to exercise motivation and adherence within applied settings. Initially, socio-technical considerations of exercise technology are outlined. Subsequently, an overview of how different hi-tech modalities have been incorporated into exercise settings is presented. Finally, new frontiers for technological development in exercise settings are discussed, and practical recommendations are offered.

SOCIO-TECHNICAL CONSIDERATIONS

Advanced exercise technology derives from novel engineering designs as well as technological transfer among various domains (e.g., ergonomics, chemical of materials, medicine; see Gowland, 2012). Nonetheless, it is the socio-technical integration among people and technology that determines whether a technological advancement will be adopted by the society (Clegg, 2000; Shani & Sena, 1994). More specifically, according to an integrative socio-technological view, technology can only be integrated within a society when considering human needs as related to a desired activity and situated in a given context (Clegg, 2000). Thus, it is essential to capture the needs of exercisers engaged in a specific physical activity within a given context, as this consideration most often precedes the development of new technologies.

Person-Task-Context

The "person-task-context" triad is important to consider when discussing the development and uses of exercise technology. To this extent, action theory purports that performance and learning are determined by a myriad of variables related to the (1) person, (2) task, and (3) context (Schack & Hackfort, 2007). According to action theory, coaches and trainers should consider person-task-context factors when prescribing training regimes to exercisers and athletes. Action theory is particularly relevant for exercisers, practitioners, and scholars interested in using technological modalities to increase exercise motivation and adherence in physical activity contexts.

Person

The person aspect entails considering the idiosyncratic needs of every person when using technological tools and designing ergonomic assets related to exercise and sports. For instance, technological equipment for people with disabilities is often adapted to a person's particular needs. Burkett (2010) posited that lower-limb amputees rely on tailored prosthetic limbs designed for their specific needs and condition. Furthermore, males and females, as well as other population groups (e.g., elderly, children), are likely to differ in their preferences for "active" video game (Floros & Siomos, 2012). Specifically, men report a preference for sport games, whereas women commonly opt for racing and dancing games (Terlecki et al., 2011). Thus, in general, screening and need assessment remain important elements to consider prior to prescribing any technological instrumentation to exercisers.

Task

The nature of the task is crucial when considering the use of technologies within exercise settings. For instance, GPS data are more reliable for longer duration events (e.g., marathon running) than for short, high-speed movements (e.g., sprint tests in soccer; see Aughey, 2011). Also, from an engineering developmental standpoint, the aerodynamic rigidity of a football helmet is markedly different than that of a cyclist. Likewise, sports wheelchair technologies vary, with racing wheelchairs prioritizing lightweight construction and sport wheelchairs focusing on stability and maneuverability (Burton et al., 2011). Therefore, a task-specific analysis should also be a factor in prescribing technological tools in exercise and sport settings.

Context

Context is particularly relevant in the design of footwear and clothing aimed at preventing injury and overheating in such activities as hiking and running (Millet, Perrey, Divert, & Foissac, 2006). Furthermore, the design and choice of skis, swimsuits with imbibed accelerometers, and ultra-light racquets and snowboards are context dependent (Stamm et al., 2013). Most recently, exercise and sport technology has been used to create virtual reality environments in order to diminish the risk of injury in contact sports (Hahn, Helmer, Mackintosh, Staynes, & Blanchonette, 2011). Technology has also been used to ensure environmental sustainability in large-scale international events (Fuss, Subic, & Mehta, 2008). Altogether, environmental factors as well as personal and task variables should be considered when assessing the use and potentials of technologies in exercise and sport settings.

Technological Features

Consideration of technological characteristics specific to the exercise or sport of choice is not a new topic in the literature. Three decades ago, McKenzie and Carlson (1984) noted that computer technology for exercise and sport should (1) allow for immediate feedback to the user, (2) communicate with external storage devices via a modem, and (3) be both portable and cost-effective. Other authors have since commented on the topic, each emphasizing the importance of equipment being light and portable, cost-effective, and capable of real-time processing (Chadwick, 2006; Fuss et al., 2008). Multimodal channels and ecologically valid equipment are also important features of new technological tools geared toward exercisers as well as recreational and elite athletes (Anderson & Collins, 2004).

Portability and Weight

Landmark developments in the sport and exercise domain (e.g., titanium golf clubs, carbon fiber skis, LZR swimsuits) are the direct result of the advancement of equipment and materials (Fuss et al., 2008). Although initially targeted to professional athletes, lighter, hi-tech equipment is also currently used by recreational athletes and exercisers (Hautanen, 2007). For example, many individuals are now accustomed to portable heart rate monitors once used primarily by professional athletes. iPods and iPads are additional examples of light, portable gear offering a variety of technological commodities (i.e., MP3 music, caloric expenditure applications). Hence, it is essential that individuals consider the portability and weight of novel technological advances when engaging in exercise.

Ecological Validity

Ecologically valid equipment allows for unencumbered monitoring and thus does not interfere with the natural movement patterns of exercisers and fitness practitioners (Anderson & Collins, 2004). Accordingly, cables and bulky equipment should be avoided when seeking ecologically valid training and research protocols for outdoor activities. Long-distance hikers and climbers must be particularly attentive to the characteristics of their sport and exercise gear, as ecologically valid apparatuses are also aimed at preventing injury and minimizing health hazards (e.g., impermeable and dri-fit technology to prevent thermal traumas; see McCann, 2005). From a research stance, scholars interested in ecologically valid studies should look for equipment with wireless and Bluetooth technology. Although some research questions remain tied to the laboratory setting, there are technological resources that allow for ecologically valid assessments in exercise psychology (Edmonds & Tenenbaum, 2011). For instance, maximal oxygen uptake equipment is currently available in portable backpacks, facilitating the acquisition of reliable data in the natural athletic environment (Maiolo, Melchiorri, Iacopino, Masala, & De Lorenzo, 2003).

Real-Time Processing

Instant replay in American football, the Hawk-Eye in tennis, and goal-line technology in soccer are examples of the increasing importance of real-time processing in sport settings (Singh Bal & Dureja, 2012). Active video game playing, an increasingly popular trend among both teenagers and adults (Russell & Newton, 2008), is also based on real-time information processing. Indeed, dancing or playing tennis in online video game interactions requires one to respond "on the fly" to a variety of stimuli. Accelerometers and GPS devices used by mountain bikers, kayakers, and recreational sailors are also capable of instantaneous data acquisition and information processing and display (Robinson, Holt, Pelham, & Furneaux, 2011). Furthermore, archers and cricket players use highly specific technology to gain immediate, real-time, augmented and kinematic feedback of their performance. In sum, systems capable of immediately acquiring and processing information might be of interest to individuals looking for augmented feedback devices.

Multimodal Assessment

Smartphones have the capability to store accelerometers and eHealth applications (Grassi et al., 2007). Likewise, modern shoes are often equipped with walking-gate technology linked to corresponding online applications. Standard bio-neurofeedback hardware suites and software are able to process over 30 channels of information, including brain waves, electro-cardiogram, galvanic skin response, and reaction-time data. Recreational runners now wear advanced chronometers that estimate and derive target-training zones and lactate threshold. Hence, equipment flexibility and the ability to integrate a number of different data types (e.g., channels of information, sampling rates, and bandwidths) are important factors to be considered by individuals interested in exercise and sport technology.

Cost

Newer hi-tech products are often expensive, as they carry development and merchandise costs (Fuss et al., 2008). Nonetheless, it is an economic fact that over time the price of a given product is a nexus between supply and demand (Hilletofth, 2011). As previously mentioned, chronometers and heart rate monitors were once used only by top-level athletes but now are readily available to the average individual. From a pragmatic standpoint, one should consider the choices available in the market in light of a clearly defined goal and budget. For instance, industrial practice (e.g., gyms, personal trainers) and professional teams may be willing to invest a greater amount financially in an attempt to ensure a performance edge over competitors. Scholars may also be willing to pay more, and find congruent funding alternatives, if their research question is related to hi-tech exercise applications. Exercisers and recreational athletes may favor user-friendly devices and consider the life expectancy, storage, and processing speed capabilities of technological equipment.

Altogether, before selecting a specific technological device, one should consider "person-task-context" factors, as well as (1) weight and portability, (2) ecological validity, (3) real-time processing capability, (4) multimodal assessment alternatives, and (5) cost (see Figure 10.1). With a variety of technological apparatuses targeting different groups (e.g., exercisers, athletes, and scholars), it is important to evolve a rationale to develop and use hi-tech exercise devices and methods. The next section provides an overview of different hi-tech modalities that have been incorporated into exercise settings.

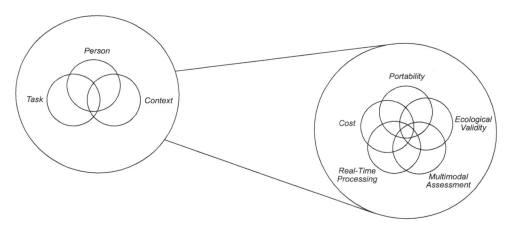

Figure 10.1 An Overview of Person-Task-Context and Technological Features to Inform the Selection of Hi-Tech Exercise Equipment

HI-TECH EXERCISE MODALITIES

Technology is the practical application of knowledge (Clegg, 2000). As such, it has infinite possibilities, ranging from nuclear chemistry to genetic engineering. Therefore, the overview offered herein does not cover each and every exercise specific technology. Rather, the focus is on presenting established modalities as well as recent trends and newly developed applications. Specifically, the following modalities are presented: (a) psycho-physiological monitoring, (b) positioning monitoring, and (c) everyday technology.

Psycho-Physiological Monitoring

Psycho-physiological monitoring relies on multimodal and non-invasive sensors to acquire signals from a living organism (Paul, Garg, & Sandhu, 2012). Three monitoring modalities have been widely used by regular exercisers and fitness professionals, as well as elite and recreational athletes (Perry, 2012). Electromyography (EMG), electrocardiography (ECG), and electroencephalography (EEG) are safe and relatively portable signal processing modalities. Advanced Neurotechnology, Bioharness, Nexus, and Thought Technology are companies currently offering these modalities for practitioners and clinicians in the exercise sciences and medical domains.

Electromyography (EMG)

EMG registers and processes electrical changes within the muscle membrane. This neuro-muscular technique is useful in assessing body tone, posture, and contraction chain. Given its multitude of applications, gyms and physical therapy clinics are now incorporating EMG in their assessment and prescription of exercise protocols. Recreational golfers, football players, and triathletes, as well as yoga and pilates practitioners, are among the groups interested in EMG for both training and recovery reasons. Furthermore, scholars from various domains are interested in using EMG in both laboratory and ecological settings (Drost, Stegeman, Van Engelen, & Zwarts, 2006).

Electrocardiography (ECG)

ECG records the electrical activity of the heart through the use of skin-surface electrodes. This technique is particularly useful in detecting abnormalities in the heart, such as atrial arrhythmia. A beneficial test to conduct prior to beginning a workout routine, ECG has also been used to monitor psycho-physiological responses of individuals interested in bio-neurofeedback training (e.g., heart rate variability; see Edmonds & Tenenbaum, 2011). Rather than undergoing an ECG, recreational athletes and exercisers are more likely to opt for a heart rate monitor, currently available from a variety of companies and offered in a wide price range. These hi-tech monitors carry "smart coach functions," thus allowing the user to set endurance tests, individualized training zones, and recovery protocols.

Electroencephalography (EEG)

EEG is a non-invasive method used to record brain electrical activity. Although EEG is predominantly used by clinicians and scholars, various mental coaches and sport and exercise psychologists offer similar neurofeedback training to exercisers interested in better controlling their mental states (Edmonds & Tenenbaum, 2011). Furthermore, recent ultra-mobile EEG products have become available, and exercisers may be able to use headsets to assess their psycho-physiological states. Recently, Samsung released a tablet controlled by the brain (Thought Launch), which intends to read one's thinking and revolutionize how humans walk, talk, and interact with their surrounding environment (MIT Technological Review, 2013).

Positioning Monitoring

Other promising hi-tech modalities include the ones geared for "positioning monitoring." Positioning monitoring pertains to the assessment of navigation and location information (Misra & Bednarz, 2004). GPS, accelerometers, and kinematic products are among the most common positioning systems adopted by exercisers, athletes, and kinesiologists (Stamm et al., 2013). Increasingly portable, these systems offer immediate feedback on location and acceleration, while also being able to transfer and store large chunks of aggregated information, which may be potentially useful for periodization protocols and detailed technical assessments.

Global Positioning System (GPS)

The ability to use a GPS is the result of the invention of the atomic clock. GPS works through the emission of radio signals from satellites to the GPS receiver on Earth. The exact location and distance traveled of the receiver can be determined if three or more satellites are in communication (Aughey, 2011). Among other applications, GPS is commonly used by a variety of exercisers and recreational athletes (e.g., runners, sailors, cyclists, rally drivers) to estimate distance covered and determine geographical location in relation to a predetermined route. Most recently, GPS has been used to determine activity profiles (e.g., player movements during matches) of sport teams. For instance, soccer and rugby players use GPS to estimate distance covered and field positioning in order to gather information on their idiosyncratic training and competition needs (Vescovi, 2012). Importantly, GPS data are not as reliable in explosive events, such as a 50-meter sprint in soccer (Aughey, 2011). However, this potential limitation may soon be rectified as atomic clocks are now incorporating quantum timekeeping mechanisms, thus allowing for accurate recording of dynamic, explosive movements (Ball, 2013).

Accelerometers

Accelerometers use microprocessors to quantify movement dynamics in different planes and axes (e.g., x, y, z). Tri-axial accelerometers are frequently used by physical therapists interested in analyzing walking gait patterns, particularly as related to acceleration and angular velocity around predefined x, y, z planes (Stamm et al., 2013). Impact reduction, ground contact time, and running and sprint technique are also of interest to scholars and athletes (Kratky & Müller, 2013). A variety of sport-specific accelerometers are available, including equipment designed for swimmers, bowlers, and cricket players. As technology develops, accelerometers are becoming increasingly lighter and more durable, and thus may become more readily used by the wider fitness population.

Kinematic Analysis

Kinematic analysis relies on accelerometers, while incorporating reaction-time devices and both online and slow-video recording. A multimodal modality in essence, kinematic analysis has numerous applications linked to technical analysis (Ansari, Paul, & Sharma, 2012).

Specifically, golfers, boxers, and dancers are all able to gain detailed insight about their movements using kinematic analysis (Marta, Silva, Castro, Pezarat-Correia, & Cabri, 2012). Furthermore, hi-tech flooring with synchronized lighting and sound can be incorporated in group-exercise classes (e.g., step aerobics, Zumba). Additionally, the usually imbibed reaction times may also be of interest to scholars studying anticipation mechanisms (Barris & Button, 2008). Finally, the increasing sophistication of kinematic hardware and software is at the core of a growing trend of active video game playing.

Everyday Modalities

Video Game Technology

Active video game playing aims to emulate real-life exercise through virtual reality animations and technology tracking body movement and reactions (Orvis, Moore, Belanich, Murphy, & Horn, 2010; Russell & Newton, 2008). With a variety of fitness, sport, and dance games available (e.g., Fitness Fun, Nintendo Wii; Kinetic Sports, Xbox; Everybody Dance, Playstation 3), active video game playing has become a target of scientific inquiry. In fact, extant empirical evidence exists indicating that active video game playing increases energy expenditure when compared to both resting values and non-active playing (Lyons et al., 2014). For instance, Smallwood, Morris, Fallows, and Buckley (2012) reported that Kinetic Sports Boxing and Dance Central increased energy expenditure by 263% and 150%, respectively, when compared to resting values.

As such, active video game playing has been viewed as a contemporary alternative to engage children and teenagers in physical activity. Older adults also engage in various video game modalities (Taylor et al., 2012) and have benefited from playing them (e.g., gains in balance control, cardiovascular fitness). Overall, integration of gaming technology in training routines and periodization programs is a natural advancement within the exercise sciences domain. Finally, internet-based interactions, such as online fitness coaching, virtual personal training, and client-oriented fitness applications, are a new and growing trend. A variety of eHealth and other online applications are also available with the increasingly widespread, global smartphone technology.

Smartphones

Smartphones are user-friendly technological devices, built around a high-definition and multitouch interface, offering an array of applications, such as music and video playing, computer processing capabilities, and wi-fi internet (Grassi et al., 2007). In fact, smartphones (and tablets) are expected to surpass the commercialization of personal computers in future years (Arthur, 2011). Smartphones are relatively affordable and thus accessible by a large group of individuals, including exercisers, health practitioners, and amateur and elite athletes (Stevens & Bryan, 2012).

Besides being cost-efficient and portable, smartphones are attractive due to their multimodal technological nature. Accelerometers and GPS are available on most smartphones and, when supported by wi-fi, 4G, and Bluetooth technology, are able to transfer motion information to a remote repository. The streaming capabilities are also important, as research has shown that music and video stimuli may positively alter one's perception of psycho-physiological effort and subsequent willingness to sustain physical effort (Razon, Basevitch, Land, Thompson, & Tenenbaum, 2009). Furthermore, the number of online applications linked to exercise and healthy living are seemingly limitless, including topics on running, fitness, nutrition, and weight control (Stevens & Bryan, 2012). The fusion of technology and portability characteristics common to the smartphone is likely to remain in vogue for years to come (Hautanen, 2007).

APPLIED IMPLICATIONS AND FUTURE AVENUES OF HI-TECH EXERCISE PSYCHOLOGY

The literature overview above aimed to equip practitioners, exercisers, athletes, and scholars with important applied information to use when selecting a technology modality within physical activity settings. Here, we summarize the importance of considering "person-task-context" information and technological factors in the prescription of hi-tech equipment to exercisers. To conclude, we forecast potential avenues of development for hi-tech modalities related to exercise psychology applications.

Applied Implications

Personal needs, task characteristics, and contextual foci associated with the use of hi-tech equipment should be taken into account by exercise practitioners and health professionals. Given that most hi-tech equipment offers multisensorial feedback and/or stimulation (e.g., audio, video, text, and graphic animations) to its users, it is crucial that health professionals consider individuals' preferred learning style (e.g., auditory, kinematic, visual) when choosing a particular hi-tech equipment (Filho, 2015; Tenenbaum & Filho, 2014). Furthermore, as previously discussed, *portability, ecological validity, real-time processing, multimodal assessment,* and *cost* are important factors to consider when selecting hi-tech equipments for practice, exercise, or scientific research. Specifically, *psycho-physiological* and *positioning monitoring* are components of leading hi-tech exercise and sport modalities, and should be considered closely by professionals, exercisers, and athletes. *Active video games* establish modern, virtual-reality scenarios, thus constituting a promising opportunity for fitness agendas and training. *Portable smartphones* are powerful devices and can support exercise planning, execution, and analysis. Additional technologies exist, and we invite the reader to actively search for advancements in clothing technology, as they vary tremendously by fitness modality and sport type. Large-scale hi-tech instruments (e.g., treadmills) are also seemingly limitless, but, as a general recommendation, practitioners should favor the continued development of lighter and multifunctional apparatuses.

Future Avenues

New materials and multifunctional products, especially linked to nanotechnology, will remain an avenue for future hi-tech advancement (Fuss et al., 2008). In addition to lighter and multifunctional apparatuses, professionals interested in the development of novel hi-tech modalities should seek inspiration from other domains within and outside the exercise sciences. Indeed, developments in society in general, and the exercise sciences in particular, have been linked to cross-fertilizations of ideas (Clegg, 2000). More specifically, ideas targeting the fields of neuroscience and DNA engineering are particularly warranted.

The recently launched "Brain Research through Advancing Innovative Neurotechnologies" (BRAIN) aims at mapping and reconstructing the activity of every neuron in a variety of important brain circuits, including those linked to memory encoding and emotional control (Insel, Landis, & Collins, 2013). This project promises technological advancements (in nano, optical, and biochemical technology) that may lead to sophisticated new products in the health and movement sciences. Furthermore, various other studies targeting the human brain (e.g., artificial intelligence, computer simulation) have been conducted in an attempt to evolve applied technologies in the health sector (Garlick, 2003). As such, neuroscience is an expansive avenue for industrial practitioners and scientists interested in advancing technology in exercise sciences.

Since the conclusion of the genome project, a number of technologies, from digital information (e.g., forensic techniques) to molecular medicine, have been proposed and implemented. DNA ancestry testing is among the most novel applications within the sport and exercise sciences (Hauser & Johnston, 2009). Numerous companies currently offer DNA ancestry testing, which provides promising information on physical capabilities and disease predispositions (see Wagner & Royal, 2012). While the predictive validity of these tests has yet to be determined, nature-consistent exercise and medical protocols have now become a reality (Balsevich, 2007). Social and ethical debate must accompany technological discoveries, so that genetic engineering (and any other technology) may be used to the betterment rather than the potential harm of humankind.

REFERENCES

Anderson, R. R., & Collins, D. J. (2004). Are wireless technologies the future for augmented feedback? *Engineering of Sport*, 5, 561–567.

Ansari, N. W., Paul, Y., & Sharma, K. (2012). Kinematic analysis of competitive sprinting. *African Journal for Physical, Health Education, Recreation & Dance*, 18, 662–671.

Arthur, C. (2011). How the Smartphone is killing the PC. *The Guardian*. Retrieved from www.theguardian.com/technology/2011/jun/05/smartphones-killing-pc

Aughey, R. J. (2011). Applications of GPS Technologies to field sports. *International Journal of Sports Physiology & Performance*, 6, 295–310.

Ball, P. (2013). Precise atomic clock may redefine time. *Nature News* (July). Retrieved from www.nature.com/news/precise-atomic-clock-may-redefine-time-1.13363. doi: 10.1038/nature.2013.13363

Balsevich, V. (2007). Nature-consistent strategy of sports training. *Research Yearbook*, 13, 11–16.

Barris, S., & Button, C. (2008). A review of vision-based motion analysis in sport. *Sports Medicine*, 38, 1025–1043.

Burkett, B. (2010). Technology in Paralympic sport: Performance enhancement or essential for performance? *British Journal of Sports Medicine*, 44, 215–220.

Burton, M., Fuss, F. K., & Subic, A. (2011). Sports wheelchair technologies. *Sports Technology*, 3, 154–166. doi.org/10.1080/19346182.2011.564286

Chadwick, S. (2006). Editorial: Technology and the future of sport. *International Journal of Sports Marketing & Sponsorship*, 8, 6.

Clegg, C. W. (2000). Sociotechnical principles for system design. *Applied Ergonomics*, 31, 463–477.

Drost, G., Stegeman, D. F., van Engelen, B. M., & Zwarts, M. J. (2006). Clinical applications of high-density surface EMG: A systematic review. *Journal of Electromyography & Kinesiology*, 16, 586–602.

Edmonds, W. A., & Tenenbaum, G. (Eds.) (2011). *Case studies in applied psychophysiology: Neurofeedback and biofeedback treatments for advances in human performance*. Hoboken, NJ: Wiley-Blackwell.

Filho, E. (2015). Bio-feedback learning environments. In M. Spector (Ed.), *Encyclopedia of educational technology*. Thousand Oaks, CA: Sage.

Floros, G., & Siomos, K. (2012). Patterns of choices on video game genres and internet addiction. *Cyberpsychology, Behavior, and Social Networking*, 15, 117–424. doi:http://dx.doi.org/10.1089/cyber.2012.0064

Fuss, F. K., Subic, A., & Mehta, R. (2008). The impact of technology on sport—new frontiers. *Sports Technology*, 1, 1–2. doi: 10.1002/jst.5

Garlick, D. (2003). Integrating brain science research with intelligence research. *Current Directions in Psychological Science*, 12, 185–189. doi:http://dx.doi.org/10.1111/14678-721.01257

Gowland, S. (2012). Knowledge transfer in the age of technology. *Journal of Orthopaedic & Sports Physical Therapy*, 42, A30–A33.

Grassi, A., Preziosa, A., Villani, D., & Riva, G. (2007). A relaxing journey: The use of mobile phones for well-being improvement. *Annual Review of Cyber Therapy and Telemedicine, 5*, 123–131.

Hahn, A. G., Helmer, R. J. N., Mackintosh, C., Staynes, L. M., & Blanchonette, I. (2011). Technological foundations and current status of a modified, low-risk form of competitive boxing. *Journal of Sports Technology, 4*, 178–184. http://dx.doi.org/10.1080/19346182.2012.725413

Hauser, S. L., & Johnston, S. C. (2009). Personalized genetic scans: With gifts like these . . . *Annals of Neurology, 65*, A7–A9. doi:http://dx.doi.org/10.1002/ana.21709

Hautanen, J. (2007). Basing planning on the needs of exercisers produces new technology. *Motion-Sport in Finland, 1*, 33–34.

Hilletofth, P. (2011). Demand-supply chain management: Industrial survival recipe for new decade. *Industrial Management + Data Systems, 111*, 184–211. doi:http://dx.doi.org/10.1108/0263557111 1115137

Insel, T. R., Landis, S. C., & Collins, F. S. (2013). The NIH BRAIN initiative. *Science, 340*(6133), 687–688.

Kratky, S., & Müller, E. (2013). Spring running with a body-weight supporting kite reduces ground contact time in well-trained sprinters. *Journal of Strength & Conditioning Research, 27*(5), 1215–1222.

Lyons, E. J., Tate, D. F., Ward, D. S., Ribisl, K. M., Bowling, J. M., & Kalyanaraman, S. (2014). Engagement, enjoyment, and energy expenditure during active video game play. *Health Psychology, 33*(2), 174–181.

Maiolo, C. C., Melchiorri, G. G., Iacopino, L. L., Masala, S. S., & De Lorenzo, A. A. (2003). Physical activity energy expenditure measured using a portable telemetric device in comparison with a mass spectrometer. *British Journal of Sports Medicine, 37*, 445–447.

Marta, S., Silva, L., Castro, M., Pezarat-Correia, P., & Cabri, J. (2012). Electromyography variables during the golf swing: A literature review. *Journal of Electromyography & Kinesiology, 22*, 803–813.

McCann, J. (2005). Material requirements for the design of performance sportswear. In R. Shishoo (Ed.) *Textiles in sport* (pp. 44–70). Cambridge, UK: Woodhead Publishing.

McKenzie, T., & Carlson, B. (1984). Computer technology for exercise and sport pedagogy: Recording, storing, and analyzing interval data. *Journal of Teaching in Physical Education, 3*, 17–27.

Millet, G., Perrey, S., Divert, C., & Foissac, M. (2006). The role of engineering in fatigue reduction during human locomotion—a review. *Sports Engineering, 9*, 209–220.

Misra, P., & Bednarz, S. (2004). Navigation for precision approaches: Robust integrity monitoring using GPS+Galileo. *GPS World, 15*, 42.

MIT Technological Review. (2013, September). Retrieved from www.technologyreview.com/news/513861/samsung-demos-a-tablet-controlled-by-your-brain/

Orvis, K. A., Moore, J. C., Belanich, J., Murphy, J. S., & Horn, D. B. (2010). Are soldiers gamers? Videogame usage among soldiers and implications for the effective use of serious videogames for military training. *Military Psychology, 22*, 143–157. doi:http://dx.doi.org/10.1080/08995600903417225

Paul, M., Garg, K., & Sandhu, J. (2012). Role of biofeedback in optimizing psychomotor performance in sports. *Asian Journal of Sports Medicine, 3*, 29–40.

Perry, F. D. (2012). Biofeedback & neurofeedback applications in sport psychology. *Sport Psychologist, 26*, 313–314.

Razon, S., Basevitch, I., Land, W., Thompson, B., & Tenenbaum, G. (2009). Perception of exertion and attention allocation as a function of visual and auditory conditions. *Psychology of Sport and Exercise, 10*, 636–643. doi:http://dx.doi.org/10.1016/j.psychsport.2009.03.007

Reinecke, K., Cordes, M., Lerch, C., Koutsandréou, F., Schubert, M., Weiss, M., & Baumeister, J. (2011). From lab to field conditions: A pilot study on EEG methodology in applied sports sciences. *Applied Psychophysiology and Biofeedback, 36*, 265–271.

Robinson, M. G., Holt, L. E., Pelham, T. W., & Furneaux, K. (2011). Accelerometry measurements of sprint kayaks: The coaches' new tool. *International Journal of Coaching Science, 5*, 45–56.

Russell, W. D., & Newton, M. (2008). Short-term psychological effects of interactive video game technology exercise on mood and attention. *Educational Technology & Society, 11*, 294–308.

Schack, T., & Hackfort, D. (2007). An action theory approach to applied sport psychology. In G. Tenenbaum & R. C. Eklund (Eds.), *Handbook of sport psychology* (3rd ed., pp. 332–351). New York, NY: John Wiley.

Shani, A. B., & Sena, J. A. (1994). Information technology and the integration of change: Sociotechnical system approach. *Journal of Applied Behavioral Science, 30,* 247–270.

Singh Bal, B., & Dureja, G. (2012). Hawk Eye: A logical innovative technology use in sports for effective decision making. *Sport Science Review, 21,* 107–119.

Smallwood, S. R., Morris, M. M., Fallows, S. J., & Buckley, J. P. (2012). Physiologic responses and energy expenditure of kinect active video game play in schoolchildren. *Archives of Pediatrics & Adolescent Medicine, 166,* 1005–1009. doi: 10.1001/archpediatrics

Stamm, A., James, D., & Thiel, D. (2013). Velocity profiling using inertial sensors for freestyle swimming. *Sports Engineering, 16,* 1–11.

Stevens, C. J., & Bryan, A. D. (2012). Rebranding exercise: There's an app for that. *American Journal of Health Promotion, 27,* 69–70. doi:http://dx.doi.org/10.4278/ajhp.120711-CIT-338

Taylor, L. M., Maddison, R., Pfaeffli, L. A., Rawstorn, J. C., Gant, N., & Kerse, N. M. (2012). Activity and energy expenditure in older people playing active video games. *Archives of Physical Medicine & Rehabilitation, 93,* 2281–2286.

Tenenbaum, G., & Filho, E. (2014). Cognitive styles. In R. C. Eklund & G. Tenenbaum (Eds.), *Encyclopedia of sport and exercise psychology* (Vol. 3, pp. 141–143). Thousand Oaks, CA: Sage.

Terlecki, M., Brown, J., Harner-Steciw, L., Irvin-Hannum, J., Marchetto-Ryan, N., Ruhl, L., & Wiggins, J. (2011). Sex differences and similarities in video game experience, preferences, and self-efficacy: Implications for the gaming industry. *Current Psychology: A Journal for Diverse Perspectives on Diverse Psychological Issues, 30,* 22–33. doi:http://dx.doi.org/10.1007/s121440-109-0955-

Vescovi, J. D. (2012). Uncovering the demands of women's soccer using GPS technology. *Soccer Journal, 57,* 5–6.

Wagner, J. K., & Royal, C. D. (2012). Field of genes: An investigation of sports-related genetic testing. *Journal of Personalized Medicine, 2,* 119–137. doi:10.3390/jpm2030119

11 Exergaming

Edson Filho, Selenia di Fronso, Claudio Robazza, and Maurizio Bertollo

The miniaturization of computer hardware, particularly gaming joysticks and controls, along with the advent of new wireless systems, has allowed for the creation of "exergames," derived from the combination of "exercise" and "digital gaming" (Di Tore & Raiola, 2012). Indeed, exergames combine exercise with game play by emulating real-life fitness, exercise, and sport situations through motion-sensor technology and virtual-reality animations (Russell & Newton, 2008; Staiano & Calvert, 2011a). This relatively new video game modality requires physical exertion during game play and measures players' movements and motor skills through a series of technological devices, such as accelerometers and gyroscopes, cameras, pads and mats, and pressure and optical sensors (Rizzo, Lange, Suma, & Bolas, 2011; Russell & Newton, 2008).

Accordingly, the interaction with the video game is not solely based on traditional joysticks and hand-eye coordination, but involves the whole body through the use of non-standard controllers, such as the Nintendo Wiimote and Balance Board or the Microsoft Kinect sensor. Noteworthy, the exergames movement has redefined the video game industry and represents one of the leading technological trends in the sport and exercise sciences (Staiano & Calvert, 2011b). The purpose herein is to offer an overview of the target population, principles, types, benefits, and educational perspectives of exergaming. First, the target population of exergames is outlined. Next, the governing principles of exergame systems are presented as well as a description of the different types of exergames. Subsequently, the physical and psychosocial benefits of playing exergames are discussed in light of empirical research. Finally, educational applications and future perspectives on exergaming are discussed.

TARGET POPULATION

Video game play is prevalent, nearly universal, among children and adolescents in the United States and various Western countries (Staiano & Calvert, 2011b). Recently, Lenhart et al. (2008) conducted a comprehensive national survey in the United States and observed that 94% of girls and 99% of boys between 12 to 17 years old play video games. Video game play is also prevalent among young adults and middle-age individuals, and has gained popularity among older adults as well (Brach et al., 2012). Since the late 1980s, when Nintendo introduced the Nintendo Entertainment System and its alternative video game consoles, active video game playing has increased among adults and the elderly (Taylor et al., 2012). Currently, exergames represent an alternative to traditional and sedentary video game playing (Staiano & Calvert, 2011b).

Although an array of individuals play exergames, game preferences exist by age and gender. Specifically, children favor richer designs, while the elderly prefer simpler screen layouts (Brox, Fernadez-Luque, & Tollesfsen, 2011). Gender differences exist in game preference, with men favoring sport games, whereas women tend to prefer racing and dancing games (Terlecki et al., 2011). Notwithstanding these differences, it is important to note that exergames are designed for numerous reasons and thus can be applied to various subpopulation groups (see Brox et al., 2011). For instance, children and teenagers enjoy learning motor skills through health exergames (e.g., *Dance Dance Revolution*; see Lenhart et al., 2008). The military and airline pilots use gaming technology to simulate domain-specific procedures (Orvis, Moore, Belanich, Murphy, & Horn, 2010). Athletes in general and golfers in particular may play video games to improve fine motor skills (Fery & Ponserre, 2001), while children with attention deficit hyperactivity disorder learn how to sustain attention using multimedia gaming technology (Rizzo et al., 2011). Children with developmental disorders can improve motor competence and mental health by playing virtual reality games (Straker et al., 2011). The elderly engage in video gaming for various reasons, including to improve coordination and balance, socialize with friends, increase heart rate, and burn calories (Brach et al., 2012). Altogether, different video game modalities are played in an array of domains (e.g., academia, military, special education, sports, and physical rehabilitation) for entertainment, health, learning, or clinical reasons. Accordingly, this literature overview is not limited to a given subpopulation group or applied context, but rather focuses on the principles common to various types of exergames.

PRINCIPLES OF EXERGAMING DESIGN

Exergames are characterized by two important characteristics (see Figure 11.1). First, exergame development stems from a solid theoretical basis, deriving many of its principles from mainstream psychology as well as sport and human movement sciences. Furthermore, exergames rely on interactive features, particularly real-time feedback, multimedia channels, and dynamic interfaces.

Theoretical Basis

Video game technology relies on software engineering, logics, and artificial intelligence concepts (see Ghaoui, 2006). In addition to these computer programming requirements, video

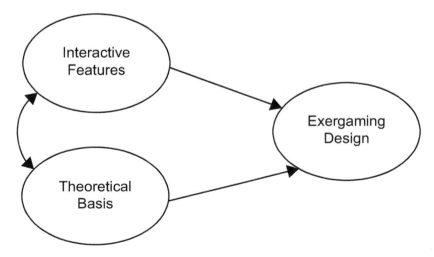

Figure 11.1 Principles of Exergaming Design

game technology is based on psychological and sport science frameworks (Hardy, Göbel, Gutjahr, Wiemeyer, & Steinmetz, 2012; Papastergiou, 2009; Schultze, 2010). Several main psychological and sport and exercise science concepts employed by exergame designers are discussed next.

Psychological Concepts

Concepts inherent in behaviorism are particularly evident in video game software and applications (Song & Kim, 2012). Games reward proper behaviors and actions with points, bonuses, and status promotions (i.e., phase advancement). Conversely, if a player fails to adhere to the game's rules, punishment occurs in the form of point deduction and stage blockage. Motivational constructs are also an element of video game design (Lenhart et al., 2008; Staiano & Calvert, 2011b). For instance, intrinsic motivation is established by allowing a player to create his/her own player profile, thus fostering a sense of identity and ownership during play. Extrinsic motivation derives from the outcome goals and competitive feelings associated with video gaming in general and exergaming in particular (see Brox et al., 2011).

Another psychological anchor to exergame designs is the flow-feeling theory (see Csikszentmihalyi & Csikszentmihalyi, 1993). In effect, players are able to balance challenge and skill by adjusting built-in configuration controls (e.g., rhythm of music play, level of opponent in tennis or golf), thus advancing a sense of control while experiencing intense involvement in the exergame (Hardy et al., 2012; Sinclair, Hingston, & Masek, 2007). Moreover, Bandura's (1997) social cognitive theory is linked to video game design. Players are able to master a new skill by "taking risks" and are allowed "repetition" of a stage until successfully advancing to a more challenging level. Vicarious experiences, operationalized through modeling behaviors by virtual personal trainers, are also part of exergame applications (e.g., *My Fitness Coach* or *Daisy Fuentes Pilates* by Wii). Furthermore, applied research on ergonomic and situated cognition concepts has been used to develop games to simulate sport and military scenarios (e.g., *America's Army*, see Goodman, Bradley, Paras, Williamson, & Bizzocchi, 2006; Orvis, Horn, & Belanich, 2009; Orvis et al., 2010). Finally, sport and exercise science constructs in general, and exercise physiology models in particular, are important in designing active video game applications.

Sport and Exercise Science Concepts

Similar to psychology, sport and exercise science is a vast domain with numerous applications to exergames (Papastergiou, 2009; Wilson, Darden, & Meyler, 2010). Of particular importance to exergame design are the sub-domains of exercise physiology as well as motor control and learning. The notion of periodization, broadly conceived as the balance between training volume and intensity aimed at ensuring overcompensation (see Issurin, 2010), is present in exergames such as *Yourself!Fitness* and *The Biggest Loser* by Xbox 360—THQ. Consideration of anthropological and anthropometric covariates (e.g., age, gender, height, and weight) is a critical feature of video game playing aimed at emulating real-life fitness and exercise agendas (Brach et al., 2012; Graves et al., 2010; Terlecki et al., 2011). Noteworthy, exergames also rely on the concept of "embodiment" in the sense that our moving bodies serve as an interface with the video game being played: "the senses act as communication channels to the actual world absorbing its energy field as they impinge on the body" (see Schultze, 2010, p. 436). Perhaps more subtle to the average player or individual unfamiliar with the sport science literature is the influence of different practice schedules (e.g., constant, random, blocked; see Bertollo, Berchicci, Carraro, Comani, & Robazza, 2010) on performance and learning of games with a strong motor skill requirement (e.g., *Dance Dance Revolution*, *Wii Sports Bowling*, *Tennis*, *Boxing*, and *NBA Wii*). Furthermore, feedback, a concept vastly studied in motor learning, is an important interactive feature of exergames.

Interactive Features

Real-Time Feedback

Exergames are designed to provide real-time augmented extrinsic information. In effect, a key feature of exergames is to initially measure a variable of interest (e.g., players' reaction time, force) and subsequently offer related information to the player (Giggins, Persson, & Caulfield, 2013). More specifically, information provided to the player can be either (1) *direct feedback*, by showing numerical values in regards to one's reaction time or power output, for instance, or (2) *transformed feedback* in the form of a sensorial stimulus, such as tactile information, sound, or visual image (Rizzo et al., 2011). The real-time feedback property common to exergames is essential to capture and sustain the players' motivation during gameplay (Courts & Tucker, 2012). Multisensorial stimuli are another important governing principle of exergames.

Multimedia Applications

Exergame playing is an immersive experience as it generates multisensorial impressions that create a feeling of being present in a simulated world (Filho, 2015; Hardy et al., 2012; Russell & Newton, 2008). In fact, multimedia stimuli are thought to enhance individuals' engagement and learning experiences (Courts & Tucker, 2012). To this extent, empirical evidence suggests that people remember approximately 20% of what they hear, 40% of what they hear and see, and 75% of what they hear, see, and interact with (Eskicioglu & Kopec, 2003). Accordingly, the multimedia channels common to exergames embrace different types of learners, thus allowing players with different cognitive and learning styles (e.g., kinesthetic, visual) to appreciate and manage their own gaming experience.

Dynamic Interfaces

A key feature of exergaming technology is its reliance on innovative exertion interfaces, rather than traditional game controllers, such as a joystick, gamepad, or mouse (Papastergiou, 2009). These dynamic interfaces (e.g., bicycle ergometers, electronic dance pads, tracking cameras, musical instruments) are crucial to exergaming technology as, without them, electronic games are primarily sedentary activities (Russell & Newton, 2008; Staiano & Calvert, 2011a). Thus, the development of dynamic interfaces allows exergames to exist. Wilson et al. (2010) noted that "exergaming is associated with participants becoming *human joy sticks* as they must move their bodies instead of just their thumbs in order to play the games" (p. 14). Noteworthy, the Nintendo Wii sold 24.5 million consoles in 2008, whereas the recently launched Xbox One (by Microsoft) and the PlayStation 4 (by Sony) are attempting to win customers by marketing their consoles as "the best gaming console possible" and the "media device that can do it all," respectively (Business Insider, 2013). This technological and marketing trend aimed at making better gaming consoles is ultimately increasing the applicability of exergames to both practitioners and researchers interested in the benefits of different types of active video game playing.

TYPES OF EXERGAMES AND HEALTH GAMING

Exergames can be categorized according to their methodological features, which may be primarily based on control, rhythm, machines, workout, or sensory parameters. Exergames are also linked to a larger gaming movement labeled "health gaming" (Brox et al., 2011; Lee, 2012).

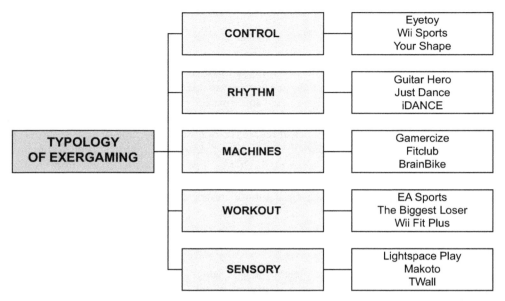

Figure 11.2 Typology of Exergaming and Applied Examples

Types of Exergames

A typology common to most exergames pertains to its "entertainment-first approach," meaning exergames are designed to create movement in immersive and cognitively enjoyable experiences (Lenhart et al., 2008; Papastergiou, 2009; Staiano & Calvert, 2011b). A more operational typology for exergaming has been proposed by the Exergame Network (http://exergamenetwork.blogspot.com; see Figure 11.2).

This typology, used by practitioners interested in developing exergaming facilities (Wilson et al., 2010), is based on the notion that exergames can be classified according to their extrinsic methodological feature into several categories: (a) control exergaming, (b) rhythm exergaming, (c) exergaming machines, (d) workout exergaming, and (e) sensory exergaming. Control exergaming includes those games in which the players' body movements are captured by the game, thus literally serving as the "control" for any action. Rhythm exergaming requires that players follow the beat of the music while the exergame registers their timing and dance steps. Exergaming machines use real fitness equipment (e.g., stationary bikes, "cybercycles") while people play interactive games aimed at diverting their attention from the exertive task. Workout exergames are built around the figure of a virtual personal trainer, who provides feedback and stores individual training progress. Lastly, sensory exergaming utilizes motion sensor technology to convert jumps, air punches, and runs to points. It is important to note that although practically and conceptually appealing, this typology is descriptive in nature and primarily based on face validity. Accordingly, sport and exercise psychologists should conduct further research pertaining to exergame classification systems and operational frameworks. Movement science professionals should also be aware, and make use of, health gaming aimed at promoting active lifestyles.

Health Gaming

Exergames are part of a larger movement labeled "health gaming" (Brox et al., 2011; Goodman et al., 2006; Russell & Newton, 2008; Staiano & Calvert, 2011a). Although health games may neither merge exercise movement with gaming technology nor ascribe to the "entertainment-first approach," they are important educational tools. In fact, health games have been used to develop clinical applications for specific sub-population groups, as well as "whole-person wellness" programs for people of all ages (Sinclair et al., 2007).

Clinical Applications

There are several health games specifically designed for clinical conditions, including blindness (e.g., *Eyes-Free Yoga*), autism (e.g., *Nurfland*), and diabetes (e.g., *Escape from Diab*), as well as asthma, cerebral palsy, dementia, and hypertension (for a review, see Staiano & Flynn, 2014). Although many games are designed with a particular clinical condition in mind, all health games are created to allow for *self-paced learning* and *in-home therapy* (see Lee, 2012). In fact, most newly developed health games use easy touchscreen interfaces (e.g., iPad), thus allowing people with disabilities to better control (i.e., self-pace) their learning experience. Moreover, health games are multisensorial experiences and include motivating graphics and sound effects. As a result, health games are more likely to be incorporated into one's everyday life (particularly children) and thus serve the purpose of an in-home therapy practice.

Whole-Person Wellness Programs

In terms of general well-being across age cohorts, health gaming has been used to educate individuals on dietary choices, hygiene habits, and injury and illness prevention. Indeed, there are a number of games directed at teaching children about healthy nutritional choices (e.g., *My Plate*; *Escape from Obez City*) and hygiene habits (e.g., *Grush*; *The Kids Corner*). Furthermore, there is evidence suggesting that video gaming can be used to educate children about injury prevention in contact sports (Goodman et al., 2006). Also, health gaming has been increasingly used to educate teenagers on sensitive topics such as sexuality (e.g., *Play it Safe*; *Freedom HIV*) and drug use and abuse (e.g., *Trauma*).

For adults, there are numerous games aimed at promoting behavioral change and self-awareness. For instance, those dealing with a smoking addiction may benefit from playing *My Stop Smoking Coach with Allen Carr*. People experiencing anxiety symptoms may consider playing *Never-Mind* or *Zenytime* to gain awareness on how to deal with cognitive and somatic anxiety-related responses. Finally, several health games have been developed to address the needs of older adults (Van Riet, Crutzen, & Shirong, 2014). For instance, *The Step Kinnection* and *Brain Fitness* have been tested as potential tools to diminish falling accidents and memory decay among older adults (Miller et al., 2013; Staiano & Flynn, 2014). Furthermore, *Sun Safety* and *IronPigs* aim to teach older adults behaviors to diminish the likelihood of skin and prostate cancer, respectively.

Additional games for clinical and non-clinical applications exist, such as games on safe cross-walking and wheel-chair use (see Brox et al., 2011). Thus, the applicability of gaming technology in health and exercise settings is likely to increase in the years to come as researchers and practitioners continue to unravel the physical and psychosocial benefits of mixing health and exercise with active digital gaming (Adkins et al., 2013; Fogel, Miltenberger, Graves, & Koehler, 2010; Papastergiou, 2009).

BENEFITS OF EXERGAMING

Although research on exergaming is in the initial stages, growing evidence suggests positive physical and psychosocial outcomes of active video game playing. The physical benefits include increased caloric expenditure, improved cardiovascular fitness, and gains in coordination and balance. The psychosocial gains of exergaming include enhanced motivation, self-esteem and self-efficacy, and opportunities for positive social interaction.

Physical Outcomes

Energy Expenditure and Heart Rate Increase

While traditional video games contribute to sedentary behaviors, exergames promote exercise during game play (Giggins et al., 2013; Graves et al., 2010; Klein & Simmers, 2009). In fact, exergames are seen as a potential tool to combat childhood obesity, which is increasingly associated with a lack of physical activity (Daley, 2009; Fogel et al., 2010). According to Sinclair et al. (2007), exergames are particularly important to decelerate obesity rates given the trend of "increased screen time and decreased physical activity" (p. 289). In fact, the majority of studies on the physical outcomes of exergaming have been focused on energy expenditure (Papastergiou, 2009). Recently, Smallwood, Morris, Fallows, and Buckley (2012) reported that *Kinetic Sports Boxing* and *Dance Central* increased energy expenditure by 263% and 150%, respectively, when compared to resting values. Other scholars have also empirically demonstrated that exergaming increases energy expenditure when compared to sedentary video gaming (Adkins et al., 2013; Duncan & Dick, 2012; Fogel et al., 2010).

Additionally, exergaming has been found to increase heart rate, an important dimension of aerobic fitness (Graves et al., 2010; Kloos, Fritz, Kostyk, Young, & Kegelmeyer, 2013). For instance, Siegel, Haddock, Dubois, and Wilkin (2009) observed that participants playing 30 minutes of a boxing exergame reached 60% or more of their heart rate reserve, a value within the American College of Sports Medicine's recommendation for daily physical activity. Garn, Baker, Beasley, and Solmon (2012) studied the physical implications of playing *Run Wii Fit* and concluded that the "game provided opportunities to accumulate moderate to vigorous physical activity" (p. 311). Importantly, different exergames are associated with different heart rate and caloric expenditure demands (Duncan & Dick, 2012; Smallwood et al., 2012). For instance, boxing, running, and dancing exergames require more physical demand than golfing. Movement professionals should also be aware of the fact that exergames are not a substitute for more traditional physical activity behaviors (e.g., pick-up basketball games), which lead to significantly greater energy expenditure and neurophysiological benefits (Nye, 2011; O'Leary, Pontifex, Scudder, Brown, & Hillman, 2011).

Coordination and Balance

There is initial evidence suggesting that exergaming may lead to gains in coordination and balance (Byrne, Roberts, Squires, & Rohr, 2012). Fery and Ponserre (2001) reported a positive transfer of golf video playing to actual putting skill. Specifically, they concluded that exergaming may be a useful training tool to teach people how to adjust force in order to successfully putt in golf. In regards to balance, Kosse, Caljouw, Vuijk, and Lamoth (2011) observed gains in dynamic balance among elderly participants in a six-week training using *SensBalance Fitness Board* as a training platform (Sensamove, the Netherlands). Nintendo *Wii Fit* exercises have also been found to be effective training tools to improve static postural sway and dynamic balance among college students (Gioftsidou et al., 2013). Furthermore, in an experimental protocol, Byrne et al. (2012) noticed significant post-training improvements in dynamic balance among young adults playing *Wii Fit*. It is important to add that, congruent with research on skill acquisition and expert performance in sport sciences (Williams & Ericsson, 2008), gains in balance through exergaming were found to be specific to the muscle groups involved in the task (Byrne et al., 2012; Gioftsidou et al., 2013). Additional research is needed to determine the applications and implications of exergaming for motor skill acquisition in general and coordination and balance in particular.

Psychosocial Outcomes

Motivation and Enjoyment

Exergames elicit a strong motivational response from participants (Lenhart et al., 2008; Staiano & Calvert, 2011b). The "novelty factor" associated with exergaming also carries an inherently motivational component. Furthermore, the balance of challenge and skill level, along with interactive features unique to exergames (i.e., multimedia and dynamic interfaces), fosters engagement, enjoyment, and "flow-feeling" states (Hardy et al., 2012; Sinclair et al., 2007). Empirical evidence echoes the notion that exergames are engaging and enjoyable experiences. For instance, Graves et al. (2010) observed higher enjoyment rates for Wii aerobics in comparison to treadmill and walking exercise for adolescents, young adults, and older adults. Sun (2012) found that interest for exergaming was higher than for regular fitness lessons among elementary children participating in physical education classes. Garn et al. (2012) studied the benefits of playing *Run Wii Fit* and concluded that exergaming provides motivational benefits to its players, particularly to those classified as obese. In this regard, Hepler, Wang, and Albarracin (2012) averred that exergames are a home-modality virtual media and therefore may provide an exercise alternative for people lacking motivation to join a gym or engage in more traditional exercise modalities and routines. The possibility of using exergames at home may also prevent self-presentation concerns common to gyms in general and group exercise classes in particular (Lee, 2012).

Self-Esteem and Self-Efficacy

Self-presentation concerns are a common barrier to physical activity, particularly for overweight individuals (Prapavessis, Grove, & Eklund, 2004). Exergaming may reduce body self-consciousness while increasing self-esteem and efficacy beliefs in obese adolescents (Staiano & Calvert, 2011b). In effect, exergame players are required to direct their focus outward during play (to the visual, tactile, and sonic effects proper to exergaming). Staiano, Abraham, and Calvert (2013) examined the influence of a 20-week exergame intervention on weight loss and psychosocial outcomes among overweight and obese adolescents. Results indicated positive outcomes in both self-esteem and self-efficacy as measured at baseline and at the conclusion of the program. The authors highlighted the benefits of cooperative exergaming, which was found to promote weight loss when compared to a control group.

Social Benefits

Excessive traditional video game playing is associated with social isolation (Sublette & Mullan, 2012), while playing violent games is considered a causal risk for increased aggressive behavior (Anderson et al., 2010). In contrast, exergaming is thought to promote positive social outcomes through multiplayer modes (Papastergiou, 2009). Indeed, social interaction is a primary reason why young adults play *Dance Dance Revolution* (Staiano & Calvert, 2011b). Multiplayer games are also common among adolescents. Lenhart et al. (2008) reported that 76% of teenagers play multiplayer games at least occasionally, with 65% of them playing in the same room. Playing exergames against peers has been found to produce greater exercise intensities and energy expenditure when compared to no-competition or competing against a virtual competitor (fictional, computer-generated; see Snyder, Anderson-Hanley, & Arciero, 2012; Staiano et al., 2013). The numerous social benefits of exergaming are an important argument for schools and teachers interested in developing physical education curriculum while advancing pedagogical principles applied to exergaming (Hall, 2012; Hardy et al., 2012).

APPLIED PERSPECTIVES ON EXERGAMING

Exergaming can be used as an educational tool in physical education, as well as in other disciplines and classroom environments (Hall, 2012; Hardy et al., 2012). According to Eskicioglu and Kopec (2003), the focus of technological education in general, and of exergaming curriculums in particular, should be on procedural knowledge ("hands and minds on education"). Specifically, the focus should be on education *with technology* rather than education *about technology*. Accordingly, students should learn how to apply knowledge through the management of their own multimedia experience. In effect, exergaming creates multisensorial experiences, allowing individuals with different preferred learning styles (e.g., auditory, kinesthetic, visual) to acquire and retain new and complex information (Filho, 2015). Bearing in mind that people have different learning styles, teachers and practitioners should include both competitive and cooperative exergames in their classrooms and applied practice (for a review, see Marker & Staiano, 2015). Competitive exergames lead to greater energy expenditure when compared to playing alone. Engaging in cooperative play helps develop empathy as the players must consider other's actions to succeed in the game. Overall, educators should remember that one of the greatest benefits of exergaming is its ability to balance change and skill, in that users have the opportunity to pace their own learning experience (e.g., competition vs. cooperation, difficulty level, mode of play).

Exergaming education should also be both holistic and systemic in nature (Kim, Hannafin, & Bryan, 2007). In particular, teachers and instructors should expose students to a multitude of different concepts (holistic) while explaining how these various concepts are simultaneously inter-connected (systemic). For instance, a physical education teacher may lecture on how the various physiological systems (e.g., neuromuscular, cardiovascular, endocrinal) are inter-related during endurance exercise. Students may also be taught periodization training, or how to use mental skills to control attentional focus during an exertive task. Overall, educators should not only offer instrumental feedback to their students, but also assume multiple critical roles, serving as motivators, models, collaborators, experimenters, guides, and innovators (Crawford, 2000). The importance of advancing pedagogical principles on technological literacy shall remain an area of future research interest.

FUTURE DIRECTIONS FOR RESEARCH AND PRACTICE

From a research standpoint, it is important to continue advancing experimental trials targeting the bio-psycho-social outcomes of exergaming. Clinical trials are essential for health games aimed at promoting a healthier lifestyle. Longitudinal studies are also warranted, as the long-term effects of exergaming, as well as the sustainability of whole-person wellness programs, have not been established yet. Legal issues and the licensing of active video gaming technology are also growing fields of research. From a broader perspective, scholars should report null results and address the negative effects of game playing, such as aggression and anti-social behaviors. Indeed, acknowledging null findings and recognizing the negative aspects of active video game playing can help establish guidelines for safe exergaming (Kato, 2012). It is thus important to note that exergaming may offer an alternative, but not necessarily a substitute, for traditional vigorous physical activities (e.g., running, swimming). In this regard, the American College of Sports Medicine (ACSM, 2013) recently published a commentary discussing exergaming within its physical activity (aerobic and strength training) guidelines.

Basic scientific approaches, particularly the ones with a neuro-scientific focus, are welcomed areas of research, as scant studies on brain imaging in exergaming exist. Of note, the Massachusetts Institute of Technology and the Max Planck Institute are currently leading a large-scale and promising neuro-scientific study on active video game playing. Specifically, the EyeWire project aims to map neurons in 3D by drawing data from a large sample of video game players (180,000 as of April, 2015). The findings from the study might help to elucidate how billions of neurons connect to process visual information.

From an applied standpoint, practitioners should continue to advance curriculum ideas on exergaming. Furthermore, interested practitioners should move from knowledge application to knowledge creation. Advancing knowledge on how to maintain and design new technological products and systems is also under the auspices of movement scientists and sport and exercise psychologists. Additionally, establishing biofeedback learning environments integrated within exergaming contexts would also be a step forward in the practice of sport and exercise psychology. Overall, exercise psychologists should continue to use exergaming and other technological tools to promote exercise engagement and adherence.

REFERENCES

Adkins, M. M., Brown, G. A., Heelan, K. K., Ansorge, C. C., Shaw, B. S., & Shaw, I. I. (2013). Can dance exergaming contribute to improving physical activity levels in elementary school children? *African Journal for Physical, Health Education, Recreation & Dance, 19*, 576–585.

American College of Sports Medicine Information on Exergaming. (2013). Retrieved from www.acsm. org/docs/brochures/exergaming.pdf?sfvrsn=6

Anderson, C. A., Shibuya, A., Ihori, N., Swing, E. L., Bushman, B. J., Sakamoto, A., . . . Saleem, M. (2010). Violent video game effects on aggression, empathy, and prosocial behavior in eastern and western countries: A meta-analytic review. *Psychological Bulletin, 136*, 151–173. doi:http://dx.doi. org/10.1037/a0018251

Bandura, A. (1997). *Self-efficacy: The exercise of control.* New York, NY: W.H. Freeman.

Bertollo, M., Berchicci, M., Carraro, A., Comani, S., & Robazza, C. (2010). Blocked and random practice organization in the learning of rhythmic dance step sequences *Perceptual and Motor Skills, 110*, 77–84.

Brach, M., Hauer, K., Rotter, L., Werres, C., Korn, O., Konrad, R., & Göbel, S. (2012). Modern principles of training in exergames for sedentary seniors: Requirements and approaches for sport and exercise sciences. *International Journal of Computer Science in Sport, 11*, 86–99.

Brox, E., Fernadez-Luque, X., & Tollesfsen, T. (2011). Health gaming—Video game design to promote health. *Applied Clinical Informatics, 27*, 128–142. doi:10.4338/ACI-2010-10-R-0060

Business Insider. (2013, December). Retrieved from www.businessinsider.com/gamers-prefer-playstation-4-to-xbox-one-20136–

Byrne, J. M., Roberts, J., Squires, H., & Rohr, L. E. (2012). The effect of a three-week Wii Fit™ balance training program on dynamic balance in healthy young adults. *International SportMed Journal, 13*, 170–179.

Courts, V., & Tucker, J. (2012). Using technology to create a dynamic classroom experience. *Journal of College Teaching & Learning, 9*, 121–127.

Crawford, B. A. (2000). Embracing the essence of inquiry: New roles for science teachers. *Journal of Research in Science Teaching, 37*, 916–937. doi:10.1002/1098-2736

Csikszentmihalyi, M., & Csikszentmihalyi, I. S. (1993). Family influences on the development of giftedness. In I. Selega (Ed.), *The origins and development of high ability* (pp. 187–206). Oxford: John Wiley & Sons.

Daley, A. J. (2009). Can exergaming contribute to improving physical activity levels and health outcomes in children? *Pediatrics, 124,* 763–771. doi:http://dx.doi.org/10.1542/peds.20082-357

Di Tore, P. A., & Raiola, G. (2012). Exergames in motor skill learning. *Journal of Physical Education and Sport, 12,* 358–361.

Duncan, M. J., & Dick, S. (2012). Energy expenditure and enjoyment of exergaming: A comparison of the Nintendo Wii and the Gamercize Power Stepper in young adults. *Medicina Sportiva, 16,* 92–98.

Eskicioglu, A. M., & Kopec, D. (2003). The ideal multimedia-enabled classroom: Perspectives from psychology, education, and information science. *Journal of Educational Multimedia and Hypermedia, 12,* 199–221.

Fery, Y. A., & Ponserre, S. (2001). Enhancing the control of force in putting by video game training. *Ergonomics, 44,* 1025–1037.

Filho, E. (2015). Bio-feedback learning environments. In M. Spector (Ed.), *Encyclopedia of educational technology.* Thousand Oaks, CA: Sage.

Fogel, V. A., Miltenberger, R. G., Graves, R., & Koehler, S. (2010). The effects of exergaming on physical activity among inactive children in a physical education classroom. *Journal of Applied Behavior Analysis, 43,* 591–600. doi:http://dx.doi.org/10.1901/jaba.2010.435-91

Garn, A. C., Baker, B. L., Beasley, E. K., & Solmon, M. A. (2012). What are the benefits of a commercial exergaming platform for college students? Examining physical activity, enjoyment, and future intentions. *Journal of Physical Activity & Health, 9,* 311–318.

Ghaoui, C. (2006). *Encyclopedia of human computer interaction.* Hershey, PA: Idea Group Reference/ IGI Global.

Giggins, O. M., Persson, U. M., & Caulfield, B. (2013). Biofeedback in rehabilitation. *Journal of Neuroengineering and Rehabilitation, 10,* 3–11. doi:10.1186/17430-0031-06-0

Gioftsidou, A., Vernadakis, N., Malliou, P., Batzios, S., Sofokleous, P., Antoniou, P., . . . Godolias, G. (2013). Typical balance exercises or exergames for balance improvement? *Journal of Back & Musculoskeletal Rehabilitation, 26,* 299–305.

Goodman, D., Bradley, N. L., Paras, B., Williamson, I. J., & Bizzochi, J. (2006). Video gaming promotes concussion knowledge acquisition in youth hockey players. *Journal of Adolescence, 29,* 351–360. doi:http://dx.doi.org/10.1016/j.adolescence.2005.07.004

Graves, L. E. F., Ridgers, N. D., Williams, K., Stratton, G., Atkinson, G., & Cable, N. T. (2010). The physiological cost and enjoyment of wii fit in adolescents, young adults, and older adults. *Journal of Physical Activity & Health, 7,* 393–401.

Hall, T. (2012). Emplotment, embodiment, engagement: Narrative technology in support of physical education, sport and physical activity. *Quest, 64,* 105–115.

Hardy, S., Göbel, S., Gutjahr, M., Wiemeyer, J., & Steinmetz, R. (2012). Adaptation model for indoor exergames. *International Journal of Computer Science in Sport, 11,* 73–85.

Hepler, J., Wang, W., & Albarracin, D. (2012). Motivating exercise: The interactive effect of general action goals and past behavior on physical activity. *Motivation and Emotion, 36,* 365–370.

Issurin, V. B. (2010). New horizons for the methodology and physiology of training periodization. *Sports Medicine, 40,* 189–206.

Kato, P. M. (2012). Evaluating efficacy and validating games for health. *Games for Health Journal, 1,* 74–76. doi:10.1089/g4h.2012.1017.

Kim, M., Hannafin, M., & Bryan, L. (2007). Technology-enhanced inquiry tools in science education: An emerging pedagogical framework for classroom practice. *Science Education, 96,* 1010–1030. doi:10.1002/sce

Klein, M. J., & Simmers, C. S. (2009). Exergaming: Virtual inspiration, real perspiration. *Young Consumers, 10,* 35–45. doi:http://dx.doi.org/10.1108/17473610910940774

Kloos, A., Fritz, N., Kostyk, S., Young, G., & Kegelmeyer, D. (2013). Video game play (Dance Dance Revolution) as a potential exercise therapy in Huntington's disease: A controlled clinical trial. *Clinical Rehabilitation, 27,* 972–982.

Kosse, N. M., Caljouw, S. R., Vuijk, P., & Lamoth, C. J. C. (2011). Exergaming: Interactive balance training in healthy community-dwelling older adults. *Journal of CyberTherapy and Rehabilitation, 4,* 399–407.

Lee, S. (2012). Project Injini: Developing cognitive training games for children with special needs. *Games for Health Journal, 1,* 69–73. doi:10.1089/g4h.2012.1016

Lenhart, A., Kahne, J., Middaugh, E., Macgill, A. R., Evans, C., & Vitak, J. (2008). Teens, video games, and civics: Teens' gaming experiences are diverse and include significant social interaction and civic engagement. *Pew Internet & American Life Project*. 1615 L Street NW Suite 700, Washington, DC 20036.

Marker, A. M., & Staiano, A. E. (2015). Better together: Outcomes of cooperation versus competition in social exergaming. *Games for Health Journal, 4*, 25–30. doi:10.1089/g4h.2014.0066.

Miller, K. J., Dye, R. V., Kim, J., Jennings, J., O'Toole, E., Wong, J., & Siddarth, P. (2013). Effect of a computerized brain exercise program on cognitive performance in older adults. *The American Journal of Geriatric Psychiatry, 21*, 655–663. doi:http://dx.doi.org/10.1016/j.jagp.2013.01.077

Nye, S. B. (2011). Exergaming and physical education: Do these game consoles get kids active. *Virginia Journal, 32*, 7–8.

O'Leary, K. C., Pontifex, M. B., Scudder, M. R., Brown, M. L., & Hillman, C. H. (2011). The effects of single bouts of aerobic exercise, exergaming, and videogame play on cognitive control. *Clinical Neurophysiology, 122*, 1518–1525. doi:http://dx.doi.org/10.1016/j.clinph.2011.01.049

Orvis, K. A., Horn, D. B., & Belanich, J. (2009). An examination of the role individual differences play in videogame-based training. *Military Psychology, 21*, 461–481. doi:http://dx.doi.org/10.1080/08995600903206412

Orvis, K. A., Moore, J. C., Belanich, J., Murphy, J. S., & Horn, D. B. (2010). Are soldiers gamers? Videogame usage among soldiers and implications for the effective use of serious videogames for military training. *Military Psychology, 22*, 143–157. doi:http://dx.doi.org/10.1080/08995600903417225

Papastergiou, M. (2009). Exploring the potential of computer and video games for health and physical education: A literature review. *Computers & Education, 53*, 603–622. doi:http://dx.doi.org/10.1016/j.compedu.2009.04.001

Prapavessis, H., Grove, R., & Eklund, R. C. (2004). Self-presentational issues in competition and sport. *Journal of Applied Sport Psychology, 16*, 19–40.

Rizzo, A., Lange, B., Suma, E., & Bolas, M. (2011). Virtual reality and interactive digital game technology: New tools to address obesity and diabetes. *Journal of Diabetes Science and Technology, 5*, 256–264.

Russell, W. D., & Newton, M. (2008). Short-term psychological effects of interactive video game technology exercise on mood and attention. *Educational Technology & Society, 11*, 294–308.

Schultze, U. (2010). Embodiment and presence in virtual worlds: A review. *Journal of Information Technology, 25*, 434–449.

Siegel, S. R., Haddock, B. L., Dubois, A. M., & Wilkin, L. D. (2009). Active video/arcade games (exergaming) and energy expenditure in college students. *International Journal of Exercise Science, 2*, 165–174.

Sinclair, J., Hingston, P., & Masek, M. (2007). *Considerations for the design of exergames*. Paper presented at the Proceedings of the 5th international conference on computer graphics and interactive techniques in Australia and Southeast Asia.

Smallwood, S. R., Morris, M. M., Fallows, S. J., & Buckley, J. P. (2012). Physiologic responses and energy expenditure of kinect active video game play in schoolchildren. *Archives of Pediatrics & Adolescent Medicine, 166*, 1005–1009. doi:10.1001/archpediatrics

Snyder, A. L., Anderson-Hanley, C., & Arciero, P. J. (2012). Virtual and live social facilitation while exergaming: Competitiveness moderates exercise intensity. *Journal of Sport & Exercise Psychology, 34*, 252–259.

Song, S., & Kim, M. (2012). Five models of players' rule behavior for game balance. *Cyberpsychology, Behavior & Social Networking, 15*, 498–502. doi:10.1089/cyber.2011.0504

Staiano, A. E., Abraham, A. A., & Calvert, S. L. (2013). Adolescent exergame play for weight loss and psychosocial improvement: A controlled physical activity intervention. *Obesity, 21*, 598–601.

Staiano, A. E., & Calvert, S. L. (2011a). The promise of exergames as tools to measure physical health. *Entertainment Computing, 2*, 17–21. doi:10.1016/j.entcom.2011.03.008

Staiano, A. E., & Calvert, S. L. (2011b). Exergames for physical education courses: Physical, social, and cognitive benefits. *Child Development Perspectives, 5*, 93–98. doi:http://dx.doi.org/10.1111/j.17508-606.2011.00162.x

Staiano, A. E., & Flynn, R. (2014). Therapeutic uses of active videogames: A systematic review. *Games for Health Journal, 3*, 351–365. doi:10.1089/g4h.2013.0100

Straker, L. M., Campbell, A. C., Jensen, L. M., Metcalf, D. R., Smith, A. J., Abbott, R. A., . . . Piek, J. P. (2011). Rationale, design and methods for a randomised and controlled trial of the impact of virtual reality games on motor competence, physical activity, and mental health in children with developmental coordination disorder. *BMC Public Health, 11*, 654. doi:10.1186/14712-4581-16-54.

Sublette, V. A., & Mullan, B. (2012). Consequences of play: A systematic review of the effects of online gaming. *International Journal of Mental Health and Addiction, 10*, 3–23.

Sun, H. (2012). Exergaming impact on physical activity and interest in elementary school children. *Research Quarterly For Exercise & Sport, 83*, 212–220.

Taylor, L. M., Maddison, R., Pfaeffli, L. A., Rawstorn, J. C., Gant, N., & Kerse, N. M. (2012). Activity and energy expenditure in older people playing active video games. *Archives of Physical Medicine & Rehabilitation, 93*, 2281–2286.

Terlecki, M., Brown, J., Harner-Steciw, L., Irvin-Hannum, J., Marchetto-Ryan, N., Ruhl, L., & Wiggins, J. (2011). Sex differences and similarities in video game experience, preferences, and self-efficacy: Implications for the gaming industry. *Current Psychology: A Journal for Diverse Perspectives on Diverse Psychological Issues, 30*, 22–33. The Exergame Network. Retrieved from http://exergamenetwork.blogspot.com

Van Riet, J., Crutzen, R., & Shirong, L. A. (2014). How effective are active videogames among the young and the old? Adding meta-analyses to two recent systematic reviews. *Games for Health Journal, 3*, 311–318. doi:10.1089/g4h.2014.0005.

Williams, A., & Ericsson, K. (2008). From the guest editors: How do experts learn? *Journal of Sport & Exercise Psychology, 30*, 653–662.

Wilson, S., Darden, G. F., & Meyler, T. (2010). Developing an "Exergaming" facility: Top 10 considerations and lessons learned. *Virginia Journal, 31*, 11–15.

12 Measuring Interventions' Effects—Assessment of Perceived Barriers, Enjoyment, and Adherence of Physical Activity

Claudio R. Nigg and Zoe Durand

OVERVIEW

"It is impossible to change things that cannot be measured"

—Nigg et al., 2012

Physical activity interventions lead to several psychological and behavioral outcomes. This chapter will discuss measurement approaches used for these outcomes and will provide examples and sample measurement tools. In the psychological domain, approaches to the measurement of barriers and enjoyment will be described. In the behavioral domain, adherence will be presented. Adherence is important, as we need to know not only whether individuals are physically active, but also whether or not their physical activity routine is sustained outside of the intervention. This allows researchers to gain insight on the long-term effects of the intervention. This chapter will illustrate why researchers and practitioners should consider measuring beyond the specific physical activity behavior when evaluating the impact of their physical activity interventions or programs.

PHYSICAL ACTIVITY DEFINED

The American College of Sports Medicine (ACSM) and Centers for Disease Control and Prevention (CDC) guidelines recommend a total of 150 minutes a week of moderate or higher intensity physical activity (or 75 minutes for vigorous exercise). The activity can be performed in bouts of 10 or more minutes as part of daily living or as part of a fitness program. (United States Department of Health and Human Services [USDHHS], 2008) Aerobic activity should be complemented with moderate- or high-intensity strengthening activities, involving all major muscles groups, on two or more days per week (USDHHS, 2008).

There are several categories of physical activity measurements most common among researchers and practitioners: (1) intensity, (2) duration, (3) frequency, (4) mode, and (5) adherence.

The first three of these categories are inter-dependent with the mode or type of activity, and understanding their impact on health can only be effective if the normal fluctuations in adherence are considered. The FIT formula illustrates the components for optimizing physical fitness (ACSM, 2014):

F for frequency—The number of times an activity is performed in a day or a week is its frequency. Personal exercise prescriptions vary; typically a minimum of three alternating days a week (more if possible) is sufficient to improve overall health. In 2007, ACSM improved their physical activity recommendations by acknowledging that longer, less frequent sessions of aerobic exercise provide no clear advantage over shorter, more frequent sessions of activity.

I for intensity—The amount of effort the individual expends at the activity corresponds to its intensity. It may be assessed through perceived exertion scales or physiological indicators, such as heart rate or self-report questionnaires addressing involvement in activity at different intensity levels. Scaled measures for intensity are not unique and may include ordinal categories (e.g., mild, moderate, vigorous) or continuous (e.g., heartbeats per minute). Physical activity performed at an intensity that increases the heart rate into a target heart rate zone (THRZ) of 55% to 90% of an individual's maximum heart rate (MHR) or 40% to 85% of their maximal amount of oxygen uptake (VO_{2max}) provides optimal cardiovascular health benefits. The formula of $[208 - (.7 \times age)]$ is used to calculate MHR. In order to maintain or improve aerobic fitness, an individual's THRZ must be calculated by multiplying the MHR by a percentage between 55% and 90% to find out the necessary total number of beats per minute (Ratamess, 2011). Intuitively, in order to achieve desired outcomes, individuals should increase intensity when performing strength exercises but decrease intensity for endurance exercises (Ratamess, 2011). Intensity of exercise must also consider the fitness goals, age, capabilities, and current fitness level of the individual.

T for time (or duration)—The length of an activity session is equivalent to its time or duration. Current recommendations suggest that health can be improved with an accumulation of 30 minutes or more of moderate physical activity on most, preferably all, days of the week. The accumulated fitness time can be achieved all at once or in multiple bouts of shorter duration throughout the day (e.g., 10-minute sessions × 3 times a day) (USDHHS, 2008). Duration can be determined through direct observation, using objective activity monitors, or through self-reports, and data usually take the form of minutes/hours.

Two additional concepts are mode and adherence (Nigg et al., 2012).

Mode (or type)—Mode describes the type of activity being measured. Mode can be summarized in categories such as leisure time, occupational, and transport, or by physiologically determined categories, such as aerobic or anaerobic (Smith & Biddle, 2008). More descriptive classifications may reference the major physiological benefits incurred, including cardiovascular (e.g., walking, cycling, and step aerobics), strengthening (e.g., stair climbing and free weights), or flexibility (e.g., yoga and Pilates) activities. As a result, measurement of mode is inherently nominal and descriptive.

Adherence—Adherence describes how faithfully a person conforms to a standard of behavior that has been set as part of a negotiated agreement (Buckworth & Dishman, 2002). This has been measured as exercise class attendance (Marcus & Stanton, 1993; McAuley & Jacobson, 1991; Weber & Wertheim, 1989), weekly distance or time goals (Wood, Stefanick, Williams, & Haskell, 1991), and responses to questionnaires, such as retrospective self-report instruments of physical activity (Svendsen, Hassager, & Christiansen, 1994) or stage of exercise behavior (Cardinal & Sachs, 1996; Marcus et al., 1992; Nigg, 2001). Exercise diaries or self-reported logs are increasingly popular and allow individuals to track their adherence online or in places that can be monitored, updated, and referenced (Sylvia, Bernstein, Hubbard, Keating, & Anderson, 2014).

In order to minimize negative influences that can result from the lack of consistent exercise, ACSM (2014) recommends frequent modification of physical activities and increasing motivational strategies within exercise programs for long-term adherence. Frequent modifications include varying the intensity levels between moderate and vigorous and alternating among activities, including endurance, strength, flexibility, and balance. Variations are also recommended within a specific type of activity (e.g., endurance), for example, jogging, brisk walking, soccer, or hiking. Motivational strategies to address long-term adherence include self-monitoring, goal setting, contracting, reinforcement, and social support among others (USDHHS, 2008).

The various indicators of physical activity include physiological measures, such as blood pressure, heart rate, VO_{2max}, lung capacity, and immune function; physical fitness measures, such as muscular strength, muscular endurance, neuromuscular coordination, and flexibility; and biometric measures, such as body mass index (BMI), skinfolds, bioelectric impedance, waist-to-hip ratio, and hydrostatic weighing (Lippke, Voelcker-Rehage, & Bültmann, 2013; Nigg, Jordan, Atkins, 2012). Similarly, there are numerous psychological correlates of physical activity, which include stress, depression, self-efficacy, pros/cons/attitude/outcome expectations, intention, enjoyment, well-being, quality of life, and general health (Biddle & Mutrie, 2003; Carron, Hausenblas, & Estabrooks, 2003; Lox, Martin Ginis, Petruzzello, 2006; Smith & Biddle, 2008). This chapter focuses on barriers, enjoyment, and adherence.

ASSESSING PERCEIVED BARRIERS, ENJOYMENT, AND ADHERENCE

Attention to measurement is paramount, especially in the planning stages of program development. Neglecting appropriate measurement means there is no way of knowing the effectiveness, reach, and impact of the program. To maximize resources used to develop and implement a physical activity program (be it strength training for employees of a company, aerobics for high school students, or a flexibility program for older adults, etc.), it is recommended that researchers and practitioners measure what the program is trying to change or promote. With measurements related to the program's goals, conclusions can be made about the program's effectiveness, and areas for improvement can be identified. There are several resources that present more comprehensive summaries of psychosocial measures (Biddle & Mutrie, 2003; Carron et al., 2003; Lox et al., 2006; Nigg et al., 2012; Nigg, Rhodes, & Amato, 2013; Smith & Biddle, 2008) and physical activity measures (Lippke et al., 2013; Nigg et al., 2012); the reader is encouraged to explore these more in depth.

The goal of physical activity–related measurements is to accurately assess the behavior and correlates, such as barriers and enjoyment of physical activity. These measures can be used for optimally designing and modifying health interventions for each individual. Furthermore, these measures can be used to evaluate interventions and programs beyond physical activity. Tools that are useful for assessment are presented in this chapter. These tools generally originate from validated questionnaires published in research papers, and references to these studies are provided throughout the chapter.

Perceived Barriers

Perceived barriers are defined as obstacles that an individual perceives to get in the way of physical activity. These barriers can be psychological, such as stress, loneliness, and depression; social, such as negative peer pressure; or environmental, such as bad weather, crime, and lack of physical activity opportunities. It is important to underline that perception is the key. If someone perceives that there is a lot of crime in the neighborhood, then this is a barrier, even if actually there is no crime in the neighborhood.

The importance of barriers has been documented in a meta-analysis that showed that individuals who adopt certain health behaviors (including physical activity) decrease their perceived barriers during the process of adopting that behavior (Hall & Rossi, 2008). Identifying and addressing perceived barriers may aid in increasing physical activity by tailoring a health program to an individual or group (Nigg & Riebe, 2002). Perceived barriers may be measured qualitatively, by asking people to identify their barriers to physical activity, or quantitatively, by presenting people with a list of common barriers and asking them to rate how much each potential barrier applies to them. The cons aspect of decisional balance is a common way of quantitatively measuring perceived barriers to physical activity.

The cons scale measures barriers that influence individuals' determinations about whether to begin or increase physical activity. The cons scale is a survey of five items. Some studies drop the last item of the cons to make a four-item scale. This may be appropriate to do when studying a population, such as children, where item 5, "Exercise puts an extra burden on my significant other," is not applicable. The scale has been validated in an ethnically diverse population (Paxton et al., 2008).

The cons scale (presented below) is a Likert-type scale where individuals are asked to rate how important each statement in a list of statements is to their decision to do physical activity. Importance levels range from "not important" to "extremely important."

Scores on the cons scale are calculated by averaging the numerical answers to all of the questions. Higher scores indicate greater importance of these perceived barriers to physical activity, and lower scores indicate lesser importance of these perceived barriers to physical activity. As people begin to engage in physical activity more, they tend to increase their pros in the early stages of behavior change and decrease their cons in the later stages (Hall & Rossi, 2008). The cons scale has also been shown to predict levels of adherence to physical activity, with people who score higher having poorer adherence than people who score lower (Nigg & Riebe, 2002).

The cons scale has been used for physical activity programs. A randomized effectiveness trial among overweight and obese adults with no intention of exercising used the cons scale to tailor the exercise portion of a multiple behavior change intervention for weight management. Participants who received the tailored intervention were more likely to move from pre-action to the action/maintenance phase of exercising (Johnson et al., 2008), as well as increase other non-targeted health behaviors (Johnson et al., 2008). Another descriptive study found that people who do not engage in any physical activity have higher perceived barriers to exercise than people who engage in physical activity regularly (Fahrenwald & Walker, 2003).

Other scales for measuring perceived barriers include the Exercise Benefits/Barriers Scale (EBBS) and the Physical Activity Benefits and Barriers Scale (PABBS). The EBBS (Brown,

---

Cons Scale

Using the 5-point scale provided, how important are the following opinions in your decision to exercise or not to exercise?

1	2	3	4	5
Not important	Slightly important	Moderately important	Very important	Extremely important

Questionnaire items

1. I would feel embarrassed if people saw me exercising.
2. Exercise prevents me from spending time with my friends.
3. I feel uncomfortable or embarrassed in exercise clothes.
4. There is too much I would have to learn to exercise.
5. Exercise puts an extra burden on my significant other.**

** This item may be inappropriate for some people or populations.

Source: Nigg, Rossi, Norman, & Benisovich, 1998; Paxton et al., 2008

2005) and PABBS (Brown et al., 2006) are both Likert-type scales made of up two component scales, a benefits scale and a barriers scale, that can be used separately or in conjunction. Like the cons scale, the higher a person's score on the EBBS or PABBS, the greater that person perceives barriers to exercise. EBBS is recommended for use in middle-class adult populations (Brown, 2005), and PABBS is recommended for use in college populations (Brown et al., 2006).

Enjoyment

Enjoyment is an agreeable feeling that may be a positive correlate of or motivator for physical activity (Paxton et al., 2008). The importance of enjoyment has been documented by a study that showed that enjoyment may mediate the effects of physical activity (Dishman et al., 2005). Enjoyment may be measured qualitatively, by asking people to identify what they enjoy about physical activity, or quantitatively, by presenting people with a list of statements describing different aspects of enjoyment and asking them to rate how much each statement applies to them. The Physical Activity Enjoyment Scale (PACES) is a common way of quantitatively measuring enjoyment of physical activity (Paxton et al., 2008).

PACES measures how much an individual enjoys physical activity, or the extent to which an individual has agreeable feelings when engaging in physical activity. The full PACES is an 18-item survey that begins with a sentence stem of "When I am active . . .," followed by a variety of responses describing different aspects of enjoyment. Like the cons scale, PACES

Physical Activity Enjoyment Scale (PACES) 18-items
Using the 5-point scale provided, how important are the following opinions in your decision to exercise or not to exercise?

1	2	3	4	5
Strongly disagree	Somewhat disagree	Neither agree nor disagree	Somewhat agree	Strongly agree

Questionnaire item

When I am active . . .

1 I enjoy it.
2 I feel interested.
3 I like it.
4 I find it pleasurable.
5 I am very absorbed in this activity.
6 It's a lot of fun.
7 I find it energizing.
8 It makes me happy.
9 It's very pleasant.
10 I feel good physically while doing it.
11 It's very invigorating.
12 I am not at all frustrated by it.
13 It's very gratifying.
14 It's very exhilarating.
15 It's very stimulating.
16 It gives me a strong sense of accomplishment.
17 It's very refreshing.
18 I felt as though there was nothing else I would rather be doing.

Source: Motl et al., 2001; Mullen et al., 2001

(presented previously) is a Likert-type scale where respondents are asked to rate their agreement with each statement. Unlike the cons scale, responses for PACES measure agreement, not importance (Paxton et al., 2008).

Scores on the PACES are calculated by averaging the numerical answers of all of the questions. Higher scores indicate greater levels of enjoyment while doing physical activity, and lower scores indicate lesser levels of enjoyment while doing physical activity. The PACES is sometimes shortened or re-worded to better fit the needs of the population it's being used on. For example, in a population of children with limited vocabulary, item 11, "It's very invigorating," may be changed to "It's very exciting" without losing its factorial validity (Motl et al., 2001).

The use of the PACES in physical activity interventions has shown that enjoyment can affect people's adoption of and adherence to physical activity. One study of girls in a school-based intervention showed that girls who reported high enjoyment of physical activity at baseline increased their physical activity during the intervention, while girls who had low enjoyment did not change their physical activity (Schneider & Cooper, 2011). Other studies showed that a person who increases their enjoyment of physical activity can also increase their adherence (Jekauc, 2015) and frequency (Hagberg et al., 2009). Additionally, physical activity intensity may be increased without compromising enjoyment (Crisp et al., 2012). Enjoyment can be increased by having agency in decision making about physical activity, receiving positive feedback, and having access to a diverse range of physical activity options (Hagberg et al., 2009; Jekauc, 2015).

Adherence

Adherence and duration both measure an individual's commitment to maintaining physical activity. The U.S. government's *Healthy People 2010* identified physical activity as one of the leading indicators of preventive health behaviors and emphasized the need for behavior health professionals to develop and provide more effective interventions and programs designed to promote and *maintain* healthy behaviors (http://www.healthypeople.gov/2010/). Although the physical activity adherence literature is scant, there is evidence that the predictors of adoption are different from those of adherence. Thus, it follows that physical activity adherence requires unique measurement approaches.

Although some researchers have studied theories and their application to physical activity maintenance, (e.g., transtheoretical model [TTM], Cardinal & Sachs, 1996; self-management, Martin & Dubbert, 1982), this area of research is quite limited. There is also a lack of measurement tools specific to maintenance and a lack of experimental interventions addressing maintenance in the physical activity literature. Reviewing the literature, Nigg (2014) recommended the following for preparing individuals and their environments for maintenance: prepare the client for long-term commitment; help the client anticipate and cope with high-risk situations; arrange conditions to foster self-responsibility; provide training in coping with setbacks; and encourage supportive lifestyle and environmental changes. This is confirmed by physical activity studies (e.g., Martin et al., 1984; McAuley, Morris, Motl, Hu, Konopack & Elavsky, 2007).

There are unique challenges associated with the measurement of physical activity adherence, including whether to emphasize amount of time over amount of effort or actual health benefit. Essentially all of these things are important, but balancing motivation and maintenance can sometimes prove difficult. Two critical factors in any exercise program are duration and adherence. While they are often seen as interchangeable, they are in fact two very different components. *Adherence* is the term used to describe how well an individual sticks to a prescribed exercise regimen. *Duration* refers to the time an individual has actually spent exercising during one bout or session (Nigg et al., 2012).

Typical adherence rates range from 50% to 80% for most research studies (Martin, Bowen, Dunbar-Jacob, & Perri, 2000); in part because there is little consistency in how adherence is defined and measured. For example, adherence comprises frequency, duration, and intensity, and it can be measured at specific time points or using self-report or objective instruments. Many factors influence any one individual's adherence to a regular exercise program, including demographics (e.g., age, gender), environment (e.g., nearby facilities, transportation options), social/cultural considerations (e.g., family role, customs), and behavior (e.g., smoking). In general, physical activity interventions should focus on factors that are potentially modifiable, while acknowledging how moderator variables influence the system.

Diary methods involve having an individual regularly record or log her physical activity, and may include such information as duration, intensity, mode, emotional state, environment, and so on (Sylvia et al., 2014). The diary or log technique requires very little expense, and information can be gathered from many individuals at once. There are several shortcomings to this particular method, which make it less desirable as a form of measurement and more useful as a motivational tool. First and foremost, the quality of the logged data is reliant solely on the cooperation and precision of the participant's reporting. Secondly, coding diary entries is not only time-consuming but tedious, and often requires more than one analyst to maximize inter-rater reliability. Finally, this method is only appropriate for persons who are not limited by any physical or cognitive challenges that could prevent them from writing.

Physical activity questionnaires are subjective measures of physical activity, and they are the most commonly used method in population studies. Questionnaires are ideal tools since they are cost effective, can be adapted to a variety of settings and populations, and possess higher validity and reliability compared to laboratory and field methods, as well as health outcomes (Kriska & Caspersen, 1997). Physical activity questionnaires can be used to rank individuals or subgroups of individuals in a population and then compare them with standardized physiological measures (e.g., body composition, aerobic capacity) and disease outcomes (Kriska & Caspersen, 1997). Physical activity questionnaires differ on several attributes: complexity, time frame, type of activity, adherence, and scoring. The choice of questionnaire for any particular application must take each of these factors into consideration with regard to the study hypotheses, population of interest (e.g., gender, age, and ethnicity), time, financial resources, and a myriad of other factors (Kriska & Caspersen, 1997).

It is important to keep in mind that older adults may not engage in the same physical activity intensity as young adults; therefore, any instruments that are used need to reflect and detect very specific changes for a broad range of physical activities. For example, there are several physical activity questionnaires that have been developed for and validated in older adults (Caspersen et al., 1991; DiPietro et al., 1993; Stewart, 1998; Washburn, Smith, Jette, & Janney, 1993). The Modified Baeke Questionnaire (Caspersen et al., 1991) and the Zutphen Questionnaire were both designed for European older adults, whereas the Yale Physical Activity Survey (YPAS) (Di Pietro et al., 1993) and the Community Healthy Activities Model Program for Seniors (CHAMPS) (Stewart, 1998) questionnaires have been carefully validated and are used more commonly with American older adults.

Challenges of self-report questionnaires include bias, such as recall or reporting bias, whereby answers rely on the respondent's memory or honesty, and social desirability or response bias, in which respondents answer what they think the researcher wants to know or in a way that makes them appear more favorable. The potential for missing data is high where self-report methods are concerned, since respondents may systematically, intentionally, or unintentionally not provide answers. As there is no gold standard for measuring adherence to physical activity in a general population, pedometers, exercise class attendance, or repeated frequency questionnaires over time may be used for interventions.

CONCLUSION

This chapter illustrates that researchers and practitioners should consider measuring beyond the specific behavior when evaluating the impact of their physical activity interventions or programs. This will ensure that the potential effects of an intervention or program, which likely are broader than one aspect, are able to be captured and documented. Of special importance are measuring motivational factors, such as barriers and enjoyment of physical activity, in order to tailor interventions to individuals for maximum effect and measuring adherence after the intervention to evaluate long-term effects.

REFERENCES

American College of Sports Medicine (2014*). ACSM's guidelines for exercise testing and prescription* (9th ed.). Baltimore, MD: Lippincott Williams and Wilkins.

Biddle, S. J. H., & Mutrie, N. (2003). *Psychology of physical activity determinants, well-being and interventions.* New York, NY: Routledge.

Brown, S. A. (2005). Measuring perceived benefits and perceived barriers for physical activity. *American Journal of Health Behavior, 29*(2), 107–116.

Brown, S. A., Huber, D., & Bergman, A. (2006). A perceived benefits and barriers scale for strenuous physical activity in college students. *American Journal of Health Promotion, 21*(2), 137–140.

Buckworth, J., & Dishman, R. K. (2002). Interventions to change physical activity behavior. In J. Buckworth (ed.), *Exercise psychology* (pp. 229–53). Champaign, IL: Human Kinetics.

Cardinal, B. J., & Sachs, M. L. (1996). Effects of mail-mediated, stage-matched exercise behavior change strategies on female adults' leisure-time exercise behavior. *The Journal of Sports Medicine and Physical Fitness, 36*(2), 100–107.

Carron, A. V., Hausenblas, H. A., & Estabrooks, P. A. (2003). *The psychology of physical activity.* New York, NY: McGraw-Hill.

Caspersen, C. J., Bloemberg, B. P. M., Saris, W. H. M., Merrit, R. K., & Kromhout, D. (1991). Physical activity questionnaires for older adults. *Journal Sport Medicine, 29*(6), 141–145.

Crisp, N. A., Fournier, P. A., Licari, M. K., Braham, R., & Guelfi, K. J. (2012). Optimising sprint interval exercise to maximize energy expenditure and enjoyment in overweight boys. *Applied Physiology, Nutrition, & Metabolism, 37*(6), 1222–1231.

DiPietro, L., Caspersen, C. J., Ostfeld, A. M., & Nadel, E. R. (1993). A survey for assessing physical activity among older adults. *Medicine & Science in Sports & Exercise, 25*(5), 628–643.

Dishman, R. K., Motl, R. W., Saunders, R., Felton, G., Ward, D. S., Dowda, M., & Pate, R. R. (2005). Enjoyment mediates effects of a school-based physical activity intervention. *Medicine & Science in Sports & Exercise, 37*(5), 403–408.

Fahrenwald, N. L., & Walker, S. N. (2003). Application of the Transtheoretical Model of Behavioral Change to the physical activity behavior of WIC mothers. *Public Health Nursing, 20*(4), 307–317.

Hagberg, L. A., Lindahl, B., Nyberg, L., & Hellenius, M. L. (2009). Importance of enjoyment when promoting physical exercise. *Scandinavian Journal of Medicine & Science in Sports, 19,* 740–747.

Hall, K. L., & Rossi, J. S. (2008). Meta-analytic examination of the strong and weak principles across 48 health behaviors. *Preventive Medicine, 46*(3), 266–274.

Jekauc, D. (2015). Enjoyment during exercise mediates the effects of an intervention on exercise adherence. *Psychology, 6,* 48–54.

Johnson, S. S., Paiva, A. L., Cummins, C. O., Johnson, J. L., Dyment, S. J., Wright, J. A., . . . Sherman, K. (2008). Transtheoretical model-based multiple behavior intervention for weight management: effectiveness on a population basis. *Preventive medicine, 46*(3), 238–246.

Kriska, A. M., & Caspersen, C. J. (1997). Introduction to a collection of physical activity questionnaires. *Medicine & Science in Sports & Exercise, 29*(6), 5–9.

Lippke, S., Voelcker-Rehage, C., & Bültmann, U. (2013). Assessing your client's physical activity behavior, motivation, and individual resources. In C. R. Nigg (Ed.), *ACSM's behavioral aspects of physical activity and exercise.* Philadelphia, PA: Wolters Kluwer/Lippincott Williams & Wilkins.

Lox, C. L., Martin Ginis, K. A., & Petruzzello, S. J. (2006). *The psychology of exercise: integrating theory and practice.* Scottsdale, AZ: Holcomb Hathaway.

Marcus, B. H., Rakowski, W., & Rossi, J. S. (1992). Assessing motivational readiness and decision making for exercise. *Health Psychology, 11*(4), 257–261.

Marcus, B. H., & Stanton, A. L. (1993). Evaluation of relapse prevention and reinforcement interventions to promote exercise adherence in sedentary females. *Research Quarterly for Exercise and Sport, 64*(4), 447–752.

Martin, J. E., & Dubbert, P. M. (1982). Exercise applications and promotion in behavioral medicine: Current status and future directions. *Journal of Consulting and Clinical Psychology, 50*(6), 1004–1017.

Martin, J. E., Dubbert, P. M., Katell, A. D., Thompson, J. K., Raczynski, J. R., Lake, M., . . . Cohen, R. E. (1984). Behavioral control of exercise in sedentary adults: Studies 1 through 6. *Journal of Consulting and Clinical Psychology, 52*(5), 795–811.

Martin, K. A., Bowen, D. J., Dunbar-Jacob, J., & Perri, M. G. (2000). Who will adhere? Key issues in the study and prediction of adherence in randomized controlled trials. *Controlled Clinical Trials, 21*(5), S195-S199.

McAuley, E., & Jacobson, L. (1991). Self-efficacy and exercise participation in sedentary adult females. *American Journal of Health Promotion, 5*(3), 185–207.

McAuley, E., Morris, K. S., Motl, R. W., Hu, L., Konopack, J. F., & Elavsky, S. (2007). Long-term follow-up of physical activity behavior in older adults. *Health Psychology, 26*(3), 375–380.

Motl, R. W., Dishman, R. K., Saunders, R., Dowda, M., Felton, G., & Pate, R. R. (2001). Measuring enjoyment of physical activity in adolescent girls. *American Journal of Preventive Medicine, 21*(2), 110–117.

Mullen, S. P., Olson, E. A., Phillips, S. M., Szabo, A. N., Wójcicki, T. R., Mailey, E. L., . . . McAuley, E. (2011). Measuring enjoyment of physical activity in older adults: invariance of the physical activity enjoyment scale (paces) across groups and time. *International Journal of Behavioral Nutrition and Physical Activity, 8*(1), 103.

Nigg, C. R. (2001). Explaining adolescent exercise behavior change: a longitudinal application of the transtheoretical model. *Annals of Behavioral Medicine, 23*(1), 11–20.

Nigg, C. R. (2014). *ACSM's behavioral aspects of physical activity and exercise.* Philadelphia: Wolters Kluwer.

Nigg, C. R., Jordan, P. J., & Atkins, A. (2012). Behavioral measurement in exercise psychology. In G. Tenenbaum, R. C. Eklund, & A. Kamata (Eds.), *Measurement in sport and exercise psychology* (pp. 455–464). Champaign, IL: Human Kinetics.

Nigg, C. R., Rhodes, R., & Amato, K. R. (2013). Determinants of physical activity: Research to application. In *Lifestyle medicine* (2nd ed., pp. 1435–1443). Oxford, UK: Taylor & Francis Group.

Nigg, C. R., & Riebe, D. (2002). The transtheoretical model: Research review of exercise behavior and older adults. In P. Burbank & D. Riebe (Eds.), *Promoting exercise and behavior change in older adults: Interventions with the transtheoretical model* (pp. 147–180). Springer Publishing Company.

Nigg, C. R., Rossi, J. S., Norman, G. J., & Benisovich, S. V. (1998). Structure of decisional balance for exercise adoption. *Annals of Behavioral Medicine, 20*, S211.

Paxton, R. J., Nigg, C. R., Motl, R. W., McGee, K., McCurdy, D., Matthai, C. H., & Dishman, R. K. (2008). Are constructs of the transtheoretical model for physical activity measured equivalently between sexes, age groups, and ethnicities? *Annals of Behavioral Medicine, 35*, 308–318.

Ratamess, N. (2011). *ACSM's foundations of strength training and conditioning.* Philadelphia: Wolters Kluwer.

Schneider, M., & Cooper, D. M. (2011). Enjoyment of exercise moderates the impact of a school-based physical activity intervention. *International Journal of Behavioral Nutrition and Physical Activity, 8*(1), 64.

Smith, A. L., & Biddle, S. J. H. (2008). *Youth physical activity and inactivity: Challenges and solutions.* Champaign, IL: Human Kinetics.

Stewart, A. L. (1998). *Community Health Activities Model Program for Seniors.* Institute for Health and Aging, University of California San Francisco.

Svendsen, O. L., Hassager, C., & Christiansen, C. (1994). Six months' follow-up on exercise added to a short-term diet in overweight postmenopausal women--effects on body composition, resting metabolic rate, cardiovascular risk factors and bone. *International Journal of Obesity and Related Metabolic Disorders: Journal of the International Association for the Study of Obesity, 18*(10), 692–698.

Sylvia, L. G., Bernstein, E. E., Hubbard, J. L., Keating, L., & Anderson, E. J. (2014). A practical guide to measuring physical activity. *Journal of the Academy of Nutrition and Dietetics, 114*(2), 199–208.

U.S. Department of Health and Human Services. (2008). *Physical activity guidelines for Americans.* Retrieved from August 6, 2014, www.health.gov/paguidelines/pdf/paguide.pdf

Washburn, R. A., Smith, K. W., Jette, A. M., & Janney, C. A. (1993). The Physical Activity Scale for the Elderly (PASE): development and evaluation. *Journal of clinical epidemiology, 46*(2), 153–162.

Weber, J., & Wertheim, E. H. (1989). Relationships of self-monitoring, special attention, body fat percent, and self-motivation to attendance at a community gymnasium. *Journal of Sport and Exercise Psychology, 11*(1), 105–114.

Wood, P. D., Stefanick, M. L., Williams, P. T., & Haskell, W. L. (1991). The effects on plasma lipoproteins of a prudent weight-reducing diet, with or without exercise, in overweight men and women. *New England Journal of Medicine, 325*(7), 461–466.

13 The Physical Environment and Public Policy

Rebecca E. Lee, Scherezade K. Mama, Heather Leach, Erica G. Soltero, and Nathan H. Parker

The physical environment refers to the context or setting in which people spend the majority of their time (Barker, 1968; Lee, McAlexander, & Banda, 2011). Multiple physical environments, such as the home, neighborhood, school, and workplace, can influence physical activity (Craig et al., 2003; Lee & Cubbin, 2009; Lee et al., 2011a, b; Van Cauwenberg et al., 2011). Features found within a physical environment can significantly affect physical activity. These features can be natural, such as lakes, hills, or open meadows, or manmade, such as bike lanes, trails, fields, or gyms (Sallis et al., 2006). The physical environment can influence multiple forms of physical activity, including active transportation, leisure-time physical activity, and household and occupational physical activity (Sallis et al., 2006). Factors within the physical environment, such as sidewalks, bike lanes, street connectivity, and land use, significantly influence active transportation. For example, streets with wider sidewalks and bike lanes can encourage physical activity by providing safe pathways for people to walk or bicycle to work, school, or other nearby destinations. Public media prompts for physical activity, such as signs that encourage the use of stairs and guide pedestrians to stairs as alternatives to elevators or escalators, may positively affect public spaces by increasing awareness and recognition of physical activity opportunities (Andersen, Franckowiak, Snyder, Bartlett, & Fontaine, 1998; Coleman & Gonzalez, 2001; McKinnon, Bowles, & Trowbridge, 2011).

Policy as an abstract concept can be difficult to define. Collectively, policy encompasses the rules, procedures, resource allocations, and strategies implemented to regulate human behavior or the environments in which humans live and interact (Centers for Disease Control and Prevention, 2014; Lee et al., 2011a, b). Policies can occur at all levels, including federal, state, and local governments, but can also be found in environments themselves, such as worksites, schools, and other environments where people spend their time. Policies shape behavior through regulation, legislation, funding priorities, and other actions (Centers for Disease Control and Prevention, 2014). For any policy to be effective, it must be implemented, enforced, evaluated, and revised to accommodate unexpected consequences, technological innovations, and other societal trends (Lee et al., 2011a, b). Many policies shape physical activity; however, the implementation of policies specifically aimed at increasing physical activity is a relatively recent historical development. Many scholars believe that policy may be the key to increasing and sustaining levels of physical activity on a large scale or population level. Policies can be used to directly or indirectly generate more opportunities for engaging in physical activity by improving access to physical activity resources, altering the built environment, or increasing transportation and commuting options that promote physical activity.

ECOLOGICAL MODEL OF PHYSICAL ACTIVITY (EMPA)

Conceptualizing how environmental and policy determinants of physical activity are defined, operate, and interact can be complex and confusing. Therefore, it is helpful to categorize these factors in a conceptual or theoretical model. The ecological model of physical activity (EMPA) offers a dynamic framework for describing many levels of environment and policy that directly and indirectly affect physical activity (Spence & Lee, 2003). The EMPA is organized into micro-, meso-, exo-, and macro-level environments and accounts for the dynamic interactions within and among levels. The EMPA also reflects grand influences on the larger ecological milieu that are forces of change on all levels of the framework. In this section, we will describe each level briefly while using specific examples. We will discuss cross-level interactions, illustrated by specific examples of particular interest to health researchers and promoters.

Micro-Level Environment

Micro-level environments of the EMPA include all locations in which someone lives, works, and spends time (Lee & Cubbin, 2009; Spence & Lee, 2003). Micro-level environments have significant impacts on physical activity. An example of a micro-level environment with abundant opportunities for physical activity is the physical activity resource. Physical activity resources are public and private settings, facilities, or programs that encourage and support physical activity, such as parks, running trails, neighborhood centers, school yards, gyms, and fitness clubs (Lee, Booth, Reese-Smith, Regan, & Howard, 2005). Residence near physical activity resources that are plentiful and high quality can help people achieve physical activity milestones and prevent chronic diseases and health conditions (Leach et al., 2016; Lee, Cubbin, & Winkleby, 2007; Lee, Mama, Adamus-Leach, & Soltero, 2015; Lee, Mama, Banda, Bryant, & McAlexander, 2009). For example, someone who lives next to a park with a trail may achieve more physical activity due to the proximity of the trail. In this case, the trail is a feature of the micro-level physical environment that encourages and supports physical activity.

Additional micro-level physical environments, such as a home or workplace, can contribute to household and occupational physical activity. For example, living in a house with a spacious yard presents homeowners with opportunities to engage in household physical activities, such as raking, lawn mowing, or gardening. The work environment can also have a significant impact on physical activity. Working in a building that has multiple levels presents the opportunity to use the stairs instead of the escalator or elevator for vertical transportation. Stair climbing readily integrates physical activity into daily life and does not require any special equipment (Lewis & Eves, 2012). Daily stair use has been associated with significant increases in energy expenditure and can have significant health benefits (Bassett et al., 1997; Lee & Paffenbarger, 1998; Lee et al., 2011b).

Policies that influence the micro-level environment can be very effective for helping people to get more physical activity (Lee, Hallett, Parker, Kao, Modelska, Rifai, & O'Connor, 2015). Policies that foster an equitable distribution of physical activity resources, as well as safe and attractive options, can encourage and promote physical activity. Effective and enforced policies can also improve neighborhood walkability. Examples include improving street cleanliness by prohibiting littering, increasing path and sidewalk connectivity through sidewalk zoning, and improving attractiveness and aesthetics via planting and maintenance. Policies can also reduce loitering and "quality of life" crimes, such as the presence of drug dealers and gang members, by implementing stronger enforcement (Zieff, Guedes, & Eyler, 2012). Policies may also address land use in neighborhoods through zoning laws that increase diversity of residential and commercial destinations, while encouraging walking for transportation (Saelens, Sallis, Black, & Chen, 2003). Policies that increase the availability and access of free or low-cost parks, playgrounds, recreation facilities, and programming for adults and children are also valuable assets for promoting physical activity among neighborhood residents (Zieff et al., 2012). In a 2008 longitudinal study involving residents who had moved between neighborhoods, researchers found that relocating to neighborhoods with more attractive physical activity options with additional social opportunities promoted increases in self-reported leisure-time physical activity (Handy, Cao, & Mokhtarian, 2008).

Policy can influence factors in the workplace, which is another important micro-level environment found to consistently affect the behavior of most adults on a daily basis. Most policies in the workplace are created and enacted within specific businesses or work environments. In a 2008 study, researchers found that workplace policies and provisions, such as accessible stairways, showering facilities, and the delivery of personal services, such as fitness testing and counseling, were associated with higher self-reported physical activity among American adults (Dodson, Lovegreen, Elliott, Haire-Joshu, & Brownson, 2008). Newer trends, such as policies that increase access to standing or walking work-stations, have also grown in popularity (Lee et al., 2011b). Given the increasingly sedentary nature of employment in the United States, workplace provisions have become increasingly important (Crespo, Sallis, Conway, Saelens, & Frank, 2011).

Policies enacted at the state and federal levels have served to improve school environments. Because children and adolescents spend a sizeable proportion of their weekday waking hours in school (Carlson et al., 2013), the school environment is a vital micro-level environment for physical activity promotion. The vast majority of states have policies requiring physical education classes in elementary schools (43 states), middle schools (40 states), and high schools (46 states) (Carlson et al., 2013). Simply requiring physical education, however, is insufficient for meeting physical activity recommendations for children and adolescents. National organizations, such as the Centers for Disease Control and Prevention, the American Heart Association, and the National Association for Sport and Physical Education, recommend that schools provide at least 150 minutes of physical activity per week for elementary school students and 225 minutes per week for middle and high school students (Centers for Disease Control and Prevention, 2011; National Association for Sport and Physical Education, 2008; Pate et al., 2006). A 2012 study found that only three states met the elementary school minutes per week recommendation based on physical education class requirements, one state met the middle school recommendation, and none met the high school recommendation (Carlson et al., 2013). Requiring physical education classes also does not ensure that children are engaging in moderate-to-vigorous physical activity. Clearly, there is a need for policies to set more stringent standards for childhood and adolescent physical activity in schools. In addition, policies that increase the existence of facilities and trained staff that can aid in the planning and implementation of curricula that incorporate physical activities, participation in sports, physical activity breaks, active recess, physical education classes, and before- and after-school activities are needed in many states. Such policies should include specific strategic recommendations, and policy makers must plan for frequent assessments to gauge compliance, as well as to spread best practices.

Meso-Level Environment

The meso-level environment includes the dynamic connections, pathways, and linkages among an individual's micro-environments (Lee & Cubbin, 2009; Spence & Lee, 2003). Meso-level environments can be either physical or social in nature, but for the purposes of this chapter, we will focus primarily on the physical connections, pathways, and linkages (social meso-environmental determinants, such as access to high-quality and safe physical activity resources that provide people with the opportunity to interact with others and build social linkages that in turn promote physical activity, are discussed in other chapters in this book). Transportation between micro-level environments is a primary component of the meso-level environment and should be an important focus for policies encouraging physical activity. Local policies can expand and improve public transportation options to effectively increase physical activity, as the use of buses, subways, and light rails typically involves active transportation to and from established stops or stations (Gordon-Larsen, Nelson, & Beam, 2005). Policies that affect roadway improvements, such as the addition or improvement of bike lanes, pedestrian pathways, and way-finding signage, can also improve the transportation-related meso-level environment by increasing physical activity via enhancing safety (McKinnon et al., 2011), which, in turn, can help promote active transportation.

Exo-Level Environment

The exo-level environment is similar to the meso-level environment in that it is a dynamic pathway or linkage that connects micro-level environments with other micro-level environments. However, the exo-level connection is the pathway that shows how physical activity can be promoted between micro-level environments that do not include the same people (Lee & Cubbin, 2009). Exo-level environments can be physical or social in nature. For example, the shared commute to school between a parent and a child can transfer things that happen at the work micro-level environment with the parent to the school micro-level environment with the child, and vice versa. Policies affecting an adult's work micro-environment may inspire changes in parenting practices that subsequently increase physical activity among children at school. Alternatively, the implementation and enforcement of school policies to increase students' physical activity may lead to conversations that inspire adults to do the same.

Macro-Level Environment

The macro-level environment includes the physical and social environments that form and encompass the micro-, meso-, and exo-level environments. Policies at the national or state level are classic examples of macro-level environmental factors that include and influence micro-, meso-, and exo-level environments and the behaviors that occur within them. For example, many states have adopted policies aimed to increase physical activity in schools by requiring students to meet minimum physical activity guidelines. In addition, teachers in those schools were assigned to enforce participation according to the recommended amounts of daily physical activity (Barroso et al., 2009). In other cases, policies are developed and maintained for reasons that have nothing to do with increasing physical activity, but rather unexpectedly promote physical activity in the micro-level environments that observe them. For example, an initiative known as the "Complete Streets Policy" alters the design of neighborhood streets to accommodate not only automobile traffic, but also public transit, bicycles, and pedestrians (National Complete Streets Coalition, 2014). This policy recommends that street design improve *safety*, rather than physical activity, for all users by allowing pedestrians to safely cross busy streets, reducing left-turning motorist crashes to zero, and creating designated bike lanes. However, the "Complete Streets Policy" can also encourage beneficial health behaviors by creating more walkable neighborhoods, which are associated with more physical activity and lower likelihood of being overweight or obese (Frank, Greenwald, Winkelman, Chapman, & Kavage, 2010; Frank, Sallis, et al., 2010; Lee, Mama, McAlexander, Adamus, & Medina, 2011). In addition, this policy may reduce carbon emissions and save fuel by encouraging short-distance trips to be made by walking, biking, bus or train, instead of by automobile. Reduction in carbon emissions, in turn, improves air quality, which can, in turn, help make outdoor physical activities more enjoyable (Lee et al., 2011b; National Complete Streets Coalition, 2014).

Along with policy, other macro-level environmental factors can significantly affect the enactment and sustainability of physical activity policies. For example, institutionalized discrimination or inequalities, embedded deeply within the histories of neighborhoods that affect minority groups in the United States, can help guide policy priorities but may also pose obstacles to their enactment and implementation. The historical and current lack of health-promoting urban planning in deprived neighborhoods—those most often inhabited by people with lower socioeconomic status, ethnic minorities, and immigrants—makes them top priorities for policies focused on improving the built environment. Due to financial considerations, residents may have limited choices in neighborhood selection compared to populations with better access to resources. Effective enforcement of policies against crime in these neighborhoods may be lacking, posing a significant obstacle to physical activity safety in these neighborhoods (Lee & Cubbin, 2009). Another example of macro-level environment factors affecting the enactment of policies occurs within schools. Federal policies regulating physical activity and physical education may be hampered in schools with lower resource allocation (e.g., lack of funding for teachers, training, or equipment) or those struggling to achieve academic standards, which can complicate effective policy implementation.

Forces of Change

The EMPA posits that peripheral, sometimes unpredictable or nebulous forces, such as globalization, technological innovation, and immigration, can enter the ecologic milieu to change factors at all levels of the environment (Lee & Cubbin, 2009; Spence & Lee, 2003). For example, globalization has led to profound increases in international manufacturing, trade, and communication, trickling down to increased automobile availability, residential relocation to suburban areas, and trends toward desk-based, sedentary jobs (Lee 2011b). Changes in these macro- and micro-level environments increase the need for effective policies that promote physical activity as part of transportation systems, schools, workplaces, and neighborhoods. Technological innovation, particularly the increasing power of computers and the Internet, plays a major role in the increasingly sedentary nature of work and leisure time. Telecommuting, or "working from home," along with ready access to the Internet, television, and video games, are increasing the popularity of sedentary activities among people of all ages (Lee et al., 2011b). As leisure time transitions from time spent outdoors to time spent sitting in front of screens, important avenues for policies enacted by local, state, and federal governments emerge to affect physical activity at the micro-environment level. Changes in immigration patterns can introduce cultural traditions into new environments, in turn leading to changes in physical activity patterns and opportunities. For example, the increase in Latino immigrants in the United States over the past 50 years has contributed to an increasing interest in popular dances and sports, such as Latin dance styles and soccer, a sport that is popular in Latin American countries. Understanding and enjoyment of these activities have developed along with meso- and exo-level environmental linkages to increased interest and popular demand. This has, in turn, influenced micro-level environment settings to include space and programming for these activities, thus demonstrating how the levels of the environment can interact dynamically to result in increases in physical activity.

EXAMPLES OF POLICY CHANGES BY SETTING

Policies implemented at the macro-environment level often directly influence individual-level behaviors like physical activity, but they can also influence behavior indirectly by influencing micro-level environment structures. Policies can be implemented within micro-level environments and can be small scale, such as at a neighborhood, school, or workplace level, or large scale, such as at the district, state, or national level. Policies to increase mixed land use (Dill & Howe, 2011), improve urban design and street-scale elements (Carlson et al., 2011), improve parks and physical activity resources (Gotschi, 2011), and increase physical education in schools (Hoelscher, Springer, Menendez, Cribb, & Kelder, 2011) are examples of macro-environmental policies that improve micro-level environments in an effort to influence physical activity. This next section discusses how policy and the environment work together to influence physical activity participation with specific setting illustrations.

Neighborhoods

A growing wealth of literature suggests that street connectivity (Kaczynski, Koohsari, Stanis, Bergstrom, & Sugiyama, 2014; Koohsari, Sugiyama, Lamb, Villanueva, & Owen, 2014; Saelens, Sallis, & Frank, 2003) and the mix of land use (McConville, Rodriguez, Clifton, Cho, & Fleischhacker, 2011; Moudon et al., 2007; Rodriguez, Evenson, Diez Roux, & Brines, 2009) are important determinants of physical activity for transportation in industrialized, higher income countries. Street connectivity at the micro-level environment refers to the manner in which travel destinations are linked in transportation systems and is determined by zoning and urban planning factors at the macro-level (Lee et al., 2011a). A neighborhood with high connectivity offers pedestrians and cyclists multiple routes for reaching multiple destinations. Land-use mix refers to the various types of uses of the land found within a particular area, as described above. A mix of land use contributes to active transportation by providing pedestrians and cyclists with a broad range of destinations to which they might travel (Lee et al., 2011a). For example, the land found within a neighborhood may be used for residential housing as well as restaurants and stores. Land use diversity in a neighborhood can give residents the opportunity to walk or bike from their home to a nearby destination, rather than using a vehicle for transportation.

Active transportation involves the use of physical activity (e.g., walking, cycling, skating) to transport from one micro-level destination to another, resulting in increased daily physical activity, while improving health and reducing fuel costs (Gotschi, 2011). Enacting transportation policies, such as those that increase active transportation via walking or bicycling, requires the involvement of multiple government levels, from local or city ordinances to national support, in order to improve the availability of options and infrastructure. At the local level, city council members, transportation board members, and city planning members must work together to create pedestrian and bicycling infrastructure, including designated lanes and paths, reduced traffic speed near these lanes, buffers between dedicated lanes and roads, rights on the road for bicyclists (e.g., yield signs for bicyclists or designated traffic lights), and adequate and convenient bicycle parking (e.g., safe and secure bicycle racks) at popular destinations, such as parks, workplaces, convenience and grocery stores, and fitness facilities (Suminski, Wasserman, Mayfield, Freeman, & Brandl, 2014). At the national level, legislation might help provide adults and children with affordable bicycles through employer- or government-subsidized programs.

Zoning laws are used for urban planning and may regulate other aspects of land use, such as building heights and their relationships to streetscapes or sidewalks. These policies can be implemented at the neighborhood or city level as well. Zoning laws require local governments to regulate land use, potentially increasing access to recreational facilities (e.g., parks, recreation centers, and open spaces), while limiting access to commercial destinations that contribute to the obesogenic environment (e.g., fast food restaurants and tobacco or liquor retailers). In addition to promoting mixed land use, zoning laws can regulate other aspects of land use, such as speed limits in residential and school areas, and lighting and shading within pedestrian facilities (Johnson Thornton et al., 2013; Lindholm, 2011; Schilling & Linton, 2005).

There are several advantages to zoning laws. Zoning may require cities and communities to provide buffer land uses, such as parks or playgrounds, between residential and commercial spaces, or between schools and commercial spaces. This not only increases access to physical activity resources, but it can also decrease access to goods and services contributing to the obesogenic environment, such as fast food restaurants and convenience stores. Zoning laws may also have the potential to reduce crime around physical activity resources and residential areas, thus alleviating safety concerns, including those related to traffic, in residential areas (Johnson Thornton et al., 2013; Lindholm, 2011; Schilling & Linton, 2005).

Although zoning laws may increase access to physical activity resources, increased maintenance costs are a potential challenge. Studies have shown access alone is not sufficient to increase physical activity participation (Lee, Mama, Adamus-Leach, & Soltero, 2015; Lee et al., 2009). Quality of physical activity resource features and amenities is important as well, as these require maintenance and upkeep. Costs associated with purchasing, maintaining, and replacing poor quality equipment may be high. Landscaping and grounds maintenance costs associated with physical activity resources may also be a limitation. Another disadvantage of zoning laws is that commercial business owners who profit from having their businesses located in close proximity to a residential area or school, such as fast food restaurant owners and liquor or convenience store owners, may resist passing and enforcing zoning laws. Thus, zoning may have long-term financial consequences worth investigating.

Schools

Policies are often implemented within the education system and school environment. The majority of policies implemented within schools have to do with physical activity opportunities available to children and students during the school day. Information distributed in schools has the potential for wide scale reach, since more than 95% of American children age 5 to 17 are enrolled in school, attending at least 180 days per year (Kaphingst & Story, 2009). One example of an effective school-based policy is Senate Bill 42 (SB42), which requires public middle school students, grades 6–8, to participate in 30 minutes of structured physical activity per day (Barroso et al., 2009). Key informant interviews with school principals, physical education instructors, and nurses indicate that SB42 affected the frequency of physical education classes and led to increased self-reported physical activity by children (Barroso et al., 2009).

Other school-based policies may be targeted at enhancing the physical activity environment in schools. For example, New York bill S587-2011 requires the Chancellor of the New York City School District to compile an inventory of the outdoor schoolyards and prepare a report on the condition and use of playgrounds. The goal of the bill is to help improve compliance with New York state laws on schoolyard spaces and reduce inequities among schools with regard to outdoor play space ("An act to amend the education law, in relation to directing the chancellor of a city school district in a city having a population of one million or more to inventory and report upon the outdoor schoolyards within such district.," 2011). Additional policies targeting the school environment may increase funding to schools by helping to enhance and fund daily physical education and sports programs in primary and secondary schools, in turn extending the school day if necessary. Although the policies presented above are state policies, many of the more specialized school-based policies and costly policy fixes, such as school wellness policies, may occur at the local level rather than at a state or federal level.

Worksites

The worksite environment has also been the focus of policy, with recent calls for multilevel strategies to increase supportiveness of worksite environments for health and well-being. Since US adults spend a majority of their waking hours at work, the worksite can be an effective venue to promote physical activity (Anderson et al., 2009). Increasing seminar occurrence and facilitating experiences that build skills and strategies that focus on providing reinforcement and social support to coworkers have been helpful for increasing physical activity along with improving other health behaviors. The American Heart Association has placed increased importance on creating a healthy work environment, or "Fit-Friendly Worksite," and encourages worksites and employers to meet worksite requirements to be recognized at the gold or platinum levels for community innovation (American Heart Association, 2014). Nearly two-thirds, 65%, of the working age (16 years or older) population in the United States works in a traditional worksite setting, making it an ideal setting to reach adults of all ages (Clark, Iceland, Palumbo, Posey, & Weismantle, 2003).

Worksite wellness legislation and initiatives may include insurance premium discounts or rebates for participation in wellness policies or programs, awareness campaigns, tax credits, transportation-related initiatives, or other wellness legislation (National Conference of State Legislatures, 2014). Although several states have established workplace health programs for state employees that are showing positive results (Mattke et al., 2013), establishing incentives for private sector employers to invest in workplace health programs continues to be a challenge. As part of wellness initiatives and programs, employers may invest in fitness, grooming, and locker facilities, while allowing flexible schedules with time to complete physical activity during the workday (Phipps, Madison, Pomerantz, & Klein, 2010; Pratt et al., 2007). In place of coffee and/or smoking breaks, physical activity breaks involving stretches, short bursts of cardio activity, yoga, or tai-chi may be implemented to help provide interesting physical activity opportunities in the work setting. Short physical activity breaks can transform work place culture, so that management supports and encourages physical activity in a workday. This would allow groups of co-workers to regularly participate in physical activity together to increase social support and enjoyment during the work day (Taylor, 2005).

Regardless of the strategy used to promote worksite wellness, it is clear that changing the worksite environment is an important part of obesity prevention and control along with other chronic health conditions that are reduced with increased physical activity participation (Aldana, Merrill, Price, Hardy, & Hager, 2005; Chapman, 2012). Worksite wellness programs have been shown to significantly reduce sick days and improve worker productivity. In addition, employees with access to worksite services, such as fitness counseling, gyms, and equipment, are approximately two times more likely to meet daily physical activity goals (Dodson et al., 2008).

Worksites, along with other micro-level environments, provide valuable opportunities to increase physical activity through point-of-decision prompting, as discussed previously in regard to climbing stairs (Andersen et al., 1998; Blamey, Mutrie, & Aitchison, 1995). Municipal codes require that multistory structures provide stairwells, yet workers accustomed to riding elevators and escalators may not know their locations. Directional signs and motivational messages (e.g., "Burn some calories, take the stairs!") may improve awareness of stairwells and increase motivation to use them. Companies and worksites can also increase use of stairwells by adding features or amenities, such as music, artwork, and welcoming décor (Kerr et al., 2012).

RECOMMENDATIONS FOR RESEARCH, POLICY, AND PRACTICE

This section is organized by level of the EMPA to emphasize the endless possible combinations of built environments and policies that can co-exist to promote physical activity.

Research, policy, and practice at the micro-, meso-, exo-, and macro-environment levels have the potential to greatly shape individual behavior and health.

Micro-Level Environment

Micro-level interventions aim to increase physical activity by changing the context in which people live their day-to-day lives, such as communities, schools, and worksites. Community-level interventions are sometimes called public health interventions, because of their focus on populations, rather than on individuals, as well as on prevention, rather than on more reactive treatment-focused interventions. They focus on enhancing health and preventing chronic conditions. One hope of these strategies is to shift the population average so that their impact is broader than individually focused strategies that focus on those most in need. One promising strategy is to link micro-level environments by using a coordinated care strategy (Valdovinos, Srikantharajah, Panares, Cohen, & Cantor, 2011) to create multiple channels of influence and opportunity for physical activity across a panoply of settings. For example, opportunities for physical activity during the work day for adults, during the school day for children, and then in communities in the evenings and weekends would make physical activity much more convenient. It is often the case that worksites are not necessarily near physical activity opportunities, and the potential for long commutes to worksites may further decrease time and opportunity for physical activity. Yet, worksites can improve matters by including physical activity opportunities during breaks or before or after work, while allowing the use of facilities for changing and bathing.

A recent review by the Guide to Community Preventive Services task force found that increasing access to places that provide opportunities for physical activity helps to increase physical activity; however, most of these efforts also included some level of education and training on physical activity, suggesting that strategies at all levels are needed (Kahn et al., 2002). Some data suggest that merely having places to do physical activity, like parks or gyms, may be sufficient, although other data suggest that quality, convenience, and programming of physical activity resources may be more important, in turn emphasizing the need for coordination across ecologic environmental levels. It is not entirely clear whether the "if you build it, they will come" mentality is completely accurate, although several studies have shown that having nearby physical activity resources is associated with increased physical activity (Cutumisu & Spence, 2012; Lee et al., 2007; Sallis et al., 1990).

Researchers need to partner with communities to determine whether improvements to existing structures would increase physical activity. It is not clear from the existing literature whether there is a single magic recipe that suits all communities. Communities are not homogeneous, and a specific combination of zoning, physical activity resources, and active transportation in one community might not be as effective in another community. For example, the city of Philadelphia is about the same size in terms of population as the city of Phoenix; however, the design of the two cities is radically different. Because these cities are very differently designed and have very different climates and sociopolitical cultures, it is likely that what works in one city to promote physical activity might not be effective in the other.

Meso- and Exo-Level Environments

The dynamic linkages between micro-environments that drive behavior are complex, difficult to quantify, and not extensively described in the research literature. However, technology, strategies derived from research on ecologic momentary assessment (EMA), and innovations in social networking show some promise for promoting social and physical interactions. In EMA, people carry hand-held communication devices, such as smartphones (Rofey et al., 2010). Periodic prompts ask people to document publically what they are doing, where they are doing it, with whom they are doing it, and what feelings they are experiencing while doing it (e.g., Facebook "Check in"). Others can access these posts throughout the day and use them to create social opportunities around physical activity experiences or as inspiration to go to a particularly appealing location for physical activity later. This kind of exo- or meso-level environmental linkage demonstrates how people in one micro-level built environment can influence behaviors in other people in that same or a different micro-level built environment.

Combining EMA data with global positioning system (GPS) tracking and accelerometer-measured physical activity monitoring devices provides detailed objective information on daily activities that can be used by researchers and practitioners in health promotion. For example, GPS and accelerometry together can detect whether people are riding bikes, walking, or driving between locations (Chaix et al., 2014; Kerr et al., 2012). Many smartphones contain GPS tracking, and practitioners can use mobile apps to encourage people to go to specific micro-level built environments to do physical activity or acquire information or resources to improve their physical activity experience. For example, when consumers enter stores, retailers can send messages to consumers offering information about products available and promotions at the point of purchase. This information could also be used by practitioners to help motivate people to try new physical activities when in an appropriate environment. In addition, combining approaches at multiple levels of the environment can help to produce the greatest opportunity for physical activity participation.

Just as meso- and exo-level environmental factors can influence micro-level environmental factors, macro-level environment strategies also can be combined to help influence meso- and exo-environmental change. Changing norms and environments in order to facilitate healthy choices in the workplace or school environment can help increase communication about physical activity participation as well as the behavior itself. In addition, word of mouth and lay information gathering (e.g., watercooler conversations) can contribute to decisions about when, where, and with whom to do physical activity.

Municipal transportation networks can also serve as physical meso- and exo-level environmental factors. Time spent in the transportation network can be active (e.g., walking to transit, cycling to work), or it can be sedentary (e.g., driving, sitting). Strategies that reduce sprawl, improve roads to accommodate multiple modes of transportation, and improve the visual appeal and safety for non-motorized transport can make transit more likely to foster physical activity. Reducing reliance on automobiles, improving air quality, and increasing active transportation are additional priorities for increasing physical activity (Smart Growth America, 2002; Vandegrift & Yoked, 2004). Strategies to improve roads and making more complete streets increases the transportation system's capacity to support all potential users, including automobile drivers, transit users, walkers, and cyclists. One model example can be seen in the city of Moses Lake, Washington, which has implemented a comprehensive community plan to make all streets complete streets like the policy example presented above in the initial description of the micro-level environment. Both secular trends and data suggest that people who are able to live in walkable neighborhoods tend to walk and cycle more, leading to increases in physical activity (National Complete Streets Coalition, 2014). A secondary improvement from increased active transportation is the reduction of reliance on automobiles and corresponding improvements in air quality. Improved air quality cycles back around to help promote active transportation, creating a symbiotic relationship between urban planning focused on active transportation and planning focused on air-quality improvement.

Macro-Level Environment

At the macro-level, policies and leadership that affect physical activity could be much stronger. For example, it is often the case that funding from the national government for local road improvements may be linked to the state increasing the capacity of the transportation system to support more rapid transit and active commuting. This is a sneaky, yet effective strategy for increasing physical activity. It is uncommon for states to turn down federal monies, and often small improvements made in response to these federal "requirements" inspire additional improvements from local resources.

Although zoning laws have been implemented at the local level, broad implementation is needed in states and cities that do not currently have initiatives to enhance the built environment for physical activity. Zoning laws could increase access to physical activity resources by regulating land use in order to have the greatest influence on individual physical activity behavior. Although this policy option may cost money initially, there is potential for long-term financial and health gains.

Increasing the visibility of the importance of physical activity at the national level is also an important area requiring improvement. The enactment of the National Physical Activity Plan has been a big step forward in this arena, but there is room for greater resources, implementation of recommendations, and measurable outcomes, such as a National Physical Activity Report Card for people of all ages and all walks of life (National Physical Activity Plan, 2010). Along with this national visibility, physical activity has to be championed as an agenda item for the federal administration. Thus, high-ranking leaders, such as the President, the First Lady, Congressional representatives, and state government officials must not only include physical activity as part of their message for the health of all Americans, but must also be role models themselves.

CONCLUSIONS

Policies can be powerful determinants of individual health behavior choices, including physical activity. Policies can change behavior either indirectly, by influencing environments where behavior occurs, or directly, by regulating the behavior itself. Environments can be improved to promote physical activity by increasing pedestrian or cyclist safety, by promoting consumer enjoyment, or simply by making physical activity more convenient, economical, or pleasurable compared to other choices. Broad-scale, coordinated efforts to regulate the built environment and improve the availability of resources and opportunities for physical activity have been suggested by experts as the best way to increase and maintain physical activity at a population level. The promise of policy and environmental approaches to increase physical activity has spawned a new field of research in the past few decades; however, research is still needed to understand how this information can be implemented and disseminated in order to emphasize the sustainability of human power over machines.

REFERENCES

Aldana, S. G., Merrill, R. M., Price, K., Hardy, A., & Hager, R. (2005). Financial impact of a comprehensive multisite workplace health promotion program. *Preventive Medicine, 40*(2), 131–137. doi: 10.1016/j.ypmed.2004.05.008

American Heart Association. (2014). *Fit-friendly worksites: Get your company or school the healthy recognition it deserves.* Retrieved October, 27, 2014, from http://mystartonline.org/start_workplace_fit_friendly.jsp

Andersen, R. E., Franckowiak, S. C., Snyder, J., Bartlett, S. J., & Fontaine, K. R. (1998). Can inexpensive signs encourage the use of stairs? Results from a community intervention. *Annals of Internal Medicine, 129*(5), 363–369.

Anderson, L. M., Quinn, T. A., Glanz, K., Ramirez, G., Kahwati, L. C., Johnson, D. B., . . . Katz, D. L. (2009). The effectiveness of worksite nutrition and physical activity interventions for controlling employee overweight and obesity: A systematic review. *American Journal of Preventive Medicine, 37*(4), 340–357. doi: 10.1016/j.amepre.2009.07.003

Barker, R. G. (1968). *Ecological psychology: Concepts and methods for studying the environment of human behavior*. Palo Alto, CA: Stanford University Press.

Barroso, C. S., Kelder, S. H., Springer, A. E., Smith, C. L., Ranjit, N., Ledingham, C., & Hoelscher, D. M. (2009). Senate Bill 42: Implementation and impact on physical activity in middle schools. *Journal of Adolescent Health, 45*(3 Suppl), S82–90. doi: 10.1016/j.jadohealth.2009.06.017

Bassett, D. R., Vachon, J. A., Kirkland, A. O., Howley, E. T., Duncan, G. E., & Johnson, K. R. (1997). Energy cost of stair climbing and descending on the college alumnus questionnaire. *Medicine and Science in Sports and Exercise, 29*(9), 1250–1254.

Blamey, A., Mutrie, N., & Aitchison, T. (1995). Health promotion by encouraged use of stairs. *British Medical Journal, 311*(7000), 289–290.

Carlson, J. A., Sallis, J. F., Norman, G. J., McKenzie, T. L., Kerr, J., Arredondo, E. M., . . . Saelens, B. E. (2013). Elementary school practices and children's objectively measured physical activity during school. *Preventive Medicine, 57*(5), 591–595. doi: 10.1016/j.ypmed.2013.08.003

Carlson, S. A., Guide, R., Schmid, T. L., Moore, L. V., Barradas, D. T., & Fulton, J. E. (2011). Public support for street-scale urban design practices and policies to increase physical activity. *Journal of Physical Activity & Health, 8*(Suppl. 1), S125–134.

Centers for Disease Control and Prevention. (2011). School health guidelines to promote healthy eating and physical activity. *MMWR Recommendations and Reports, 60*(Rr-5), 1–76.

Centers for Disease Control and Prevention. (2014). *Definition of policy*. Retrieved October, 23, 2014, from www.cdc.gov/policy/process/definition.html

Chaix, B., Kestens, Y., Duncan, S., Merrien, C., Thierry, B., Pannier, B., . . . Meline, J. (2014). Active transportation and public transportation use to achieve physical activity recommendations? A combined GPS, accelerometer, and mobility survey study. *International Journal of Behavioral Nutrition and Physical Activity, 11*(1), 124. doi: 10.1186/s12966-014-0124-x

Chapman, L.S. (2012). Meta-evaluation of worksite health promotion economic return studies: 2012 update. *American Journal of Health Promotion, 26*(4), 1–12. doi: 10.4278/ajhp.26.4.tahp

Clark, S. L., Iceland, J., Palumbo, T., Posey, K., & Weismantle, M. (2003). *Comparing employment, income, and poverty: Census 2000 and the current population survey*. Bureau of the Census, US Department of Commerce, September.

Coleman, K. J., & Gonzalez, E. C. (2001). Promoting stair use in a US-Mexico border community. *American Journal of Public Health, 91*(12), 2007–2009.

Craig, C. L., Marshall, A. L., Sjostrom, M., Bauman, A. E., Booth, M. L., Ainsworth, B. E., . . . Oja, P. (2003). International physical activity questionnaire: 12-country reliability and validity. *Medicine and Science in Sports and Exercise, 35*(8), 1381–1395. doi: 10.1249/01.MSS.0000078924.61453.FB

Crespo, N. C., Sallis, J. F., Conway, T. L., Saelens, B. E., & Frank, L. D. (2011). Worksite physical activity policies and environments in relation to employee physical activity. *American Journal of Health Promotion, 25*(4), 264–271. doi: 10.4278/ajhp.081112-QUAN-280

Cutumisu, N., & Spence, J. C. (2012). Sport fields as potential catalysts for physical activity in the neighbourhood. *International Journal of Environmental Research and Public Health, 9*(1), 294–314. doi: 10.3390/ijerph9010294

Dill, J., & Howe, D. (2011). The role of health and physical activity in the adoption of innovative land use policy: Findings from surveys of local governments. *Journal of Physical Activity & Health, 8* (Suppl. 1), S116–124.

Dodson, E. A., Lovegreen, S. L., Elliott, M. B., Haire-Joshu, D., & Brownson, R. C. (2008). Worksite policies and environments supporting physical activity in midwestern communities. *American Journal of Health Promotion, 23*(1), 51–55. doi: 10.4278/ajhp.07031626

Frank, L. D., Greenwald, M. J., Winkelman, S., Chapman, J., & Kavage, S. (2010). Carbonless footprints: Promoting health and climate stabilization through active transportation. *Preventive Medicine, 50*(Suppl 1), S99–105. doi: 10.1016/j.ypmed.2009.09.025

Frank, L. D., Sallis, J. F., Saelens, B. E., Leary, L., Cain, K., Conway, T. L., & Hess, P. M. (2010). The development of a walkability index: Application to the neighborhood quality of life study. *British Journal of Sports Medicine, 44*(13), 924–933. doi: 10.1136/bjsm.2009.058701

Gordon-Larsen, P., Nelson, M. C., & Beam, K. (2005). Associations among active transportation, physical activity, and weight status in young adults. *Obesity Research*, *13*(5), 868–875. doi: 10.1038/oby.2005.100

Gotschi, T. (2011). Costs and benefits of bicycling investments in Portland, Oregon. *Journal of Physical Activity & Health*, 8 (Suppl. 1), S49–58.

Handy, S. L., Cao, X., & Mokhtarian, P. L. (2008). The causal influence of neighborhood design on physical activity within the neighborhood: Evidence from Northern California. *American Journal of Health Promotion*, *22*(5), 350–358. doi: 10.4278/ajhp.22.5.350

Hoelscher, D. M., Springer, A., Menendez, T. H., Cribb, P. W., & Kelder, S. H. (2011). From NIH to Texas schools: Policy impact of the Coordinated Approach to Child Health (CATCH) program in Texas. *Journal of Physical Activity & Health*, 8 (Suppl. 1), S5–7.

Johnson Thornton, R. L., Greiner, A., Fichtenberg, C. M., Feingold, B. J., Ellen, J. M., & Jennings, J. M. (2013). Achieving a healthy zoning policy in Baltimore: Results of a health impact assessment of the TransForm Baltimore zoning code rewrite. *Public Health Reports*, 128 (Suppl. 3), 87–103.

Kaczynski, A. T., Koohsari, M. J., Stanis, S. A., Bergstrom, R., & Sugiyama, T. (2014). Association of street connectivity and road traffic speed with park usage and park-based physical activity. *American Journal of Health Promotion*, *28*(3), 197–203. doi: 10.4278/ajhp.120711-QUAN-339

Kahn, E. B., Ramsey, L. T., Brownson, R. C., Heath, G. W., Howze, E. H., Powell, K. E., . . . Corso, P. (2002). The effectiveness of interventions to increase physical activity. A systematic review. *American Journal of Preventive Medicine*, *22*(4 Suppl), 73–107.

Kaphingst, K. M., & Story, M. (2009). Child care as an untapped setting for obesity prevention: State child care licensing regulations related to nutrition, physical activity, and media use for preschool-aged children in the United States. *Preventing Chronic Disease*, *6*(1), A11.

Kerr, J., Norman, G., Godbole, S., Raab, F., Demchak, B., & Patrick, K. (2012). Validating GPS data with the PALMS system to detect different active transportation modes. *Medicine and Science in Sports and Exercise*, *44*, 647.

Koohsari, M. J., Sugiyama, T., Lamb, K. E., Villanueva, K., & Owen, N. (2014). Street connectivity and walking for transport: Role of neighborhood destinations. *Preventive Medicine*, *66*, 118–122. doi: 10.1016/j.ypmed.2014.06.019

Leach, H. J., O'Connor, D. P., Mama, S. K., Simpson, R., Rifai, H., & Lee, R. E. (2016). The built environment for physical activity and prediction of cardiovascular disease risk factors in African American women—an exploratory decision tree analysis. *Health Psychology*, *35*, 397–402. doi: 10.1037/hea0000267.PubMedPMID:27018731

Lee, I. M., & Paffenbarger, R. S., Jr. (1998). Physical activity and stroke incidence: The Harvard Alumni Health Study. *Stroke*, *29*(10), 2049–2054.

Lee, R. E., Booth, K. M., Reese-Smith, J. Y., Regan, G., & Howard, H. H. (2005). The Physical Activity Resource Assessment (PARA) instrument: Evaluating features, amenities and incivilities of physical activity resources in urban neighborhoods. *International Journal of Behavioral Nutrition and Physical Activity*, *2*, 13. doi: 14795-8682-13 [pii]

Lee, R. E., & Cubbin, C. (2009). Striding toward social justice: The ecologic milieu of physical activity. *Exercise and Sport Science Reviews*, *37*(1), 10–17. doi: 10.1097/JES.0b013e318190eb2e

Lee, R. E., Cubbin, C., & Winkleby, M. (2007). Contribution of neighbourhood socioeconomic status and physical activity resources to physical activity among women. *Journal of Epidemiology and Community Health*, *61*(10), 882–890. doi: 61/10/882 [pii]

Lee, R. E., Hallett, A. M., Parker, N. H., Kao, D., Modelska, M. J., Rifai, H. S., & O'Connor, D. P. (2015). Physical activity policies in Childhood Obesity Research Demonstration (CORD) Communities. *Health Behavior & Policy Review*, *2*(4), 284–295.

Lee, R. E., Mama, S. K., Adamus-Leach, H. J., & Soltero, E. G. (2015). Contribution of neighborhood income and access to quality physical activity resources to physical activity in ethnic minority women over time. *American Journal of Health Promotion*, *29*(4), 210–216. doi: 10.4278/ajhp.130403-QUAN-148

Lee, R. E., Mama, S. K., Banda, J. A., Bryant, L. G., & McAlexander, K. P. (2009). Physical activity opportunities in low socioeconomic status neighbourhoods. *Journal of Epidemiology and Community Health*, *63*(12), 1021. doi: 10.1136/jech.2009.091173

Lee, R. E., Mama, S. K., McAlexander, K. P., Adamus, H., & Medina, A. V. (2011a). Neighborhood and PA: Neighborhood factors and physical activity in African American public housing residents. *Journal of Physical Activity & Health, 8* (Suppl 1), S83–90.

Lee, R. E., McAlexander, K. M., & Banda, J. A. (2011b). *Reversing the obesogenic environment* (H. Kinetics, Ed.). Champaign, IL: Human Kinetics.

Lewis, A., & Eves, F. (2012). Prompt before the choice is made: Effects of a stair-climbing intervention in university buildings. *British Journal of Health Psychology, 17*(3), 631–643. doi: 10.1111/j.2044-8287.2011.02060.x

Lindholm, R. (2011). Combating childhood obesity: A survey of laws affecting the built environments of low-income and minority children. *Reviews on Environmental Health, 26*(3), 155–167.

Mattke, S., Liu, H., Caloyeras, J., Huang, C. Y., Van Busum, K. R., Khodyakov, D., & Shier, V. (2013). Workplace wellness programs study. *Rand Health Quarterly, 3,* 7.

McConville, M. E., Rodriguez, D. A., Clifton, K., Cho, G., & Fleischhacker, S. (2011). Disaggregate land uses and walking. *American Journal of Preventive Medicine, 40*(1), 25–32. doi: 10.1016/j.amepre.2010.09.023

McKinnon, R. A., Bowles, H. R., & Trowbridge, M. J. (2011). Engaging physical activity policymakers. *Journal of Physical Activity & Health, 8* (Suppl 1), S145–147.

Moudon, A. V., Lee, C., Cheadle, A. D., Garvin, C., Rd, D. B., Schmid, T. L., & Weathers, R. D. (2007). Attributes of environments supporting walking. *American Journal of Health Promotion, 21*(5), 448–459.

National Association for Sport and Physical Education. (2008). *Comprehensive school physical activity programs* [position statement]. Reston, VA: American Alliance for Health, Physical Education, Recreation, and Dance.

National Complete Streets Coalition. (2014). *Changing policy.* Retrieved October, 27, 2014, from www.smartgrowthamerica.org/complete-streets/changing-policy

National Conference of State Legislatures. (2014). *State wellness legislation, 2006–2010.* Retrieved October, 27, 2014, from www.ncsl.org/research/health/state-wellness-legislation.aspx

National Physical Activity Plan. (2010). *The plan.* Retrieved October 27, 2014, from www.physicalactivityplan.org/theplan.php

Pate, R. R., Davis, M. G., Robinson, T. N., Stone, E. J., McKenzie, T. L., & Young, J. C. (2006). Promoting physical activity in children and youth: A leadership role for schools: A scientific statement from the American Heart Association Council on Nutrition, Physical Activity, and Metabolism (Physical Activity Committee) in collaboration with the Councils on Cardiovascular Disease in the Young and Cardiovascular Nursing. *Circulation, 114*(11), 1214–1224. doi: 10.1161/circulationaha.106.177052

Phipps, E., Madison, N., Pomerantz, S. C., & Klein, M. G. (2010). Identifying and assessing interests and concerns of priority populations for work-site programs to promote physical activity. *Health Promotion Practice, 11*(1), 71–78. doi: 10.1177/1524839908318165

Pratt, C. A., Lemon, S. C., Fernandez, I. D., Goetzel, R., Beresford, S. A., French, S. A., . . . Webber, L. S. (2007). Design characteristics of worksite environmental interventions for obesity prevention. *Obesity, 15*(9), 2171–2180. doi: 10.1038/oby.2007.258

Rodriguez, D. A., Evenson, K. R., Diez Roux, A. V., & Brines, S. J. (2009). Land use, residential density, and walking. The multi-ethnic study of atherosclerosis. *American Journal of Preventive Medicine, 37*(5), 397–404. doi: 10.1016/j.amepre.2009.07.008

Rofey, D. L., Hull, E. E., Phillips, J., Vogt, K., Silk, J. S., & Dahl, R. E. (2010). Utilizing ecological momentary assessment in pediatric obesity to quantify behavior, emotion, and sleep. *Obesity, 18*(6), 1270–1272. doi: 10.1038/oby.2009.483

Saelens, B. E., Sallis, J. F., Black, J. B., & Chen, D. (2003). Neighborhood-based differences in physical activity: An environment scale evaluation. *American Journal of Public Health, 93*(9), 1552–1558.

Saelens, B. E., Sallis, J. F., & Frank, L. D. (2003). Environmental correlates of walking and cycling: Findings from the transportation, urban design, and planning literatures. *Annals of Behavioral Medicine, 25*(2), 80–91.

Sallis, J. F., Cervero, R. B., Ascher, W., Henderson, K. A., Kraft, M. K., & Kerr, J. (2006). An ecological approach to creating active living communities. *Annual Review of Public Health, 27,* 297–322. doi: 10.1146/annurev.publhealth.27.021405.102100

Sallis, J. F., Hovell, M. F., Hofstetter, C. R., Elder, J. P., Hackley, M., Caspersen, C. J., & Powell, K. E. (1990). Distance between homes and exercise facilities related to frequency of exercise among San Diego residents. *Public Health Reports, 105*(2), 179–185.

Schilling, J., & Linton, L. S. (2005). The public health roots of zoning: In search of active living's legal genealogy. *American Journal of Preventive Medicine, 28*(2 Suppl 2), 96–104. doi: 10.1016/j. amepre.2004.10.028

Smart Growth America. (2002). *Measuring Sprawl and its impact.* Retrieved October, 27, 2014, from www.smartgrowthamerica.org/research/measuring-sprawl-and-its-impact/

Spence, J. C., & Lee, R. E. (2003). Toward a comprehensive model of physical activity. *Psychology of Sport and Exercise, 4,* 7–24.

Suminski, R. R., Wasserman, J. A., Mayfield, C. A., Freeman, E., & Brandl, R. (2014). Bicycling policy indirectly associated with overweight/obesity. *American Journal of Preventive Medicine, 47*(6), 715–721. doi: 10.1016/j.amepre.2014.07.048

Taylor, W. C. (2005). Transforming work breaks to promote health. *American Journal of Preventive Medicine, 29*(5), 461–465. doi: 10.1016/j.amepre.2005.08.040

Valdovinos, E., Srikantharajah, J., Panares, R., Cohen, L., & Cantor, J. (2011). Community-centered health homes: Bridging the gap between health services and community prevention. Retrieved October, 27, 2014, from www.preventioninstitute.org/component/jlibrary/article/id-298/127.html

Van Cauwenberg, J., De Bourdeaudhuij, I., De Meester, F., Van Dyck, D., Salmon, J., Clarys, P., & Deforche, B. (2011). Relationship between the physical environment and physical activity in older adults: A systematic review. *Health & Place, 17*(2), 458–469. doi: 10.1016/j.healthplace.2010.11.010

Vandegrift, D., & Yoked, T. (2004). Obesity rates, income, and suburban sprawl: An analysis of US states. *Health & Place, 10*(3), 221–229. doi: 10.1016/j.healthplace.2003.09.003

Zieff, S. G., Guedes, C. M., & Eyler, A. (2012). Policy-makers' responses to neighborhood focus group outcomes on physical activity. *Journal of Physical Activity & Health, 9*(8), 1056–1064.

14 Cross-Cultural Considerations in Exercise Promotion

A Cultural Sport Psychology Perspective

Kerry R. McGannon and Robert J. Schinke

Sport and exercise psychology researchers have recently focused attention on the topic of culture to facilitate contextualized understandings of cultural identities in physical activity contexts (Ryba, Schinke, & Tenenbaum, 2010; Schinke & Hanrahan, 2009; Schinke, McGannon, Parham, & Lane, 2012). Known as *cultural sport psychology* (CSP), scholars within this genre challenge mainstream sport and exercise psychology's assumptions, particularly assumptions concerning conceptions and meanings of cultural identities (McGannon, Curtin, Schinke, & Schweinbenz, 2012; Ryba, Stambulova, Si, & Schinke, 2013; Schinke & Hanrahan, 2009). A central reason for focusing on cultural identities is because physical activity practitioners are increasingly working with people from a variety of cultural backgrounds (Gill & Kamphoff, 2009; Ryba et al., 2013; Schinke & Hanrahan, 2009). Moreover, considerable scholarship supports the fact that culture shapes how we think, feel, and behave; we cannot step outside culture, thus to ignore it would be to ignore a key matter that shapes us (see McGannon et al., 2012; McGannon & Smith, 2015; Smith, 2010; Sparkes & Smith, 2005). The consequences of denying or ignoring cultural identities can result in decreased physical activity participation (McGannon & Schinke, 2013; Resnicow, Jackson, Braithwaite et al., 2002), alienation and distress (Schinke, Hanrahan, Eys, et al., 2008; Smith, 2013), and reduced physical performance and/or failure to meet one's performance potential (Blodgett, Schinke, Smith, Peltier, & Pheasant, 2011; Schinke et al., 2012).

The above presents challenges for practitioners lacking in cultural awareness concerning cultural identity diversity and/or for those seeking to gain cultural competence but unsure of where to begin (Gill & Kamphoff, 2009; McGannon et al., 2014; Ryba et al., 2013). As the term is used here, *cultural competence* refers to "possessing cultural knowledge and skills of a particular culture to deliver effective interventions to members of that culture" (Sue, 2006, p. 237). Challenges related to cultural competence include, but are not limited to, misinterpreting cultural norms (e.g., emotional expressions, communication styles) (Parham, 2005), reducing cultural identities and/or cultural practices to overgeneralizations or stereotypes (Chiu & Hong, 2005), physical activity attrition due to reliance on a monocultural view (e.g., White Eurocentric, male, individualistic, middle class) (Ryba & Schinke, 2009; Ryba et al., 2013), or a denial that cultural identities matter within the physical activity context (see Butryn, 2002; Parham, 2005).

Given the above challenges, cultural awareness and cultural competence are essential parts of quality program delivery and effective practice to address the needs of culturally diverse physical activity participants (Gill & Kamphoff, 2009; McGannon et al., 2014; Parham, 2005; Ryba et al., 2013). How might physical activity practitioners' cultural competence be facilitated? Within the present chapter this complex question is explored by first outlining three CSP tenets and their link to cultural competence. To further illustrate the tenets "in use," research pertaining to motherhood and physical activity participation from a social constructionist perspective is discussed. Through discussing this research, we draw attention to the usefulness of focusing on cultural discourses as potential pathways for raising cultural awareness concerning cultural identities (i.e., motherhood and exerciser identities) and exercise behavior. Drawing on additional research grounded in social constructionism, we further exemplify CSP tenets through discussion of the often taken-for-granted ways that women's bodies and exercise are "constructed" and "represented" in fitness discourse, and why such constructions/representations can be problematic for exercise and fitness identities, with behavioral implications. We conclude by summarizing key points from CSP for practitioners to consider, as opposed to definitively follow, when seeking to raise cultural awareness and create opportunities for individuals as cultural beings in physical activity contexts.

CULTURAL SPORT PSYCHOLOGY AND CULTURAL COMPETENCE: THREE KEY TENETS

Within clinical and counseling psychology, the inclusion of cultural aspects affecting therapeutic relationships, intervention strategies, and intervention outcomes with clients has been embraced (see American Psychological Association, 2003, for multicultural education and practice guidelines). Health education researchers have also advocated for the development of culturally competent practitioners to enhance program delivery and effectiveness (see Kreuter, Lukwago, Bucholtz, Clark, & Sanders-Thompson, 2002; Selig, Tropiano, & Greene-Moton, 2006). Cultural competence from these perspectives emphasizes reflective cultural awareness (e.g., understanding one's own identities and values as culturally constituted), cultural knowledge (e.g., understanding others' world views), and cultural skills (e.g., using communication and interventions that align with clients' world views) (see American Psychological Association, 2003). In line with these views, Schinke and Moore (2011, p. 288) outlined that a culturally competent sport psychology professional not only values diversity, but undertakes active engagement and commitment to the following:

> (a) formally gaining knowledge of cultures and cultural differences; (b) imbedding this knowledge into the employment of techniques and strategies; (c) understanding how issues of diversity can impact the interpersonal (and thus therapeutic) dynamic; (d) willingly being reflective practitioners; (e) warding against taking cultural considerations too far, over-generalizing, and making assumptions that because a client has certain cultural affiliations, they *surely* live by them and need them to be addressed and this is stereotyping too isn't it?; and (f) maintaining a commitment to staying abreast of the evolving literature and engaging in ongoing self-assessment and growth in this area.

The central assumptions of CSP align with the above notions concerning cultural competence, with the ultimate goals through cultural research being able to "(a) reveal the cultural standpoint of each participant; (b) understand the role of the researcher/practitioner and what cultural lens s/he infused into a project; and (c) create a transparent place for the aforementioned" (Ryba et al., 2013, p. 129–130). Although sport psychology has been slower to include and/or consider culture in the applied/practice realm (see Martens, Mobily, & Zizzi, 2000), a rich dialogue within CSP advocates for cultural competence and culturally sensitive practice (e.g., Gill & Kamphoff, 2009; Ryba et al., 2013; Schinke & Moore, 2011; Schinke et al., 2012). We recently contributed toward this growing dialogue by outlining three key CSP tenets that align with cultural competence in sport and exercise psychology for practitioners to consider. In the following, each of these tenets are briefly reiterated and discussed in relation to cultural competence.

Tenet I: People Have Intersecting Identities

One CSP tenet aligned with cultural competence—particularly in terms of cultural self-awareness and understanding others' world views—is that people have cultural identities composed of more than a single meaningful cultural characteristic (Gill & Kamphoff, 2009). From a CSP perspective, cultural identity is conceptualized as fluid and complex, rather than as a fixed entity, an oppositional binary (e.g., male/female, straight/gay), or static qualities reflecting the mind (see McGannon & Spence, 2010; Smith, 2010). The composition of one's cultural identity thus includes intersecting and socially constructed components, such as race, ethnicity, socioeconomic status, physicality, sexual orientation, and gender (Gill & Kamphoff, 2009; McGannon et al., 2012; Ryba et al., 2013). Adding to this complexity is that practitioners have intersecting cultural identities and that some people (e.g., sport and exercise practitioners, researchers) are afforded more power and privilege than others within physical activity contexts, depending on those identities (Butryn, 2002; Fisher, Butryn, & Roper, 2003; McGannon & Johnson, 2009; Ryba et al., 2013; Schinke et al., 2012; Smith, 2013).

For practitioners seeking to expand their awareness of their own and others' cultural identities and the implications, the above point is central because it means that difference and cultural diversity are embraced rather than omitted, ignored, or denied (Ryba et al., 2013; Schinke & Moore, 2011). Thus, while guidelines to raise cultural awareness and improve cultural competence can be provided, there are no definitive approaches (nor should there be) for working with participants based on skin color, gender, sexual orientation, physicality, or cultural, socioeconomic, and/or religious backgrounds (Parham, 2005). People cannot be reduced to a single monolithic, fixed, and static cultural category that directs them to behave in certain ways (see Chiu & Hong, 2005). Seeking generalities and oversimplification can lead to stereotyping, silencing, and/or marginalizing cultural identities, which, as noted, can lead to a disengagement, or less enjoyment, from physical activity (see Blodgett et al., 2011; Parham, 2005; Schinke et al., 2008).

Underscoring this point concerning embracing cultural diversity as complex and fluid is that CSP has a broader goal of challenging mainstream sport psychology's adherence to a monocultural or singular approach that privileges White, and largely male, heterosexual, middle-to-upper-class, Eurocentric views and experiences within physical activity contexts (Butryn, 2002; Parham, 2005; Ryba et al., 2013; Schinke et al., 2012). Culturally aware and culturally competent sport and exercise psychology practitioners thus do not seek to generalize across cultures or engage in stereotyping; they strive for ways to reduce and avoid such stereotyping (see Anderson, 1993; Gill & Kamphoff, 2009; Parham, 2005; Ryba et al., 2013).

Tenets II and III: Recognizing Power and Privilege, and Cultural Praxis

Recognizing one's own power, privilege, and beliefs as a practitioner in light of the social and cultural identity categories to which one belongs (and at times may even take for granted) is another CSP tenet that affects being a culturally competent practitioner (Fisher et al., 2003; McGannon & Johnson, 2009; Ryba et al., 2013). For example, a White male exercise psychology consultant working with minority exercise participants might ask himself the following: In what ways do my social class, social position, education, and White male privilege produce particular power hierarchies? (see Butryn, 2002) Toward what end do these power hierarchies structure my assumptions about, interactions with, and interpretations of the participants in the consulting context? (see Schinke et al., 2012). By asking these self-related questions, one looks inward to reflect on one's own power and privilege within the exercise context, and in turn practitioners begin to work toward what has been called the "heart" of CSP—cultural praxis (Ryba & Schinke, 2009; Ryba & Wright, 2005). The goal of cultural praxis is to blend theory, lived culture, and social justice with a "self-reflexive sensibility" to raise awareness as to how one's own values, biases, social position, and self-identity categories affect participants within the research and/or consulting realms (McGannon & Johnson, 2009; McGannon & Smith, 2015; Ryba & Schinke, 2009). Through cultural praxis, CSP practitioners strive to be culturally competent by highlighting issues of sociocultural difference, within the context of power and ethical issues, to facilitate contextualized understanding of cultural identities (Ryba et al., 2013; Schinke et al., 2012).

In order to realize the goals of cultural praxis (and, implicitly, cultural competence goals) practitioners need to reflect on how clients' backgrounds and their own backgrounds (e.g., education, gender, sexuality, age, physicality, ethnicity) infuse with practices (e.g., communication strategies, approaches to problem solving) (Schinke et al., 2012). Within applied sport psychology, Anderson, Knowles, and Gilbourne (2004) defined reflective practice as "an approach to training and practice that can help practitioners explore their decisions and experiences in order to increase their understanding of (self) and manage themselves and their practice" (p. 189). While little empirical research exists within the applied exercise psychology realm on reflective practice, a specific example of reflective tenets "in action" comes from Schinke and colleagues (2008) who considered their identities as outsiders (i.e., sport scientists, academics, White) to explore how they could enlist Canadian Aboriginal communities as co-participants who actively partake in the research process. Rather than imposing research goals on the community, these researchers worked with and for the community to identify what they viewed as important issues pertaining to physical activity within their reserve and how such issues could be linked to the research. This work is a form of self-reflective practice because it shows that an important effect of conscious self-reflexivity (i.e., acknowledging the social categories, values, and differences between one's self and community participants) is the acknowledgement of power differences. By acknowledging power via self-reflective practices, research participants were repositioned as co-participants rather than as people of a "different culture" to be "studied." In turn, a marginalized community became the centralized voice in designing the research questions and the (re)presentation of results, which may result in more cultural inclusion for the participants (McGannon & Smith, 2015; Ryba et al., 2013).

Self-reflective practices thus provide a pathway for power relationships between participants and practitioners to be acknowledged, an important step in facilitating marginalized cultures to speak for themselves and have their cultural identities recognized (McGannon & Johnson, 2009; McGannon & Smith, 2015; Schinke et al., 2012). To further illustrate some of these tenets "in use" we next discuss research pertaining to motherhood and physical activity participation from a social constructionist perspective, drawing particular attention to cultural discourses as potential pathways toward raising cultural awareness regarding cultural identities and physical activity. To further show the utility of focusing on cultural discourses as pathways to cultural identity construction and exercise behavior, we discuss research on the (often) taken-for-granted ways that women's bodies and exercise are "constructed" and "represented" in fitness discourse. The implications of this socially constructed "fit female body" and the implications for self-identity, psychological experiences, and exercise behavior will also be outlined.

MOTHERHOOD AND PHYSICAL ACTIVITY RESEARCH: ENHANCING CULTURAL AWARENESS THROUGH SOCIAL CONSTRUCTIONISM

Mothers of young children have been suggested as one subgroup upon which to focus research efforts due to an inverse relationship between motherhood and physical activity (PA) participation (Bellows-Riecken & Rhodes, 2008; McIntyre & Rhodes, 2009; Miller &

Brown, 2005). To understand motherhood and PA determinants, researchers have used theoretical approaches, such as social cognitive theory (Bandura, 1989) and the theory of planned behavior (Ajzen, 1991). While a great deal has been learned from these theoretical perspectives, the determinants of PA participation for mothers of young children are only beginning to be understood (Hamilton & White, 2010; McIntyre & Rhodes, 2009). In addition to "traditional" forms of theorizing, theoretical perspectives that conceptualize motherhood as a culturally constructed identity are needed to further understand the influences of mothers' physical activity participation within the context of society and culture (Lewis & Ridge, 2005; McGannon & Busanich, 2016; McGannon et al., 2012; Miller & Brown, 2005).

Social Constructionism: Three Central Points

A theoretical perspective relevant for understanding motherhood and physical activity within a sociocultural context, and within the CSP genre, is social constructionism (see Gergen, 1994; McGannon et al., 2012). From a social constructionist perspective, there are three central points pertinent to understanding motherhood as a culturally constructed identity with implications for exercise behavior. The first of these points is that, in line with CSP tenets highlighted earlier, self-identity is conceptualized as *simultaneously* social and cultural, rather than reduced to decontextualized mechanisms within the mind, as with mainstream sport and exercise psychology (McGannon & Mauws, 2000; McGannon & Spence, 2010; Smith, 2010). This recognition of self-identity (e.g., mother) as multiple, fluid, and socially constructed is an important step in working toward the goals of cultural competence, particularly those outlined by Schinke and Moore (2011). Following from this point, is a second point, which is that motherhood identity is viewed as the product of individual, social, and cultural discourses that interact to create particular meanings concerning cultural identities (McGannon & Schinke, 2013; Smith & Sparkes, 2008). *Discourse* is a broad concept used to refer to different ways of constituting meaning specific to particular groups, cultures, and historical contexts and provides the meanings that constitute people's behaviors/practices (Harré & Gillett, 1994; McGannon & Mauws, 2000). There are multiple ways of speaking with and about ourselves available for use within different discourses, which construct how we think, feel, and behave in light of the social and behavioral practices tied to them. In any context where decision making is required, people negotiate their behavior (e.g., to exercise or not to exercise) via language and conversations (e.g., saying "I need to care for my children before exercising; they come first.") to decide what is appropriate for them to do, say, and feel (e.g., caring for children instead of exercising, experiencing guilt if one exercises instead of spending time with children), given who they are (e.g., a good mother, bad mother) (McGannon, Gonsalves, Schinke, & Busanich, 2015; McGannon & Schinke, 2013; McGannon & Spence, 2010).

Because self-identities and the meanings that we take from them are the product of cultural discourses, the third point relevant for understanding motherhood as a sociocultural identity is that in order to raise cultural awareness of the subtle and taken-for-granted ways identities are linked to behaviour, a focus on cultural discourses is necessary (McGannon & Mauws, 2000; McGannon & Smith, 2015; McGannon & Spence, 2010; Smith, 2010, 2013). Such a focus, we propose, is a potential pathway toward becoming more culturally aware as practitioners, particularly in terms of understanding the complexity of cultural identities and their link to behavior. Moreover, such awareness is an important step toward realizing central goals of cultural competence: cultural reflection, increasing cultural knowledge, and increasing cultural skills. Central to the notion that discourse is linked to self-identity and behavior is the concept of a *subject position* (see Davies & Harré, 1990; McGannon & Mauws, 2000; McGannon & Spence, 2010). People acquire a sense of self-identity and interpret the world from a particular perspective (i.e., subject position) by participating in narrative practices that allocate meanings to particular categories and images (e.g., good mother, bad mother, exerciser). Identities are then positioned in relation to particular storylines articulated around categories and images, and people may have specific psychological experiences associated with that world view (Davies & Harré, 1990; McGannon & Mauws, 2000, McGannon & Spence, 2010; Smith, 2013).

While people may be constituted in one subject position or another, in one narrative or another within a story, research has shown that individuals are not passive recipients of discourse(s), as they can (re)negotiate subject positions by refusing the ones articulated by taking up alternatives within new and different cultural discourses/narratives (McGannon & Schinke, 2013; McGannon & Spence, 2010; Smith, 2013). The concept of a subject position thus suggests the potential for human agency, resistance, and change by virtue of drawing upon different cultural discourses by increasing the discursive/narrative resources at one's disposal (McGannon & Spence, 2010; Smith, 2013). Despite the possibility for agency and change of self-related views and behavior(s) by virtue of the tactical usage of discourses, discourses that people may draw upon to make sense of who they are as well as others are not characterized by infinite possibility, as local practices/choices (i.e., identity-talk about motherhood, behaviors such as caring for children and taking time to exercise) are made within a larger web of discourses held in place by social and institutional practices (McGannon & Schinke, 2013; McGannon & Spence, 2010). The implication of these ideas for raising the cultural awareness of practitioners is that if we wish to understand the links between cultural identities pertaining to motherhood and physical activity behavior, and even change self-related views and behaviors, it is advantageous to focus on the local narratives/conversations and the cultural discourses within which identities and local narratives are formed and framed (McGannon & Mauws, 2000; McGannon & Smith, 2015; Smith & Sparkes, 2008; Sparkes & Smith, 2005).

Social Constructionism "In Use": Motherhood and Physical Activity Research

To further illustrate these social constructionist points and the implications for enhancing cultural awareness concerning motherhood identity and physical activity behavior, it is useful to more explicitly discuss empirical research. Research pertinent to understanding motherhood and physical activity from a social constructionist perspective has revealed that certain social and cultural practices perpetuated by dominant discourses (e.g., a patriarchal discourse of the family that places men at the head of the household and women as subordinate) are linked to gender ideologies that are less likely to encourage women's physical activity participation (Currie, 2004; McGannon et al., 2015; McGannon & Schinke, 2013; Miller & Brown, 2005; Thomsson, 1999). A gender ideology pertaining to motherhood and what it means to "be" a mother is that women's "true" calling is to have children and care for them (Weedon, 1997). However, cultural discourses and cultural ideals, rather than biology, "tell" us what it means to be a mother, what behaviors and attitudes are appropriate for mothers, and how motherhood shapes a woman's identity (see Douglas & Michaels, 2004; Petrassi, 2012). These cultural ideals are made known and reinforced through the cultural ideals that men are supposed to uphold as well, with men's identities as husbands and fathers being viewed as that of providers and working outside the home, leaving domestic duties to women (Dixon & Wetherell, 2004; Petrassi, 2012).

Despite the suggestion that equal leisure access for both partners and shared responsibility of domestic work and the well-being of children would enhance physical activity opportunities (see Hamilton & White, 2010), when particular discourses dominate within a person's life (e.g., patriarchal discourse of the family), gender ideologies are circulated that structure motherhood identity and behavioral practices in ways that constrain physical activity (Lewis & Ridge, 2005; McGannon & Schinke, 2013; Miller & Brown, 2005). The foregoing childcare and domestic practices for "mothers" and "fathers" are partly reinforced as natural and taken-for-granted "facts" in concrete institutional practices (e.g., unpaid or lower pay for domestic labor, maternity leave offered only for women or less time offered for paternity leave for men, media constructions that reinforce gendered roles) (Dixon & Wetherell, 2004; Douglas & Michaels, 2004; Johnston & Swanson, 2003; Weedon, 1997). When certain discourses and institutional practices such as these are more prevalent and/or have endured over time, we find that expansion of discursive resources (and implicitly how one thinks, feels, and behaves), while possible, is more difficult for some women (McGannon et al., 2015; McGannon & Schinke, 2013; McGannon & Spence, 2010; Petrassi, 2012).

Further reinforcing the taken-for-granted notion that women are the primary caregivers within the family is *an ethic of care*, which is a cultural expectation and a cultural discourse that women sacrifice their own needs to take care of others. Intertwined with an ethic of care is the subject position of a "good mother," which when taken up within an ethic of care discourse, links the meaning of motherhood identity to selfless sacrificing and the experience of joy and fulfillment when doing so (Choi, Henshaw, Baker, & Tree, 2005). Originally proposed as an integral component of women's moral development (see Gilligan, 1982), an ethic of care has been linked in research to women's lack of a sense of entitlement to physical activity and/or lack of time to do physical activity (see Lewis & Ridge, 2005; McGannon & Schinke, 2013; Miller & Brown, 2005). Women negotiating both motherhood and careers may be especially vulnerable to experiencing guilt when engaging in physical activity for fear of not adhering to an ethic of care and living up to good mother identities and associated ideals perpetuated within this discourse (McGannon et al., 2012; McGannon & Schinke, 2013; Miller & Brown, 2005; Thomsson, 1999).

Qualitative research grounded in social constructionism has also allowed researchers to further reveal the nuances of motherhood and physical activity participation, as some women (re)negotiate gender ideologies to facilitate physical activity participation (Appleby & Fisher, 2009; Currie, 2004; Lewis & Ridge, 2005; McGannon et al., 2012; McGannon & Schinke, 2013; Miller & Brown, 2005). In particular, studies outside of sport and exercise psychology (e.g., sport sociology, sport management, leisure studies) have revealed that motherhood may give athletes an additional perspective on sport, decreasing pressure to perform and providing fulfillment in another life sphere (Palmer & Leberman, 2009; Spowart, Burrows, & Shaw, 2010). Qualitative research on athlete-mothers who are negotiating the "dual" cultural identities has also found that women reposition themselves as role models for others (e.g., children, other women) rather than as selfish when constructing their identities as athlete-mothers, making physical activity participation more likely (Freeman, 2008; Leberman & Palmer, 2009; Palmer & Leberman, 2009).

At the same time, consistent with research on physical activity and motherhood previously discussed, the relationship among the notion of guilt, motherhood, and athletics is complex, with time away from children identified as a cause of guilt despite a sense of control and well-being gained through athletics (Freeman, 2008; McGannon et al., 2015; McGannon et al., 2012). Results of one of the few studies in sport and exercise psychology on this subject revealed that, on the one hand, elite distance runners experienced an integration of their identities through the negotiation of sociocultural stereotypes concerning motherhood versus competitive athletics (Appleby & Fisher, 2009). But, on the other hand, those athlete-mothers who accepted such stereotypes within an ethic of care discourse/narrative adopted a good mother identity involving selfless care, which led to psychological distress and fatigue (see Currie, 2004; Miller & Brown, 2005). Some athletes resisted the good mother ideal/identity by viewing sport as pleasure and a way to enhance mental health, and thus did more sport training and experienced less psychological distress. This new perspective on sport as pleasure and health is a novel cultural discourse/narrative that holds potential for resisting dominant cultural ideals concerning athletics and motherhood that create psychological distress and constrain performance and/or sport participation (Appleby & Fisher, 2009; McGannon et al., 2012; McGannon et al., 2015; Spowart et al., 2010).

The above research on athletic and motherhood identities has also shown that important to accomplishing a sport-integrated identity was having significant others provide opportunities for these women to be active (e.g., helping with childcare), likely reinforcing particular discourses with behavioral practices linked to sport-integrated identities for athlete-mothers (see Appleby & Fisher, 2009; McGannon et al., 2012; McGannon et al., 2015). Other qualitative researchers have uncovered that women with children are physically active by reconfiguring physical activity as a time-out for themselves and an important part of their identities as women as well as mothers, which benefits the family as well as themselves (Lewis & Ridge, 2005; Miller & Brown, 2005). Together, this research reveals previously unrecognized opportunities for physical activity promotion by focusing on cultural discourses and the associated identities, with physical activity (re)positioned as a way to challenge gender ideologies by reconfiguring the meaning of motherhood and physical activity in women's lives (Lewis & Ridge, 2005; McGannon & Busanich, 2016; McGannon et al., 2012; McGannon et al., 2015; McGannon & Schinke, 2013; Palmer & Leberman, 2009; Spowart et al., 2010).

THE SOCIALLY CONSTRUCTED FIT FEMALE BODY: ANOTHER EXAMPLE OF CULTURAL DISCOURSES AS PATHWAYS TO CULTURAL AWARENESS

The utility of the preceding social constructionist points regarding how discourse functions with respect to self-identity construction and the promotion of physical activity behavior can be further illustrated in relation to another example pertaining to women's exercise: the promotion of a particular version of the "fit" female body. When promoting physical activity, popular culture sources (e.g., newspapers, magazines) often invoke stereotypical images and ideals concerning gender (Markula, 1995, 2003; McGannon & Busanich, 2010; Mutrie & Choi, 2000). In turn, physical activity discourses (i.e., what women may say to themselves about physical activity, what the media says physical activity) tend to rely upon narrowly defined images of femininity, which are linked to the ideologies of individualism, consumerism, and heteronormativity (Dworkin & Wachs, 2009; Krane, Stiles-Shipley, Waldron, & Michaelnok 2001a; Krane, Choi, Baird, Aimar, & Kauer, 2004; McGannon & Spence, 2012). These ideologies and discourses construct an "ideal version" of the fit female body that is slim, with toned and sculpted musculature. Bodies that look this way are promoted as moving with grace and ease in social space, which is linked to impossible ideals and standards for women to attain by promoting a narrow version of beauty and femininity (Dworkin & Wachs, 2009; Maguire & Mansfield, 1998; Markula, 2003; McGannon, Johnson, & Spence, 2011).

To further illustrate these points in relation to discourse and women's exercise, consider the following personal example of author Kerry McGannon to illustrate her physical self and physical activity experiences (see McGannon, 2012 or McGannon & Busanich, 2010 for an expanded discussion) Kerry notes:

> *As a physically active woman, the journey of understanding my physical self through exercise—both as a recreational exerciser and a fitness instructor—has spanned over 25 years. During my nine years (1994–2002) as a group fitness leader, women would draw upon*

weight loss and appearance discourses to ask me questions about their bodies: "how can I get rid of THIS?" (pointing at abdominals or thighs), "how many calories did we burn?," or "I've been doing this exercise for a year, why isn't the weight coming off?" And many of us—participants and fitness leaders alike—despite trying to attain a particular version of a "fit female body" via the gendered practice of aerobics, were aware of the futility of obtaining the socially constructed ideal fit female body (Markula, 1995, 2003; McGannon, 2012; Mutrie & Choi, 2000). Some fitness participants and my fitness instructor colleagues went beyond awareness and/or verbal acknowledgment of the socially constructed ideal fit female body and challenged its narrow construction. For example, one of my fitness instructor colleagues taught boxing and viewed her muscularity and athleticism as a tool for sport and recreational endeavors. She strove to be strong and imparted that knowledge to fitness participants through how she structured her boxing classes (e.g., emphasizing skill and correct form; deemphasizing body-shaping motives and practices). Another group of participants I taught in a class for overweight women reclaimed the terms fit *and* fat *and openly appreciated their curvier, fleshier bodies, emphasizing instead the empowering and positive features of their exercise (e.g., it was a tool for enjoyment, it was a way to connect with others in a non-judgmental space).*

In 2003, when I moved to the United States and could no longer teach group exercise, I took up recreational running. I continued to primarily draw upon weight management and appearance discourses to experience my running as a way to control how my body looked. In turn, I experienced what were at times psychologically distressing experiences in relation to my running (e.g., I felt guilty when I didn't run; I felt fat if I ate too much and/or if I didn't run far enough). Contradictory experiences continued when I began to resist weight loss and appearance discourses by changing how I viewed physical activity by (re)constructing its meaning within health and wellness discourses (Busanich, McGannon, & Schinke, 2012; Markula, 2001) to experience my running as empowering and my body as fit apart from how it looked. Healthy psychological experiences (e.g., enjoyment, a sense of accomplishment) and behavioral practices (e.g., not using running as a punishment but as a tool for energy and well-being) followed when I drew upon alternative discourses.

(McGannon, 2012)

The preceding brief example reveals the power and complexity of the way(s) that female bodies and physical activity are (re)presented and experienced, depending upon the particular cultural discourses that are drawn upon to construct them. Such representations have power and complexity because they become commonsense ways of understanding and relating to ourselves as embodied beings, which is further linked to health and well-being (McGannon & Busanich, 2010). Neither a neutral nor a benign process, "commonsense" representations of the fit female body and physical activity—whether at the level of culture (e.g., media, a particular fitness club or class) or the individual (e.g., what people say exercise "is" and can do for them)—are often connected to weight loss and appearance discourses perpetuating a pervasive theme of thinness conflated with an ideal suggesting that a thin body—no matter how attained—is healthy and fit (Markula, 1995, 2003; McGannon & Spence, 2012; Mutrie & Choi, 2000).

Researchers in sport and exercise psychology and sport sociology have drawn upon the key social constructionist tenets concerning the role discourse in the construction of self-identity and behavior outlined earlier to problematize the notion that "thin is fit and healthy." Highlighting this notion as problematic is important because when women's bodies do not meet appearance ideals—and the ideal cannot be attained (Markula, 2001; Mutrie & Choi, 2000)—women feel dissatisfied with their bodies and experience psychological distress (Krane et al., 2004; Markula, 1995, 2003; McGannon & Spence, 2010). Feeling dissatisfied with one's body is linked to unhealthy behaviors for female recreational exercisers and athletes. Behaviors include avoidance of particular forms of physical activity (e.g., weight training) or overexercising (Busanich et al., 2012; Maguire & Mansfield, 1998; McGannon & Spence, 2010), withdrawal from exercise when appearance-related goals are not attained (McGannon & Spence, 2010), and athletic performance concerns related to appearance concerns (e.g., toned but not too muscular) (Krane et al., 2001b). Exercisers and athletes who experience the perception that others are judging their bodies (i.e., social physique anxiety) are also vulnerable to disordered eating and disordered exercise patterns (Krane et al., 2004; Krane et al., 2001a).

The example of Kerry's personal physical activity experiences within this section aligns with the preceding literature findings that women do not always experience the liberating, positive self-related benefits of exercise promoted and desired by sport and exercise psychology researchers and practitioners. However, a more nuanced look at Kerry's personal narrative through a social constructionist lens also illustrates that weight loss and appearance discourses and associated meanings (e.g., thin is fit, exercise leads to weight loss) and practices (e.g., disordered eating, avoiding particular forms of exercise, feeling guilty about one's lack of exercise or amount of exercise) can be actively challenged/resisted to reconfigure and reposition one's identity as a 'female exerciser' or 'fit woman' as strong and healthy apart from appearance aspirations (Haravon Collins, 2002; Markula, 1995, 2003; McGannon, 2012; McGannon & Busanich, 2010).

Overall, the foregoing shows that it is important for sport and exercise psychology practitioners to be aware of cultural discourses—what they are and how they can form and frame certain identities that may limit more adaptive psychological experiences and/or constrain physical activity behavior. In turn, both practitioners and participants can be made aware of how certain dominant discourses construct and frame exercise in particular ways because such discourses are ubiquitous and often taken for granted as truth (McGannon & Spence, 2010). Moreover, such knowledge allows further awareness to be raised that such discourses are politically charged by the ideologies of consumerism and economic interests (e.g., the diet and fitness industry). Social and institutional practices (e.g. the way health and fitness are marketed and promoted) and the broader health and fitness discourses have to change for women to experience new and different views of their physical selves and experience the benefits of physical activity more often (Dworkin & Wachs, 2009; McGannon & Spence, 2012).

Apart from larger institutional changes, people's individual resistance practices—as exemplified in Kerry's narrative and other forms of empirical research highlighted within this section—draw attention to the power of individual action in the process of resisting dominant discourses and reconfiguring the discourse/power nexus. Such resistance points to sport and exercise psychology practitioners and female exercise participants becoming politically aware and literally *actively* resistant, questioning the limits of "natural" identities and practices in exercise formed through the games of truth that may disempower women (see Markula, 2003; McGannon, 2012). Thus dominant cultural discourses can be resisted through certain practices and the meanings associated with exercise and what constitutes a fit, female body. Such practices might include practitioners and women exercise participants *consciously* embracing their shape as fit and feminine regardless of weight/size, building a muscular body apart from appearance aspirations, changing the meaning of the term "exercise" to movement, enjoying the freedom and fun that comes from movement apart from appearance, and reconfiguring dominant discourses that construct a narrow version of a "fit, female body" (Dworkin & Wachs, 2009; Haravon Collins, 2002; Markula, 1995, 2003; McGannon, 2012; McGannon & Spence, 2010). In this regard, sport and exercise psychology researchers and practitioners have much to gain by focusing on cultural discourse as an "entry point" to the tools of self-identity (re)construction and behavior change.

CONCLUSIONS

Despite the established rationale for culturally informed sport and exercise psychology research and practice (see Ryba et al., 2010; Schinke & Hanrahan, 2009), the movement toward cultural competence within the domain has been slow to progress. But it can no longer be ignored (McGannon & Smith, 2015; Ryba et al., 2013). When considering the contents of this chapter (i.e., cultural competence parameters, CSP tenets and research on social constructionism, motherhood and physical activity, representations of women's bodies in relation to exercise), it becomes clear there is much more to any cultural context than might first meet the eye. While this can be overwhelming and sometimes unsettling, we hope that the reader is left with the sense that culture is, in fact, rich, complex, and difficult to fully understand due its fluid, dynamic nature (see McGannon & Smith, 2015; Ryba et al., 2013). Indeed, a key point of CSP from a social constructionist perspective is that no cultural identity, experience, interpretation, or view point within the social and cultural world is ever final or definitive (McGannon et al., 2015; McGannon et al., 2012; Schinke, McGannon, Battochio, & Wells, 2013; Smith, 2013). Despite this complexity of meaning concerning cultural identity, cultural awareness, and cultural competence, we leave the reader with five "take-home points" we sought to draw attention to, which readers may find useful in moving forward to (re)create culturally inclusive physical activity spaces/contexts that offer the potential for encouraging physical activity participation and enhanced well-being of participants:

- Every physical activity participant and practitioner brings a unique mélange of cultural identities, values, and inclinations into the physical activity context. As such, the physical activity context can become a psychologically healthy and enriched, or an unhealthy and depleted, environment, depending upon on how members' multifaceted identities are encouraged or subverted and silenced.
- Combined with the CSP tenets of multiple identities, power and privilege, and cultural praxis, cultural awareness and cultural competence are essential parts of quality program delivery and effective practice that may begin to acknowledge, and address, the complex needs of culturally diverse sport and physical activity participants.
- Through key ideas grounded in social constructionism, multiple intersecting identities as (re)negotiated processes and products of cultural discourses/narratives linked to certain ideologies and behavioral practices are acknowledged. In turn, practitioners have a focal point/pathway toward cultural awareness and potential behavior change: the cultural discourses within which identities and local self-related narratives are formed, fashioned, and framed.
- By raising awareness of cultural discourses as "entry points" of resistance from dominant discourses that may be less encouraging of physical activity behavior, practitioners can be key facilitators of "discursive resource expansion" (e.g., discussing 'exercise' within health and well-being discourses as opposed to weight loss and appearance discourses). By virtue of expanding discursive resources, exercise participants are offered additional conditions of possibility to reconfigure who they are, with the possibility of new or different identities emerging that are more encouraging of adaptive psychological experiences and well-being.
- CSP tenets, when adopted from a social constructionist perspective, provide the potential means to encourage diverse, intersecting, and richer views of cultural identities to be embraced and come forward, using sport and physical activity as sites for empowerment, inclusivity, and a means for achieving inclusion and social justice.

REFERENCES

Ajzen, I. (1991). The theory of planned behavior. *Organizational Behavior and Human Decision Processes, 50,* 179–211.

American Psychological Association. (2003). Guidelines on multicultural education, training, research, practice and organizational change for psychologists. *American Psychologist, 58,* 377–402.

Anderson, A., Knowles, Z., & Gilbourne, D. (2004). Reflective practice for sport psychologists: Concepts, models, practical implications, and thoughts on dissemination. *The Sport Psychologist, 18,* 188–203.

Anderson, M. B. (1993). Questionable sensitivity: A comment on Lee and Rotella. *The Sport Psychologist, 7,* 1–3.

Appleby, K. M., & Fisher, L. A. (2009). Running in and out of motherhood: Elite distance runners' experiences of returning to competition after pregnancy. *Women in Sport and Physical Activity Journal, 18,* 3–17.

Bandura, A. (1989). Human agency in social cognitive theory. *American Psychologist, 44,* 159–172.

Bellows-Riecken, K., & Rhodes, R. E. (2008). The birth of inactivity? A review of physical activity and parenthood. *Preventive Medicine, 46,* 99–110.

Blodgett, A., Schinke, R. J., Smith, B., Peltier, D., & Pheasant, C. (2011). Exploring vignettes as a narrative strategy for co-producing the research voices of Aboriginal Community. *Qualitative Inquiry, 17,* 522–533.

Busanich, R., McGannon, K. R., & Schinke, R. J. (2012). Expanding understandings of the body, food and exercise relationship in distance runners: A narrative approach. *Psychology of Sport and Exercise, 13,* 582–590.

Butryn, T. M. (2002). Critically examining white racial identity and privilege in sport psychology consulting. *The Sport Psychologist 16,* 316–336.

Chiu, C. Y., & Hong, Y. Y. (2005). Cultural competence: Dynamic processes. In A. J. Elliot & C. S. Dweck (Eds.), *Handbook of competence and motivation* (pp. 489–505). New York, NY: Guilford Press.

Choi, P., Henshaw, C., Baker, S., & Tree, J. (2005). Supermum, superwife, supereverything: Performing femininity in the transition to motherhood. *Journal of Reproductive and Infant Psychology, 23,* 167–180.

Currie, J. (2004). Motherhood, stress and the exercise experience: Freedom or constraint? *Leisure Studies, 23,* 225–242.

Davies, B., & Harré, R. (1990). Positioning: The discursive production of selves. *Journal for the Theory of Social Behaviour, 20,* 43–63.

Dixon, J., & Wetherell, M. (2004). On discourse and dirty nappies: Gender, the division of household labour and the social psychology of distributive justice. *Theory and Psychology, 14,* 167–189.

Douglas, S. J., & Michaels, M. W. (2004). *The mommy myth: The idealization of motherhood and how it has undermined all women.* New York, NY: Free Press.

Dworkin, S. L., & Wachs, F. L. (2009). *Body panic: Gender, health and the selling of fitness.* New York, NY: New York University Press.

Fisher, L. A., Butryn, T. M., & Roper, E. A. (2003). Diversifying (and politicizing) sport psychology through cultural studies: A promising perspective. *The Sport Psychologist; 17,* 391–405.

Freeman, H. V. (2008). *A qualitative exploration of the experiences of mother-athletes training for and competing in the Olympic games* (Doctoral dissertation). Temple University, Philadelphia.

Gergen, K. J. (1994). *Realities and relationships: Soundings in social construction.* Cambridge, MA: Harvard University Press.

Gill, D. L., & Kamphoff, C. S. (2009). Cultural diversity in applied sport psychology. In R. J. Schinke & S. J. Hanrahan (Eds.), *Cultural sport psychology* (pp. 45–56). Champaign, IL: Human Kinetics.

Gilligan, C. (1982). *In a different voice.* Cambridge, MA: Harvard University Press.

Hamilton, K., & White, K. M. (2010). Understanding parental physical activity: Meanings, habits, and social role influence. *Psychology of Sport and Exercise, 11,* 275–285.

Haravon Collins, L. (2002). Working out the contradictions: Feminism and aerobics. *Journal of Sport and Social Issues, 26,* 85–109.

Harré, R., & Gillett, G. (1994). *The discursive mind*. Washington, DC: Sage Publications.

Johnston, D., & Swanson, D. (2003). Invisible mothers: A content analysis of motherhood ideologies and myths in magazines. *Sex Roles, 49*, 21–33.

Krane, V., Choi, P. Y. L., Baird, S. M., Aimar, C. M., & Kauer, K. J. (2004). Living the paradox: Female athletes negotiate femininity and muscularity. *Sex Roles, 50*, 315–329.

Krane, V., Stiles-Shipley, J., Waldron, J., & Michaelnok, J. (2001a). Relationships among body satisfaction, social physique anxiety, and eating behaviors in female athletes and exercisers. *Journal of Sport Behavior, 24*, 247–264.

Krane, V., Waldron, J., Michaelnok, J., & Stiles-Shipley, J. (2001b). Body image concerns in female exercisers and athletes: A feminist cultural studies perspective. *Women in Sport and Physical Activity Journal, 10*, 17–34.

Kreuter, M. W., Lukwago, S. N., Bucholtz, D. C., Clark, E. M., & Sanders-Thompson, V. (2002). Achieving cultural appropriateness in health promotion programs. *Health Education and Behavior, 30*, 133–146.

Leberman, S., & Palmer, F. (2009). Motherhood, sport leadership and domain theory: Experiences from New Zealand. *Journal of Sport Management, 23*, 305–334.

Lewis, B., & Ridge, D. (2005). Mothers reframing physical activity: Family oriented politicism, transgression and contested expertise in Australia. *Social Science and Medicine, 60*, 2295–2306.

Maguire, J., & Mansfield, L. (1998). "No-body's perfect": Women, aerobics, and the body beautiful. *Sociology of Sport Journal, 15*, 109–137.

Markula, P. (1995). Firm but shapely, fit but sexy, strong but thin: The post-modern aerobicizing female bodies. *Sociology of Sport Journal, 12*, 424–453.

Markula, P. (2001). Beyond the perfect body: Women's body image distortion in fitness magazine discourse. *Journal of sport and social issues, 25*(2), 158–179.

Markula, P. (2003). Post-modern aerobics: Contradiction and resistance. In A. Bolin & J. Granskog (Eds.), *Athletic intruders: Ethnographic research on women, culture and exercise* (pp. 53–78). Albany: State University of New York Press.

Martens, M. P., Mobley, M., & Zizzi, S. J. (2000). Multicultural training in applied sport psychology. *The Sport Psychologist* 14, 81–97.

McGannon, K. R. (2012). Am "I" a work of art(?): Understanding exercise and the self through critical self-awareness and aesthetic self-stylization. *Athletic Insight, 4*, 79–95.

McGannon, K. R., & Busanich, R. (2010). Rethinking subjectivity in sport and exercise psychology: A feminist post-structuralist perspective on women's embodied physical activity. In T. Ryba, R. J. Schinke, & G. Tenenbaum (Eds.), *The cultural turn in sport psychology* (pp. 203–229). Morgantown, WV: Fitness Information Technology.

McGannon, K. R., & Busanich, R. (2016). Athletes and motherhood. In R. J. Schinke, K. R. McGannon, & B. Smith (Eds.), *Routledge international handbook of sport psychology* (pp. 286–295). London: Routledge.

McGannon, K. R., Curtin, K., Schinke, R. J., & Schweinbenz, A. N. (2012). (De)Constructing Paula Radcliffe: Exploring media representations of elite athletes, pregnancy and motherhood through cultural sport psychology. *Psychology of Sport and Exercise, 13*, 820–829.

McGannon, K. R., Gonsalves, C. A., Schinke, R. J., & Busanich, R. (2015). Negotiating motherhood and athletic identity: A qualitative analysis of Olympic athlete mother representations in media narratives. *Psychology of Sport and Exercise, 20*, 51–59.

McGannon, K. R., & Johnson, C. R. (2009). Strategies for reflective sport psychology research. In R. J. Schinke & S. J. Hanrahan (Eds.), *Cultural sport psychology* (pp. 57–78). Champaign, IL: Human Kinetics.

McGannon, K. R., Johnson, C. R., & Spence, J. C. (2011). I am (not) BIG . . . it's the pictures that got small: Examining cultural and personal exercise narratives and the fear of fat. In P. Markula & E. Kennedy (Eds.), *Women and exercise: The body, health and consumerism* (pp. 101–120). London: Routledge.

McGannon, K. R., & Mauws, M. K. (2000). Discursive psychology: An alternative approach for studying adherence to exercise and physical activity. *Quest, 52*, 148–165.

McGannon, K. R., & Schinke, R. J. (2013). "My first choice is to work out at work; then I don't feel bad about my kids": A discursive psychological analysis of motherhood and physical activity participation. *Psychology of Sport and Exercise, 14*, 179–188.

McGannon, K. R., Schinke, R. J., & Busanich, R. (2014). Cultural sport psychology: Considerations for enhancing cultural competence of practitioners. In L. S. Tashman & G. Cremades (Eds.), *Becoming a sport, exercise, and performance psychology professional: International perspectives* (pp. 135–142). London: Routledge.

McGannon, K. R., & Smith, B. (2015). Centralizing culture in cultural sport psychology research: The potential of narrative inquiry and discursive psychology. *Psychology of Sport and Exercise, 17*, 79–87.

McGannon, K. R., & Spence, J. C. (2010). Speaking of the self and physical activity participation: What discursive psychology can tell us about an old problem. *Qualitative Research in Sport and Exercise, 2*, 17–38.

McGannon, K. R., & Spence, J. C. (2012). Exploring news media representations of women's exercise and subjectivity through critical discourse analysis. *Qualitative Research in Sport, Exercise and Health, 4*, 32–50.

McIntyre, C. A., & Rhodes, R. E. (2009). Correlates of leisure-time physical activity during transitions to motherhood. *Women and Health, 49*, 66–83.

Miller, Y. D., & Brown, W. J. (2005). Determinants of active leisure for women with young children— an "ethic of care" prevails. *Leisure Sciences, 27*, 405–420.

Mutrie, N., & Choi, P. (2000). Is "fit" a feminist issue? Dilemmas for exercise psychology. *Feminism and Psychology, 10*, 544–551.

Palmer, F. R., & Leberman, S. I. (2009). Elite athletes as mothers: Managing multiple sport identities. *Sport Management Review, 12*, 241–254. doi:10.1016/j.smr.2009.03.001

Parham, W. D. (2005). Raising the bar: Developing an understanding of athletes from racially, culturally and ethnically diverse backgrounds. In M. B. Anderson (Ed.), *Sport psychology in practice* (pp. 201–215). Champaign, IL: Human Kinetics.

Petrassi, D. (2012). "For me, the children come first": A discursive psychological analysis of how mothers construct fathers' roles in childrearing and childcare. *Feminism & Psychology, 22*, 518–527.

Resnicow, K., Jackson, A., Braithwaite, R., DiIorio, C., Blisset, D., Rahotep, S., & Periasamy, P. (2002). Healthy body/health spirit: A church based nutrition and physical activity intervention. *Health Education Research, 17*, 562–573.

Ryba, T. V., & Schinke, R. J. (2009). Methodology as a ritualized eurocentrism: Introduction to the special issue. *International Journal of Sport and Exercise Psychology, 7*, 263–274.

Ryba, T. V., Schinke, R. J., & Tenenbaum, G. (Eds.). (2010). *The cultural turn in sport and exercise psychology*. WV: Fitness Information Technology.

Ryba, T. V., Stambulova, N., Si, G., & Schinke, R. J. (2013). ISSP position stand: Culturally competent research and practice in sport and exercise psychology. *International Journal of Sport and Exercise Psychology, 11*, 123–142.

Ryba, T. V., & Wright, H. K. (2005). From mental game to cultural praxis: A cultural studies model's implications for the future of sport psychology. *Quest, 57*(2), 192–212.

Schinke, R. J., & Hanrahan, S. J. (Eds.). (2009). *Cultural sport psychology*. Champaign, IL: Human Kinetics.

Schinke, R. J., Hanrahan, S. J., Eys, M. A., Blodgett, A., Peltier, D., Ritchie, S., et al. (2008). The development of cross-cultural relations with a Canadian Aboriginal community through sport research. *Quest, 60*, 357–369.

Schinke, R. J., McGannon, K. R., Battochio, R. C., & Wells, G. (2013). Acculturation in elite sport: A thematic analysis of immigrant athletes and coaches. *Journal of Sports Sciences, 15*, 1676–1686.

Schinke, R. J., McGannon, K. R., Parham, W. D., & Lane, A. (2012). Toward cultural praxis: Strategies for self-reflexive sport psychology practice. *Quest, 64*, 34–46.

Schinke, R. J., & Moore, Z. (2011). Culturally informed sport psychology: An introduction to the special issue. *Journal of Clinical Sport Psychology, 5*, 283–294.

Selig, S., Tropiano, E., & Greene-Moton, E. (2006). Teaching cultural competence to reduce health disparities. *Health Promotion Practice, 7*, 247S–255S.

Smith, B. (2010). Narrative inquiry: Ongoing conversations and questions for sport and exercise psychology research. *International Review of Sport and Exercise Psychology, 3*, 87–107.

Smith, B. (2013). Disability, sport, and men's narratives of health: A qualitative study. *Health Psychology, 32*, 110–119.

Smith, B., & Sparkes, A. C. (2008) Contrasting perspectives on narrating selves and identities: An invitation to dialogue. *Qualitative Research, 8*, 5–35.

Sparkes, A., & Smith, B. (2005). When narratives matter. *Medical Humanities, 31*, 81–88.

Spowart, L., Burrows, L., & Shaw, S. (2010). I just eat, sleep and dream of surfing: When surfing meets motherhood. *Sport in Society, 13*, 1186–1203.

Sue, S. (2006). Cultural competency: From philosophy to research and practice. *Journal of Community Psychology, 34*, 237–245.

Thomsson, H. (1999). Yes, I used to exercise, but . . . a feminist study of exercise in the life of Swedish women. *Journal of Leisure Research, 31*, 35–56.

Weedon, C. (1997). *Feminist practice and poststructuralist theory* (2nd ed.). Oxford: Blackwell.

15 Gender
Important Terms and Concepts

Emily A. Roper

It is initially important to outline terms central to the study of gender. Of primary importance is the distinction between sex and gender. According to the American Psychological Association (APA, 2011), sex refers to the biological distinction between males and females, whereas gender refers to socially constructed roles, behaviors, activities, and attributes. Gender identity refers to the degree to which a person sees themself as masculine or feminine given society's definition of what it means to be a man or woman. Society decides what being male or female means, with males generally defining themselves as masculine and females defining themselves as feminine.

Gender socialization is the process by which people learn to behave in a certain way, as dictated by societal beliefs, values, attitudes, and norms. These gender norms are learned through a variety of socializing agents, including parents and caregivers, mass media, educators, school curriculum, extracurricular activities, religion, and peers. Early research has indicated that by age two children are beginning to understand the difference between being a boy and being a girl, and by five years of age are already forming rigid gender stereotypes and gender norms (Pidgeon, 1994). Gender is often described as a "performance" or a set of expectations projected onto and demanded of an individual (Butler, 1990). This "performance" is dictated by societal attitudes and gender norms associated with gender-appropriate behavior and appearance.

Masculinity and femininity are constructed in relationship to each other and placed on contrasting poles on the gender continuum. In Western culture, hegemonic masculinity, the culturally normative ideal of male behavior, is commonly associated with aggression, dominance, competitiveness, strength, and (hyper)heterosexuality (Anderson, 2008). By demonstrating physical, social, and psychological attributes associated with hegemonic masculinity, men gain status in most male groups (Anderson, 2008). According to Knight and Giuliano (2003), men who participate in activities that are considered "non-masculine" by Western societal standards are often subject to harassment, ridicule, and the homosexual label.

Hegemonic femininity is defined as the socially privileged form of femininity (Krane, 2001). In contrast to hegemonic masculinity, the characteristics of hegemonic femininity include being passive, emotional, dependent, gentle, and compassionate (Krane, 2001). Whereas males gain status in many physical pursuits, physically active females must attempt to balance "masculine" athleticism/physicality with "feminine" appearance in order to conform to traditional notions of femininity (Krane, 2001).

GENDER AND EXERCISE

Studying gender and its role in exercise is important for a number of reasons. It is of primary importance due to the multitude of health benefits associated with regular exercise. Exercise plays an essential role in the maintenance of an overall healthy well-being by lowering cholesterol levels; reducing the incidence of heart disease, diabetes, and some cancers; and improving body image, self-esteem, and overall mental well-being (U.S. Department of Health and Human Services, 2008).

Despite the benefits of engaging in regular exercise, research has consistently found differences in exercise behaviors among males and females. Fewer females take part in regular exercise programs compared to males. Garcia, Broda, Frenn, Coviak, Pender, and Ronis (1995) examined gender and developmental differences in exercise-related beliefs and exercise behaviors of 286 racially diverse youth. Compared to males, females reported less prior and current exercise, lower self-esteem, poorer health status, and lower exercise self-schema. Among college students, female students have been found to engage in less exercise/physical activity than male students (Buckworth & Nigg, 2004). While females tend to engage in less physical activity than males, physical inactivity is also a serious problem for males. According to the 2000 National College Health Assessment, 57% of male and 61% of female college students reported that they had not engaged in vigorous or moderate exercise at least three times during the previous week. Also, for adolescent and early adult males, despite being more physically active and engaging in more vigorous physical activity/exercise than females, males tend to engage in more sedentary behaviors (e.g., video games, watching television) than females (Buckworth & Nigg, 2004).

Sedentarism has also been found to be high among racial and ethnic minority women. The low levels of physical activity/exercise have been shown to begin as early as eight years of age among Black and Hispanic girls (Gletsu & Tovin, 2010). The rates of inactivity among Black and Hispanic females are even more pronounced during the college years (Suminski, Petosa, Utter, & Zhang, 2002). As a result, Black and Hispanic females are at an increased risk for development of chronic illnesses, such as cardiovascular disease, cancer, and diabetes, all of which are associated with a sedentary lifestyle (D'Alonzo & Fischetti, 2008).

THE IDEAL (GENDERED) BODY

Throughout history, the ideal feminine and masculine body, each defined and evaluated differently, has varied to reflect the aesthetic standard of the period. Current masculine body ideals prescribe strength and muscularity, while the feminine (usually White) ideal emphasizes thinness (Choi, 2000). The focus for males has been "bulking up" and for White females "slimming down" (LaCaille et al., 2011). Such standards, reinforced by the mass media and other socializing agents, influence the ways in which males and females perceive and use their bodies (Kwan & Trautner, 2009).

While the dominant ideal for White females has historically emphasized thinness, today's female body has become a site of constant self-scrutiny. The quest for the ideal body has become an ongoing and often never-ending journey. The ideal feminine body requires continuous improvement, as the ideal can never be reached completely (Markula, 1995). As Markula explained, "now it is not enough to eliminate the excess, soft fat from our bodies; we are also required to achieve an athletic, tight look as well" (p. 426). For today's White woman, her "beautiful body is not just thin; it is firm, well-toned and sexy" (Mutrie & Choi, 2000, p. 545). In an attempt to achieve this unobtainable feminine ideal, many women become dissatisfied with their body and develop a preoccupation with their body fat, size, and shape (Cash & Pruzinsky, 2002; McAllister & Caltabiano, 1994). This dissatisfaction has the potential to lead to unhealthy eating behaviors, a negative relationship with exercise, and negative affective states (Striegel-Moore, McAvay, & Rodin, 1986). Markula (1995) described the feminine body ideal as a confusing contradiction that women are expected to understand and work toward—"firm but shapely, fit but sexy, strong but thin" (p. 424). The female ideal body (i.e., being thin) is also seen by many as being synonymous with health. As a result, exercise becomes a tool with which to achieve this "healthy" ideal body (Mutrie & Choi, 2000). As Mutrie and Choi (2000) argued, exercise has become "the latest commodity in the highly commercialized beauty culture" (p. 545).

D'Alonzo and Fischetti (2008) found that the Hispanic and Black women viewed their bodies as distinctly different from White women. While the Hispanic and African American women in their study conceptualized exercise as a means to enhance their appearance, both groups did acknowledge a distinct difference from the ideal White female body ideal. Some research has suggested that the desire to be thin is not viewed as attractive or healthy among Black women (Bledman, 2011). However, research has also suggested that Black women feel pressure to conform to "White standards" of beauty and feel uncomfortable comparing their bodies to White women. This finding is in contrast to Frisby's (2004) findings which suggested that Black women were not influenced by idealized images of White women. D'Alonzo and Fischetti (2008) suggested that exercise programs should acknowledge these potential differences when designing programs for racially and ethnically diverse groups of women, and more research is needed to understand racial and ethnic differences among women.

While women's concerns have focused on being too large, men have been found to be preoccupied with areas of their body being too small. Males associate their attractiveness with increased muscle definition and are concerned about body shape and increasing their muscle mass (Pope, Philips, & Olivardia, 2000). Drummond and Drummond (2010) found that 5- to 12-year-old boys already believed that a man should be highly muscular and strong. Research suggests that males are becoming as dependent on image as females, and there is greater social acceptance for males to express concern and dislike of their bodies and overall appearance (Loland, 2000). Research shows that college men are reporting greater levels of body dissatisfaction, which is resulting in more men engaging in practices to improve their appearance (Garner, 1997; Loland, 2000). Furthermore, because men are socialized not to discuss their body image concerns, it is possible that their silence may lead to feelings of distress, isolation, depression, and anxiety.

EXERCISE AS GENDERED ACTIVITY

The divergent gendered body ideals for women and men demand divergent exercise regiments. In 1992, Leary suggested that an individual's selection of exercise type may be influenced by self-presentational concerns; individuals will be reluctant to participate in activities that they think will lead to negative stereotypes. Gender stereotypes in particular may influence the form of exercise that males and females select; men may be reluctant to participate in aerobics, yoga, or dance for fear of being labeled feminine or gay, and women may not lift weights or participate in boxing classes for fear of being labeled unfeminine (Leary, 1992; Salvatore & Marecek, 2010). Running, jogging, and cycling are often considered gender-neutral forms of exercise (Drouin, Varga, & Gammage, 2008).

Activities that are gender coded as feminine are those that tend to emphasize physical appearance and socially accepted standards of beauty, whereas masculine activities are those that are associated with power, strength, and aggression (Drouin, Varga, & Gammage, 2008). For example, Salvatore and Marecek (2010) found that female members of a fitness facility identified the StairMaster as a primarily female exercise and the bench press as male, and *not* female exercise. Drummond and Drummond (2010) found that young boys recognized the gendered nature of exercise, indicating that activities emphasizing strength and toughness were "more for males than females" (p. 497). Hispanic women, particularly those born outside the United States, were found to define vigorous exercise as "unfeminine" and were more likely to adhere to culturally constructed "rules" about what physical activities are appropriate for women and girls (D'Alonzo & Fischetti, 2008).

Some researchers have described the gym as a sex-segregated environment. Nast and Pile (1998) argued that the segregated masculine and feminine space of the gym effects the time of day women go to the gym and the space they occupy or move through. Dworkin (2003) and Ostgaard (2006) both found that the women in their research reported feeling "out of place" and "intimidated" in co-ed fitness facilities because they were dominated by men.

Weight lifting is one form of exercise that is highly gendered (Salvatore & Marecek, 2010). Due to the fear of "getting big" or looking too muscular, often considered an undesirable outcome of weight lifting for women, many women neglect lifting weights altogether (Angier, 1999). As Dworkin (2003) stated, "the proportion of men to women in the weight room at any given time is approximately eighty/twenty or ninety/ten" (p. 132). Salvatore and Marecek (2010) describe a self-perpetuating cycle that occurs within the weight training area of a gym: "first, women may avoid gyms (or weight training areas of gyms) because they see them as masculine spaces; the absence of women reaffirms the gender coding of those spaces and thus, serves to perpetuate women's avoidance of them" (p. 565). In addition to the societal stigma attached to weight training, Dworkin (2003) addressed additional factors influencing why women neglect weight training:

> The territory is also intimidating because of the knowledge gap . . . those who enter the weight room with a lack of knowledge are more likely to be women . . . women must therefore "catch-up" in the space upon entering—find out the "how-tos" of the equipment, formal and informal rules, etc. Some of the gap may be due to women having less encouragement to use their body physically in childhood.
>
> (p. 140)

Such neglect of weight training has significant health consequences for women, as lifting weights has physical and mental benefits specific to women. Not only do well-toned muscles contribute to increased metabolism, cushion the body from the effects of illness, and slow the normal process of aging, but for women, lifting weights is also known to help to prevent or forestall osteoporosis (Layne & Nelson, 1999), which women are especially prone to post-menopause. Psychologically, weight lifting has also been found to diminish body dissatisfaction and increase body satisfaction among women (Williams & Cash, 2001). Despite the multitude of benefits associated with weight lifting, women are underrepresented among users who lift weights (Gruber, 2007). Some have suggested that due to changing attitudes and ideals regarding women's bodies, weight training may be becoming more acceptable, as ideals move from being thin to including *some* muscle tone and definition (Gruber, 2007). However, this shift is not due to a desire among females to reap the health benefits of weight training, but rather to sculpt the body into the ever-changing ideal (Mutrie & Choi, 2000).

Aerobics, often defined as a "feminine domain" (Loland, 2000), is one space that has garnered considerable attention among sociocultural scholars, particularly those who study gender. As Loland indicated, "the aerobic context is not just a place for exercise, it is a place where particular gender identities are constructed, it is a gendered space" (p. 115). During the 1970s and 1980s, women were being encouraged to engage in regular physical activity. Aerobics became one of the primary forms of movement marketed to women at that time and continues to maintain its popularity (Mutrie & Choi, 2000; Schroeder & Friesen, 2008). In addition to a predominately female population, the majority of aerobics instructors are also female (Collins, 2002). In 1970, Kenneth Cooper, the father of the aerobics running program, suggested that aerobics provides women with a "double payoff" in that it not only improves their appearance, but also gives them "fitness and health as fringe benefits" (p. 134).

It is clear in Cooper's statement that the primary focus was on women's physical appearance, with the health and fitness benefits being secondary. While group exercise has evolved, aerobics is still today marketed and presented as a feminine domain (Schroeder & Friesen, 2008).

As a way to counter some of the negative aspects associated with co-ed fitness facilities, women's-only fitness facilities began to emerge and have continued to grow in popularity in the United States. To that end, Ostgaard (2006) posed the question: "are they [women's-only fitness facilities] truly empowering and supportive to women or do they replicate hegemonically-defined masculinity and femininity seen in male-dominated gyms?" (p. 9). Grounded in feminist cultural studies and feminist geography, Ostgaard conducted an ethnography examining the experiences and perceptions of members and staff of a women's-only gym, as well the role of social space in creating these experiences. While the women's-only space was empowering to the women, the influence of hegemonic masculinity and femininity were still evident. The women in Ostgaard's study "could not escape the influence of hegemonically-defined femininity, which influenced how the women viewed their bodies as well as what they thought of as the ideal feminine form" (p. 70–71). As such, Ostgaard explained the women's-only facility as a contested space.

> On the one hand, the women felt empowered to exercise and move their bodies because of the lack of an overt male gaze and traditional expectations of femininity. On the other hand, they also expressed a certain degree of apprehension about exercising and their bodies due to the internalization of hegemonically defined femininity. The result was that The Gym [women's-only facility] was a contested space.
>
> (p. 78)

In response to some female students, including female students from certain faith groups, several US colleges have implemented women-only exercise time at their university fitness facilities (Supiano, 2008). The request for a women-only time was spearheaded by the desire to decrease anxiety and increase women's level of comfort in the male-defined gym space. Dunlop and Beauchamp (2011) examined preferences for exercising in gender-segregated and gender-integrated groups among male and female adult exercisers. Their findings revealed a greater preference for gender-segregated groups rather than gender-integrated ones among both males and females. Furthermore, D'Alonzo and Fischetti (2008) have suggested that Hispanic and African American women preferred to exercise in gender-segregated places where there were women that looked like them, both in terms of body shape/size and race/ethnicity.

Being described as an "exerciser" has also been found to have a positive effect on the impressions that others form of a person. Drouin, Varga, and Gammage (2008) examined if the positive exerciser stereotype exists for men and women when participating in gender-stereotyped activities and in opposite gender-stereotyped activities. Their findings revealed that the positive exerciser stereotype was maintained for those engaged in gender-neutral or gender-appropriate activities. The researchers also found that exercisers engaged in opposite gender-stereotyped activities were favorably evaluated, suggesting that individuals may not be influenced by gender stereotypes. Additional research is needed to examine the effect of gender on the exerciser stereotype.

FEMINIST PERSPECTIVES ON EXERCISE

Feminism places women's and girls' experiences and knowledge at the center of analysis. Feminist research, grounded in critical theory, recognizes the oppressed and marginalized status of women and girls and seeks to understand their varied experiences. The aim of feminist research is to (a) expose the structures and conditions that contribute to the present situation for women and girls, (b) enlighten the community to the factors that generate this phenomenon, (c) propose ways that can help alleviate the problem, (d) empower women and give them a voice to speak about social life from their perspective, and (e) ultimately contribute toward social change and reconstruction (Sarantakos, 2005). While the female body has been central to feminism, feminists have not always paid attention to active female bodies, "nor have they always seen the relevance of physicality, or empowerment through physical activity, to feminist politics" (Hall, 1996, p. 50). Much of the focus on fitness among feminists has focused on the ways in which "fitness discourses, spaces, and practices are means of 'disciplining' bodies seen as unruly and of (re)producing hegemonic and heteronormative regimes" (Scott-Dixon, 2008, p. 23).

Within sport studies, a significant amount of feminist attention has focused on aerobics. Mutrie and Choi (2000) argued that aerobics "has become beauty-related exercise" that both "empowers and enslaves [women]" (p. 544). The organization and purpose of aerobics is, as Loland (2000) indicated, set up to appeal to "people's dissatisfaction with, and concern for, bodily appearance" (p. 113). Even the names of classes, Body Sculpting and Body Shaping, emphasize spot reduction of women's "problem areas" (e.g., thighs, stomach), suggesting that women's "natural" bodies and shape are somehow unacceptable or not good enough. As Loland (2000) stated, "aerobicizers work on parts of their body to improve their look, more than to have some quality time with themselves as persons" (p. 120). Women are led to believe that through spot reduction exercises, their "problem areas" will no longer be problematic, according to societal definitions of the feminine body ideal. However, physiological evidence indicates that such exercises do very little to reduce the fat in a specific area, working the underlying group of muscles instead (Mutrie & Choi, 2000). Certainly involvement in aerobics can produce physical and psychological health benefits, but the exploitation of women by the fitness industry is worthy of analysis and discussion. To that extent, as Mutrie and Choi (2000) suggested, "women are being exploited to attend such classes on a false premise and this makes it an issue for feminists" (p. 546).

At the center of the debate surrounding aerobics is whether it is/can be an empowering form of exercise for women. Many critics argue that women, due to societal pressures, use aerobics primarily as a means to achieve the "ideal" body rather than to empower and strengthen their bodies (Choi & Mutrie, 1997; Loland, 2000). Markula (1995) found that some women involved in aerobics indicated being strong was more important than looking strong. The women interviewed in her study questioned the body ideal, indicating that they "find the whole process ridiculous" (p. 450). Despite their awareness, the participants in Markula's study did not actively resist the patriarchal body ideal or challenge the gendered body norms inherent within aerobics. Loland examined how male and female aerobics participants use and experience their bodies. All of the participants used aerobics to improve their bodily appearance and work toward the body ideals for women and men, respectively. The female participants used aerobics as a way in which to reduce their body weight, while the male participants used it as a method to increase their muscle size. D'Abundo (2007) examined the health messages conveyed by aerobics instructors and found an overemphasis on physical health (i.e., appearance, weight loss). As a result, the other dimensions of health and wellness were rarely addressed. D'Abundo discussed the potential for aerobics to become a site of empowerment and improved health and wellness, but argued that to do so, modifications in the traditional class were necessary. Even the design of the aerobics studio emphasizes objectification of the predominately female occupants of the room. The wall-to-wall mirrors promote constant scrutiny of the room's occupants, and glass partitions contribute to a "culture of display" by allowing club members to view the classroom and its occupants (Loland, 2000, p. 121). Collins (2002) examined the extent to which women can exert agency within the gendered constraints of aerobics. Through interviews with 10 self-identified feminist women who participate in aerobics, Collins found that the participants used a variety of strategies to downplay the oppressive aspects and enhance their personal empowerment and enjoyment in aerobics. Specifically, the participants would distance themselves from the components that did not fit with their feminist ideology. For example, several of the participants would tune out the sexist lyrics in much of the music played in their aerobics classes, not wear the prescribed clothing by the aerobics industry, or not follow the instructor's chorography.

MOTIVATIONS TO EXERCISE AND GENDER

Motivation has been found to be one of the most important and consistent predictors of exercise (Guerin, Bales, Sweet, & Fortier, 2012). Research indicates that males and females differ with regard to their motivation toward exercise (Egli, Bland, Melton, & Czech, 2011; Guerin et al., 2012).

Evaluation concerns refer to people's interest in what others think of them. Such concerns have been found to affect how a person presents themself (Baumeister & Leary, 1995). Generally, people want to make a desirable impression on others. While both males and females use exercise as a way in which to improve their bodily appearance (Loland, 2000), females have been found to experience stronger social evaluation concerns than males. Egli, Bland, Melton, and Czech (2011) found that males tend to be motivated by intrinsic factors and females by extrinsic factors. For females, the external desirable impression they seek is highly influenced by the cultural ideals concerning the female body (Krane et al., 2002). To be accepted and perceived positively, females are socialized to believe they must present a body that is in line with the cultural feminine ideal. Research suggests that females are motivated to exercise in order to acquire the ideal female body, exercising to reduce their weight and body fat and increase their muscle tone (Gill & Overdorf, 1994; Teregerson & King, 2002). This motivation is often rooted in dissatisfaction and/or disapproval of their current bodily appearance. Teregerson and King (2002) found that adolescent females in their study were motivated to exercise in order to "lose weight" and "stay in shape," whereas the adolescent males were motivated to "become strong" and "stay in shape." Kilpatrick, Hebert, and Bartholomew (2005) found that college-age men are more highly motivated by performance and ego-related factors, including challenge, endurance, competition, and strength. Older males have also been found to be motivated to exercise for the "challenging nature of exercise," whereas older females report "health concerns" as a primary reason to exercise (Newson & Kemps, 2007, p. 480). Research suggests that exercisers who are motivated by social pressures or external standards have been found less likely to develop long-term motivational patterns (Wilson & Rodgers, 2002).

Support from others has been found to influence exercise behavior through encouragement and role modeling (Darlow & Xu, 2011). Walcott-McQuigg and Prohaska (2001) found that having a network of friends and family members was important for the initiation and maintenance of an exercise program. As females tend to connect with their social networks more than males, social support (e.g., partner/spouse, family, friends) has been noted as a significant source of motivation for females. Teregerson and King (2002) found that adolescent females felt more strongly than adolescent males that encouragement from friends was an important motivator for physical activity. As Teregerson and King (2002) stated, "one of the strongest predictors for physical activity among girls is having a best friend who is physically active" (p. 377). As such, a "buddy system" in which adolescents monitor each other's progress and provide support and motivations for physical activity may be helpful for females. Social support has been found to be especially important for minority females (D'Alonzo &

Fischetti, 2008). D'Alonzo and Fischetti (2008) found that social support was a primary factor related to why African American and Hispanic women initiated and maintained a regular exercise program.

Exposure to physically active roles models has also been found beneficial for both males and females (Teregerson & King, 2002) and may serve as a way in which to improve activity levels (Teregerson & King, 2002). Males receive widespread encouragement and support about being physically active across the lifespan. Females, due to the stereotypes and barriers associated with femininity and physical activity, are exposed to role models who are less physically active (Roper & Clifton, 2013). Physically active female role models serve as important sources of inspiration and encouragement and have the potential to debunk restrictive stereotypes often associated with female physicality. Active female role models are especially important during adolescence, a time with many transitions and developmental changes and a marked drop in physical activity and sport among females (Kimm et al., 2002).

Research has addressed the influence of cultural differences on exercise motives. D'Alonzo and Fischetti (2008) addressed the role musical preferences play in the motivations to attend exercise classes among Hispanic and African American women. As a participant in D'Alonzo and Fischetti's (2008) study noted, "I don't want to go into a class and hear the Dave Matthews Band. I'd like to hear rap music or even a mix of music" (179). In addition, it was noted that the forms of exercise and movement women may prefer may differ across cultures. For example, D'Alonzo and Fischetti (2008) found that dancing was a preferred form of exercise among Hispanic women in their study.

While external goals have been identified as a prevalent motive for exercise among females, an additional motivator to exercise among girls is enjoyment and meeting challenges (Gillison, Sebire, & Stanage, 2012). Exercise has been found to provide a context for females to obtain direct competence feedback relating to their skills and fitness, as well as a platform to experience success at meeting challenges (Gillison, Sebire, & Stanage, 2012). In a study assessing approximately 2,000 adolescent White and Black girls, Dishman et al. (2005) found that girls were more motivated to exercise for enjoyment rather than for weight loss when given (a) gender-separate activities, (b) gender-separate sports instruction, (c) an expanded choice of activities that included more "female-favored activities" (e.g., tennis, aerobics); (d) when competition was deemphasized; and (e) when girls worked in smaller groups. While these findings are promising and provide helpful information about how to develop programs for some females, it is also important to consider that catering to "female-favored activities" and "de-emphasizing competition" play into the societal stereotypes associated with what females enjoy and are capable of doing physically. Such a program, while important, assumes that males and females have different ways in which they approach physical activity, rather than working to open up all forms of movement/exercise to all.

GENDERED BARRIERS TO EXERCISE

In order to increase physical activity levels, it is important to determine the barriers that individuals face for engaging in regular physical activity. Gender has been found to play a role in the nature and type of barriers faced by an individual.

Women are more likely than men to report barriers to exercise (The Tucker Center, 2007). Girls and women tend to be responsible for more domestic responsibilities (e.g., taking care of children/siblings, elderly, housework or chores, expectation for girls to be at home) even if they also work outside of the home. These responsibilities leave little time for exercise and may even be perceived as "less important" than their other responsibilities (The Tucker Center, 2007). African American and Hispanic women identify that they are the main caretakers, which provides further evidence for women's perceiving greater barriers to exercise (Gletsu & Tovin, 2010). As Gletsu and Tovin stated, "these women felt tremendous responsibility for their families and communities before themselves" (p. 406). Earlier research (Young, He, Harris, & Mabry, 2002) has also found that becoming a mother results in a dramatic drop in exercise among urban African American women. Consequently, lack of childcare clearly serves as a significant barrier for women's participation in exercise.

The cost of and accessibility to safe, quality fitness facilities/spaces is an additional barrier for girls and women. Researchers have found that women may limit their leisure and exercise patterns due to feelings of fear and concerns for safety (Roper, 2008; Whyte & Shaw, 1994). Gender-related feelings of objectification, vulnerability, and fear limit women's participation. This fear has been found to be greater when women participate in outdoor, solitary activities (e.g., running, hiking, cycling) and is especially heightened in unpopulated and concealed natural settings (e.g., trails, wooded areas). Such environments are commonly identified as spaces where women are more susceptible to attacks and, therefore, are often perceived as unsafe for women. Researchers have also found that women's experiences may be hindered as a result of concerns for safety (Roper, 2008); due to their feelings of fear and concerns for safety while exercising outdoors, their level of enjoyment may be reduced. When asked "how would things be different if she had nothing to fear?," one female runner whom Burton Nelson (1991) interviewed indicated:

> I would run with abandon . . . certainly without fear. I'm very tight when I run. When somebody honks to get my attention, I tense inside . . . were I to feel perfectly safe, I wouldn't do that. I wouldn't avoid the bushes. All those precautionary things I wouldn't do; therefore I'd be far more relaxed.
>
> (p. 121)

Eyler and Vest (2002) found that women enjoy beautiful scenery and safe places to walk outdoors. However, street harassment, safety issues in neighborhoods, and unleashed dogs were noted as environmental characteristics that discouraged exercise in both rural and urban neighborhoods (Eyler & Vest, 2002; Roper, 2008). For female adolescents, Teregerson and King (2002) indicated that safe and accessible places to engage in physical activity outside of school are needed. Wesley and Gaarder (2004) found that women struggle with their appreciation of nature and their need to feel safe in this environment. As such, an ongoing negotiation exists for women as they attempt to balance choice and concerns related to their outdoor recreation.

Physical barriers such as having a low fitness level or lack of physical fitness literacy have also been found to limit women and girls' participation in regular physical activity. LaCaille et al. (2011) found that female college students indicated feeling intimidated by unfamiliar equipment and/or by working out with men. Newson and Kemps (2007) found that older adult females reported lack of exercise facilities and exercise-specific knowledge as factors that prevent them from exercising. O'Brien Cousins (2000) found that older women would limit their exercise/physical activity because of a perceived risk of harming themselves. While they were aware of the health benefits associated with regular exercise, they still held major concerns for their health and safety. As O'Brien Cousins (2000) explained,

> lack of youth sport opportunities for girls, the low social status given to women's physical activities, and the habitual and strong social commitment of women to their families mean that by later life most older women lack the confidence, encouragement, and even the discretionary time to allow them to participate without undue stress.
>
> (p. 290)

Just as evaluation concerns may motivate women and men to exercise, evaluation concerns also restrict and limit the activities and forms of exercise that they participate in. Evaluation concerns have been found to discourage women and men from participating in non-gender-appropriate activities due to fear of not fitting in with the socially accepted cultural norms of the ideal body (Salvatore & Marecek, 2010). When activities are eliminated from the "acceptable" list of activities because they do not fit the criteria for appropriate gender roles, males and females are prevented the opportunity to engage in a range of activities that have long-term health implications. As Drummond and Drummond (2010, p. 500) indicated,

> It could be argued that this hegemonic position that boys adopt with respect to their bodies and the types of activities in which they engage is ultimately problematic for them as they are given the limitations it creates surrounding alternative activity pursuits.

Research has suggested that hair management during exercise may serve to limit some African American women's exercise habits (Barnes, Goodrick, Pavlik, Markesino, Laws, & Taylor, 2007; Gletsu & Tovin, 2010). Barnes et al. (2007) found that African American women use a number of hairstyle management solutions, including adopting manageable hairstyles (e.g., ponytails, braids, afros), setting aside a necessary amount of time to style their hair after working out, or avoiding exercise if their hair had recently been styled. The role of hairstyle management and exercise adherence among African American women is an area in need of further examination.

VIGNETTE: CYNTHIA

In the following vignette, Cynthia provides us with an understanding of her experiences working in the fitness industry, and specifically working as a personal trainer with female clients. Cynthia is a 30-year-old, Caucasian female currently finishing her undergraduate degree in kinesiology. Upon graduation, she will pursue a master's degree in exercise science. She is also the mother of a four-year-old son. Cynthia has approximately 10 years of work experience in the fitness industry, mostly in commercial gym settings. She is presently in the process of developing her own personal training company to exclusively train female clients.

Cynthia is 6′2″. Her height is significant, as it was in many ways the impetus for pursuing a career in the fitness industry. When younger, Cynthia indicated that she struggled to fit in, often "not feeling like a girl" because of her height. She indicated that sport became the only space she felt "comfortable to be herself," developing a strong athletic identity. Despite feeling "at home" within the athletic setting, Cynthia continued to struggle with feeling "feminine." As Cynthia explained,

> When I was in high school I did not want to be tall . . . I didn't accept myself. After I had my child, a very womanly thing to do, I put on a little more make-up to make sure no one thought I was a man. I actually thought—when I have my child everyone will know I am a woman and I would look feminine. Now being older I have accepted being tall. I have used it to my advantage. It is a large part of my identity.

At the age of 24, Cynthia was hired to work the front desk at a commercial fitness center and eventually became a fitness trainer. While she had always been involved in athletics, this was her first exposure to the fitness industry. After several years, Cynthia worked her way up to fitness manager of a commercial fitness center. She was responsible for leading trainers (on average 7–10 male trainers), hiring and firing employees, making monthly sales quotas, and marketing to local clients. She described it as a demanding 60–70-hour work week. After several years, she made the decision to leave the commercial gym setting because she "was never going to be heard" as the only female manager. As she explained,

> It wasn't that they [males] discredited me, but that I had nothing in common with them. They were friends and would "hang out" together—talk business. I had a child and other responsibilities and didn't share the same interests. I also felt I had to be three times on top of things [compared to her male counterparts]. I had to always prove myself.

Still interested in working in the fitness industry, she committed to developing her own personal training business focused specifically on training female clients, describing herself as "a woman training women." Cynthia felt strongly about wanting to serve as an active role model for women and girls. She believes that the gym (and exercise/physical activity in general) can serve as a source of empowerment for women and girls and sees her role as helping to equip women and girls with the necessary knowledge to not only know how to use fitness equipment, but also feel comfortable within the fitness setting. When asked about why she chose to train women exclusively she indicated the following,

> I feel that there will always be too many factors that are involved with women training men, too many potential problems for females. Because of societal beliefs associated with men being typically stronger [than women], they [men] see women as not equal. In training, you pay money to follow someone, it just doesn't work well—they [men] don't take women seriously from my experience. Also, I've trained men, and it often leads to sexual innuendos. There are just too many factors. Now I train only women. I focus on the whole package—it's a lifestyle change. And I didn't want to be flirted with.

Cynthia described her clients as women and girls of varying fitness levels. The one commonality Cynthia noted was that most of her clients are motived by a specific number (e.g., dress size or goal weight) rather than overall health and wellness goals. Cynthia sees it as her role to reorient this way of thinking and encourage a healthy, holistic approach to health and wellness, indicating that her job goes well beyond physical training. As she explained,

> When women come in [to see me], I almost get a biography during their work-up at the beginning. I want to understand who they are. I have found that every woman has a number involved—"When I was 21, I was a size 4." Everyone wants to go back to when they weren't married, or when they were in high school; they say, "I want to lose this . . ." It's very emotional for them. They often equate weight loss with happiness or happier times.

From her experience working in the commercial fitness industry, Cynthia discussed some of her observations related to gender in the gym setting. Cynthia described the gym as a gender-segregated space, with specific areas gender marked for males (e.g., weight training) and areas for females (aerobics studio, cardiovascular equipment). She noted that while she has always felt comfortable occupying all areas of the gym, most women do not; most women are "intimidated" and "unsure of themselves" when they leave the female-dominated areas of the gym. Cynthia felt strongly that gender roles and societal expectations associated with how women are expected to look severely limit the health benefits women can attain. In addition, Cynthia suggested that a lack of knowledge, childcare and domestic responsibilities, and limited role models are some of the factors contributing to why women fail to engage in regular exercise.

As a trainer focusing exclusively on female clients, we spoke about the emergence of women's-only fitness settings, which she described as a "double-edged sword." Cynthia suggested that while these settings can be positive, many fail to provide women with the full gamut of fitness and training possibilities. As Cynthia suggested, "many of the women's-only spaces have broken machines, older machines. It becomes the area with the hand-me-downs of fitness equipment. They do not provide women with top of the line equipment or appropriate space because they [fitness industry] do not take them seriously as gym members."

Cynthia's experiences echo many of the findings presented within this chapter and also raise several important points regarding women's status and role in the fitness industry. While she has chosen to develop her own personal training company to work exclusively with female clients, it is important that women's voices are at the table within the commercial and corporate fitness world. Having women involved in the design and layout of fitness spaces and recreational areas, as well as represented at higher levels of management, is critical to ensuring that women feel comfortable, safe, and represented within these environments.

REFERENCES

American Psychological Association. (2011). *Definition of terms: Sex, gender, gender identity and sexual orientation*. Retrieved from www.apa.org/pi/lgbt/resources/sexuality-definitions.pdf

Anderson, E. (2008). "Being masculine is not about who you sleep with . . .:" Heterosexual athletes contesting masculinity and the one-time rule of homosexuality. *Sex Roles, 58*, 104–115.

Angier, N. (1999). *Woman: An intimate geography*. New York, NY: Anchor Books

Barnes, A. S., Goodrick, G. K., Pavlik, V., Markesino, J., Laws, D. Y., & Taylor, W. C. (2007). Weight loss maintenance in African–American women: Focus group results and questionnaire development. *Journal of General Internal Medicine, 22*(7), 915–922.

Baumeister, R. F., & Leary, M. R. (1995). The need to belong: Desire for interpersonal attachments as a fundamental human motivation. *Psychological Bulletin, 117*, 497–529.

Bledman, R. (2011). *The ideal body shape of African American/Black college women*. (Unpublished Doctoral Dissertation). University of Missouri, Columbia, Missouri.

Buckworth, J., & Nigg, C. (2004). Physical activity, exercise, and sedentary behavior in college students. *Journal of American College Health, 53*, 28–34.

Burton Nelson, M. (1991). *Are we winning yet? How women are changing sports and sports are changing women*. New York, NY: Random House.

Butler, J. (1990). *Gender trouble: Feminism and the subversion of identity*. New York, NY: Routledge.

Cash, T., & Pruzinsky, T. (2002). *Body image: A handbook of theory, research, and clinical practice*. New York, NY: Guilford Press.

Choi, P., & Mutrie, N. (1997). The psychological benefits of physical exercise for women: Improving employee quality of life. In J. Kerr, A. Griffiths, & T. Cox (Eds.), *Workplace health: Employee fitness and exercise* (pp. 83–100). London: Taylor and Francis.

Choi, P. Y. L. (2000). *Femininity and the physically active woman*. London: Routledge.

Collins, L. H. (2002). Working out the contradictions: Feminism and aerobics. *Journal of Sport and Social Issues, 26*, 85–109.

D'Abundo, M. L. (2007). How "healthful" are aerobics classes? Exploring the health and wellness messages in aerobics classes for women. *Health Care for Women International, 28*, 21–46.

D'Alonzo, K., & Fischetti, N. (2008). Cultural beliefs and attitudes of Black and Hispanic college-age women toward exercise. *Journal of Transcultural Nursing, 19*, 175–183.

Darlow, S., & Xu, X. (2011). The influence of close others' exercise habits and perceived social support on exercise. *Psychology of Sport and Exercise, 12*, 575–578.

Dishman, R., Dunn, A., Sallis, J., Vandenberg, R., & Pratt, C. (2005). Social-cognitive correlates of physical activity in a multi-ethnic cohort of middle-school girls: Two-year prospective study. *Journal of Pediatric Psychology, 35*, 188–198.

Drouin, B., Varga, H., & Gammage, K. (2008). The positive exerciser stereotype: The role of gender stereotype of the activity. *Journal of Applied Biobehaviornal Research, 13*, 143–156.

Drummond, M., & Drummond, C. (2010). Interviews with boys on physical activity, nutrition and health: Implications for health literacy. *Health Sociology Review, 19*, 491–504.

Dunlop, W. L., & Beauchamp, M. R. (2011). En-gendering choice: Preferences for exercising in gender-segregated and gender-integrated groups and consideration of overweight status. *International Journal of Behavioral Medicine, 18*, 216–220.

Dworkin, S. (2003). A woman's place is in the . . . cardiovascular room. Gender relations, the body and the gym. In A. Bolin & J. Granskog (Eds.), *Athletic intruders: Ethnographic research on women, culture and exercise* (pp. 131–158). New York, NY: Suny Press.

Egli, T., Bland, H., Melton, B., & Czech, D. (2011). Influence of age, sex, and race on college students' exercise motivation of physical activity. *Journal of American College Health, 59*, 399–406.

Eyler, A., & Vest, J. (2002). Environmental and policy factors related to physical activity in rural white women. *Women and Health, 36*, 111–121.

Frisby, C. M. (2004). Does race matter? Effects of idealized images on African American women's perceptions of body esteem. *Journal of Black Studies, 34*, 323–347.

Garcia, A. W., Broda, M., Frenn, M., Coviak, C., Pender, N. J., & Ronis, D. L. (1995). Gender and developmental differences in exercise beliefs among youth and prediction of their exercise behavior. *Journal of School Health, 65*, 213–219.

Garner, D. M. (1997). The 1997 body image survey results. *Psychology Today, 30*(1), 30–44.

Gill, D., & Overdorf, V. (1994). Incentives for exercise in younger and older women. *Journal of Sport Behavior, 17*, 87–97.

Gillison, F., Sebire, S., & Stanage, M. (2012). What motivates girls to take up exercise during adolescence? Learning from those who succeed. *British Journal of Health Psychology, 17*, 536–550.

Gletsu, M., & Tovin, M. (2010). African American women and physical activity. *Physical Therapy Reviews, 15*, 405–409.

Gruber, T. (2007). Ontology of folksonomy: A mash-up of apples and oranges. *International Journal on Semantic Web and Information Systems (IJSWIS), 3*(1), 1–11.

Guerin, E., Bales, E., Sweet, S., & Fortier, M. (2012). A meta-analysis of the influence of gender on self-determination theory's motivational regulations for physical activity. *Canadian Psychology, 53*, 291–300.

Hall, M. A. (1996). *Feminism and sporting bodies: Essays on theory and practice*. Champaign, IL: Human Kinetics.

Kilpatrick, M., Hebert, E., & Bartholomew, J. (2005). College students' motivation for physical activity: Differentiating men's and women's motives for sport participation and exercise. *Journal of American College Health, 54*, 87–94.

Kimm, S. Y., Glynn, N. W., Kriska, A. M., Barton, B. A., Krönsberg, S. S., Daniels, S., . . . Liu, K. (2002). Decline in physical activity in Black and White girls during adolescence. *New England Journal of Medicine, 347*, 709–715.

Knight, J. L., & Giuliano, T. A. (2003). Blood, sweat, and jeers: The impact of the media's heterosexist portrayals on perceptions of male and female athletes. *Journal of Sport Behavior, 26*(3), 272–284.

Krane, V. (2001). We can be athletic and feminine, but do we want to? Challenging hegemonic femininity in women's sport. *Quest, 53*(1), 115–133.

Krane, V., Stiles-Shipley, J., Waldron, J., & Michalenok, J. (2002). Relationships among body satisfaction, social physique anxiety and eating behaviors in female athletes and exercisers. *Journal of Sport Behavior, 24*, 247–264.

Kwan, S., & Trautner, M. N. (2009). Beauty work: Individual and institutional rewards, the reproduction of gender, and questions of agency. *Sociology Compass, 3*(1), 49–71.

LaCaille, L., Dauner, K., Krambeer, R., & Pedersen, J. (2011). Psychosocial and environmental determinants of eating behaviors, physical activity, and weight change among college students: A qualitative analysis. *Journal of American College Health, 59*, 531–538.

Layne, J. E., & Nelson, M. E. (1999). The effects of progressive resistance training on bone density: A review. *Medicine and Science in Sports and Exercise, 31*, 25–30.

Leary, M. (1992). Self-presentational processes in exercise and sport. *Journal of Sport and Exercise Psychology, 14*, 339–351.

Loland, N. W. (2000). The art of concealment in a culture of display: Aerobicizing women's and men's experiences and use of their own bodies. *Sociology of Sport Journal, 17*, 111–129.

Markula, P. (1995). Firm but shapely, fit but sexy, strong but thin: The postmodern aerobicizing female bodies. *Sociology of Sport Journal, 12*, 424–453.

McAllister, R., & Caltabiano, M. (1994). Self-esteem, body image, and weight in non-eating disordered women. *Psychological Reports, 75*, 1339–1343.

Mutrie, N., & Choi, P. (2000). Is 'fit' a feminist issue?: Dilemmas for exercise psychology. *Feminism and Psychology, 10*, 544–551.

Nast, H., & Pile, S. (1998). Everyday places bodies. In H. Nast & S. Pile (Eds.), *Places through the body* (pp. 405–416). London: Routledge

Newson, R., & Kemps, E. (2007). Factors that promote and prevent exercise engagement in older adults. *Journal of Aging and Health, 19*, 470–481.

O'Brien Cousins, S. (2000). "My heart couldn't take it": Older women's beliefs about exercise benefits and risks. *Journal of Gerontology: Psychological Sciences, 55B*(5), 283–P294.

Ostgaard, G. D. (2006). *For "women only:" Understanding the cultural space of a women's gym through feminist geography* (Master's Thesis). Retrieved from Ohio Link ETD Center. (Document number: bgsu1155218461).

Pidgeon, S. (1994). Learning reading and learning gender. In M. Barrs & S. Pidgeon (Eds.), *Reading the difference: Gender and reading in elementary classrooms* (pp. 20–34). York, ME: Stenhouse Publishing.

Pope, H. G., Philips, K., & Olivardia, R. (2000). *The adonis complex: The secret crisis of male body obsession*. New York, NY: Simon & Schuster.

Roper, E. A. (2008, October). *Perceptions of fear and concerns for safety among female recreational runners*. Paper presented at the annual Association for Applied Sport Psychology conference, Saint Louis, MI.

Roper, E. A., & Clifton, A. (2013). The representations of physically active girls in children's picture books. *Research Quarterly for Exercise and Sport, 84*, 147–156.

Salvatore, J., & Marecek, J. (2010). Gender in the gym: Evaluation concerns as barriers to women's weight lifting. *Sex Roles, 63*, 556–567.

Sarantakos, S. (2005). *Social research*. London: Palgrave Macmillan.

Schroeder, J. M., & Friesen, K. (2008, July–August). 2008 IDEA fitness programs and equipment survey: Overview. *IDEA Fitness Journal*, 22–28.

Scott-Dixon, K. (2008). Big girls don't cry: Fitness, fatness, and the production of feminist knowledge. *Sociology of Sport Journal, 25*, 22–47.

Striegel-Moore, R. H., McAvay, G., & Rodin, J. (1986). Psychological and behavioral correlates of feeling fat in women. *International Journal of Eating Disorders, 5*, 935–947.

Suminski, R. R., Petosa, R., Utter, A. C., & Zhang, J. J. (2002). Physical activity among ethnically diverse college students. *Journal of American College Health, 51*, 75–80.

Supiano, B. (2008). *In college gyms, a time for women only*. Retrieved from http://chronicle.com/article/In-College-Gyms-a-Time-for/11702

Teregerson, J. L., & King, K. A. (2002). Do perceived cues, benefits, and barriers to physical activity differ between males and female adolescents? *Journal of School Health, 72*, 374–380.

The Tucker Center for Research on Girls & Women in Sport (2007). *Executive summary*.

U.S. Department of Health and Human Services. (2008). *Physical activity guidelines for Americans*. Retrieved from www.health.gov/paguidelines/

Walcott-McQuigg, J., & Prohaska, T. (2001). Factors influencing participation of African American elders in exercise behavior. *Public Health Nursing, 18*, 194–203.

Wesley, J. K., & Gaarder, E. (2004). The gendered "nature" of the urban outdoors: Women negotiating fear of violence. *Gender and Society, 18*, 645–663.

Whyte, L. B., & Shaw, S. M. (1994). Women's leisure: An exploratory study of fear of violence as a leisure constraint. *Journal of Applied Recreation Research, 19*, 5–21.

Williams, P., & Cash, T. F. (2001). Effects of a circuit weight training program on the body images of college students. *International Journal of Eating Disorders, 30*, 75–82.

Wilson, P. M., & Rodgers, W. M. (2002). The relationship between exercise motives and physical self-esteem in female exercise participants: An application of self-determination theory. *Journal of Applied Biobehavioral Research, 7*, 30–43.

Young, D. R., He, X., Harris, J., & Mabry, I. (2002). Environmental, policy, and cultural factors related to physical activity in well-educated urban African American women. *Women & Health, 36*(2), 29–41.

16 Swimming Upstream

Addressing Barriers to Exercise and Physical Activity in Women of Color

Leeja Carter, Kisha Grady, and Jardana Silburn

Overweight and obesity-related conditions affect more than one-third of American adults (CDC, 2013). The World Health Organization (WHO, 2013) has found common obesity-related conditions to be cardiovascular disease, musculoskeletal disorders (e.g., osteoarthritis), diabetes, and certain types of cancer. Obesity has been reported to be the second leading preventable cause of death (CDC, 2013). Begley (2012) found that obesity in America is now adding an astounding $190 billion to the annual national healthcare cost, with obese men accounting for an additional $1,152 a year in medical spending and women accounting for an extra $3,613. It is important for health professionals to know the unfortunate consequences that overweight and obese adults suffer daily, specifically as they battle their weight; obese adults are more likely to suffer with depression, anxiety, type-2 diabetes, asthma, and lowered self-esteem than any other medical population (Landers & Arent, 2012). To further complicate the matter, obesity also comes with many comorbid medical conditions (e.g., high blood pressure, elevated insulin levels, or hyperlipidemia) as well as orthopedic problems (Pi-Sunyer, 2009).

The National Institutes of Health (NIH, 2013) has found that an improvement in health can be accomplished, more often than not, by lifestyle changes, including participating in physical activity and maintaining a healthy weight. However, "weight loss can be difficult to achieve and weight maintenance even more elusive" (DiLillo, Siegfried, & West, 2003, p. 120). Strategies to enhance the adoption of positive health behaviors have increasingly become apparent for long-term weight reduction and maintenance (Jeffery, Wing, Sherwood, & Tate, 2003; National Heart, Lung, and Blood Institute and North American Association for the Study of Obesity, 2000; Perri, McAdoo, McAllister, Lauer, & Yancey, 1986). Moreover, applied research and practice within the fields of public health, health psychology, and exercise psychology are now addressing health disparities in minority women.

According to the Centers for Disease Control and Prevention (CDC, 2010), the contributing factors for obesity differences among racial and ethnic groups are threefold. First, racial and ethnic groups differ in behaviors that contribute to weight gain (CDC, 2010). Second, there are differences in individual attitudes and cultural norms related to body weight. For example, Grundy (1998) explains that cultural differences in weight and economic status are interdependent, whereby "in some developing countries, obesity is a symbol of affluence, and thus is to be desired; the most affluent therefore are the most obese. In the United States and Western Europe, in contrast, affluent people usually shun obesity" (p. 567S). A third factor is differences in access to affordable, healthy nutrition and safe locations to be physically active.

CAUSES OF OBESITY

Research supports previous assumptions that genetic and biological factors are not the primary contributing factors to obesity (CDC, 2011). Factors such as sedentary behavior, psychological factors, access to community-based intervention programs, and parental socialization behaviors point to childhood and adult obesity as a complex health issue that requires a multifaceted intervention approach (CDC, 2011). The Obesity and Socioeconomic Status in Adults report (CDC, 2011) found that women whose income was below the poverty level were more likely to be obese compared to women whose income was at or above the poverty level (CDC, 2011). Findings from the report suggest a need for the medical community to focus on the socioeconomic factors that affect obesity in adult women.

Unfortunately, obesity in childhood is correlated to obesity in adulthood, and the cycle of overweight and obese populations is becoming increasingly prevalent (Guo, Wu, Chumlea, & Roche, 2002). Pugliese and Tinsley (2007) postulated that health-related behaviors are first learned within the family and home environments, and it is necessary to study how much of an impact parents' behaviors have on their children's physical activity.

RACIAL AND ETHNIC DIFFERENCES IN EXERCISE ADHERENCE

African American Women

Among all women, 30 percent are overweight, and 36.5 percent are obese (State of Obesity, 2014). Among Black women, 25.4 percent are overweight and 56.6% are obese (State of Obesity, 2014). Furthermore, African American women report increased rates of mental health issues (e.g., depression) and preventable chronic illnesses, including cardiovascular disease and diabetes (Woods-Gisombé, 2010).

African American women's health is an important topic to explore as reports show that African American women have higher rates of overweight and obesity than White women (Gletsu & Tovin, 2010). Researchers have proposed various hypotheses to understand the higher rates of obese and overweight African American women, including exploring the role of sedentary living, metabolic disorders, and lack of convenient areas and opportunities for exercise. According to Rowe (2010), African American women, particularly those who work in a professional setting, avoid regular physical activity during lunch hours because of concerns about messing up their hair and a dislike for using public showers.

Furthermore, Rowe (2010) found that African American women believe that their perceptions of weight and health diverged from that of White society. Such divergence may be due in part to parental influences and cultural constructs. The notion that African American women "see" their bodies, health, and food differently raises questions regarding the possibility of African American women's perception of the ideal weight being higher or heavier than that typified by the media or suggested by health professionals. Understanding why African American women perceive food, health, and physical activity in ways that diverge from other racial or ethnic groups is still in need of exploration.

Moreover Rowe (2010) found that African American women reported eating larger amounts of food as adults (and perhaps as children) due to rituals and beliefs surrounding food within the African American community:

> Like my grandfather, his peach cobbler is good and I know that I shouldn't eat it, I know in my heart I shouldn't eat it, but I do every time I go home . . . That's how African Americans show their love . . . My grandma's a good cook and always wants you to eat, and you know, eat a little bit, no that's not enough, eat some more.

(p. 795)

Participants reported food serving as a symbol within their family. Therefore, not eating food, specifically certain foods, would be seen as disrespectful to their family.

In addition, prior health-related interventions and studies have focused on sedentary behaviors in African American women through church-based interventions (Campbell, Resnicow, Carr, Wang, & Williams, 2009), reframing perceptions of their community as a safe place to exercise (Zenk, Wilbur, Wang, McDevitt, Oh, Block, McNeil, & Savar, 2009), and exploring women's definitions of health.

Woods-Giscombé (2010) explored the role of the Superwoman schema: the characterization of "the strong Black woman" in understanding Black women's daily coping strategies. Woods-Giscombé (2010) researched how African American women characterize the Superwoman role, what they believe to be the contributing contextual factors, and what women describe as the benefits and liabilities of this role in relation to their general well-being. Eight focus groups involving 43 African American women were conducted for the purpose of this study. The women reported that obligations to manifest strength, suppress emotions, resist being vulnerable or be dependent, succeed despite limited resources, and help others were key themes within understanding the Superwoman concept as it relates to African American women's health deregulation, mood, and familial interactions (Woods-Giscombé, 2010). Thus, Black women's perception that "superwomen" are those who suppress emotions, resist vulnerability, appear strong, and help others provides a preliminary explanation of physical activity rates within this population. Black women forfeit sustaining an active physical activity regimen due to definitions of strength, womanhood, and blackness.

With such culturally significant belief systems circulating within the collective of African American women, implementing an intervention that works to debunk the idea of "we" over "me," promoting exercise as a positive form of self-care and coping with daily stress, and mediating women's current beliefs regarding barriers to daily physical activity are essential. In order to effectively decrease the rising rate of preventable illness related to sedentariness and maladaptive coping processes among African American women, an effective exercise intervention applicable to the cultural staples of the Black community and sensitive to the attitudes and physical and psychological barriers to exercise among African American women is needed.

Hispanic Women

Hispanic Americans (i.e., persons of Hispanic descent who reside within the United States) are the largest minority group in the United States and have not been impervious to the obesity epidemic. Similar to African American women, rates of obesity and inactivity among Hispanic American women compared to non-Hispanic White women are alarming: The Office of Minority Health (2013) reports that 78% of Hispanic American women are overweight and 53.6% are inactive. Furthermore, Hispanic Americans, regardless of gender, have a higher rate of end-stage renal failure than any other ethnic group (National Institute of Diabetes and Digestive and Kidney Diseases, 2014).

Barriers for Hispanic Women

According to the Robert Wood Johnson Foundation (RWJF, 2008), "health differences across income and education groups are seen in a range of health conditions from the beginning of life to old age" (p. 16). There is evidence to suggest that those who fall lower in the socioeconomic hierarchy experience a higher prevalence of unhealthy behaviors and higher rates of mortality (Adler et al., 1993; Stringhini et al., 2010). Furthermore, Hispanic Americans may experience environmental barriers, such as food deserts (i.e., an area where affordable healthy food options are unavailable) and lack of physical activity facilities (Baker et al., 1998). Beyond a person's residence, poverty also increases the risk for obesity. Limited purchasing power makes it more difficult to buy lower-calorie, nutrient-rich foods, which tend to be more expensive than higher-calorie, nutrient-deficient foods even when healthy foods are available (Latino Coalition for a Healthy California, 2006).

Evenson, Sarmiento, Macon, Tawney, and Ammerman (2002) performed focus groups with Latina women who report English as a second language and found that their limited English proficiency presented another barrier to participating in community physical activity programs. Policy makers and researchers are starting to understand that some individuals experience difficulty in effectively communicating with health professionals, which has been coined "health literacy." In short, health literacy can be defined as the individual's ability to obtain, process, and understand basic health information and services needed to make appropriate health decisions and adopt positive health behavior factors (Williams et al., 2002). Similarly, educational background (e.g., years or levels of overall schooling) was also linked with adoption of health behaviors. Specifically, the Robert Wood Johnson Foundation (Robert Wood Johnson Foundation, 2009) suggested that an individual's educational level influences health behavior by means of (1) health knowledge and behaviors, such as exercise, eating healthy, and eliminating tobacco and alcohol use; (2) employment and income (i.e., correlation between income level and health condition); and (3) social and psychological factors (e.g., sense of control, social standing, and social support). As previously mentioned, language and environmental barriers can deter a person from seeking information from others and adhering to exercise. The Latino Coalition for a Healthy California (LCHC, 2006) describes Hispanic culture as a collective one, meaning Hispanics tend to place family concerns and social cohesiveness above individual needs and desires. Thus, for those who have immigrated to the United States, social isolation can influence eating and physical activity.

Typically, Hispanic women's children, husband, and household duties come before their personal needs. Moreover, the husband's value on physical activity is a contributing factor to whether Hispanic women participate in leisure-time exercise (Evenson et al., 2002). Therefore, Hispanic women whose husbands' do not place a high value on physical activity might perceive household and caregiving duties as exercise (Eyler et al., 2002b). Additionally, low socioeconomic status, inflexible work schedules, and transportation difficulties were shown as important barriers to physical activity for Hispanic women (Austin, Smith, Gianini, & Campos-Melady, 2013).

Native American Women

The epidemic of obesity has also reached the Native American community. Welty (1991) notes that obesity has only become a major health problem in Native Americans within the past two generations, due to massive feeding programs that were made available to the community after reports of malnutrition began to circulate. The food provided in these programs was laden with calories and low in fiber. A rapid change from an active to a sedentary lifestyle has also been found to greatly contribute to obesity among Native Americans (Office of Women's Health, 2010).

Barriers for Native American Women

Documentation is limited on barriers for Native American women to adhere to physical activity or other positive health behaviors. However, Eyler et al. (2002b) noted that "planned time to participate in recreations exercise did not fit with the identity of Native American women" (p. 248).

Asian American Women

It has been reported that Asian Americans are often delineated as the "healthy minority," as Asian Americans have a higher life expectancy than any other group in the United States

(Measure of America, 2011). However, the grouping of Asian Americans may possibly hide health risks for specific subgroups (Office of Women's Health, 2012). The Office of Women's Health (2012) reports that the common health conditions in Asian American women are heart disease, high cholesterol, osteoporosis, mental health problems, and various cancers.

Barriers for Asian American Women

Similar to barriers found in English as a Second Language (ESL)–speaking Hispanic women, ESL Asian American women also face limitations in adherence to healthy lifestyles (Office of Women's Health, 2012). Moreover, Asian American women's cultural beliefs may conflict with the Western health paradigm, resulting in non-compliance with protective health-related behaviors. In a focus group, Eyler et al. (2002b) found that Asian American women "perceived themselves to be physically active enough just doing their daily tasks, such as housework and walking for transportation" (p. 249). The researchers also found that peer non-acceptance due to cultural beliefs was a barrier to physical activity in this population.

BARRIERS TO SUCCESS

Despite the success of most weight-loss intervention programs, it has been found that these programs may not be effective across all ethnic and racial groups, because the traditional Eurocentric paradigm for health-related behavioral strategies may not apply in other populations (Austin, Smith, Gianini, & Campos-Melady, 2013). As Rucker and Cash (1992) state, "if individually internalized . . . cultural standards shape the individual's body-image experiences and his/her adjustive behaviors (e.g., dieting, exercising, grooming, avoiding, etc.) to manage these body-image experiences," then culturally valid intervention strategies for behavioral programs should be considered (p. 292). Similarly, Eyler et al. (2002a) note that cultural influences are proximal in relationship to societal norms (e.g., acceptance of a heavier size) and institutional barriers (e.g., lack of access to exercise facilities and local food markets).

EXERCISE INTERVENTIONS

In the past, behavioral interventions for obesity primarily focused on changes in dietary consumption. However, in correlational studies involving clinical and normative samples, an increase in physical activity was noted to be among the best predictors of long-term success in weight reduction (Jeffery et al., 2003). Additionally, exercise has been found to be a positive mechanism for coping with daily stress (Anxiety and Depression Association of America, 2008). Yet within the field of public health and exercise psychology, effective interventions to combine culturally specific exercise techniques with positive coping to transition sedentary minority women into long-term exercise is lacking.

Pan et al. (2009) noted that there are differences in attitudes and cultural norms regarding body weight. They have found that African American and Hispanic American women are more satisfied with their body size than White women. This in turn may cause those women to present higher vulnerability to health-risk behaviors, including physical inactivity and unhealthy eating (Millstein et al., 2008). In sum, understanding different attitudinal norms about women's body composition can aid health professions with intervention strategies. Campbell et al. (2009) found that using preexisting staples within the community (e.g., using the church to promote positive eating habits) may help decrease fat consumption and increase fruit and vegetable intake in African American men and women churchgoers. Campbell et al. (2009)

also concluded that successful interventions must develop culturally and socially relevant community-based programs.

Another important barrier to exercise adherence and engagement in sedentary African American women is education on the benefits of exercise. Campbell et al. (2009) found that using preexisting staples within the community (e.g., using the church to promote positive eating habits) may help decrease fat consumption and increase fruit and vegetable intake in African American men and women churchgoers. Campbell et al. (2009) also concluded that successful interventions must develop culturally and socially relevant community-based programs.

FUTURE RESEARCH

There are multiple areas for future research and practice. First, culturally specific or community-based programs should focus on implementing strategies for physical activity that educate, motivate, and promote adherence for both parents and children of color. Second, through understanding cultural and community barriers reported by women, research can assist health professionals in developing tailored health interventions to motivate women of color to engage in healthier lifestyles. Third, investigating barriers to physical activity engagement and adherence that involve change at the community level warrants deeper investigation as these barriers influence the health and well-being of persons of color.

CONCLUSION

Women of color have higher rates of overweight and obesity than White women. Researchers propose various reasons for these rates, and successful clinical interventions for women of color are yet to be implemented in a long-term fashion. Research exploring racial and ethnic minority women's perceptions of food, health, physical activity, and barriers to healthy living is needed to further understand such disparities as well as to create successful, clinically tailored interventions. A successful exercise intervention is one tailored to address women's perceptions of physical activity, coping, and strength through a convenient, culturally sensitive program.

Culturally specific or community-based programs should focus on implementing strategies for physical activity that educate, motivate, and promote adherence to exercise within women of color. Such interventions should look to (1) include effective exercise programs applicable to other racial and ethnic groups for whom traditional methods of exercise intervention have proven unsuccessful and (2) provide health professionals with a guide to exercise promotion within racial and ethnic minority groups whose beliefs of physical activity, body, and health diverge from those commonly found within the frequently researched racial majority.

REFERENCES

Adler, N. E., Boyce, T., Chesney, M. A., Folkman, S., & Syme, L. (1993). Socioeconomic inequalities in health. *The Journal of the American Medical Association, 269*(24), 3140–3145.

Anxiety and Depression Association of America. (2008). *Physical activity reduces stress.* Retrieved from www.adaa.org/understanding-anxiety/related-illnesses/other-related-conditions/stress/physical-activity-reduces-sta.org/understanding-anxiety/related-illnesses/other-related-conditions/stress/physical-activity-reduces-st

Austin, J. L., Smith, J. E., Gianini, L., & Campos-Melady, M. (2013). Attitudinal famialism predicts weight management adherence in Mexican—American women. *Journal of Behavioral Medicine, 36*(3), 259–269. doi: 10.1007/s108650-129-4206-

Baker, E., Brownson, C. R., Cromer, L., Donatelle, J. R., Eyler, A. A., & King, C. A. (1998). Physical activity and minority women: A qualitative study. *Health Education & Behavior, 25*(5), 640–652.

Begley, S. (2012, April 30). As America's waistline expands, costs soar. *Reuters*. Retrieved from www.reuters.com/article/2012/04/30/us-obesity-idUSBRE83T0C820120430

Campbell, M. K., Resnicow, K., Carr, C., Wang, T., & Williams, A. (2009). Process evaluation of an effective church-based diet intervention: Body & soul. *Health, Education, and Behavior, 34*(6), 8648–80. doi: 10.1177/1090198106292020

Center for Disease Control and Prevention. (2010). *Obesity rate*. Retrieved November 22, 2013, from www.cdc.gov/Features/dsObesityAdults/

Center for Disease Control and Prevention. (2011). *Obesity and socioeconomic status in adults*. Retrieved from www.cdc.gov/nchs/data/databriefs/db50.pdf

Centers for Disease Control and Prevention. (2013). *Overweight and obesity*. Retrieved October 27, 2013, from www.cdc.gov/obesity/data/adult.html

DiLillo, V., Siegfried, N. J., & West, D. S. (2003). Incorporating motivational interviewing into behavioral obesity treatment. *Cognitive and Behavioral Practice, 10*(2), 120–130.

Evenson, K. R., Sarmiento, O. L., Macon, M. L., Tawney, K. W., & Ammerman, A. S. (2002). Environmental, policy, and cultural factors related to physical activity among Latina immigrants. *Women & health, 36*(2), 43–56.

Eyler, A. A., Matson-Koffman, D., Vest, J. R., Everson, K. R., Sanderson, B., Thompson, J. L., Wilbur, J., Wilcox, S., & Young, D. R. (2002a). Environmental, policy, and cultural factors related to physical activity in a diverse sample of women: The women's cardiovascular health network project—summary and discussion. In A. A. Eyler (Ed.), *Environmental, policy, and cultural factors related to physical activity in a diverse sample of women: The women's cardiovascular health network project* (pp. 123–134). Binghamton, NY: The Haworth Press, Inc.

Eyler, A. E., Wilcox, S., Matson-Koffman, D., Evenson, K. R., Sanderson, B., Thompson, J., Wilbur, J., & Rohm-Young, D. (2002b). Correlates of physical activity among women from diverse racial/ethnic groups. *Journal of Women's Health & Gender-Based Medicine, 11*(3), 239–253.

Gletsu, M., & Tovin, M. (2010). African American women and physical activity. *Physical Therapy Reviews, 15*(5): 405–409.

Grundy, S. M. (1998). Multifactorial causation of obesity: Implications for prevention. *The American Journal of Clinical Nutrition, 67*(3), 563S–572S.

Guo, S. S., Wu, W., Chumlea, W. C., & Roche, A. F. (2002). Predicting overweight and obesity in adulthood from body mass index values in childhood and adolescence. *The American journal of clinical nutrition, 76*(3), 653–658.

Jeffery, R. W., Wing, R. R., & Latino Coalition for a Healthy California. (2006). *Obesity in Latino communities*. Retrieved November 22, 2013, from www.lchc.org/documents/ObesityLatinosLCHC

Jeffery, R. W., Wing, R. R., Sherwood, N. E., & Tate, D. F. (2003). Physical activity and weight loss: does prescribing higher physical activity goals improve outcome? *American Journal of Clinical Nutrition, 78*(4), 684–690.

Landers, D. M., & Arent, S. M. (2012). Physical activity and mental health. In G. Tenenbaum & R. C. Eklund (Eds.), *Handbook of sport psychology* (3rd ed.) (pp. 469–491).

Measure of America (2011). The measure of America 20102–011: Mapping risks and resilience. Retrieved from http://ssrc-static.s3.amazonaws.com/moa/AHDP-HEALTH-FACT-SHEET-12.21.10.pdf

Millstein, R. A., Carlson, S. A., Fulton, J. E., Galuska, D. A., Zhang, J., Blanck, H. M., & Ainsworth, B. E. (2008). Relationships between body size satisfaction and weight control practices among US adults. *The Medscape Journal of Medicine, 10*(5), 119.

National Heart, Lung, and Blood Institute and North American Association for the Study of Obesity. (2000). *Practical guide to the identification, evaluation, and treatment of overweight and obesity in adults*. Retrieved from www.nhlbi.nih.gov/guidelines/obesity/prctgd_c.pdf

National Institute of Diabetes and Digestive and Kidney Diseases. (2014). *Race, ethnicity, and kidney disease*. Retrieved from www.niddk.nih.gov/health-information/health-communication-programs/nkdep/learn/causes-kidney-disease/at-risk/race-ethnicity/Pages/race-ethnicity.aspx

National Institutes of Health. (2013). *Understanding adult overweight and obesity*. Retrieved from http://win.niddk.nih.gov/publications/understanding.htm

The Office of Minority Health. (2013). *Obesity and hispanic Americans.* Retrieved November 22, 2013, from http://minorityhealth.hhs.gov/templates/content.aspx?ID=6459

Office of Women's Health. (2010). *Overweight and obesity.* Retrieved from www.womenshealth.gov/minority-health/american-indians/obesity.html

Office of Women's Health. (2012). *Asian-Americans.* Retrieved from www.womenshealth.gov/minority-health/asian-americans/index.html

Pan, L., Galuska, D. A., Sherry, B., Hunter, A. S., Rutledge, G. E., Dietz, W. H., & Balluz, L. S. (2009). Differences in prevalence of obesity among black, white, and Hispanic adults-United States, 2006–2008. *Morbidity and Mortality Weekly Report, 58*(27), 740–744.

Perri, M. G., McAdoo, W. G., McAllister, D. A., Lauer, J. B., & Yancey, D. Z. (1986). Enhancing the efficacy of behavior therapy for obesity: Effects of aerobic exercise and a multicomponent maintenance program. *Journal of Consulting and Clinical Psychology, 54*(5), 670.

Pi-Sunyer, X. (2009). The medical risks of obesity. *Postgraduate Medicine, 121*(6), 21–33.

Pugliese, J., & Tinsley, B. (2007). Parental socialization of child and adolescent physical activity: A meta-analysis. *Journal of Family Psychology, 21*(3), 331–343. doi: 10.1037/0893-3200.21.3.331

Robert Wood Johnson Foundation. (2008). *Overcoming obstacles to health.* Retrieved December 11, 2013, from www.commissiononhealth.org/PDF/ObstaclesToHealth-Report.pdf

Robert Wood Johnson Foundation. (2009). *Education matters for health.* Retrieved from www.commissiononhealth.org/PDF/c270deb3-ba424–fbd

Rowe, J. (2010). Voices from the inside: African American women's perspectives on healthy lifestyles. *Health, Education, and Behavior, 37*(6), 789–800. doi: 10.1177/1090198110365992

Rucker III, C. E., & Cash, T. F. (1992). Body images, body-size perceptions, and eating behaviors among African-American and white college women. *International Journal of Eating Disorders, 12*(3), 291–299.

The State of Obesity. (2014). *Special report: Racial and ethnic disparities in obesity.* Retrieved from http://stateofobesity.org/disparities/

Stringhini, S., Sabia, S., Shipley, M., Brunner, E., Nabi, H., Kivimaki, M., & Singh-Manoux, A. (2010). Association of socioeconomic position with health behaviors and mortality: The Whitehall II study. *The Journal of the American Medical Association, 303*(12), 1159–1166.

Welty, T. K. (1991). Health implications of obesity in American Indians and Alaska Natives. *The American Journal of Clinical Nutrition, 53*(6), 1616S–1620S.

Williams, M. V., Davis, T., Parker, R. M., Weiss, B. D. (2002). The role of health literacy in patient-physician communication. *Family Medicine, 34*(5), 383–389.

Woods-Giscombé, C. L. (2010). Superwoman schema: African American women's views on stress, strength, and health. *Qualitative Health Research, 20*(5), 668–683. doi:10.1177/1049732310361892

World Health Organization. (2013). *Obesity and overweight.* Retrieved October 27, 2013, from www.who.int/mediacentre/factsheets/fs311/en/

Zenk, S., Wilbur, J., Wang, E., McDevitt, J., Oh, A., Block, R., McNeil, S., Savar, N. (2009). Neighborhood environment and adherence to a walking intervention in African-American women. *Health, Education, and Behavior, 36*(1), 167–181. doi:10.1177/1090198108321249

17 Socioeconomic Status

Amanda M. Perkins

WHAT IS SOCIOECONOMIC STATUS?

According to the American Psychological Association (APA, 2007), socioeconomic status (SES) is defined as the social standing or class of an individual or group, taking into account three related, but distinct, indicators: social, economic, and work statuses. Of these, social status is measured by education, economic status by income, and work status by occupation (Adler et al., 1994; Adler & Newman, 2002; APA, 2007). It is important to note that the term *low SES* is not limited to one region, gender, or ethnic group. Often, a low SES community is composed of one or more segments of the following populations:

- Recent immigrants
- The homeless
- Veterans
- Victims of domestic violence
- Women
- The working poor
- Ethnic minorities
- The elderly
- Relocated disaster victims
- Single-parent families
- And many others (DeNavas-Walt & Proctor, 2014; Kipke, 2008)

There are typically three ways in which SES is conceptualized: (1) materialist approaches, which focus on access to resources and information (e.g., education, health care); (2) gradient approaches, which characterize SES as a continuous variable and highlight inequalities among individuals' (or groups of individuals') positions; and (3) class approaches, which stress the reproduction of power and privilege among some groups (i.e., high SES) and subordination of others (i.e., low SES) (APA, 2007). Though SES may be conceptualized in a number of ways, the materialist and gradient approaches are particularly relevant to the study of health behavior.

The materialist perspective focuses on the attainment of resources, taking into account measurable constructs such as income. Research adopting a materialist approach underscores the association between low SES and undesirable physical and mental health outcomes, such as smoking, poor diet, reduced frequency of health screenings, and a sedentary lifestyle at large (Adler & Newman, 2002; Cohen, Kaplan, & Salonen, 1999; Wardle & Steptoe, 2003). Materialist research additionally identifies the conditions contributing to these health disparities, including unemployment, lack of health insurance, and limited access to healthy grocery stores (APA, 2007).

Research focusing on SES and health-related gradients, on the other hand, highlights a positive relationship between SES and health; that is, as SES improves, so does health (Adler et al., 1994; Marmot, 2006). Further, these research findings reveal an inverse relationship between SES and morbidity as well as between SES and mortality. As SES improves, morbidity and mortality lessen (Adler et al., 1994; McDonough, Duncan, Williams, & House, 1997). Furthermore, work from the Centers for Disease Control and Prevention (CDC) also reveal a positive correlation between level of education (an indicator of SES) and physical activity participation.

The 2008 Physical Activity Guidelines for Americans (PAG), which have been adopted for use in the Healthy People 2020 objectives, are the current guidelines for Americans age six and older to improve their health through physical activity (CDC, 2008). The Guidelines are similar to, but less stringent than American Heart Association (AHA)/American College of Sports Medicine (ACSM) physical activity guidelines (i.e., accumulating 150 min/wk of moderate-intensity activity, compared to 30 min/day x 5 days/wk to obtain 150 min) (Haskell et al., 2007; CDC, 2008). The PAG can be found online at www.health.gov/paguidelines/.

For example, in the United States, adults with a graduate degree are over two times more likely than adults with less than a high school diploma (63.6% compared to 28.9%) to meet the 2008 PAG recommendations (Schoenborn, Adams, & Peregoy, 2013). A positive relationship also exists between physical activity and income (another indicator of SES). Adults living in higher SES households (i.e., ≥ 4x the poverty level) are almost two times more likely (57.8% compared to 32.4%) to meet 2008 PAG recommendations for aerobic activities than adults with household incomes below the poverty level (Schoenborn, Adams, & Peregoy, 2013).

Regardless of how one conceptualizes SES, it has implications for exercise psychologists and practitioners. Individuals with a lower SES are less likely to be healthy than their counterparts with a higher SES (Adler et al., 1994; Adler & Newman, 2002; Baum, Garofalo, & Yali, 1999; Steenland, Hu, & Walker, 2004). Community-based physical activity programs experience greater difficulty recruiting participants from low-SES groups and experience higher attrition rates among these participants (Withall, Jago, & Fox, 2011, 2012). Further, individuals from low-SES backgrounds may be less successful in achieving desired behavior change following participation in intervention programs than their high-SES counterparts (Adler & Newman, 2002; Michie, Jochelson, Markham, & Bridle, 2009).

Consequently, reducing health disparities and increasing exercise behavior among low-SES individuals is dependent upon the development of effective interventions to increase desired behaviors targeted for those individuals. In order to do so, exercise psychologists should first identify the potential barriers to exercise that may be uniquely influencing their clients with low SES.

BARRIERS TO EXERCISE

The most commonly cited barriers to exercise include lack of time, lack of energy, and lack of motivation (Weinberg & Gould, 2015, p. 430). These barriers are common among low-SES populations (Bragg, Tucker, Kaye, & Desmond, 2009). However, low-SES individuals may experience further challenges related to the dimensions of SES: education, income, and occupation. These barriers include lack of accessibility, location of residence, lack of knowledge, social norms, time orientation, work demands, lack of leisure time, lack of economic resources, stress, poor health, low personal functioning, and many others (Bragg et al., 2009; Burton, Turrell, & Oldenburg, 2003; Parks, Houseman, & Brownson, 2003; Schrop et al., 2006).

By examining each of the three SES indicators, the exercise psychologist can uncover various resources that may be utilized in order to promote physical activity participation. Similarly, each component of SES may also provide insight into a range of barriers that, if not addressed, may hinder participation. In the present chapter, the link between exercise adherence and each of the three SES indicators (i.e., education, income, and occupation) will be discussed. Further, common barriers, including time orientation, attitudes, lack of accessibility, and lack of social support, will be discussed in relation to the SES indicators.

Education

Educational attainment is a major dimension of SES and social class because education itself is symbol of status. Furthermore, education is closely related to the other dimensions, income and occupation. Higher levels of education allow individuals to enter professional or "white-collar" jobs and increase their earning potential (Adler & Newman, 2002; APA, 2007; Ross & Wu, 1995). Despite the importance of education in achieving social status and increasing opportunities, it is not always easily obtained. In 2013, nearly 24.5 million people over the age of 25 living in the United States (nearly 13%) did not graduate from high school (US Census, 2014).

In addition to its relationship to income and occupation, education provides individuals with increased knowledge, as well as better cognitive and life skills, which in turn allows them to gain greater access to information and resources to promote health (Adler & Newman, 2002). Further, education is associated with fewer health-risk behaviors, which is reinforced by an inverse relationship between educational attainment and mortality, even after controlling for other demographic factors (Muller, 2002). Additionally, exercise and physical activity research consistently shows a positive correlation between level of education and adherence to exercise (Trost, Owen, Bauman, Sallis, & Brown, 2002).

Lower educational attainment is a predictor of low exercise participation and limits access to health-promoting resources; however, lack of exercise-related knowledge is a substantial barrier to participation as well (Moore, Fulton, Kruger, & McDivitt, 2010; Morrow, Krzewinski-Malone, Jackson, Bungum, & Fitzgerald, 2004). Studies have suggested that physicians are less likely to discuss exercise with low-income and less-educated patients than with higher-income and more well-educated patients (Taira, Safran, Seto, Rogers, & Tarlov, 1997; Wee, McCarthy, Davis, & Phillips, 1999). In a study evaluating adults' knowledge of previous 1998 ACSM guidelines for aerobic physical activity (i.e., a minimum of 30 minutes of moderate-intensity most days of the week), 25.6 percent of respondents were able to correctly identify the guideline, but those earning less than $15,000 annually were less likely to identify the guideline than those making greater than $60,000 (Moore et al., 2010).

Income

Income, another component of SES, can be a considerable barrier to exercise participation for low-SES individuals. Income provides access to goods and services that can facilitate access to exercise participation, as well as other valuable resources, such as health care, healthy foods, adequate housing, and recreation (Adler & Newman, 2002). According to 2013 census information, 14.5 percent of individuals in the United States live in poverty (approximately 45.3 million), and 42 million people in the United States were without health insurance coverage in 2013. The average household income in the United States in 2013 was $52,250 (US Census, 2014).

Socioeconomic status dictates the type of neighborhood in which an individual resides. Individuals living in low-income neighborhoods may experience several environmental barriers related to their exercise behavior, such as neighborhood safety, traffic, lack of recreational facilities, and inadequate transportation (Estabrooks, Lee, & Gyuresik, 2003; Moore, Diez Roux, Evenson, McGinn, & Brines, 2008). Low- and medium-SES neighborhoods may have physical activity resources, such as fitness centers (Estabrooks et al., 2003); however, they may have fewer free physical activity resources (e.g., public pools, sports areas, bike lanes, green spaces) (Estabrooks et al., 2003; Powell, Slater, Chaloupka, & Harper, 2006) relative to higher-SES neighborhoods (Estabrooks et al., 2003). Although neighborhood parks may be equally distributed across levels of income (Moore et al., 2008), one may contend that the parks seem visibly less attractive in lower-SES neighborhoods, with trash, traffic noise, crime, and equipment in disrepair (Duke, Huhman, & Heitzler, 2003; Neckerman et al., 2009).

Residents of lower-income neighborhoods may also perceive less availability of recreational facilities in their neighborhoods. It is important to realize, however, that availability does not necessarily mean that the resource is accessible (Powell et al., 2006). For example, a commercial fitness center is located in a low-SES community, but that does not mean the cost of membership is realistic for individuals residing in that neighborhood. According to the International Health, Racquet, and Sportsclub Association (IHRSA) Health Club Consumer Report (2012), the average monthly health club membership for an individual is $42.55, which is approximately $500 per year. These health club memberships may prove too costly for low-SES individuals and families.

In addition to inaccessibility of physical activity resources, low-income residents face barriers to resources that complement a physically active lifestyle, such as a lack of full-service grocery stores and farmers' markets and an abundance of fast food restaurants (Larson, Story, & Nelson, 2009). Finally, some segments of the low-SES population may be transient, moving often due to unstable income and housing arrangements (Kipke, 2008). This may influence accessibility of resources.

Occupation

Occupational status is a complex component of SES and a significant barrier to exercise for low-SES individuals. Whether or not one is employed affects their earnings (Muller, 2002); further, type of employment (e.g., blue-collar, white-collar, full-time, part-time) dictates whether or not one receives health and wellness benefits. Occupational characteristics also include number of hours worked, level of job stress, enjoyment, job security, level of prestige, and rewards (Ross & Wu, 1995), each of which may directly or indirectly influence a person's exercise behavior. Finally, lower-SES occupations generally provide less autonomy, may involve shift work, have a higher risk of injury, and offer lower or hourly wages (Muller, 2002).

Occupational status has been linked with several negative outcomes, including job strain and increased risk of cardiovascular and metabolic risk factors (APA, 2007). Individuals in blue-collar occupations are more likely to be physically inactive than those in white-collar occupations (Burton & Turrell, 2000; Trost et al., 2002). Finally, there is a well-documented correlation between occupation and mortality (APA, 2007; Muller, 2002).

ADDITIONAL BARRIERS TO EXERCISE

Time Orientation

Time orientation, a psychological construct that refers to an individual's tendency to think and act according to consequences that are short or long term, is a proposed mediator of

SES and health (Krueter, Lukwago, Bucholtz, Clark, & Sanders-Thompson, 2003; Ward, Guthrie, & Butler, 2009). An individual's perspective of time can be characterized as being primarily present-oriented, where one tends to focus on the "here and now," or future-oriented, where one tends to make decisions based upon the long-term outcome. Time orientation, or time perspective, is associated with SES, where high-SES groups tend to possess a future perspective, and low-SES groups tend to be present-oriented (Wardle & Steptoe, 2003; Ward et al., 2009). Time orientation has been linked to a number of health behaviors (e.g., smoking, alcohol abuse, sexual risk-taking behavior); however, this construct has been explored little in the exercise realm. A future time orientation is associated with health behaviors and improved health outcomes, whereas present time orientation is linked with engaging in unhealthy behaviors (Ward et al., 2009). Time orientations, however, are not limited to influencing behavior; they may also be related to expectations about one's life span (Wardle & Steptoe, 2003).

Time orientations are particularly significant in the exercise realm, because few benefits of exercise and physical activity are immediately realized (e.g., lower disease risk, weight loss). Orientations toward the future may encourage a physically active lifestyle (i.e., the individual is motivated by the long-term benefits of physical activity). As a result, promoting long-term health behaviors may be less successful among low-SES individuals, because their thinking about the future may be limited. Low-SES individuals may focus their attention on what requires immediate attention (e.g., finances, family) and ascribe lesser importance to behaviors resulting in long-term benefits (e.g., exercise). Time orientation may also be related to actual and perceived lack of time, both of which are negatively correlated with adherence to exercise (Trost et al., 2002). Similarly, having other priorities (e.g., work or family responsibilities) may contribute to low-SES individuals' lack of time for participating in physical activity (Bragg, Tucker, Kaye, & Desmond, 2009).

Lack of Social Support

In addition to the exercise barriers related to the physical environment mentioned earlier (e.g., lack of facilities, traffic, crime), low-SES individuals might experience barriers related to the social environment. Social support from friends, peers, and family members has a positive effect on the initiation and maintenance of physical activity (Trost et al., 2002). Further, research shows that individuals with high levels of social support recover faster after illness (Holahan, Holahan, Moos, & Brennan, 1995), report fewer depressive symptoms (Cairney, Boyle, Offord, & Racine, 2003; Frasure-Smith et al., 2000), and have lower mortality rates (Brummett et al., 2001; Frasure-Smith et al., 2000).

Unfortunately, lack of support is a commonly cited barrier to participation across populations (Sallis, Hovell, & Hofstetter, 1992) and is negatively associated with leisure-time physical activity among low-SES populations (Parks et al., 2003; Wilcox, Castro, King, Houseman, & Brownson, 2000). Lack of support may come in various forms: a spouse who feels exercise takes away from taking care of the household, friends who engage in sedentary activities, or family members who are unwilling to praise another's effort.

Attitudes

Low SES is associated with attitudes and expectations that might undermine exercise and other health behaviors, including less health consciousness (i.e., trying to be healthy), an external health locus of control (i.e., believing one's health is left up to chance), and lower life expectancies (i.e., expecting not to live long lives) (Wardle & Steptoe, 2003).

SUMMARY OF BARRIERS TO PHYSICAL ACTIVITY PARTICIPATION

Low-SES populations face a number of psychological, social, economic, environmental, and structural barriers that may limit their physical activity participation. These include, but are not limited to

- Financial insecurity
- Homelessness/unstable housing
- Unemployment or underemployment
- Food insecurity
- Lack of transportation
- Lack of healthcare
- Crime and unsafe neighborhoods
- Depression
- Chronic stress
- Social or cultural norms
- Exposure to violence, including domestic violence
- Fatigue, physical discomfort, and fitness level

(Bragg et al., 2009; Burton et al., 2003; Duke et al., 2003; Estabrooks et al., 2003; Larson et al., 2009; Neckerman et al., 2009; Parks et al., 2003; Powell, Slater, Chaloupka, & Harper, 2006; Schrop et al., 2006; Taira et al., 1997). Given the numerous barriers that low-SES clients may face, exercise psychologists must be able to identify the barriers for the individual with whom they are working and endeavor to address them.

STRATEGIES FOR WORKING WITH LOW-SES CLIENTS

A number of evidence-based strategies are available to the exercise psychologist providing counseling to low-SES individuals. These strategies include cognitive and behavioral techniques, such as offering information, facilitating goal setting, and modifying behavior, which may be particularly helpful for low-income exercisers (Michie et al., 2009). Additional approaches include environmental, decision-making, reinforcement, and social support approaches. The exercise psychologist should first assess their client's motivators and barriers to exercise in order to determine which approaches may be most useful for the individual (or group of clients) (Bragg et al., 2009). Research findings suggest that using more focused interventions (i.e., those utilizing a few select techniques) may more effectively change behavior than using many different techniques (Michie et al., 2009). It is important to note, however, that prior to working with a low-SES client, the practitioner should cultivate a level of cultural competence. Cultural competence is a "process that takes effort over time" (Watson, Etzel, & Loughran, n.d., para. 5) and consists of (1) being aware of one's own assumptions about behavior, values, and biases; (2) attempting to understand the differing worldview of the client without negative judgments; and (3) seeking to develop relevant and culturally sensitive skills for working with one's clients of different cultures (Sue, Arredondo, & McDavis, 1992).

Rapport

The first strategy, building rapport, is essential for effectively working with any clients (Kottler, 1992; LeBeauf, Smaby, & Maddox, 2009). This is particularly true when working with low-SES clients. It is important to be mindful of the individual's social position, and while it is important to be professional, the exercise psychologist should make the client feel comfortable and not create a hierarchical relationship in excess of the dynamics that already exist (i.e., do not forget about the intimidation factor) (Kipke, 2008; LeBeauf et al., 2009). Furthermore, according to Payne, DeVol, and Smith (2001), low-SES populations may have an innate distrust or suspicion of authority figures. A simple way to address this is to permit the client to call you by your name and not your title (e.g., "Hi, I'm Dr. Gregory Thompson, but please call me Greg."). Additional ways to build rapport include discussing things that are important to the client, asking the client open-ended questions, and allowing the client to elaborate on any questionnaire items you may ask during the initial consultation. As a suggestion, if the practitioner is not sure of the client's level of literacy, he or she should ask questions rather than asking the client to complete written questionnaires (National Cancer Institute, 1995). Actively building a relationship with clients from the beginning allows for gaining insight into their experiences as well as their barriers and motivators to exercise, thereby increasing the effectiveness of the clinician (Andersen & Hanrahan, 2015).

Education

The second evidence-based strategy for counseling low-SES individuals is providing education (Atkinson et al., 2007). Knowledge is necessary, but not all that is required, for successfully changing behavior. Providing information alone has little effect on people's knowledge about their own health; however, when combined with professional consultation or advice, its effectiveness increases (Michie et al., 2009). Low-SES individuals, as well as other disadvantaged populations, may experience a substantial benefit through education, because they initially may have a limited knowledge base in regard to exercise and physical activity. Further, health information is generally written at advanced reading levels (National Cancer Institute, 1995), leading to the possibility that some low-SES individuals may not be able to understand the content. To that end, the exercise psychologist should provide appropriate educational resources to their client.

Educational strategies should be tailored to, and appropriate for, the individual. The exercise psychologist should consider the client's level of education when planning educational approaches for promoting exercise behavior. When providing written or verbal communication, use simple language and avoid wordiness or jargon (Kipke, 2008). Sample educational approaches include handouts, pamphlets, lists of contacts, maps, brochures, videos, and exercise demonstrations. The following organizations provide a variety of the aforementioned resources online:

- American Heart Association: www.heart.org/HEARTORG/GettingHealthy/Physical Activity/Physical-Activity_UCM_001080_SubHomePage.jsp
- American College of Sports Medicine: www.acsm.org/access-public-information
- Centers for Disease Control and Prevention: www.cdc.gov/physicalactivity/basics/vid eos/index.htm
- U.S. Department of Health and Human Services, Office of Disease Prevention and Health Promotion: www.health.gov/paguidelines/guidelines/#resources

It is important to educate clients about the benefits of exercise, as well as the current exercise recommendations. For example, Atkinson and colleagues (2007) found that low-income rural women had little knowledge about physical activity recommendations and considered childcare a physical activity. Educating low-SES clients about physical activity opportunities is equally important. One of the barriers to exercise among low-SES individuals is lack of accessibility; however, in some instances, this lack of resources may be a perception, rather than a reality (Duncan, Duncan, Strycker, & Chaumeton, 2002). The practitioner can provide the low-SES client with a list of local resources available to them. Included in this list may be parks, free-for-use recreation facilities, community centers that offer free classes, playgrounds for children, and low-cost supermarkets to help the client complement their new healthy lifestyle. The following are examples of educational strategies that may be helpful for low-SES clients (McNeill & Emmons, 2012, CDC, 2008):

- A list of free or low-cost facilities and community centers offering exercise programs
- Testimonials from similar others about the benefits of exercise
- A map of nearby parks
- A pamphlet debunking common exercise myths
- A handout (accompanied by an explanation) of the current physical activity recommendations
- A demonstration of exercises that can be done at home with no or little equipment

One should carefully consider the best method for delivering an educational strategy before implementation. For example, developing a website, embedding a link in an email directing individuals to parks, or sending exercise reminders via text message may not be the best methods for reaching this population, many of whom may have limited or no access to computers and other technologies (Smith, 2013).

"Pros and Cons" Table

Another strategy that the exercise psychologist working with low-SES clients may utilize is the decisional balance table. The decisional balance table, originally developed by Janis and Mann (1977), is used to aid in decision making and is commonly used in behavior change counseling. Decisional balance theory has been incorporated into such theories as the transtheoretical model (Prochaska & Velicer, 1997) and is premised on the idea that people engage in a behavior based on the positive and negative outcomes derived from the behavior. If an individual believes the pros of engaging in a behavior outweigh the cons, he will continue to engage in the behavior. However, if the cons of the behavior outweigh the pros, the individual will be more inclined to change his behavior. It is important to consider that some low-SES clients may have difficulty evaluating the consequences of their decisions (i.e., the cons of their behavior), particularly if some of their lower-level needs (e.g., food, clothing, shelter) are unmet (i.e., "other things are more important") (LeBeauf et al., 2009).

In order to help clients evaluate their behaviors, decisional balance (or "pro/con") sheets may be used (Prochaska & Velicer, 1997). Decisional balance sheets may be configured a number of ways; however, low-SES clients may benefit from including a temporal component in this strategy. As noted earlier in the chapter, low-SES individuals tend to focus on the present; therefore, sustaining behavior change that yields few immediate positive outcomes may be particularly challenging. The exercise psychologist could configure the decisional balance sheet to have eight cells consisting of the short-term and long-term pros and cons of engaging in the current (sedentary) behavior and of the changed (physically active) behavior. Doing so may help the client see greater value in a physically active lifestyle. Also, the exercise psychologist can use this as an additional opportunity to educate the client about the immediate benefits of exercise (e.g., improved mood, reduced blood pressure, and greater self-efficacy).

Goal Setting

Goal setting, perhaps the most common behavior change technique, is an integral component of evidence-based behavior change theories (see Bandura, 1977). A number of goal-setting methodologies are used in exercise behavior change interventions (Duncan & Pozehl, 2002; Shilts, Horowitz, & Townsend, 2004; Weinberg, 1994), and further research may be needed to identify the best practices for goal setting in health behavior change (Shilts et al., 2004). Nonetheless, setting goals appears to be most effective when it is a collaborative process, where the client and practitioner work together to develop realistic goals (Shilts et al., 2004, Weingberg & Gould, 2015, p. 361), tailored to the individual client. Goals should also be developed in ways that address the client's barriers to exercise. For example, if a client cites lack of time as a barrier to exercise, a "traditional" program consisting of longer (30 minutes or more) exercise sessions may be less effective than a goal of "walking five days a week, three 10-minute bouts each day."

Exercise psychologists should work with clients to develop both long-term and short-term goals. Developing short-term goals is particularly important, because achieving those goals helps foster self-efficacy and feelings of control among individuals (Shilts et al., 2004). Additionally, goals should be challenging but should not be so challenging that the likelihood of meeting the goal is slim (Weinberg & Gould, 2015, pp. 357–358). After setting a goal, the practitioner should ask their clients how confident they are in their ability to accomplish their proposed behavior change. One way to do this is to have the client rate his or her confidence using a scale of 1–10. If a client lacks confidence in his ability to achieve the goal, the goal should be amended in order to increase self-efficacy. Finally, having clients track their progress toward their goals, a process called self-monitoring (Weinberg & Gould, 2015, p. 441), can aid in their behavior change. Incremental successes, which can be achieved through proper goal setting, may be vital in getting members of low-SES and other disadvantaged populations to exercise by increasing their self-efficacy for exercise and motivation (Michie et al., 2009).

Another important part of the goal-setting process is to determine an appropriate reward for when clients attains their short- and long-term goals. The client and practitioner should work together to implement a reward system. Rewards, which serve as motivators toward goal progress and attainment, may be intrinsic or extrinsic. Intrinsic rewards, such as feelings of pride and enjoyment, may motivate individuals to adhere to their exercise programs (Ekkekakis, Parfitt, & Petruzello, 2011; Weinberg & Gould, 2015, p. 453); however, most individuals are more motivated by extrinsic rewards, such as recognition, in the adoption stage of their behavior change (Weinberg & Gould, 2015, p. 453). The practitioner's role is to help clients develop appropriate, yet motivating rewards for themselves. Rewards should not be monetary rewards, particularly when working with low-SES clients. Additionally, if the exercise intervention is fueled by the incentive desire of participants, one should teach clients how to develop appropriate rewards.

Social Support

Another important strategy to include in interventions developed for low-SES individuals is social support. Social support strategies are typically grounded in coping theories and provide ways for individuals to cope with stressful events and changing behavior through networking and developing social relationships. There are four types of social support: emotional, informational, instrumental, and appraisal (House, 1981). Emotional support entails the provision of "empathy, caring, love, and trust" (House, 1981, p. 24) and is particularly important because it provides individuals with the perception of being supported (House, 1981). Examples of emotional support are giving someone praise for their hard work as well as listening and empathizing with a client. Informational support is the provision of information or advice (House, 1981; Langford, Bowsher, Maloney, & Lillis, 1997) and is used to help individuals solve problems. Examples include demonstrating exercises for a client and providing a list of neighborhood resources. The third type of support, instrumental support, is the provision of tangible goods and services, such as providing childcare, transit passes, or financial assistance.

Finally, while appraisal support is similar to informational support, in that one provides information, the intent of appraisal support is to have the individual evaluate their circumstances (House, 1981). For example, a psychologist may provide a client with information about the health consequences of physical inactivity, which allows the client to make a decision regarding exercise on their own. Exercise companionship, which is both emotional and instrumental in nature, may be particularly meaningful to low-SES individuals (Bragg et al., 2009; Parks et al., 2003); therefore, practitioners should encourage clients to elicit this tangible support from friends and family.

SUMMARY

There are a number of strategies that an exercise psychologist can use when working with low-SES clients. Rapport building, education, "pros and cons" tables, goal-setting, and social support strategies are among those that may be particularly useful when working with this disadvantaged population. Developing exercise counseling strategies that are developed for, and tailored to, the individual are also effective. Working with low-SES clients is both a challenging and a rewarding experience. Best results are typically garnered when the client and practitioner work together to identify barriers to exercise, develop strategies to address those barriers, and ultimately improve the behavior.

REFERENCES

Adler, N., Boyce, T., Chesney, M., Cohen, S., Folkman, S., Kahn, R., & Syme, S. (1994). Socioeconomic status and health: The challenge of the health gradient. *American Psychologist, 49*(1), 15–24.

Adler, N., & Newman, K. (2002). Socioeconomic disparities in health: Pathways and policies. *Health Affairs, 21*(2), 60–76.

American Psychological Association, Task Force on Socioeconomic Status. (2007). *Report of the APA Task Force on Socioeconomic Status.* Washington, DC: American Psychological Association.

Andersen, M., & Hanrahan, S. (Eds.). (2015). *Doing sport psychology.* Champaign, IL: Human Kinetics.

Atkinson, N., Billing, A., Desmond, S., Gold, R., & Tournas-Hardt, A. (2007). Assessment of the nutrition and physical activity education needs of low-income, rural mothers: Can technology play a role? *Journal of Community Health, 32*(4), 245–267.

Bandura, A. (1977). Self-efficacy: Toward a unifying theory of behavioral change. *Psychological Review, 84*(2), 191–215.

Baum, A., Garofalo, J., & Yali, A. (1999). Socioeconomic status and chronic stress: Does stress account for SES effects on health? *Annals of the New York Academy of Sciences, 896,* 131–144.

Bragg, M., Tucker, C., Kaye, L., & Desmond, F. (2009). Motivators of and barriers to engaging in physical activity: Perspectives of low-income culturally diverse adolescents and adults. *American Journal of Health Education, 40*(3), 146–154.

Brummett, B., Barefoot, J., Siegler, I., Clapp-Channing, N., Lytle, B., Bosworth, H., . . . Mark, D. (2001). Characteristics of socially isolated patients with coronary artery disease who are elevated risk for mortality. *Psychosomatic Medicine, 63*(2), 267–272.

Burton, N., & Turrell, G. (2000). Occupation, hours worked, and leisure-time physical activity. *Preventive Medicine, 31*(6), 673–681.

Burton, N., Turrell, G., & Oldenburg, B. (2003). Participation in recreational physical activity: Why do socioeconomic groups differ? *Health Education & Behavior, 30*(2), 225–244.

Cairney, J., Boyle, M., Offord, D., & Racine, Y. (2003). Stress, social support and depression in single and married mothers. *Social Psychiatry & Psychiatric Epidemiology, 38,* 442–449.

Centers for Disease Control and Prevention. (2008). *2008 Physical activity guidelines for Americans.* Retrieved June 29, 2013, from www.health.gov/paguidelines/pdf/paguide.pdf

Cohen, S., Kaplan, G., & Salonen, J. (1999). The role of psychological characteristics in the relation between socioeconomic status and perceived health. *Journal of Applied Social Psychology, 29*(3), 445–468.

DeNavas-Walt, C., & Proctor, B. (2014). Income and poverty in the United States: 2013. *U.S. Census Bureau Current Population Reports,* 60–249. Retrieved from www.census.gov/content/dam/Census/library/publications/2014/demo/p602-49.pdf

Duke, J., Huhman, M., & Heitzler, C. (2003). Physical activity levels among children aged 9–13 years—United States, 2002. *Morbidity and Mortality Weekly Report, 52*(33), 785–788.

Duncan, K. A., & Pozehl, B. (2002). Staying on course: The effects of an adherence facilitation intervention on home exercise participation. *Progress in Cardiovascular Nursing, 17*(2), 59.

Duncan, S., Duncan, T., Strycker, L., & Chaumeton, N. (2002). Neighborhood physical activity opportunity: A multilevel contextual model. *Research Quarterly on Exercise and Sports, 73,* 457–463.

Ekkekakis, P., Parfitt, G., & Petruzzello, S. J. (2011). The pleasure and displeasure people feel when they exercise at different intensities. *Sports Medicine, 41*(8), 641–671.

Estabrooks, P., Lee, R., & Gyuresik, N. (2003). Resources for physical activity participation: Does availability and accessibility differ by neighborhood socioeconomic status? *Annals of Behavioral Medicine, 25*(2), 100–104.

Frasure-Smith, N., Lesperance, F., Gravel, G., Masson, A., Juneau, M., Talajic, M., & Bourassa, M. (2000). Social support, depression, and mortality during the first year after myocardial infarction. *Circulation, 101*(16), 1919–1924.

Haskell, W., Lee, I., Pate, R., Powell, K., & Blair, S. (2007). Physical activity recommendations and public health: Updated recommendations for adults from the American College of Sports Medicine and the American Heart Association. *Circulation, 166*(9), 1081–1093.

Holahan, C., Holahan, C., Moos, R., & Brennan, P. (1995). Social support, coping, and depressive symptoms in a late-middle-aged sample of patients reporting cardiac illness. *Health Psychology, 14*(2), 152–163.

House, J. (1981). *Work stress and social support.* Reading, MA: Addison-Wesley.

International Health Racquet & Sportsclub Association. (2012). *The IHRSA health club consumer report: 2012 health club activity, usage, trends, & analysis.* Boulder, CO: Leisure Trends Group.

Janis, I., & Mann, L. (1977). *Decision making: A psychological analysis of conflict, choice, and commitment.* New York, NY: Free Press.

Kipke, R. (2008). *Culture in evaluation #6: Low-socioeconomic status populations in California.* UC Davis: Tobacco Control Evaluation Center. Retrieved July 19, 2013, from http://programeval.ucdavis.edu

Kottler, J. A. (1992). *Compassionate therapy.* San Francisco: Jossey-Bass.

Krueter, M., Lukwago, S., Bucholtz, D., Clark, E., & Sanders-Thompson, V. (2003). Achieving cultural appropriateness in health promotion programs: Targeted and tailored approaches. *Health Education & Behavior, 30*(2), 133–146.

Langford, C., Bowsher, J., Maloney, J., & Lillis, P. (1997). Social support: A conceptual analysis. *Journal of Advanced Nursing, 25,* 95–100.

Larson, N., Story, M., & Nelson, M. (2009). Neighborhood environments: Disparities in access to health foods in the U.S. *American Journal of Preventive Medicine, 36*(1), 74–81.

LeBeauf, I., Smaby, M., & Maddux, C. (2009). Adapting counseling skills for multicultural and diverse clients. In G. R Waltz, J. C. Bleuer, & R. K. Yep (Eds.), *Compelling counseling interventions: VISTAS 2009* (pp.33–42). Alexandria, VA: American Counseling Association.

Marmot, M. (2006). Health in an unequal world. *Lancet, 368,* 2081–2094.

McDonough, P., Duncan, G., Williams, D., & House, J. (1997). Income dynamics and adult mortality in the United States, 1972–1989. *American Journal of Public Health, 87,* 1476–1483.

McNeill, L., & Emmons, K. (2012). GIS walking maps to promote physical activity in low-income public housing communities: A qualitative examination. *Preventing Chronic Disease, 9*(1). doi: 10.5888/pcd9.110086

Michie, S., Jochelson, K., Markham, W., & Bridle, C. (2009). Low-income groups and behavior change interventions: A review of intervention content, effectiveness and theoretical frameworks. *Journal of Epidemiology & Community Health, 63,* 610–622.

Moore, L., Diez Roux, A., Evenson, K., McGinn, A., & Brines, S. (2008). Availability of recreational resources in minority and low socioeconomic status areas. *American Journal of Preventive Medicine, 34*(1), 16–22.

Moore, L., Fulton, J., Kruger, J., & McDivitt, J. (2010). Knowledge of physical activity guidelines among adults in the United States, health styles 2003–2005. *Journal of Physical Activity & Health, 7*(2), 141–149.

Morrow, J., Krzewinski-Malone, J., Jackson, A., Bungum, T., & Fitzgerald, S. (2004). American adults' knowledge of exercise recommendations. *Research Quarterly for Exercise and Sport, 75*(3), 231–237.

Muller, A. (2002). Education, income inequality, and mortality: A multiple regression analysis. *British Medical Journal, 324,* 23–25.

National Cancer Institute. (1995). *Clear & simple: Developing effective print materials for low-literate readers* (Pub. No. NIH 95–3594). Washington, DC: Department of Health and Human Services.

Neckerman, K., Lovasi. G., Purciel, M., Wuinn, J., Raghunath, N., Wasserman, B., & Rundle, A. (2009). Disparities in urban neighborhood conditions: Evidence from GIS measures and field observation in New York City. *Journal of Public Health Policy, 20*(S1), S264–S285.

Parks, S., Houseman, R., & Brownson, R. (2003). Differential correlates of physical activity in urban and rural adults of various socioeconomic backgrounds in the United States. *Journal of Epidemiology & Community Health, 57,* 29–35.

Payne, R., DeVol, P., & Smith, T. (2001). *Bridges out of poverty: Strategies for professionals and communities.* Highlands, TX: aha! Process, Inc.

Powell, L., Slater, S., Chaloupka, F., & Harper, D. (2006). Availability of physical activity-related facilities and neighborhood demographic and socioeconomic characteristics: A national study. *American Journal of Public Health, 96,* 1676–1680.

Prochaska, J., & Velicer, W. (1997). The transtheoretical model of health behavior change. *American Journal of Health Promotion, 12*(1), 38–48.

Ross, C., & Wu, C. (1995). The links between education and health. *American Sociological Review, 60*(5), 719–745.

Sallis, J., Hovell, M., & Hofstetter, R. (1992). Predictors of adoption and maintenance of vigorous physical activity in men and women. *Preventive Medicine, 21*(2), 237–251.

Schoenborn, C., Adams, P., & Peregoy, J. (2013). Health behaviors of adults: United States, 2008–2010. National Center for Health Statistics. *Vital and Health Statistics, 10*(257).

Schrop, S., Pendleton, B., McCord, G., Gil, K., Stockton, L., McNatt, J., & Gilchrist, V. (2006). The medically underserved: Who is likely to exercise and why? *Journal of Health Care for the Poor and Underserved, 17*(2), 276–289.

Shilts, M., Horowitz, M., & Townsend, M. (2004). Goal setting as a strategy for dietary and physical activity behavior change: A review of the literature. *Journal of Health Promotion, 19*(2), 81–93.

Smith, A. (2013). *Technology adoption by lower income populations.* Paper presented at the American Public Health Human Services—IT Solutions Management Annual Conference, San Diego, CA. Presentation retrieved from www.pewinternet.org/2013/10/08/technology-adoption-by-lower-income-populations/

Steenland, K., Hu, S., & Walker, J. (2004). All-cause and cause-specific mortality by socioeconomic status among persons employed in 27 US states, 1984–1997. *American Journal of Public Health, 94,* 1037–1042.

Sue, D., Arredondo, P., & McDavis, R. (1992). Multicultural counseling competencies and standards: A call to the profession. *Journal of Counseling & Development, 70,* 477–486.

Taira, D., Safran, D., Seto, T., Rogers, W., & Tarlov, A. (1997). The relationship between patient income and physician discussion of health risk behaviors. *Journal of the American Medical Association, 278*(17), 1412–1417.

Trost, S., Owen, N., Bauman, A., Sallis, J., & Brown, W. (2002). Correlates of adults' participation in physical activity: Review and update. *Medicine & Science in Sports & Exercise, 34*(12), 1996–2001.

U.S. Census Bureau. (2014). *Current population survey: Annual social and economic supplement.* Retrieved June 16, 2015, from www.census.gov/cps/data/

Ward, M., Guthrie, L., & Butler, S. (2009). Time perspective and socioeconomic health status: A link to socioeconomic disparities in health? *Social Science & Medicine, 68*(12), 2145–2151.

Wardle, J., & Steptoe, A. (2003). Socioeconomic differences in attitudes and beliefs about healthy lifestyles. *Journal of Epidemiology & Community Health, 57,* 440–443.

Watson, J., Etzel, E., & Loughran, M. (n.d.). *Ethics and cultural competence.* Association for Applied Sport Psychology. Retrieved August 7, 2013, from www.appliedsportpsych.org/resource-center/professionals/articles/competence

Wee, C. C., McCarthy, E. P., Davis, R. B., & Phillips, R. S. (1999). Physician counseling about exercise. *Jama, 282*(16), 1583–1588.

Weinberg, R. (1994). Goal setting and performance in sport and exercise settings: A synthesis and critique. *Medicine & Science in Sports & Exercise, 26*(4), 469–477.

Weinberg, R., & Gould, D. (2015). *Foundations of sport and exercise psychology* (6th ed.). Champaign, IL: Human Kinetics.

Wilcox, S., Castro, C., King, A., Houseman, R., & Brownson, R. (2000). Determinants of leisure time physical activity in rural compared with urban older and ethnically diverse women in the United States. *Journal of Epidemiology & Community Health, 54,* 667–672.

Withall, J., Jago, R., & Fox, K. (2011). Why some do but most don't. Barriers and enablers to engaging low-income groups in physical activity programmes: A mixed methods study. *BMC Public Health, 11,* 507.

Withall, J., Jago, R., & Fox, K. (2012). The effect of a community-based social marketing campaign on recruitment and retention of low-income groups into physical activity programmes: A controlled before-and-after study. *BMC Public Health, 12,* 836.

18 Playing the Field

Experiences With Sexual Orientation and Gender in Sport and Physical Activity

Leslee A. Fisher, Allison Daniel Anders, and James M. DeVita

INTRODUCTION

> Spectators watch with wonder. He quickly crosses the space with precision, technique, and control. With sharp, focused movements, he spins, pivots, and pushes forward. Rising from the wood floor without a sound, he extends his body across those below him slicing through the air and completing a 360-degree rotation. He flashes a smile as he lands. He knows his execution was perfect as the crowd erupts into applause.

Before moving into our discussion, we invite you to reflect on the paragraph above: What images are evoked by the description? Do you imagine Mikhail Baryshnikov completing a dynamic solo at the conclusion of a ballet performance? Or do you see Michael Jordan driving down the court, spinning away from his opponents and slamming a dunk for the win? Can you imagine both? Which one is more difficult for you to imagine? Why do you think that is? And why should sport and exercise psychology professionals care?

In this chapter, we seek to describe how everyday understandings of the ways in which sex assignment at birth (often referred to as "sex" or "biological sex" historically), gender identity, gender expression, and sexual orientation are embodied by athletes, scripted across binary gender norms, and inspected by others through surveillance. We address the following questions: What are sexual orientation and gender? What is heteronormativity and binary gender expression? And why should sport and exercise psychology professionals wrestle with these constructs? First, we briefly describe theory related to gender identity and expression based on a brief theoretical review. Definitions are given for relevant constructs, such as female and male assignment at birth, gender identity, gender expression, and sexual orientation, as well as binary gender expression, LGBT spectrum, heteronormativity, and cisgender privilege. Next, we explicate why lesbian/gay/bisexual/transgender (LGBT) issues are important to consider in general and why they matter in physical activity contexts. Following that, we offer a narrative to illustrate some of the identity issues that may be associated with being a gay male, an athlete, a dancer, and a researcher. Specifically, we document four intersecting components or understandings of identity that affect performances and interpretations of the body: (a) assignment at birth (e.g., female assignment at birth [FAAB] and male assignment at birth [MAAB]), (b) gender identity (e.g., female, male, queer, or transgender), (c) gender expression (e.g., "feminine," "masculine," and "androgynous"), and (d) sexual orientation (e.g., asexual, bisexual, heterosexual, or homosexual). Our aim is to analyze the heteronormative narrative that falsely collapses gender expression into sexual orientation. We end the chapter with implications for sport and exercise psychology professionals even as we learn to better navigate these deeply entrenched social patterns ourselves.

BRIEF REVIEW OF THEORY RELATED TO GENDER IDENTITY AND EXPRESSION

A mixture of theories have been used to explore gender identity and expression in the sport and physical activity domain, including feminist sport studies (e.g., Markula, 2005), gender studies (e.g., Heywood & Dworkin, 2003), and queer theory (e.g., Sykes, 1998, 2001). Central categories of analysis employed have consisted of gender identity and gendered representation (e.g., Krane, Choi, Baird, Aimar, & Kauer, 2004), to name a few. In addition, a useful organizing framework that those in cultural studies, feminist studies, and LGBT studies, as well as some in sport and exercise psychology studies, have taken up is Butler's (1993) work on everyday discourse as performance. Butler proposed that the speech we use to communicate with others every day is a performative act, including speech that conjures and cites issues of gender and sexual orientation.

From a sport science perspective, Coakley (2009) asserted that in US culture, *gender* is what is considered to be "feminine" or "masculine." In this model, individuals are assumed to experience gender identity reflective of female or male assignment at birth. For example, if one is assigned as male at birth then "he" is assumed to identify as "male." Additionally, individuals are assumed to express gender in two gender categories, or binary gender expression, based on the assumed relationship across assignment at birth and gender identity. This means that the individual given a "male" assignment at birth is expected to express gender through a "masculine" performance. Not only do these assumptions and expectations reflect the idea of binary gender expression, but they also reflect cisgender privilege—resonance between one's assignment at birth and one's gender identity. The assumption—that assignment at birth will resonate with an individual's sense of his or her own gender identity—is false (Sedgwick, 1993). Individuals who experience congruity and resonance between assignment at birth and gender identity have cisgender privilege. The privilege is the experience of congruity. Individuals who do not experience this congruity do not experience this privilege. In fact, many individuals may identify as transgender.

These two constructs (e.g., assignment and gender identity) are intertwined within a gender binary system. In any binary system, categories are also set up to be "opposites" as well as hierarchical. According to Coakley (2009), for example, in the case of US assignment and gender, when females act "feminine" and males act "masculine," it is interpreted as "normal" and "natural." In addition, Coakley suggested that in the United States, "male" and "masculine" are thought to be *better than* (e.g., afforded more cultural status and privilege to) "female" and "feminine," because males control "a disproportionate share of power and resources":

> All people in the male category are believed to be naturally different from all people in the female category, and they are held to different normative expectations when it comes to feelings, thoughts, and actions . . . The two-category gender classification model is so central to the way people see the world that they resist thinking about gender critically and are likely to feel uncomfortable when people don't fit neatly into one assignment category or the other.
>
> (p. 258)

It is also taken for granted that *assignment* and *gender* are the same thing; therefore, they are frequently and incorrectly used interchangeably. According to definitions by the American Psychological Association (APA, 2011), *sex* (e.g., what we are calling *assignment*) represents an individual's biological status, identified by "assignment chromosomes, gonads, internal reproductive organs, and external genitalia," while *gender* represents "the attitudes, feelings, and behaviors that a given culture associates with a person's biological sex" (www.apa.org/pi/lgbt/resources/assignmentuality-definitions.pdf).

In a parallel vein, *sexual orientation* is regularly defined within a binary system based in the two categories of "heterosexual" or "homosexual." Just like with assignment and gender in a binary system, these categories are politically and socially policed and reinforced. However, sexual orientation is experienced as far more fluid by most individuals than these two categories. In fact, the APA (2011) defined *sexual orientation* as falling along a continuum or spectrum (the LGBT spectrum), ranging from "exclusive homosexuality" to "exclusive heterosexuality." The LGBT spectrum is (partially) represented for the purposes of this chapter as follows:

Lesbian: A woman who is primarily sexually and romantically attracted to women
Gay: A person who is primarily sexually and romantically attracted to persons of the same gender
Bisexual: A person who is primarily sexually and romantically attracted to persons of the same gender, other genders, or regardless of gender
Transgender: A person whose gender identity differs from the societally defined gender the person was assigned at birth (LGBT Union, 2013)

As a final point, *heteronormativity* has been defined as "the cultural bias in favor of opposite-assignment relationships of a sexual nature, and against same-assignment relationships of a sexual nature" (Head, 2013, p. 1). Because of the particular histories of discourse and power cited and deployed/redeployed about gender (Butler, 1993) in the United States, heterosexual relationships are viewed as "normal" and "natural," while LGBT relationships are not; those in LGBT relationships are then more likely to be targeted for heteronormative bias. Some examples of heteronormativity in social contexts include using religion to justify the denial of equal rights to LGBT individuals, such as marriage and adoption, and the stereotyping in the media of LGBT individuals as deviant or abnormal (Head, 2013).

However, like sexism and racism, for example, heteronormativity cannot be eliminated through the legal system; it is a bias that can only be eradicated culturally. As Kate Bornstein (2004) wrote:

> If we're truly going to develop a politic that's going to dismantle the gender binary, we need to rid ourselves of binary thinking as our sole way of thinking and our own binary methodology as our sole way of doing things.
>
> (p. 777)

In the next section, we share parts of James's narrative. One of the main points of sharing this is to follow it with an analysis of what assignment at birth, gender identity, gender expression, and sexual orientation mean to an *actual sport and physical activity participant*. Specifically, we argue that too often people in both heterosexual as well as LGBT communities collapse gender expression into sexual orientation; this can prove to have devastating consequences on the sport and physical activity participant.

WHY GENDER IDENTITY AND EXPRESSION SHOULD MATTER TO SPORT AND PHYSICAL ACTIVITY PROFESSIONALS

To situate gender-identity constructs historically is beyond the scope of this chapter. This said, it is important to note that structural and institutional discrimination and violence against

LGBT-identified individuals, as well as straight individuals redefining binary gender expression, is the historical pattern. Confronting discourses that reify binary categories of identity, expression, and relationships, Sedgwick (1993) lamented that gay and lesbian teenagers were two to three times more likely to attempt and complete suicide than their straight counterparts. Writing in *Tendencies*, Sedgwick shared: "I look at my adult friends and colleagues doing lesbian and gay work and I feel that the survival of each one is a miracle. Everyone who survived has stories about how it was done" (p. 1).

In the 1990s, the U.S. election of President Bill Clinton brought issues of sexual orientation in the military to the forefront. Clinton's "Don't Ask, Don't Tell" (DADT) policy implemented in December 1993 served to simultaneously acknowledge the presence of LGBT folks in the military while also silencing their right to openly serve (Human Rights Campaign, 2006). The policy dominated the national discourse for almost 18 years. The highly publicized 1998 fatal beating perpetrated by Russell Henderson and Aaron McKinney against Matthew Shepard, a gay University of Wyoming student, affected families across the country and generated grassroots demands for non-discrimination laws that included LGBT people and systemic education about LGBT issues (Clark, 1999). By the turn of the 21st century, LGBT discussions had begun to include gay marriage and parenting rights, among others (Eleveld, 2009).

More recently, the performance of masculinity in particular has been changed by the birth of the "metrosexual," defined as "young, urban, straight men [who] are appropriating certain elements of style and culture from the gay community and marketing executives" (Flocker, 2003, p. xiii). The rise of the metrosexual has blurred the distinction between gay and straight men's performance of gender and has become especially popular among younger generations of males in Western societies (Flocker, 2003; Miller, 2005). Multiple, fluid definitions of maleness have appeared in society and allowed for more effeminate representations (e.g., fashionable clothing, manicured appearance, etc.) to be accepted as masculine.

Unfortunately, anti-gay hate speech in the United States is still creating hostility and fostering violence. According to the Southern Poverty Law Center (SPLC, 2014), political representatives like former congresswoman Michele Bachmann (R-MN), believe that "it isn't that some gay will get some rights. It's that everyone else in our state will lose rights" (p. 1). The SPLC reported also that Pat Robertson, an evangelical preacher, stated, "[T]he union of two men doesn't bring forth anything except disease and suffering, and the same thing with the union of two women" (p. 1). Moreover, a recent report from the National Institute of Health (NIH, 2011) titled *The Health of Lesbian, Gay, Bisexual, and Transgender People: Building a Foundation for Better Understanding* cited numerous mental and physical health–related issues for LGBT individuals associated with their marginalization in society. The report asserted that LGBT youth are at greater risk for physical violence, harassment, alcohol abuse, and depression or suicide, among other health-related issues. These health concerns extend into adulthood, with LGBT individuals more likely than their heterosexual peers to be targets of discrimination and violence, experience mood and anxiety disorders, and engage in substance abuse. The report also critiqued historic misconceptions, misrepresentations, and stereotypes of individuals who identify as lesbian, gay, bisexual, and transgender individuals.

The NIH is not alone in identifying the negative consequences of targeted discrimination encountered by LGBT individuals. A 2007 publication that included the data analyzed from the National Longitudinal Study of Adolescent Health found that teenagers who identified as LGB were three times more likely than their straight peers to both have suicidal ideations and to attempt suicide (Silenzio et al., 2007). In addition, approximately 85 percent of transgender individuals report being verbally harassed, over one-third report being physically harassed, and over half report employment discrimination (Transgender Law, n.d.).

These reports highlight the fact that binary conceptions of "female" and "male" and "feminine" and "masculine" are politically and socially policed and reinforced, which can lead to dangerous physical and mental health consequences. Due to deeply entrenched gendered and heteronormative social patterns and the perpetuation of homophobia (i.e., the irrational fear of gay people), sexism, transphobia (i.e., the irrational fear of trans people), and cisgender privilege (the privilege of experiencing congruency between one's gender identity and the assignment they were given at birth, i.e., "female," "male"), LGBT community members face "a profound and poorly understood set of additional health risks largely due to social stigma" (NIH, 2011, p. 14). Perhaps most importantly, these are risks from which their heterosexual counterparts are spared. Additionally, it is important to note that LGBT youth are coming out with their sexual orientation at the median age of about 16 years (Grov et al., 2006). In order to combat hostile campus climates, administrators, faculty, and staff in higher education must implement policies and practices in academic and student affairs as well as athletics that are celebratory, inclusive, and productive (Anders, DeVita, & Oliver, 2012).

In physical activity and athletic contexts, LGBT individuals face discrimination that mirrors larger society. For example, although she and her partner, Alisa Scott, had been in a relationship for seven years, it was not until 2005 that three-time Olympic gold medalist and reigning Women's National Basketball Association's Most Valuable Player Sheryl Swoopes came out (Swoopes, 2006). In 2007, John Amaechi came out three years after he had retired from the NBA (Sheridan, 2007). More recently, numerous hetero-normative and homophobic examples abound, ranging from the firing of a high school coach and physical educator who openly disclosed her lesbian identity (Wright, 2012) to the physical violence and harassment experienced by an openly gay male coach and his straight players (Anderson, 2012). A pervasive climate of homophobia and heterosexism is prevalent, with recent examples occurring at Rutgers University, where the former men's basketball coach used homophobic slurs while demeaning players at practice (Jones, 2013); in addition, Indiana Pacers' Roy Hibbert used a homophobic slur in a post-game news conference (Greenberg, 2013). An unwelcoming environment for LGBT individuals in physical education/exercise and athletic contexts means that they must endure harassment and marginalization, remain closeted, or avoid engagement in sport and physical activity–related experiences. The last option means that these individuals may fail to reap any of the positive benefits of these contexts, including increased physical health, increased self-esteem, leadership development, and teamwork.

PERFORMING GENDER AND SEXUAL ORIENTATION: JAMES'S NARRATIVE

Before presenting selected parts of James's narrative, we describe how Butler (1993) offered an analytical framework related to the constitution of identity via language that we can use to analyze this narrative. We believe that this framework is capable of positioning the aforementioned tension between gender expression and sexual orientation. Butler's (1993) work on performative acts reminds us that as we use language to communicate prior discourse as well as context and history and that both affect the enactment of our words. Butler argued that in provisional ways we are always already constituted by language, before and as we speak. To describe these phenomena, she employed the idea of a "citational chain" (p. 29). The citational chain—which is conjured and deployed in the moment of speech—serves as a referent to prior acts or "reiteration of acts" (p. 29). As such, an analysis of discourse provides us with opportunities to interrogate both the citational chain that is conjured and the utterance that is deployed, or rather redeployed. Since the collapse of gender expression into sexual orientation is pervasive, particularly among heterosexual males (e.g., when effeminate men are targeted with "gay-baiting") (e.g., Kite & Deaux, 1987; Madon, 1997; Sakalli, 2002), the process of discrimination demands that we invest in understanding how misconception and misrepresentation work. Here, we hope such an analysis will render everyday speech participation regarding LGBT issues more inclusive, productive, and supportive, particularly within physical activity and sport domains.

What follows is an excerpt from James's narrative about being a ballet dancer and a soccer player. The focus is on the intersection of gender identity and expression across ballet, soccer, and public high school spaces.

I recall many fond memories from my early experiences in dance: the joy of mastering a double pirouette and a grande jeté; the feel of shiny costumes that draped my body as I danced; performing for family and friends; and receiving praise from teachers after demonstrating a new step. These are the memories that make me smile. They are also things that kept me involved in the activity as I matured, despite a burgeoning anxiety during my adolescence. While most of the boys I knew practiced sports after school, I practiced ballet. While many boys socialized with brothers, fathers, and male classmates, I spent hours with my sister, mother, and female classmates in dance. When the football teams dressed in pads and helmets, I performed in tights and makeup.

For a great deal of my young childhood, these differences went largely unnoticed for both me and my male peers. I enjoyed my experience in dance and had become quite good at it. As a male dancer, in fact, I was strongly encouraged by many individuals to stick with it. My initial involvement in dance was actually due to poorly developed feet and legs, flat feet and bowed legs that multiple doctors had wanted to "break and re-set." Dance was a form of physical therapy for me as much as it was a form of expression until around age 10. At that point, as the only male in my company, I was offered classes free of charge in exchange for my commitment to perform. This opportunity highlighted my unique characteristic inside of dance class: my male identity.

My experiences inside of dance class, however, were not what led me to question my involvement as I entered my teenage years. Rather, it was my classmates who performed on the field—not on the stage—who raised doubts in my mind. When I first became active in sports with males only, I felt insecure about my "masculinity." My mannerisms, gestures, and movements were markedly more "feminine" than my male peers, which made me concerned about how I would be accepted by my teammates.

Ironically, at dance, my performance of "masculinity" sharply contrasted with my female peers even as our bodies were subjected for well over a decade to similar foundational trainings. However, my definitively "masculine" gender expression in dance spaces did not translate to the soccer field. My same embodiments were scripted as "masculine" in one space (dance) and markedly "feminine" in the other space (soccer).

"Effeminate," or more precisely "less masculine," was a title I was willing to accept, but "gay" was not an ascription I was willing to accept at this point in my life. Looking back it would have felt like too many "strikes" against me. Because dance had disciplined my body in particular ways and led me to be named by others as "effeminate," I never fully allowed myself to consider thoughts about my sexual orientation.

Although never physically harassed about my sexual orientation during high school, occasional teasing and taunting by bullies or foes made me aware of others' perceptions. I responded by performing the role of a straight male to the best of my abilities. My gender expression on the soccer field reflected my study of my male peers.

My relationships with women at dance also made my performance easier. Since I was the only male in my age group enrolled in dance at both of the studios at which I studied, the close relationships I developed with female dancers became romantic ones as we spent considerable time together away at competitions or during summer intensives. Dance provided me with years of opportunity to socialize with females and to learn to appreciate their equal commitment to dance. In high school I dated a number of company members as well as young women at school. Through the process of repeated denial of my sexual orientation to my classmates I was allowed to use my performances to convince myself of a heterosexual identity. I marvel that I did not know then what I know now: that I was and am gay.

(DeVita, 2010, unpublished)

OUR NARRATIVE ANALYSIS OF JAMES'S EXPERIENCE

For Butler (1993), "performative acts are forms of authoritative speech" (p. 17). She argued that most performative acts "are statements which, in the uttering, also perform a certain action and exercise a binding power" (p. 17). As previously stated, Butler distinguished between the enactment of language and the "citational chain" (p. 29). The performative is "thus one domain in which power acts *as* discourse" (p. 17). The subject, however, does not execute her or his "will through discourse" (p. 18). Even as they are provisional, discourse and citational chains are always already present.

Here, as we turn toward James's narrative, we witness his responsiveness to the always already present discourses around male assignment, gender identity, gender expression, and sexual orientation. At dance, in a predominantly female setting, James performs three embodiments. First, there is a performance of the physical, *male assignment at birth*, or what some might call the "biological" male. In ballet, the physical embodiment of the male body is rare and, therefore, highly valued. Here, he practices and performs diligently across 15 years of childhood into adolescence with much success. He is valued for his skill and his embodiment and performance at the intersection of assignment and gender identity. In ballet, males are required to lift and partner their female counterparts. This kind of hierarchical partnership based on binary gender norms privileges James as he was one of the only male dancers.

Second, there is the performance of *gender identity*. Although the aim in this section is to analyze the narrative James wrote, and, therefore, to understand his performances as a once-closeted young gay male with multiple performances of gender expression, we would be remiss if we did not underscore his cisgender privilege. For James—who has cisgender privilege—experiences of discontinuity did not exist between the assignment given to him at birth as male and his experience and performance of gender identity. He identified as male and, when he did so, he experienced a self-identification resonance with the assignment given to him at birth. James's sense that the assignment at birth as male reflected who he experienced himself to be is an incredible privilege.

Third, there is a performance of *gender expression*. The performance of binary gender expression, the way James expressed himself through movement and speech, exists in relationship to both the entrenchment of social patterns scripted for the gender expression of men and women, and, specifically, for this relationship in the space of ballet. Indeed, as Butler (1993) argues, "gender is performative insofar as it is the effect of a regulatory regime of gender differences in which genders are divided and hierarchized under constraint" (p. 21). For example, when James first joined all-male sport teams, he recognized that he needed a comprehensive understanding of the social norms already present and governing male sport in order to navigate what felt like a "hyper-masculine," heteronormative space. In contrast to his experiences at school, James navigated his experiences with dance from a dominant position as a male dancer who performed male-only moves, and therefore, performed coveted moves through a body assigned male at birth and situated as male through both self-identification and discourse.

Becoming a star athlete for his team, school, and community created layered performances of gender expression, that is, athletic prowess in dance with grace, agility, and strength through his male body for male roles in a predominantly female setting, and athletic prowess in soccer with speed, balance, and strength through his male body in an all-male setting.

We think it is important to note here that James's achievements in both dance and soccer make the deconstruction of his performance of "masculine" gender expression along a gender binary an impossibility. We argue that his success as an athlete was tightly coupled (Weick, 1976) to his performances and that his success reinforced those same binary gender norms. That is to say, in sport and physical activity, athletes are expected to perform well with the aim of winning. James did this and did it well. Not only did he meet the demands of soccer, but he contributed to his team's success too, an achievement that we argue solidified evidence of a successful performance of "masculinity" or "legitimacy" under the questioning gaze of his teammates and classmates. Dating young women from his company and from high school transformed this questioning, too.

Working against entrenched social patterns of gender expression, our aim here was to investigate the layers of performance and the particular contexts in which they occur (Noblit, 1999). Most importantly, the reification of binary conceptions of gender expression fore-closes opportunities to understand experience at the intersections of assignment, gender identity, and gender expression and different experiences across different contexts. At school, the classroom and hallway performances of gender expression reflected the false binary of "feminine" and "masculine."

Recently during a performance, as James still dances and now teaches dance, the father of one of his dance students approached him with a smile and exclaimed, "White men *can* jump!" The man shook James's hand and talked about how powerful and impressive his leaps were. His focus was squarely on the athleticism in James's movements rather than the technique, grace, or control. As an adult, this comment did not surprise James. He has come to understand the ways binary gender expression and gay baiting limit both male consumption of athleticism and male-to-male communication about athleticism. Remembering his training from childhood, he knew that it would not help if he critiqued the man's compliment, not only for its inverted racism, but also for the absence of compliment regarding technique, grace, and control.

The particular mastery that James had over his sport and physical activity experience generated two co-occurring strategies for him: it helped him succeed in soccer, a space of deeply entrenched heteronormative and binary gender social patterns, and it helped him silence the interpretation of a gay identity when teammates and classmates would collapse binary gender expression into sexual orientation.

Finally, the performance of *sexual orientation* comes late in James's adolescence. Indeed, James was a junior in high school when he went to New York City for a ballet intensive with Joffrey Ballet. While there, he was introduced for the first time in his 14 years of dance to some gay male dancers. It was not until his junior year in high school that James remembers having romantic feelings toward male peers. Before then, sexual orientation was something he thought about only as heterosexual; this is what heteronormative and binary gender norms demanded of him. James explained that his performance of heterosexuality kept questions about his sexual orientation at bay.

Although one can interpret gender expression from visual witnessing, one cannot interpret sexual orientation in the same way. Sexual orientation exists in relationship to another. In other words, you cannot see sexual orientation except through relationship to another, and sometimes not even then. Isolated, the sharing of mutual attention and care, emotional vulnerability, intimacy, and physical affection is an impossibility. Certainly there is as well relationality that is emotional, psychological, and spiritual that may not be physically expressed in romantic or sexual expression. Most often, to visually witness sexual orientation is to witness someone in relation to another. Sexual orientation is not scripted in binary gender norms of expression named "feminine" or "masculine." Nor is it likely without disclosure to be ascribed to an individual alone. Its consumption is dependent on its relationality. This is not to say that a gay man cannot speak of his partner and share through such disclosure that he is gay. It is to say that such witnessing is contingent on disclosure and not on one's carriage, gate, or step. Collapsing the latter into the former is what classmates and teammates did at James's high school. In response to the threat of that collapse, James repressed his own feelings and performed a heterosexual "masculine" male identity. His sense of "success" at passing as straight on the field and in the hallways mutually reinforced and unproductively obstructed his coming out to himself and others. Ultimately, the cultural regimes of heteronormativity and binary gender expression postponed James's coming out.

SO WHAT? IMPLICATIONS FOR SPORT AND EXERCISE PSYCHOLOGY PROFESSIONALS

What we hoped to illustrate with James's experience and our subsequent analysis—and what is important for sport and exercise psychology professionals to take away from this chapter—is that we need to speak, teach, and coach with specificity and thoughtfulness. We have provided definitions of assignment at birth, gender identity, cisgender privilege, gender expression, and sexual orientation, and we have argued that these concepts are distinct even as they intersect with one another. Attuning to these distinctions is paramount in working with lesbian, gay, bisexual, and transgender students and athletes. Moreover, practicing discernment between gender expression (androgyny, femininity, masculinity) and sexual orientation is essential. One must guard against collapsing gender expression into sexual orientation.

As professionals, it is critical that we attune to differences across context for athletes or exercisers navigating more than one competition space; for example, for James, dance and soccer were spaces in which he found achievement and success, but they required very different accommodations on his part, soccer so much so that he pursued the continual dating of girls to keep the threat of gay baiting at bay. For many sport and exercise psychology professionals, the idea of cisgender privilege may also be new. As a gay male, James's still articulated cisgender privilege because of the sense of congruency and pride he experienced in having the ascription of a male identity correspond to his male assignment at birth. We believe that cisgender privilege needs to be included in any study of LGBT issues; it is a potential layer of identity often overlooked in both heterosexual and LGBT communities. James's experience demands that we pay more attention to its importance.

As a final point, we hoped to highlight the everyday navigation that we are all subjected to with regard to heteronormative and binary gender expression social patterns and the damage they can do. We believe it is necessary to rewrite performative acts in ways that challenge their dominance and also dismantle their citational chain. New ones must be created if we are to celebrate and provide resources for targeted groups in any context, but most importantly, for those of us working in sport and physical activity contexts.

REFERENCES

American Psychological Association. (2011). Definition of terms: Assignment, gender, gender identity, sexual orientation. *The Guideline for Psychological Practice with Lesbian, Gay, and Bisexual Clients.* Retrieved from www.apa.org/pi/lgbt/resources/assignmentuality-definitions.pdf and www.apa.org/topics/assignmentuality/sorientation.pdf

Anders, A. D., DeVita, J. M., & Oliver, S. T. (2012). Southern predominantly white institutions, targeted students, and the intersectionality of identity: Two case studies. In C. Clark, M. Brimhall-Vargas, & K. Fasching-Varner (Eds.), *Just how important is diversity in higher education? Stories from the front-lines* (pp. 71–81). Lanham, MD: Rowman & Littlefield Publishers, Inc.

Anderson, E. (2012). The changing relationship between men's homosexuality and sport. In G. B. Cunningham (Ed.), *Sexual orientation and gender identity in sport: Essays from activists, coaches, and scholars* (pp. 35–45). College Station, TX: Center for Sport Management Research and Education.

Bornstein, K. (2004). This quiet revolution. In L. Heldke & P. O'Connor (Eds.), *Oppression, privilege, and resistance: Theoretical perspectives on racism, sexism, and heterosexism* (pp. 767–786). Boston, MA: McGraw Hill.

Butler, J. (1993). Critically queer. *GLQ: A Journal of Gay Lesbian Studies, 1*, 17–32.

Clark, T. (1999, April 5). *First defendant gets life in gay student killing: Sentence comes after guilty plea.* Retrieved March 1, 2010, from http://cnn.com/US/9904/05/gay.attack.trial.03/

Coakley, J. (2009). *Sports in society: Issues and controversies.* New York, NY: McGraw-Hill.

DeVita, J. M. (2010). *Positionality draft.* Unpublished essay. The University of Tennessee.

Eleveld, K. (2009, June 17). Hate crimes passes, faces veto. *Advocate.com.* Retrieved from www.advocate.com/news_detail_ektid98991.asp

Flocker, M. (2003). *The metrosexual guide to style: A handbook for the modern man.* Cambridge, MA: Da Capo Press.

Greenberg, C. (2013). Roy Hibbert apologizes, tweets at Jason Collins after saying 'no homo' at press conference. *Huffington Post.* Retrieved from www.huffingtonpost.com/2013/06/02/roy-hibbert-apologizes-gay-slur-cursing_n_3375101.html.

Grov, C., Bimbi, D. S., Nanin, J. E., & Parsons, J. T. (2006). Race, ethnicity, gender, and generational factors associated with the coming-out process among gay, lesbian, and bisexual individuals. *The Journal of Sex Research, 43*(2), 115–121.

Head, T. (2013, June 12). *Definition of heteronormativity from About.com.* Retrieved from http://civil-liberty.about.com/od/gendersexuality/g/heteronormative.htm

Heywood, L., & Dworkin, S. (2003). *Built to win: The female athlete as cultural icon.* Minneapolis, MN: University of Minnesota Press.

Human Rights Campaign [HRC] website. (2006). *Don't ask, don't tell, don't pursue, don't harass.* Retrieved from www.hrc.org/Content/NavigationMenu/HRC/Get_Informed/Issues/Military2/Fact_Sheets_Dont_Ask_Dont_Tell/Dont_Ask,_Dont_Tell_Fact_Sheet.htm

Jones, D. (2013, April 3). Rutgers fires basketball coach after abuse video surfaces. *Reuters.* Retrieved from www.reuters.com/article/2013/04/03/us-usa-rutgers-coach-idUSBRE93200V20130403

Kite, M. E., & Deaux, K. (1987). Gender belief systems: Homosexuality and the implicit inversion theory. *Psychology of Women Quarterly, 11*, 83–96.

Krane, V., Choi, P. Y. L., Baird, S. M., Aimar, C. M., & Kauer, K. J. (2004). Living the paradox: Female athletes negotiate femininity and muscularity. *Sex Roles, 50*(5/6), 315–329.

LGBT Union. (2013, June 12). *LGBTQI definitions & information.* University of Akron Center for Service and Leadership. Retrieved from http://uakronstudentlife.orgsync.com/org/lgbtu/lgbtqi_definitions

Madon, S. (1997). What do people believe about gay males? A study of stereotype content and strength. *Sex Roles, 37*(9/10), 663–685.

Markula, P. (2005). *Feminist sport studies: Sharing experiences of joy and pain.* New York, NY: SUNY Press.

Miller, T. (2005). A metrosexual eye on queer eye. *GLQ: A Journal of Lesbian and Gay Studies, 11*(1), 112–117.

National Institute of Health. (2011). *The health of lesbian, gay, bisexual, and transgender people: Building a foundation for better understanding.* Washington, DC: The National Academies Press.

Noblit, G. W. (1999). *Particularities: Collected essays on ethnography and education.* New York, NY: Peter Lang Publishing, Inc.

Sakalli, N. (2002). Pictures of male homosexuals in the heads of Turkish college students: The effects of sex difference and social contact on stereotyping. *Journal of Homosexuality, 43*(2), 111–126.

Sedgwick, E. K. (1993). *Tendencies.* Durham: NC: Duke University Press.

Sheridan, C. (2007). Amaechi becomes first NBA player to come out. *ESPN NBA*. Retrieved April 1, 2009, from http://sports.espn.go.com/nba/news/story?id=2757105

Silenzio, V. M. B., Pena, J. B., Duberstein, P. R., Cerel, J., & Knox, K. L. (2007). Sexual orientation and risk factors for suicidal ideation and suicide attempts among adolescents and young adults. *American Journal of Public Health*, *97*(11), 2017–2019. doi: 10.2105/AJPH.2006.095943

Southern Poverty Law Center. (Spring, 2014). *Hate in the mainstream*. Retrieved from https://www.splcenter.org/fighting-hate/intelligence-report/2015/hate-mainstream-2

Swoopes, S. (2006). Outside the arc. *ESPN The Magazine*. Retrieved April 1, 2009, from http://sports.espn.go.com/wnba/news/story?id=2204322

Sykes, H. (1998). Turning the closets inside/out: Towards a queer-feminist theory in women's physical education. *Sociology of Sport Journal*, *15*, 154–173.

Sykes, H. (2001). Understanding and overstanding: Feminist-poststructural life histories of physical education teachers. *Qualitative Studies in Education*, *14*, 13–31.

Transgender Law. (n.d.). *Transgender issues: A fact sheet*. Retrieved from www.transgenderlaw.org/resources/transfactsheet.pdf

Weick, K. E. (1976). Educational organizations as loosely coupled systems. *Administrative Science Quarterly*, *21*, 2–18.

Wright, J. (2012, January 12). *Coach settles with Waxahachie school that allegedly fired her for being gay*. Retrieved from www.dallasvoice.com/breaking-coach-settles-waxahachie-charter-school-allegedly-fired-gay-1098798.html

19 Persons With Disabilities

Stephanie J. Hanrahan

The title of this chapter is "Persons With Disabilities." Although it is a basic title, for some people I have already taken a stand. To use the term *disabled person* instead of *person with a disability* is thought by many to be politically incorrect because *disabled person* suggests that the only thing worth mentioning about the person is the disability. The American Psychological Association (APA, 2010) advocates the use of person-first language to maintain the integrity of all individuals as human beings and avoid inferring that the whole person is disabled. Putting the person first is standard practice within the medical model of disability. The medical (and dominant) model of disability locates the problem of disability within the individual. Health professionals diagnose and attempt to treat or otherwise address the impairments that people "have." The social model of disability, however, locates the problem of disability within society. Developed within the civil and human rights movements, the social model indicates that impairments do not cause disabilities. Instead, any problems arise from a society that is unaccommodating. Societies disable people through such avenues as poor building design, limited access to information (e.g., documents not available in Braille), unequal opportunities, and prejudiced attitudes. Because it is society that places limits on what people with impairments can achieve, according to the social model the term *disabled person* is not derogatory; it is a commentary on society, not the person. Nevertheless, whether it is because of my indoctrination in the medical model or my years of abiding by APA format, I have chosen to use person-first terminology, even though I agree that there would be fewer issues with disabilities if the world was a completely accommodating place.

COPING WITH DISABILITY

In addition to dealing with various degrees of an unaccommodating society, individuals with disabilities have to cope with the impairments themselves. One would think that those with more severe disabilities would have greater psychological distress, but research indicates that this assumption is not always true. In a study of individuals with congenital spina bifida, less disability was associated with greater psychologist distress and more emotional problems (Padua et al., 2002). Therefore, as practitioners we want to avoid assuming that those with severe disabilities are in need of greater psychological support compared to those with mild disabilities.

Approximately 17 percent of physical disabilities are congenital (i.e., the individuals were born with the impairments; Papworth Trust, 2013). The remaining 83 percent of physical disabilities are acquired through either traumatic injuries or progressive diseases over time. Acquired disabilities obviously require physical and psychological adjustment. The emotional distress from acquired disabilities, however, may not always follow the expected trajectory of decreasing as time passes. In a longitudinal study of individuals experiencing amputations, individuals reported greater distress four to six months post-amputation then they did just a few weeks after the amputations (Fisher & Price, 2003). Support needs to be available to those who previously may have been determined to be effectively coping. Individuals who quickly initiate involvement in, or return to, exercise and physical activity post-amputation may experience delayed psychological reactions (Fisher & Price, 2003). The context of the amputation or other acquired impairment may also influence adaptation. For example, a limb amputated because of cancer may involve ongoing treatment for the illness and the fear of additional body parts being surgically removed in the future, whereas an amputation as a result of a motorcycle accident may lead to anxiety when around motorcycles or even when being the passenger in a car.

People with acquired disabilities often also have to deal with relational changes. They sometimes have difficulty relating to old friends and may experience rejection by friends (Lyons, Ritvo, & Suliivan, 1995). In addition, familial relations can be affected; disability is a risk factor for divorce. Although pre-existing relationships may alter or disappear, social support can help individuals cope with disabilities and can be critical in determining the quality of their lives. Nevertheless, not all social support is helpful. Even though it may be well intended, social support in the forms of encouraging quicker coping, giving inappropriate advice, minimizing the importance of the traumatic event, or avoiding open communication about the event is unhelpful (Rees, Smith, & Sparks, 2003). Individuals usually want to be proactive in seeking support, with the security that it is available if needed.

Social factors not only influence people with disabilities; they also relate to the onset of functional disability (i.e., difficulty in performing activities of daily living). In a four-year prospective study in Japan, women who lived in communities with social environments involving mistrust and lack of social participation were more likely to experience the onset of disability, even after adjusting for age, income, education, and baseline health status (Aida et al., 2013).

EFFECTS OF PARTICIPATING IN PHYSICAL ACTIVITY

People with physical disabilities are much more likely than the general population to experience preventable and treatable health conditions, such as obesity, fatigue, chronic pain, depression, anxiety, pain, sleep problems, and urinary tract infections (Kinne, Partich, & Doyle, 2004; Liou, Pi-Sunyer, & Laferrère, 2005; Nosek et al., 2006). Many of these conditions can be ameliorated by participation in regular physical activity (Warburton, Nicol, & Bredin, 2006). In an extensive review of both random and non-random controlled trails, the Physical Activity Guidelines Advisory Committee (2008) found that people with physical disabilities who engaged in physical activity showed significant improvements in muscle strength, cardiorespiratory fitness, bone mineral content and density, flexibility, depression, quality of sleep, anxiety, interpersonal relationships, self-esteem, functional independence, pain, triglycerides, total cholesterol, and quality of life.

In addition to aiding physical (and psychological) factors, participation in physical activity also enhances social aspects of the self (Blinde & McClung, 1997). People with physical disabilities who participated in physical activity reported that their involvement in the activities expanded their social interactions and experiences, and helped them initiate social activities in other contexts. Participation in physical activity has also been found to provide opportunities for empowerment for individuals with physical or sensory disabilities. That empowerment can be in terms of goal attainment, social integrations, and perceived competence as a social actor (Blinde & Taub, 1999).

Through interviews with children with physical disabilities ages 10–17, Taub and Greer (2000) found that physical activity is a normalizing experience for them because it legitimates their social identities as children and strengthens social ties. The school students indicated that being physically active strengthened their perceptions of improving life situations and increased their feelings of control over life events.

Not only do individuals with physical and sensory disabilities benefit from physical activity, people with intellectual disabilities also profit from participation. Adults with intellectual disabilities who were randomly assigned to a five-week physical activity program reported increased perceptions of competence, self-esteem, and internal locus of control as compared to those in a control group (Mactavish & Searle, 1992). Physical activity positively affects muscle strength, balance, and quality of life in individuals with intellectual disabilities (Bartlo & Klein, 2011). The positive effects of physical activity programs, however, are dependent upon the quality of the programs. Coaches or teachers who block participants' aspirations for autonomy (e.g., because of a tendency to overprotect participants with disabilities) typically limit many of the potential benefits of participation (Dluzewska-Martyniec, 2002; Hanrahan, 2007).

OPPORTUNITIES TO PARTICIPATE

Although the evidence of the physical, psychological, and social benefits of physical activity for people with disabilities is overwhelming, the majority of individuals with disabilities are sedentary. Most people with disabilities are insufficiently physically active (Centers for Disease Control and Prevention, 2007). In addition to obstacles to participation experienced by the general public (e.g., lack of time, limited financial resources, low exercise efficacy, little motivation), individuals with disabilities are confronted with additional barriers (Latimer, Martin-Ginis, & Carven, 2004). These additional barriers include the scarcity of accessible facilities and transportation, adapted equipment, and personnel trained about disabilities and exercise. Gyms, for example, often have limited space between pieces of exercise equipment, making it extremely difficult (or impossible) for those in wheelchairs or those using white canes to get around. Some gyms and recreational clubs deny access to potential members with disabilities because of liability fears (Smeltzer, 2010; Smith, 2013).

Although many children with disabilities attend regular schools together with their able-bodied peers, some children with disabilities attend separate schools or separate support units within regular schools. The disabling effects on children differ between mainstream and specialized educational programs (Gaskin, Andersen, & Morris, 2012). Even well-intentioned educational policy can result in less-than-ideal actions in terms of inclusion, environments, and attitudes of others (Graham & Spandagou, 2011). Some students are excluded from participating in physical education and after-school sporting activities, and this exclusion can be highly distressing (Gaskin et al., 2012). The attitudes of teachers, fitness instructors, coaches, family members, and able-bodied peers influence participation in physical activity by individuals with disabilities of all ages (Hutzler, 2003). When opportunities to participate are limited, it becomes even more difficult for people to acquire physical skills or develop exercise self-efficacy. Getting general members of the community to engage in regular physical activity is challenging enough without the added obstacles of exclusion, inaccessibility, and stigma that many individuals with disabilities face.

INTEGRATION/SEGREGATION

There has been ongoing debate as to whether it is better to have integrated physical activity programs where people with and without disabilities participate together, or whether people with disabilities benefit more from programs tailor-made for them. Inclusive (i.e., integrated) programs can be perceived as either freeing or constraining (Devine, 2003). The perceived meaning of being included with able-bodied participants depends on the context and the role of the social group. The setting may be constraining if participants feel they are excluded from the group for either ability or social reasons. Nevertheless, environments (both social and physical) that allow individuals to engage on an equal footing with able-bodied participants or provide opportunities for social integration and achievement can be perceived as freeing (Devine, 2003). If minor accommodations are not made for impairments (e.g., using a bright ball when a person with a visual impairments is participating in a soccer activity), then the experience will probably be constraining rather than freeing (Nixon, 1988).

Research within physical education classes indicates that, whether or not children have disabilities, the social experiences within integrated physical education classes are determined by the physical education teachers, the social substance of the activities, and the cultural backgrounds and social skills of the students (Suomi, Collier, & Brown, 2003).The primary positive influence on the social experiences of all students is the physical education teacher (i.e., the quality of adult leadership). Obrusnikova, Valkova, and Block (2003) investigated the effects of the presence of a student in a wheelchair with no direct support in a volleyball module within a fourth-grade physical education class. One class included a student in a wheelchair, and a second class did not. There were no significant differences between the classes in terms of the acquisition of volleyball knowledge and skills. In addition, the able-bodied students tended to have positive attitudes toward the student with a disability. It would be interesting if future research were to determine whether able-bodied participants in integrated classes experience positive effects, such as the development of acceptance, tolerance, and open-mindedness.

Unlike in physical education classes, where integration may be mandated, in community physical activity programs instructors often decide for themselves how open (or not) their activities will be to individuals with disabilities. Conatser, Block, and Gansneder (2002) found that swim instructors were more favorable toward including individuals with mild disabilities than those with severe disabilities. The instructors' attitudes and perceived behavioral control predicted their intentions to include participants with disabilities, and their intentions predicted the actual inclusion of swimmers with disabilities in their programs (Conatser et al., 2002). Education about the practical issues of involving people with disabilities might result in more instructors and coaches being open to the inclusion of individuals with disabilities in physical activity programs. In a study of caregivers for people with intellectual disabilities, Martin, McKenzie, Newman, Bowden, and Morris (2011) found that perceived control over the ability to support clients with intellectual disabilities in their physical activity was the strongest predictor of reported physical activity levels of the people they supported.

PSYCHOSOCIAL ISSUES THAT MAY ARISE IN EXERCISE ENVIRONMENTS

As mentioned previously, the attitudes of teachers, instructors, family members, and able-bodied peers influence the participation of individuals with disabilities in physical activity (Hutzler, 2003). There is a flip side to attitudes, though. Individuals with disabilities who exercise may influence the attitudes of others. People hold more positive attitudes toward active people with physical disabilities compared to those who are inactive (Dionne, Gainforth, O'Malley, & Latimer-Cheung, 2013).

Within many exercise environments, relatively little clothing is typically worn. For example, many people experience anxiety when appearing in a bathing suit in front of others.

This anxiety may be exacerbated for individuals with physical disabilities. Self-esteem and self-identity predicted social physique anxiety in adolescent swimmers with physical disabilities (Martin, 1999). It is possible that allowing or modelling less-revealing clothing (as done in some physical activity programs for Muslim girls and women) might make some participants feel more comfortable within exercise settings.

For some individuals with physical disabilities, exercise and physical activity programs may bring up unpleasant memories of physiotherapy sessions. Physical activity is a part of some physiotherapy sessions for people with physical disabilities, particularly for children (Anttila, Autti-Rämö, Suoranta, Mäkelä, & Malmivaara, 2008). Although the intention of physiotherapists is to maintain or restore physical functioning, some individuals find these therapy sessions to be painful. Children, in particular, may not understand the purpose of engaging in these physical exercises, and this minimal understanding combined with associated pain, fatigue, and physical distress may deter individuals from whole-heartedly enjoying participation in physical activities (Gaskin et al., 2012; Redmond & Parrish, 2008).

Participation in exercise sessions may not only bring about associations related to pain; they may also be perceived as punishing due to the experience of negative evaluations of physical competencies (particularly compared to able-bodied peers) and the occurrence of being excluded (or at least not fully included). Children with disabilities may internalise ableism (i.e., incorporate prejudices against people who are not able-bodied), identify with their able-bodied classmates, and therefore develop feelings of inferiority (Hutzler, Fliess, Chacham, & Van den Auweele, 2002). Although some individuals downplay labels of normality or abnormality, others regard able-bodied people as normal and themselves as abnormal. Their inability to do some things in a physical activity setting may spark these feelings of inferiority (Gaskin & Hanrahan, 2015). Obviously, these evaluations and feelings may influence psychological well-being.

Psychological well-being can also be negatively affected by individuals being excluded from some activities or entire programs. Unfortunately, routine exclusion of people with disabilities from social and physical activities is the norm in some schools and clubs (McMaugh, 2011).

Some individuals with disabilities may attempt to normalize their bodies through physical exercise (Gaskin, Andersen, & Morris, 2011). Engaging in structured physical activity gives them the opportunity to align (or realign) themselves with society's body-beauty ideals of attractiveness (Guthrie & Castelnuovo, 2001). Having muscles or other signs of being exercisers, or even just being seen to be participating in culturally valued pursuits of fitness, can allow individuals with disabilities to feel they are a part of normal physical culture.

FACTORS AFFECTING EXERCISE BEHAVIOR

As mentioned previously, participating in regular physical activity can have many benefits for people with disabilities. Just as with the general population, however, knowing that one should engage in regular exercise and actually doing so are two different things. As described in Chapter 5 of this volume, the theory of planned behavior indicates that attitudes, subjective norms, and perceived behavioral control predict intentions to exercise, which in turn predicts actual exercise behavior (with some research suggesting that perceived behavioral control also directly predicts behavior; Blue, 1995; De Bruijn, 2011).

In a study testing the theory of planned behavior in individuals with physical disabilities, Latimer et al. (2004) found that perceived behavioral control was the only variable from the theory that predicted exercise intentions and behavior in people with quadriplegia. Within the same study, however, none of the variables from the theory of planned behavior predicated the exercise intentions or behaviors for people with paraplegia. The results may not have fully supported the theory of planned behavior because of the additional barriers to exercise that many people with disabilities confront. In addition to the commonly experienced barriers of limited time, financial resources, motivation, and energy, women with disabilities have reported additional barriers to exercise, including poor social support, low confidence in the ability to exercise, health limitations, and environmental barriers (Rauzon, 2002). Few people without disabilities probably have to deal with the barriers of accessible facilities, adapted equipment, and staff knowledgeable about disabilities and exercise. It may be that these additional barriers play such a significant role that the variables within the theory of planned behavior pale in comparison.

CONSIDERATIONS WHEN WORKING WITH PEOPLE WITH DIFFERENT DISABILITIES

When exercise practitioners work with people with disabilities, the disability is rarely the main focus. Whatever a nutritionist, physiologist, or psychologist generally tries to achieve when working with clients does not dramatically change just because a client has a disability. The disability should not be ignored if it influences what practitioners are doing, but it should not be the main focus. If information about the disability is needed, with the exception of young children and people with intellectual disabilities, clients with disabilities are often the best source of information regarding the disability. It is not unusual for two people with the same disability (and even degree of disability) to have notably different experiences of disability. What follows are suggestions for practitioners to keep in mind when working with people with a variety of different disabilities. These considerations are only guidelines, because individual circumstances may alter ideal practice. These suggestions are designed to introduce readers to some of the exercise, communication, and psychological skill issues they may encounter when working with clients with disabilities.

Amputees

- Exercise can result in muscle imbalances in individuals with single-limb amputations. For example, a single-arm amputee doing upper-body strength training may end up with back and chest problems if only one side of the body is used when exercising. Creative use of aids such as pulleys and straps can help the side with a stump engage in similar activity to the side with the complete limb.
- Particularly in people with a single-leg amputation, the existing limb may be more susceptible to overstressing or overuse injuries compared to able-bodied exercisers. Keep in mind the extra work that a single limb might be required to do (e.g., when moving between different stations in a weights circuit).
- Amputees who choose sport as a form of exercise may benefit from learning (and ensuring that those involved in able-bodied sporting clubs also learn) about rule differences that may exist. For example, at a local swim carnival a girl who lost her arm in a farming accident was disqualified in her breaststroke race because she did not finish with a two-hand touch on the wall. The rule is that the shoulders must be square to the wall when finishing.
- A prosthesis can influence body awareness and imagery. Generally, if individuals wear their prosthesis while exercising, then it should be worn if they engage in body awareness or imagery exercises relevant to that activity. On the other hand, if the prosthetic device is removed for participation (e.g., swimming), then it should also be removed for related body awareness and imagery exercises (Hanrahan, 1995).
- Studying the relationship between body awareness or imagery and phantom limb experiences of amputee exercisers could be an interested topic for future research.

Blind and Visually Impaired

- Identify yourself when you begin or join a conversation, and similarly, never leave a conversation without saying so. Many blind people I know get rightfully irritated when they begin talking to someone they think is there, but who has left.
- Avoid background noise. With no (or little) information being obtained through sight, there is an increased reliance on sound. Making the sound as clear as possible can be helpful.
- Speak directly to the person and maintain eye contact. Some individuals fail to maintain eye contact because they are not receiving eye contact. Once eye contact is lost, there is a tendency to no longer face the person. Even without sight, it is easy to tell when someone is not speaking directly to you.
- The acquisition of many physical skills relies on visual feedback. When visual feedback is not available, verbal feedback becomes even more important.
- Provide accurate and specific instructions and directions. To that end, teachers of physical skills may need to improve their teaching abilities when working with people who cannot see. Instead of relying on visual demonstrations, precise verbal instructions are required. Improving verbal instructions can be beneficial for many sighted learners who may not be primarily visual learners.
- Avoid rearranging furniture. If circumstances require a change in location of furniture, be sure to inform people who are blind or visually impaired of any changes.
- If providing written information to clients, consider Braille, large-font handouts, or recorded information (e.g., electronic, CD). Braille handouts can frequently be printed at a local school for the blind or a related community organization. Be sure to write on any Braille handouts what they are, so people who are not capable of reading Braille can identify the topics of the handouts. It is worth noting here, however, that many people who are blind do not read Braille.
- Self-talk during relaxation sessions may be more disruptive for people who are blind compared to people who are sighted. Sighted people may have a signal to begin the relaxation process just by closing their eyes and blocking out visual distractions. People who are blind do not have this cue and therefore may need extra practice in calming the mind during relaxation (Hanrahan, Grove, & Lockwood, 1990).
- Imagery is effective. Individuals who are blind typically have better movement or kinaesthetic imagery than they do visual imagery, but even visual imagery tends to be reasonably good. Because imagery is based on past experience, some visual images may be difficult or impossible for individuals who have never been able to see.

Cerebral Palsy

- Cerebral palsy is a variety of neuromuscular conditions caused by damage to the part of the brain that controls and coordinates muscle tone, reflexes, and action. The muscles that control speech are frequently affected. It is important not to assume that an intellectual disability is present because of the different speech patterns of people with cerebral palsy.
- Individuals with severe forms of cerebral palsy are frequently confined to motorized wheelchairs and are often accompanied by caregivers. Because caregivers are often experienced at deciphering what these individuals are trying to say, there can be a tendency for less-experienced individuals to communicate through the caregiver. Even if a caregiver is playing the role of interpreter, it is still important to speak directly to the individual.
- Two people with the same classification of cerebral palsy may vary in the control of various muscles. Determining which muscles each individual can and cannot control can be helpful when engaging in various physical activities.

- If using progressive muscular relaxation, consider skipping the tension phase because increasing tension to a muscle or groups of muscles may increase spasticity in people with cerebral palsy, which is obviously not conducive to relaxation (Page & Wayda, 2001).

Deaf

- There is a difference between being *deaf* and being *Deaf*. The lowercase *deaf* refers to people with a medical condition that affects their hearing. The uppercase *Deaf* refers to individuals who were born deaf, socialize mainly within the Deaf community, and primarily communicate through sign language (which is different in different countries, but is also different than the spoken languages in those countries). People who self-identify as being Deaf would likely take offense at deafness being considered a disability.
- Speak naturally. Some individuals make the mistake of exaggerating their lip movements, thinking it will make them more easily understood. It doesn't.
- Face individuals when speaking and avoid chewing gym, smoking, blocking your face, leaning your cheek or chin on your hand, or doing anything else that might obstruct the view of your face and lips.
- Make sure the sun or other light source is in front or to the side of you. If the light is coming from behind you, the view of your lips and face will be poor.
- If you are not being understood, rephrase instead of repeating what you are saying.
- If individuals are hard of hearing (and not deaf or Deaf), eliminating background noise will be beneficial to communication.
- Use visual demonstrations and communication tools (e.g., text messaging, written instructions, white/chalk boards, PowerPoint). Just as working with blind people can enhance communication skills, so too can working with people who are deaf.

Intellectual Disabilities

- There is a wide range of ability levels within this population, but generally speaking, people with intellectual disabilities find it difficult to think in abstract terms, struggle to make decisions, have poor short-term memory, possess limited literacy and numeracy skills, hold inconsistent concentration spans, and have learning difficulties.
- Although usually beneficial for most participants, it is perhaps even more important to keep sessions fun and enjoyable when working with people with intellectual disabilities.
- Keep practice time on specific activities short.
- Keep instructions simple.
- Confirm that you have been understood by asking open-ended questions. Simply asking, "Do you understand?" will often result in an affirmative response even if nothing has been understood.
- Be specific in praise, criticism, and encouragement.
- Be aware of need to teach things that we may take for granted (e.g., that one needs to wait for play to finish on a neighboring tennis court before going onto the court to retrieve a ball).
- The field of exercise psychology could benefit from research that investigates the most effective techniques for teaching mental skills to individuals with intellectual disabilities.

Wheelchair Participants

- The first issue most people think of when mentioning people in wheelchairs is accessibility. Accessibility, however, does not only refer to ramps and lifts instead of stairs. From an exercise point of view, additional accessibility issues include access to fitness classes, space for wheelchairs around fitness equipment, and the provision of grips/pulleys/Velcro to be able to use exercise equipment when limbs are affected by partial paralysis.

- Many individuals with spinal cord injuries have difficulty dealing with heat and cold.
- Get on the individual's level. Use a chair or squat, but avoid standing and talking down to people in wheelchairs.
- Be aware of rules for sporting activities that may be unique to participants in wheelchairs. For example, in tennis two bounces are allowed instead of one.
- Help people with incomplete spinal lesions to harness all even partially usable muscles. Sometimes individuals who are unable to walk but have partial use of their trunk or lower limbs become accustomed to not using those muscles at all. In water-based activities especially, these individuals can learn to make use of the muscle function they do have.
- Consider that leaning on someone's wheelchair (while they are in it) may be perceived as having someone lean on the person and interpreted as an invasion of personal space.
- Abdominal breathing can be a useful relaxation/centering activity, even when individuals do not have use of abdominal muscles.
- If using progressive muscular relaxation, offer participants two recorded scripts: one that contains directions for tensing and relaxing all the different muscle groups in the body, and a second one that only includes the muscle groups over which the individual has control. Some individuals prefer the long version because focusing on the muscles they do not control still improves their body awareness (or in the case of quadriplegics, the tailor-made scripts may be perceived to be too short). Other individuals prefer the tailor-made version because the full version causes them to get frustrated and angry when they are asked to tense muscles they cannot control (Hanrahan, 1995).
- Under-activation is often of greater concern than over-activation (perhaps due to low blood pressure).

CONCLUSION

Practitioners who work with individuals with disabilities enhance their professional effectiveness no matter with whom they end up working in the long term. Working with people with sensory impairments often strengthens communication skills, and adapting to various physical impairments can result in greater creativity. Working with people with disabilities might also enhance empathy in practitioners who have limited people skills. Regardless of ability or disability, individuals benefit from regular participation in physical activity. As practitioners we need to do our best to enhance the experience for all participants. Some practitioners are uncomfortable or fearful when first working with clients with disabilities. Usually this discomfort or fear is due to inexperience or lack of familiarity with different populations. Approaching new clients as opportunities for professional growth may help some individuals overcome any initial reticence.

REFERENCES

Aida, J., Kondo, K., Kawachi, I., Subramanian, S. V., Ichida, Y., Hirai, H., . . . Watt, R. G. (2013). Does social capital affect the incidence of functional disability in older Japanese? A prospective population-based cohort study. *Journal of Epidemiology & Community Health, 67*, 42–47.

American Psychological Association. (2010). *Publication manual of the American Psychological Association* (6th ed.). Washington, DC: Author.

Anttila, H., Autti-Rämö, I., Suoranta, J., Mäkelä, M., & Malmivaara, A. (2008). Effectiveness of physical therapy interventions for children with cerebral palsy: A systematic review. *BMC Pediatrics, 8,* 14. doi:10.1186/14712-4318-14

Bartlo, P., & Klein, J. K. (2011). Physical activity benefits and needs in adults with intellectual disabilities: Systematic review of the literature. *American Journal on Intellectual and Developmental Disabilities, 116,* 220–232. doi 10.1352/1944-7558-116.3.220

Blinde, E. M., & McClung, L. R. (1997). Enhancing the physical and social self through recreational activity: Accounts of individuals with physical disabilities. *Adapted Physical Activity Quarterly, 14,* 327–344.

Blinde, E. M., & Taub, D. E. (1999). Personal empowerment through sport and physical fitness activity: Perspective from male college students with physical and sensory disabilities. *Journal of Sport Behavior, 22,* 181–202.

Blue, C. L. (1995). The predictive capacity of the theory of reasoned action and the theory of planned behaviour in exercise research: An integrated literature review. *Research in Nursing & Health, 18,* 105–121.

Centers for Disease Control and Prevention. (2007). Physical activity among adults with a disability—United Sates, 2005, *Morbidity and Mortality Weekly Report, 56,* 1021–1024.

Conatser, P., Block, M., & Gansneder, B. (2002). Aquatic instructors' beliefs toward inclusion: The theory of planned behaviour. *Adapted Physical Activity Quarterly, 19,* 172–187.

De Bruijn, G. (2011). Exercise habit strength, planning and the theory of planned behaviour: An action control approach. *Psychology of Sport and Exercise, 12*(2), 106–114. doi: 10.1016/j.psychsport.2010.10.002

Devine, M. A. (2003). Constraining and freeing: The meaning of inclusive leisure experiences for individuals with disabilities. *Journal of the Canadian Association for Leisure, 28,* 24–47. doi:10.1080/14927713.2003.9649938

Dionne, C. D., Gainforth, H. L., O'Malley, D. A., & Latimer-Cheung, A. E. (2013). Examining implicit attitudes towards exercisers with a physical disability. *The Scientific World Journal, 2013,* Article ID 621596, 8 pages. doi:10.1155/2013/621596

Dluzewska-Martyniec, W. (2002). The need of autonomy in Special Olympics athletes and its satisfying through sports activity. *Gymica, 32,* 53–58. Abstract retrieved May 15, 2013 from SPORT Discus database.

Fisher, K., & Price, E. M. (2003). The use of a standard measure of emotional distress to evaluate early counseling intervention in patients with amputations. *Journal of Prosthetics and Orthotics, 15,* 31–34.

Gaskin, C. J., Andersen, M. B., & Morris, T. (2011). Physical activity and fantasies in the life of an adult with cerebral palsy: The motivator, looking for love. *Qualitative Research in Sport, Exercise and Health, 3,* 238–262. doi:10.1080/2159676X.2011.572178

Gaskin, C. J., Andersen, M. B., & Morris, T. (2012). Physical activity in the life of a woman with cerebral palsy: Physiotherapy, social exclusion, competence, and intimacy. *Disability and Society, 27,* 205–218.

Gaskin, S. J., & Hanrahan, S. J. (2015). Enabling activity and conquering prejudices when working with disabled people. In M. Andersen & S. J. Hanrahan (Eds.), *Doing exercise psychology* (pp. 201–215). Champagne, IL: Human Kinetics.

Graham, L. J., & Spandagou, I. (2011). From vision to reality: Views of primary school principals on inclusive education in New South Wales, Australia. *Disability & Society, 26,* 223–237. doi: 10.1080/09687599.2011.544062

Guthrie, S. R., & Castelnuovo, S. (2001). Disability management among women with physical impairments: The contribution of physical activity. *Sociology of Sport Journal, 18,* 5–20.

Hanrahan, S. J. (1995). Psychological skills training for competitive wheelchair and amputee athletes. *Australian Psychologist, 30*(2), 96–101.

Hanrahan, S. J. (2007). Athletes with disabilities. In G. Tenenbaum & R. C. Eklund (Eds.), *Handbook of sport psychology* (3rd ed., pp. 845–858). Hoboken, NJ: Wiley.

Hanrahan, S. J., Grove, J. R., & Lockwood, R. J. (1990). Psychological skills training for the blind athlete: A pilot program. *Adapted Physical Activity Quarterly, 7*(2), 143–155.

Hutzler, Y. (2003). Attitudes toward the participation of individuals with disabilities in physical activity: A review. *Quest, 55*, 347–373. doi:10.1080/00336297.2003.10491809

Hutzler, Y., Fliess, O., Chacham, A., & Van den Auweele, Y. (2002). Perspectives of children with physical disabilities on inclusion and empowerment: Supporting and limiting factors. *Adapted Physical Activity Quarterly, 19*, 300–317.

Kinne, S., Partrich, D. L., & Doyle, D. L. (2004). Prevalence of secondary conditions among people with disabilities. *American Journal of Public Health, 94*, 443–445. doi:10.2105/AJPH.94.3.443

Latimer, A. E., Martin-Ginis, K. A., & Craven, B. C. (2004). Psychosocial predictors and exercise intentions and behaviour among individuals with spinal cord injury. *Adapted Physical Activity Quarterly, 21*, 71–85.

Liou, T.-H., Pi-Sunyer, F. X., & Laferrère, B. (2005). Physical disability and obesity. *Nutrition Reviews, 63*, 321–331. doi:10.1301/nr.2005.oct.321-331

Lyons, R. F., Ritvo, P. G., & Sullivan, M. J. L. (1995). *Relationships in chronic illness and disability*. Thousand Oaks, CA: Sage.

Mactavish, J. B., & Searle, M. S. (1992). Older individuals with mental retardation and the effect of a physical activity intervention on selected social psychological variables. *Therapeutic Recreation Journal, 26*, 38–47.

Martin, E., McKenzie, K., Newman, E., Bowden, K., & Morris, P. G. (2011). Care staff intentions to support adults with an intellectual disability to engage in physical activity: An application of the theory of planned behaviour. *Research in Developmental Disabilities, 32*, 2535–2541. doi: 10.1016/j.ridd.2011.07.006

Martin, J. J. (1999). Predictors of social physique anxiety in adolescent swimmers with physical disabilities. *Adapted Physical Activity Quarterly, 16*, 75–85.

McMaugh, A. (2011). En/countering disablement in school life in Australia: Children talk about peer relations and living with illness and disability. *Disability & Society, 26*, 853–866. doi: 10.1080/09687599.2011.618740

Nixon, H. L. (1988). Getting over the worry hurdle: Parental encouragement and the sports involvement of visually impaired children and youths. *Adapted Physical Activity Quarterly, 5*, 29–43.

Nosek, M. A., Hughes, R. B., Petersen, N. J., Taylor, H. B., Robinson-Whelen, S., & Byrne, M. (2006). Secondary conditions in a community-based sample of women with physical disabilities over a 1-year period. *Archives of Physical Medicine and Rehabilitation, 87*, 320–327. doi:10.1016/j.apmr.2005.11.003

Obrusnikova, I., Valkova, H., & Block, M. E. (2003). Impact of inclusion in general physical education on students without disabilities. *Adapted Physical Activity Quarterly, 20*, 230–245.

Padua, L., Rendeli, C., Rabini, A., Girardi, E., Tonali, P., & Salvaggio, E., (2002). Health-related quality of life and disability in young patients with spina bifida. *Archives of Physical Medicine and Rehabilitation, 83*, 1384–1388. doi: 10.1053/apmr.2002.34599

Page, S. J., & Wayda, V. K. (2001). Modifying sport psychology services for athletes with cerebral palsy. *Palaestra, 17*, 10–14.

Papworth Trust. (2013). *Disability in the United Kingdom 2013: Facts and figures*. Author.

Physical Activity Guidelines Advisory Committee. (2008). *Physical activity guidelines advisory committee report, 2008*. Washington, DC: US Department of Health and Human Services.

Rauzon, T. A. (2002). *Barriers to participation in physical activity/exercise for women with physical disabilities*. Eugene, OR: Kinesiology Publications, University of Oregon microfiche. Abstract retrieved June 3, 2013 from SPORT Discus database.

Redmond, R., & Parrish, M. (2008). Variables influencing physiotherapy adherence among young adults with cerebral palsy. *Qualitative Health Research, 18*, 1501–1510. doi:10.1177/1049732308325538

Rees, T., Smith, B., & Sparks, A. C. (2003). The influence of social support on the lived experiences of spinal cord injured sportsmen. *The Sport Psychologist, 17*, 135–156.

Smeltzer, S. C. (2010). Improving health and wellness of people with disabilities. In J. H. Stone & M. Blouin (Eds.), *International encyclopedia of rehabilitation*. Retrieved from http://cirrie.buffalo.edu/encyclopedia/en/article/300/

Smith, S. E. (2013, April 13). Gym turns away customer with Down Syndrome. *Care2*. Retrieved from www.care2.com/causes/gym-turns-away-customer-with-down-syndrome.html

Suomi, J., Collier, D., & Brown, L. (2003). Factors affecting the social experiences of students in elementary physical education classes. *Journal of Teaching in Physical Education, 22*, 186–202.

Taub, E. E., & Greer, K. R. (2000). Physical activity as a normalizing experience for school-age children with physical disabilities. *Journal of Sport and Social Issues, 24*, 395–414. doi: 10.1177/0193723500244007

Warburton, D. E. R., Nicol, C. W., & Bredin, S. S. D. (2006). Health benefits of physical activity: The evidence. *Canadian Medical Association Journal, 174*, 801–809. doi:10.1503/cmaj.051351

20 Applied Exercise Psychology
Children and Adolescents

Lindsey C. Blom, Amanda J. Visek, and Brandonn S. Harris

CHAPTER OVERVIEW

Using Welk's (1999a) Youth Physical Activity Promotion Model (YPAP) as the guide, the main objective of this chapter is to provide information regarding children and adolescents' current physical activity patterns, share known explanations for these patterns, and review methods for engaging children and adolescents in physical activity. Moderators (i.e., personal sociodemographic factors) and mediating factors known to foster and sustain physical activity participation are discussed. Emphasis is placed on how to provide opportunities for fun experiences so that physical activity habits acquired during childhood and adolescence become lifelong health behaviors.

BENEFITS OF PHYSICAL ACTIVITY AND CONSEQUENCES OF PHYSICAL INACTIVITY

The 2008 Physical Activity Guidelines for Americans (USDHHS, 2008a) recommends that young persons between the ages of 6 and 17 accumulate 60 minutes or more of moderate-to-vigorous physical activity daily, of which the majority should be aerobic (e.g., bicycling, brisk walking, rollerblading, jumping rope, playing sports) as well as some muscle- and bone-strengthening activities (e.g., games of tug-of-war, push-ups, sit-ups, swinging on playground equipment, hopping, skipping, jumping). Physical activity is in fact a critical component to the healthy growth and development of children and adolescents (Hills, King, & Armstrong, 2007). There is strong scientific evidence that regular physical activity results in a number of biological and physical improvements in children and adolescents, namely bone health, cardiorespiratory and muscular fitness, lower body fat composition, and improved cardiovascular and metabolic health biomarkers (e.g., DeBoer, 2013; USDHHS, 2008b). There is also growing evidence that regular physical activity is associated with improved mental health (e.g., Weichselbaum & Buttriss, 2011), as well as enhanced academic performance in young persons (e.g., Singh, Uijtdewilligen, Twisk, Mechelen, & Chinapaw, 2012). Moreover, participation in organized physical activities, such as sport, is linked with psychosocial benefits, including increased self-esteem, confidence, character building, socialization, and life skills (e.g., Andreann et al., 2012; Smoll & Smith, 1996). In addition, participating in team sports has also been found to act as a moderator, reducing the negative psychological effects associated with bullying in 8–10-year-old children (Andreann et al., 2012). Indeed, both organized sport and unstructured play result in substantive biopsychosocial benefits for children and adolescents (Bailey, Hillman Arent, & Petitpas, 2013; Perron et al., 2012), and the physical activity habits developed in early childhood typically carryover into adulthood

(Dodge & Lambert, 2009). Therefore, children's physical activity is a significant investment not only for their present health and development, but also for their continued health and development across their lifespan.

Collectively, the positive outcomes that result from sustained engagement in regular physical activity can be described as human capital; that is, physical activity is an investment in the physical, emotional, intellectual, social, individual, and future financial health and well-being of children and adolescents (Bailey et al., 2013). As noted previously, this investment is recommended daily. However, despite the health benefits physical activity is known to yield (Bailey et al., 2013), a large proportion of children and adolescents do not meet recommended guidelines. In fact, physical activity levels decline as children age (CDC, 2014).

In the United States, 77 percent of children ages 9–13 report participating in free-time physical activity (CDC, 2010). However, only 29 percent of high school students report engaging in at least 60 minutes per day of physical activity (CDC, 2014), and 15.2 percent report participating in no physical activity (CDC, 2014). With respect to physical education classes, the percentage of students who participate in physical education classes also declines during adolescence. In an average week, less than half of high school students attended physical education classes; participation was highest in 9th grade (64%) and significantly declined by 12th grade (35%). Those participating in daily physical education classes are even lower— just 42 percent of 9th graders and only 20 percent of 12th graders (CDC, 2014).

Worldwide, the prevalence of physical inactivity varies from a low of 18.7 percent to a staggering high of 90.6 percent, with a median of 79.7 percent among adolescents (Moraes, Guerra, & Menezes, 2013). Physical inactivity is a global pandemic (Kohl et al., 2012) and is the fourth-leading risk factor for mortality (World Health Organization, 2009). Insufficient amounts of physical activity, combined with poor dietary intake, has led to one of the most serious public health challenges of the 21st century, chiefly overweight and obesity. Recent estimates indicate that 17 percent of children (6–11 years old) and adolescents (12–19 years old) are obese (BMI ≥ 95th percentile), and 31.8 percent are considered overweight or obese (BMI ≥ 85th percentile; Ogden, Carroll, Kit, & Flegal, 2012). Worldwide, it is estimated that over 43 million children under the age of five are overweight (de Onis, Blossner, & Borghi, 2010). These numbers are of great significance because overweight and obesity leads to cardiometabolic consequences (e.g., hypertension, diabetic dyslipidemic syndrome, increased cardiovascular inflammation) in children and adolescents (CDC, 2011; DeBoer, 2013; Friedemann et al., 2012; National Center for Health Statistics, 2009; Rodrigues et al., 2013; Wilkinson, 2008). If children remain obese in their childhood, they are also at the highest risk of continued obesity as an adult, and therefore at future risk for developing many chronic diseases, including cardiovascular disease morbidity and mortality (Goldhaber-Fiebert et al., 2013; Sowers, 2001). Consequently, it is commonly reported that today's generation of youth may be the first generation to not outlive their parents (Olshansky, 2005). Chronic diseases that were once adult-onset conditions, such as type-2 diabetes, are now being diagnosed in child and adolescent populations. Subsequently, in the United States, reports indicate that one-third of children possess at least one of the risk factors for metabolic syndrome (Bailey et al., 2013), which will have devastating effects on an already overburdened healthcare system if left untreated (Finkelstein et al., 2012).

In regards to government-based initiatives, within the US Department of Health and Human Services (USDHHS), the Office of Disease Prevention and Health Promotion (ODPHP) manages a collaborative, evidence-based, and federally funded public health effort known as "Healthy People." Healthy People envisions a society in which all people live long, healthy lives (USDHHS, 2002). Every decade, Healthy People provides an agenda with specific public health objectives, including measurable outcome targets for each objective.

Improving health, fitness, and quality of life through daily physical activity is one of the many public health goals of Healthy People 2020. The physical activity objectives identified by Healthy People 2020 are based on the aforementioned 2008 Physical Activity Guidelines for Americans. As such, Healthy People 2020 includes 15 overarching physical activity objectives, of which the majority aim to increase child and adolescent physical activity through a multidisciplinary approach (e.g., schools, childcare, physician visits, active transport, built environment) and reduce the amount of time spent in sedentary activities (e.g., screen time). For example, one of the Healthy People physical activity objectives is to improve the proportion of adolescents that participate in school-based daily physical education from 33.3 percent to 36.6 percent by the year 2020. Similarly, by 2020, Healthy People aims to increase the number of states that require regularly scheduled elementary recess from 7 to 17 states (see www.healthypeople.gov for a review). In addition to these government-initiated efforts, a large array of physical activity promotion programs exist at local, regional, and national levels. Table 20.1 provides descriptive examples of select physical activity promotion programs with a special focus on children and adolescents within the United States.

YOUTH PHYSICAL ACTIVITY PROMOTION MODEL

Given the aforementioned benefits from engaging in lifelong physical activity, coupled with the health-related disparities associated with the growing global pandemic of physical inactivity among young persons, the promotion of healthy lifestyles among children and adolescents remains a significant area of interest for professionals in various health-related domains. Indeed, programs such as Healthy People continue to provide clinicians and researchers with targeted markers to better enhance participation in physical activity among youth. For this and other programs to remain successful in their efforts, a better understanding of the motives for physical activity participation becomes increasingly important. Toward this effort, Welk (1999a) proposed an integrated and specific multidimensional conceptual model referred to as the Youth Physical Activity Promotion Model (YPAP). Welk's model is highlighted in this chapter for two reasons. First, unlike other theoretical approaches that largely address adult physical activity behavior, the YPAP accounts for the developmental differences in motives for physical activity as experienced by children and adolescents. To that end, research has found that the YPAP accounts for a significant proportion of the variance in physical activity participation for children and adolescents (Joens-Matre, 2007). Second, the comprehensive nature of the YPAP model provides a thorough framework for detailing the known moderators and psychosocial mediators of physical activity participation among children and adolescents. More specifically, the YPAP model suggests that three different sets of factors influence physical activity behaviors among youth: enabling, predisposing, and reinforcing (see Figure 20.1).

Based on YPAP, *enabling* factors include the biological or environmental determinants that facilitate children and adolescents to be physically active. Examples of these are fitness levels, physical skill sets, and access to physical activity equipment and environments. *Predisposing* factors address the likelihood that youth will be physically active on a consistent basis. Examples of these are perceptions of ability and the cost-benefit analysis of being physically active. Finally, *reinforcing* factors denote those social or familial variables that reinforce youth's physical activity behaviors. Examples of these include parent-, peer-, and coach-related behaviors and the interactions between youth and each of these groups. Additionally, Welk also notes that each of these three factors are influenced by various personal sociodemographic characteristics or moderators, including gender, age, socioeconomic status, and ethnicity.

Table 20.1 Select Examples of Efforts to Promote Physical Activity in Children and Adolescents

	Purpose	Programming and Resources Offered
American Alliance for Health, Physical Education, Recreation and Dance	To enhance knowledge, improve professional practices, and increase support for quality physical education, sport, and physical activity programs.	Sets national and state standards for physical education and sport programs, provides professional development opportunities via conferences and workshops, provides grant opportunities for research to expand evidence-based practice. www.aahperd.org/naspe/about/
America Scores	To inspire urban youth to lead healthy lives, engage as students, and develop confidence and character.	A unique programming approach, combining soccer, poetry, and service learning, designed to improve students' health, scholastic achievement, and positive civic engagement. http://www.americascores.org/
Boys and Girls Club of America	To provide community-based and building-centered clubs and programming that are safe, affordable sites for youth during non-school hours to play, learn, and reach their potential.	Sport, fitness, and recreation-focused programming offers programs in partnership with the Professional Golf Association and Major League Baseball, such as the PGA Sports Academy, Wanna Play, Jr. RBI, and RBI: Reviving Baseball in Inner Cities. http://www.bgca.org
CANFIT (Communities, Adolescents, Nutrition, Fitness)	To connect communities and policy makers to focus on improving the healthy eating and physical activity environments for low-income adolescents of color.	Provides an active guide to make it easier to promote physical activity in youth, provides a physical activity pyramid for active school programs, and offers physical activity trainings for youth-serving organizations; California based. http://canfit.org/
KaBOOM!	To create playspaces through the participation and leadership of communities.	Program focuses on three major efforts: building playgrounds, taking action for play, and mapping the state of play (and play deserts). http://kaboom.org
Let's Move!	To enrich children's health through nutrition and physical activity; focused on active kids at play through active families, schools, and communities; initiative of former First Lady Michelle Obama.	The Let's Move! initiative includes programs around the country designed to mobilize physical activity and nutrition efforts in cities, towns, schools, and communities. Provides a variety of tips and factsheets online. www.letsmove.obamawhitehouse.archives.gov
National Basketball Association and Women's National Basketball Association Wellness Programs	To provide national programming and partnerships toward physical activity and healthy living through workouts, programs, events, and products to encourage physical activity for children and families.	Physical activity and health-related programming such as the Fit Pledge, Dribble to Stop Diabetes, the Gatorade Training Center, and Live Healthy Week. www.nba.com/nbafit/

NFL Play 60	To aid the next generation of youth in becoming the most active and healthy generation by encouraging them to be active for at least 60 minutes each day.	NFL Play 60 connects players and coaches with schools and communities for in-school, after-school, and team-based programs. www.nfl.com/play60
President's Council on Fitness, Sports, and Nutrition	To build partnerships with public, private, and non-profit sectors to promote efforts to adopt healthy lifestyles; made up of 25 volunteer citizens who serve in an advisory capacity through the Secretary of Health and Human Services.	Presidential youth fitness program (school-based), Let's Move! Active Schools (school-based), I Can Do It, You Can Do It! (for persons with disabilities), Physical Activity Initiative (public service announcements). www.fitness.gov
Playworks, Inc.	To increase opportunities for physical activity and safe and meaningful play at recess and throughout the school day.	Provides a direct-services model with onsite coaches at low-incomes schools to facilitate positive recess and play experiences in order to maximize learning opportunities throughout the school day; has full-time coaches in 360 schools in 22 cities. www.playworks.org
The First Tee	To provide educational programming focused on values and life skills development to promote healthy choices through the sport of golf.	Provides chapter enrichment programs beginning at age 7, professional development training and lesson plans for physical educators in elementary schools, after-school programs, and military programs for children of servicemen and women, including National Guardsmen and Reservists. www.thefirsttee.org
YMCA of the USA	To improve, as an inclusive, community-based organization, the spiritual, mental, and physical health of its members.	Fitness and health programming is based on preventive health activities. Youth development physical activities include a Swim, Sports & Play program; also offers a variety of other healthy-living programming focused on children and families. http://www.ymca.net/

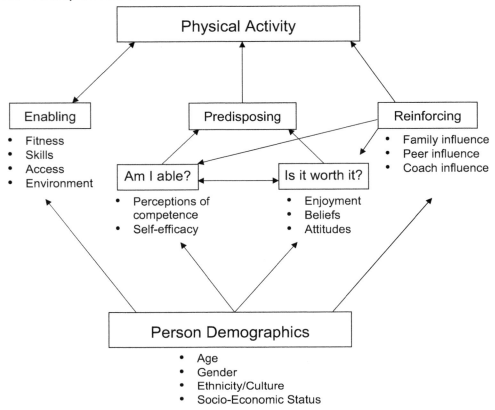

Figure 20.1 Welk's Youth Physical Activity Promotion Model

PHYSICAL ACTIVITY MODERATORS

In order to understand and improve the current physical activity patterns of children and adolescents, it is important first to examine sociodemographic variables that moderate these behaviors (i.e., *reinforcing factors* and *personal demographic factors* from Welk's model). Research has identified a considerable number of physical activity moderators for adults (e.g., Amireault, Godin, & Vézina-IM, 2013; Trost, Owen, Bauman, Sallis, & Brown, 2002); however, these same results have not necessarily been found nor yet studied as extensively in younger populations. Specifically, moderators such as gender, age, self-efficacy, and parental support have been consistently confirmed for children and adolescents. Conversely, other moderators commonly known for adult populations, including socioeconomic status (SES), show mixed results for children and adolescents (Ferreira et al., 2006; Gustafson & Rhodes, 2006; Van der Horst et al., 2007). Table 20.2 provides a synthesis of the current scientific evidence for these moderators. This information can be used to direct future research as well as aid practitioners in designing intervention strategies.

Gender

Typically, among children and adolescents, more boys than girls meet the physical activity recommendations, which is consistent across ethnicities as well as SES. Further, the magnitude

Table 20.2 Select Moderators Associated With Physical Activity in Children and Adolescents

Factor	Operationalization	Children	Adolescents	Select References
Age	Children: ages 6–11; Adolescents: 12–19	Younger more likely to be active	Younger more likely to be active	Belcher et al. (2010); Stanley et al. (2012); Van der Horst et al. (2007)
Ethnicity	A group with cultural characteristics in common	Non-Hispanic Black most active, compared to Mexican American and non-Hispanic White	Differences in physical activity decline with age	Belcher et al. (2010)
Gender		Boys more likely to be active	Boys more likely to be active	Belcher et al. (2010); Floyd et al. (2008); Pearson et al. (2009); Stanley et al. (2012)
SES	Family income	Not applicable	Positive relationship	Ferreira et al. (2006)
	Parental education	Mixed results	Positive relationship, especially with mother's education	Ferreira et al. (2006); Gustafson & Rhodes (2006); Van der Horst et al. (2007)
Parents' Physical Activity	Parental physical activity	Inconclusive	Inconclusive	Ferreira et al. (2006); Gustafson & Rhodes (2006)
	Father's physical activity	Probable positive relationship, especially for boys	Inconclusive	Ferreira et al. (2006); Van der Horst et al. (2007)
	Mother's physical activity	Mostly unrelated	Mostly unrelated	Ferreira et al. (2006); Van der Horst et al. (2007)
Parental Support	Parental support	Positive relationship (stronger for younger children)	Positive relationship	Ferreira et al. (2006); Gustafson & Rhodes (2006); Limstrand (2008)
	Household physical activity policy	Positive relationship		Ferreira et al. (2006)
Peer Support	Significant others	Positive relationship	Positive relationship	Ferreira et al. (2006); Limstrand (2008); Van der Horst et al. (2007); Veitch, Salmon, & Ball (2010)
Time Spent Outdoors		Positive relationship		Ferreira et al. (2006)
School Physical Activity Policy	Inclusion of physical education, recess, teacher modeling	Positive relationship		Ferreira et al. (2006)

(Continued)

Table 20.2 (Continued)

Factor	Operationalization	Children	Adolescents	Select References
Type of School	High school vs vocational or alternative	Not applicable	Positive relationship for high school	Ferreira et al. (2006)
Self-Efficacy	Belief in ability to be active	Positive relationship	Positive relationship	Fisher et al. (2010); Van der Horst et al. (2007); Welk & Schaben (2004)
Environment Structure	Presence of sidewalks	Positive relationship	Positive relationship	Davison & Lawson (2006); Limstrand (2008)
Access to Neighborhood Play Areas	Having a destination Playgrounds, play space	Positive relationship Mixed results	Positive relationship Mixed results	Davison & Lawson (2006); Limstrand (2008) Davison & Lawson (2006); Ferreira et al. (2006); Limstrand (2008); Veitch, Salmon & Ball (2010)

Note. *Inconclusive* indicates that there is not enough evidence to make a strong conclusion. *Mixed results* indicates the there are several research studies that had contradictory findings. *Not applicable* indicates that no research currently exists.

of this difference between boys and girls becomes greater in adolescence (e.g., Belcher et al., 2010; Loucaides, Plotnikoff, & Bercovitz, 2007; Stanley, Ridley, & Dollman, 2012). Boys also participate in more vigorous physical activity than do girls (Belcher et al., 2010; Zach & Netz, 2007) and are more active in structured and unstructured physical activity settings (Rosenkranz, Welk, Hastmann, & Dzewaltowski, 2011). Generally speaking, researchers hypothesize that gender differences may be due to biological characteristics, sociocultural norms, and differential expectations placed upon the two genders (Prentice-Dunn & Prentice-Dunn, 2012; Stanley et al., 2012).

Age

Specific tendencies within age groups are often hard to ascertain because of sampling or methodological choices made by researchers, as well as the number of factors that influence physical and social maturity within the same age group (Craggs et al., 2011). However, regardless of gender, race, ethnicity, or SES, data most frequently indicate that physical activity does decline with age and through adolescence, as it does in adulthood (Belcher et al., 2010; Stanley et al., 2012). For example, in one study, youth in the 6–11 age group had higher levels of activity than both the 12–15 and the 16–19 age groups, while the 12–15 group displayed more activity than the oldest group (Belcher et al., 2010). For age-related differences, maturation seems to be an important factor to consider, as disparities exist between children and adolescents on other known correlates (Craggs et al., 2011). Other possible reasons for age-related differences include common changes that occur as children become adolescents, including, but not limited to: (a) changes in physical activity–related goals, (b) increased interest in screen-based activities, (c) decreased parental control and influence, (d) decreased physical activity opportunities in school (e.g., recess, physical education), and (e) more selective sport participation in general.

Ethnicity

Ethnicity, as defined by a group with cultural characteristics in common (Woods, 2011), has shown to be related to physical activity levels in youth (Belcher et al., 2010). Recent research indicates that, overall, non-Hispanic White youth are less active than both non-Hispanic Black and Mexican American youth, with non-Hispanic Blacks, ages 6–11, being the most likely group to achieve physical activity recommendations (Belcher et al., 2010). This differs from earlier research, which indicated that non-Hispanic Black youth were the least active group (Sirard, Pfeiffer, Dowda, & Pate, 2008). Researchers have hypothesized that the results are different because more recent research uses objective measures of physical activity rather than self-report, which allows for all domains of physical activity, including active transportation, household work, and leisure and sport activities to be considered (Sirard et al., 2008). Consequently, more research is needed to better indicate an accurate pattern of physical activity based on ethnic groups.

Socioeconomic Status

The correlation of SES with physical activity levels is also challenging to explain, because of the inconsistent ways in which it has been measured thus far. For example, oftentimes SES is a measure of family income alone, while other times it includes household income and/or parents' education level. Therefore, because of the varying operational definitions, data are often not comparable, which is important to consider. Furthermore, many researchers have not found SES as a relevant correlate for children (e.g., Ferreira et al., 2006; Stanley et al.,

2012; Whitt-Glover et al., 2009), while some relevance of SES was indicated in adolescents (de Vet et al., 2011). Perhaps income becomes a more restrictive factor when children reach adolescence because many physical activity choices and opportunities require greater monetary expenses as children age as well as become more competitive (Ferreira et al., 2006).

When individually examining specific factors that are often considered in determining SES, more definitive findings have been identified. For example, mothers' education level has been found to be positively associated with adolescents' physical activity levels, but not in children (Ferreira et al., 2006). Other researchers have found that SES may be a stronger differentiating factor in urban settings than in rural settings (Loucaides et al., 2007).

Familial Support

Families (e.g., parents, guardians, and siblings) can socialize and support children to be active through encouragement (verbal and non-verbal), involvement (direct assistance), facilitation (transportation and financial support), and role-modeling (see Welk [1999b] for a full discussion of parental support). While it is challenging to directly measure family support, researchers are increasingly interested in better understanding the role of family support in children and adolescents' physical activity (see Gustafson & Rhodes, 2006; Welk, 1999b). Thus far, research indicates that the father-figure in a child's life is one of the most important socialization agents. In fact, the father's physical activity level has been shown to be a probable and positive correlate for children (e.g., Ferreira et al., 2006; Gustafson & Rhodes, 2006), particularly for sons (Gustafson & Rhodes, 2006). Physical activity behavior related to the mother-daughter relationship has also been established (Gustafson & Rhodes, 2006); however, this relationship seems to weaken as children get older (Ferreira et al., 2006; Gustafson & Rhodes, 2006). Subsequently, parents' overall physical inactivity has also been shown to predict children's physical inactivity (Fogelholm et al., 1999).

Parental support, as defined through encouragement, involvement, and facilitation, can directly and indirectly correlate with children's physical activity. The latter is especially true for younger children when they are offered encouragement, involvement, and facilitation (Gustafson & Rhodes, 2006), but the specifics of this support are unknown. Scant research, however, suggests that parents are more supportive in promoting boys' physical activity choices, which could in turn explain some of the physical activity differences between the two genders (Gustafson & Rhodes, 2006). Another conclusive correlate is the physical activity–related policies within a household (Ferreira et al., 2006). In other words, when parents have policies for limiting screen time, promoting outdoor time, or requiring a number of hours spent in activity, children engage in higher levels of physical activity. Correlates that have not been found to be related to children and/or adolescents' physical activity time include parenting styles (Ferreira et al., 2006), family structure for children and adolescents (Ferreira et al., 2006), access to home equipment (Davidson & Lawson, 2006; Ferreira et al., 2006; Van der Horst et al., 2007), and parents' marital status (Craggs et al., 2011; Ferreira et al., 2006).

School-Based Correlates

The school environment can be a great opportunity for children to learn motor skills and have access to physical activity facilities, equipment, and activities that they might otherwise not be exposed to regularly. Furthermore, school is a way to equalize physical activity opportunities for youth from lower-SES backgrounds (Ferreira et al., 2006). Some school-based characteristics have been linked to higher physical activities levels (e.g., Ferreira et al., 2006; Stanley et al., 2012), which are important to consider when schools are implementing comprehensive programs. As such, one important correlate to consider is the overall school policy on physical activity (e.g., free time, time outdoors, physical education), which has been positively linked to children's in-school physical activity levels (Ferreira et al., 2006; Stanley et al., 2012).

Another fairly consistent finding includes the type of school. For example, youth in high schools are more active than youth in vocational schools (Ferreira et al., 2006). Studies have also indicated more specific factors that correlate with greater physical activity in children, such as school size, length of recess, and availability of balls (Zask, van Beurden, Barnett, Brooks, & Dietrich, 2001), while school size (McKenzie, Marshall, Sallis, & Conway, 2000), class size (inverse; McKenzie et al., 2000), lesson-specific context (McKenzie et al., 2000), and access to physical activity facilities seem to be particularly related to physical activity in adolescents. Nevertheless, additional research on the school-based correlates of physical activity in children and adolescents is needed.

MEDIATING FACTORS THAT FOSTER AND SUSTAIN PARTICIPATION

In addition to moderating factors of child and adolescent physical activity, researchers have also identified potential psychosocial mediators (i.e., psychosocial constructs that can lead to changes in physical activity behavior) that promote physical activity participation in young persons (e.g., Gao, Lochbaum, & Podlog, 2011; Lubans, Foster, & Biddle, 2008), of which fun, self-efficacy, and competence are accounted for as *predisposing factors* within the YPAP model (Welk, 1999a). Additionally, autonomy can also be considered a mediating factor and is thus discussed as a fourth factor. These constructs have strong theoretical foundations and practical implications for understanding and enhancing levels of physical activity.

Fun

Extensive research over decades consistently indicates that the presence (or lack) of fun or enjoyment may be one of the most important, if not the most significant, factors influencing children's continued participation in physical activity (e.g., Butcher, Linder, & Johns, 2002; Klint & Weiss, 1987; Pugh, Wolff, & DeFrancesco, 2000). Fun typically refers to activities where youth participate more than they watch, experience development toward mastery of the activity, receive positive reinforcement and encouragement, can be with their friends, and have some choices over their participation (Petlichkoff, 1992; Schwab, Wells, & Arthur-Banning, 2010). That said, fun is actually more complex than originally thought. The fun integration theory (FIT; Visek et al., 2015) offers the most recent evidence-based advancement in understanding how children view fun, positive physical activity experiences in organized sport settings. Based on a series of evidence-based FUN MAPS, FIT is the first community-based, stakeholder-derived framework that identifies and quantifies an entire array of 81 fun determinants and 11 fun factors that compose the 4 *fun*damental tenets essential to promoting the most positive, fun physical activity movement experiences in youth sport, across children and adolescents, girls and boys, and recreational and travel sport programs. Developed from data provided directly from children, parents, and coaches, FIT is also the first theoretical framework to cooperatively integrate the many theories that have independently aided in understanding children's physical activity behavior into one harmonious model (Visek et al., 2015).

Self-Efficacy

According to the YPAP model, self-efficacy (one's belief in being able to succeed in a particular situation [Bandura, 1997]) is another predisposing factor that mediates physical activity behaviors. Research indicates that children and adolescents who believe in their ability to be physically active are more active (Atkin et al., 2010; Debourdeaudhuij, Lefevre, Deforche, Wijndaele, Matton, & Philippaerts, 2005; Loucaides et al., 2007; Rosenkranz et al., 2011; Trost, Pate, Ward, Saunders, & Riner, 1999; Welk & Schaben, 2004). In fact, self-efficacy has even been shown to predict future exercise behaviors among children (Glazebrook et al., 2011).

Listed in order of their degree of influence, children's self-efficacy for physical activity can be derived from four sources: (a) their previous physical activity accomplishments (e.g., completing a season of tee ball and moving up to coach-pitch baseball), (b) verbal persuasion and encouragement from others (e.g., praise and positive reinforcement from a coach), (c) the vicarious experience of physical activity from observing others (e.g., watching an older sibling's soccer games), and (d) achieving an optimal physiological and psychological state (e.g., raised heart rate and sweating while physically active and the experience of elevated mood and ability to concentrate on homework more easily afterward; Bandura, 1997; Lee, Kuo, Fanaw, Perng, & Juang, 2012). Notably, verbal persuasion and modeling via vicarious experiences have been shown to be particularly influential in initiating and maintaining physical activity among children and adolescents (Shields, Spink, Chad, Muhajarine, Humbert, & Odnokon, 2008). Ultimately, the experience of competence and ability to perform a task will influence behavioral choices, persistence in a task, and success (Annesi, Faigenbaum, & Westcott, 2010).

Competence

Perceived competence, the perception of one's abilities in various achievement-related situations (Horn, 2004), is another predisposing factor for physical activity maintenance within the YPAP model. Competence, as a motive for physical activity behavior, has been primarily studied within competence motivation theory, originally developed by Harter (1978, 1990), which posits that people will strive to be competent in achievement-type activities.

A person's perceived competence has also been associated with whether she or he sets task- or ego-oriented goals in the pursuit of achievement (see achievement goal theory; Nicholls, 1984). For example, children with a predominantly task orientation will set goals that are self-referenced and based on their previous accomplishments (e.g., a swimmer who strives to improve her personal record for the freestyle swim at her next meet by two seconds). Contrastingly, children with greater ego orientations will typically strive to demonstrate competence by comparing their performance with that of others (Ames, 1992; Duda & Treasure, 2000). For these children, success is not defined by whether they set a new personal best, but instead is defined by whether they outperformed someone else. Children who are able to experience a sense of mastery or success during physical activity are more likely to be motivated to continue their involvement in such activities compared to those who experience frequent failure (e.g., Klint & Weiss, 1987; Weiss, 1993). Therefore, particularly for children, efforts should be made to create motivational climates that emphasize individual improvement, which can help enhance a child's competence and self-esteem, thereby maintaining their motivation to continue being physically active and ultimately fostering their autonomy in those activities (Deci & Ryan, 1985; Duda & Treasure, 2000; Standage & Treasure, 2002; Williams & Gill, 1995).

Autonomy

Physical activity behaviors that are autonomous are behaviors that are self-determined or chosen by the child or adolescent versus being determined by an adult (Deci & Ryan, 1985).

Further, the degree to which children are self-determined in their decision to engage in exercise or sport is a known mediator of sustained involvement in physical activity.

Within physical activity environments, research generally suggests that perceptions of self-determined behavior are important predictors of intrinsic motives for sustained participation and enjoyment in physical activity settings for children and adolescents (e.g., Biddle, 1999; Chatzisarantis, Biddle, & Meek, 1997; Goudas, Biddle, & Fox, 1994; Spray, John-Wang, Biddle, & Chatzisarantis, 2006) as well as in physical education environments in schools (Gillison, Standage, & Skevington, 2006; Standage & Treasure, 2002). For example, when children are required to participate in an activity and not given the opportunity to be involved in choosing one of several different physical activities, they may be likely to feel less self-determined and less intrinsically motivated to participate (see Udry, Gould, Bridges, & Tuffey, 1997). This is because individuals possess a fundamental human need to exert influence over their environment and be the determinants of their own behavior (Grandpre, Alvaro, Burgoon, Miller, & Hall, 2003). This is particularly true of adolescents, who may often exhibit behavioral reactance, rebelliously acting in the direction opposite from what was instructed (Grandpre et al., 2003). From a developmental perspective, adolescents are at the stage of development in which autonomy and the desire to behave independently becomes increasingly important (Van Petegem, Vansteenkiste, & Beyers, 2013; Weiss & Williams, 2004); therefore, opportunities for choice and selection when it comes to physical activity participation are important efforts toward fostering autonomy and personal investment in the physical activity.

PRACTICAL IMPLICATIONS AND RECOMMENDATIONS

The YPAP model identifies the enabling, predisposing, reinforcing, and personal factors that explain physical activity behaviors in children and adolescents. A thorough understanding of these factors can aid in developing effective strategies for fostering and sustaining physical activity in youth. Ideal strategies involve traditional exercise mediums as well as innovative approaches and include ways for parents, teachers, and communities to restructure daily activities with more physical activity components. The underlying goal should be to help children replace inactivity with activity whenever possible (USDHHS, 2002). In fact, small changes can make a significant difference and can lead to a change in a child's mindset about physical activity, especially for children who have a very inactive lifestyle. In order to help young people meet physical activity guidelines, it is important to be creative in developing and offering physical activity programs that are fun and that children and adolescents will enjoy.

Increasing Fun

As previously discussed, activities that are fun are more likely to be regularly engaged in than activities that are perceived as duty and drudgery (Zimmerman, 2009). Thus, parents and teachers are encouraged to (a) frame participation in physical activity as an incentive or positive experience versus as punishment to correct undesirable behaviors; (b) encourage children to competitively participate with others who are similar in development and skill level; (c) reinforce participation independent of outcomes versus comparing children's performances to one another, particularly when in the early stages of the learning process; and (d) provide specific feedback for improvement when critiquing children's participation in physical activity. The fun integration theory's FUN MAPS provide easy-to-use navigational blueprints for maximizing children's fun in sport-based settings. For a full overview see Visek et al. (2015).

Providing Opportunities for Success

Developing one's competence within the physical activity setting is an aspect of making the physical activity environment fun. More specifically, practitioners can encourage youth to set mastery-based goals and provide opportunities to demonstrate competence in the motor-learning aspects of physical activity, as well as in social and intellectual components. For example, youth could be given opportunities to engage in cooperative activities (e.g., soccer, relay running) in which social accomplishments such as teamwork and communication can be emphasized and reinforced. Cognitively, areas such as decision making and planning could be included in physical activity settings for children and adolescents.

Physical activity environments should provide children and adolescents with opportunities to experience success, early and often, when learning a new task. Learning and improving is a major factor in children's fun experiences (e.g., Visek et al., 2015), and even small successes are helpful in building a child's self-efficacy. For example, providing positive and specific feedback for self-referenced improvements of "correct" performances can help foster self-efficacy. Other ways to build efficacy are to help children establish realistic goals regarding their skill development, demonstrate ways to complete the skill, and provide ample opportunity of skill learning before moving on to more complex tasks.

Empowering Youth

In addition to fun, competence, and self-efficacy, children who have an opportunity to feel autonomous about choices related to their physical activity levels will be more likely to continue. Thus, fostering opportunities for children and adolescents to exert choice and decision making when engaged in physical activity is an important effort toward sustaining their engagement in physical activities. For example, youth could be provided with several modes of physical activity, such as running, jumping rope, or step aerobic activities, each of which target cardiovascular health, and allowed to choose which activity they would prefer to complete. This can facilitate their autonomy and increase the fun they experience participating in those exercises while enhancing the likelihood of continuing them in the future. Similarly, in organized sport settings, coaches could allow their players to choose from a set of drills when structuring individual training sessions and team practices.

Using Technology

In the attempt to get as many children and adolescents involved in physical activity as possible, it is important to be creative and current with technological advances that can be used to facilitate physical activity. Children increasingly have more and more technology-based devices at their fingertips. As a result, there is an increased effort to take popular activities among children and adolescents, such as video games and other devices, and use them to engage youth in more physical activities.

Physical Activity–Based Video Games

Because children and adolescents enjoy and value screen-based activities, attempts to decrease time spent on them have been largely unsuccessful (Timperio, Salmon, & Ball, 2004). Thus, with the idea that "if you can't beat them, join them," video games involving physical activity have been manufactured; this novel technology is often referred to as exergaming, interactive gaming, and/or active video gaming (see Chapter 11 in this volume). The exergaming approach requires the user to be physically active while playing the game. Some of these opportunities include Dance Dance Revolution (DDR), Wii Fit exercise games, and Winds of Orbis, and are commonly implemented in research and physical activity promotion initiatives. Recent evidence associated with the use of these games indicates at least a moderate increase in activity levels can occur during exergaming (Sween et al., 2013). This said, research is inconclusive regarding the actual levels of activity occurring during exergaming versus traditional physical education activities. For example, Shayne, Fogel, Miltenberger, and Koehler (2012), in a case study with four boys, found exergaming produced substantially higher percentages of physical activity than traditional physical education. However, Sun (2012) found the opposite in a study with 74 9- to 12-year-old students. Recently, Sween et al. (2013) reviewed 27 studies on exergaming and indicated that dance simulation games exhibited the highest levels of energy expenditure (EE) compared to other video games. Furthermore, Sween et al. (2013) suggested that moderate-to-vigorous intensity exercise and significant EE could be achieved after short durations, while longer durations could have higher benefits. On the other hand, Miller, Vaux-Bjerke, McDonnell, and DiPietro (2013) found that overall energy expenditure was significantly greater from involvement in physical education compared to DDR and Orbis for elementary and middle school inner-city children. However, Miller et al. (2013) also found that the EE amounts among the three activities were similar for girls as well as for children with obesity, indicating that subgroups may benefit from non-traditional exergaming activities. Nevertheless, further exergaming research is needed, with special attention applied to sociodemographic subgroups.

Devices

Recently, mobile exergames and portable means of providing immediate physical activity feedback are becoming commonplace. One of the least expensive types of technology are pedometers, which are portable motion/step-counting devices that typically are attached to the hip and provide tangible feedback to youth about their activity levels. Although they vary in cost, they can be a practical, easy-to-use, and inexpensive method of encouraging youth to monitor their own physical activity (Robinson & Wadsworth, 2010). Through the use of pedometers, users can, for instance, quickly learn that they accumulate more steps playing tag than playing in the sandbox (Robinson & Wadsworth, 2010). Research also has demonstrated that this feedback can lead to increased physical activity levels in children (e.g., Goldfield et al., 2006; Oliver, Schofield, & McEvoy, 2006). More expensive and alternative devices include accelerometers, FitBit, UpBand, Sqord, Nike Plus, and the Nike Fuel band, for example.

Smartphones and tablets are additional types of devices that can make exercise-related technology mobile and easy to use. Global positioning system (GPS), geosocial, and exergaming applications can be installed on smartphones and tablets, allowing children and adolescents to use them outside and away from home and school. In fact, health and fitness applications installed on these devices are among the most frequently used applications and remain popular facilitators of physical activities (Boulos & Yang, 2013).

Creating an Active Home

Children are more likely to develop enjoyment and interest in physical activities when parents encourage physical activity, participate in active play with their children, and provide active options when trying to increase children's involvement (Gustafson & Rhodes, 2006; Welk, 1999b). Thus, one of the most helpful strategies is for adults to establish and promote a positive norm and expectation for physical activity at home. Ideally, both parents need to be more than just active, indirect role models, as expressed through their own physical activity choices; they also need to promote and encourage children's and adolescents' activity by providing, participating in, financing, observing, and reinforcing these activities (Ferreira et al., 2006). One positive role model is better than two negative models (Gustafson & Rhodes, 2006), yet the more family and friends who are active, the more active the child is likely to be (Loucaides et al., 2007).

Other strategies for families can happen in the backyard. Families can work to promote safe, fun options in the yard, as the yard is the most common place for children to play (Veitch et al., 2010). Furthermore, increasing neighborhood social networks for children can assist physical activity opportunities, as children who have playmates within walking distance are more likely to be active than their peers who do not (Veitch et al., 2010). While the research is inconclusive about how parents' own levels of physical activity relate to their children's physical activity, we do know that providing options for children to be active at home can be helpful in fostering autonomy and motivation.

Utilizing After-School Opportunities

Many schools do not offer daily physical education during the school day; therefore, after-school programs and community sports can be used to offer more opportunities for youth to be active. In fact, after-school programs can be effective in improving physical activity levels, accounting for as much as one-third of the recommended daily activity (Trost, Rosenkranz, & Dzewaltowski, 2008).

After-School Programs

After-school programs can occur on site at schools or even off site at community centers or through private organizations. Participation in after-school programs has been shown to be most effective when: (a) attendance is emphasized, thus allowing for a stronger dose-response (Beets et al., 2009); (b) transportation is organized for the program participants (Robinson, Killen, Kraemer, et al., 2003); (c) activities are tailored to the target audience to increase enjoyment (Beets et al., 2009); (d) the curriculum lasts at least 12 weeks (Atkin et al., 2010; Kriemler, Meyer, Martin, van Sluijs, Anderson, & Martin, 2011); and (e) the program is school-based (Atkin et al., 2010; Kriemler et al., 2011). Other specific components of after-school programming are inconclusive to date, largely due to the high degree of variability across programs in their intended goals, duration, intensity, and target population (Atkin et al., 2010; Beets et al., 2009).

Youth Sports

Organized sport provides a wide variety of opportunities for youth to be active, and this environment can be a healthy context for positive youth development. Youth sport participation has been linked to greater physical activity and sports participation in adulthood (e.g., Cleland et al., 2012; Perkins, Jacobs, Barber, & Eccles, 2004; Russell & Limle, 2013) and may be a better predictor than socioeconomic status (Scheerder et al., 2006). Furthermore, girls who participate in sports at least one time per week and boys who participate in sports at least two times per week at age 14 were more likely to be active as adults (Tammelin, Näyhä, Hills, et al., 2003). However, this correlation is more likely to hold true when adults recalled a positive youth sport experience and did not specialize early in a single sport (Cleland et al., 2012; Russell & Limle, 2013). Additionally, when individuals have had positive experiences in sport as children, they also report higher levels of physical activity enjoyment, which is associated with higher levels of physical activity (Russell & Limle, 2013). Consistent with these findings, Visek et al. (2015) assert that parents and coaches may benefit from organizing sport with a particular focus on promoting the many fun-determinants of (a) being a good sport,

(b) trying hard, and (c) positive coaching. In fact, according to the FUN MAPS (Visek et al., 2015), these three fun factors are most important to fun and supersede winning. Fostering these aspects of fun, versus win-at-all costs tactics, will allow children to develop positive patterns of physical activity that can be lifelong.

Promoting Active Schools

Most schools recognize a responsibility to create a school-based environment that promotes physical activity and health in large part due to Let's Move in Schools, an effort initiated through former First Lady Michelle Obama's Let's Move! campaign (see https://letsmove. obamawhitehouse.archives.gov/). As a result of this campaign and the more recent focus on comprehensive school programming, schools are developing goals and policies that are comprehensive in the desire to improve students' activity, fitness, skills, attitudes, and knowledge regarding physical activity and health. School has been found to be a successful environment for promoting physical activity because of the amount of time spent at school and the opportunity for youth to learn and master a variety of physical skills that allow them to successfully participate in a variety of activities, which will help for lifelong activity (Welk, 1999b). In order to maximize this opportunity, a full school effort, from physical education classes and recess to movement in the classroom and active transport to school, is needed, with these components immersed into the school curriculum, programming, and overall school environment.

Physical Education

In 2006, only 3.8 percent of elementary schools, 7.8 percent of middle and junior high schools, and 2.1 percent of high schools required daily physical education (Lee, Burgeson, Fulton, & Spain, 2007). Efforts to increase these numbers are among the objectives of Healthy People 2020, because effective physical education allows children and adolescents to learn motor skills that lead to physical self-efficacy and to participate in activity sessions that are mastery focused (Standage, Duda, & Ntoumanis, 2003). Two of the most effective characteristics of physical education that assist with increasing physical activity are the high compliance rates and the training of the instructor (Trudeau & Shephard, 2005). Research indicates that the long-term benefits of physical education on adult physical activity are stronger for women, who had a more lasting effect from effective and positive physical education classes than men did (Cleland et al., 2012; Trudeau, Laurencelle, Tremblay, Rajic, & Shephard, 1999; Trudeau & Shephard, 2005). Research has also found that children are more likely to adopt an active lifestyle as adults if they participate in at least 18 minutes of physical education per day in elementary school (Trudeau & Shephard, 2005).

Recess

Recess is recommended for at least 20 minutes per day, in addition to physical education classes (Mahar et al., 2009). This school-time activity allows youth to have unstructured physical activity and offers an opportunity to practice and engage needed motor skills, as well as providing the chance to socially interact with peers. Unfortunately, in 2006, only seven states and 57 percent of school districts across the nation required regularly scheduled recess for elementary schools (Lee et al., 2007). Indeed, simply offering recess does not ensure quality physical activity time (Escalante et al., 2012). It is recommended that children be provided with adequately large play areas in order to engage in physical activities, as the area of the play space for elementary-age children has been found to be linked to active time (Escalante et al., 2012); the availability of equipment, such as playground balls that require movement to be used, is important as well (Zask et al., 2001). Children in smaller play areas often have to choose sedentary activities due to the lack of space or are forced to take turns participating, which may result in idle activity (Escalante et al., 2012). Therefore, schools with smaller play areas may benefit from efforts to deliberately increase activity of the youth within the limited space (see Table 20.1 for Playworks, an example program that makes good use of small, urban play spaces).

Classroom Movement

One of the more novel and innovative approaches to facilitating children's and adolescents' physical activity during the school day is by incorporating classroom movement into the academic curriculum. Activities can be integrated into any subject in 5–10-minute bouts throughout the school day, with as few as one activity break helping to improve children's physical activity levels. To that end, a variety of resources for teachers, such as Active and Healthy Schools™ activity break cards, *Promoting Physical Activity and Health in the Classroom* activity cards, Energizers, and Take 10!® can prove helpful (Erwin, Fedewa, Beighle, & Soyeon, 2012).

Although research in this area is still in its infancy, results of a recent study showed a 6 percent improvement in physical activity levels when comparing classroom movement intervention groups to control groups (Donnelly & Lambourne, 2011). Research has also concluded that these movement-based activities enhance learning outcomes, especially for elementary school children (Erwin et al., 2012), helping them stay focused on school-related tasks (Mahar et al., 2009) as well as increasing concentration (Norlander, Moås, & Archer, 2005), among other academic benefits following each activity session. A meta-analysis of studies relating to this strategy also indicate very positive intervention effects of the strategy on physical activity outcomes (Erwin et al., 2012). Therefore, while classroom movement time will not, in and of itself, help all youth meet the physical activity guideline, it can be incorporated as a part of a comprehensive school-based physical activity program.

Active Transport to School

Healthy People 2020 Active Transport to School (ATS) objectives are established in order to increase the proportion of walking and biking trips made by 5–15 year olds who live within one mile of their school (DeBoer, 2013). Currently the numbers indicate that between 5 percent (Bungum, Lounsbery, Moonie, & Gast, 2009) and 15 percent (Barriers to children, 2004) of children walk to school, with more boys than girls using an active method. In order to increase these percentages, communities are encouraged to build and link sidewalks from neighborhoods to schools as well as build crosswalks and bike lanes. Streets should be children-friendly, and it is also recommended that school norms surrounding active transport be established (Bungum et al., 2009).

Involving the Community

When using a social ecological approach (McLeroy, Bibeau, Steckler, & Glanz, 1988; see Chapter 5, this volume, for a review of the social ecological approach) for understanding factors related to children's and adolescents' physical activity choices, it is important to consider the neighborhood area or built environment where physical activity outside of school can take place, as well as the community needs and issues. In regards to the built environment, research is mixed on various factors. For example, perceived neighborhood safety and neighborhood hazards do not seem to be related to children's or adolescents' physical activity (see

Ferreira et al., 2006 for full reviews). This said, variables including access to neighborhood facilities have been shown to be related to physical activity in some studies (e.g., see review by Stanley et al., 2012) and not in others (e.g., review by Ferreira et al., 2006). Additionally, variables such as walkable destinations to shops and restaurants (de Vet et al., 2011), more children in the neighborhood to play with (Veitch et al., 2010), and more access to play space (Stanley et al., 2012) have been shown to positively correlate with more minutes in physical activity. Thus, while some results are inconclusive, others seem more unequivocal; therefore, the built environment does need to be considered when designing effective programs for increasing physical activity in children and adolescents.

In addition, engaging strong partnerships with outside agencies and community organizations is crucial in efforts to increase physical activity among children and adolescents (Ward, Saunders, & Pate, 2007). For example, building partnerships with local schools and businesses in order to pool resources and ideas can be an effective first step toward creating a new norm for physical activity. Communities can also be strong advocates for health behavior changes by conducting community-wide campaigns designed to promote positive physical activity messages through social media, print/radio/television media, libraries, and community centers (Guide to Community, 2011). Furthermore, citizens can advocate to their community leaders for funding for walking trails, bike paths, playgrounds, and sidewalks, as well as organize opportunities where youth can be active when school is not in session (USDHHS, 2009).

CONCLUSION

Physical activity is important to health and well-being, but is critically important to the development of the child through adolescence and into adulthood. A multifaceted approach to promoting physical activity will require the active engagement of parents and families at home, at school, in after-school care, and in communities at large. Collective investment from these sources will likely yield the greatest and most healthful returns in terms of physical activity prevalence and benefits. Physical activities developed for children and adolescents should be age-appropriate; consider gender, minority status and geographical location; and promote known psychosocial mediators of physical activity behavior, namely fun, competence, self-efficacy, and autonomy. Moreover, the YPAP model provides a working framework for understanding how to promote physical activity specifically in young persons and can be applied to different physical activity settings. For more detailed information on planning, implementing, and evaluating physical activity programs for youth, see the *Physical Activity Evaluation Handbook* (USDHHS, 2002).

REFERENCES

Ames, C. (1992). Achievement goals, motivational climate, and motivational processes. In G. C. Roberts (Ed.), *Motivation in sport and exercise* (pp. 161–176). Champaign, IL: Human Kinetics.

Amireault, S., Godin, G., & Vézina-IM, L. (2013). Determinants of physical activity maintenance: A systematic review and meta-analysis. *Health Psychology Review*, 7(1), 55–91.

Andreann, P., Mara, B., Frank, V., Sylvana, M. C., Richard, E. T., & Michel, B. (2012). Moderating effects of team sports participation on the link between peer victimization and mental health problems. *Mental Health and Physical Activity*, 5, 107–115. doi:10.1016/j.mhpa.2012.08.006

Annesi, J., Faigenbaum, A. D., & Westcott, W. L. (2010). Relations of transtheoretical model stage, self-efficacy, and voluntary physical activity in African American preadolescents. *Research Quarterly for Exercise and Sport*, 81, 239–244.

Atkin, A. J., Gorely, T., Biddle, S. J. H., Cavill, N., & Foster, C. (2010). Interventions to promote physical activity in young people conducted in the hours immediately after school: A systematic review. *International Journal of Behavioral Medicine, 18*, 176–187.

Bailey, R., Hillman, C., Arent, S., & Petitpas, A. (2013). Physical activity: An underestimated investment in human capital? *Journal of Physical Activity & Health, 10*, 289–308.

Bandura, A. (1997). *Self-efficacy: The exercise of control.* New York, NY: Freeman.

Barriers to children walking to and from school, United States. (2004). *Morbidity and Mortality Weekly Report, 54*(38), 949–952.

Beets, M. W., Beighle, A., Erwin, H. E., & Huberty, J. L. (2009). After- school program impact on physical activity and fitness: A meta-analysis. *American Journal of Preventive Medicine, 36*(6), 527–537.

Belcher, B. R., Berrigan, D., Dodd, K. W., Emken, B. A., Chou, C-P., & Spuijt-Metz, D. (2010). Physical activity in US youth: Impact of race/ethnicity, age, gender, & weight status. *Medicine & Science in Sports & Exercise, 41*(12), 2211–2221. doi:10.1249/MSS.0b013e3181e1fba9

Biddle, S. (1999). Motivation and perceptions of control: Tracing its development and plotting its future in exercise and sport psychology. *Journal of Sport & Exercise Psychology, 21*, 1–23.

Boulos, M. N. K., & Yang, S. P. (2013). Exergames for health and fitness: The roles of GPS and geosocial apps. *International Journal of Health Geographics, 12*(1), 18–24.

Bungum, T. J., Lounsbery, M., Moonie, S., & Gast, J. (2009). Prevalence and correlates of walking and biking to school among adolescents. *Journal of Community Health, 34*, 129–134.

Butcher, J., Linder, K. J., & Johns, D. P. (2002). Withdrawal from competitive sport: A retrospective ten-year study. *Journal of Sport Behavior, 25*, 145–163.

Centers for Disease Control (CDC). (2010). *The association between school-based physical activity, including physical education, and academic performance.* Atlanta, GA: U.S. Department of Health and Human Services.

Centers for Disease Control [CDC]. (2014). Youth risk behavior surveillance—United States, 2013. *MMWR, 63*, SS-4.

Centers for Disease Control (CDC) and Prevention. (2011). *Obesity: Halting the epidemic by making health easier.* Retrieved from www.cdc.gov/chronicdisease/resources/publications/aag/pdf/2011/obesity_aag_web_508.pdf

Chatzisarantis, N., Biddle, S., & Meek, G. (1997). A self-determination theory approach to the study of intentions and the intention-behaviour relationship in children's physical activity. *British Journal of Health Psychology, 2*, 343–360.

Cleland, V., Dwyer, T., & Venn, A. (2012). Which domains of childhood physical activity predict physical activity in adulthood? A 20-year prospective tracking study. *British Journal of Sports Medicine, 46*, 595–602.

Craggs, C., Corder, K., van Sluijs, E. M. F., & Griffin, S. J. (2011). Determinants of change in physical activity in children and adolescents: A systematic review. *American Journal of Preventative Medicine, 40*(6), 645–658.

Davison, K. K., & Lawson, C. T. (2006). Do attributes in the physical environment influence children's physical activity? A review of the literature. *International Journal of Behavioral, Nutrition and Physical Activity, 3*, 19–35.

de Onis, M., Blossner, M., & Borghi, E. (2010). Global prevalence and trends of overweight and obesity among preschool children. *American Journal of Clinical Nutrition, 92*, 1257–1264.

de Vet, E., de Ridder, D. T. D., & de Wit, J. B. F. (2011). Environmental correlates of physical activity and dietary behaviours among young people: A systematic review of reviews. *Obesity Prevention, 12*, e130–e142.

DeBoer, M. D. (2013). Obesity, systemic inflammation, and increased risk for cardiovascular disease and diabetes among adolescents: A need for screening tools to target interventions. *Nutrition, 29*(8), 379–386.

Debourdeaudhuij, I., Lefevre, J., Deforche, B., Winjndaele, K., Matton, L., & Philippaerts, R. (2005). Physical activity and psychosocial correlates in normal weight and overweight 11 to 19 year olds. *Obesity Research, 13*, 1097–1105.

Deci, E., & Ryan, R. (1985). *Intrinsic motivation and self-determination in human behavior.* New York, NY: Plenum.

Dodge, T., & Lambert, S. (2009). Positive self-beliefs as a mediator of the relationship between adolescents' sports participation and health in young adulthood. *Journal of Youth and Adolescence, 38,* 813–825.

Donnelly, J. E., & Lambourne, K. (2011). Classroom-based physical activity, cognition, and academic achievement. *Preventative Medicine, 52,* S36–S42.

Duda, J., & Treasure, D. (2000). Toward optimal motivation in sport: Fostering athletes' competence and sense of control. In J. Williams (Ed.), *Applied sport psychology: Personal growth to peak performance* (pp. 43–62). Mountain View, CA: Mayfield Publishing Company.

Erwin, H., Fedewa, A., Beighle, A., & Soyeon, A. (2012). A quantitative review of physical activity, health, and learning outcomes associated with classroom-based physical activity interventions. *Journal of Applied School Psychologists, 28*(1), 14–36.

Escalante, Y., Backx, K., Saavedra, J. M., García-Hermoso, A., & Domínguez, A. M. (2012). Play area and physical activity in recess in primary schools. *Kinesiology, 44*(2), 123–129.

Ferreira, I., van der Horst, K., Wendel-Vos, W., Kremers, S., van Lenthe, F. J., & Brug, J. (2006). Environmental correlates of physical activity in youth—a review and update. *Obesity Reviews, 8,* 129–154.

Finkelstein, E. A., Khavjou, O. A., Thompson, H., Trogdon, J. G., Pan, L., Sherry, B., & Dietz, W. 2012. Obesity and severe obesity forecasts through 2030. *American Journal of Preventive Medicine, 42*(16), 563–570.

Fisher, A., Saxton, J., Hill, C., Webber, L., Purslow, L., & Wardle, J. (2010). Psychosocial correlates of objectively measured physical activity in children. *European Journal of Public Health, 21*(2), 145–150.

Floyd, M. F., Spengler, J. O., Maddock, J. E., Gobster, P. H., & Suau, L. (2008). Environmental and social correlates of physical activity in neighborhood parks: An observational study in Tampa and Chicago. *Leisure Sciences, 30*(4), 360–375.

Fogelholm, M., Nuutinen, O., Pasanen, M., Myöhänen, E., & Säätelä, T. (1999). Parent-child relationship of physical activity patterns and obesity. *International Journal of Obesity, 23,* 1262–1268.

Friedemann, C., Heneghan, C., Mahtani, K., Thompson, M., Perera, R., & Ward, A. M. (2012). Cardiovascular disease risk in healthy children and its association with body mass index: Systematic review and meta-analysis. *British Medical Journal, 345,* e4759.

Gao, Z., Lochbaum, M., & Podlog, L. (2011). Self-efficacy as a mediator of children's achievement motivation and in-class physical activity. *Perceptual & Motor Skills, 13,* 969–981.

Gillison, F. B., Standage, M., & Skevington, S. M. (2006). Relationships among adolescents' weight perceptions, exercise goals, exercise motivation, quality of life and leisure-time exercise behaviour: A self-determination theory approach. *Health Education Research, 21,* 836–847.

Glazebrook, C., Batty, M. J., Mullan, N., MacDonald, I., Nathan, D., Sayal, K., . . . Hollis, C. (2011). Evaluating the effectiveness of a schools-based programme to promote exercise self-efficacy in children and young people with risk factors for obesity: steps to active kids (STAK). *BMC public health, 11*(1), 830.

Goldfield, G. S., Mallory, R., Parker, T., Cunningham, T., Legg, C., Lumb, A., . . . Adamo, K. B. (2006). Effects of open-loop feedback on physical activity and television viewing in overweight and obese children: A randomized, controlled trial. *Pediatrics, 118,* 157–166.

Goldhaber-Fiebert, J. D., Rubinfeld, R. E., Bhattacharya, J., Robinson, T. N., & Wise, P. H. (2013). *Medical Decision Making, 33,* 163–175. doi: 10.1177/0272989X12447240

Goudas, M., Biddle, S., & Fox, K. (1994). Perceived locus of causality, goal orientations, and perceived competence in school physical education classes. *British Journal of Educational Psychology, 64,* 453–463.

Grandpre, J., Alvaro, E. M., Burgoon, M., Miller, C. H., & Hall, J. R. (2003). Adolescent reactance and anti-smoking campaigns: A theoretical approach. *Health Communication, 15,* 349–366.

Guide to Community Preventive Services. (2011). *Campaigns and informational approaches to increase physical activity: Community-wide campaigns.* Retrieved from www.thecommunityguide.org/pa/campaigns/community.html

Gustafson, S. L., & Rhodes, R. (2006). Parental correlates of physical activity in children and early adolescents. *Sports Medicine, 36*(1), 79–97.

Harter, S. (1978). Effectance motivation reconsidered: Toward a developmental model. *Human Development, 21,* 34–64.

Harter, S. (1990). Causes, correlates, and the functional role of global self-worth: A life-span perspective. In R. Sternberg & J. Kolligian (Eds.), *Competence considered* (pp. 67–97). New Haven, CT: Yale University Press.

Hills, A. P., King, N. A., & Armstrong, T. P. (2007). The contribution of physical activity and sedentary behaviors to the growth and development of children and adolescents: Implications for overweight and obesity. *Sports Medicine, 37*, 533–545.

Horn, T. S. (2004). Developmental perspectives on self-perceptions in children and adolescents. In M. R. Weiss (Ed.), *Developmental sport and exercise psychology: A lifespan perspective* (pp. 101–143). Morgantown, WV: Fitness Information Technology.

Joens-Matre, R. R. (2007). A social ecological analysis of physical activity promotion for overweight and normal weight youth. *Dissertation Abstracts International, 67*, 6341.

Klint, K. A., & Weiss, M. R. (1987). Perceived competence and motives for participating in youth sports: A test of Harter's competence motivation theory. *Journal of Sport Psychology, 9*, 55–65.

Kohl, H. W., Craig, C. L., Lambert, E. V., Inoue, S., Alkandari, J. R., Leetongin, G., & Kahlmeier, S. (2012). The pandemic of physical inactivity: Global action for public health. *The Lancet, 380*(9838), 294–305.

Kriemler, S., Meyer, U., Martin, E., van Sluijs, E. M., Andersen, L. B., & Martin, B. W. (2011). Effect of school-based interventions on physical activity and fitness in children and adolescents: A review of reviews and systematic update. *British Journal of Sports Medicine, 45*(11), 923–930.

Lee, L. L., Kuo, Y. C., Fanaw, D., Perng, S. J., & Juang, I. F. (2012). The effect of an intervention combing self-efficacy theory and pedometers on promoting physical activity among adolescents. *Journal of Clinical Nursing, 21*, 914–922. doi: 10.1111/j.1365-2702.2011.03881

Lee, S. M., Burgeson, C. R., Fulton, J. E., & Spain, C. G. (2007). Physical education and physical activity: Results from the School Health Policies and Program Study 2006. *Journal of School Health, 77*(8), 435–463.

Limstrand, T. (2008). Environmental characteristics relevant to young people's use of sports facilities: A review. *Scandinavian Journal of Medicine & Science of Sport, 18*(3), 275–287. doi: 10.1111/j.1600-0838.2007.00742.x

Loucaides, C. A., Plotnikoff, R. C., & Bercovitz, K. (2007). Differences in the correlates of physical activity between urban and rural Canadian youth. *Journal of School Health, 77*(4), 164–170.

Lubans, D. R., Foster, C., & Biddle, S. J. (2008). A review of mediators of behavior in interventions to promote physical activity among children and adolescents. *Journal of Preventative Medicine, 47*, 463–470.

Mahar, M. T., Murphy, S. K., Rowe, D. A., Golden, J., Shields, A., Raedeke, T. D. (2009). Effects of a classroom-based program on physical activity and on-task behavior. *Medicine and Science in Sports and Exercise, 38*(12), 2086–94.

McKenzie, T. L., Marshall, S. J., Sallis, J. F., & Conway, T. L. (2000). Student activity levels, lesson context, and teacher behavior during middle school physical education. *Research Quarterly for Exercise and Sport, 71*, 249–259.

McLeroy, K. R., Bibeau, D., Steckler, A., & Glanz, K. (1988). An ecological perspective on health promotion programs. *Health Education Quarterly, 15*, 351–377.

Miller, T. A., Vaux-Bjerke, A., McDonnell, K. A., & DiPietro, L. (2013). Can e-gaming be useful for achieving recommended levels of moderate- to vigorous-intensity physical activity in inner-city children? *Games for Health Journal, 2*(1), 1–7. doi: 10.1089/g4h.2012.0058

Moraes, A., Guerra, P., & Menezes, P. (2013). The worldwide prevalence of insufficient physical activity in adolescents: A systematic review. *Nutrition Hospital Journal, 28*(3), 575–584.

National Center for Health Statistics. (2009). *Health, United States, 2009: With special feature on medical technology.* Hyattsville, MD: U.S. Department of Health and Human Services.

Nicholls, J. (1984). Conceptions of ability and achievement motivation. In R. Ames & C. Ames (Eds.), *Research on motivation in education: Student motivation* (pp. 39–73). New York, NY: Academic Press.

Norlander, T., Moås, L., & Archer, T. (2005). Noise and stress in primary and secondary school children: Noise reduction and increased concentration ability through a short but regular exercise and relaxation program. *School Effectiveness and School Improvement, 16*(1), 91–99.

Ogden, C. L., Carroll, M. D., Kit, B. K., & Flegal, K. M. (2012). Prevalence of obesity and trends in body mass index among US children and adolescents, 1999–2010. *The Journal of the American Medical Association*, *307*(5), 483–490. doi:10.1001/jama.2012.40

Oliver, M., Schofield, G., & McEvoy, E. (2006). An integrated curriculum approach to increasing habitual physical activity in children: A feasibility study. *Journal of School Health*, *76*, 74–79.

Olshansky, S. J. (2005). Projecting the future of US health and longevity. *Health Affairs*, *24*, W5R86.

Pearson, N., Atkin, A. J., Biddle, S. J., Gorely, T., & Edwardson, C. (2009). Patterns of adolescent physical activity and dietary behaviours. *The International Journal of Behavioral Nutrition and Physical Activity*, *6*(45). doi: http://doi.org/10.1186/1479-5868-6-45

Perkins, D., Jacobs, J., Barber, B., & Eccles, J. (2004). Childhood and adolescent sports participation as predictors of participation in sports and physical fitness activities during young adulthood. *Youth & Society*, *35*, 495–520.

Perron, A., Brendgen, M., Vitaro, F., Côté, S. M., Tremblay, R. E., & Boivin, M. (2012). Moderating effects of team sports participation on the link between peer victimization and mental health problems. *Mental Health and Physical Activity*, *5*(2), 107–115. doi:10.1016/j.mhpa.2012.08.006

Petlichkoff, L. M. (1992). Youth sport participation and withdrawal: Is it simply a matter of fun? *Pediatric Exercise Science*, *4*, 105–110.

Prentice-Dunn, H., & Prentice-Dunn, S. (2012). Physical activity, sedentary behavior, and childhood obesity: A review of cross-sectional studies. *Psychology, Health & Medicine*, *17*(3), 255–273.

Pugh, S., Wolff, R., & DeFrancesco, C. (2000). A case study of elite male youth baseball athletes' perception of the youth sport experience. *Education*, *120*, 773–781.

Robinson, L. E., & Wadsworth, D. D. (2010). Stepping toward physical activity requirements: Integrating pedometers into early childhood settings. *Early Childhood Education Journal*, *38*, 95–102.

Robinson, T. N., Killen, J. D., Kraemer, H. C., Wilson, D. M., Matheson, D. M., Haskell, W. L., . . . Flint-Moore, N. M. (2003). Dance and reducing television viewing to prevent weight gain in African-American girls: The Stanford GEMS pilot study. *Ethnicity & Disease*, *13*(1S1), S65–77.

Rodrigues, A., Abreu, G., Resende, R., Goncalves, W., & Gouvea, S. (2013). Cardiovascular risk factor investigation: A pediatric issue. *International Journal Of General Medicine*, *6*, 57–66.

Rosenkranz, R. R., Welk, G. J., Hastmann, T. J., & Dzewaltowski, D. A. (2011). Psychosocial and demographic correlates of objectively measured physical activity in structured and unstructured after-school recreation sessions. *Journal of Science & Medicine in Sport*, *14*(4), 306–311. doi: 10.1016/j.jsams.2011.01.005

Russell, W. D., & Limle, A. N. (2013). The relationship between youth sport specialization and involvement in sport and physical activity in young adulthood. *Journal of Sport Behavior*, *36*(1), 82–98.

Scheerder, J., Thomis, M., Vanreusel, B., Lefevre, J., Renson, R., Vanden Eynde, B., & Beunen, G. P. (2006). Sports participation among females from adolescence to adulthood. *International Review for the Sociology of Sport*, *4*, 413–430.

Schwab, K. A., Wells, M. S., & Arthur-Banning, S. (2010). Experiences in youth sports: A comparison between players' and parents' perspectives. *Journal of Sport Administration & Supervision*, *2*(1), 41–51.

Shayne, R. K., Fogel, V. A., Miltenberger, R. G., & Koehler, S. (2012). The effects of exergaming on physical activity in a third grade physical education class. *Journal of Applied Behavior Analysis*, *45*(1), 211–215.

Shields, C. A., Spink, K. S., Chad, K., Muhajarine, N., Humbert, L., & Odnokon, P. (2008). Youth and adolescent physical activity lapsers: Examining self-efficacy as a mediator of the relationship between family social influence and physical activity. *Journal of Health Psychology*, *13*, 121–130. doi: 10.1177/1359105307084317

Singh, A., Uijtdewilligen, L., Twisk, J. W. R., Mechelen, W., & Chinapaw, M. J. M. (2012). Physical activity and performance at school: A systematic review of the literature including a methodological quality assessment. *Archives of Pediatrics & Adolescent Medicine*, *166*(1), 49–55.

Sirard, J. R., Pfeiffer, K. A., Dowda, M., & Pate, R. R. (2008). Race differences in activity, fitness, and BMI in female eighth graders categorized by sports participation status. *Pediatric Exercise Science*, *20*(2), 198–210.

Smoll, F. L., & Smith, R. E. (1996). *Children and youth in sport: A biopsychosocial perspective*. Madison, WI: Brown & Benchmark Publishers.

Sowers, J. R. (2001). Update on the cardiometabolic syndrome. *Clinical Cornerstone, 4*(2), 17–23.

Spray, C., John-Wang, C. K., Biddle, S., & Chatzisarantis, N. (2006). Understanding motivation in sport: An experimental test of achievement goal and self determination theories. *European Journal of Sport Science, 6*, 43–51.

Standage, M., Duda, J., & Ntoumanis, N. (2003). Predicting motivational regulations in physical education: The interplay between dispositional goal orientations, motivational climate, and perceived competence. *Journal of Sports Science, 21*(8), 631–647.

Standage, M., & Treasure, D. C. (2002). Relationship among achievement goal orientations and multidimensional situational motivation in physical education. *British Journal of Educational Psychology, 72*, 7–103.

Stanley, R. M., Ridley, K., & Dollman, J. (2012). Correlates of children's time-specific physical activity: A review of the literature. *International Journal of Behavioral Nutrition and Physical Activity, 9*(1), 50–62.

Sun, H. (2012). Exergaming impact on physical activity and interest in elementary school children. *Research Quarterly for Exercise and Sport, 83*(2), 212–223.

Sween, J., Wallington, S. F., Sheppard, V., Taylor, T., Llanos, A. A., & Adams-Campbell, L. L. (2013). The role of exergaming in improving physical activity: A review. *Journal of Physical Activity and Health*, (ahead of print).

Tammelin, T., Näyhä, S., Hills, A. P., & Järvelin, M. R. (2003). Adolescent participation in sports and adult physical activity. *American Journal of Preventative Medicine, 24*(1), 22–28.

Timperio, A., Salmon, J., & Ball, K. (2004). Evidence-based strategies to promote physical activity among children, adolescents and young adults: Review and update. *Journal of Science and Medicine in Sport, 7*(1), 20–29.

Trost, S. G., Owen, N., Bauman, A. E., Sallis, J. F., & Brown, W. (2002). Correlates of adults' participation in physical activity: Review and update. *Medicine & Science in Sports & Exercise, 34*, 1996–2001.

Trost, S. G., Pate, R., Ward, D. S., Saunders, R., & Riner, W. (1999). Correlates of objectively measured physical activity in preadolescent youth. *American Journal of Preventative Medicine, 17*, 120–126.

Trost, S. G., Rosenkranz, R. R., & Dzewaltowski, D. (2008). Physical activity levels among children attending after-school programs. *Medicine & Science in Sports & Exercise, 40*, 622–629.

Trudeau, F., Laurencelle, L., Tremblay, J., Rajic, M., & Shephard, R. J. (1999). Daily primary school physical education: Effects on physical activity during adult life. *Medicine & Science in Sports & Exercise, 31*(1), 111–117.

Trudeau, F., & Shephard, R. J. (2005). Contribution of school programmes to physical activity levels and attitudes in children and adults. *Sports Medicine, 35*(2), 89–106.

U.S. Department of Health and Human Services (USDHHS). (2002). *Physical activity evaluation handbook*. Atlanta, GA: US Department of Health and Human Services, Centers for Disease Control and Prevention.

U.S. Department of Health & Human Services. (2008a). *2008 Physical activity guidelines for Americans*. Washington, DC: U.S. Department of Health and Human Services. Retrieved from www.health.gov/paguidelines/pdf/paguide.pdf

U.S. Department of Health & Human Services, Physical Activity Guidelines Advisory Committee. (2008b). *Physical activity guidelines advisory committee report, 2008*. Washington, DC: U.S. Department of Health and Human Services. Retrieved from www.health.gov/paguidelines/Report/pdf/CommitteeReport.pdf

U. S. Department of Health & Human Services. Office of Disease Prevention and Health Promotion. *Healthy People 2020*. Washington, DC. Retrieved from www.healthypeople.gov

U.S. Department of Health and Human Services (USDHHS). (2009). *Youth physical activity: The role of communities*. Centers for Disease Control and Prevention. Retrieved from www.cdc.gov/HealthyYouth

Udry, E., Gould, D., Bridges, D., & Tuffey, S. (1997). People helping people? Examining the social ties of athletes coping with burnout and injury stress. *Journal of Sport & Exercise Psychology, 19*, 368–395.

Van der Horst, K., Chin, A., Paw, M. J., Twisk, J. W. R., & Van Mechelen, W. (2007). Brief review of correlates of physical activity and sedentariness in youth. *Medicine & Science in Sports & Exercise, 39*(8), 1241–1250. doi: 10.1249/mss.0b013e318059bf35

Van Petegem, S., Vansteenkiste, M., & Beyers, W. (2013). The jingle-jangle fallacy in adolescence autonomy in the family: In search of an underlying structure. *Journal of Youth and Adolescence, 42,* 994–1014. doi: 10.1007/s109640-129-8477-

Veitch, J., Salmon, J., & Ball, K. (2010). Individual, social and physical environmental correlates of children's active free-play: A cross-sectional study. *International Journal of Behavioral Nutrition and Physical Activity, 7*(1), 11–20.

Visek, A. J., Achrati, S. M., Manning, H., McDonnell, K., Harris, B. S., & DiPietro, L. (2015). The fun integration theory: Towards sustaining children and adolescents sport participation. *Journal of Physical Activity & Health, 12*(3), 424–433. doi: 10.1123/jpah.2013-0180. PMCID: PMC24770788

Ward, D. S., Saunders, R. P., & Pate, R. R. (2007). *Physical activity interventions in children and adolescents.* Human Kinetics: Champaign, IL.

Weichselbaum, E. E., & Buttriss, J. J. (2011). Nutrition, health and schoolchildren, *Nutrition Bulletin, 36*(3), 295–355. doi:10.1111/j.1467-3010.2011.01910.x

Weiss, M. R. (1993). Psychological effects of intensive sport participation on children and youth: Self-esteem and motivation. In B. Cahill & A. Pearl (Eds.), *Intensive participation in children's sports* (pp. 39–69). Champaign, IL: Human Kinetics.

Weiss, M. R., & Williams, L. (2004). The *why* of youth sport involvement: A developmental perspective on motivational processes. In M. R. Weiss (Ed.), *Developmental sport and exercise psychology: A lifespan perspective* (pp. 223–268). Morgantown, WV: Fitness Information Technology.

Welk, G. J. (1999a). The youth physical activity promotion model: A conceptual bridge between theory and practice. *Quest, 51,* 5–23.

Welk, G. J. (1999b). Promoting physical activity in children: Parental influences. *ERICDigest.* ED436480 1999-10-00.

Welk, G. J., & Schaben, J. A. (2004). Psychosocial correlates of physical activity in children—a study of relationships when children have similar opportunities to be active. *Measurement in Physical Education and Exercise Science, 8*(2), 63–81.

Whitt-Glover, M. C., Taylor, W. C., Floyd, M. F., Yore, M. M., Yancey, A. K., & Matthews, C. E. (2009). Disparities in physical activity and sedentary behaviors among US children and adolescents: Prevalence, correlates, and intervention implications. *Journal of Public Health Policy, 30,* S309–S334.

Wilkinson, K. (2008). Increasing obesity in children and adolescents: An alarming epidemic. *Journal of the American Academy of Physician Assistants, 21*(12), 31–38.

Williams, L., & Gill, D. (1995). The role of perceived competence in the motivation of physical activity. *Journal of Sport & Exercise Psychology, 17,* 363–378.

Woods, R. B. (2011). *Social issues in sport.* Champaign, IL: Human Kinetics.

World Health Organization. (2009). *Global health risks: Mortality and burden of disease attributable to selected major risks.* Geneva, Switzerland: Author. Retrieved from www.who.int/healthinfo/global_burden_disease/GlobalHealthRisks_report_full.pdf

Zach, S., & Netz, Y. (2007). Like mother like child: Three generations' patterns of exercise behavior. *Families, Systems, & Health, 25*(4), 419–434.

Zask, A., van Beurden, E., Barnett, L., Brooks, L. O., & Dietrich, U. C. (2001). Active school playgrounds—myth or reality? Results of the "Move it groove it" project. *Preventative Medicine, 33,* 402–408.

Zimmerman, F. J. (2009). Using behavioral economics to promote physical activity. *Preventive Medicine, 49,* 289–291.

21 Exercise and Aging

David Pargman and Urska Dobersek

Humans are living longer than in past millennia and even past decades. Every hour of the day 330 Americans turn 60 (Brody, 2008). By the year 2060, individuals 85 years and older are projected to reach about 4.3 percent of the total North American population (U.S. Census Bureau, 2012). Today men and women in the United States over the age of 65 compose approximately 20 percent of the population, but unfortunately this segment is among the least physically active of all age groups (Center for Chronic Disease Prevention and Health Promotion, 2013).

The purpose of this chapter is to overview research findings that bear upon aging in relation to exercise—with particular reference to psychological considerations. Commentary provided throughout the chapter takes the form of interpretation and application of information for readers whose professional commitments involve understanding and guiding the motivations and behaviors of active elderly individuals. This population might be of interest to some sport psychology consultants, as elderly persons are living longer now than ever before. Indeed, life expectancy today is close to 80 years (Petz, 2013). This chapter provides answers to some of the following questions: What are the specific mechanisms underlying the psychological correlates of health and wellness? Does exercise induce neuromolecular alterations in the central nervous system of participants and influence various psychological functions? Is the alleged augmented longevity simply a derivative of strengthened organic systems, or do psychological imperatives mediate the positive influence of exercise upon health and wellness?

The chapter is divided into four sections, the first of which explains the physiological, cognitive, and psychosocial dynamics underlying the aging process. The second section discusses the concepts of wellness, fitness, and health vis-à-vis exercise as well as exercise characteristics. In the third section, the focus shifts to exercise as a putative inhibitor of aging and to its "fountain of youth" potential, including pointed reference to the effects of physical activity upon cognitive function in older persons. The last section addresses special recommendations and cautions that apply to older persons and provides suggestions for professionals who work with such clients.

Clarification of important terms used throughout the chapter is necessary. We use the term *old* or *older* to refer to persons who have attained a chronological status of no less than 60 years. Other terms that are frequently used throughout the discussion include *physical activity*, *exercise*, and *physical fitness*. Physical activity is defined as "any bodily movement produced by the skeletal muscles that result in energy expenditure" (Caspersen, Powell, & Christenson, 1985, p. 126). Exercise refers to "planned, structured, and repetitive bodily movement done to improve or maintain one or more components of physical fitness" (Caspersen et al., 1985, p. 128). Finally, physical fitness, "is a set of attributes that people have or achieve that relates to the ability to perform physical activity" (Caspersen et al., 1985, p. 128). Even though there is a clear distinction between physical activity and exercise, for the purpose of this chapter, we use these terms interchangeably.

A MYRIAD OF CHANGES DURING THE AGING PROCESS

Physiological Changes

Moving forward developmentally over decades involves progressive growth of the body's organs and systems until a maximal status is achieved. As these processes advance, we *age*, wherein structural, psychological, and other changes occur, many of which are measurable and quantifiable (Bowen & Atwood, 2004). For the most part, such changes involve neuro-muscular deterioration beginning at about the mid- or late twenties—somewhat earlier than might be expected (Faulkner, Larkin, Claflin, & Brooks, 2007). However, some functions begin to deteriorate somewhat at a much earlier age. For instance, the immune system shows decline in the mid-teens (Bowen & Atwood, 2004). Biologically, we are not what we were ten, twenty, or thirty years ago. According to Bowen and Atwood (2004), the aging process involves any changes occurring in one's body, whether they are subtle or more blatant, that often have significant psychological ramifications. What is the basis of these alterations? What is happening on a cellular level that accounts for this sometimes slow and often barely per-ceptible deterioration? Some answers to these questions are available, one of which involves structures found in the cell's chromosomes known as *telomeres* (Aubert & Lansdorp, 2008).

Telomeres are located at the end of the chromosome in the nucleus of each animal cell and protect the chromosome from deterioration or from fusion with the adjacent chromo-somes (Aubert & Lansdorp, 2008; Cowan, Carlton, & Cande, 2001; Fossel, Blackburn, & Woynarowski, 2011). During aging, the telomeres weaken and fray, thereby compromising the integrity of the chromosomes and undermining their reproduction, which can lead to the cells' attrition or death (Sahin & DePinho, 2010). When substantial numbers of an organ's cells die, the organ's volume and capacity to function are diminished. Typically a human cell (with cardiac tissue being an exception) has the capacity to divide and reproduce about 50 to 70 times before its telomeres become so shortened that the cell dies (Blackburn, 1991). Shorter telomeres equate with reduced longevity, contributing to mortality (Cawthon, Smith, O'Brien, Sivatchenko, & Kerber, 2003); however, what remains unclear is whether this link is an indication of aging or a factor that causes aging.

Telomeres have been shown to be longer in individuals who exercise regularly than in their sedentary counterparts, thus providing those who exercise with greater protection against aging because their cells can reproduce over a comparatively longer period of time (Du et al., 2012). This is likely the rationale employed by John Ratey, who has maintained that if a fountain of youth truly exists, it is exercise (Ratey & Hagerman, 2008). Dr. Regina Benjamin, a former US Surgeon General, refers to exercise as medicine. She maintains that it is better than most pills (Benjamin, 2011).

Fat storage increases during aging (Kyle, Genton, Slosman, & Pichard, 2001), which may precipitate an increase in body weight and thus create an augmented cardiovascular burden. Another possible contributor to an increase in fat mass is a process known as *glycation*, which has been identified as a contributor to aging (Semba, Nicklett, & Ferrucci, 2010). This pro-cess involves sugar derived from eaten food combining with cellular components, resulting in changes to cells that inhibit their function. Glycation becomes more and more prevalent and problematic because of inefficient biochemical transactions during aging (Boulanger, Puisieux, Gaxatte, & Wautier, 2007), which encourages the frequently heard advice to reduce caloric intake as one gets older. Nevertheless, the scale may indicate no change in weight as one advances from middle to old age, although the ratio of lean body mass to stored body fat is likely to shift significantly (Delmonico et al., 2009), particularly if caloric intake remains stable (or increases) and physical activity decreases.

Other measurable changes may be observed during aging, such as a reduction in bone density and skeletal muscle mass (i.e., sarcopenia; Sayer et al., 2008). Significantly reduced bone density may cause a predisposition toward fracture following physical trauma (Cummings et al., 1993). This becomes additionally problematic in older persons whose static and dynamic balancing abilities may be compromised due to weakened anti-gravity musculature and overall skeletal system weakening. Muscle atrophy responsible for locomotion and maintenance of posture (the upright position) may in turn result in a predisposition to falling, a common bane in the elderly (Keskin et al., 2008). It is estimated that as many as 50 percent of people have some element of motor impairment by the age of 80 (Fried, Ferrucci, Darer, Williamson, & Anderson, 2004; Louis & Bennett, 2007). In addition to bone density and muscle atrophy, a loss of elasticity in connective tissue is commonly concomitant to aging (Barros et al., 2002; Sargon, Doral, & Atay, 2004). Ligaments and tendons enable movement of limbs and account for the manner in which they interact in joints. When their structure is altered and their function inhibited, agility and flexibility are undermined (Dunkman et al., 2013).

Brain and Cognitive Functioning

Among the earliest and most important publications pertinent to psychological and cognitive advantages of exercise are those by Spirduso and colleagues (Spirduso, 1975; Spirduso & Clifford, 1977). Their systematic approaches to hypothesis testing and sound methodological strategies have generated a host of valuable findings in the area of aging and physical exercise, with notable implications for cognitive function.

The preponderance of contemporary scientific thinking holds that the brain has the capacity to change throughout life and that its neural communication mechanisms are constantly being restructured or established anew (Pascual-Leone, Amedi, Fregni, & Merabet, 2005). The brain's ability to carry out meaningful anatomical and physiological change refers to *plasticity* (Kolb & Whishaw, 1998). This remarkable capacity may exert a positive effect upon cognitive vitality (brain output), especially in learning and memory (Cotman & Berchtold, 2002). Among the changes occurring during experience-related plasticity are dendrite length, synapse formation, and metabolic activity—all of which change negatively during adult aging (Kolb & Whishaw, 1998). The inevitable process of aging brings with it loss of acuity in many intellectual capacities (Schaie, Willis, & Cask, 2004).

Neurotransmitters and Brain Functioning

A large portion of brain function deals with electrochemical stimulation of the nervous system, including dopamine, serotonin, and norepinephrine, all of which increase during exercise (Meeusen & De Meirleir, 1995). Dopamine depletion has been indicted in the development of Parkinson's Disease—a condition that affects approximately 1 percent of the North American population over the age of 65 (Ratey & Hagerman, 2008). In their popular book *Spark*, Ratey and Hagerman (2008) defend the assertion that regular exercise has a profound effect on the brain and permanently changes its anatomy and function.

Advanced aging is accompanied by brain volume shrinkage, including the temporal cortex, hippocampus, and frontal cortex (Andrews-Hanna et al., 2007; Brans et al., 2010; Fjell et al., 2009). This is a consequence of neurons that can no longer reproduce and replenish themselves (Morrison & Hof, 1997). When this occurs, blood capillaries designed to nourish and service the neurons atrophy and disappear, thus the decrease in brain volume. After age 40, the rate at which this necrosis occurs accelerates (Henkenius, Peterson, Sowell, Thompson, Toga, & Welcome, 2003), and functions associated with particular sections of the brain (e.g., cognition, memory, etc.) are severely compromised.

Older individuals may have experiential advantages that enable avoidance of complete cognitive deficits, but they routinely demonstrate comparatively poorer performances on memory and learning tasks than younger individuals, which may be attributed to brain tissue decrease (Reuter-Lorenz & Park, 2010). Research has shown that the deterioration and resulting decrease in brain volume during aging may be delayed or even partially reversed as a result of exercise (Whitbourne, Neupert, & Lachman, 2008), especially in the cerebral cortex and hippocampus (Erickson, Gildengers, & Butters, 2013; Erickson, Miller, Weinstein, Akl, & Banducci, 2012). A significant association between fitness level and performance on certain memory tests has been reported along with the finding that elderly subjects (between ages 59 and 81) with comparatively higher fitness levels had a larger hippocampus—a part of the brain involved in the development of memories (Erikson et al., 2011).

A high level of fitness and social activity has been shown to correlate inversely with deterioration of certain kinds of cognitive (Churchill, Galveza, Colcombea, Swaine, Kramera, & Greenough, 2002; Colcombe & Kramer, 2003; Erikson et al., 2011) and motor function (James, Boyle, Buchman, & Bennett, 2011). For example, elderly individuals who are fit tend to perform better than their unfit counterparts on many mental tasks, particularly those that emphasize speed and attention (Spirduso, Francis, & MacRae, 2005).

In addition, voluntary aerobic fitness training seems to positively influence the brain's executive control processes (Colcombe & Kramer, 2003). In their study of 18,766 women who were 70 and older, Weuve, Kang, Manson, Breteler, Ware, and Grodstein (2004) reported that regular physical activity (i.e., walking) was associated with higher levels of cognitive function and less cognitive decline. The more vigorous the walking and the greater the distance regularly walked, the greater the strength in cognitive performance. Among elderly participants, those who exercise regularly do better on short-term memory assessment, general information processing, and executive brain function than do those who are sedentary (Geda et al., 2010).

What mechanisms account for such observations? Why does exercise seem to exert a salubrious impact upon brain structure and function? One possible answer is offered by Cotman and colleagues (Cotman & Berchtold, 2002; Cotman, Berchtold, & Christie, 2007), who make a case for exercise acting directly on the "molecular machinery of the brain itself." Exercise, they suggest, stimulates an increase in brain chemicals generically known as *neurotrophic factors*, which stimulate brain tissue growth or *neurogenisis* that counters age-related brain tissue damage. Cotman et al. (2007) speculate that exercise may also reduce inflammatory agents in the brain that tend to interfere with tissue growth and health.

Exercise has been attributed to the prevention of or reduction in severity of cognitive impairment and dementia among elderly men and women (Kemoun et al., 2010). Research also supports a link between muscular strength (thus suggesting regular exercise as a contributing factor) and Alzheimer's disease (AD) in older individuals (M_{age} = 80.3; Buchman, Wilson, Boyle, Bienias, & Bennett, 2007). This is to say, the greater the amount of muscular strength, the lower the probability of cognitive decline as well as a lower likelihood of developing AD (Arnold et al., 2013). Once again, explanations for this connection presently remain speculative, but this is not to say that the relationship does not exist.

Although a good deal of the beneficial effects of exercise upon brain function derives from animal studies (Albeck, Sano, Prewitt, & Dalton, 2006; van Praag, Shubert, Zhao, & Gage, 2005), a considerable amount of supportive evidence has been recently accruing from investigations utilizing elderly human subjects, as noted above. A reasonable conclusion from these studies is that exercise enhances not only general health, but also various aspects of brain function, particularly functions associated with the hippocampus referred to as *executive function* (Churchill et al., 2002; Colcombe & Kramer, 2003; Cotman & Berchtold, 2002; Cotman et al., 2007; Weuve et al., 2004).

Personality and Exercise

Personality is a well-recognized but certainly controversial hypothetical psychological construct. Various robust questions relative to personality have been deliberated upon by scholars as well. For example, if behavioral tendencies indeed exist, as is implied by the very application of the term personality, are they inherited or acquired? (Schuett, Dall, Wilson, & Royle, 2013). Are these proclivities subject to situational or psychodynamic influences? (Tett & Murphy, 2002). How many factors actually exist within an individual's personality, and are they enduring? (Eysenck, 1991). Are certain traits more deeply embedded in the personality framework (i.e., core traits) and therefore more resistant to modification? (Matthews, Deary, & Whiteman, 2003).

One additional and controversial issue is whether or not the personality of older adults is able to change (McCrae & Costa, 2008; Roberts, 2009), and if so, whether exercise and/or cognitive training are among the interventions that might encourage this. Some recent research indicates that the answer to the first question is yes. Jackson, Hill, Payne, Roberts, and Stine-Morrow (2012) have reported that in response to inductive-reasoning training conducted over a 16-week period, certain dimensions of personality supposedly linked to cognitive processes were modified in their sample of men between the ages of 60 and 94 years, notably openness.

Various dimensions of personality vis-à-vis exercise have been studied (Erfle, 2014; Rhodes & Courneya, 2001; Yap & Lee, 2013). Possible connections between personality traits and certain exercise variables, such as degree of adherence, exercise type, level of fitness of the exerciser, intensity and duration of exercise, and motivation for exercise have been investigated, with inconsistent degrees of methodological rigor and results (Ekkekakis, Hall, & Petruzzello, 2005; Flegal, Kishiyama, Zajdel, Haas, & Oken, 2007; Ingledew & Markland, 2008). However, these connections do not necessarily suggest causal relationships.

One area that has received considerable attention in the scientific literature is the relationship between personality and fitness level (Chen & Lee, 2007; Gurven, von Rueden, Stieglitz, Kaplan, & Rodriguez, 2014; Hogan, 1989) and, therefore, ultimately health, considering that physical fitness is a significant component of overall health. Physical fitness, or the degree of preparedness to satisfy the physical demands of daily living (Caspersen et al., 1985; Greenberg & Pargman, 1986), has been shown to be linked to some personality traits (Rhodes & Smith, 2006). For instance, physical disability and skeletal muscle inadequacy are associated with certain personality traits in older persons (Jaconelli, Stephan, Canada, & Chapman, 2012). Tolea and her colleagues report associations between such personality traits as neuroticism, extraversion, and conscientiousness and knee muscular strength in older men and women (Tolea et al., 2012a, 2012b). Negative traits, including high neuroticism, depression, anxiety, hostility, low extraversion, and low agreeableness, were negatively correlated with muscular strength scores. The explanation for this finding offered by the studies' authors posits that such behavioral tendencies contribute to an unhealthy lifestyle in the elderly, discourage participation in regular physical activity, and deter required levels of adherence, which may account for comparatively low strength. The authors also speculate that these traits may even predispose individuals to compromised mobility since they move the body less.

Research (Terracciano et al., 2008; Wilson, Krueger, Gu, Bienias, Mendes de Leon, & Evans, 2005) suggests that the more extraverted and conscientious, and the less neurotic, older persons are—components of what Terracciano et al. (2013) refer to as a resilient personality profile—the more physically active they are. This in turn may account for higher aerobic capacities being observed in older exercisers in comparison to their sedentary counterparts, who also have slower walking speeds (Terraccinao et al., 2013). Further, this may clarify the observed link between strength scores and certain personality traits. Tolea et al. (2012b) found that low scores on extraversion, which is associated with a weak inclination to interact socially with others, appear to be negatively correlated with strength scores. Those with high extraversion tendencies tend to be inclined toward participation in a broad range of positive behaviors, including physical activity. Thus, the planning and construction of prevention and intervention programs may beneficially take into consideration personality typology.

It may be possible to identify elderly persons with certain personality types who, for whatever reason, tend to have relatively low muscular strength. However, this finding relative to extraversion and knee strength is in conflict with results reported by Jorm et al. (1993), who found no association between extraversion and strength in dominant hand grip. Perhaps this discrepancy is due to the incorporation of different muscle groups in the above-cited studies. The connection between extraversion and muscle strength, although seductive, remains undetermined at this time.

Psychosocial Factors

Regular participation in exercise, especially aerobic exercise, seems to recruit physiological mechanisms that provide protection from various forms of stress reactions (Salmon, 2001). Albeit a vital function, and one that facilitates distinctions among animals of various orders, cognitive activity is but one aspect of human psychology. There are other *psychosocial factors* one can consider.

The positive effects of acute as well as chronic bouts of exercise upon various mood components and perceptions of well-being in elderly participants are well established (Netz, Wu, Becker, & Tenenbaum, 2005). Li, Duncan, Duncan, McAuley, Chaumeton, and Harmer (2001) provide findings from their study that support a case for positive effects of Tai Chi on measures of depression and life satisfaction for elderly participants immediately after exercise.

Both satisfactory and satisfying human existence are dependent upon social interaction (Spiro, 1994). They particularly merit consideration when elderly individuals are concerned, since opportunities for social contacts may have been significantly reduced or lost all together due to illness, injury, or death among friends and acquaintances (Dury, 2014). Exercise has the potential to provide opportunities for building and maintaining interpersonal relations since it offers occasions for meeting and interacting with others (Estabrooks & Carron, 1999). This is obvious when considering team or group physical activities where participants gather to engage, but is also common in so-called individual forms of exercise. For example, running, jogging, or walking are often done in group settings, despite the fact that participants perform individually within their cohorts.

Attendance at gyms or places where exercise sets, repetitions, and routines are executed also encourages social intercourse. Participants speak to one another, inquire about others, and share thoughts and experiences (Resnick, Orwig, Magaziner, & Wynne, 2002). Acquaintances become friends, and friendships may generate non-exercise-related activities. The exercise location may become an opportune gathering place for elderly persons with limited options for social interactions. Elderly individuals, notably those who have retired from their careers but nonetheless profess a desire to temporarily change their milieu, may satisfy their wish to "get out of the house" by going to the gym, golf and tennis courses, or senior activity center, where persons of similar age and interests are to be found.

WORKING WITH THE ELDERLY

Wellness, Fitness, and Health

Structural and functional changes in organs and systems during aging may impinge upon the quality of life, as noted throughout this chapter. Although of equal importance and to some degree overlapping in their definitions, *wellness, fitness,* and *health* are conceptually different. In order to clarify these differences, a good beginning point is the identification of five basic categories or elements underlying human existence and inherent in the above-mentioned concepts, namely social, mental, emotional, physical, and spiritual entities (not listed here in order of criticality). Greenberg and Pargman (1986) offer a more detailed perspective of these concepts in their book. In the following, we provide a brief overview of these categories.

Social Entity

The social component of life refers to the interactions between an individual and other persons in their sphere of human relationships. The number and quality of friendships, acquaintances, kinships, and interpersonal connections are determinants of the strength of the social component. A key element in the social category is the notion of *satisfaction*—the implication being that if the relationships do not generate comfort or contentment, they miss the mark.

Mental Entity

The mental element refers to perceptions one maintains about one's intellectual abilities. This, in turn suggests the ability to learn, to understand the intricacies of the multiple challenges and problems one regularly confronts, and to develop strategies for their resolution.

Emotional Entity

Emotions may be understood as tones of feelings, and the emotional side of self is an integral aspect of overall health and wellness. Control of emotions is essential; however, emotion regulation does not necessarily suggest eradication. In the healthy and well individual, the appropriate expression of feelings in gradated amounts is a positive attribute. Representation of emotions is thereby managed in order to conform to societal ethos and standards.

Physical Entity

The physical dimension of health and wellness brings to mind organic and structural integrity. Physical fitness may be interpreted as preparedness to fulfill the motor and strength demands associated with daily living. If and when individuals are prepared to efficiently deal with their regular physical challenges, they are deemed to be of adequate fitness. Training or systematic conditioning of the various physical capacities (e.g., muscular strength, muscular power, muscular and respiratory endurance, agility, flexibility) may improve this readiness, thus elevating the capacity to satisfy daily physical demands.

Spiritual Entity

Spirituality refers to a belief in some unifying force that is credited with regulatory power, be it a godly, metaphysical entity; nature itself; or some inanimate model or figure. A person imbued with a strong spiritual component is invested in the influence of these forces upon their destiny. Deeply religious persons maintain a strong spiritual sense, but atheists, who are strongly impressed with natural beauty—with the magic and wonder of mountains, forests, and glistening bodies of water—also may make claim to a well-developed spirituality.

Health might be simplistically understood as the absence of illness, but it is rather a state of complete physical, mental, and social well-being (World Health Organization, 2014). Implicit in this approach is that the extent of one's health is contingent upon the degree of organic malfunction; the greater the physiological vulnerability, the lower the health. However, this relationship is not limited to physicality. One may be structurally or physiologically sound, but spiritually, emotionally, or mentally deficient. Conversely, one may be *well* despite being ill or in poor health because the measure of wellness equates with successful integration of all five elements described above. An individual who is high in spirituality, mental function, or sociality may claim a very high level of wellness despite serious infirmity. Therefore, terminally ill persons may be very well, and physically sound individuals may be entirely unwell. Of essence is balance and integration of the five components of life (Greenberg & Pargman, 1986). Exercise and aging significantly interrelate with all five of the above-delineated categories.

The process of aging carries the potential to affect the five elements of life. As one progresses chronologically, significant changes are likely to occur to the social, mental, emotional, spiritual, and physical components of health and wellness (Birren, Cohen, & Sloane, 2013). Decade after decade of existence is accompanied by shifting internal and external environmental forces that bear upon these elements. Relationships are altered due to geographic relocation or death of friends and relatives, and physical abilities gradually weaken. Learning and knowledge accumulation occurring throughout the years generates different perspectives about environmental stimuli of all sorts, thereby altering emotional responses, values, and beliefs in such things as metaphysical entities. Needless to say, in sundry ways we are quite different at age 60 than we are at age 20.

Motivation for Exercise in Older Persons

Motivation may be understood as (the extrinsic as well as intrinsic) forces acting on or within an individual that energize and direct overt behavior (Sage, 1977). Its dynamics are known to vary according to developmental stages, culture, gender, and ethnicity (Dergance et al., 2003; Marx, Cohen-Mansfield, & Guralnik, 2003; Schutzer & Graves, 2004). The forces that impel human behavior or serve as barriers to behavior are not necessarily the same in children, young adults, and elderly adults. It is true that some motives do cut across all age groups to some extent, notably the health motive (Gavin, McBrearty, & Seguin, 2006). Distinctions according to age do exist, though. Members of age cohorts are characterized by different basic needs and interests (Molanorouzi, Khoo, & Morris, 2015), and as such, different strategies are required to stimulate them to embark upon or maintain exercise regimens. For instance, the fun motive is paramount in children if they are to enter and remain in a particular physical activity. When a perception of "no fun" prevails, children do not adhere (Gottfried, 1983).

The enjoyment motive, although prominent in children, is not necessarily exclusive to this developmental group. The enjoyment factor is also involved, but perhaps to a lesser degree, in older exercisers (Titze, Stronegger, & Owen, 2005). Young adults, especially those still in the work force, are likely to be influenced in their exercise-related decisions by scheduling demands and by proximity of exercise venues to home or workplace (Reed & Phillips, 2005). Body weight regulation enters the motivational framework more for the young adult than the elderly (Gavin et al., 2006). The importance of physical appearance declines as a motivational force with increasing age (Trujillo, Brougham, & Walsh, 2004). Elderly individuals are likely to be motivated to participate in programmatic physical activity because of perceived health benefits, a desire for independence, or a physician's recommendation (Hirvensalo, Heikkinen, Lintunen, & Rantanen, 2003). An important observation that exercise psychology specialists should acknowledge is that intrinsically motivated individuals are more likely to embark upon exercise regimens than those who are encouraged to do so by external stimulants (Dacey, Baltzell, & Zaichkowsky, 2008).

Exercise psychology consultants should be cognizant of commonly identified barriers to exercise reported by elderly individuals. These issues must be addressed and somehow resolved if physical activity is to be inspired in elderly clients. Barriers perceived and commonly expressed by the elderly include chronic health problems, too much pain, being already active enough, no self-discipline, nobody to exercise with, lack of knowledge, lack of time, a perception that exercise is for young people, limited access/transportation, unsafe neighborhoods, difficult weather conditions, fear of injury, or limited financial resources (Clark, 1999; Grossman & Stewart, 2003; Nied & Franklin, 2002; Schuler, Roy, Vinci, Philipp, & Cohen, 2006; Whaley & Ebbeck, 1997). Other perceived barriers include cultural expectations and social factors (Rasinaho, Hirvensalo, Leinonen, Lintunen, & Rantanen, 2006). From personal experiences, it is often difficult to convince elderly individuals to engage in regular physical activity and to sustain participation. Resolution of these barrier-related issues may pose more of a challenge to the exercise psychology professional than will the design and implementation of the exercise program itself.

Recommendations for Professionals Working With Older Clients

Exercise psychology professionals would do well to consider the following caveats and recommendations that relate to the safety and effectiveness of physical activity and exercise programs as well as to motivation for their clients' initial program entry.

Regularity

The beneficial impact of exercise upon the various psychological components of elderly persons enumerated in this chapter will be entirely elusive or at least less than optimal if participation is irregular. Although some research reveals that even casual participation generates some psychological and physiological benefits (Paffenbarger, Hyde, Wing, & Hsieh, 1986), for best outcomes, exercise should be conducted according to a predetermined schedule with emphasis on regularity (Burdette & Hill, 2008). Schedule construction should be consensual and predicated upon the client's input and demands of their personal scheduling requirements and idiosyncrasies. Sleep and waking patterns of older individuals are likely to be well established (Evans & Rogers, 1994), and many older persons have highly preferred times of the day for physical activity. To countermand such preferences is to invite additional barriers to exercise. The clients' needs and preferences for their schedule deserve primary consideration, rather than those of the exercise psychology specialist. Although regularity is of essence, the same routine need not be pursued during each and every exercise session. Cross-training (e.g., strength training, aerobic exercise, etc.) options should be explored in order to avoid staleness and motivational depreciation (McDermott & Mernitz, 2006; Nied & Franklin, 2002).

Rigor

Older persons are understandably obliged to confront daily physical challenges that differ markedly from those of younger exercisers. Their needs are usually not the same, since many older persons are retired from their careers, are close to retirement, or have strategically altered their lifestyle. Rigor is an essential ingredient of physical activity done with the intent of deriving psychological benefit (Lampinen, Heikkinen, & Ruoppila, 2000). Older persons may be insecure about what their physical activity safety limitations are, or expressed alternatively, how much rigor is satisfactory. Their strong desire to avoid injury (Nied & Franklin, 2002) and even temporary incapacitation tends to foster a conservative cut-off demarcation, one that may fall short of the mark for rigorous physical activity. Here lies the rub, as it does for exercisers of all ages, but particularly for elderly individuals: What constitutes the least degree of rigor, that is, the minimal essential level of physical activation? Caution should be exercised by exercise leaders whose professional responsibility is to provide guidance in determining an appropriate level of exercise intensity (McDermott & Mernitz, 2006). Miscalculation of this bottom line is likely to result in decreased motivation for adherence or anxiety about injury in clients. Target heart rate training may be the answer (Pargman, 2012).

Target Heart Rate

Target heart rate (THR) addresses the question of how much exercise is appropriate by predicating the answer exclusively upon the number of heart beats per minute during exercise. Chronological age is subtracted from the number 220 (i.e., the highest heart rate usually achieved by humans). Next, an exerciser would identify the degree to which he or she wishes to expend effort during exercise (e.g., 60, 70, or 80%). Persons selecting 80 percent are committing to a considerably higher level of effort than those who choose 60 percent. A THR for a 70-year-old man or woman would therefore be 220 minus 70, multiplied by the degree of effort he or she wishes to exert throughout an aerobic exercise bout, which should be 20 to 30 minutes long (for high effort: $220 - 70 = 150$; $150 \times 0.80 = 105$). For a beginning exerciser, three bouts per week while operating within the zone should suffice (American College of Sports Medicine—ACSM, 2013). A person with a low beginning fitness level—someone who has not partaken of rigorous physical activity in a while—should be advised to use a relatively low-intensity goal in calculating the THR, namely 50 percent. Exercisers should be encouraged to attend to their impressions about the effort expended during exercise necessary to stay within the zone. Recalibration of the target is in order when the elderly exerciser testifies to an exceptionally high perception of pain or discomfort (i.e., perceived exertion). In this case, the exercise leader would be injudicious to insist upon continuation of effort and intensity. This approach to identifying the appropriate degree of exercise rigor takes into account person-specific levels of readiness for exercise as well as individual fitness goals.

Metabolic Equivalent of Task

An alternative to THR is Metabolic Equivalent of Task or metabolic equivalency (MET; Ainsworth et al., 2011). This strategy for determining exercise rigor is predicated upon the basic or *basal metabolic rate* of the exerciser. Basal metabolic rate is the rate at which the body burns calories during complete rest—calories necessary to produce energy for vital bodily functions. Conventionally a MET of about one equates with metabolism at rest for an average person (depending upon a few factors, such as body mass). The intensity of effort, be it exercise or non-exercise-related work, may be expressed in terms of number of METs. Thus, an assigned value of two, three, or four METs indicates that an activity requires two, three, or four times the resting metabolic rate to be sustained during the 20 to 30 minutes of exercise. Various exercise activities have been assigned METs. For instance, singles tennis would equate with more than six METs; cycling in excess of 10 miles per hour would also score more than six METS. Slow walking would represent about two METS, whereas running could be assessed at 23 METs, depending upon speed and distance. Energy cost of the same activity would be different for persons of varying body weight. Generally, three to six METs is considered to constitute moderate exercise (Haskell et al., 2007). With age, level of fitness, body mass, and duration of exercise participation per bout factored in, number of METs could be used to assign levels of rigor.

Idiosyncratic Needs and Interests of Clients

The exercise program for older persons should take into consideration desired personal outcomes. Not all individuals of similar age seek identical programmatic results. A thorough overview of each participant's individual goals and aspirations should be conducted prior to attempting enrollment of elderly clients in an exercise program. Although certain generalizations about motives for elderly persons were made in previous sections of this chapter, exercise psychology professionals should probe the motivations of their clients and avoid assumptions about what may inspire all members of an exercise group.

Despite the existence of probable motivations for elderly persons relative to exercise, there may exist within a particular person or cohort a disproportionate emphasis upon one factor rather than more widespread ones. An example would be the motive to regulate body weight in compliance with a physician's recommendation. Four categories should definitely be included in a structured exercise program for older persons, namely aerobic exercise, balance training, flexibility, and stretching exercises. Progressive resistance training should also be incorporated, but to a lesser degree (Latham, Bennett, Stretton, & Anderson, 2004). The emphasis of each of these suggested components would be predicated upon the individual needs and interests of participants. For instance, a client preparing to enter a road race (e.g., a fun run) would incorporate more aerobic activity than someone motivated to increase range of motion and reduce stiffness after gardening.

Overuse and Injury

When entering or contemplating entry into an exercise regimen, older persons may bring with them anxiety about discomfort and injury. This concern is not fanciful in that the probability of experiencing these two consequences increases with regular participation in rigorous physical activity. However, discomfort and injury are not inevitable outcomes of exercise, and the likelihood of their occurrence may be reduced through sensible approaches. The exercise psychology specialist should take note of such anxieties and discuss related issues with clients at the onset of their participation (Lee et al., 2015). A participant's history of injury should be reviewed in an effort to determine whether the client has frequently been injured or is vulnerable to injury. The approach to exercise in older populations should be gradual and represent a shared effort between client and exercise specialist.

SUMMARY

This chapter is primarily concerned with exercise as it relates to older individuals. To this end, we began by defining the term exercise and acknowledging the physical and psychological changes that occur during the aging process. We specifically focused on chromosomal and biochemical factors that are known to contribute to the organic and structural sequence of aging. Changes in central nervous system function due to aging and their implications for various psychological aspects, such as cognition and personality, were discussed next.

Wellness, health, and fitness were then presented as critical concepts underlying physical and psychological stability. Following this, dimensions of motivation as applied to exercise participation were presented. Having provided foundational material for the reader, we proceeded with a discussion of recommendations for those professionals whose efforts are directed toward elderly clients. Among these are the importance of regularity and rigor as components of well-designed exercise programs, assessment of physical fitness, the importance of exercise as a mechanism for addressing social needs, and measures to be taken in an effort to reduce the probability of injury.

REFERENCES

Ainsworth, B. E., Haskell, W. L., Herrmann, S. D., Meckes, N., Bassett, D. R. J., Tudor-Locke, C., . . . Leon, A. S. (2011). 2011 compendium of physical activities a second update of codes and MET values. *Medicine and Science in Sports and Exercise*, *43*(8), 1575–1581. doi: 10.1249/MSS.0b013e31821ece12

Albeck, D. S., Sano, K., Prewitt, G. E., & Dalton, L. (2006). Mild forced treadmill exercise enhances spatial learning in the aged rat. *Behavioural Brain Research*, *168*(2), 345–348. doi:10.1016/j.bbr.2005.11.008

American College of Sports Medicine. (2013). *ACSM issues new recommendations on quantity and quality of exercise*. Retrieved from www.acsm.org/about-acsm/media-room/news-releases/2011/08/01/acsm-issues-new-recommendations-on-quantity-and-quality-of-exercise

Andrews-Hanna, J. R., Snyder, A. Z., Vincent, J. L., Lustig, C., Head, D., Raichle, M. E., & Buckner, R. L. (2007). Disruption of large-scale brain systems in advanced aging. *Neuron*, *56*(5), 924–935. doi: 10.1016/j.neuron.2007.10.038

Arnold, S. E., Louneva, N., Cao, K., Wang, L., Han, L., Wolk, D. A., . . . Bennett, D. A. (2013). Cellular, synaptic, and biochemical features of resilient cognition in Alzheimer's disease. *Neurobiology of Aging*, *34*(1), 157–168. doi: 10.1016/j.neurobiolaging.2012.03.004

Aubert, G., & Lansdorp, P. M. (2008). Telomeres and aging. *Physiological Reviews*, *88*(2), 557–579. doi: 10.1152/physrev.00026.2007

Barros, E. M., Rodrigues, C. J., Rodrigues, N. R., Oliveira, R. P., Barros, T. E., & Rodrigues, A. J. (2002). Aging of the elastic and collagen fibers in the human cervical interspinous ligaments. *The Spine Journal*, *2*(1), 57–62. doi: 10.1016/s1529-9430(01)00167-x

Benjamin, R. (2011, January 7). Doctor's order. *The New York Times*. Retrieved from www.nytimes.com/2011/01/09/magazine/09FOB-Q4-t.html?_r=0

Birren, J. E., Cohen, G. D., & Sloane, R. B. (Eds.). (2013). *Handbook of mental health and aging*. San Diego, CA: Academic Press.

Blackburn, E. H. (1991). Structure and function of telomeres. *Nature*, *350*(6319), 569–573. doi: 10.1038/350569a0

Boulanger, E., Puisieux, F., Gaxatte, C., & Wautier, J. L. (2007). Aging: Role and control of glycation. *La Revue de Médecine Interne*, *28*(12), 832–840. doi: http://dx.doi.org/10.1016/j.revmed.2007.05.019

Bowen, R. L., & Atwood, C. S. (2004). Living and dying for sex. *Gerontology*, *50*(5), 265–290. doi: 10.1159/000079125

Brans, R. G. H., Kahn, R. S., Schnack, H. G., van Baal, G. C. M., Posthuma, D., van Haren, N. E. M., . . . Hulshoff Pol, H. E. (2010). Brain plasticity and intellectual ability are influenced by shared genes. *The Journal of Neuroscience*, *30*(16), 5519–5524. doi: 10.1523/jneurosci.5841-09.2010

Brody, J. E. (2008, June 24). Fit, not frail: Exercise as a tonic for aging. *The New York Times*. Retrieved from www.nytimes.com/2008/06/24/health/24brod.html?_r=0

Buchman, A. S., Wilson, R. S., Boyle, P. A., Bienias, J. L., & Bennett, D. A. (2007). Change in motor function and risk of mortality in older persons *Journal of the American Geriatrics Society*, *55*(1), 11–19. doi: 10.1111/j.1532-5415.2006.01032.x

Burdette, A. M., & Hill, T. D. (2008). An examination of processes linking perceived neighborhood disorder and obesity. *Social Science & Medicine*, *67*, 38–46. doi:10.1016/j.socscimed.2008.03.029

Caspersen, C. J., Powell, K. E., & Christenson, G. M. (1985). Physical activity, exercise, and physical fitness: Definitions and distinctions for health-related research. *Public Health Reports (1974)*, *100*(2), 126–131. doi: 10.2307/20056429

Cawthon, R. M., Smith, K. R., O'Brien, E., Sivatchenko, A., & Kerber, R. A (2003). Association between telomere length in blood and mortality in people aged 60 years or older. *Lancet*, *361*(9355), 393–395. doi: 10.1016/s0140-6736(03)12384-7

Centers for Disease Control and Prevention (2013). *The state of aging and health in America*. Retrieved from www.cdc.gov/features/agingandhealth/state_of_aging_and_health_in_america_2013.pdf

Chen, L. S., & Lee, Y. (2007). Association between personality traits and attending a fitness center. *Social Behavior and Personality: An International Journal*, *35*(10), 1323–1324. doi:10.2224/sbp.2007.35.10.1323

Churchill, J., Galveza, R., Colcombea, S., Swaine, R. A., Kramera, A. F., & Greenough, W. T. (2002). Exercise, experience and the aging brain. *Neurobiology of Aging, 23*(5), 941–955. doi: 10.1016/s0197-4580(02)00028-3

Clark, D. (1999). Identifying psychological, physiological, and environmental barriers and facilitators to exercise among older low income adults. *Journal of Clinical Geropsychology, 5*(1), 51–62. doi: 10.1023/a:1022942913555

Colcombe, S., & Kramer, A. F. (2003). Fitness effects on the cognitive function of older adults: A meta-analytic study. *Psychological Science, 14*(2), 125–130. doi: 10.2307/40063782

Cotman, C. W., & Berchtold, N. C. (2002). Exercise: A behavioral intervention to enhance brain health and plasticity. *Trends in Neurosciences, 25*(6), 295–301. doi: http://dx.doi.org/10.1016/S01662-236(02)021434-

Cotman, C. W., Berchtold, N. C., & Christie, L. A. (2007). Exercise builds brain health: Key roles of growth factor cascades and inflammation. *Trends in Neurosciences, 30*(9), 464–472.

Cowan, C. R., Carlton, P. M., & Cande, W. Z. (2001). The polar arrangement of telomeres in interphase and meiosis. Rabl organization and the bouquet. *Plant Physiology, 125*(2), 532–538.

Cummings, S. R., Browner, W., Black, D. M., Nevitt, M. C., Genant, H. K., Cauley, J., . . . Vogt, T. M. (1993). Bone density at various sites for prediction of hip fractures. *The Lancet, 341*(8837), 72–75. doi:10.1016/0140-6736(93)92555-8

Dacey, M., Baltzell, A., & Zaichkowsky, L. (2008). Older adults' intrinsic and extrinsic motivation toward physical activity *American Journal of Health Behavior, 32*(6), 570. doi: 10.5993/ajhb.32.6.2

Delmonico, M. J., Harris, T. B., Visser, M., Won Park, A., Conroy, B. M., . . . Goodpaster, B. H., (2009). Longitudinal study of muscle strength, quality, and adipose tissue infiltration. *American Journal of Clinical Nutrition, 90*, 1579–1585. doi: 10.3945/ajcn.2009.28047

Dergance, J. M., Calmbach, W. M., Dhanda, R., Miles, T. P., Hazuda, H. P., & Mouton, C. P. (2003). Barriers to and benefits of leisure time physical activity in the elderly: Differences across cultures. *Journal of the American Geriatrics Society, 51*(6), 863–868. doi: 10.1046/j.1365-2389.2003.51271.x

Du, M., Prescott, J., Kraft, P., Han, J., Giovannucci, E., Hankinson, S. E., & De Vivo, I. (2012). Physical activity, sedentary behavior, and leukocyte telomere length in women. *American Journal of Epidemiology, 175*(5), 414–422. doi: 10.1093/aje/kwr330

Dunkman, A. A., Buckley, M. R., Mienaltowski, M. J., Adams, S. M., Thomas, S. J., Satchell, L., . . . Soslowsky, L. J. (2013). Decorin expression is important for age-related changes in tendon structure and mechanical properties. *Matrix Biology, 32*(1), 3–13. doi: http://dx.doi.org/10.1016/j.matbio.2012.11.005

Dury, R. (2014). Social isolation and loneliness in the elderly: An exploration of some of the issues. *British Journal of Community Nursing, 19*(3), 125–128. Retrieved from www.magonlinelibrary.com/action/showCategory?categoryCode=internurse

Ekkekakis, P., Hall, E. E., & Petruzzello, S. J. (2005). Variation and homogeneity in affective responses to physical activity of varying intensities: An alternative perspective on dose — response based on evolutionary considerations. *Journal of Sports Sciences, 23*(5), 477–500. doi: 10.1080/02640410400021492

Erfle, S. E. (2014). Persistent focal behavior and physical activity performance. *Measurement in Physical Education & Exercise Science, 18*(3), 168–183. doi:10.1080/1091367X.2014.905946

Erickson, K. I., Gildengers, A. G., & Butters, M. A. (2013). Physical activity and brain plasticity in late adulthood. *Dialogues in Clinical Neuroscience, 15*(1), 99.

Erickson, K. I., Miller, D. L., Weinstein, A. M., Akl, S. L., & Banducci, S. (2012). Physical activity and brain plasticity in late adulthood: A conceptual and comprehensive review. *Gastroenterology Insights, 3*(1), e6. doi: 10.4081/ar.2012.e6

Erickson, K. I., Voss, M. W., Prakashd, R. S., Basake, C., Szabof, A., Chaddockb, L., . . . Kramerb, A. F. (2011). Exercise training increases size of hippocampus and improves memory. *Proceedings of the National Academy of Sciences, 108*(7), 3017–3022. doi: 10.1073/pnas.1015950108

Estabrooks, P., & Carron, A. V. (1999). The influence of the group with elderly exercisers. *Small Group Research, 30*(4), 438–452. doi: 10.1177/104649649903000403

Evans, B. D., & Rogers, A. E. (1994). 24-hour sleep/wake patterns in healthy elderly persons. *Applied Nursing Research, 7*(2), 75–83. doi: http://dx.doi.org/10.1016/08971-897(94)900361-

Eysenck, H. J. (1991). *Dimensions of personality* (pp. 87–103). Philadelphia: PA, Springer.

Faulkner, J. A., Larkin, L. M., Claflin, D. R., & Brooks, S. V. (2007). Age-related changes in the structure and function of skeletal muscles. *Clinical and Experimental Pharmacology & Physiology, 34*(11), 1091–1096. doi: 10.1111/j.1440-1681.2007.04752.x

Fjell, A. M., Westlye, L. T., Amlien, I., Espeseth, T., Reinvang, I., Raz, N., . . . Walhovd, K. B. (2009). High consistency of regional cortical thinning in aging across multiple samples. *Cerebral Cortex, 19*(9), 2001–2012. doi: 10.1093/cercor/bhn232

Flegal, K., Kishiyama, S., Zajdel, D., Haas, M., & Oken, B. (2007). Adherence to yoga and exercise interventions in a 6-month clinical trial. *BMC Complementary and Alternative Medicine, 7*(1), 37. doi: 10.1186/14726-8827-37

Fossel, M., Blackburn, G., & Woynarowski, D. (2011). *The immorality edge: Realize the secrets of your telomeres for a longer, healthier life.* Hoboken, NJ: John Wiley & Sons, Inc.

Fried, L. P., Ferrucci, L., Darer, J., Williamson, J. D., & Anderson, G. (2004). Untangling the concepts of disability, frailty, and comorbidity: Implications for improved targeting and care. *Biological Sciences and Medical Sciences, 59*(3), M255–M263. doi: 10.1093/gerona/59.3.M255

Gavin, J., McBrearty, M., & Seguin, D. (2006). The psychology of exercise. *IDEA Health & Fitness Source, 3,* 2.

Geda, Y. E., Roberts, R. O., Knopman, D. S., Christianson, T. J. H., Pankratz, V. S., Ivnik, R. J. . . . Rocca, W. A. (2010). Physical exercise, aging, and mild cognitive impairment: A population-based study. *Archives of Neurology, 67*(1), 80–86. doi:10.1001/archneurol.2009.297

Gottfried, A. E. (1983). Intrinsic motivation in young children. *Young Children, 39*(1), 64–73. www.jstor.org/stable/42658350

Greenberg, J. S., & Pargman, D. (1986). *Physical fitness: A wellness approach.* Englewood Cliffs, NJ: Prentice Hall Bailey.

Grossman, M. D., & Stewart, A. L. (2003). "You aren't going to get better by just sitting around": Physical activity perceptions, motivations, and barriers in adults 75 years of age or older. *American Journal of Geriatric Cardiology, 12,* 33–37.

Gurven, M., von Rueden, C., Stieglitz, J., Kaplan, H., & Rodriguez, D. E. (2014). The evolutionary fitness of personality traits in a small-scale subsistence society. *Evolution and Human Behavior, 35*(1), 17–25. doi: 10.1016/j.evolhumbehav.2013.09.002

Haskell, W. L., Lee, I.-M., Pate, R. R., Powell, K. E., Blair, S. N., Franklin, B. A., . . . Bauman, A. (2007). Physical activity and public health: Updated recommendation for adults from the American College of Sports Medicine and the American Heart Association. *Medicine and Science in Sports and Exercise, 39*(8), 1423.

Henkenius, A. L., Peterson, B. S., Sowell, E. R., Thompson, P. M., Toga, A. W., & Welcome, S. E. (2003). Mapping cortical change across the human life span. *Nature Neuroscience, 6*(3), 309–315. doi: 10.1038/nn1008

Hirvensalo, M., Heikkinen, E., Lintunen, T., & Rantanen, T. (2003). The effect of advice by health care professionals on increasing physical activity of older people. *Scandinavian Journal of Medicine and Science in Sports, 13,* 231–236.

Hogan, J. (1989). Personality correlates of physical fitness. *Journal of Personality and Social Psychology, 56*(2), 284–288. doi: 10.1037/0022-3514.56.2.284

Ingledew, D. K., & Markland, D. (2008). The role of motives in exercise participation. *Psychology & Health, 23*(7), 807–828. doi: 10.1080/08870440701405704

Jackson, J. J., Hill, P. L., Payne, B. R., Roberts, B. W., & Stine-Morrow, E. A. L. (2012). Can an old dog learn (and want to experience) new tricks? Cognitive training increases openness to experience in older adults. *Psychology and Aging, 27*(2), 286–292. doi: 10.1037/a0025918

Jaconelli, A., Stephan, Y., Canada, B., & Chapman, B. P. (2012). Personality and physical functioning among older adults: The moderating role of education. *The Journals of Gerontology Series B: Psychological Sciences and Social Sciences.* doi: 10.1093/geronb/gbs094

James, B. D., Boyle, P. A., Buchman, A. S., & Bennett, D. A. (2011). Relation of late-life social activity with incident disability among community-dwelling older adults. *The Journals of Gerontology. Series A, Biological Sciences and Medical Sciences, 66A*(4), 467–473. doi: 10.1093/gerona/glq231

Jorm, A. F., Christensen, H., Henderson, S., Korten, A. E., Mackinnon, A. J., & Scott, R. (1993). Neuroticism and self-reported health in an elderly community sample. *Personality and Individual Differences, 15*(5), 515–521. doi: http://dx.doi.org/10.1016/01918-869(93)90334-Y

Kemoun, G., Thibaud, M., Roumagne, N., Carette, P., Albinet, C., Toussaint, L., . . . Dugué, B. (2010). Effects of a physical training programme on cognitive function and walking efficiency in elderly persons with dementia. *Dementia and Geriatric Cognitive Disorders, 29*(2), 109–114.

Keskin, D., Borman, P., Ersöz, M., Kurtaran, A., Bodur, H., & Akyüz, M. (2008). The risk factors related to falling in elderly females. *Geriatric Nursing, 29*(1), 58–63. doi: 10.1016/j.gerinurse.2007.06.001

Kolb, B., & Whishaw, I. Q. (1998). Brain plasticity and behavior. *Annual Review of Psychology, 49*(1), 43–64. doi: doi:10.1146/annurev.psych.49.1.43

Kyle, U. G., Genton, L., Slosman, D. O., & Pichard, C. (2001). Fat-free and fat mass percentiles in 5225 healthy subjects aged 15 to 98 years. *Nutrition, 17*(7–8), 534–541. doi: 10.1016/s0899-9007(01)00555-x

Lampinen, P., Heikkinen, R., & Ruoppila, I. (2000). Changes in intensity of physical exercise as predictors of depressive symptoms among older adults: An eight-year follow-up. *Preventive Medicine, 30*(5), 371–380.

Latham, N. K., Bennett, D. A., Stretton, C. M., & Anderson, C. S. (2004). Systematic review of progressive resistance strength training in older adults. *Journal of Gerontology: Medical Sciences, 59*(1), 48–61. doi: 10.1093/gerona/59.1.M48

Lee, D. A., Day, L., Finch, C. F., Hill, K., Clemson, L., McDermott, F., & Haines, T. P. (2015). Investigation of older adults' participation in exercises following completion of a state-wide survey targeting evidence-based falls prevention strategies. *Journal of Aging and Physical Activity, 23,* 256–263.

Li, F., Duncan, T. E., Duncan, S. C., McAuley, E., Chaumeton, N. R., & Harmer, P. (2001). Enhancing the psychological well-being of elderly individuals through Tai Chi exercise: A latent growth curve analysis. *Structural Equation Modeling, 8*(1), 53–83. doi: 10.1207/s15328007sem0801_4

Louis, E. D., & Bennett, D. A. (2007). Mild Parkinsonian signs: An overview of an emerging concept. *Movement Disorders, 22*(12), 1681–1688. doi: 10.1002/mds.21433

Marx, M. S., Cohen-Mansfield, J., & Guralnik, J. M. (2003). Recruiting community-dwelling elderly at risk for physical disability into exercise research. *Journal of Aging and Physical Activity, 11*(2), 229–241.

Matthews, G., Deary, I. J., & Whiteman, M. C. (2003). *Personality traits.* Cambridge: Cambridge University Press.

McCrae, R. R., & Costa, P. T. Jr., (2008). The five-factor theory of personality. In O. P. John, R. W. Robins, & L. A. Pervin (Eds.), *Handbook of personality theory and research* (pp. 159–181). New York, NY: Guilford Press.

McDermott, A. Y., & Mernitz, H. (2006). Exercise and older patients: Prescribing guidelines. *American Family Physician, 74*(3), 437–444. Retrieved from http://search.proquest.com/docview/68756391?accountid=4840

Meeusen, R., & De Meirleir, K. (1995). Exercise and brain neurotransmission. *Sports Medicine 20*(3), 160–188. doi: 10.2165/00007256-199520030-00004

Molanorouzi, K., Khoo, S., & Morris, T. (2015). Motives for adult participation in physical activity: Type of activity, age, and gender. *BMC Public Health, 15*(1), 66. doi: 10.1186/s128890-151-4297-.

Morrison, J. H., & Hof, P. R. (1997). Life and death of neurons in the aging brain. *Science, 278*(5337), 412–419. doi: 10.1126/science.278.5337.412

Netz, Y., Wu, M. J., Becker, B. J., & Tenenbaum, G. (2005). Physical activity and psychological well-being in advanced age: A meta-analysis of intervention studies. *Psychology and Aging, 20*(2), 272–284. doi: 10.1037/0882-7974.20.2.272

Nied, R., & Franklin, B. (2002). Promoting and prescribing exercise for the elderly. *American Family Physician, 65*(3), 419–426. Retrieved from www.aafp.org/afp

Paffenbarger, R. S., Hyde, R., Wing, A. L., & Hsieh, C. C. (1986). Physical activity, all-cause mortality, and longevity of college alumni. *New England Journal of Medicine, 314*(10), 605–613. doi:10.1056/NEJM198603063141003

Pargman, D. (2012). *Boomercise: Exercising as you age.* Morgantown, WV: Fitness Information Technology.

Pascual-Leone, A., Amedi, A., Fregni, F., & Merabet, L. B. (2005). The plastic human brain cortex. *Annual Review of Neuroscience, 28*(1), 377–401. doi: 10.1146/annurev.neuro.27.070203.144216

Petz, B. (2013). *Ecology today.* Retrieved May 27, 2013, from www.ecology.com/2013/04/01/us-life-expectancy-mortality-rates/

Rasinaho, M, Hirvensalo, M., Leinonen, R. Lintunen, T., & Rantanen, T. (2006). Motives for and barriers to physical activity among older adults with mobility limitations. *Journal of Aging and Physical Activity, 15*, 80–102. Retrieved from www.humankinetics.com/home

Ratey, J. J., & Hagerman, E. (2008*). Spark: The revolutionary new science of exercise and the brain.* New York, NY: Little, Brown and Company.

Reed, J. A., & Phillips, D. A. (2005). Relationships between physical activity and the proximity or exercise facilities and home exercise equipment used by undergraduate university students. *Journal of American College Health, 53*(6), 285–290.

Resnick, B., Orwig, D., Magaziner, J., & Wynne, C. (2002). The effect of social support on exercise behavior in older adults. *Clinical Nursing Research, 11*(1), 52–70. doi: 10.1177/105477380201100105

Reuter-Lorenz, P. A., & Park, D. C. (2010). Human neuroscience and the aging mind: A new look at old problems. *The Journals of Gerontology Series B: Psychological Sciences and Social Sciences, 65B*(4), 405–415. doi: 10.1093/geronb/gbq035

Rhodes, R., & Courneya, K. (2001). Personality and exercise preferences. *Journal of Sport & Exercise Psychology, 23*, S45–S45.

Rhodes, R. E., & Smith, N. E. I. (2006). Personality correlates of physical activity: A review and meta-analysis. *British Journal of Sports Medicine, 40*(12), 958–965. doi:10.1136/bjsm.2006.028860

Roberts, B. W. (2009). Back to the future: Personality and assessment and personality development. *Journal of Research in Personality, 43*, 137–145. doi:10.1016/j.jrp.2008.12.015

Sage, G. (1977). *Introduction to motor behavior: A neuropsychological approach* (2nd ed.). Reading, MA: Addison-Wesley.

Sahin, E., & DePinho, R. A. (2010). Linking functional decline of telomeres, mitochondria and stem cells during ageing. *Nature 464*(7288), 520–528. doi:10.1038/nature08982

Salmon, P. (2001). Effects of physical exercise on anxiety, depression, and sensitivity to stress. *Clinical Psychology Review, 21*(1), 33–61. doi: 10.1016/s0272-7358(99)00032-x

Sargon, M. F., Doral, N. M., & Atay, Ö. A. (2004). Age-related changes in human PCLs: A light and electron microscopic study. *Knee Surgery, Sports Traumatology, Arthroscopy, 12*(4), 280–284. doi: 10.1007/s00167-003-0427-y

Sayer, A. A., Syddall, H., Martin, H., Patel, H., Baylis, D., & Cooper, C. (2008). The developmental origins of sarcopenia. *The Journal of Nutrition Health and Aging, 12*(7), 427–432. doi: 10.1007/bf02982703

Schaie, K. W., Willis, S. L., & Cask, G. I. L. (2004). The Seattle longitudinal study: Relationship between personality and cognition. *Aging, Neuropsychology, and Cognition, 11*(2–3), 304–324. doi: 10.1080/13825580490511134

Schuett, W., Dall, S. R. X., Wilson, A. J., & Royle, N. J. (2013). Environmental transmission of a personality trait: Foster parent exploration behaviour predicts offspring exploration behaviour in zebra finches. *Biology Letters, 9*(4), 20130120. doi: 10.1098/rsbl.2013.0120

Schuler, P. B., Roy, J. P., Vinci, D., Philipp, S. F., & Cohen, S. J. (2006). Barriers and motivations to exercise in older African American and European American women. *Californian Journal of Health Promotion, 6*(4), 3. 128–134

Schutzer, K., & Graves, B. S. (2004). Barriers and motivations to exercise in older adults. *Preventive Medicine, 39*(5), 1056–1061. doi: 10.1016/j.ypmed.2004.04.003

Semba, R. D., Nicklett, E. J., & Ferrucci, L. (2010). Does accumulation of advanced glycation end products contribute to the aging phenotype? *The Journals of Gerontology. Series A, Biological Sciences and Medical Sciences, 65A*(9), 963–975. doi: 10.1093/gerona/glq074

Spirduso, W. W. (1975). Reaction and movement time as a function of age and activity level. *Journal of Gerontology, 30*, 435–440.

Spirduso, W. W., & Clifford, P. (1977). Replication of age and physical activity effects on reaction and movement time. *Journal of Gerontology, 33*, 26–30.

Spirduso, W. W., Francis, K. L., & MacRae, P. G. (2005). *Physical dimensions of aging* (2nd ed.). Champaign, IL: Human Kinetics.

Spiro, M. (1994). *Culture and human nature.* New Brunswick, NJ: Transaction Publishers.

Terracciano, A., Löckenhoff, C. E., Zonderman, A. B., Ferrucci, L., & Costa, P. T. (2008). Personality predictors of longevity: Activity, emotional stability, and conscientiousness. *Psychosomatic Medicine, 70*(6), 621–627. doi:10.1097/PSY.0b013e31817b9371

Terracciano, A., Schrack, J. A., Sutin, A. R., Chan, W., Simonsick, E. M., & Ferrucci, L. (2013). Personality, metabolic rate and aerobic capacity. *PloS one, 8*(1), e54746. doi: 10.1371/journal.pone.0054746

Tett, R. P., & Murphy, P. J. (2002). Personality and situations in co-worker preference: Similarity and complementarity in worker compatibility. *Journal of Business and Psychology, 17*(2), 223–243.

Titze, S., Stroneggerb, W., & Owen, N. (2005). Prospective study of individual, social, and environmental predictors of physical activity: Women's leisure running. *Psychology of Sport and Exercise, 6*(3), 363–376. doi: 10.1016/j.psychsport.2004.06.001

Tolea, M. I., Costa Jr., P. T., Terracciano, A., Ferrucci, L., Faulkner, K., Coday, M. C., . . . Simonsick, E. M. (2012a). Associations of openness and conscientiousness with walking speed decline: Findings from the health, aging, and body composition study. *The Journals of Gerontology. Series B, Psychological Sciences and Social Sciences, 67*(6), 705–711. doi: 10.1093/geronb/gbs030

Tolea, M. I., Terracciano, A., Simonsick, E. M., Metter, E. J., Costa Jr., P. T., & Ferruccic, L. (2012b). Associations between personality traits, physical activity level, and muscle strength. *Journal of Research in Personality, 46*(3), 264–270. doi: 10.1016/j.jrp.2012.02.002

Trujillo, K. M., Brougham, R. R., & Walsh, D. A. (2004). Age differences in reasons for exercising. *Current Psychological Research & Reviews, 22*(4), 348–367. doi: 10.1007/s12144-004-1040-z

U.S. Census Bureau. (2012). *Profile America facts for features.* Retrieved from www.census.gov/newsroom/releases/archives/facts_for_features_special_editions/cb12-ff07.html

van Praag, H., Shubert, T., Zhao, C., & Gage, F. (2005). Exercise enhances learning and hippocampal neurogenesis in aged mice. *Journal of Neuroscience, 25*(38), 8680–8685. doi:10.1523/jneurosci.1731-05-2005

Weuve, J., Kang, J. H., Manson, J. E., Breteler, M. M. B., Ware, J. H., & Grodstein, F. (2004). Physical activity, including walking, and cognitive function in older women. *The Journal of the American Medical Association, 292*(12), 1454–1461. doi: 10.1001/jama.292.12.1454

Whaley, D., & Ebbeck, V. (1997). Older adults' constraints to participation in structured exercise classes. *Journal of Aging and Physical Activity, 5*(3), 190–212.

Whitbourne, S. B., Neupert, S. D., & Lachman, M. E. (2008). Daily physical activity: Relation to everyday memory in adulthood. *Journal of Applied Gerontology, 27*(3), 331–349. doi: 10.1177/0733464807312175

Wilson, R. S., Krueger, K. R., Gu, L., Bienias, J. L., Mendes de Leon, C. F., & Evans, D. A. (2005). Neuroticism, extraversion, and mortality in a defined population of older persons. *Psychosomatic medicine, 67*(6), 841–845. Retrieved from journals.lww.com/psychosomaticmedicine/pages/default.aspx

World Health Organization. (2014). *Mental health: A state of well-being.* Retrieved from www.who.int/features/factfiles/mental_health/en/

Yap, S., & Lee, C. K. C. (2013). Does personality matter in exercise participation? *Journal of Consumer Behaviour, 12*(5), 401–411. doi:10.1002/cb.1442

22 Communication Style

Kate L. Nolt

The purpose of this chapter is to establish various methods to help communicate and build rapport with a client. Of course, this rapport and relationship building will solidify over time. However, rushing this process to demonstrate an expert level of knowledge can be damaging not only to practice growth and professional reputation, but also, and more importantly, to a client's belief in their ability to be successful in exercise and/or sport. The chapter begins with various communication styles and behaviors, as well as examples to demonstrate their appropriate application. The chapter will also address the importance and relevance of understanding the factors that may influence clients' exercise habits and health behaviors, such as their cultural background. The chapter will end with a discussion of the basics of an interviewing technique as a structural framework for how to conduct a productive, respectful, and person-centered conversation with a client.

COMMUNICATION STYLE AND BEHAVIOR

Communication *style* and communication *behavior* can mean the difference between what is heard by someone and what is absorbed and understood, which can then translate into long-term behavior change. For the practitioner of exercise psychology, utilizing an effective communication style and behavior is as important as having a comprehensive understanding of the skills one is attempting to apply. In other words, the "how" of what is said to clients is as important as "what" is actually said. Presented in this chapter are various communication styles and behaviors, along with suitable examples of how to apply each. Styles will include direct versus indirect, clear versus masked styles, the use of "I" messages, and sending versus receiving messages. The techniques that one uses to facilitate open and productive dialogue are also important. Effective techniques in communication are necessary in order to ensure that a client remains open to continued exploration of motivation and sustains adherence to exercise. *Motivational interviewing* is a communication technique used to explore a client's motivation to change. The constructs of motivational interviewing and their appropriate application will also be presented.

Let us begin the discussion of communication style by considering fashion styles from the 1970s. Bell-bottom pants, platform shoes, and jumpsuits were the *style*. This type of clothing defined the era. Even the language used in the 1970s was different than it is today. Frequently used in conversation in the 1970s were statements like "groovy, man," "keep on truckin'," "dynamite," and "awesome" to communicate that something is exciting and well liked. Much like the fashion and language style that defined the 1970s, communication style used by a practitioner of exercise psychology can help to define that practitioner as a thoughtful communicator, determine how well a client will understand what is communicated by the practitioner, and facilitate a better understanding of the presented issue.

The importance of attention to personal communication style is highlighted when considering a conversation that resulted in a complete misunderstanding. A classic example of this occurs when a parent is communicating with a child. Oftentimes, the child misunderstands the meaning of and intent behind what the parent is saying. One simple explanation for this mishap is that the information sent to the brain of a child is processed and interpreted differently than it was in the brain of the parent who sent the communication in the first place. According to the American Psychological Association (APA, 2015) successful conversations between parents and their kids result from, among other things, parents who soften strong reactions, resist arguing about who is right, and listen to and talk with their children as a way to form a connection between parent and child. A parent whose communication style is directing, interfering, opinionated, and critical runs the risk of fostering a child who grows to be an adult who communicates the same way. Communication style may be one of many reasons why relationships are in jeopardy of failing (APA, 2015). Unless the communication style matches very closely with the person one is in conversation with, it is difficult to know whether what is said and what is intended are received and clearly understood without bias by the other in the conversation (HM Management Space, 2008, p. 101).

Communication style is defined as *a way of thinking and behaving*. This is one's own preferred way of communicating, whether it is patient or passive, cautious or compromising, accommodating or assertive or aggressive. It can include intonation, accent, and/or the use of gestures. Being self-aware of one's own personal communication style can enhance communication with clients. Sometimes adjusting communication style to match that of clients can engender a higher level of trust, reduce communication bias, and create a more productive working relationship (HM Management Space, 2008). According to Whitehurst (1976), this adjustment refers to when a speaker of a message formulates said message to be compatible with "the listener's knowledge and capabilities" (p. 473). Robinson (2009) refers to incompatibility in conversation as *counter informing*. Counter informing occurs when "one speaker responds to another in a way that [publicly] exposes that the two speakers hold an incompatible [position] (e.g. knowledge and belief) on the same subject matter" (p. 581) and one of the speakers is in a position of authority over the other speaker with respect to the subject matter. This situation can be contained by equalizing the perceived power differential between, for our purposes, the client and the exercise psychologist. Conversational strategies may include as affirming statements, which refers to accepting aloud that a difference may exist by saying "okay" or "that's right." A practitioner would want to avoid creating an exchange with a client in which it would appear to be a "one-up" or domineering conversation. In this way, dispute is avoided and reconciling the positional difference can move the conversation forward (Robinson, 2009, p. 582). There are many different ways to communicate with clients. What follows are a few basic communication styles or methods of communicating that can be used, or should be avoided, in an effort to build strong and effective communication skills.

Clear and Direct

The communication style of *clear and direct* is the healthiest form of communication (Joyce, 2012). In this style, the conveyed message is "clearly and directly" stated to the client.

Example: A client expresses she has failed to maintain exercise adherence beyond three weeks for years. She explains how anxious she becomes at sustaining her exercise schedule around the three-week mark. Failure to adhere to exercise is a common occurrence and can happen for many reasons that vary considerably according to individual circumstances (Shizue et al., 2015). Direct and clear communication might include such statements as "Let us take a look at your exercise history as a whole, and see if we can figure out what is happening as a trend around the three week mark. Is that OK?" This statement clearly states the *intention* of the practitioner, as well as the goal for the work to be completed. While this form of communication may cause some anxiety for the client at first, it is still the most direct way of beginning the process of exploring this client's issue further. By asking the client if it is okay to continue, the practitioner is playing more of a supportive role in exploring the issue of adherence, rather than a directing, power role over the client (Rollnick, Miller, & Butler, 2008). This type of technique is called motivational interviewing and will be discussed later in this chapter.

Clear and Indirect

The exercise psychologist who practices using the communication style of *clear and indirect* clearly states what is *intended* to be directed at the client, but leaves the client uncertain as to whether or not the statement is really directed at them.

Using the previous scenario, a response to the client's assertion that she cannot sustain exercise beyond three weeks in this communication style would be "There are many reasons why people cannot adhere to exercise, and it is really disappointing when that happens." The first part of this statement is clear and relevant. Factually, there are many reasons why people cannot adhere to exercise. However, the second part of this statement *implies*, but the client may not be sure, that the practitioner is disappointed in *her* for failing to adhere to her exercise regimen beyond three weeks.

The intent of this statement is to be supportive and validating, as obviously the client is disappointed in herself. However, the exercise psychologist would need to explain the intent to avoid the client interpreting the statement above as an expression of disappointment by the exercise psychologist. According to Sanchez-Burks, Lee, Choi, Nisbett, Zhao, and Koo (2003), indirectness refers to how a speaker conveys a message and affects how a listener interprets the messages of others. Further, Sanchez-Burks et al. indicate that indirectness occurs when there is a "discrepancy between sentence meaning and speaker meaning." The difference here refers to the literal meaning of the sentence spoken and what the speaker of the sentence actually intended to accomplish with the remark (p. 364).

Masked and Direct

In the *masked and direct* style of communicating, the content of the message is unclear (masked), but it is directed toward the client. In our example, the client's issue receives a response of "Susan, people just don't exercise like they used to." This statement is obviously directed to the client, but the message is unclear. Is the exercise psychologist implying that people in general do not exercise with the same devotion and intensity as they did during the fitness craze of the 1980s, or is the exercise psychologist asserting that Susan herself may not be exercising today as perhaps she did at a younger age? The message in this statement is unclear, and therefore its intent is "masked" (Peterson & Green, 2009).

Masked and Indirect

Masked and indirect comments are not directed toward anyone in particular. These comments appear to be off-handed or "off the cuff." Continuing with our example, a statement such as "Most people today tend to be lazy when it comes to exercise" made during a client session can lead the client to believe that she is lazy, even though this may be just an expression of personal observation by the exercise psychologist of "most people." A better method would be to state this clearly and directly (see "Clear and Direct" above), stating the relevance of the observation to the client's situation, or to simply avoid making statements such as these all together.

USING "I" MESSAGES

The importance of using "I" messages is to demonstrate an ability to assertively express feelings. Simply put, "I" messages allow for stating the problem without blaming someone else for it. According to Dr. Robert C. Nielsen at North Dakota State University (personal communication, 2014), there are four components to an "I" message:

1.   State exactly what was said or done that triggered your feelings.
2.   State the feelings that you have.
3.   Provide an explanation for why you feel the way you do.
4.   If appropriate, make a request stating what you need.

   An appropriate use for "I" messages in conversations with clients includes, for example, "I really appreciate it when you call if you are going to be late. This way I do not worry about you." Another example may be when summarizing back to a client what was heard in an effort to clarify what they said. The exercise psychologist may say something like, "I think what I heard you say is that after you have started exercising regularly, you can only be consistent for three weeks. Is that correct?" In the absence of the "I" statement in this example, any statement may sound more accusatory to a client, rather than supportive.

SENDING VERSUS RECEIVING MESSAGES

The person who is speaking in a conversation is the *sender* of a message. The person to whom the message is spoken (the listener) is the *receiver* of a message. Within a conversation of two or more people, these roles will switch back and forth. In a session with a client, during the initial stages of informing and educating, the messages that are sent as the practitioner can either result in positive outcomes, such as meeting the goals of the client, or place the relationship in jeopardy, which may result in a complete breakdown of communication. Therefore, being mindful of one's own personal communication style, tonality, and body language and carefully constructing the message to be sent increase the likelihood of a positive outcome at the end of the session. Minimally, this effort on the part of the practitioner will establish a healthy rapport with clients and foster a sense of comfort for clients to discuss their issue(s) freely (Windover, Boissy, Rice, Gilligan, Velez, & Merlino, 2014, p. 9).

CULTURAL SENSITIVITY AND LISTENING MISCONCEPTIONS

Oftentimes, the assumption is that whoever is listening within a conversation hears and understands the same message that the sender intended. In fact, each person will respond to a message uniquely. Many factors influence what a client may hear and interpret in a session. Social roles, personal interests, needs, and culture will shape how a client interprets an exercise psychologist's counsel. According to Adler and Rodman (1994), there are three erroneous assumptions that create listening misconceptions (p. 117). The first is "thinking that, because you were hearing a message, you were listening to it." Listening is a *proactive* skill requiring a practitioner of exercise psychology to ensure that all distractions are minimized and that the environment being used for a session is conducive to effective reflective listening.

   Reflective listening refers to when a practitioner has been intently listening to what the client is saying and can narratively reflect back or summarize what they heard in an effort to clarify the client's statement (Windover et al., 2014, p 11). There is a difference in communication when conducted within a formal office environment as opposed to at a local café or coffee shop. One location can foster strong reflective listening (less distraction), whereas the other, more public setting can produce many distractions and therefore reduce the quality of reflective listening that occurs.

The second assumption is "believing that listening effectively is natural and effortless." The third assumption is "assuming that other listeners understand a message in the same way as [you]" (Adler & Rodman, 1994, p. 117).

Nowhere are these assumptions more prevalent than in conversations between people from different cultures. Americans live in an *individualistic* culture where, according to Adler and Rodman (1994), group memberships are based on similar interests and activities, placing high value on autonomy, change, youth, and equality (p. 51). Conversely, there are *collectivist* cultures wherein people belong to groups that are more like extended families and where people would take care of their extended family before taking care of themselves. These extended family groups have a great deal of influence over a person. There is a high value placed on duty, tradition, group security, and hierarchy (p. 51).

The relevance of this to communication style is knowing what customs and taboos may be relevant for your clients. For example, in some Asian cultures, it is traditional to address one another by surname, rather than informally by the first name, as within American culture. According to Spector (2000), younger people in Asian cultures will address elders first and "will show great respect by looking away when talking to avoid a [physician's] eyes" (p. 1). Additionally, Spector suggests that in Asian cultures, "sitting with legs crossed, or leaning on a table or desk, or pointing at anything with the foot when talking are considered signs of contempt toward the person one is addressing" (p. 1). These behaviors are characteristic of American culture. Further, it is important to note that some Asian clients, even though they may appear to understand and accept your recommendations, may fail to comply. This may be attributable, according to Spector (2000), to a belief in harmony and saving "face." Within the Asian culture, there is a cultural respect for harmony, and Asian patients who do not understand a recommendation or may even disagree with it may try to avoid any conflict and suppress negative thoughts and emotions. An Asian client who voices non-acceptance would be disrupting harmony. In order to save "face," both for the practitioner and themselves, the client may avoid saying they do not understand or even disagree with the plan. Therefore, practitioners should learn to observe indirect and/or nonverbal communication signs that could indicate disagreement or displeasure. Spector (2000) suggests that rather than asking Asian clients whether they understand the recommendations, it is better to ask them to describe what was heard as the recommended plan (p. 1).

These communication nuances among some people from Asian cultures are only a few examples in which understanding cultural diversity within the practice of exercise psychology is imperative to creating a good rapport with a client. While the practitioner of exercise psychology may not encounter cultural differences in a typical day, this section is meant to emphasize the importance of understanding and clarifying a client's cultural influences, thereby ensuring the likelihood of compliance. Maintaining a high level of cultural competence within the application of skills reflects a willingness to understand the cultural influences that may play a role in why the client is seeking help from an exercise psychology professional. To expound on this a bit more, let us examine the Hispanic population and the possible influences of this culture on the practice of exercise psychology.

According to the US Census, there are more than 50 million people who identify as Hispanic or Latino living in the United States. It is possible, if not likely, that clients from this ethnicity will in fact bring to their sessions some cultural influences that will inform the degree to which outcomes are successful. For example, a 30-something male of Hispanic descent is seeking help to enhance his motivation to engage in exercise more often. He describes himself as being a strong family man, with many children and a stressful job. He is overweight and expresses that he wants to be healthier through exercise, but he emphasizes that his family comes first. Exploring and understanding the role of this client's ties to his heritage and culture while obtaining a historical perspective of exercise habits and beliefs provides the opportunity for the practitioner to build a profile of this potential client that encompasses everything about this person's life. Taking the time to explore a client's cultural background demonstrates that as a practitioner you are interested in your client's values, concerns, perceptions, and motivations (Rollnick et al., 2008, p. 9).

Knowing the following information with respect to the culture presented by this potential client demonstrates cultural competency and sensitivity. The term Hispanic "has traditionally been used to describe Americans who identify themselves as being of Spanish-speaking background and, regardless of race, trace their origin to Spanish-speaking countries including Mexico, Puerto Rico, Cuba, Central and South America, and others" (Herrara, Owens, & Mallinckrodt, 2013, p. 22). Male gender roles are deep rooted in the Hispanic culture and are traditional in nature. *Machismo* is associated with the "stereotypical male characteristics" of domination over women, hyper-masculinity, and other predominantly negative male behaviors. This belief is linked to restricted emotional expression, depression, aggression, and other anti-social behaviors (Herrara et al., 2013).

Another male gender-role belief within this culture is called *caballerismo*. This is a term coined by Arciniega, Anderson, Tovar-Blank, and Tracey in 2008 (as reported in Herrara et al., 2013). *Caballerismo* is essentially the opposite of machismo and dates back to medieval times as a code of honor. This role "embodies positive male images of the nurturing provider who is respectful, defends the weak, and lives by an ethical code of chivalrous values" (Herrara et al., 2013, p. 24). It is also associated with caretaking, chivalry, and deepened family involvement, which may inform the level of family support a client may possess. Close adherence to either of these norms can inform the approach to take when working with a client from this culture. Carefully and respectfully exploring a client's beliefs about gender roles can mean the difference between a more positive outcome, including an increase in ability to express concerns and proactive participation, and negative outcomes, such as non-compliance, conflict, reduced self-esteem, and anxiety.

As part of the initial intake process, inquiring as to one's cultural heritage and how it may influence or inform why the client is seeking your guidance also demonstrates a willingness to apply exercise psychology skills in a humanistic and holistic approach. Using a questionnaire such as the Heritage Assessment Tool (see Form 1.0) can assist in obtaining the necessary information. The information gleaned from this form will provide some insight as to the degree of attachment to their heritage a client might have. It can also be used as a conversation starter on health and exercise beliefs in general. As a practitioner of exercise psychology, understanding that gender roles may differ between your own culture and that of a client's can strengthen rapport and establish that you are a culturally sensitive and culturally competent practitioner.

This tool is used to describe your own ethnic, cultural, and religious background. This form is to assist in identifying your ties to traditional heritage and how those ties may help enhance your experience within this practice. This helps to set the stage for understanding a person's health and illness beliefs and practices, and assists with tapping into community resources that can provide support when needed. This form can be used for any family circumstance (e.g., LGBT, adoption). Please feel free to interview family members, neighbors, and friends who may be able to assist in the completion of this form.

Form 1.0 Heritage Assessment Tool

The greater the number of positive responses, the higher the degree of connection to one's heritage.

1. Where was your mother (or the person you identify with as your mother—the same will apply for the rest of the form) born?_____

2. Where was your father (or the person you identify with as your father—the same will apply for the rest of the form) born?_____

3. Where were your grandparents born?

    a. Your mother's mother?_____

    b. Your mother's father?_____

    c. Your father's mother?_____

    d. Your father's father?_____

4. How many brothers and/or sisters do you have?

    Brothers: _____

    Sisters: _____

5. What setting did you grow up in? Urban _____ Rural _____

6. What country did your parents grow up in?

    1. Father _____

    2. Mother_____

7. How old were you when you came to the United States?_____

8. How old were your parents when they came to the United States?

    1. Mother _____

    2. Father _____

9. When you were growing up, who lived with you?

    _____

10. Have you maintained contact with

    1. Aunts, uncles, cousins?   1. Yes   2. No (circle one)

    2. Brothers and sisters?   1. Yes   2. No (circle one)

    3. Parents?   1. Yes   2. No (circle one)

    4. Your own children?   1. Yes   2. No (circle one)

11. Did most of your aunts, uncles, cousins live near your home?

    1. Yes _____   2. No _____

12. Approximately how often did you visit family members who lived outside of your home?

    1. Daily _____   2. Weekly _____   3. Monthly _____

    4. Once a year or less _____   5. Never _____

13. Was your original family name changed?

    1. Yes _____   2. No _____

Form 1.0 (Continued)

14. What is your religious preference?

    1. Catholic _____   2. Jewish _____

    3. Protestant _____ Denomination _____

    4. Other _____   5. None _____

15. Is your spouse/partner the same religion as you?

    1. Yes _____   2. No _____

16. Is your spouse/partner the same ethnic background as you?

    1. Yes _____   2. No _____

17. What kind of school did you go to?

    1. Public _____   2. Private _____   3. Parochial _____

18. As an adult, do you live in a neighborhood where the neighbors are the same religion and ethnic background as yourself? 1. Yes _____ 2. No _____

19. Do you belong to a religious institution? 1. Yes _____ 2. No _____

20. Would you describe yourself as an active member? 1. Yes _____ 2. No _____

21. How often do you attend your religious institution?

    1. More than once a week _____   2. Weekly _____   3. Monthly _____

    4. Special Holidays only _____   5. Never _____

22. Do you practice your religion in your home? 1. Yes _____ 2. No _____ (if yes, please specify) 3. Praying _____ 4. Bible reading _____

    5. Diet _____

    6. Celebrating religious holidays _____

23. Do you prepare foods special to your ethnic background? 1. Yes _____ 2. No _____

24. Do you participate in ethnic activities? 1. Yes _____ 2. No _____ (if yes, please specify) 3. Singing _____ 4. Holiday celebrations _____

    5. Dancing _____

    6. Festivals _____   7. Costumes _____   8. Other _____

25. Are your friends from the same religious background as you?

    1. Yes ____   2. No _____

26. Are your friends from the same ethnic background as you?

    1. Yes _____   2. No _____

27. What is your native language? _____

28. Do you speak this language? 1. Prefer _____ 2. Occasionally _____

    3. Rarely _____

29. Do you read your native language? 1. Yes _____ 2. No _____

(Adapted with permission from the Heritage Assessment Tool created by Rachel Spector, 2000)

Form 1.0 (Continued)

MOTIVATIONAL INTERVIEWING TECHNIQUE

The motivational interviewing (MI) technique is a multifaceted process of how to ask questions of a client to elicit their motivation for behavior change. What follows is a brief introduction to the MI technique and is by no means a comprehensive discussion of this client-centered approach. There are many easy-to-read books on this technique, and it is recommended that a practitioner of exercise psychology use these resources to develop and practice MI skills.

Drs. Stephen Rollnick and William Miller have used MI successfully since its inception in 1983. Their focus for MI was on patients whose problems with alcohol had ruined their lives and their ambivalence to changing their behavior. "We quickly learned that lecturing, arguing, and warning did not work well with ambivalent people, and over time developed the more gentle approach that would come to be called motivational interviewing" (Rollnick et al., 2008, p. viii). The focus, according to Rollnick et al. (2008), was to "evoke conversation about changing one's behavior, resolving his or her own ambivalence to changing, and to do so using his or her own motivation and energy to do it" (p. viii).

With MI's intent focused on reducing ambivalence or indifference to change, through years of utilization it became apparent that this technique could apply to almost any circumstance where ambivalence reduces the likelihood of positive behavior change. Ambivalence refers to when positive and negative feelings, in this case regarding exercise, exist together. The successful use of MI is predicated on an understanding of its five basic principles: express empathy, develop discrepancy, avoid arguments, roll with resistance, and support self-efficacy (Rollnick et al., 2008). Self-efficacy refers to someone's belief in their own ability to accomplish a task (Bandura, 1977).

For the practitioner of exercise psychology, using MI can mean the difference between being successful in identifying a client's motivation toward exercise and not. Similar to the use of MI with problem drinkers, the time it will take to evoke behavior change in a client has shown to be less when using a technique such as MI than without this technique. To begin the process of understanding MI, one must have an understanding of the nature of MI.

Nature or Spirit of MI

MI is a collaborative effort between practitioner and client. It is a cooperative partnership in exploring a specific situation where behavior change is needed on the part of the client. The process involves joint decision making, and there is no power relationship at play. The practitioner does not direct the client as to what to do, but rather guides the client through discussion that could evoke talk about change. Such talk is called *change talk*. MI evokes motivation in the client toward changing behaviors. As a practitioner, you will guide rather than direct, using acquired knowledge in applied exercise psychology as a tool to activate resourses the client already has to motivate themselves and adhere to exercise goals. These things might be values, aspirations, dreams, goals in life, or anything that they may care about as their own values and concerns. In the end, the client has the autonomy to decide not to change, and honoring that autonomy is also in the nature or spirit of MI. It is important to recognize that not all clients are in a stage of readiness to change and to respect that choice; referring them elsewhere may be what is required.

According to Rollnick et al. (2008), there are three core communication skills that are basic to understanding the nature of how to speak with clients. These skills are *asking*, *informing*, and *listening*. Knowing how to ask questions in a guiding style can lead to a better understanding of a client's problems. Good listening is a learned skill and is essential in order to convey to a client that the problem has been heard and understood correctly. The practitioner would then express a desire to hear more in order to explore the problem further. In a guiding style such as MI, listening may be the core skill (Rollnick et al., 2008, p. 19).

Informing refers to when the practitioner conveys their knowledge of facts, theory, and recommendations in a way that the client can understand. In this way, the client will most likely be more interested in staying engaged in the session and more motivated to participate in recommended changes.

MI Strategies

Miller and Rollnick (2002) established four strategies for the use of MI in the early stages with a client: open-ended questions, affirm, reflective listening, and summarize. The acronym OARS reminds MI users to engage in these strategies to evoke talk that may indicate a readiness to make changes on the part of a client. Asking *open-ended* questions, for instance, means the client will offer up more information about their problem as they see it. The answer to an open-ended question requires more of a response than a simple "yes" or "no" answer would. An open-ended question may start with words such as "how," "describe," or "tell me about" (Windover et al., 2014, p. 10). Here are some examples of brief questions that may serve the practitioner's purpose more efficiently than asking many closed questions. If as a practitioner you are skillfully using reflective listening, more information will be gleaned from questions such as these (Rollnick et al., 2008).

1. *What is worrying you the most about your exercise adherence?* This question should take the practitioner to the heart of the client's concerns, and if the practitioner responds respectfully, can build a good rapport for launching new topics that are on the agenda.
2. *What concerns you the most about your situation?* This type of question can reveal a lot about a client's attitude and behavior as well as where the problem lies.
3. *What exactly happens when you . . . (e.g., stop exercising or lose motivation; complete the question with whatever is the presented issue)?* This is the opening for the client to tell their story. According to Rollnick et al. (2008), the use of the word *exactly* indicates your intention to "get to the bottom" of the client's concern. Again, skillful use of reflective listening may reveal factual information, and other questions may surface.
4. *What did you first notice about this issue when you realized what was going on?* The word *notice*, as suggested by Rollnick et al (2008), can be very useful. They suggest, "[People] usually respond well, because this word invites them to be the expert commentator about their experiences of events and behavior. Information often comes flooding out, and they feel heard" (p. 49).
5. *"Tell me more about . . ."* or *"please describe for me . . ."*

To *affirm* means to show support of what the client is discussing, and this *must* be done with authenticity and sincerity. This effort will validate the client's experience and feelings. Affirming statements such as "you must have been proud of yourself" or "that took a lot of courage to do" can prevent discouragement over past failures and can help to redefine past experiences as successes and demonstrations of strength. Affirmations can also acknowledge the difficulties a client has experienced and overcome.

Reflective listening is an active and ongoing process during a client session. Rollnick et al. (2008) state that it is a way of thinking and "includes an interest in what the person has to say and a desire to truly understand how the person sees things" (p. 70). What the practitioner thinks a person means may in fact *not* be what the person means. Reflective listening means that the practitioner is listening in such a manner that they will be able to repeat in simplest form what was heard, rephrase what was heard, paraphrase the salient points, and reflect the feelings that have been expressed by the client. There is a clear effort on the part of the practitioner to understand the perspective of the client. There is no intent to fix anything, but simply to understand the problem through the client's lens.

Summarizing reinforces what has been said. This is a demonstration that the practitioner has been listening to the client and prepares the client to move on in the discussion. This can be where in the discussion the practitioner can begin to establish any discrepancies that may exist between the client's current behaviors and their exercise goals. A strong summary tells the client that the practitioner has been listening carefully to what has been said and can serve to strengthen the rapport between the practitioner and the client. Essentially, the main themes captured are being drawn together and reflected back to the client to ensure that all the salient points were absorbed by the practitioner. Rollnick et al. (2008) suggest that this is a good time to change direction, draw the period of listening to a close, and move on to the next task at hand (p. 75).

Periodic summaries are done throughout a client session and should emphasize those statements that might lead in guiding the client to changing their behavior. A summary might start with "let me see if I've heard you right . . ." and then continue with a "recap" of the main themes of what has been heard so far. The words should be well chosen, with attention to the details and nuances of the feeling behind what was said as well. The very act of empathy on the practitioner's part will be appreciated by the client, thus increasing the likelihood that they will feel free to resolve any ambivalence to changing their behaviors (Rollnick et al., 2008).

Principles of MI

According to Rollnick et al. (2008) the collaborative and client-centered nature of MI is supported by the use of five principles. The first principle is to *express empathy*. This refers to the extent to which the practitioner puts forth the effort to understand and grasp the client's perspective and experiences. By expressing empathy, the practitioner is demonstrating a non-judgmental understanding of the client's perspective. As the guided discussion continues, there should be opportunity to *develop discrepancy* between what the client has established as their exercise goals and the current behaviors that are preventing them from achieving those goals.

Let us take for example the scenario of Susan from the beginning of this chapter. Susan has expressed that she struggles to adhere to her exercise goals after three weeks of being consistent. She expresses that she has done this on and off for years, and wishes to resolve why this happens. While in conversation with Susan, the practitioner hears that her goal is to exercise every day for one hour. The practitioner also hears that Susan volunteers a lot, has children, and works a full-time job. While using reflective listening skills, the practitioner will summarize what was heard and then might suggest to Susan that perhaps her exercise goal is at odds with her busy life, thereby developing discrepancy between her exercise goal and the attainability of that goal. The next step would be to explore setting goals that are easier to attain and adhere to given Susan's busy lifestyle. At this point, the practitioner and Susan have developed a discrepancy within her life, broadly, that may be contributing to her inability to adhere to her exercise goals for more than a three-week period.

Avoiding argument refers to when the client makes the argument for behavior change, not the practitioner. MI is intended to *guide* a client to suggesting that change is possible, thereby eliciting talk of change through their own intrinsic motivation. The practitioner must avoid falling into the trap of being the one whose argument for change evokes resistance in the client (Rollnick et al., 2008, p. 8). One helpful tool for avoiding argument is a decisional balance sheet, sometimes referred to as benefits and costs sheet, for changing the desired behavior(s). This tool assists in avoiding argument against change from the client and reduces the urge on the practitioner's part to insist or persuade a client that if they just follow the practitioner's advice, change is inevitable. Through establishing the benefits and costs of current behavior using this tool, a more meaningful and value-added conversation can be had regarding the likelihood of change, the foundation of which is rooted in associating the costs of continuing with the current behavior and the benefits of making change.

Should resistance to change surface, the fourth principle, *rolling with resistance*, is applicable. Rolling with resistance refers to responding to client's resistance with flexibility and being creative in that response. Some classic signs of resistance include (but are not limited to) interrupting, arguing, denying, blaming, and disagreeing. To creatively sidestep resistance, a practitioner might use a simple reflection to acknowledge a client's disagreement. Clarification of a client's perception, and ensuring it matches that of the practitioner, also demonstrates flexibility in responding to resistance. This clarification verifies that that practitioner's understanding of the resistance matches the client's perception. Lastly, shifting the client's focus away from the source of contention can sidestep the obstacle to change and can always be revisited as part of another session's agenda (Rollnick et al., 2008, p. 79).

Earlier in the chapter, self-efficacy was defined as one's belief in their own ability to successfully accomplish something (Bandura, 1977). According to Hayden (2009), "Efficacious people set challenging goals and maintain a strong commitment to them. In the face of impending failure, they increase, and sustain their efforts to be successful. They [efficacious people] approach difficult or threatening situations with confidence that they have control [over those situations]" (p. 7). *Supporting self-efficacy* of a client is realized when affirmation statements are used to empower the client to take an active interest in their own healthy behaviors. By helping clients to explore how they can actually make a difference in their own lives and health a practitioner is supporting the client's self-efficacy.

There are many books, videos, articles, and websites available that can support a practitioner's desire to learn the nuances of the practice of MI, and some are listed at the end of this chapter. These resources are easy to follow, providing case studies that afford many opportunities for a learner to practice the skills discussed above. There are several other skills that are not discussed within this chapter, and a practitioner should engage in a more in-depth reading of MI before attempting to practice these skills with a client.

People who study and practice exercise psychology usually do so because they wish to provide people with solutions to solve their problems with exercise. While offering a solution can be valuable, the way in which that solution is communicated can mean the difference between solving the problem and frustrating a situation further. Becoming a competent communicator takes time and practice, vigilance, and patience. Effective communicators are able to choose their actions and style from a wide range of behaviors. Sometimes saying nothing is appropriate, telling jokes may be fitting, or being clear and direct is suitable. Knowing exactly when and how to apply these communication behaviors can be the key to a successful and long-lasting rapport with a client. Remember, being self-aware of one's own personal communication style can enhance communication with clients. Sometimes adjusting communication style to more closely match that of a client's can engender a higher level of trust, reduce communication bias, and create a more productive working relationship with a client (HM Management Space, 2008).

The use of the motivational interviewing (MI) technique is one way in which a strong rapport can be built with a client. Using MI demonstrates support of a client's belief in their ability to make positive changes with respect to exercise adherence and motivation. Engaging in this type of interviewing is further demonstrating a client-centered approach to exercise psychology, one that engages in a guiding style of communication, rather than directing change or using persuasion to elicit change. Tapping into the core values of a client and attaching meaning to those values as they relate to current behaviors and exercise goals are more likely to reap the outcomes sought by a client, and in turn, ensure a long and healthy relationship between a practitioner and a client.

CONCLUSION

Effective communicators are able to choose their actions from a wide range of behaviors, sometimes integrating more than one approach. Knowing how to pick the one that stands the best chance of success is a skill in and of itself and takes time and practice to master. Simply possessing the knowledge does not guarantee effectiveness. It is important to be able to discern which of these behaviors will work best in a particular situation. Adler and Rodman (1994) state, "choosing the best way to send a message is rather like choosing a gift: What is appropriate for one person won't suit another one at all. This ability to choose the best approach is essential, since a response that works well in one setting would flop miserably in another one" (p. 21). People who seem to care about the relationship they have with other people, who are naturally warm and curious about how to help others, demonstrate a commitment to relationships that people without these characteristics cannot. Proactively practicing communication style and skills, self-monitoring, and being aware of one's own communication style increases competence and enables the practitioner to communicate more effectively.

REFERENCES

Adler, R. B., & Rodman, G. (1994). *Understanding human communication* (5th ed.). Fort Worth, TX: Harcourt Brace College Publishers.

American Psychological Association. (2015) *Parenting: Communication tips for parents.* Downloaded March 30, 2015 from www.apa.org/helpcenter/communication-parents.aspx

Bandura, A. (1977). Self-efficacy: Toward a unifying theory of behavioral change. *Psychological Review*, *84*(2), 191–215.

Hayden, J. (2009). Self-efficacy theory. In A. Flagg (Ed.), *Introduction to health behavior theory* (p. 7). Sudbury, MA: Jones and Bartlett Publishers.

Herrara, C. J., Owens, G. P., & Mallinckrodt, B. (2013, January). Traditional machismo and caballerismo as correlates of posttraumatic stress disorder, psychological distress, and relationship satisfaction in Hispanic veterans. *Journal of Multicultural Counseling and Development, 4*, 21–24.

HM Management Space. (2008). Downloaded from resource.mccneb.edu/HMR/files/hmrl/metronhmrl.text (pp. 100–127)

Joyce, C. (2012). The impact of direct and indirect communication. *Independent Voice.* November Issue of the newsletter of the International Ombudsman Association, North Dakota State University (personal communication, 2014)

Miller, W. R., & Rollnick, S. (2002). Preparing people for change. *Motivational Interviewing.* New York, NY: Guilford Press.

Peterson, R., & Green, S. (2009) *Families first—keys to successful family functioning: Communication.* Department of Human Development, Virginia Tech. Retrieved from www.ext.vt.edu/pubs/family/350092/350092.html

Robinson, J. D. (2009). Managing counterinformings. *Human Communication Research, 35*, 561–587.

Rollnick, S., Miller, W., & Butler, C. (2008), *Motivational interviewing in health care: Helping patients change behavior.* New York, NY: The Guilford Press.

Sanchez-Burks, J., Lee, F., Choi, I., Nisbett, R., Zhao, S., & Koo, J. (2003). Conversing across cultures: East-west communication styles in work and nonwork contexts. *Journal of Personality and Social Psychology, 85*(2), 363–372.

Shizue, M., Masayuki, M., Yasuharu, T., Akihiro, S., Shigenari, H., Mayuko, M., Miyagawa, K., Sumiyoshi, E., Tetsuro, M., Keiichi, H., & Hiroshi, N. (2015). Shinshu University genetic research consortium. *Journal of Applied Physiology, 118*, 595–603. First published December 24, 2014; doi:10.1152/japplphysiol.00819.2014

Spector, R. (2000). *Cultural diversity in health and illness* (3rd ed.). Upper Saddle River, NJ: Pearson Prentice Hall. Chapter 1—Building Cultural and Linguistic Competence.

Whitehurst, G. J. (1976). The development of communication: Changes with age and modeling. *Child Development, 47*, 473–482.

Windover, A., Boissy, A., Rice, T., Gilligan, T., Velez, V., & Merlino, J. (2014). The REDE model of healthcare communication: Optimizing relationship as a therapeutic agent. *Journal of Patient Experience*, 1(1), 8–12.

RECOMMENDED MI RESOURCES

Books

Rollnick, S., Miller, W. R., & Butler, C. C. (2008). *Motivational Interviewing in Health Care: Helping Patients Change Behavior*. New York, NY: Guilford Press

Rosengren, D. B. (2009). *Building Motivational Interviewing Skills: A Practitioner Workbook*. New York, NY: Guilford Press.

Miller, W. R., & Rollnick, S. (2012). *Motivational interviewing. Helping people change* (3rd ed.). New York, NY: Guilford Press.

Websites

www.motivationalinterviewing.org/

23 Exercise in Obesity From the Perspective of Hedonic Theory

A Call for Sweeping Change in Professional Practice Norms

Panteleimon Ekkekakis, Zachary Zenko, and Kira M. Werstein

Two thirds of American adults, as well as the majority of adults in most other western countries, are considered overweight, and up to one third are obese (Finucane et al., 2011; Flegal, Carroll, Kit, & Ogden, 2012; Ng et al., 2014; von Ruesten et al., 2011). The average client that exercise practitioners are likely to face in the United States today has a body mass index of 28.7 kg/m^2, just short of the threshold for being designated "obese." In some clinical settings, such as cardiac rehabilitation (Bader, Maguire, Spahn, O'Malley, & Balady, 2001) or osteoarthritis clinics (Frieden, Jaffe, Stephens, Thacker, & Zaza, 2011), half of the patients are classified as obese and almost all are overweight.

Regular physical activity is an essential component of lifestyle interventions recommended for weight management (Jensen et al., 2014), having been shown to significantly improve long-term weight loss beyond what can be achieved by diet-only programs (Johns, Hartmann-Boyce, Jebb, & Aveyard, 2014). The problem is that very few adults with obesity participate in physical activity at the recommended levels (Ekkekakis, Vazou, Bixby, & Georgiadis, 2016).

At the same time, if one peruses the reference lists of exercise psychology textbooks, it becomes apparent that the evidence base of this field consists mainly of studies conducted with young, healthy, and active undergraduate students of exercise science programs. If one specifically searches for research investigating the psychological concerns, challenges, or barriers faced by obese adults as they contemplate or engage in exercise, the search will turn up very few usable leads. Moreover, while examining guideline documents issued by exercise science organizations about the prevention and treatment of obesity (e.g., Donnelly et al., 2009; Fogelholm, Stallknecht, & Van Baak, 2006; Jensen et al., 2014), one discovers that these documents are exclusively prescriptive; while they specify how much exercise obese individuals should be doing, they include no guidance for professionals on how to support their clients in carrying out the prescribed amount of exercise and no advice for the obese individuals themselves on how to cope with barriers.

In the absence of a foundation of empirical research and evidence-based clinical guidance, the field of exercise practice dealing with obesity has largely depended on non-scientific sources of information, such as dogma, tradition, expert opinion, and intuition. As a result, many entrenched elements of professional practice in this field can be shown to be problematic or downright fallacious, consequently driving obese individuals away from exercise rather than drawing them in. For example, think of any infomercial for an exercise machine or contraption, anything from a belt with electrodes that stimulate the abdominal muscles to a stair climber. Most likely, the sales presentation that came to your mind included "before and after" pictures or stories of people transformed from fleshy to trim. Visualize an advertisement for any health or fitness club and the image would probably be very similar. Now, try to remember your last five fitness instructors, exercise leaders, or personal trainers. Would it be safe to guess that each one had minimal body fat, was tan, and was usually dressed in shape-revealing attire? Think of the interior of any aerobics, stepping, spinning, or weightlifting room you have ever seen in your life. The room had wall-to-wall mirrors, correct? Now, think of an episode of any television show in which participants miraculously metamorphose from obese to slim and svelte over the course of a few weeks. It is probably a safe bet that any memory from such shows includes images of participants nearly collapsing of exhaustion, suffering injuries, or grimacing in apparent pain and discomfort. It is also safe to assume that, in each case, the "trainers" (a fuzzy category that includes former marine drill sergeants, former professional sports stars, and personal trainers to Hollywood celebrities) acted "tough" and attributed all failures by participants to carry out the exercise they were instructed to do to lack of willpower or self-discipline. Regular viewers of such shows have probably watched these trainers offer numerous monologues about the need of obese individuals to "take control of their lives."

All the images described in the previous paragraph have become ingrained components of exercise practice and, as such, they are rarely questioned and tend to be perpetually emulated. We have all heard the reasoning behind each of these. "Before and after" pictures, the argument goes, boost motivation because people aspire to look like the "after" picture. Exercise leaders are supposed to look exceptionally fit because clients look up to them for inspiration. As role models, they should seem as if they do not just talk the talk but also walk the walk. Thus, most fitness clubs prefer to hire individuals who look exceptionally fit rather than "average," often overlooking professional credentials, experience, or skill, allegedly because they want to project "the right image." Mirrors are reportedly necessary in exercise facilities because they allow people to check and correct their form. The same "folk wisdom" also evidently dictates that exercise for the treatment of obesity should be intense and prolonged, so that it can dramatically elevate caloric expenditure and yield visible "results" quickly. Likewise, many exercise professionals apparently assume that obesity is the result of character flaws, such as an inherent propensity for indolence or overindulgence. Consequently, many "fit" personal trainers feel justified in lecturing their "fat" clients, imparting lessons on life and living.

Because, at least on the surface, these points seem to have a semblance of logic, many students and graduates of exercise science programs are apt to accept them as time-honored components of the professional knowledge base that is passed down from one generation of practitioners to the next. However, as we explain in this chapter, each of these points has been shown through research to have negative consequences on the exercise motivation and adherence of participants. "Before and after" pictures, by focusing on statistical outliers, create unrealistic outcome expectations (e.g., Foster, Wadden, Vogt, & Brewer, 1997). In turn, expectancy violations raise the risk of dropout (Sears & Stanton, 2001). Exercise leaders who appear exceptionally fit are unlikely to serve as effective models for individuals who are obese, because they are generally not perceived as empathetic and/or relatable (Dunlop & Schmader, 2014; Martin Ginis, Prapavessis, & Haase, 2008). Although wall-to-wall mirrors in exercise facilities may serve the practical function of allowing exercisers to check their form, this one positive effect is overshadowed by the significant adverse effects on people who have concerns about their physical appearance (Focht & Hausenblas, 2006; Martin Ginis, Burke, & Gauvin, 2007). Mirrors act as reminders that physiques are on public display and exposed to potentially negative evaluations. Thus, people exercising in front of mirrors report that they experience more self-presentational concerns and more anxiety about being negatively evaluated by critical observers (Focht & Hausenblas, 2003). Exercise programs designed to yield rapid and visible changes in physical appearance by maximizing caloric expenditure within a short period may occasionally produce the desired result, but this always comes at the cost of substantial displeasure and discomfort (da Silva et al., 2011; Ekkekakis, Lind, & Vazou, 2010). In the long run, these experiences diminish intrinsic motivation for exercise, increase the chances of exercise avoidance, and raise the risk of relapse into a sedentary lifestyle and weight regain (Jackson, Gao, & Chen, 2014; Miller & Miller, 2010). Finally, explicit or implicit signs of anti-obesity bias on the part of exercise professionals, including unsubstantiated assumptions about the causes of obesity, are likely to induce personally salient negative emotions, such as embarrassment or guilt (Dimmock, Hallett, & Grove, 2009; Hare, Price, Flynn, & King, 2000). These are more likely to result in resentment of the overall exercise experience than to serve as a stimulus for positive behavior change.

Against this backdrop, the purposes of this chapter are the following. First, we document the often underappreciated magnitude of the problem of exercise non-participation and avoidance among individuals who are obese. Second, we present the basic postulates of hedonic theory as the general conceptual framework from which we approach the empirical evidence and derive practice recommendations. Third, we review research demonstrating how specific components of the exercise stimulus and the social environment in which it is embedded may generate negative affective and emotional experiences for obese participants. We conclude with specific recommendations for exercise and health practitioners.

THE CARDINAL FALLACY: MARKETING EXERCISE SOLELY AS AN ANTI-OBESITY TREATMENT

Exercise scientists and practitioners have allowed marketers to dictate how exercise is promoted to the public. Marketers, who have little interest in the research evidence and whose sole purpose is to sell exercise machines or club memberships, have decided that the message with the highest potential impact is the equation of exercise with weight loss. Indeed, in the minds of most people, the notions of "exercise" and "weight loss" have become tautological (Guess, 2012). For example, anecdotally, it is common to hear some members of the public say that they do not need to exercise because they "have always been thin" and others refer to exercise as the punishment they must endure for being "bad" over the holidays (i.e., eating more than usual). Even among physicians and other health professionals, it is often assumed that the benefits of exercise are either limited to or fully mediated by weight loss.

The equation of the concepts of "exercise" and "weight loss" has far-reaching implications for exercise promotion. For one thing, the narrow emphasis on weight loss does not allow many individuals to recognize the numerous other health benefits of exercise that are independent of weight loss. More importantly, research shows that exercise alone (i.e., without monitoring or restricting caloric intake) does not have the advertised effects on body weight, a fact that can have devastating consequences for exercise motivation (Södlerlund, Fischer, & Johansson, 2009).

On August 17, 2009, *Time* magazine shocked exercise proponents worldwide with a cover story titled "The Myth About Exercise" and subtitled "Of Course It's Good for You but It Won't Make You Lose Weight." In the opening paragraph of the article itself, author John Cloud described his weekly exercise routine:

> On Wednesday a personal trainer will work me like a farm animal for an hour, sometimes to the point that I am dizzy—an abuse for which I pay as much as I spend on groceries in a week. Thursday is 'body wedge' class, which involves another exercise contraption, this one a large foam wedge from which I will push myself up in various hateful ways for an hour. Friday will bring a 5.5-mile run, the extra half-mile my grueling expiation of any gastronomical indulgences during the week.

The retort by the then-President of the American College of Sports Medicine (ACSM), James Pivarnik, published in the August 31, 2009, issue of the magazine, reminded readers of one

incontrovertible point: "The key concept is a simple equation of energy balance: calories expended throughout the day must exceed calories consumed as food."

So, who is right? The answer is not simple. Although this may come as a surprise to many ardent proponents of exercise, interventions focusing exclusively on exercise (i.e., those that do not include a parallel component focusing on dietary restriction) result in minimal weight loss. One review found that the average weight loss was 2.4 kg at 6 months and 1.0 kg at 24 months (Franz et al., 2007). A meta-analysis found that the average weight loss was 1.6 kg at 6 months and 1.7 kg at 12 months (Thorogood et al., 2011). These figures are unlikely to be perceived as representing a worthwhile investment of time and effort by most people. Likewise, these reductions in body weight are of limited clinical meaningfulness, as their magnitude is such that they are unlikely to have an appreciable beneficial effect on overall health.

These results illustrate that, while weight management ultimately depends on a "simple equation of energy balance," marketing exercise as a weight loss intervention is somewhat misleading, as this "simple equation" is only part of the story. The reasons why regular exercise does not result in much larger reductions in weight are still not fully understood (Boutcher & Dunn, 2009; Donnelly et al., 2014; Thomas et al., 2012).

One commonly proposed explanation (and the only one highlighted in the *Time* magazine article) is that people who exercise subsequently compensate by eating more. However, most studies have not uncovered evidence that the prevalence and extent of such compensation can adequately explain the lower-than-predicted weight loss (King et al., 2012a). Nevertheless, some types of compensation do occur (King et al., 2007; King, Hopkins, Caudwell, Stubbs, & Blundell, 2008; Melanson, Keadle, Donnelly, Braun, & King, 2013).

Interestingly, the discrepancy between the weight loss that is predicted on the basis of the amount of exercise performed and the weight loss actually achieved increases as the amount of exercise increases (Church et al., 2009). One possible explanation for this phenomenon is that the compensation does not consist of an increase in energy intake but a decrease in energy expenditure the rest of the day, an effect that would presumably be more pronounced with larger doses of exercise, such as those that leave one exhausted (Manthou, Gill, Wright, & Malkova, 2010). A second possibility is that a larger amount of exercise is perceived as "license to eat." When people are led to believe that they spent more calories during an exercise session (McCaig, Hawkins, & Rogers, 2016) or the exercise is described as "fat-burning" as opposed to endurance-promoting (Fenzl, Bartsch, & Koenigstorfer, 2014), they tend to consume more calories post-exercise. A third, exceptionally intriguing possibility is that the post-exercise compensation is hedonic at its core. Preliminary evidence shows that those who experience an exercise session as less pleasant or less enjoyable are likely to consume more calories, especially "hedonic" calories (e.g., dessert) after exercise (Schneider, Spring, & Pagoto, 2009; Unick, Michael, & Jakicic, 2012). Even framing a walk as an "exercise walk" as opposed to a "scenic walk" seems to have the same effect (Werle, Wansink, & Payne, 2015). Collectively, these results suggest that any push to accelerate or amplify the weight-loss effect by increasing the amount of exercise performed may trigger compensatory behaviors that can adversely affect both the intake and the expenditure sides of the equation, and ultimately negate the potential benefit of any additional investment of time and/or effort in exercise.

Besides compensatory behaviors, another possible explanation is that exercise adherence among obese individuals tends to be low, and, as a result, research participants complete considerably smaller amounts of exercise than what was prescribed or specified in experimental protocols (Colley et al., 2008). This possibility is supported by the findings of several clinical trials (e.g., Borg, Kukkonen-Harjula, Fogelholm, & Pasanen, 2002) and systematic reviews (Catenacci & Wyatt, 2007; Fogelholm & Kukkonen-Harjula, 2000; Thorogood et al., 2011; Wing, 1999).

Regardless of the exact mechanisms, it is well established that, for most people, exercise does not produce the weight loss that one would expect based on energy expenditure. Thus, a growing number of experts are calling for a radical change in how exercise is promoted to the public, shifting the focus from weight loss to other, weight-independent but nonetheless crucial benefits for cardiometabolic health (Blair & LaMonte, 2006; King, Hopkins, Caudwell, Stubbs, & Blundell, 2009; Ross & Bradshaw, 2009; Ross & Janiszewski, 2008; Vartanian, Wharton, & Green, 2012). Epidemiologic evidence demonstrates that the risk of all-cause mortality associated with body mass is only elevated for those with obesity class II/III (i.e., body mass index of at least 35 kg/m²). Obesity class I (i.e., body mass index from 30 to < 35 kg/m²) is not associated with elevated risk, while the range considered "overweight" (i.e., body mass index from 25 to < 30 kg/m²) is associated with lower risk compared to "normal weight" (Flegal, Kit, Orpana, & Graubard, 2013), a finding considered "paradoxical" but nonetheless reliable. Moreover, the risk associated with obesity (all classes) may be superseded by the risk associated with inactivity and low cardiorespiratory fitness (Blair, 2009; Lee, Sui, & Blair, 2009; McAuley & Blair, 2011).

Taking the calls for a reorientation of the messaging strategy further, a growing number of researchers insist that the focus of promotion efforts should be neither on weight loss nor on health but rather on the immediate benefits of exercise for enjoyment and well-being (Gellert, Ziegelmann, & Schwarzer, 2012; Marttila, Laitakari, Nupponen, Miilunpalo, & Paronen, 1998; Segar, Eccles, & Richardson, 2008, 2011). Consistent with this suggestion, it has been found that body shape–related motives for exercise participation (e.g., weight loss or toning) are not associated with actual participation, whereas having a negative affective reaction to the thought of exercise (e.g., feeling guilty) is inversely related to participation (Segar, Spruijt-Metz, & Nolen-Hoeksema, 2006). Although it remains to be seen whether the new approaches will be adopted and implemented by exercise and health professionals, there can be little doubt that the psychological implications of the proposed changes in messaging strategy can be profound. If people stop using their bathroom scales as the sole gauge of the effectiveness of exercise, the number of individuals abandoning exercise because it "doesn't work" could be greatly reduced.

HOW BADLY ARE WE FAILING?

To put it bluntly, the failure of the field of exercise science to develop and implement effective, evidence-based strategies to promote exercise participation and adherence among obese individuals has been nearly absolute. No other domain of public health has seen rates of compliance with recommendations as low as those pertaining to physical activity in obesity (Ekkekakis et al., 2016).

According to current guidelines on the application of exercise for weight management, at least 60–90 minutes per day, performed at least at moderate intensity, are necessary (Andersen & Jakicic, 2009; Goldberg & King, 2007). Experts have cautioned, however, that this amount of activity may be "too daunting" (Hill & Wyatt, 2005, p. 769) or "too ambitious" (Davis, Hodges, & Gillham, 2006, p. 2264) and may, therefore, act as a deterrent. Indeed, in a nationwide study in the United States, among obese individuals trying to lose weight, only 6 percent of men and 3 percent of women reported at least 420 minutes of physical activity per week (i.e., 60 minutes per day on average; Bish et al., 2005). Self-reports of activity, however, are prone to considerable measurement error, mainly in the direction of overreporting (Troiano et al., 2008). Objective assessments with accelerometers in a nationally representative sample show that fewer than 2 percent of obese adults in the United States are physically active at the level recommended for health promotion (Tudor-Locke et al., 2010). Obese men average 23.4 minutes of moderate-intensity and 36.0 seconds of vigorous-intensity activity daily, whereas obese women average 13.8 minutes and 10.8 seconds, respectively (Archer et al., 2013). Among obese adults, the almost complete avoidance of vigorous-intensity activity, in particular, appears to be a global phenomenon (Hansen, Holme, Anderssen, & Kolle, 2013; Scheers, Philippaerts, & Lefevre, 2012).

Especially interesting from a psychological perspective is the phenomenon of dropout. While a higher body mass index has been found to predict an earlier stage of behavior change (e.g., precontemplation, contemplation; Marcus, Rossi, Selby, Niaura, & Abrams, 1992), numerous obese individuals do initiate exercise attempts. This presents an opportunity and a challenge for exercise professionals and the exercise science field as a whole. Presumably, well-prepared exercise professionals should be able to support participants in raising their level of motivation and, consequently, reducing dropout and increasing adherence. Although ecologically valid evidence is scant, the extant data are not encouraging. For example, according to an observational study of exercise-on-prescription programs in the United Kingdom, among participants with an average body mass index of 38.75 kg/m² (range from 29 to 58 kg/m²), 26.5 percent dropped out during the first month, and 18.4 percent dropped out during the second month. Another 4.1 percent were still exercising after three months but did not comply with the exercise prescription they had been given (Edmunds, Ntoumanis, & Duda, 2007).

THE HEDONIC PERSPECTIVE

When the level of non-compliance with a recommendation exceeds 98 percent, this is a good indication that a radically different approach is needed. Consistent with the dominant paradigm in the field of exercise psychology, the main approach underlying the promotion of exercise in obesity is based on the principles of cognitivism. In this framework, the decision to engage in or disengage from a health behavior, such as exercise, depends on the rational evaluation of information that one has in relation to this behavior (Ekkekakis & Zenko, 2016). For example, it is assumed that individuals with obesity will decide to engage in exercise and adhere over the long haul if they appraise the available information and concludes that the perceived benefits outnumber the perceived barriers, the perceived capabilities suffice given the perceived demands, and there is an adequate support system in place to assist in the endeavor (Dalle Grave, Calugi, Centis, El Ghoch, & Marchesini, 2011; Gallagher, Jakicic, Napolitano, & Marcus, 2006; Marchant, 2011). Thus, from this perspective, the exercise professional should counsel the obese client on the health benefits to be gained from exercise (e.g., on blood glucose or arterial pressure), increase the dose of exercise gradually (duration, frequency, intensity) to allow the development of a sense of self-efficacy, and secure the approval and encouragement of important others, such as family and friends.

These factors are important and, if these interventions were to be properly implemented by exercise practitioners on a large scale, they would likely make a difference. However, the extant evidence from intervention trials indicates that the positive effects, although statistically reliable, are neither large nor sustained (Bélanger-Gravel, Godin, Vézina-Im, Amireault, & Poirier, 2011; Gourlan, Trouilloud, & Sarrazin, 2011). The less-than-spectacular effects of interventions based on cognitivist theories have been described as "somewhat surprising, given that the use of theoretical frameworks should increase the likelihood of developing more effective interventions" (Bélanger-Gravel et al., 2011, p. 436). The reason why these results are deemed "surprising" is because they stand in contrast to generally stronger effects that similar interventions have been shown to have in the promotion of other health behaviors, such as smoking cessation or responsible sexual practices. This discrepancy raises the possibility that exercise in obesity is controlled by mechanisms that are largely distinct from those driving other health behaviors. Collectively, the evidence that is available to date suggests that, even under the best of circumstances, the effectiveness of activity-promotion interventions relying solely on changing cognitive appraisals would be modest (Bélanger-Gravel et al., 2011).

Thus, in this chapter, we propose a different approach. We assume that the decision to engage in or disengage from exercise depends not only on the rational cognitive appraisal of information but also, to a large extent, on affective experiences (pleasure versus displeasure) derived from prior exercise attempts. In essence, this represents the application to the domain of exercise of the theory of psychological hedonism, an idea that has persisted in various forms in psychological thought for over 25 centuries (Ekkekakis & Dafermos, 2012). The core postulate of this theory is that, because pleasure evolved to signify utility and displeasure evolved to signify danger, people have a strong inherent propensity to seek out and repeat pleasant experiences and avoid unpleasant ones. In the long run, people consistently gravitate toward behavioral options that, on previous occasions, yielded pleasure and stay clear of those that yielded displeasure. Recent evidence has demonstrated that the pleasure or displeasure experienced during or after exercise (Berger, Darby, Owen, & Carels, 2010; Carels, Berger, & Darby, 2006; Williams et al., 2008; Williams, Dunsiger, Jennings, & Marcus, 2012) and the degree to which people regard exercise as enjoyable (Rhodes, Fiala, & Conner, 2009) are significantly predictive of physical activity behavior. In open-ended responses to interviews, which allow respondents the freedom to express their thoughts and feelings unconstrained by the theoretical framework of the researcher, "fun" and "enjoyment" are "reported more often as predictors of participation and non-participation than perceived health benefits" (Allender, Cowburn, & Foster, 2006, p. 832).

Thus, after years of neglect under the influence of cognitivist models, a growing number of experts now recognize the importance of affect in exercise motivation. According to Rhodes and Nigg (2011), "the affective qualities of [physical activity] are the driving factor of [physical activity] motivation" (p. 116). Importantly, the role of affect in exercise motivation is also recognized by the ACSM; in its latest guidelines for exercise prescription, it states that "feelings of fatigue and negative affect . . . can act as a deterrent to continued participation" (ACSM, 2013, p. 374).

Furthermore, the version of hedonic theory we espouse is one specifically tailored to the unique challenges of the exercise stimulus and the unique attributes of the exercise environment. Thus, we fully endorse the suggestion that "there is adequate, if not overwhelming, evidence to suggest that unique theories of [physical activity] should be pursued" (Rhodes & Nigg, 2011, p. 114). We believe that "exercise is a multifaceted stimulus [and] as such, it has the capacity to induce affective responses emerging from any level of affective processing, from basic affect to specific emotions" (Ekkekakis & Petruzzello, 2000, p. 78; see Figure 23.1). For example, on one end of the spectrum, an obese individual may experience pleasure associated with a sense of somatic energy and revitalization following an appropriately tailored exercise bout or the displeasure of fatigue and exhaustion after a draining hour-long session. These varieties of pleasure and displeasure, included under the rubric of "core affect," do not require a cognitive appraisal; they can emanate directly from the body in an automatic, reflex-like fashion. On the opposite end of the spectrum, an obese individual may experience the pleasure of pride and accomplishment after reaching an important milestone (e.g., lowering systolic arterial pressure by 10 mmHg) or the displeasure of embarrassment and anger after appraising a remark by a personal trainer as insensitive or offensive. These varieties of pleasure and displeasure, which fall under the rubric of "emotions," differ from the previous ones in that their elicitation requires an antecedent cognitive appraisal of a specific social-environmental stimulus. Thus, emotions are heavily influenced by prior experiences

Figure 23.1 Obese individuals may derive negative affective experiences from multiple sources. These include
negative forms of core affect (e.g., displeasure, discomfort, pain, fatigue, exhaustion) and negative
appraisal-dependent emotions (e.g., fear, embarrassment, disappointment, guilt, anger).

(individual developmental histories) and are embedded within the sociocultural context (e.g.,
may depend greatly on the importance ascribed to "thinness").

In the application of hedonic theory to exercise behavior (Ekkekakis, 2013; Ekkekakis &
Dafermos, 2012), it is assumed that repeated unpleasant experiences from exercise, regardless
of their exact nature (core affect or emotions), create a negative association for exercise (see
Figure 23.2). When the notion of exercise is later recalled as one, consciously or subcon-
sciously, weighs different behavioral options (e.g., exercising or watching television), the negativity or positivity attached to the notion of exercise will tilt the balance of decision making
toward or away from exercise. The theory, of course, acknowledges that "reason" (the rational cognitive appraisal of information) also plays an important role in decision making and
that many decisions may involve a conflict between affect and reason. It is easy to imagine, for
example, that for many obese individuals, who are constantly reminded by their physicians or
family members that exercise would be highly beneficial, the decision to not exercise would
probably involve a conflict between reason and affect. In these situations, hedonic theory
presents an entirely new path for interventions by suggesting that the appropriate avenue is
not to attempt to make people *even* more convinced of the health benefits of exercise or *even*
more confident about their ability to be active but rather to make exercise more pleasant or
at least less unpleasant.

Thus, in the hedonic approach, the exercise professional should be mindful of all possible
sources of displeasure, including those associated with the exercise stimulus itself (i.e., its

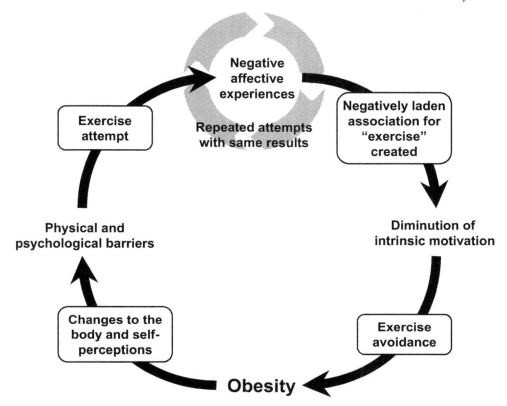

Figure 23.2 From the perspective of hedonic theory, obesity, presumably through the combination of physical and psychological challenges it poses, increases the likelihood that obese individuals will derive unpleasant affective experiences from exercise. Over multiple attempts, this may result in the formation of a negative association for exercise. In turn, a negatively charged concept of "exercise" acts to bias subsequent behavioral decisions against exercise and in favor of other, more pleasant options, thus setting in motion a vicious cycle of avoidance.

dose characteristics and the totality of its demands on the body), the exerciser (i.e., attitudes, personality), and the social and physical environment in which exercise takes place (i.e., the presence of mirrors and other evaluative cues, the number and behavior of others, the communication style and focus of the exercise professional). Research on the factors that contribute to the pleasant and unpleasant experiences that obese individuals derive from exercise is growing but remains scant (Ekkekakis et al., 2016). Thus, the full range of factors that may play a role is not known.

As illustrated in Figure 23.1, we speculate that a conglomeration of physiological (e.g., inability to maintain lactate steady state, thermoregulatory difficulties), biomechanical (e.g., pain from excessive impacts on joints, uncomfortable gait patterns), and psychological factors (e.g., self-presentational concerns, perceptions of anti-obesity bias) associated with obesity can contribute to making the exercise experience less pleasant overall for obese individuals than for their non-obese counterparts. Each of these categories present opportunities for interventions, and it is important for practitioners working with obese individuals to be aware of the unique challenges that obesity poses for exercise motivation and adherence. For example, conscientious practitioners should know that, in obese individuals, walking a little slower can reduce the potential for musculoskeletal injuries (Browning & Kram, 2007) or that dyspnea and respiratory muscle fatigue can develop even at intensities considered "moderate" (Dreher & Kabitz, 2012). Nevertheless, due to space constraints, this chapter focuses on psychological factors.

Affective and Emotional Responses

A standard adage in exercise psychology textbooks, which are mainly based on studies of young, healthy, active, and physically fit participants, is that "exercise makes people feel better." Given the homogeneity of the samples involved in these studies and the general inattention to individual variation, an implicit assumption has developed that this effect probably applies to all individuals or at least to the vast majority of them. Thus, when researchers find that exercise interventions involving formerly sedentary, elderly, or overweight and obese individuals *reduce* pleasure and enjoyment, the findings are characterized as "surprising" or "contrary to expectations" (e.g., Castro, Sallis, Hickmann, Lee, & Chen, 1999; Stevens, Lemmink, van Heuvelen, de Jong, & Rispens, 2003). Then, upon reflection, researchers come to the realization that, for individuals who are middle-age or older, physically inactive, with high body mass and low cardiorespiratory fitness, exercise is "unlikely to be construed as inherently pleasurable or enjoyable" (Wilson, Rodgers, Blanchard, & Gessell, 2003, p. 2375). Authors recognize that this combination of characteristics makes it "unrealistically optimistic" to expect that exercise can be enjoyable because "even mild physical activity can be physically demanding when one is not used to it" (Castro et al., 1999, p. 290). Findings that responses to items like "doing leisure-time physical activities makes me feel good" or "gives me satisfaction" show large decreases over the course of an intervention are attributed to the fact that, for "sedentary people unfamiliar with leisure-time physical activity," expecting that the enjoyment of the program will be "51" on a 70-point scale is "unrealistically high" (Stevens et al., 2003, p. 566).

Until a few years ago, there were no studies on how obesity may influence the subjective experience of exercise. Thus, practitioners had no reliable information about the challenges that obese individuals may face while trying to comply with exercise guidelines. This absence of information probably contributed to many exercise scientists and practitioners operating under the assumption that it is sufficient to develop exercise prescriptions solely based on mathematical formulas (e.g., to produce a daily deficit of X calories, one must exercise for Y minutes at Z intensity). Moreover, the absence of evidence on how an obese person may feel while exercising made it easier for exercise professionals to shift the burden of responsibility for any failure to carry out the prescribed exercise to the clients or patients (e.g., to their presumed lack of commitment, willpower, persistence, conscientiousness, or sense of personal responsibility).

In actuality, obesity changes the affective and emotional experience of exercise in several profound ways. One important, but often overlooked, issue is how the exercise itself feels. Although it is well-established that obesity limits exercise capacity (Lafortuna, 2013), the severity of this limitation has been greatly underappreciated. In the early 1990s, Donnelly et al. (1992) noted that efforts to field-test the cardiorespiratory capacity of obese women using a one-mile walk test failed because only 3 of 17 women could walk the full mile. Moreover, those who finished the mile took at least 20 minutes and subsequently reported feeling exhausted. They also complained of soreness in their legs for several days. A few years later, Mattsson, Evers Larsson, and Rössner (1997) raised the issue again, pointing out that "not many authors have analyzed the experience of the patients" (p. 380). They asked obese women, who were 44 years of age on average and had a body mass index of 37 kg/m², to "walk at a self-selected, comfortable speed" for four minutes. They were surprised to find that, although the obese women chose to walk significantly more slowly than normal-weight women, they raised their oxygen uptake 50 percent higher. One quarter of the obese women required from 64 percent to 98 percent of their maximal aerobic capacity. One in five women reported pain, mainly from the hip, knee, and ankle joints. The researchers commented that "walking for exercise may be too demanding and fatiguing for many obese women" (p. 384). Similar results were obtained by Hills, Byrne, Wearing, and Armstrong (2006), who observed that, when adults were asked to walk at a self-selected pace "consistent with walking for pleasure," the obese adults walked more slowly but raised their heart rate higher than their non-obese counterparts (70 percent versus 59 percent of maximal heart rate).

Mattsson et al. (1997) attributed the problems to the very low functional aerobic capacity associated with obesity (i.e., maximal aerobic capacity divided by body weight). For example, in a sample of 225 obese but otherwise healthy women who averaged 40.2 years of age and had a body mass index of 38.1 kg/m^2, Hulens, Vansant, Lysens, Claessens, and Muls (2001) found a maximal aerobic capacity of only 15.8 ml of O_2 per kg of body weight per min. To put this figure in perspective, a maximal aerobic capacity of 14 ml of O_2 per kg of body weight per min is suggested as an appropriate criterion for referring heart failure patients for cardiac transplantation (Mancini et al., 1991). The results of Hulens et al. (2001) are not unique; other studies have also found maximal aerobic capacity values in the teens (e.g., Misquita et al., 2001).

The problem of low exercise capacity is exacerbated further as the degree of obesity rises. For example, King et al. (2012) conducted a study in which they asked candidates for bariatric surgery (N = 2,458), with a body mass index averaging 45.9 kg/m^2, to walk 400 meters at their "usual pace" along a straight, level, uncluttered, and well-lit corridor. Upon screening, 13 percent were deemed ineligible to participate for medical reasons. Another 15 percent, despite being medically eligible, elected not to participate, invoking such reasons as uncomfortable shoes, pain, injury, medical conditions, lightheadedness, and fear of falling. Those who completed the walk took between 3 minutes 22 seconds and 13 minutes 22 seconds. More than half (56 percent) reported physical discomfort (foot, knee, or hip pain, shortness of breath, back pain, muscle pain, numbness or tingling in legs, and chest pain).

From the perspective of hedonic theory, whether an obese adult *can* walk 400 meters or one mile is not the main question of interest. Instead, the more crucial question is what an obese person can do while still deriving an experience that is pleasant or at least not unpleasant. This requirement increases the challenge of exercise prescription in obesity even further. A decade of research on the relationship between exercise intensity and affective responses has demonstrated that most individuals begin to feel worse once the intensity exceeds the ventilatory threshold (VT), the level at which the volume of exhaled CO_2 is larger than the volume of O_2 being consumed (Ekkekakis, Parfitt, & Petruzzello, 2011). The VT, however, typically occurs at 50–60 percent of maximal aerobic capacity in non-athletic adults. For example, in the sample of 225 obese women tested by Hulens et al. (2001), the VT occurred at 56 percent of maximal aerobic capacity on average.

Given a maximal capacity of 15.8 ml of O_2 per kg of body weight per min, this means that the average participant could raise her oxygen uptake to approximately 2.5 metabolic equivalent units (METs) before exceeding the VT. To illustrate the practical significance of this figure, consider these examples. Activities estimated to correspond to 2.5 METs (not exceeding VT) include moving about indoors within a radius of just a few steps (e.g., while preparing a meal in the kitchen), mild stretching, fishing from a seated position, light dusting, washing dishes, placing dishes on shelves, watering flower pots, or playing the piano or the violin (Ainsworth et al., 2011). On the other hand, examples of activities estimated to correspond to 3.0 METs and would, therefore, exceed the VT of this sample of obese women include walking slowly, waltzing, fishing from a standing position, cleaning windows, sweeping or mopping floors, washing the car, painting walls, picking fruit from trees, carrying trash to the trash bin, bowling, and golfing.

The challenge faced by obese adults—and exercise professionals—should be apparent, as the range of (weight-bearing) activity options available to them without incurring a reduction in pleasure appears to be extremely limited. Indeed, studies have shown that obese adults report feeling significantly worse than their non-obese counterparts not only at intensities exceeding the VT (da Silva et al., 2011) but throughout most of the range of exercise intensity (Ekkekakis et al., 2010). Moreover, the affective rebound phenomenon (i.e., the quick reversal from feeling worse to feeling better) that is common and robust among most individuals once strenuous exercise is terminated appears to be absent in obesity (Ekkekakis et al., 2010).

Findings that obese adults experience diminished pleasure responses to exercise, particularly at higher exercise intensities, are consistent with the results of studies showing that, among overweight and obese adults with low cardiorespiratory capacity, higher intensity results in lower adherence (Perri et al., 2002) and retention (Cox, Burke, Gorely, Beilin, & Puddey, 2003). Collectively, these results suggest that obese adults may have a particular sensitivity to higher levels of intensity (i.e., obesity may strengthen the inverse relationship between exercise intensity and affective responses).

This represents an especially timely observation given that high-intensity interval training is being promoted as a weight-loss intervention (Boutcher, 2011). Such calls are based exclusively on two considerations, namely effectiveness (i.e., acceleration of the rate of weight or fat loss compared to moderate intensity) and safety (i.e., low rate of adverse events, mainly among young and healthy participants). However, it should be clear that an intervention that is effective and safe may still have limited public-health relevance if the rates of avoidance, non-adherence, and dropout are high. It is, therefore, important to note that, when given a choice between lower walking intensity (but longer duration) or shorter duration (but higher intensity), most obese adults "requested a reduction, rather than an increase, of walking intensity" (Fogelholm, Kukkonen-Harjula, Nenonen, & Pasanen, 2000, p. 2182). Higher perceptions of exercise intensity at the end of a weight-management intervention have been found to predict weight regain and (marginally) lower exercise behavior during the subsequent 12 months (Brock et al., 2010).

Of the methods for enhancing the affective experience of exercise that have been tested so far, the easiest to implement and one of the most effective is the promotion of self-selected intensity (Ekkekakis, 2009). One study simulated a scenario in which a personal trainer sets the exercise intensity for a client at a level slightly higher than what the client would have self-selected (Ekkekakis & Lind, 2006). When allowed to self-select their intensity, previously sedentary overweight and obese women (average body mass index of 31.06 kg/m²) chose to walk at an intensity well within the range recommended by the ACSM for the development and maintenance of cardiorespiratory fitness (69–70% of peak aerobic capacity, 85–87% of peak heart rate). Over 20 minutes, the women maintained their oxygen uptake below their VT (up to 97% of the oxygen uptake associated with the VT). Importantly, they also reported ratings of pleasure that remained stable between "I feel fairly good" and "I feel good" for the duration of the walk. On the other hand, when the walking speed was set by the investigators to exceed the self-selected by only 10 percent (from ~3.4 to ~3.8 miles per hour), the intensity rose to 83 percent of peak oxygen uptake, 93–94 percent of peak heart rate, and up to 115 percent of the oxygen uptake associated with the VT. Compared to the stable ratings of pleasure during the bout at self-selected intensity, reports of pleasure during the imposed-intensity condition showed a large decline ($d = -0.90$).

Besides core affective responses, such as pleasure and displeasure, obesity influences the overall exercise experience by prompting individuals to make a range of cognitive appraisals leading to negative emotions. In particular, various forms of fear appear to be a common accompaniment of exercise for many obese individuals. These fears reflect worry and apprehension about the possible adverse effects of exercise on both psychological and physical well-being (Leone & Ward, 2013). In terms of psychological well-being, obese adults, often burdened by negative self-evaluations, are concerned that critical observers may evaluate their physical appearance and exercise ability negatively (Bain, Wilson, & Chaikind, 1989). Especially when exercising in the presence of others that they perceive as more physically fit, obese adults tend to feel embarrassment and intimidation (Miller & Miller, 2010), two salient negative emotions that may "override the knowledge that exercise is healthful" (p. 7). In terms of physical well-being, obese adults fear that exercise may cause physical injury, mainly to the musculoskeletal and cardiovascular systems, and this fear is a reliable predictor of inactivity, exercise avoidance, and perceived disability (Sallinen et al., 2009; Vincent et al., 2011; Wingo et al., 2011, 2013; Wouters, van Nunen, Vingerhoets, & Geenen, 2009). Perceptions of distress are especially elevated during exercise among individuals who have a combination of high body mass index and a tendency to interpret bodily symptoms as signs of danger (e.g., "When I notice that my heart is beating rapidly, I worry that I might have a heart attack," "It scares me when I become short of breath"; Smits, Tart, Presnell, Rosenfield, & Otto, 2010).

Unrealistic Weight-Loss Expectations

In a classic study, Foster et al. (1997) illustrated the perils inherent in allowing the perceived success of an intervention to depend solely on weight loss. They asked 60 obese women (average body mass index of 36.3 kg/m²) entering a weight-loss program to indicate what they considered "dream weight," "happy weight," "acceptable weight," and "disappointed weight." They found that their goal weight corresponded to a 32-percent reduction in body weight on average (32 kg or 70.5 lbs). Losing 17 kg (37.5 lbs) was considered "disappointed" ("not successful in any way") and 25 kg (55 lbs) was considered merely "acceptable" ("not one that I would be particularly happy with"). After 48 weeks of treatment and a large average weight loss (16 kg or 35 lbs), nearly half (47%) of the women did not even achieve what they considered "disappointed weight." Another 20 percent reached "disappointed weight," and 24 percent reached an "acceptable weight." Only 9 percent reached a "happy weight," while none reached "dream weight." Even after this experience, what the women considered "disappointed" and "acceptable" weights remained the same. Their satisfaction with the result of the intervention was closely and inversely ($r = -0.67$) related to the discrepancy between the weight loss they wanted to achieve and the one they actually achieved.

Research suggests that, although high initial weight-loss expectations may motivate one to begin exercise, motivation can be dramatically diminished once these high initial expectations are violated. An expectancy violation occurs when, for example, a desired amount of weight is not lost at the rate and with the ease that was anticipated. When expectations are not met, negative emotions are experienced (e.g., sadness, disappointment, resentment, guilt), resulting in a reduction in the motivation to continue with the behavior change. Thus, expectancy violations have long been known to predict dropout from exercise programs (Desharnais, Bouillon, & Godin, 1986). Sears and Stanton (2001) found that formerly sedentary enrollees in a women's health club, 50 percent of whom were overweight (33%) or obese (17%), were more likely to drop out during weeks 7–12 if they had larger expectancy violations for weight loss during weeks 1–6. Likewise, in obese patients entering a weight-loss program, the higher the expectations for weight loss, the higher the likelihood of attrition a year later (Dalle Grave et al., 2005). Conversely, individuals who completed an exercise program had more modest expectations than those who failed to adhere (Jones, Harris, & Waller, 1998; Jones, Harris, Waller, & Coggins, 2005).

Dysfunctional Attitudes

An attitude is defined as a "summary evaluation of a psychological object captured in such attribute dimensions as good-bad, harmful-beneficial, pleasant-unpleasant, and likable-dislikable" (Ajzen, 2001, p. 28). Attitudes are malleable; they are shaped through life experiences and are influenced by the social and cultural context. However, once formed, they are relatively stable. So, they are conceptualized as *"dispositions* to evaluate psychological objects" (p. 29) favorably or unfavorably. Attitudes are theorized to influence the formation of behavioral intentions (Ajzen, 2001), so positive attitudes can be a significant motivational force, whereas negative attitudes can impede and diminish motivation.

Therefore, understanding the attitudes that obese individuals hold toward exercise could shed light on the reasons behind the phenomenon of exercise avoidance. In approaching this topic, however, it is first important to appreciate the complexity of the construct of attitude and, in particular, the fact that it is possible for someone to hold two conflicting (but qualitatively different) attitudes about the same object (Ajzen, 2001; Wilson, Lindsey, & Schooler, 2000). For example, in what is called an expression of *explicit* attitude, obese individuals, when asked, may readily offer a list of perceived benefits of exercise that exceeds the list of perceive barriers (Smith, Griffin, & Fitzpatrick, 2011). At the same time, however, an *implicit* negative attitude, which may not be reflected in responses to a questionnaire or an interview, may preclude someone from exercising. Implicit attitudes may reflect past negative affective experiences with exercise, such as pain, exhaustion, embarrassment, or guilt. Miller and Miller (2010) have noted that obese adults exhibit a peculiar co-occurrence of a strong appreciation of the benefits of exercise and a strong intention to be active with very low levels of past and present actual exercise behavior. This seemingly paradoxical phenomenon may be explained by a conflict between explicit and implicit attitudes. Moreover, emerging evidence suggests that evaluations of exercise along the dimension ranging from "not enjoyable" to "enjoyable" predict exercise intention and behavior better than evaluations along the dimension ranging from "harmful" to "beneficial" (Lawton, Conner, McEachan, 2009). Thus, while most interventions to increase exercise participation among obese individuals continue to focus on raising the awareness of health benefits, little attention is directed at what might be a more powerful mechanism, namely making exercise experiences more pleasant or enjoyable.

Research on the attitudes of obese individuals toward exercise, although still limited, suggests that several dysfunctional attitudes may contribute to the overall experience of exercise as unpleasant. One common theme is the belief that exercise should only be performed by people who "look the part" by appearing fit or athletic and, conversely, that someone can be "too fat" or "too overweight" to be seen exercising (Atlantis, Barnes, & Ball, 2008; Ball, Crawford, & Owen, 2000). The consequences of this belief are reflected in reports of obese individuals feeling "emotionally uncomfortable or publicly humiliated" in exercise environments (Thomas, Hyde, Karunaratne, Kausman, & Komesaroff, 2008, p. 6), "too shy or embarrassed to exercise" or "not the sporty type" (Ball et al., 2000, p. 331), and "uncomfortable with appearing in public wearing exercise clothing" (Wiklund, Olsén, & Willén, 2011, p. 179).

A second common theme is the belief that exercise is or should be extremely prolonged and/or intense to be truly effective (Timperio, Cameron-Smith, Burns, Salmon, & Crawford, 2000). Obese individuals overwhelmingly perceive dieting to be easier than exercise; compared to diet, exercise is described as "extremely difficult" as it requires significant "emotional and physical effort" (Thomas et al., 2008, p. 6). According to an insightful qualitative study, obese women perceived displeasure to be an integral and unavoidable part of exercise: "the pain and discomfort were interpreted as something they had to endure" (Groven & Engelsrud, 2010, p. 8). Exercise was equated to "hard work" and portrayed as the antithesis of "fun." For example, one woman, expressing her admiration for other women in the group, described them as "hard working . . . they really wish to get into better shape and lose weight. They are not here for the fun of it. No, they aren't" (p. 8).

As described earlier in this chapter, obesity imposes added stress on the joints (Browning & Kram, 2007) and the cardiorespiratory system (Lafortuna, 2013). Nevertheless, when given the autonomy to self-regulate the intensity, it is still possible for obese and formerly inactive individuals to "feel good" during exercise (Ekkekakis & Lind, 2006). When exercise feels manageable, obese individuals tend to express surprise: "I can actually exercise if I want to . . . it isn't as hard as I thought" (Daley, Copeland, Wright, & Wales, 2008, p. 816). The source of the belief that exercise is supposed to be difficult or painful can probably be traced to culturally imposed norms and social models. In an interesting study, students watched an episode of the television show *The Biggest Loser*, in which obese participants are subjected to grueling workouts and often berated by the trainers for their lack of effort (Berry, McLeod, Pankratow, & Walker, 2013). After the show, the students reported lowered affective attitude toward exercise (they rated the idea of exercising every day during the next month as less pleasant, enjoyable, and pleasurable or more unpleasant, unenjoyable, and painful). The students commented on how "painful and stressing" the exercise appeared to be, causing the researchers to speculate that "negative depictions of exercise as hard work may result in diminished exercise behavior, mediated by lowered exercise-related attitudes" (p. 101). While this chain of causation has yet to be fully tested, it appears to be corroborated by the narratives in qualitative studies. According to Groven and Engelsrud (2010), one of the women they interviewed said: " 'I pushed myself to go, even though I hated it.' But after 2 months of regular training, she decided to quit" (p. 7).

Self-Presentational Concerns, Social Comparisons, and Social Physique Anxiety

Being overweight or obese is a risk factor for non-adherence and dropout from exercise programs but being overweight or obese *and* exercising in a group setting raises the risk even further (King et al., 1997; Perri, Martin, Leermakers, Sears, & Notelovitz, 1997). This suggests that the social-psychological environment of exercise may contain elements that repel and deter, rather than attract, individuals with a high body mass. Indeed, experiencing negative social emotions, such as feeling "ashamed and uncomfortable" as a result of being "stared at" while exercising, is a ubiquitous theme in interviews of obese participants, especially women (Groven & Engelsrud, 2010, p. 7). The displeasure associated with the perceived critical gaze of others appears to be even more personally significant than any pain or discomfort associated with the exercise itself. Investigating the sources of this concern, researchers commonly invoke the concept of "self-objectification," the idea that girls and women may tend to internalize the view of the female body as a sexual object to be gazed upon and evaluated against cultural standards of "beauty" or "perfection" (Fredrickson & Roberts, 1997). Learning to place a high value on appearance results in constant self-surveillance and, consequently, increased risk of experiencing body dissatisfaction, appearance-related anxiety, and shame. As alluded to in the introduction, because of lack of awareness of or sensitivity to this important social-psychological phenomenon, exercise facilities include many features that promote the process of self-objectification and its negative consequences (Miller & Miller, 2010). According to Prichard and Tiggemann (2005), "the fitness center environment contains a large number of clearly objectifying features: multiple full-length mirrors, posters that idealize the female body, the opportunity for direct comparison with other women, scanty and revealing aerobic clothing, and the presence of men observing women exercising" (p. 20).

Prichard and Tiggemann (2008) focused on the implications of promises made by the exercise and fitness industry that the female body is an indefinitely malleable object that can be "sculpted" by exercise to reach a level of culturally dictated "perfection." These researchers found that time spent in an exercise facility was positively related to self-objectification and exercising for weight loss, body tone, and attractiveness rather than health. "Cardio" exercise, in particular, which is perceived as more conducive to weight loss than other types of exercise (e.g., yoga), was related to lower body esteem and a higher likelihood of disturbed eating. Prichard and Tiggemann (2008) postulated that promoting exercise as a means of transforming the female body may lead to disappointment, a sense of failure, and guilt because, in actuality, exercise is a "slow and challenging means of appearance improvement that does not instantly change a woman's shape" (p. 856).

The type of social anxiety that develops when someone perceives that his or her physical appearance is being critically evaluated by others is called social physique anxiety (Hart, Leary, & Rejeski, 1989). Social physique anxiety tends to be correlated with body mass index (e.g., $r = 0.34$) and body fat (e.g., $r = 0.31$), although these correlations are far from perfect (Treasure, Lox, & Lawton, 1998). In most studies, social physique anxiety has been found to be inversely related to exercise participation (Hausenblas, Brewer, & Van Raalte, 2004), presumably because, as Leary (1992) noted, "social anxiety detracts from the emotional rewards of exercising" (p. 346). Indeed, studies have shown that social physique anxiety burdens exercisers with concerns that would make it very difficult to derive pleasure and enjoyment, including seeking ways to hide their body and avoid the gaze of others (Brewer, Diehl, Cornelius, Joshua, & Van Raalte, 2004).

Research has made progress in identifying the elements of the exercise environment that promote self-objectification, trigger self-surveillance, and induce a fear of negative evaluation by critical observers. First, particularly among women with a predisposition to worry about their physical appearance being judged by others, exercising in front of mirrors has been found to induce lower exercise self-efficacy (Katula, McAuley, Mihalko, & Bane, 1998), increased state anxiety (Focht & Hausenblas, 2003), and less positive affective responses (Focht & Hausenblas, 2006; Martin Ginis, Jung, & Gauvin, 2003). The negative effect of mirrors is exacerbated when others are present, presumably because the participants become more self-conscious and make more social comparisons (Martin Ginis et al., 2007).

Second, the goals emphasized by the exercise leader can also trigger self-surveillance, with negative consequences on how exercise is experienced. In general, placing emphasis on appearance over health increases body dissatisfaction and lowers body esteem (Vartanian et al., 2012). When the exercise leader gives instructions that focus on appearance (e.g., "stand tall, you'll look five pounds lighter," "let's get your legs toned so they look good," "burn calories") rather than health (e.g., "shoulders back for good posture," "let's get fit and healthy"), participants feel worse after exercise (Raedeke, Focht, & Scales, 2007).

Third, contrary to the assumption that watching others who are lean and fit will have a motivating effect, research shows that perceiving a negative discrepancy between one's own body and the body of an exercise leader who seems exceptionally fit and is dressed in revealing clothes results in reduced body satisfaction and increased anxiety about the appearance of one's physique, without any effect on motivation (Martin Ginis et al., 2008). Likewise, overweight and obese individuals who are concerned about the negative judgment of others prefer to exercise in environments in which most other exercisers are also overweight, with individuals who appear to be "in shape" representing only a small minority (Dunlop & Schmader, 2014).

Perceptions of Stigmatization and Anti-Obesity Bias

It is a generalized perception that obese individuals became obese through a combination of two characteristics, namely gluttony and sloth. Society at large views these characteristics as reflecting a failure of personal responsibility and, therefore, as morally objectionable (Yoo, 2013). In actuality, however, the etiology of obesity is multifactorial, complex, and still poorly understood (McAllister et al., 2009). As such, it does not lend itself to simplistic assumptions. Based on estimates from national statistics, for 90 percent of the population, weight gain over time is a slow process resulting from a surplus in caloric balance of no more than 100 calories per day (Hill, Wyatt, Reed, & Peters, 2003). Nevertheless, as long as the narrative that attributes the cause of obesity to personal responsibility remains prevalent in contemporary culture (Ata & Thompson, 2010; Greenberg, Eastin, Hofschire, Lachlan, & Brownell, 2003), a bias against obese individuals will likely continue. According to Puhl and Heuer (2009): "Weight bias translates into inequities in employment settings, health-care facilities, and educational institutions, often due to widespread negative stereotypes that overweight and obese persons are lazy, unmotivated, lacking in self-discipline, less competent, noncompliant, and sloppy" (p. 941).

Strong negative bias and baseless stereotypes are also prevalent among health professionals from multiple fields who are called to play important roles in the prevention and treatment of obesity. Studies demonstrating various forms of anti-obesity bias have been conducted with physicians, pharmacists, and other healthcare professionals (Sabin, Marini, & Nosek, 2012; Teachman & Brownell, 2001), nurses (Poon & Tarrant, 2009), clinicians specializing in obesity (Schwartz, Chambliss, Brownell, Blair, & Billington, 2003), dieticians (Berryman, Dubale, Manchester, & Mittelstaedt, 2006; Puhl, Wharton, & Heuer, 2009), physical educators (Greenleaf & Weiller, 2005; O'Brien, Hunter, & Banks, 2007), exercise science students (Chambliss, Finley, & Blair, 2004; Rukavina, Li, Shen, & Sun, 2010), fitness professionals, and regular exercisers (Dimmock et al., 2009; Hare et al., 2000; Robertson & Vohora, 2008).

Living in a cultural environment replete with anti-obesity stereotypes and coming in contact with professionals who endorse these stereotypes results, at least in some cases, in internalization of the bias among obese individuals. Thus, although there is an inverse relationship between one's own weight and anti-obesity bias (Schwartz, Vartanian, Nosek, & Brownell, 2006), many overweight and obese people still endorse several negative stereotypes associated with body weight (Wang, Brownell, & Wadden, 2004). This endorsement is both explicit (i.e., reporting on a questionnaire that obese people are "lazier" than non-obese people) and implicit (i.e., pairing the concepts "fat" and "overweight" more frequently with negative attributes such as "lazy" or "sluggish" in a timed association test). In turn, having experienced stigmatization and having internalized anti-obesity biases are associated with avoidance of lifestyle changes such as adopting exercise (Carels et al., 2009; Vartanian & Novak, 2011; Vartanian & Shaprow, 2008). While the mechanisms underlying this phenomenon are still not fully understood, early findings suggest that negative feelings toward the self (i.e., self-blame, low self-esteem, body dissatisfaction) may be responsible. According to Vartanian and Novak (2011), "one possibility is that experiences with weight stigma lead individuals to want to avoid exercise situations out of embarrassment or out of fear of being further stigmatized" (p. 761).

Once formed, bias, prejudice, and stigmatizing attitudes may be hard to change. A variety of approaches have been proposed (Puhl & Wharton, 2007), ranging from modifying the exercise environment (e.g., ensuring privacy for assessments and consultations, using appropriately sized equipment, allowing diversity of body size among staff, encouraging comfortable but not revealing professional attire among staff), being aware of communication style (e.g., becoming sensitized to the use of descriptors perceived as having negative connotations, such as "fat," "weight problem," and "morbidly obese," and preferring neutral terms, such as "weight" or "BMI"), and changing beliefs about etiology (e.g., raising awareness of the important role of pharmacological, endocrine, or genetic contributors that are beyond personal control). Although such interventions are generally successful in improving knowledge and reducing explicit forms of bias (e.g., Puhl & Wharton, 2007; Rukavina, Li, & Rowell, 2008), implicit bias is more entrenched and resistant to change (Daníelsdóttir, O'Brien, & Ciao, 2010; Rukavina et al., 2010; Teachman, Gapinski, Brownell, Rawlins, & Jeyaram, 2003), and may, therefore, require more extensive intervention (O'Brien, Puhl, Latner, Mir, & Hunter, 2010).

RECOMMENDATIONS FOR PRACTICE

The hedonic perspective summarized in this chapter is a radically different approach from the current standard of professional practice. It calls for an overhaul of the way that exercise in obesity is conceptualized, a drastic reformulation and reorientation of promotion strategies, and a comprehensive reengineering of the way that exercise environments are designed.

First, weight loss should be dethroned from its current position as the sole or the chief purpose of exercise. The narrow focus on weight loss, to the exclusion of other valuable benefits of exercise, is unjustified by the evidence. Moreover, using weight loss as the sole criterion for evaluating the effects of exercise, particularly in the presence of cultural influences causing individuals to expect unrealistic amounts of weight loss, can be causally linked to disappointment and dropout. This makes this focus not only unjustified but also detrimental. The focus of promotion campaigns should be shifted instead to improved health and well-being, with the understanding that, based on evidence, neither health nor well-being is inherently incompatible with the range of body mass labeled "overweight" and "obese."

Second, in the hedonic approach, the rate of accrual of health or weight-loss benefits is a secondary concern, far behind the prime objective of maintaining long-term, ideally life-long, exercise adherence by ensuring that exercise is experienced as pleasant and enjoyable. Attempting to amplify or accelerate "results," however defined, will likely entail increasing the intensity and/or duration of exercise beyond the range that most obese participants would find pleasant or even tolerable. "Results" of any type will not occur, and those that do occur will be quickly reversed, if exercise is not adopted as a permanent component of lifestyle. Short-term adaptations, such as those that may result from a regimen of high-intensity training, represent an entirely misleading criterion of the efficacy of an exercise intervention inasmuch as a regimen of this type is aversive and, therefore, unsustainable in the long run. In this sense, the hedonic perspective is fully compatible with the "small changes" approach (Hill, 2009; Hill et al., 2003; Hills, Byrne, Lindstrom, & Hill, 2013) and the "health at every size" approach (Bacon & Aphramor, 2011; Brown, 2009). Both the former (Paxman, Hall, Harden, O'Keeffe, & Simper, 2011) and the latter (Gagnon-Girouard et al., 2010) encourage autonomy in selecting the dose of exercise (i.e., intensity, duration) and, consistent with the evidence presented in this chapter, both approaches have been found to have positive effects on indices of well-being.

Third, an exercise facility designed on the basis of the hedonic approach is a welcoming environment, not a threatening one, for obese exercisers. The sources of fear and intimidation that have been identified through research (i.e., mirrors, emphasis on appearance, comparisons to realistically unattainable standards of fitness or athleticism, shape-revealing attire, excessive physiological demands, staff lacking empathy or sensitivity to the challenges associated with obesity) should be removed. Their effect on motivation is demonstrably negative.

Therefore, the presence of these elements in the exercise environment, when considered through the prism of the prime objective (i.e., ensuring lifelong adherence), makes no sense. Along the same lines, exercise professionals should not be hired and retained on the basis of the "image" they project. Far more meaningful criteria are their professional competence (including knowledge of the unique physiological and biomechanical challenges that obesity poses) and sensitivity (including awareness of the impact that their verbal and non-verbal behavior can have on participant motivation and adherence, as well as their acceptance of exercisers with diverse needs).

Despite the unquestionable growth of exercise science, its track record in developing interventions that promote and facilitate exercise among individuals with obesity is not positive. This is largely because, for far too long, the field has relied on unfounded assumptions and has overlooked evidence from psychological research on the processes underlying non-adherence and dropout. This must change. The hedonic perspective outlined in this chapter targets adherence as the prime objective and represents an evidence-based path forward.

REFERENCES

Ainsworth, B. E., Haskell, W. L., Herrmann, S. D., Meckes, N., Bassett, D. R. Jr., Tudor-Locke, C., . . . Leon, A. S. (2011). 2011 compendium of physical activities: A second update of codes and MET values. *Medicine and Science in Sports and Exercise, 43*(8), 1575–1581.

Ajzen, I. (2001). Nature and operation of attitudes. *Annual Review of Psychology, 52*, 27–58.

Allender, S., Cowburn, G., & Foster, C. (2006). Understanding participation in sport and physical activity among children and adults: A review of qualitative studies. *Health Education Research, 21*(6), 826–835.

American College of Sports Medicine. (2013). *ACSM's guidelines for exercise testing and prescription* (9th ed.). Philadelphia, PA: Lippincott Williams & Wilkins.

Andersen, R. E., & Jakicic, J. M. (2009). Interpreting the physical activity guidelines for health and weight management. *Journal of Physical Activity and Health, 6*(5), 651–656.

Archer, E., Hand, G. A., Hébert, J. R., Lau, E. Y., Wang, X., Shook, R. P., . . . Blair, S. N. (2013). Validation of a novel protocol for calculating estimated energy requirements and average daily physical activity ratio for the US population: 2005–2006. *Mayo Clinic Proceedings, 88*(12), 1398–1407.

Ata, R. N., & Thompson, J. K. (2010). Weight bias in the media: A review of recent research. *Obesity Facts, 3*(1), 41–46.

Atlantis, E., Barnes, E. H., & Ball, K. (2008). Weight status and perception barriers to healthy physical activity and diet behavior. *International Journal of Obesity, 32*(2), 343–352.

Bacon, L., & Aphramor, L. (2011). Weight science: Evaluating the evidence for a paradigm shift. *Nutrition Journal, 10*, 9.

Bader, D. S., Maguire, T. E., Spahn, C. M., O'Malley, C. J., & Balady, G. J. (2001). Clinical profile and outcomes of obese patients in cardiac rehabilitation stratified according to National Heart, Lung, and Blood Institute criteria. *Journal of Cardiopulmonary Rehabilitation, 21*(4), 210–217.

Bain, L. L., Wilson, T., & Chaikind, E. (1989). Participant perceptions of exercise programs for overweight women. *Research Quarterly for Exercise and Sport, 60*(2), 134–143.

Ball, K., Crawford, D., & Owen, N. (2000). Too fat to exercise? Obesity as a barrier to physical activity. *Australian and New Zealand Journal of Public Health, 24*(3), 331–333.

Bélanger-Gravel, A., Godin, G., Vézina-Im, L. A., Amireault, S., & Poirier, P. (2011). The effect of theory-based interventions on physical activity participation among overweight/obese individuals: A systematic review. *Obesity Reviews, 12*(6), 430–439.

Berger, B. G., Darby, L. A., Owen, D. R., & Carels, R. A. (2010). Implications of a behavioral weight loss program for obese, sedentary women: A focus on mood enhancement and exercise enjoyment. *International Journal of Sport and Exercise Psychology, 8*(1), 10–23.

Berry, T. R., McLeod, N. C., Pankratow, M., & Walker, J. (2013). Effects of Biggest Loser exercise depictions on exercise-related attitudes. *American Journal of Health Behavior, 37*(1), 96–103.

Berryman, D. E., Dubale, G. M., Manchester, D. S., & Mittelstaedt, R. (2006). Dietetics students possess negative attitudes toward obesity similar to nondietetics students. *Journal of the American Dietetic Association, 106*(10), 1678–1682.

Bish, C. L., Blanck, H. M., Serdula, M. K., Marcus, M., Kohl, H. W. 3rd, & Khan, L. K. (2005). Diet and physical activity behaviors among Americans trying to lose weight: 2000 behavioral risk factor surveillance system. *Obesity Research, 13*(3), 596–607.

Blair, S. N. (2009). Physical inactivity: The biggest public health problem of the 21st century. *British Journal of Sports Medicine, 43*(1), 1–2.

Blair, S. N., & LaMonte, M. J. (2006). Current perspectives on obesity and health: Black and white, or shades of grey? *International Journal of Epidemiology, 35*(1), 69–72.

Borg, P., Kukkonen-Harjula, K., Fogelholm, M., & Pasanen, M. (2002). Effects of walking or resistance training on weight loss maintenance in obese, middle-aged men: A randomized trial. *International Journal of Obesity, 26*(5), 676–683.

Boutcher, S. H. (2011). High-intensity intermittent exercise and fat loss. *Journal of Obesity,* 868305.

Boutcher, S. H., & Dunn, S. L. (2009). Factors that may impede the weight loss response to exercise-based interventions. *Obesity Reviews, 10*(6), 671–680.

Brewer, B. W., Diehl, N. S., Cornelius, A. E., Joshua, M. D., & Van Raalte, J. L. (2004). Exercising caution: Social physique anxiety and protective self-presentational behaviour. *Journal of Science and Medicine in Sport, 7*(1), 47–55.

Brock, D. W., Chandler-Laney, P. C., Alvarez, J. A., Gower, B. A., Gaesser, G. A., & Hunter, G. R. (2010). Perception of exercise difficulty predicts weight regain in formerly overweight women. *Obesity, 18*(5), 982–986.

Brown, L. B. (2009). Teaching the "health at every size" paradigm benefits future fitness and health professionals. *Journal of Nutrition Education and Behavior, 41*(2), 144–145.

Browning, R. C., & Kram, R. (2007). Effects of obesity on the biomechanics of walking at different speeds. *Medicine and Science in Sports and Exercise, 39*(9), 1632–1641.

Carels, R. A., Berger, B., & Darby, L. (2006). The association between mood states and physical activity in postmenopausal, obese, sedentary women. *Journal of Aging and Physical Activity, 14*(1), 12–28.

Carels, R. A., Young, K. M., Wott, C. B., Harper, J., Gumble, A., Oehlof, M. W., & Clayton, A. M. (2009). Weight bias and weight loss treatment outcomes in treatment-seeking adults. *Annals of Behavioral Medicine, 37*(3), 350–355.

Castro, C. M., Sallis, J. F., Hickmann, S. A., Lee, R. E., & Chen, A. H. (1999). A prospective study of psychosocial correlates of physical activity for ethnic minority women. *Psychology and Health, 14*(2), 277–293.

Catenacci, V. A., & Wyatt, H. R. (2007). The role of physical activity in producing and maintaining weight loss. *Nature Clinical Practice: Endocrinology and Metabolism, 3*(7), 518–529.

Chambliss, H. O., Finley, C. E., & Blair, S. N. (2004). Attitudes toward obese individuals among exercise science students. *Medicine and Science in Sports and Exercise, 36*(3), 468–474.

Church, T. S., Martin, C. K., Thompson, A. M., Earnest, C. P., Mikus, C. R., & Blair, S. N. (2009). Changes in weight, waist circumference and compensatory responses with different doses of exercise among sedentary, overweight postmenopausal women. *PLoS One, 4*(2), e4515.

Colley, R. C., Hills, A. P., O'Moore-Sullivan, T. M., Hickman, I. J., Prins, J. B., & Byrne, N. M. (2008). Variability in adherence to an unsupervised exercise prescription in obese women. *International Journal of Obesity, 32*(5), 837–844.

Cox, K. L., Burke, V., Gorely, T. J., Beilin, L. J., & Puddey, I. B. (2003). Controlled comparison of retention and adherence in home- vs center-initiated exercise interventions in women ages 40-65 years: The S.W.E.A.T. study (Sedentary Women Exercise Adherence Trial). *Preventive Medicine, 36*(1), 17–29.

da Silva, S. G., Elsangedy, H. M., Krinski, K., de Campos, W., Buzzachera, C. F., Krause, M. P., . . . Robertson, R. J. (2011). Effect of body mass index on affect at intensities spanning the ventilatory threshold. *Perceptual and Motor Skills, 113*(2), 575–588.

Daley, A. J., Copeland, R. J., Wright, N. P., & Wales, J. K. (2008). "I can actually exercise if I want to; it isn't as hard as I thought": A qualitative study of the experiences and views of obese adolescents participating in an exercise therapy intervention. *Journal of Health Psychology, 13*(6), 810–819.

Dalle Grave, R., Calugi, S., Centis, E., El Ghoch, M., & Marchesini, G. (2011). Cognitive-behavioral strategies to increase the adherence to exercise in the management of obesity. *Journal of Obesity, 2011,* 348293.

Dalle Grave, R., Calugi, S., Molinari, E., Petroni, M. L., Bondi, M., Compare, A., & Marchesini, G. (2005). Weight loss expectations in obese patients and treatment attrition: An observational multi-center study. *Obesity Research*, *13*(11), 1961–1969.

Daníelsdóttir, S., O'Brien, K. S., & Ciao, A. (2010). Anti-fat prejudice reduction: A review of published studies. *Obesity Facts*, *3*(1), 47–58.

Davis, J. N., Hodges, V. A., & Gillham, M. B. (2006). Physical activity compliance: Differences between overweight/obese and normal-weight adults. *Obesity*, *14*(12), 2259–2265.

Desharnais, R., Bouillon, J., & Godin, G. (1986). Self-efficacy and outcome expectations as determinants of exercise adherence. *Psychological Reports*, *59*(3), 1155–1159.

Dimmock, J. A., Hallett, B. E., & Grove, J. R. (2009). Attitudes toward overweight individuals among fitness center employees: An examination of contextual effects. *Research Quarterly for Exercise and Sport*, *80*(3), 641–647.

Donnelly, J. E., Blair, S. N., Jakicic, J. M., Manore, M. M., Rankin, J. W., & Smith, B. K. (2009). American College of Sports Medicine Position Stand: Appropriate physical activity intervention strategies for weight loss and prevention of weight regain for adults. *Medicine and Science in Sports and Exercise*, *41*(2), 459–471.

Donnelly, J. E., Herrmann, S. D., Lambourne, K., Szabo, A. N., Honas, J. J., & Washburn, R. A. (2014). Does increased exercise or physical activity alter ad-libitum daily energy intake or macronutrient composition in healthy adults? A systematic review. *PLoS One*, *9*(1), e83498.

Donnelly, J. E., Jacobsen, D. J., Jakicic, J. M., Whatley, J., Gunderson, S., Gillespie, W. J., . . . Tran, Z. V. (1992). Estimation of peak oxygen consumption from a sub-maximal half mile walk in obese females. *International Journal of Obesity and Related Metabolic Disorders*, *16*(8), 585–589.

Dreher, M., & Kabitz, H. J. (2012). Impact of obesity on exercise performance and pulmonary rehabilitation. *Respirology*, *17*(6), 899–907.

Dunlop, W. L., & Schmader, T. (2014). For the overweight, is proximity to in-shape, normal-weight exercisers a deterrent or an attractor? An examination of contextual preferences. *International Journal of Behavioral Medicine*, *21*(1), 139–143.

Edmunds, J. K., Ntoumanis, N., & Duda, J. L. (2007). Adherence and well-being in obese patients referred to an exercise on prescription scheme: A self-determination theory perspective. *Psychology of Sport and Exercise*, *8*(5), 722–740.

Ekkekakis, P. (2009). Let them roam free? Physiological and psychological evidence for the potential of self-selected exercise intensity in public health. *Sports Medicine*, *39*(10), 857–888.

Ekkekakis, P. (2013). Redrawing the model of the exercising human in exercise prescriptions: From headless manikin to a creature with feelings! In J. M. Rippe (Ed.), *Lifestyle medicine* (2nd ed., pp. 1421–1433). Boca Raton, FL: CRC Press.

Ekkekakis, P., & Dafermos, M. (2012). Exercise is a many-splendored thing but for some it does not feel so splendid: Staging a resurgence of hedonistic ideas in the quest to understand exercise behavior. In E. O. Acevedo (Ed.), *The Oxford handbook of exercise psychology* (pp. 295–333). New York, NY: Oxford University Press.

Ekkekakis, P., & Lind, E. (2006). Exercise does not feel the same when you are overweight: The impact of self-selected and imposed intensity on affect and exertion. *International Journal of Obesity*, *30*(4), 652–660.

Ekkekakis, P., Lind, E., & Vazou, S. (2010). Affective responses to increasing levels of exercise intensity in normal-weight, overweight, and obese middle-aged women. *Obesity*, *18*(1), 79–85.

Ekkekakis, P., Parfitt, G., & Petruzzello, S. J. (2011). The pleasure and displeasure people feel when they exercise at different intensities: Decennial update and progress towards a tripartite rationale for exercise intensity prescription. *Sports Medicine*, *41*(8), 641–671.

Ekkekakis, P., & Petruzello, S. J. (2000). Analysis of the affect measurement conundrum in exercise psychology: I. Fundamental issues. *Psychology of Sport and Exercise*, *1*(2), 71–88.

Ekkekakis, P., Vazou, S., Bixby, W. R., & Georgiadis, E. (2016). The mysterious case of the public health guideline that is (almost) entirely ignored: Call for a research agenda on the causes of the extreme avoidance of physical activity in obesity. *Obesity Reviews*, *17*(4), 313–329.

Ekkekakis, P., & Zenko, Z. (2016). Escape from cognitivism: Exercise as hedonic experience. In M. Raab, P. Wylleman, R. Seiler, A. M. Elbe, & A. Hatzigeorgiadis (Eds.), *Sport and exercise psychology research from theory to practice* (pp. 389–414). London: Academic Press.

Fenzl, N., Bartsch, K., & Koenigstorfer, J. (2014). Labeling exercise fat-burning increases post-exercise food consumption in self-imposed exercisers. *Appetite, 81*, 1–7.

Finucane, M. M., Stevens, G. A., Cowan, M. J., Danaei, G., Lin, J. K., Paciorek, C. J., . . . Ezzati, M. (2011). National, regional, and global trends in body-mass index since 1980: Systematic analysis of health examination surveys and epidemiological studies with 960 country-years and 9.1 million participants. *Lancet, 377*(9765), 557–567.

Flegal, K. M., Carroll, M. D., Kit, B. K., & Ogden, C. L. (2012). Prevalence of obesity and trends in the distribution of body mass index among US adults, 1999–2010. *Journal of the American Medical Association, 307*(5), 491–497.

Flegal, K. M., Kit, B. K., Orpana, H., & Graubard, B. I. (2013). Association of all-cause mortality with overweight and obesity using standard body mass index categories: A systematic review and meta-analysis. *Journal of the American Medical Association, 309*(1), 71–82.

Focht, B. C., & Hausenblas, H. A. (2003). State anxiety responses to acute exercise in women with high social physique anxiety. *Journal of Sport and Exercise Psychology, 25*(2), 123–144.

Focht, B. C., & Hausenblas, H. A. (2006). Exercising in public and private environments: Effects on feeling states in women with social physique anxiety. *Journal of Applied Biobehavioral Research, 11*(3–4), 147–165.

Fogelholm, M., & Kukkonen-Harjula, K. (2000). Does physical activity prevent weight gain: A systematic review. *Obesity Reviews, 1*(2), 95–111.

Fogelholm, M., Kukkonen-Harjula, K., Nenonen, A., & Pasanen, M. (2000). Effects of walking training on weight maintenance after a very-low-energy diet in premenopausal obese women: A randomized controlled trial. *Archives of Internal Medicine, 160*(14), 2177–2184.

Fogelholm, M., Stallknecht, B., & Van Baak, M. (2006). ECSS position statement: Exercise and obesity. *European Journal of Sport Sciences, 6*(1), 15–24.

Foster, G. D., Wadden, T. A., Vogt, R. A., & Brewer, G. (1997). What is a reasonable weight loss? Patients' expectations and evaluations of obesity treatment outcomes. *Journal of Consulting and Clinical Psychology, 65*(1), 79–85.

Franz, M. J., VanWormer, J. J., Crain, A. L., Boucher, J. L., Histon, T., Caplan, W., . . . Pronk, N. P. (2007). Weight-loss outcomes: A systematic review and meta-analysis of weight-loss clinical trials with a minimum 1-year follow-up. *Journal of the American Dietetics Association, 107*(10), 1755–1767.

Fredrickson, B. L., & Roberts, T.-A. (1997). Objectification theory: Toward understanding women's lived experiences and mental health risks. *Psychology of Women Quarterly, 21*(2), 173–206.

Frieden, T. R., Jaffe, H. W., Stephens, J. W., Thacker, S. B., & Zaza, S. (2011). Prevalence of obesity among adults with arthritis: United States, 2003–2009. *Morbidity and Mortality Weekly Report, 60*(16), 509–513.

Gagnon-Girouard, M. P., Bégin, C., Provencher, V., Tremblay, A., Mongeau, L., Boivin, S., & Lemieux, S. (2010). Psychological impact of a "health-at-every-size" intervention on weight-preoccupied overweight/obese women. *Journal of Obesity, 2010*, 928097.

Gallagher, K. I., Jakicic, J. M., Napolitano, M. A., & Marcus, B. H. (2006). Psychosocial factors related to physical activity and weight loss in overweight women. *Medicine and Science in Sports and Exercise, 38*(5), 971–980.

Gellert, P., Ziegelmann, J. P., & Schwarzer, R. (2012). Affective and health-related outcome expectancies for physical activity in older adults. *Psychology and Health, 27*(7), 816–828.

Goldberg, J. H., & King, A. C. (2007). Physical activity and weight management across the lifespan. *Annual Review of Public Health, 28*, 145–170.

Gourlan, M. J., Trouilloud, D. O., & Sarrazin, P. G. (2011). Interventions promoting physical activity among obese populations: A meta-analysis considering global effect, long-term maintenance, physical activity indicators and dose characteristics. *Obesity Reviews, 12*(7), e633–e645.

Greenberg, B. S., Eastin, M., Hofschire, L., Lachlan, K., & Brownell, K. D. (2003). Portrayals of overweight and obese individuals on commercial television. *American Journal of Public Health, 93*(8), 1342–1348.

Greenleaf, C., & Weiller, K. (2005). Perceptions of youth obesity among physical educators. *Social Psychology of Education, 8*(4), 407–423.

Groven, K. S., & Engelsrud, G. (2010). Dilemmas in the process of weight reduction: Exploring how women experience training as a means of losing weight. *International Journal of Qualitative Studies on Health and Well-being, 5*, 2.

Guess, N. (2012). A qualitative investigation of attitudes towards aerobic and resistance exercise amongst overweight and obese individuals. *BMC Research Notes, 5*, 191.

Hansen, B. H., Holme, I., Anderssen, S. A., & Kolle, E. (2013). Patterns of objectively measured physical activity in normal weight, overweight, and obese individuals (20–85 years): A cross-sectional study. *PLoS One, 8*(1), e53044.

Hare, S. W., Price, J. H., Flynn, M. G., & King, K. A. (2000). Attitudes and perceptions of fitness professionals regarding obesity. *Journal of Community Health, 25*(1), 5–21.

Hart, E. A., Leary, M. R., & Rejeski, W. J. (1989). The measurement of social physique anxiety. *Journal of Sport and Exercise Psychology, 11*(1), 94–104.

Hausenblas, H. A., Brewer, B. W., & Van Raalte, J. L. (2004). Self-presentation and exercise. *Journal of Applied Sport Psychology, 16*(1), 3–18.

Hill, J. O. (2009). Can a small-changes approach help address the obesity epidemic? A report of the Joint Task Force of the American Society for Nutrition, Institute of Food Technologists, and International Food Information Council. *American Journal of Clinical Nutrition, 89*(2), 477–484.

Hill, J. O., & Wyatt, H. R. (2005). Role of physical activity in preventing and treating obesity. *Journal of Applied Physiology, 99*(2), 765–770.

Hill, J. O., Wyatt, H. R., Reed, G. W., & Peters, J. C. (2003). Obesity and the environment: Where do we go from here? *Science, 299*(5608), 853–855.

Hills, A. P., Byrne, N. M., Lindstrom, R., & Hill, J. O. (2013). 'Small changes' to diet and physical activity behaviors for weight management. *Obesity Facts, 6*(3), 228–238.

Hills, A. P., Byrne, N. M., Wearing, S., & Armstrong, T. (2006). Validation of the intensity of walking for pleasure in obese adults. *Preventive Medicine, 42*(1), 47–50.

Hulens, M., Vansant, G., Lysens, R., Claessens, A. L., & Muls, E. (2001). Exercise capacity in lean versus obese women. *Scandinavian Journal of Medicine and Science in Sports, 11*(5), 305–309.

Jackson, T., Gao, X., & Chen, H. (2014). Differences in neural activation to depictions of physical exercise and sedentary activity: An fMRI study of overweight and lean Chinese women. *International Journal of Obesity, 38*(9), 1180–1185.

Jensen, M. D., Ryan, D. H., Apovian, C. M., Ard, J. D., Comuzzie, A. G., Donato, K. A., . . . Tomaselli, G. F. (2014). 2013 AHA/ACC/TOS guideline for the management of overweight and obesity in adults: A report of the American College of Cardiology/American Heart Association Task Force on Practice Guidelines and The Obesity Society. *Circulation, 129*(25, Suppl 2), S102–S138.

Johns, D. J., Hartmann-Boyce, J., Jebb, S. A., & Aveyard, P. (2014). Diet or exercise interventions vs combined behavioral weight management programs: A systematic review and meta-analysis of direct comparisons. *Journal of the Academy of Nutrition and Dietetics, 114*(10), 1557–1568.

Jones, F., Harris, P., & Waller, H. (1998). Expectations of an exercise prescription scheme: An exploratory study using repertory grids. *British Journal of Health Psychology, 3*(3), 277–289.

Jones, F., Harris, P., Waller, H., & Coggins, A. (2005). Adherence to an exercise prescription scheme: The role of expectations, self-efficacy, stage of change and psychological well-being. *British Journal of Health Psychology, 10*(3), 359–378.

Katula, J. A., McAuley, E., Mihalko, S. L., & Bane, S. M. (1998). Mirror, mirror on the wall . . . Exercise environment influences on self-efficacy. *Journal of Social Behavior and Personality, 13*(2), 319–332.

King, A. C., Kiernan, M., Oman, R. F., Kraemer, H. C., Hull, M., & Ahn, D. (1997). Can we identify who will adhere to long-term physical activity? Signal detection methodology as a potential aid to clinical decision making. *Health Psychology, 16*(4), 380–389.

King, N. A., Caudwell, P., Hopkins, M., Byrne, N. M., Colley, R., Hills, A. P., . . . Blundell, J. E. (2007). Metabolic and behavioral compensatory responses to exercise interventions: Barriers to weight loss. *Obesity, 15*(6), 1373–1383.

King, N. A., Hopkins, M., Caudwell, P., Stubbs, R. J., & Blundell, J. E. (2008). Individual variability following 12 weeks of supervised exercise: Identification and characterization of compensation for exercise-induced weight loss. *International Journal of Obesity, 32*(1), 177–184.

King, N. A., Hopkins, M., Caudwell, P., Stubbs, R. J., & Blundell, J. E. (2009). Beneficial effects of exercise: Shifting the focus from body weight to other markers of health. *British Journal of Sports Medicine, 43*(12), 924–927.

King, N. A., Horner, K., Hills, A. P., Byrne, N. M., Wood, R. E., Bryant, E., . . . Blundell, J. E. (2012a). Exercise, appetite and weight management: Understanding the compensatory responses in eating behaviour and how they contribute to variability in exercise-induced weight loss. *British Journal of Sports Medicine, 46*(5), 315–322.

King, W. C., Engel, S. G., Elder, K. A., Chapman, W. H., Eid, G. M., Wolfe, B. M., & Belle, S. H. (2012b). Walking capacity of bariatric surgery candidates. *Surgery for Obesity and Related Diseases, 8*(1), 48–59.

Lafortuna, C. L. (2013). Physiological bases of physical limitations during exercise. In P. Capodaglio, J. Faintuch, & A. Liuzzi (Eds.), *Disabling obesity: From determinants to health care models* (pp. 21–38). New York, NY: Springer.

Lawton, R., Conner, M., & McEachan, R. (2009). Desire or reason: Predicting health behaviors from affective and cognitive attitudes. *Health Psychology, 28*(1), 56–65.

Leary, M. R. (1992). Self-presentational processes in exercise and sport. *Journal of Sport and Exercise Psychology, 14*(4), 339–351.

Lee, D. C., Sui, X., & Blair, S. N. (2009). Does physical activity ameliorate the health hazards of obesity? *British Journal of Sports Medicine, 43*(1), 49–51.

Leone, L. A., & Ward, D. S. (2013). A mixed methods comparison of perceived benefits and barriers to exercise between obese and nonobese women. *Journal of Physical Activity and Health, 10*(4), 461–469.

Mancini, D. M., Eisen, H., Kussmaul, W., Mull, R., Edmunds, L. H., Jr., & Wilson, J. R. (1991). Value of peak exercise oxygen consumption for optimal timing of cardiac transplantation in ambulatory patients with heart failure. *Circulation, 83*(3), 778–786.

Manthou, E., Gill, J. M., Wright, A., & Malkova, D. (2010). Behavioral compensatory adjustments to exercise training in overweight women. *Medicine and Science in Sports and Exercise, 42*(6), 1121–1128.

Marchant, D. (2011). Obese individuals and exercise participation. In J. A. Waumsley (Ed.), *Obesity in the UK: A psychological perspective* (pp. 16–25). Leicester, UK: British Psychological Society.

Marcus, B. H., Rossi, J. S., Selby, V. C., Niaura, R. S., & Abrams, D. B. (1992). The stages and processes of exercise adoption and maintenance in a worksite sample. *Health Psychology, 11*(6), 386–395.

Martin Ginis, K. A., Burke, S. M., & Gauvin, L. (2007). Exercising with others exacerbates the negative effects of mirrored environments on sedentary women's feeling states. *Psychology and Health, 22*(8), 945–962.

Martin Ginis, K. A., Jung, M. E., & Gauvin, L. (2003). To see or not to see: Effects of exercising in mirrored environments on sedentary women's feeling states and self-efficacy. *Health Psychology, 22*(4), 354–361.

Martin Ginis, K. A., Prapavessis, H., & Haase, A. M. (2008). The effects of physique-salient and physique non-salient exercise videos on women's body image, self-presentational concerns, and exercise motivation. *Body Image, 5*(2), 164–172.

Marttila, J., Laitakari, J., Nupponen, R., Miilunpalo, S., & Paronen, O. (1998). The versatile nature of physical activity: On the psychological, behavioural and contextual characteristics of health-related physical activity. *Patient Education and Counseling, 33*(Suppl. 1), S29–S38.

Mattsson, E., Evers Larsson, U., & Rössner, S. (1997). Is walking for exercise too exhausting for obese women? *International Journal of Obesity and Related Metabolic Disorders, 21*(5), 380–386.

McAllister, E. J., Dhurandhar, N. V., Keith, S. W., Aronne, L. J., Barger, J., Baskin, M., . . . Allison, D. B. (2009). Ten putative contributors to the obesity epidemic. *Critical Reviews in Food Science and Nutrition, 49*(10), 868–913.

McAuley, P. A., & Blair, S. N. (2011). Obesity paradoxes. *Journal of Sports Sciences, 29*(8), 773–782.

McCaig, D. C., Hawkins, L. A., & Rogers, P. J. (2016). License to eat: Information on energy expended during exercise affects subsequent energy intake. *Appetite, 107*, 323–329.

Melanson, E. L., Keadle, S. K., Donnelly, J. E., Braun, B., & King, N. A. (2013). Resistance to exercise-induced weight loss: Compensatory behavioral adaptations. *Medicine and Science in Sports and Exercise, 45*(8), 1600–1609.

Miller, W. C., & Miller, T. A. (2010). Attitudes of overweight and normal weight adults regarding exercise at a health club. *Journal of Nutrition Education and Behavior, 42*(1), 2–9.

Misquita, N. A., Davis, D. C., Dobrovolny, C. L., Ryan, A. S., Dennis, K. E., & Nicklas, B. J. (2001). Applicability of maximal oxygen consumption criteria in obese, postmenopausal women. *Journal of Women's Health and Gender-Based Medicine, 10*(9), 879–885.

Ng, M., Fleming, T., Robinson, M., Thomson, B., Graetz, N., Margono, C., . . . Gakidou, E. (2014). Global, regional, and national prevalence of overweight and obesity in children and adults during 1980–2013: A systematic analysis for the Global Burden of Disease Study 2013. *Lancet, 384*(9945), 766–781.

O'Brien, K. S., Hunter, J. A., & Banks, M. (2007). Implicit anti-fat bias in physical educators: Physical attributes, ideology and socialization. *International Journal of Obesity, 31*(2), 308–314.

O'Brien, K. S., Puhl, R. M., Latner, J. D., Mir, A. S., & Hunter, J. A. (2010). Reducing anti-fat prejudice in preservice health students: A randomized trial. *Obesity, 18*(11), 2138–2144.

Paxman, J. R., Hall, A. C., Harden, C. J., O'Keeffe, J., & Simper, T. N. (2011). Weight loss is coupled with improvements to affective state in obese participants engaged in behavior change therapy based on incremental, self-selected "small changes". *Nutrition Research, 31*(5), 327–337.

Perri, M. G., Anton, S. D., Durning, P. E., Ketterson, T. U., Sydeman, S. J., Berlant, N. E., . . . Martin, A. D. (2002). Adherence to exercise prescriptions: Effects of prescribing moderate versus higher levels of intensity and frequency. *Health Psychology, 21*(5), 452–458.

Perri, M. G., Martin, A. D., Leermakers, E. A., Sears, S. F., & Notelovitz, M. (1997). Effects of group- versus home-based exercise in the treatment of obesity. *Journal of Consulting and Clinical Psychology, 65*(2), 278–285.

Poon, M. Y., & Tarrant, M. (2009). Obesity: Attitudes of undergraduate student nurses and registered nurses. *Journal of Clinical Nursing, 18*(16), 2355–2365.

Prichard, I., & Tiggemann, M. (2005). Objectification in fitness centers: Self-objectification, body dissatisfaction, and disordered eating in aerobic instructors and aerobic participants. *Sex Roles, 53*(1/2), 19–28.

Prichard, I., & Tiggemann, M. (2008). Relations among exercise type, self-objectification, and body image in the fitness centre environment: The role of reasons for exercise. *Psychology of Sport and Exercise, 9*(6), 855–866.

Puhl, R. M., & Heuer, C. A. (2009). The stigma of obesity: A review and update. *Obesity, 17*(5), 941–964.

Puhl, R. M., & Wharton, C. M. (2007). Weight bias: A primer for the fitness industry. *ACSM's Health and Fitness Journal, 11*(3), 7–11.

Puhl, R., Wharton, C., & Heuer, C. (2009). Weight bias among dietetics students: Implications for treatment practices. *Journal of the American Dietetic Association, 109*(3), 438–444.

Raedeke, T. D., Focht, B. C., & Scales, D. (2007). Social environmental factors and psychological responses to acute exercise for socially physique anxious females. *Psychology of Sport and Exercise 8*(4), 463–476.

Rhodes, R. E., Fiala, B., & Conner, M. (2009). A review and meta-analysis of affective judgments and physical activity in adult populations. *Annals of Behavioral Medicine, 38*(6), 180–204.

Rhodes, R. E., & Nigg, C. R. (2011). Advancing physical activity theory: A review and future directions. *Exercise and Sport Sciences Reviews, 39*(3), 113–119.

Robertson, N., & Vohora, R. (2008). Fitness vs. fatness: Implicit bias towards obesity among fitness professionals and regular exercisers. *Psychology of Sport and Exercise, 9*(4), 547–557.

Ross, R., & Bradshaw, A. J. (2009). The future of obesity reduction: Beyond weight loss. *Nature Reviews Endocrinology, 5*(6), 319–325.

Ross, R., & Janiszewski, P. M. (2008). Is weight loss the optimal target for obesity-related cardiovascular disease risk reduction? *Canadian Journal of Cardiology, 24*(Suppl. D), 25D-31D.

Rukavina, P. B., Li, W., & Rowell, M. B. (2008). A service learning based intervention to change attitudes toward obese individuals in kinesiology pre-professionals. *Social Psychology of Education, 11*(1), 95–112.

Rukavina, P. B., Li, W., Shen, B., & Sun, H. (2010). A service learning based project to change implicit and explicit bias toward obese individuals in kinesiology pre-professionals. *Obesity Facts, 3*(2), 117–126.

Sabin, J. A., Marini, M., & Nosek, B. A. (2012). Implicit and explicit anti-fat bias among a large sample of medical doctors by BMI, race/ethnicity and gender. *PLoS One, 7*(11), e48448.

Sallinen, J., Leinonen, R., Hirvensalo, M., Lyyra, T. M., Heikkinen, E., & Rantanen, T. (2009). Perceived constraints on physical exercise among obese and non-obese older people. *Preventive Medicine, 49*(6), 506–510.

Scheers, T., Philippaerts, R., & Lefevre, J. (2012). Patterns of physical activity and sedentary behavior in normal-weight, overweight and obese adults, as measured with a portable armband device and an electronic diary. *Clinical Nutrition, 31*(5), 756–764.

Schneider, K. L., Spring, B., & Pagoto, S. L. (2009). Exercise and energy intake in overweight, sedentary individuals. *Eating Behavior, 10*(1), 29–35.

Schwartz, M. B., Chambliss, H. O., Brownell, K. D., Blair, S. N., & Billington, C. (2003). Weight bias among health professionals specializing in obesity. *Obesity Research, 11*(9), 1033–1039.

Schwartz, M. B., Vartanian, L. R., Nosek, B. A., & Brownell, K. D. (2006). The influence of one's own body weight on implicit and explicit anti-fat bias. *Obesity, 14*(3), 440–447.

Sears, S. R., & Stanton, A. L. (2001). Expectancy-value constructs and expectancy violation as predictors of exercise adherence in previously sedentary women. *Health Psychology, 20*(5), 326–333.

Segar, M. L., Eccles, J. S., & Richardson, C. R. (2008). Type of physical activity goal influences participation in healthy midlife women. *Women's Health Issues, 18*(4), 281–291.

Segar, M. L., Eccles, J. S., & Richardson, C. R. (2011). Rebranding exercise: Closing the gap between values and behavior. *International Journal of Behavioral Nutrition and Physical Activity, 8*, 94.

Segar, M., Spruijt-Metz, D., & Nolen-Hoeksema, S. (2006). Go figure? Body-shape motives are associated with decreased physical activity participation among midlife women. *Sex Roles, 54*(3–4), 175–187.

Smith, D. W., Griffin, Q., & Fitzpatrick, J. (2011). Exercise and exercise intentions among obese and overweight individuals. *Journal of the American Academy of Nurse Practitioners, 23*(2), 92–100.

Smits, J. A., Tart, C. D., Presnell, K., Rosenfield, D., & Otto, M. W. (2010). Identifying potential barriers to physical activity adherence: Anxiety sensitivity and body mass as predictors of fear during exercise. *Cognitive Behaviour Therapy, 39*(1), 28–36.

Södlerlund, A., Fischer, A., & Johansson, T. (2009). Physical activity, diet and behaviour modification in the treatment of overweight and obese adults: A systematic review. *Perspectives in Public Health, 129*(3), 132–142.

Stevens, M., Lemmink, K. A., van Heuvelen, M. J., de Jong, J., & Rispens, P. (2003). Groningen Active Living Model (GALM): Stimulating physical activity in sedentary older adults; validation of the behavioral change model. *Preventive Medicine, 37*(6), 561–570.

Teachman, B. A., & Brownell, K. D. (2001). Implicit anti-fat bias among health professionals: Is anyone immune? *International Journal of Obesity, 25*(10), 1525–1531.

Teachman, B. A., Gapinski, K. D., Brownell, K. D., Rawlins, M., & Jeyaram, S. (2003). Demonstrations of implicit anti-fat bias: The impact of providing causal information and evoking empathy. *Health Psychology, 22*(1), 68–78.

Thomas, S. L., Hyde, J., Karunaratne, A., Kausman, R., & Komesaroff, P. A. (2008). "They all work . . . when you stick to them": A qualitative investigation of dieting, weight loss, and physical exercise, in obese individuals. *Nutrition Journal, 7*, 34.

Thomas, D. M., Bouchard, C., Church, T., Slentz, C., Kraus, W. E., Redman, L. M., . . . Heymsfield, S. B. (2012). Why do individuals not lose more weight from an exercise intervention at a defined dose? An energy balance analysis. *Obesity Reviews, 13*(10), 835–847.

Thorogood, A., Mottillo, S., Shimony, A., Filion, K. B., Joseph, L., Genest, J., . . . Eisenberg, M. J. (2011). Isolated aerobic exercise and weight loss: A systematic review and meta-analysis of randomized controlled trials. *American Journal of Medicine, 124*(8), 747–755.

Timperio, A., Cameron-Smith, D., Burns, C., Salmon, J., & Crawford, D. (2000). Physical activity beliefs and behaviours among adults attempting weight control. *International Journal of Obesity, 24*(1), 81–87.

Treasure, D. C., Lox, C. L., & Lawton, B. R. (1998). Determinants of physical activity in a sedentary, obese female population. *Journal of Sport & Exercise Psychology, 20*(2), 218–224.

Troiano, R. P., Berrigan, D., Dodd, K. W., Mâsse, L. C., Tilert, T., & McDowell, M. (2008). Physical activity in the United States measured by accelerometer. *Medicine and Science in Sports and Exercise, 40*(1), 181–188.

Tudor-Locke, C., Brashear, M. M., Johnson, W. D., & Katzmarzyk, P. T. (2010). Accelerometer profiles of physical activity and inactivity in normal weight, overweight, and obese U.S. men and women. *International Journal of Behavioral Nutrition and Physical Activity, 7*, 60.

Unick, J. L., Michael, J. C., & Jakicic, J. M. (2012). Affective responses to exercise in overweight women: Initial insight and possible influence on energy intake. *Psychology of Sport and Exercise, 13*(5), 528–532.

Vartanian, L. R., & Novak, S. A. (2011). Internalized societal attitudes moderate the impact of weight stigma on avoidance of exercise. *Obesity, 19*(4), 757–762.

Vartanian, L. R., & Shaprow, J. G. (2008). Effects of weight stigma on exercise motivation and behavior: A preliminary investigation among college-aged females. *Journal of Health Psychology, 13*(1), 131–138.

Vartanian, L. R., Wharton, C. M., & Green, E. B. (2012). Appearance vs. health motives for exercise and for weight loss. *Psychology of Sport and Exercise, 13*(3), 251–256.

Vincent, H. K., Omli, M. R., Day, T., Hodges, M., Vincent, K. R., & George, S. Z. (2011). Fear of movement, quality of life, and self-reported disability in obese patients with chronic lumbar pain. *Pain Medicine, 12*(1), 154–164.

von Ruesten, A., Steffen, A., Floegel, A., van der A. D. L., Masala, G., Tjønneland, A., . . . Boeing, H. (2011). Trend in obesity prevalence in European adult cohort populations during follow-up since 1996 and their predictions to 2015. *PLoS One, 6*(11), e27455.

Wang, S. S., Brownell, K. D., & Wadden, T. A. (2004). The influence of the stigma of obesity on overweight individuals. *International Journal of Obesity, 28*(10), 1333–1337.

Werle, C. O. C., Wansink, B., & Payne, C. R. (2015). Is it fun or exercise? The framing of physical activity biases subsequent snacking. *Marketing Letters, 26*(4), 691–702.

Wiklund, M., Olsén, M. F., & Willén, C. (2011). Physical activity as viewed by adults with severe obesity, awaiting gastric bypass surgery. *Physiotherapy Research International, 16*(3), 179–186.

Williams, D. M., Dunsiger, S., Ciccolo, J. T., Lewis, B. A., Albrecht, A. E., & Marcus, B. H. (2008). Acute affective response to a moderate-intensity exercise stimulus predicts physical activity participation 6 and 12 months later. *Psychology of Sport and Exercise, 9*(3), 231–245.

Williams, D. M., Dunsiger, S., Jennings, E. G., & Marcus, B. H. (2012). Does affective valence during and immediately following a 10-min walk predict concurrent and future physical activity? *Annals of Behavioral Medicine, 44*(1), 43-51.

Wilson, P. M., Rodgers, W. M., Blanchard, C. M., & Gessell, J. (2003). The relationship between psychological needs, self-determined motivation, exercise attitudes, and physical fitness. *Journal of Applied Social Psychology, 33*(11), 2373–2392.

Wilson, T. D., Lindsey, S., & Schooler, T. Y. (2000). A model of dual attitudes. *Psychological Review, 107*(1), 101–126.

Wing, R. R. (1999). Physical activity in the treatment of the adulthood overweight and obesity: Current evidence and research issues. *Medicine and Science in Sports and Exercise, 31*(11 Suppl.), S547–S552.

Wingo, B. C., Baskin, M., Ard, J. D., Evans, R., Roy, J., Vogtle, L., Grimley, D., & Snyder, S. (2013). Component analysis and initial validity of the Exercise Fear Avoidance Scale. *American Journal of Health Behavior, 37*(1), 87–95.

Wingo, B.C., Evans, R.R., Ard, J.D., Grimley, D.M., Roy, J., Snyder, S.W., . . . Baskin, M.L. (2011). Fear of physical response to exercise among overweight and obese adults. *Qualitative Research in Sport, Exercise and Health, 3*(2), 174–192.

Wouters, E. J., van Nunen, A. M., Vingerhoets, A. J., & Geenen, R. (2009). Setting overweight adults in motion: The role of health beliefs. *Obesity Facts, 2*(6), 362–369.

Yoo, J. H. (2013). No clear winner: Effects of The Biggest Loser on the stigmatization of obese persons. *Health Communication, 28*(3), 294–303.

24 Solvitur Ambulando
Exercise and Mental Health Conditions

Kate F. Hays

On nearly a daily basis, we encounter information regarding one or another aspect of mental health. It may be a news report concerning changes in health care accessibility. Perhaps there are yet new headlines regarding the latest challenges or treatment for a prominent public figure. It may be closer to home—a neighbor, friend, or colleague's life challenges. This increased public consciousness has been instrumental in awareness, with the potential for a gradual reduction of stigma surrounding problems in mental health (Angermeyer & Dietrich, 2006).

Mental health issues are increasingly being recognized and accepted as part of the everyday lives of millions of people. In the United States, the most common mental health disorders include anxiety and depression, estimated at 18 percent and 10 percent of the adult population per year, respectively (Kessler, Berglund, Demler, Jin, & Walters, 2005). In addition to the impact on the individuals who are directly affected, mental disorders can impair relationships, capacity for caregiving, and job productivity (e.g., NIMH, 2002).

The primary treatments for mental health conditions, recognized as generally effective, are psychotropic medication and psychotherapy (DeBoer, Powers, Utschig, Otto, & Smits, 2012). A large proportion of people, however, may experience barriers to treatment, do not receive adequate treatment, may not respond well to treatment, or relapse shortly after treatment (DeBoer et al., 2012). Exercise, whether as a treatment in itself or as a complement to or augmentation of other treatments, is receiving increased attention among researchers and practitioners (Blumenthal et al., 2007; Dunn, Trivedi, Kampert, Clark & Chambliss, 2005; Martinsen, 2008; Stathopoulou, Powers, Berry, Smits & Otto, 2006).

The Latin phrase *solvitur ambulando*, or "it is solved by walking," is an apt description of the effectiveness of physical activity in regard to a number of mental health conditions. A long and illustrious history has recognized the salutary effect of exercise in assisting recovery from mental illness, whether as a treatment in and of itself or as a concomitant or adjunct to other treatments. More than 100 years ago, Sigmund Freud held a couple of psychoanalytic sessions, while walking, with composer Gustav Mahler (Feder, 2004). In the 1970s, psychiatrist John Greist and colleagues compared the effectiveness of exercise to psychotherapy. Around the same time, a small number of psychiatrists and psychologists extolled the "positive addictive" qualities of exercise—including therapists exercising with clients (e.g., Glasser, 1976; Johnsgard, 1989; Kostrubala, 1977). Books for practitioners appeared in the 1990s (e.g., Hays, 1999; Leith, 1998). More recently, self-help books have offered research-based information directly targeted to those with mental health conditions (e.g., Baxter, 2011; Otto & Smits, 2011). Although there is a plethora of anecdotes and poorly controlled experimental evidence, it is only within recent years that systematic examination of the effectiveness of exercise in relation to mental health conditions has begun to accumulate. Much of this research is correlational in nature, but some causal relationships are beginning to be elucidated. To that end, animal studies can also help in mapping some of the brain-body mechanisms that may account for the "affective beneficence" of physical activity (Morgan, 1985).

This chapter is designed to explicate the relationship between exercise and mental health conditions through a review of relevant theories and empirical investigations. Generic information is followed by research that addresses specific mental health conditions. Information is presented concerning current understandings of the biopsychosocial reasons for the interaction between exercise and mental health. Competent practice is then articulated. This chapter concludes with some concerns and future directions for research, training, and practice. Although there are clearly psychological components to the interaction between exercise and (a) cognition, (b) weight and weight management, and (c) developmental and lifespan concerns, these issues are addressed in other chapters in this book.

EXERCISE AND MENTAL HEALTH CONDITIONS: THEORY AND RESEARCH

Research with large populations has concluded that there is a significant association between exercise and mental health. In the adolescent and adult population, exercise has been inversely related to anxiety, depression, hostility, and stress (Russell, 2002). Exercise increases health and emotional stability (Craft & Perna, 2004; Paffenbarger, Lee, & Leung, 1994). A meta-analysis of exercise studies among both general and clinical populations concluded that chronic exercise increased energy and decreased fatigue to a larger extent than cognitive-behavioral or drug treatments (Puetz, O'Connor, & Dishman, 2006).

General Well-Being and Mild Stress or Dysthymia

Within the general population, numerous studies regularly report on the mental benefits of physical activity. Research consistently indicates the connection between exercise and both physical and mental well-being (Berger & Tobar, 2011; DeBoer et al., 2012). A large-scale Scottish study of nearly 20,000 community residents, for example, noted the mental health benefits that accrued with even 20 minutes per week of any type of physical activity (Hamer, Stamatakis, & Steptoe, 2008). At higher volume or intensity, Hamer and colleagues (2008) observed a dose-response pattern among the 6 percent self-reporting distress. Experimental research and meta-analyses have both concluded that exercise is a useful method of stress relief, serves a preventive function with regard to clinical symptoms, and promotes the development of resilience or stress hardiness (DeBoer et al., 2012; Landers & Arent, 2007).

Depression

Of the various clinical conditions, research has focused in particular, for over 30 years, on the impact of exercise in relation to depression. Most recently, a Cochrane review of randomized control trials compared exercise to standardized treatment, placebo, or no-treatment conditions for patients diagnosed with depression (Mead, Morley, Campbell, Greig, McMurdo, & Lawlor, 2009). Even single bouts of exercise improved sense of well-being and vigor in patients with major depressive disorder (MDD).

Moving from correlational to causal connections, comparative effects as well as dose-response relationships have been considered. Research at Duke University concerning older adults diagnosed with clinical depression has found aerobic exercise to be as effective as psychotropic medication (sertraline) (Blumenthal et al., 1999; Blumenthal et al., 2007).

Exercise has also been considered as an augmentation treatment in regard to clinical depression. When anti-depressant medication does not result in sufficient symptom remission, physicians typically augment their treatment with further classes or types of medication. The University of Texas Southwestern Medical Center has conducted various research under the TReatment with Exercise Augmentation for Depression (TREAD) program (Trivedi et al., 2011). Moderate or intense daily exercise has shown benefits as effective as an additional medication in the remission of MDD.

In a landmark study addressing the dose-response relationship of exercise in relation to clinical depression, Dunn, Trivedi, Kampert, Clark, and Chambliss (2005) compared the effects of exercise of differing intensity and duration. Over 12 weeks, they found that exercise intensity (7.0 kcal/kg/week or 17.5 kcal/kg/week) but not frequency (3 days/week compared to 5 days/week) affected decreases in depression ratings among the exercise participants. This suggests that a greater intensity of exercise and frequency of at least three sessions per week may be most beneficial in decreasing mild or moderate clinical depression.

Anxiety

Along with clinical depression, anxiety disorders are the most frequently diagnosed clinical conditions (Kessler et al., 2005). Although research regarding exercise among those with anxiety is less robust than in regard to depression, its usefulness has been demonstrated in the general population and among clinical patients as well (DeBoer et al., 2012).

A meta-analysis of exercise in relation to clinical anxiety concluded that exercise training significantly decreased anxiety scores among patients with a chronic illness (including anxiety or depression) (Herring, O'Connor, & Dishman, 2010). The largest effects were noted among participants in programs ranging from 3 to 12 weeks with session length greater than 30 minutes.

Comparing exercise, tricyclic medication, and control (placebo pills) conditions for moderate to severe panic disorder, Broocks et al. (1998) used a randomized control design and found that running resulted in a significant decrease in symptom severity, more effective than placebo although less effective than medication. The dropout rate for exercise, however, was higher than for placebo or medication.

The use of exercise as an adjunct to other forms of treatment for anxiety, both in in-patient and out-patient settings, has been explored in a number of research studies (summarized by DeBoer et al., 2012). As noted below, Hays (2015) has offered a model regarding adjunctive use of exercise in psychotherapy.

Substance Abuse and Other Addictions

Alcohol has long been linked to sport and exercise, whether used as one aspect of spectators' experience or by athletes in various sports as a reward for a hard-fought game or tough race. Along with our everyday observations, a statistical positive correlation between exercise and alcohol consumption has been documented in both collegiate (Martin, Martens, Serrao, & Rocha, 2008) and adult populations (French, Popovici, & Maclean, 2009).

Despite these connections and, perhaps, causal relations, exercise has been used as a method of treatment for addictions. For example, a 12-week moderate-intensity aerobic exercise program, developed as an adjunctive intervention for alcohol dependency, found that physical activity assisted in the maintenance of recovery and decrease in relapse (Brown et al., 2009). In another study, among a community sample of 114 adults who had experienced traumatic events and who used alcohol, those who engaged in vigorous-intensity exercise were less likely to turn to alcohol to cope with their problems. It is notable that light or moderate activity did not serve this same function, however (Medina, Vujanovic, Smits, Irons, Zvolensky, & Bonn-Miller, 2011).

In a series of experiments using drug self-administration with laboratory rats, Smith and colleagues (e.g., Smith & Lynch, 2011) found that aerobic exercise served a protective effect with regard to the development of and recovery from substance use disorders. Impressively, this reduction occurred in relation to the acquisition, maintenance, escalation, binge, and relapse after a period of abstinence with regard to cocaine, amphetamine, and methamphetamine in laboratory rats. Smith and Lynch suggested that exercise may directly decrease substance use by serving as an alternative, non-drug reinforcer and/or may decrease comorbid risk factors typically associated with substance use disorders, such as depression or anxiety.

Post-Traumatic Stress Disorder (PTSD)

In recent years, increased attention has been drawn to the delayed impact of trauma. A survey of physical activity habits of out-patients in a Brazilian program for victims of violence and stress found that there was a significant reduction in physical activity or sport participation following the onset of PTSD (Assis et al., 2008). This decrease in exercise activity among trauma victims has also been noted among college students (Rutter, Weatherill, Krill, Orazem, & Taft, 2013). That exercise may be useful in managing trauma is suggested by research with a community sample of trauma-exposed adults without other psychopathology. One of the characteristic clusters of PTSD, hyperarousal, was inversely associated with vigorous exercise in this sample (Harte, Vujanovic, & Potter, 2015).

Given the nature of combat, with its high likelihood of stress, research has addressed the role and effectiveness of exercise in the military. Self-report regarding extreme military stress suggested that physical fitness of soldiers may buffer stress symptoms and that aerobic fitness was inversely associated with trait anxiety (Taylor et al., 2007). A systematic review of 11 studies of combat veterans noted a number of aspects of physical activity or sport that could address PTSD and enhance well-being (Caddick & Smith, 2014): "Sport and/or physical activity has the potential not only to provide enjoyable and pleasurable experiences for combat veterans, but also to help shape their personal growth and development in the aftermath of combat-acquired disability and/or psychological trauma" (p. 15). Caddick and Smith note that in the studies they reviewed, those interventions that targeted veterans diagnosed with PTSD offered non-competitive activities often associated with therapeutic qualities, whereas those that involved injured or physically disabled veterans focused more on competitive or elite sports.

Serious and Persistent Mental Illness (SPMI)

The financial and human costs of serious and persistent mental illness (SPMI) are staggering, whether in regard to individuals, families, or our society at large. On average, those with SPMI are at greater risk for unhealthy lifestyle behaviors and chronic medical conditions, and their life span is 25 years shorter than those without mental illness:

> It is unclear to what extent this disparity is due to a common underlying health deficit (e.g., a biologic predisposition to poor health), the effects of mental illness (e.g., poor self-care), iatrogenic effects of treatment (e.g., increased risk of diabetes with some antipsychotic medications), or health care disparities for those with mental illness (e.g., their physical complaints may be taken less seriously).
>
> (Perlman et al., 2010, p. 120)

Some of the perceived barriers to physical activity were examined via focus group meetings with a total of 34 low-income, predominantly non-Caucasian agency clients with schizophrenia, psychosis, and mood disorders (McDevitt, Snyder, Miller, & Wilbur, 2006). Among the barriers identified: profound avolition (lack of initiative), anergia (lack of energy), and anhedonia (inability to feel pleasure), each of which is among the defining symptoms of SPMI; medication effects including sedation, lethargy, and weight gain, as well as a sense of vulnerability and lack of neighborhood safety, particularly in the context of being identified as having a mental illness and the stigma surrounding that condition. Despite these constraints, it is notable that all participants saw physical activity as having physical and psychological benefits, including increased energy, decreased stress, distraction from preoccupations, and improved sleep.

Although the effectiveness of exercise has been most widely studied in regard to the treatment of anxiety and depression, its use has been explored with a wide variety of psychopathological conditions. Among hospitalized psychiatric patients, including those with schizophrenia, two separate, well-designed studies noted improved mood and quality of life through the inclusion of physical exercise (Acil, Dogan, & Dogan, 2008; Haworth & Young, 2009). A pilot wellness program designed for veterans with psychiatric disorders and comorbid chronic medical conditions resulted in clinically meaningful and statistically significant changes in emotional health/interpersonal interactions as well as physical health domains (Perlman et al., 2010). A critical review of the literature noted both an increasing trend toward using exercise for patients with psychosis as well as improved mental health outcomes among those patients (Ellis, Crone, Davey, & Grogan, 2007).

Co-occurring Disorders

Although randomized clinical trials (RCTs) often try to be selective regarding particular diagnoses in order to decrease confounding variables, in actuality many clients experience a variety of symptoms and may be treated for a number of interacting disorders. For example, in the population-based study of Brazilian patients with PTSD cited earlier (Assis et al., 2008), three-quarters experienced other disorders along with PTSD. Most common were depression (58%) and anxiety (22%). The fact of co-morbidities suggests that, even if exercise has not been proven effective with one particular disorder, it may be useful within the context of the whole person.

WHY EXERCISE IS EFFECTIVE WITH MENTAL HEALTH CONDITIONS

As in many other fields, the facts regarding exercise efficacy with regard to mental or emotional conditions are considerably more advanced than the understanding of why this causal connection exists. Over the years, many hypotheses have been proposed and, increasingly, both animal and human studies have begun to clarify this complex process. Rather than being due to any one explanation, it is most likely that a number of factors may be involved, including changes in both brain function and psychological or social experiences and attributions.

A number of brain chemicals have been identified that are related to improvement in affect and cognition, whether in healthy subjects or those with specifically identified illnesses. Exercise appears to raise or adjust neurotransmitters, such as serotonin, dopamine, and norepinephrine. Serotonin synthesis is affected by exercise, along with increased thalamic gamma aminobutric acid (GABA) levels (DeBoer et al., 2012). Further, exercise affects such chemicals as brain-derived neurotrophic factor (BDNF), insulin-like growth factor (IGF-1), and fibroblast growth factor (FGF-2). These are elements of brain neuroplasticity, assisting in the maintenance of normal cognitive functioning, mood, and neuronal growth (Baxter, 2011; Ratey, 2008). BDNF has been described as a "crucial biological link between thought, emotions, and movement" (Ratey, 2008, p. 40). With aerobic exercise, BDNF levels increase, at least temporarily, among people both with and without psychiatric conditions (DeBoer et al., 2012). Initial research suggests that there may be a dose-response relationship in regard to exercise intensity (DeBoer et al., 2012).

Various psychological explanations for the relationship between exercise and mental or emotional states have been posited. Among the most widely accepted reasons for this relationship are changes in self-esteem, decreased stress reactivity, distraction, and social connection (Wolff, Gaudlitz, von Lindenberger, Plag, Heinz, & Ströhle, 2011). A sense of mastery or self-efficacy can be strengthened by accomplishing specific physical tasks and meeting particular exercise goals over time (McAuley & Blissmer, 2000). In turn, this can affect self-esteem and generalize to other aspects of one's life. Thus, self-efficacy can be understood as both a predictor and an outcome of exercise (McAuley & Blissmer, 2000). A meta-analysis of controlled studies of the effects of exercise on self-esteem and physical self-perception noted that 78 percent of the studies found positive changes in some aspects of physical self-esteem or self-concept (Fox, 2000). A 16-week aerobic exercise training program for subjects with major depression showed significantly improved self-esteem, equivalent to that obtained with medication or a combination of exercise and medication (Blumenthal et al., 1999).

The physiological similarity of physical activity and anxiety-related symptoms has been used experimentally to reduce fears of anxiety-related sensations (anxiety sensitivity) within a clinical population (Smits et al., 2008). Potentially, then, the positive effects of repeated exposure to somatic sensations similar to those of anxiety, via exercise, may be one of the psychological mechanisms of action (Harte et al., 2015; Smits et al., 2008). It is much like interoceptive exposure, a CBT method used in the treatment of panic disorder in particular (Wolff et al., 2011).

Exercise is regularly prescribed as an antidote to stress and as a method of increasing stress hardiness. Exercise may serve a distraction function, allowing for "time out" from stressors (Leith, 1998). An earlier account suggested that exercise may be a stress inoculator, helping people respond more effectively to psychosocial stressors (Landers & Arent, 2001).

Another important psychological aspect is the interpersonal effect of exercise. Clinical depression often results in decreased interpersonal contact. Thus, exercise involving interaction with others can decrease social isolation, whether that social support is the necessary ingredient or the mediator of other factors (Otto & Smits, 2011). For others, perhaps women overwhelmed by "people demands" in particular, exercise can become a rationale for intentional alone time, offering the opportunity for reflection, self-nurturance, or differentiation (Hays, 1999).

Baxter (2011) suggested that exercise is especially effective with clinical populations because it offers "a reciprocal loop between . . . brain, muscles, and bones" (p. 111). Psychotropic medications begin their activity in the brain stem, moving "up" (the brain function ladder) into the limbic system until reaching the prefrontal cortex. Anti-depressants may initially relieve the physical effects of depression, increasing energy before decreasing negative mood. Psychotherapy, on the other hand, affects mood (in CBT, presumably, affecting the prefrontal cortex and shifting to the limbic system) without necessarily changing how one feels physically. With exercise, a reciprocal loop is activated in the following way: The various brain chemicals affect the prefrontal cortex, shifting one's self-concept (higher-order brain functioning working "down"), while the physical act of exercise affects the bones and muscles, working "up" by increasing the growth of BDNF and decreasing cortisol.

For any particular individual, the interaction and combination of biochemical, physical, and psychological or mental effects may offer the richest explanation. Exercise may also serve as a "gateway" to other changes. From an anecdotal perspective, a person struggling with addictions, for example, may find that joining a bicycle club gives him an alternative early evening activity in the company of other people. His improved mood and sense of self-confidence may further assist him in feeling an increased sense of self-control. As he becomes more physically fit, his taste for cigarettes decreases and his interest in a nutritionally sound diet increases.

Optimal FITT for Mental Health Benefits

Whether in regard to sport performance, fitness, or physical health, considerable information is available regarding optimal frequency, intensity, duration [time], and type (known by the acronym FITT) regarding the physical benefits of exercise (American College of Sports Medicine, 2010; Garber et al., 2011). Over a couple of decades, Berger has been refining a model to describe the relevant exercise characteristics regarding the mental benefits of exercise. This evolving taxonomy overlaps in some ways with physical fitness exercise guidelines, but it is focused on the goal of enhanced subjective well-being. This sense of "feeling good" is characterized by desirable changes in level of arousal, mood (increased positive affect and decreased negative affect), and emotion (Berger & Tobar, 2011).

Berger, Pargman, and Weinberg (2007) suggested that subjective well-being is enhanced if the following characteristics are met: the activity is experienced as enjoyable; the mode involves aerobic conditioning or abdominal, rhythmical breathing; there is an absence or decreased focus on interpersonal competition; the activity is "closed" or predictable; and the frequency is at least three times per week of moderate intensity with a duration of approximately 20–30 minutes.

This framework may be useful as a general structure or guideline to increase positive sense of self. When working with clinical populations, it is important to take into account some specific modifications. Are particular types of exercise or frequency, intensity, or duration of exercise of assistance in dealing with specific emotional problems? This line of research is just beginning to be developed, and attention to level of intensity seems to be especially relevant. Higher-intensity exercise is often perceived as less comfortable within the general population and adherence to exercise is more likely with low or moderate intensity exercise (Buckworth & Dishman, 2007). In an experimental design, young men with less fitness, matched with regard to trait anxiety, experienced decreased anxiety immediately after 20 minutes of light intensity cycling but an increase in anxiety after hard intensity cycling (Tieman, Peacock, Cureton, & Dishman, 2002). On the other hand, both clinical anecdotal and experimental evidence suggests that higher-intensity physical activity may positively affect depression (e.g., Dunn et al., 2005; Hays, 1999; Otto & Smits, 2011) and perhaps anxiety. For individuals with panic disorder, moderate to hard exercise, compared with very light exercise, resulted in fewer panic attacks and decreased anxiety (Esquivel, Díaz-Galvis, Schruers, Berlanga, Lara-Muñoz, & Griez, 2008). Among a community sample with PTSD, vigorous intensity exercise was significantly related to a decrease in hyperarousal (Harte, Vujanovic, & Potter, 2015).

Some research has addressed the issue of the most effective mode or type of exercise in relation to mental health conditions. Most frequently, research in regard to exercise and mental health has used aerobic exercise as the measure of physical activity. Berger's extension of beneficial effects derived from yoga practice underscores the importance of rhythmic, diaphragmatic breathing, perhaps especially in terms of the calming effect that may be experienced by those with anxiety. For others with mental health conditions, various forms of anaerobic exercise, such as weight lifting, can offer shifts in perceived mental or emotional strength as well as serve anxiolytic and affective effects (Arent, Alderman, Short, & Landers, 2007).

In addition to the specific ways in which physical activity may relate to particular clinical syndromes, some of the more generic effects can be relevant to a number of clinical conditions. Robert Thayer (2003) described the effect of exercise as creating a condition of "calm energy." Increased calmness can address anxiety, while increased energy can help counteract depression. Exercise allows enhanced capacity for attention and memory and may be instrumental in, for example, reducing the types of repetitive thought and rumination that at times characterize depression or panic (Otto & Smits, 2011).

EXERCISE AND MENTAL HEALTH CONDITIONS: PRACTITIONER KNOWLEDGE AND SKILLS

Practitioner Training and Role

Practitioners working with people with mental health conditions, especially in the intersection of mental illness and exercise, may take on a variety of roles (Hays, 2015). Ideally, practitioners would have training in both exercise science and psychotherapy. Few formal programs currently exist (Pasquariello, 2011), however, and many therapists end up "prescribing" based on their own personal experience (Rosenblatt, 2012).

Psychotherapists working with clients with regard to the mental benefits of exercise will likely serve in one or another of three roles (Hays, 2015; Hays & Sime, 2014). Most often, they are "consultants" concerning exercise. In this role, the psychotherapist or counselor may offer resources or support to assist the mental health client in understanding, appreciating, and choosing to exercise. Some may actively "prescribe" exercise as part of the treatment model. In addition to recommending exercise, they may serve as or be experienced as "role models" who exercise regularly and directly attest to the importance of physical activity to mental well-being. Finally, the therapist occasionally may participate in physical activity with the client, such that the activity becomes the medium in which the psychotherapy is conducted (DeAngelis, 2013; Hays, 1994).

Some practitioners will have primary training in health psychology, fitness, or athletic therapy. Their knowledge and skills with regard to physical activity may be high but their knowledge of psychopathology and psychotherapy low. These practitioners may find it most useful to work within interdisciplinary settings when encountering clients with mental health needs. Alternatively, they may develop independent collaborative relationships with psychotherapists who are open to informal "team" approaches.

Critical Components for Effective Use of Exercise With People With Mental Health Conditions

When working with clinical populations in regard to exercise, certain factors should be taken into consideration. Most obvious are the requisite ingredients of psychotherapy, such as rapport, relational factors, treatment orientation, and timing of interventions. Similarly, exercise FITT needs to be developed and discussed. It will be important to address the potential impact of physiological side-effects of psychotropic medication, such as weight gain and sluggishness, in planning shifts in physical activity. Additionally, the competent practitioner will find it useful to understand both the literature and applications related to motivational factors and goals, reinforcement, and maintenance of change, while keeping in mind the central value of individual differences.

Motivational Factors

When working with a client, particularly in relation to the development of a new, complex, and self-directed behavior, it is critically important to understand both *why* the client might be interested in change as well as the client's readiness to make that change (Ajzen, 2001).

Clients are most likely to change, that is, begin exercising, if they have intrinsic reason to do so (e.g., "It will help me feel better") as compared with extrinsic reasons, such as "My spouse/parent/therapist thinks I should" (Deci & Ryan, 2002).

The person's readiness to change is also inextricably tied to the process. The well-known transtheoretical or "stage of change" model (Prochaska, Norcross, & DiClemente, 1995) offers a useful framework for both therapist and client: with regard to exercise initiation, is the client pre-contemplative (not even thinking of exercising), contemplating (intending to change within the next six months), preparing (trying it out), or active (meaningfully committed within the past 6 six months)? For each stage of change, certain activities and supports are especially useful and meaningful (Marcus & Forsyth, 2008). In contrast to some other change efforts in which specific processes are most effective at different stages of change, a variety of processes may be useful throughout the initiation of exercise (Marcus, Rossi, Selby, Niaura, & Abrams, 1992).

Related to the "why" of motivation, relevant goals within the change framework are very important. Goals and goal review assist a person in setting direction and being able to evaluate progress (see, e.g., Weinberg & Gould, 2011).

Often, specific issues related to their clinical disorder will need to be addressed when working with clients with mental health conditions. For example, the most obvious and at times dramatic can be the pessimism, hopelessness, and inertia often associated with depression.

Reinforcement, Exercise Adherence, and Maintenance

Another major component of successful behavior change will be various forms of reinforcement of change. In this instance, reinforcement can be most useful if it links the relationship between exercise effects and the targeted symptoms. Keeping a log or record is one way to assist clients in developing intrinsic motivation for exercise. One simple method is a before exercise/after exercise mood rating on a 1 [low mood] to 10 [high mood] scale. This awareness helps clients recognize the "acute," that is, immediate, effects of exercise. Tracking and review also can be instrumental in helping clients appreciate the "chronic" effects of exercise. One of this author's clients provides a striking example of this method: Moderately clinically depressed, she tracked her moods in response to using a treadmill. Although she did not like walking on the treadmill, by seeing visual proof of her pre-post shift in mood, she came to see the utility of this activity in affecting her level of depression.

Exercise initiation can be challenging, for clinical populations no less than the general public (Buckworth & Dishman, 2007). Adherence and, ultimately, maintenance (within the Prochaska et al. framework, exercising for more than six months) may be equally—or more—challenging. In addition to typical recommendations for exercise adherence, with clinical populations it is especially important to take into account patient history and preference (Lin et al., 2005). Critically important awareness and interventions include attention to small but significant changes and review and modification of cognitions and goals (Hays & Sime, 2014; Otto & Smits, 2011; Seime & Vickers, 2006). The application of information concerning lapse and relapse in regard to other behavioral change (e.g., alcohol) (Witkiewitz, & Marlatt, 2004) can be used to anticipate and prepare for lapse and help prevent relapse.

Individualization

All of the components mentioned above are important, but they will be minimally effective if not applied at an individualized level. Evidence-based practice in psychology suggests that optimal practice involves a combination of research, the practitioner's knowledge and expertise, and the client's own characteristics, culture, and preferences in the context of environmental influences (Goodheart, Kazdin, & Sternberg, 2006). With regard to this final practice component, when considering exercise and mental health, it is particularly important to take into account age, gender, gender socialization regarding physical activity, fitness level, and beliefs about exercise.

FUTURE DIRECTIONS

Over the past few decades, increased attention has focused on the important role that exercise can play in treating issues in mental health. We no longer ask *whether* exercise is useful; rather, more nuanced and specific explorations address types and conditions of exercise in relation to particular aspects of mental health or illness. This is an exciting moment for understanding and learning, whether through research, practice, or training.

At the same time, many questions and issues remain. Meta-analyses routinely point to the lack of agreement regarding terminology and the wide variability in research design. Methodologically more-robust research can more adequately address the risks and costs of treatments using exercise. Research should address a number of issues, including the FITT components and their interaction with various types of mental illness. For example, what are the potential mental health benefits of resistance training? How and under what conditions is anaerobic exercise more or less effective than aerobic exercise? What level of intensity and duration affects which clinical conditions, and how does that affect exercise adherence? To what extent can research with non-clinical populations inform practice for clinical populations? What are the similarities and differences between various clinical populations? What are the best methods to address motivation, exercise initiation, and maintenance of physical activity among those with particular emotional problems? What non-specific factors, such as therapeutic contact, therapist-client interaction, social support, and distraction account for which proportion of effects with whom? Issues around perceived exertion, exercise matching with preference, and exercise adherence need further exploration. Greater understanding of brain and intra- and interpersonal mechanisms of effect requires additional work as well.

With regard to practice, two possible options exist regarding this particular knowledge intersection, that is, relevant physical activity in relation to mental health conditions. Preferably, psychotherapists will have training and knowledge regarding (minimally) (a) the physiology of exercise, (b) various types and benefits of physical activity, (c) the current literature on the relationship between exercise and mental health conditions, and (d) issues of motivation and adherence regarding behavior change. Alternatively, psychotherapists can partner with exercise physiologists in planning and monitoring optimal physical activity for specific clients.

Currently, a wide gap exists with regard to practitioner training regarding the mental health benefits of physical activity, specifically in regard to clinical populations. Considering the undisputable fact that exercise is at least correlated with, if not causally related to, effective changes in mental health conditions to a degree comparable with psychotherapy or psychotropic medication, it is baffling that such training is not routinely part of the clinical or counseling curriculum. Although many psychotherapists, whether during or after graduate training, are eager and interested to incorporate aspects of exercise into their practice, little guidance currently exists as to how to do so. Graduate students should not need to fight their way, on an individual basis, to obtain the training needed to incorporate exercise into practice with clients with emotional problems. Programs in exercise science, health psychology, and counseling and clinical psychology should develop ease of access for training across departments. Similarly, post-graduates should be able to obtain training to fill in the gaps in their own knowledge.

Much can be learned from the active involvement of researchers, practitioners, and the learning environment (educational institutions, faculty, and students). Much can be done to facilitate this opportunity to more effectively assist an especially deserving segment of the public.

REFERENCES

Acil, A. A., Dogan, S., & Dogan, O. (2008) The effects of physical exercises to mental state and quality of life in patients with schizophrenia. *Journal of Psychiatric and Mental Health Nursing, 15*, 808–815. doi: 10.1111/j.1365-2850.2008.01317.x

American College of Sports Medicine. (2010). *ACSM's guidelines for exercise testing and prescription* (8th ed.). Philadelphia, PA: Lippincott, Williams & Wilkins.

Angermeyer, M. C., & Dietrich, S. (2006). Public beliefs about and attitudes towards people with mental illness: A review of population studies. *Acta Psychiatrica Scandinavica, 113*, 163–179.

Arent, S. M., Alderman, B. L., Short, E. J., & Landers, D. M. (2007). The impact of the testing environment on affective changes following acute resistance exercise. *Journal of Applied Sport Psychology, 19*(3), 364–378.

Assis, M. A. D., Mello, M. F. D., Scorza, F. A., Cadrobbi, M. P., Schooedl, A. F., Silva, S. G. D., . . . Arida, R. M. (2008). Evaluation of physical activity habits in patients with posttraumatic stress disorder. *Clinics, 63*, 473–478.

Ajzen, I. (2001). Nature and operation of attitudes. *Annual Review of Psychology, 52*, 27–58.

Baxter, J. (2011). *Manage your depression through exercise*. North Branch, MN: Sunrise River Press.

Berger, B. G., Pargman, D., & Weinberg, R. S. (2007). *Foundations of exercise psychology* (2nd ed.). Morgantown, WV: FIT.

Berger, B. G., & Tobar, D. A. (2011). Exercise and quality of life. In T. Morris & P. Terry (Eds.), *The new exercise and sport psychology companion* (pp. 483–505). Morgantown, WV: FIT.

Blumenthal, J. A., Babyak, M. A., Doraiswamy, P. M., Watkins, L., Hoffman, B. M., Barbour, K. A., . . . Sherwood, A. (2007). Exercise and pharmacotherapy in the treatment of major depressive disorder. *Psychosomatic Medicine, 69*, 587–596. doi: 10.1097/PSY.0b013e318148c19a

Blumenthal, J. A., Babyak, M. A., Moore, K. A., Craighead, W. E., Herman, S., Khatri, P., & Krishman, R. (1999). Effects of exercise training on older patients with major depression. *Archives of Internal Medicine, 159,* 2349–2356.

Broocks, A., Bandelow, B., Pekrun, G. A., Meyer, T., Bartmann, U., Hillmer-Vogel, U., & Rüther, E. (1998). Comparison of aerobic exercise, clomipramine, and placebo in treatment of panic disorder. *American Journal of Psychiatry, 155*, 603–609.

Brown, R. A., Abrantes, A. M., Read, J. P., Marcus, B. H., Jakicic, J., Strong, D. R., . . . Gordon, A. A. (2009). Aerobic exercise for alcohol recovery: Rationale, program description, and preliminary findings. *Behavior Modification, 33*, 220–249.

Buckworth, J., & Dishman, R. K. (2007). Exercise adherence. In G. Tenenbaum & R. C. Eklund (Eds.), *Handbook of sport psychology* (3rd ed., pp. 509–536). Hoboken, NJ: John Wiley.

Caddick, N., & Smith, B. (2014). The impact of sport and physical activity on the well-being of combat veterans: A systematic review. *Psychology of Sport and Exercise, 15*, 9–18.

Craft, L. L., & Perna, F. M. (2004). The benefits of exercise for the clinically depressed. *Journal of Clinical Psychiatry, 6*, 104–111.

DeAngelis, T. (2013, September). A natural fit. *Monitor on Psychology*, pp. 56–59.

DeBoer, L. B., Powers, M. B., Utschig, A. C., Otto, M. W., & Smits, J. A. J. (2012). Exploring exercise as an avenue for the treatment of anxiety disorders. *Expert Review of Neurotherapeutics, 12*, 1011–1022.

Deci, E. L., & Ryan, R. M. (Eds.) (2002). *Handbook of self-determination research*. Rochester, NY: University of Rochester Press.

Dunn, A. L., Trivedi, M. H., Kampert, J. B., Clark, C. G., & Chambliss, H. O. (2005). Exercise treatment for depression: Efficacy and dose response. *American Journal of Preventive Medicine, 28*, 1–8. doi:10.1016/j.amepre.2004.09.003

Ellis, N., Crone, D., Davey, R., & Grogan, S. (2007). Exercise interventions as an adjunct therapy for psychosis: A critical review. *British Journal of Clinical Psychology, 46*, 95–111. doi: 10.1348/014466506X122995

Esquivel, G., Díaz-Galvis, J., Schruers, K., Berlanga, C., Lara-Muñoz, C., & Griez, E. (2008). Acute exercise reduces the effects of a 35% CO_2 challenge in patients with panic disorder. *Journal of Affective Disorders, 107*, 217–220.

Feder, S. (2004). *Gustav Mahler: A life in crisis.* New Haven, CT: Yale University Press.

Fox, K. R. (2000). Self-esteem, self-perceptions and exercise. *International Journal of Sport Psychology, 31*, 228–240.

French, M. T., Popovici, I., & Maclean, J. C. (2009). Do alcohol consumers exercise more? Findings from a national survey. *American Journal of Health Promotion, 24*, 2–10.

Garber, C. E., Blissmer, B., Deschenes, M. R., Franklin, B. A., Lamonte, M. J., Lee, I. M., . . . Swain, D. P. (2011). American College of Sports Medicine position stand. Quantity and quality of exercise for developing and maintaining cardiorespiratory, musculoskeletal, and neuromotor fitness in apparently healthy adults: Guidance for prescribing exercise. *Medicine and Science in Sports and Exercise, 43*, 1334–1359.

Glasser, W. (1976). *Positive addiction.* New York, NY: Harper.

Goodheart, C. D., Kazdin, A. E., & Sternberg, R. J. (Eds.). (2006). *Evidence based psychotherapy: Where practice and research meet.* Washington, DC: American Psychological Association.

Hamer, M., Stamatakis, E., & Steptoe, A. (2008). Dose-response relationship between physical activity and mental health: The Scottish Health Survey. *British Journal of Sports Medicine, 43*, 1111–4. doi: 10.1136/bjsm.2008.046243

Harte, C. B., Vujanovic, A. A., & Potter, C. M. (2015). Association between exercise and posttraumatic stress symptoms among trauma-exposed adults. *Evaluation & the Health Professions, 38*, 42–52.

Haworth, J., & Young, C. (2009). The effects of an "exercise and education" program on exercise self-efficacy and level of independent activity in adults with acquired neurological pathologies: An exploratory, randomized study. *Clinical Rehabilitation, 23*, 371–383. doi: 10.1177/0269215508101728

Hays, K. F. (1994). Running therapy: Special characteristics and therapeutic issues of concern. *Psychotherapy, 31*, 725–734.

Hays, K. F. (1999). *Working it out: Using exercise in psychotherapy.* Washington, DC: American Psychological Association.

Hays, K. F. (2015). Let's run with that: Exercise, depression, and anxiety. In M. B. Andersen & S. J. Hanrahan (Eds.), *Doing exercise psychology* (pp. 217–230). Champaign, IL: Human Kinetics.

Hays, K. F., & Sime, W. E. (2014). Clinical applications of exercise therapy for mental health. In J. L. Van Raalte & B. W. Brewer (Eds.), *Exploring sport and exercise psychology* (3rd ed., pp. 209–239). Washington, DC: American Psychological Association.

Herring, M. P., O'Connor, P. J., & Dishman, R. K. (2010). The effect of exercise training on anxiety symptoms among patients: A systematic review. *Archives of Internal Medicine, 170*, 321–331. doi:10.1001/archinternmed.2009.530

Johnsgard, K. W. (1989). *The exercise prescription for depression and anxiety.* New York, NY: Plenum.

Kessler, R. C., Berglund, P. A., Demler, O., Jin, R., Walters, E. E. (2005). Lifetime prevalence and age-of-onset distributions of DSM-IV disorders in the National Comorbidity Survey Replication (NCS-R). *Archives of General Psychiatry, 62*, 593–602.

Kostrubala, T. (1977). *The joy of running.* New York, NY: Pocket.

Landers, D. M., & Arent, S. M. (2001). Physical activity and mental health. In R. N. Singer, H. A. Hausenblas, & C. M. Janelle (Eds.), *Handbook of sport psychology* (2nd ed., pp. 740–765). New York, NY: Wiley.

Landers, D. M., & Arent, S. M. (2007). Physical activity and mental health. In G. Tenenbaum & R. C. Eklund (Eds.), *Handbook of sport psychology* (3rd ed., pp. 469–491). Hoboken, NJ: Wiley.

Leith. L. M. (1998). *Exercising your way to better mental health.* Morgantown, WV: FIT.

Lin, P., Campbell, D. G., Chaney, E. F., Liu, C. F., Heagerty, P., Felker, B. L., & Hedrick, S. C. (2005). The influence of patient preference on depression treatment in primary care. *Annals of Behavioral Medicine, 30*, 164–173.

Marcus, B. H., & Forsyth, L. (2008). *Motivating people to be physically active*. Champaign, IL: Human Kinetics.

Marcus, B. H., Rossi, J. S., Selby, V. C., Niaura, R. S., & Abrams, D. B. (1992). The stages and processes of exercise adoption and maintenance in a worksite sample. *Health Psychology, 11*, 386–395. doi:10.1037/0278-6133.11.6.386

Martin, J. L., Martens, M. P., Serrao, H. F., & Rocha, T. L. (2008). Alcohol use and exercise dependence: Co-occurring behaviors among college students. *Journal of Clinical Sport Psychology, 2*, 381–397.

Martinsen, E. W. (2008). Physical activity in the prevention and treatment of anxiety and depression. *Nordic Journal of Psychiatry, 62* (Suppl. 47), 25–29.

McAuley, E., & Blissmer, B. (2000). Self-efficacy determinants and consequences of physical activity. *Exercise and Sport Science Review, 29*, 85–88.

McDevitt, J., Snyder, M., Miller, A., & Wilbur, J. (2006). Perceptions of barriers and benefits to physical activity among outpatients in psychiatric rehabilitation. *Journal of Nursing Scholarship, 38*, 50–55.

Mead, G. E., Morley, W., Campbell, P., Greig, C. A., McMurdo, M., & Lawlor, D. A. (2009). Exercise for depression. *Cochrane Database Systematic Review, 4*, CD004366. doi: 10.1016/j.mhpa.2009.06.001

Medina, J. L., Vujanovic, A. A., Smits, J. A., Irons, J. G., Zvolensky, M. J., & Bonn-Miller, M. O. (2011). Exercise and Coping-Oriented Alcohol Use among a Trauma-Exposed Sample. *Addictive Behaviors, 36*, 274–277.

Morgan, W. P. (1985). Affective beneficence of vigorous physical activity. *Medicine and Science in Sports and Exercise, 17*, 94–100.

NIMH (2002). *Annual total direct and indirect costs of serious mental illness*. Retrieved from www.nimh.nih.gov/health/statistics/cost/index.shtml

Otto, M. W., & Smits, J. A. J. (2011). *Exercise for mood and anxiety: Proven strategies for overcoming depression and enhancing well-being*. New York: Oxford University Press.

Paffenbarger, R. S., Jr., Lee, I. M., & Leung, R. (1994). Physical activity and personal characteristics associated with depression and suicide in American college men. *Acta Psychiatrica Scandanavia, S 377*, 16–22.

Pasquariello, C. D. (2011). *Let's get physical: The role of physical activity in the training of graduate mental health students* (Unpublished master's thesis). Virginia Commonwealth University, Richmond, VA.

Perlman, L. M., Cohen, J. L., Altiere, M. J., Brennan, J. A., Brown, S. R., Mainka, J. B., & Diroff, C. R. (2010). A multidimensional wellness group therapy program for veterans with comorbid psychiatric and medical conditions. *Professional Psychology: Research and Practice, 41*, 120–127. doi: 10.1037/a0018800

Prochaska, J. O., Norcross, J., & DiClemente, C. (1995). *Changing for good*. New York, NY: Harper.

Puetz, T. W., O'Connor, P. J., & Dishman, R. K. (2006). Effects of chronic exercise on feelings of energy and fatigue: A quantitative synthesis. *Psychological Bulletin, 132*, 866–876.

Ratey, J. J. (2008). *Spark: The revolutionary new science of exercise and the brain*. New York, NY: Little, Brown.

Rosenblatt, A. H. (2012). *Factors related to psychologists' recommendation of physical exercise to depressed clients*. (Unpublished doctoral dissertation). Adler School of Professional Psychology, Chicago, IL.

Russell, W. (2002). Comparison of self-esteem, body satisfaction, and social physique anxiety across males of different exercise frequency and racial background. *Journal of Sport Behavior, 25*, 74–90.

Rutter, L. A., Weatherill, R. P., Krill, S. C., Orazem, R., & Taft, C. T. (2013). Posttraumatic stress disorder symptoms, depressive symptoms, exercise, and health in college students. *Psychological Trauma: Theory, Research, Practice, and Policy, 5*, 56–61.

Seime, R. J., & Vickers, K. S. (2006), The challenges of treating depression with exercise: From evidence to practice. *Clinical Psychology: Science and Practice, 13*, 194–197. doi: 10.1111/j.1468-2850.2006.00022.x

Smith, M. A., & Lynch, W. J. (2011). Exercise as a potential treatment for drug abuse: Evidence from preclinical studies. *Frontiers in Psychiatry, 2*, 82. Published online 2012 January 12. doi: 10.3389/fpsyt.2011.00082

Smits, J. A. J., Berry, A. C., Rosenfield, D., Powers, M. B., Behar, E., Otto, M. W. (2008). Reducing anxiety sensitivity with exercise. *Depression and Anxiety*, 25, 689–699. http://dx.doi.org/10.1002/da.20411

Stathopoulou, G., Powers, M. B., Berry, A. C., Smits, J. A., & Otto, M. W. (2006). Exercise interventions for mental health: A quantitative and qualitative review. *Clinical Psychology: Science and Practice*, 13, 179–193. doi: 10.1111/j.14682-850.2006.00021x

Taylor, M. K., Markham, A. E., Reis, J. P., Padilla, G. A., Potterat, E. G., Drummond, S. P., & Mujica-Parodi, L. R. (2007). *Physical fitness influences stress reactions to extreme military training* (No. NHRC-07-35). San Diego, CA: Naval Health Research Center.

Thayer, R. (2003). *Calm energy: How people regulate mood with food and exercise*. New York, NY: Oxford.

Tieman, J. G., Peacock, L. J., Cureton, K. J., & Dishman, R. K. (2002). The influence of exercise intensity and physical activity history on state anxiety after exercise. *International Journal of Sport Psychology*, 33, 155–166.

Trivedi, M. H., Greer, T. L., Church, T. S., Carmody, T. J., Grannemann, B. D., Galper, D. I, . . . Blair, S. N. (2011). Exercise as an augmentation treatment for nonremitted major depressive disorder: A randomized, parallel dose comparison. *Journal of Clinical Psychiatry*, 72, 677–684. doi:10.4088/JCP.10m06743

Weinberg, R. S., & Gould, D. (2011). *Foundations of sport and exercise psychology* (5th ed.). Champaign, IL: Human Kinetics.

Witkiewitz, K., & Marlatt, G. A. (2004). Relapse Prevention for Alcohol and Drug Problems: That Was Zen, This Is Tao. *American Psychologist*, 59, 224–235. doi:10.1037/0003-066X.59.4.224

Wolff, E., Gaudlitz, K., von Lindenberger, B. L., Plag, J., Heinz, A., & Ströhle, A. (2011). Exercise and physical activity in mental disorders. *European archives of psychiatry and clinical neuroscience*, 261(Suppl 2), 186–191.

25 Exercise Addiction

Michael L. Sachs

Addiction is defined as "continued involvement with a substance or activity despite its ongoing negative consequences" (Donatelle, 2011, p. 192). Addiction is classified by the American Psychiatric Association (APA, 2013) as a mental disorder. Donatelle (2011) notes that, to be addictive, a substance or, in the case of exercise addiction, a behavior, must produce positive mood changes or reduction of pain.

In the light of this definition, addiction to exercise becomes particularly dangerous when a person develops dependence on the exercise behavior to feel normal or to be able to function adequately on a daily basis with no other activity that can replace the exercise in case the person cannot participate in it. Exercise addiction, therefore, is a condition wherein exercisers are addicted to an exercise regimen, and exercise has become the number-one priority in their lives and controls their existence.

This chapter will provide a definition as well as diagnostic elements of exercise addiction, including references for measurement tools for determining whether exercise addiction is present. A variety of counseling strategies for addressing exercise addiction in clients will be offered. These will encompass education, use of role models, and techniques for reducing the amount of exercise in which the client engages, as well as strategies for substituting other activities for some of the time usually spent exercising. While one desires not to be judgmental, the position is taken that addiction to anything, including exercise, is not desirable in that it decreases one's overall quality of life. Therefore, the goal is to move exercise from an addiction to a healthy habit, an important but considered aspect of one's existence.

The concept of addiction to exercise dates back to 1976, with two published works. The first, by William Glasser, entitled *Positive Addiction*, examined activities Glasser considered supportive of a person's psychology and physiology. These activities were meditation and running, and Glasser felt that "many people, weak and strong, can help themselves to be stronger, and an important path to strength may be positive addiction" (p. 11). Second, psychiatrist Thaddeus Kostrubala, in his book *The Joy of Running* (1976), also used the term addiction: "Slow, long distance running is addictive" (p. 140). It should be noted, for those interested in a broader historical perspective, Schreiber and Hausenblas (2015) provide a historical context for the concept of exercise addiction dating back to ancient Greece.

Although there have been occasional attempts to suggest alternative terms, such as exercise dependence (Downs & Hausenblas, 2014; Sachs & Pargman, 1984), the concept of exercise addiction has stuck since the mid 1970s. Indeed, although Downs and Hausenblas use the term "exercise dependence" in their encyclopedia entry in 2014 (as do Petitpas, Brewer, & Van Raalte, 2015), Schreiber and Hausenblas (2015) feature the term exercise addiction boldly on the front cover of their book.

Sachs and Pargman (1984) define exercise addiction as "psychological and/or physiological addiction to a regular regimen of running, characterized by withdrawal symptoms after 24 to

36 hours without the activity" (p. 233). This definition highlights that exercise addiction in general (beyond just addiction to running) includes both psychological and physiological elements. Most "true" exercise addicts will participate six to seven days a week, three to four hours a day. Importantly, when participation is not possible, withdrawal symptoms will be manifest. These may be psychological in nature (e.g., anxiety, restlessness, feelings of guilt, irritability, tension, general crabbiness as Lucy from Peanuts would say) and/or physiological in nature (e.g., bloated feeling, muscle twitching, discomfort, sleeplessness, headaches, and stomachaches). Downs and Hausenblas (2014) confirm some of these components in their definition of exercise dependence as "a craving for leisure-time physical activity that results in uncontrollable and excessive exercise behavior that manifests in physiological (e.g., tolerance) or psychological (e.g., withdrawal) symptoms" (p. 266).

In regards to withdrawal symptoms, if the exerciser is taking a scheduled rest day, one would not expect withdrawal symptoms. However, if the exerciser misses a day, then the withdrawal symptoms would manifest themselves. In most cases, if it is just a day missed, the intensity of the symptoms will be mild to moderate. However, if more than a day or two are missed (perhaps due to injury or severe illness), the symptoms can become more severe.

Hausenblas and Downs (cited in Schreiber & Hausenblas, 2015) suggest a number of criteria for a diagnosis of exercise addiction: tolerance, withdrawal, intention effects, loss of control, time, conflict, and continuance. Individuals with three of these symptoms are seen as being at a less disruptive end of the exercise addiction spectrum. Those with more symptoms are seen as "more entrenched in pathology" (p. 10). Downs and Hausenblas (2014) define these criteria:

tolerance—"need for increased exercise levels to achieve the desired effect, or diminished effects experienced from the same exercise level" (p. 267);

withdrawal—"negative symptoms are evidenced with cessation of exercise, or exercise is used to relieve or forestall the onset of these symptoms" (p. 267);

intention—"exercise is undertaken with greater intensity, frequency, or duration than was intended" (p. 267);

lack of control—"exercise is maintained despite a persistent desire to cut down or control it" (p. 267);

time—"considerable time is spent in activities essential to exercise maintenance" (p. 267);

reduction in other activities—"social, occupational, or recreational pursuits are reduced or dropped because of exercise" (p. 267); and

continuance—"exercise is maintained despite the awareness of a persistent physical or psychological problem" (p. 267).

Exercise addiction may one day make it into the APA's *Diagnostic and Statistical Manual of Mental Disorders*, currently in its fifth edition (*DSM-V*) (APA, 2013). For the moment, the APA states:

> groups of repetitive behaviors, which some term behavioral addictions, with such subcategories as 'sex addiction,' 'exercise addiction,' or 'shopping addiction,' are not included because at this time there is insufficient peer reviewed evidence to establish the diagnostic criteria and course descriptions needed to identify these behaviors as mental disorders.
>
> (p. 481)

DOES ADDICTION HAVE A NEGATIVE CONNOTATION?

While one would think the term "addiction" has a negative connotation, within certain microcultures, such as the running community, this may not be the case. If one were to ask a group of runners if they were addicted to running, many would probably say "yes." Within these communities, being addicted to running is seen as a badge of honor, a prerequisite to being part of this culture. Indeed, the best evidence for this orientation is the Addiction brand running shoe manufactured by Brooks (www.brooksrunning.com, Seattle, WA). Addiction is now in its 11th edition, suggesting a very successful name and design.

ADDICTION OR HEALTHY HABIT

While Glasser (1976) may have popularized the idea of a positive addiction, others have suggested that this is an oxymoron (Morgan, 1979a, b). Specifically, it has been argued that something cannot be an addiction and positive at the same time. Morgan (1979a, b) examined addicted runners and found a number who were consumed by the need to run. They ran when medically inadvisable to do so (e.g., serious injuries) and neglected responsibilities of work, home, and family.

If we agree that one cannot have a positive addiction and that an addiction is negative by definition, then one can think of healthy habits rather than positive addictions. Peele (1981) has suggested that addiction is a pathological habit or dependency. The addiction impairs functioning, and one can no longer make choices. In the case of exercise addiction, the exerciser has lost control—they must exercise, rather than having a choice of doing so. In short, the addiction to exercise consumes the person's life.

On the other hand, healthy habits enhance one's sense of oneself, provide feelings of perceived control, and enhance overall sense of well-being. People with healthy habits typically feel better about themselves, are better able to cope with challenges, and have increased self-esteem (Peele, 1981). As opposed to addictions, healthy habits would be seen as part of a non-addicted lifestyle, characterized by balance and moderation, with the individual having other interests, setting realistic expectations, engaging in appropriate alternatives, and socializing with a network of friends with diverse activities and realms of interests.

There may also be value in considering alternative approaches to considering exercise addiction. In their Dualistic Model of Passion framework, Vallerand et al. (2003) have proposed two distinct types of passions: harmonious passion and obsessive passion. Harmonious passion "results from an autonomous internalisation of the activity into the person's identity. An autonomous internalisation occurs when individuals have freely accepted the activity as important for them without any contingencies attached to it" (Vallerand, 2008, p. 2). Furthermore, "With this type of passion, the activity occupies a significant, but not overpowering, space in the person's identity and is in harmony with other aspects of the person's life. In other words, with harmonious passion the authentic integrating self (Ryan & Deci, 2000) is at play allowing the person to fully partake in the passionate activity with an openness that is conducive to positive experiences (Hodgins & Knee, 2002)" (p. 2).

However, Vallerand (2008) notes:

> People with an obsessive passion can thus find themselves in the position of experiencing an uncontrollable urge to partake in the activity they view as important and enjoyable. They cannot help but to engage in the passionate activity. . . . The passion must run its course as it controls the person. Consequently, they risk experiencing conflicts and other negative affective, cognitive, and behavioral consequences during and after activity engagement.
>
> (p. 2)

Bureau, Razon, Saville, Tokac, and Judge (2017) found that obsessive passion, including exercise addiction, was positively correlated with exercise addiction. Consequently, framing involvement with exercise as a harmonious passion may resonate with some individuals who are addicted to exercise and wish to move toward the healthy habit side of the continuum.

It may also be helpful to consider work that suggests the presence of primary exercise dependence and secondary exercise dependence (Downs & Hausenblas, 2014). In primary exercise dependence, the criteria for exercise dependence are met but exercise is participated in "for the psychological gratification resulting from the exercise behavior" (p. 266). Secondary exercise dependence, on the other hand, "occurs when an exercise dependent individual uses increased amount of exercise to accomplish some other end, such as weight management or body composition manipulation" (p. 266). Exercise addiction/dependence and eating disorders are known to be linked in many cases (Downs & Hausenblas, 2014), and this potential motivation behind the exerciser's participation should be determined.

Interestingly, there has been a relative paucity of books on this topic, although a few book chapters are available (along with some information in exercise and sport psychology textbooks). One potentially valuable book is *Exercise Dependence*, by Kerr, Lindner, and Blaydon (2007). Another is *The Exercise Balance*, by Powers and Thompson (2008). More recently, an excellent book by Schreiber and Hausenblas (2015), entitled *The Truth About Exercise Addiction*, may also be useful in further exploration of exercise addiction. Of book chapters, the earliest chapter is the one by Sachs and Pargman (1984), with more recent ones by Downs and Hausenblas (2014) and Petitpas at al. (2015). Other books and book chapter address exercise addiction and relevant case studies only in passing but could nevertheless prove beneficial (Acevedo, 2012; Anshel, 2016; Brewer & Petrie, 2014; Petitpas et al., 2015; Reel, 2015).

MEASURING EXERCISE ADDICTION

In regards to the measurement of exercise addiction, the first scale of exercise addiction focused on running. The "Feelings about Running" scale was developed by Mary Ann Carmack and Rainer Martens in 1979. Informal quizzes are also available (see Prussin, Harvey, & DiGeronimo, 1992), as well as a number of valid and reliable instruments, including the Exercise Dependence Scale (Schreiber & Hausenblas, 2015) and the Exercise Addiction Inventory (Terry, Szabo, & Griffiths, 2004). An open-ended intake or interview also presents unique benefits in confirming whether addiction is present and is therefore highly recommended within clinical settings.

COUNSELING STRATEGIES FOR ADDRESSING EXERCISE ADDICTION

First and foremost, it may be helpful to understand the relationship of the individual to exercise and the function exercise serves for the person. Is exercise a means toward health optimization, physically and psychologically? Is it a coping strategy for challenges the individual faces in daily life? Does it serve some other purpose? Motivational Interviewing may be helpful in working with individuals who are addicted to exercise (see Chapter 32 in this volume; see also Breckon, 2015; Clifford & Curtis, 2016). Developed by Stephen Rollnick and William Miller (1995), motivational interviewing is a communication style used in brief interventions. This is a "softer, gentler" approach to asking questions to evoke thoughts toward making changes in behavior. It is more of a "guiding" style of communication, rather than a directing style. Its purpose is to elicit change talk in individuals who suffer from addiction and are ambivalent about making behavior change.

Once one identifies addiction, the first step in addressing it is education. To that end, a case can be made that addiction to anything, wherein the person is consumed by a substance or activity, is not desirable. Beginning with this assumption, educating the individual on the nature of addiction in general, and exercise addiction in particular, is needed. We often find that individuals start exercising as a healthy habit. As they become more and more involved, for a variety of reasons (e.g., personal development, competitiveness, sense of achievement), they may start engaging in it more often, to the point where the exercise behavior may take over their lives and control them.

To that end, education can provide the individual with information about the definition and parameters of exercise addiction, and may be instrumental in initiating a process of self-reflection, wherein the person rethinks and considers their relationship with exercise. Does the person want to be controlled by exercise or be in control of it (as in healthy habits)? If the person chooses being controlled, as in exercise addiction, then the practitioner may have to honor that decision, making sure the individual understands the ramifications of it. Exploring the meaning of exercise for the individual may also be helpful, as part of a broader therapeutic process in which the individual is actively engaged. While potentially challenging, with the use of some strategies (described below), moving back along the continuum from addiction to healthy habit can certainly be accomplished.

Individuals of all ages may become addicted to exercise and could benefit from education. There are a number of books that may be helpful as part of a strategic approach known as bibliotherapy, wherein books are used as part of a therapeutic intervention. For adults, an excellent book by Prussin at al. (1992) may be helpful, as well a more recent book by Powers and Thompson (2008). For adolescents, Kaminker's work (1998, 1999) in the Teen Health Library of Eating Disorder Prevention series and Johnson's book (2000) in the Teen Eating Disorder Prevention series may prove particularly useful.

Other approaches can include the use of role models. Identifying individuals (perhaps with whom one has worked in the past and who are willing to share their experiences with others) who could serve as role models and talk about their experiences of coming back from addiction to a healthy habit can present unique benefits. There are numerous books by and about individuals who have dealt with exercise addition, as well as about the use of exercise for overcoming addiction (Crandell & Hanc, 2006; David, 2009; Friedman, 2009; Pipes, 2015; Skupien, 2006), and some of these could be of help. Finally, more recently, Schreiber and Hausenblas (2015) provide compelling "true stories" (p. 77) of exercise addicts that may resonate with some exercisers dealing with the same or similar issues.

Of more specific approaches, an essential one remains to provide the exercisers with techniques for reducing the amount of exercise in which they engage, as well as strategies for substituting other activities for some of the time usually spent exercising. This may involve developing a behavior change contract that outlines the changes to be made. For example, consider the case of an individual who is running three days a week and swimming three days a week and wishes to decrease from six days a week to five. The person could be advised to take one day off from swimming and switch to another activity, perhaps engaging in a household task on the person's to-do list, for the period of time that is typically spent swimming. A sample behavioral contract is provided in Appendix A, adapted from Donatelle (2011) by Nolt (K. Nolt, personal communication, February 14, 2017).

Although exercise addiction is not included in the *DSM-V*, the stereotypical/classic exercise addict is thought of as exercising six to seven days a week, two to three hours a day (or more). Therefore, dropping a day, as with the case example above, may not be as desirable as decreasing the time spent on one or more days. In regards to activities to substitute for the exercise behavior, "fun" alternatives, such as spending time with family and friends, can help reduce the time otherwise spent exercising. These activities may or may not include a physical activity component. Examples can include playing with one's children at the park or playground, going to the movies, reading a book, or playing chess. Nevertheless, regardless of the amount of activity involved, the focus should remain on moving the individual from an exercise framework to a recreational/leisure pursuit. The practitioner should remain cognizant that each individual is different, and programs will need to be designed to meet the specific needs of each individual.

In regards to a behavioral contract, a formal or informal contract can be developed with the idea that writing everything down presents its advantages. Specifically, once put into writing, one has a written reminder of the choice one has made, as well as a place where one can monitor and check off one's weekly commitment levels and goals. After a certain time interval, nearing a few weeks or a month, the effectiveness of the contract for behavior change can be reassessed and its content can be modified. Special emphasis should be placed upon the inquiry of whether the addiction decreased sufficiently to become a healthy habit, or is further action required? These contracts are most effective when a reward structure including positive reinforcements has been set in place for achieving certain specified outcomes.

Additionally, in cases where exercise serves as an avoidance behavior, Prussin et al. (1992) recommend helping individuals identify their stress triggers, gradually develop coping skills, and use various stress management techniques to cope with the stress that results in the avoidance behavior of exercise. More recently, Schreiber and Hausenblas (2015) identified a variety of treatment options for exercise addiction, including "cognitive behavioral therapy (CBT), acceptance and commitment therapy (ACT), medication, and alternative approaches such as nutraceuticals, mindfulness practices, and a more intuitive and natural approach to keeping fit" (p. 121). Similarly, Petitpas et al. (2015) discuss various approaches that might be effective, particularly through the lens of the biopsychosocial model—"Considering exercise dependence to be the potential product of multiple interacting biological, psychological, and social factors offers an abundance of opportunities for assessments and interventions" (p. 277).

EXERCISE ADDICTION/DEPENDENCE

Distinguishing between addiction and dependence could be useful at this point. While these terms were noted earlier in this chapter, addiction has a specific *DSM-V* definition. Dependence, on the other hand, is seen as a more general term. In cases where the person's involvement with exercise is truly an addiction, a licensed psychologist, mental health counselor, clinical social worker, or psychiatrist would be needed to provide treatment. Exercise psychologists who are not also licensed in clinical/counseling psychology should collaborate with others who are licensed to avoid working outside the ethical scope of practice.

CONCLUSION

In conclusion, exercise addiction is a real condition experienced by a small but still considerable number of regular exercisers. Some may feel comfortable with being addicted to exercise and may even see their addiction as a badge of honor. But most exercisers would prefer not to be addicted/controlled and would prefer to have exercise as a healthy habit. There are approaches, as indicated above, that one can take that will be effective in working with these individuals. Most importantly, though, regardless of what one decides to do, remember that exercise should be fun.

REFERENCES

Acevedo, E. (2012). Exercise psychology: Understanding the mental health benefits of physical activity and the public health challenges of inactivity. In E. O. Acevedo (Ed.), *The Oxford handbook of exercise psychology* (pp. 3–8). New York, NY: Oxford University Press.

American Psychiatric Association (APA). (2013). *Diagnostic and statistical manual of mental disorders—DSM-5* (5th ed.). Washington, DC: American Psychiatric Publishing.

Anshel, M. H. (2016). *Intervention strategies for changing health behavior.* New York, NY: Routledge.

Breckon, J. (2015). Motivational interviewing, exercise, and nutrition counseling. In M. B. Andersen & S. J. Hanrahan (Eds.), *Doing exercise psychology* (pp. 75–100). Champaign, IL: Human Kinetics.

Brewer, B. W., & Petrie, T. A. (2014). Psychopathology in sport and exercise. In J. L. Van Raalte & B. W. Brewer (Eds.), *Exploring sport and exercise psychology* (3rd ed.), (pp. 311–335). Washington, DC: American Psychological Association.

Bureau, A. T., Razon, S., Saville, B. K., Tokac, U., & Judge, L. W. (2017). Passion for academics and problematic health behaviors. *International Journal of Exercise Science, 10*(3), 417–433.

Clifford, D., & Curtis, L. (2016). *Motivational interviewing in nutrition and fitness.* New York, NY: The Guilford Press.

Crandell, T., & Hanc, J. (2006). *Racing for recovery: From addict to ironman.* Halcottsville, NY: Breakaway Books.

David, M. (2009). *The addicted runner.* Chandler, AZ: Marc David.

Donatelle, R. (2011). Addiction and drug abuse. In *Health—The basics* (green ed., pp. 191–192). San Francisco: Pearson Education.

Downs, D. S., & Hausenblas, H. (2014). Exercise dependence. In R. C. Eklund & G. Tenenbaum (Eds.), *Encyclopedia of sport and exercise psychology* (Vol. 1, pp. 266–269). Thousand Oaks, CA: Sage Publications.

Friedman, P. (2009). *Diary of an exercise addict.* Guilford, CT: The Globe Pequot Press.

Glasser, W. (1976). *Positive addiction.* New York, NY: Harper and Row.

Hodgins, H. S., & Knee, C. R. (2002). The integrating self and conscious experience. *Handbook of self-determination research,* 87–100.

Johnson, M. (2000). *Understanding exercise addiction.* New York, NY: The Rosen Publishing Group, Inc.

Kaminker, L. (1998). *Exercise addiction: When fitness becomes an obsession.* New York, NY: The Rosen Publishing Group, Inc. (hardcover edition)

Kaminker, L. (1999). *Exercise addiction: When fitness becomes an obsession.* New York, NY: The Rosen Publishing Group, Inc. (paperback edition)

Kerr, J. H., Lindner, K. J., & Blaydon, M. (2007). *Exercise dependence.* London: Routledge.

Kostrubala, T. (1976). *The joy of running.* Philadelphia: J. B. Lippincott.

Morgan, W. P. (1979a). Negative addiction in runners. *Physician and Sports Medicine, 7*(2), 56–63, 67–70.

Morgan, W. P. (1979b). Running into addiction. *Runner, 1*(6), 72–74, 76.

Peele, S. (1981). *How much is too much: Healthy habits or destructive addictions.* Englewood Cliffs, NJ: Prentice-Hall.

Petitpas, A. J., Brewer, B. W., & Van Raalte, J. L. (2015). Exercise dependence: Too much of a good thing. In M. B. Andersen & S. J. Hanrahan (Eds.), *Doing exercise psychology* (pp. 275–285). Champaign, IL: Human Kinetics.

Pipes, K. (2015). *The do over: My journey from the depths of addiction to world champion swimmer.* Honolulu, HI: Aquatic Edge Inc.

Powers, P., & Thompson, R. (2008). *The exercise balance: What's too much, what's too little, and what's just right for you!* Carlsbad, CA: Gurze.

Prussin, R., Harvey, P., & DiGeronimo, T. F. (1992). *Hooked on exercise: How to understand and manage exercise addiction.* New York, NY: Simon & Schuster.

Reel, J. (2015). *Working out: The psychology of sport and exercise.* Santa Barbara, CA: Greenwood.

Rollnick, S., & Miller, W. R. (1995). What is motivational interviewing? *Behavioural and Cognitive Psychotherapy, 23*(4), 325–334.

Ryan, R. M., & Deci, E. L. (2000). Intrinsic and extrinsic motivations: Classic definitions and new directions. *Contemporary Educational Psychology, 25*(1), 54–67.

Sachs, M. L., & Pargman, D. (1984). Running addiction. In M. L. Sachs and G. W. Buffone (Eds.), *Running as therapy: An integrated approach* (pp. 231–252). Lincoln, NE: University of Nebraska Press.

Schreiber, K., & Hausenblas, H. A. (2015). *The truth about exercise addiction*. Lanham, MD: Rowman & Littlefield.

Skupien, S. (2006). *Wired to run: The runaholics guide to living with running addiction*. Kansas City, MO: Andrews McMeel Publishing, LLC.

Terry, A., Szabo, A., & Griffiths, M. A. (2004). The exercise addiction inventory: A new brief screening tool. *Addiction Research and Theory, 12*, 489–499.

Vallerand, R. J. (2008). On the psychology of passion: In search of what makes people's lives most worth living. *Canadian Psychology, 49*, 1–13.

Vallerand, R. J., Blanchard, C., Mageau, G. A., Koestner, R., Ratelle, C., Léonard, M., . . . Marsolais, J. (2003). Les passions de l'aˆme: On obsessive and harmonious passion. *Journal of Personality and Social Psychology, 85*, 756–767.

APPENDIX A

Behavior Change Contract

Choose a health behavior that you would like to change, and complete the contract below. Sign the contract at the bottom to affirm your commitment to making a healthy change, and ask a friend to witness it. Select a reward that is reasonable and avoids creating obstacles to success.

My behavior change will be:

_____

My long-term goal for this behavior change is:

_____

These are three obstacles to change (things that I am currently doing or situations that contribute to this behavior or make it harder to change):

1. _____
2. _____
3. _____

The strategies I will use to overcome these obstacles are:

1. _____
2. _____
3. _____

Resources I will use to help me change this behavior include:

a friend/partner/relative: _____
a school-based resource: _____
a community-based resource: _____
a book or reputable website: _____

In order to make my goals more attainable, I have devised these short-term goals:

_____	_____	_____
short-term goal	target date	reward
_____	_____	_____
short-term goal	target date	reward

When I make the long-term behavior change described above, my reward will be:

_____ target date: _____

I intend to make the behavior change described above. I will use the strategies and rewards to achieve the goals that will contribute to a healthy behavior change.

Signed: _____   Witness: _____

Print Name: _____

26 Persons With Exercise Injuries

Monna Arvinen-Barrow and Damien Clement

The benefits of engaging in sport and exercise (e.g., Molina-Garcia, Castillo, & Queralt, 2011) are well known; however, with this participation also comes an increased risk of injury. Thus far, musculoskeletal injuries are identified as the most commonly reported adverse effect of exercise (e.g., Hootman et al., 2002; Janney & Jakicic, 2010) and appear to occur for a range of reasons. These reasons are typically classified into five main categories: (1) inappropriate exercise prescription, (2) faulty execution of movement, (3) personal psychological attributes or states (e.g., body image, perception about self), (4) subconscious factors (i.e., psychodynamic forces that underlie our thoughts, emotions, and behaviors), and (5) environmental factors (e.g., surface, weather, other participants, audience; Berger, Pargman, & Weinberg, 2007, p. 186).

A number of personal and situational factors are also potentially influential in increasing the risk of encountering an exercise-related injury. The most prominently identified personal factors that have been found to have an adverse effect on injury occurrence include history of previous injuries (e.g., Colbert, Hootman, & Macera, 2000; Hootman et al., 2002), higher body mass index (Janney & Jakicic, 2010), higher levels of fitness (Colbert et al., 2000; Hootman et al., 2002; Hootman et al., 2001), and age (Finch, Owen, & Price, 2001). As we age, both the risk of injury and the subsequent healing time will increase (Finch et al., 2001). In addition, situational factors, such as time, activity type, and activity intensity, have been found to effect injury susceptibility. The more time an individual spends on an activity, the greater the likelihood of injury risk will be. Hootman et al. (2001) have argued that spending more than 1.25 hours a week on exercise is considered a risk factor for injury susceptibility. It has also been found that in comparison to low-intensity activities (e.g., walking), more intensive and vigorous activities (e.g., running and jogging) pose higher risk of injury (Berger et al., 2007; Colbert et al., 2000; Hootman et al., 2002; Hootman et al., 2001).

Thus far, research investigating the prevalence of exercise injuries is limited. The most current available population data (albeit somewhat dated) have shown that in the United States during a one year period, approximately 20.3 million people encountered a sport and exercise–related injury, half of which required medical attention (Conn, Annest, & Gilchrist, 2003). In the UK, two million sport and exercise–related incidents occur annually (Nicholl, Coleman, & Williams, 1995), accounting for nearly one third of all injuries nationwide (Uitenbroek, 1996). These numbers are likely not to be a true reflection of all exercise-related injuries, as (1) exercise injury statistics are typically combined with sport injury statistics, with great differences in reporting methods (e.g., Burt & Overpeck, 2001; Carlson et al., 2006; Uitenbroek, 1996), and (2) due to the varied nature of exercise injuries, it is likely that not all exercise injuries are treated by medical professionals and as such may go unreported or even undetected. Indeed, it has been stated that approximately 75 percent of all people with exercise injuries will not seek treatment for their injuries (Nicholl et al., 1995).

Injuries experienced in sport and exercise contexts will have consequences that effect more than the physical area of trauma (Taylor, Stone, Mullin, Ellenbecker, & Walgenbach, 2003). In addition to obvious physical and functional impairments, sport and exercise injuries will typically have psychosocial consequences that, if not addressed appropriately, can influence an individual's rehabilitation and return to participation outcomes (Brewer, Andersen, & Van Raalte, 2002; Wiese-Bjornstal, Smith, Shaffer, & Morrey, 1998). Indeed, physiotherapists treating injuries at different levels of sport participation (recreational to international) have suggested that all injured athletes are psychologically affected by their injuries (Arvinen-Barrow, Hemmings, Weigand, Becker, & Booth, 2007). A number of psychological factors have also been found as instrumental in defining successful coping with the sport-related injury and its subsequent rehabilitation. Athletes who (1) have the ability to maintain a positive attitude (toward the injury and rehabilitation), (2) exhibit less negative mood (i.e., stress, anxiety, anger, depression), and (3) engage in positive rehabilitation behaviors (i.e., adherence/comply better with rehabilitation) are more likely to cope successfully with their injuries than those with opposite characteristics (Arvinen-Barrow et al., 2007; Clement, Granquist, & Arvinen-Barrow, 2013; Heaney, 2006; Hemmings & Povey, 2002).

The above factors are also important when considering individuals' psychological reactions to exercise injuries. Habitual exercisers consider their participation in exercise activities as low risk with regards to injury (Finch, Otago, White, Donaldson, & Mahoney, 2011) and often use exercise as a means of alleviating daily stressors (e.g., American Psychological Association, 2011; Cairney, Kwan, Veldhuizen, & Faulkner, 2014). When injured, habitual exercisers are likely to experience a sense of loss of their daily routines and self, which in itself can become a stressor and trigger additional psychological consequences. As such, they may be highly motivated to return back to participation quickly (Taylor et al., 2003), causing high levels of adherence to their rehabilitation and therefore facilitating quick recovery and return to activity. Equally, if habitual exercisers consider exercising as a big part of their identity (Whaley & Ebbeck, 2002; Yin & Boyd, 2000), there is the possibility that they may do too much during rehabilitation, or may even downplay their injuries and continue to participate, both of which can have significant negative effects on recovery outcomes and return to participation.

In a similar manner, if an injury is sustained by an individual for whom exercise is a recently adopted behavior, injury may also have significant psychosocial consequences that extend far beyond the injury and rehabilitation. For example, if the individual has not yet experienced the positive impact of exercise, and their motivation to exercise is driven by mainly external factors (i.e., for a reward or out of necessity), experiencing an exercise-related injury could be a reason to stop exercising. Sustaining an injury is frequently reported as one of the main reasons why individuals choose to cease involvement in a particular physical activity (Hootman et al., 2002), and it is often their psychological reactions to the injury that influence whether or not they will resume exercise after injury recovery (Hargreaves & Waumsley, 2013).

To date, limited research has examined the impact of injury among exercisers and physically active populations (Hargreaves & Waumsley, 2013). Within such constraints, this chapter will draw from relevant psychological theories and research with the goal of providing insight into the factors affecting persons with exercise injuries journey from motivation to adherence. Specifically, it will initially introduce key definitions, concepts, and relevant theoretical foundations for understanding individuals' reactions to exercise-related injury. The chapter will also discuss the existing research pertaining to individuals' psychological reactions to exercise injuries. Moreover, it will evaluate research to date in relation to individuals' readiness for post-injury behavior change required to maintain motivation during rehabilitation and subsequent return to physical activity. This will be followed by examples of evidence-based practice and suggestions for future research and practice. In essence, this chapter aims to provide theoretical frameworks on, and practical solutions for, the psychological process of exercise injury. By doing so, the chapter hopes to gain a better understanding of (a) individuals' reactions to injury and rehabilitation and (b) how to motivate individuals with exercise injuries throughout the process or rehabilitation, as well as facilitate a safe return to activity after injury and rehabilitation.

KEY DEFINITIONS AND CONCEPTS

With the aim of easing the navigation throughout the chapter, some of the key definitions and concepts are introduced here.

Adherence

How researchers define adherence can vary depending on the overall area in which it is used. For example, in exercise psychology, "[a]dherence refers to maintaining an exercise regimen for a prolonged period of time. . . . Central to adherence is the assumption that the individual voluntarily and independently chooses to engage in the activity" (Lox, Martin Ginis, & Petruzzello, 2006; cited in Granquist & Brewer, 2013, p. 41). Such a definition can be applied to injury rehabilitation, with the exception that there is also a need to include a short-term motivational component to the definition, as the aim of any rehabilitation program is to get better and get back to pre-injury functionality and fitness. For the purposes of this chapter, we will adopt a definition from sport injury rehabilitation literature in which "adherence is seen as the extent to which an individual completes behaviors as part of a treatment regimen designed to facilitate recovery from injury" (Granquist & Brewer, 2013, p. 42).

Exercise Injury

Given that there are number of ways in which sport and exercise injuries are classified, it is imperative to provide a framework for how injuries are defined in this chapter. In epidemiological context, exercise injury has been defined as a "physical damage that requires medical evaluation and/or diagnosis that results in loss or restricted participation in normal exercise endeavors" (Macera & Wooten, 1994, p. 425). In exercise psychology literature, however, the definitions have been broader since exercise injury is seen as "trauma to the body or its parts that result in at least temporary, but sometimes permanent physical disability and inhibition of motor function" (Berger et al., 2007, p. 186)[2]. For the purposes of this chapter, we will adopt a definition that encompasses both of the definitions above: exercise injuries are seen as a trauma to the body that result in at least temporary, but sometimes permanent physical disability/motor function and a loss or restricted participation in normal exercise endeavors.

Motivation

In the sport and exercise psychology literature, motivation has been defined as "the direction and intensity of one's effort" (Sage, 1977; cited in Weinberg & Gould, 2011, p. 51). In a simplistic way, the intensity and effort an individual is willing to invest in any given activity (be it physical activity or exercise, or exercise injury rehabilitation–related activities) can vary greatly depending on whether their sources of motivation are extrinsic (i.e., participation is seen as means to an end, such as receiving a reward and not for the activity's own sake; Vallerand, 2004) or intrinsic (i.e., participation is related to receiving personal pleasure from engaging in the activity; Vallerand & Losier, 1999).

THEORETICAL FRAMEWORKS

Using a theoretical model as a foundation when making sense of an exercise injury experience can help researchers, educators, and applied practitioners gain greater insights into how an individual may react to exercise injury, the subsequent rehabilitation, and return to activity. In the absence of exercise injury–specific literature, theoretical frameworks from both psychology of sport injury and sport and exercise psychology literature in general are important to consider. To this end, first, the integrated model of psychological response to the sport injury and rehabilitation process (Wiese-Bjornstal et al., 1998) will be introduced to provide readers with contextual background as to how individuals potentially respond psychologically upon sustaining an injury. Second, the transtheoretical model of behavior change (Prochaska & DiClemente, 1983) will be presented to facilitate an increased understanding of the thoughts and behaviors individuals may engage in when they transition into an injury rehabilitation program and post-injury activity after sustaining and recovering from an exercise injury.

Integrated Model of Psychological Response to the Sport Injury and Rehabilitation Process

The integrated model of psychological response to the sport injury and rehabilitation process (Wiese-Bjornstal et al., 1998; from now on, referred to as the integrated model) is a stress-process–based model that aims to explain the psychological processes that occur prior to sport injury, following injury, and during rehabilitation. By adopting the work of Andersen and Williams (1988), the integrated model proposes that injury occurrence is often a result of unfavorable physical and psychological reaction to a stressful situation, which is mediated by three psychosocial antecedents: the individual's personality factors (e.g., anxiety, resilience, and mood), history of stressors (e.g., prior injury, major life events, and daily hassles), and coping resources (e.g., psychological skills, coping behavior, and social support). It also proposes that a number of psychological strategies (e.g., cognitive restructuring, thought stopping, and relaxation training, to name a few) can be used to assist individuals with stress adaptation and as such, prevent the injury from occurring (for more details of the model and its constructs, please see Appaneal & Habif, 2013). The integrated model also proposes that in the event of an injury, the injury itself becomes a stressor, to which the injured individual will respond in a variety of ways. The pre-injury factors listed above can influence not only injury occurrence, but also the individual's subsequent psychological reactions to the injury.

Consistent with original cognitive appraisal models of typical adjustment to sport injury (e.g., Brewer, 1994), the integrated model proposes that following injury, an individual will cognitively appraise the situation. These appraisals will vary and can include appraisals of the meaning of injury itself (e.g., loss or a relief) and the impact of injury on self-identity, as well as forming perceptions about rate of recovery, to name a few. These cognitive appraisals will then influence the individual's emotional responses to the injury. These will typically be negative in nature and may include feelings of anxiety, confusion, tension, anger, depression, frustration, and fear of unknown; on occasion, there may be more positive feelings, such as relief. The emotional responses will in turn affect the resultant behavioral responses, for example adherence to rehabilitation, use/disuse of available social support, and engagement in risk-taking behaviors. The model also recognizes that this process of cognitive appraisals and emotional and behavioral responses is cyclical in nature and can also occur in the opposite direction (i.e., cognitive appraisals affecting behaviors, behaviors affecting emotions, and emotions affecting cognitive appraisals). Moreover, changes in direction between any of the responses during rehabilitation are possible. These reactions to the injury and rehabilitation are also influenced by a range of personal and situational factors, including but not limited to: demographics, injury characteristics, individual differences, sporting situation, and a number of social and environmental factors. Depending on the success of the appraisal process, these factors can have an impact on the overall physical and psychosocial recovery outcomes in a positive or negative way.

For example, an individual who is typically an anxious person, is dealing with increased amounts of general life stress, and perceive their coping resources to be limited or non-existent would be more likely to appraise their situation as stressful. As such, their cognitive appraisal of the situation would be relatively negative, potentially resulting in attentional changes and increased muscle tension, which would then make them more susceptible to injury. These pre-injury factors, along with other personal (e.g., age, gender, injury location) and situational (e.g., access to rehabilitation professionals, social support from those around them, and financial implications of the injury) factors, would in turn have an impact on whether they would appraise their situation as positive, negative, indifferent, or something in between. Depending on the cognitive appraisals, the person's mood and levels of anxiety, frustration, anger, and depression (i.e., emotional response) will be varied. Both their appraisals and emotional responses will in turn have an effect on their behavior, which can be favorable, unfavorable, or indifferent toward the injury and rehabilitation process.

As noted in the introduction, research investigating psychological effects of exercise injuries is sparse, and the application of the integrated model into exercise injury and rehabilitation has been limited (Hargreaves & Waumsley, 2013). However, similar to injuries encountered in athletic/sporting contexts, several personal and situational factors listed in the integrated model (Wiese-Bjornstal et al., 1998) have been proposed as potentially influencing individuals' psychological responses to exercise injuries and affecting their overall physical and psychosocial injury rehabilitation outcomes (Hargreaves & Waumsley, 2013). What follows is a brief outline of the psychological research as it relates or is applicable to exercise injuries in the context of the integrated model (Wiese-Bjornstal et al., 1998).

Self-Efficacy

Self-efficacy—that is, individuals' situation-specific confidence in their ability to perform a task (Bandura, 1977)—is one of the core underlying constructs of our self-perceptions. It is also seen as one of the strongest factors influencing exercise participation in physical activity and influences affective and cognitive outcomes of physical activity (Biddle & Mutrie, 2008). Self-efficacy can act as a significant contributor in determining whether or not an individual will believe they (a) are able to recover from the injury, (b) can complete the required rehabilitation activities successfully and adhere to the rehabilitation protocol, and (c) can return back to exercise following the rehabilitation. It is likely that due to injury an individual may experience reduction in their self-efficacy in that they may not feel able to perform activities to the same level after the injury as they did prior to injury (Hargreaves & Waumsley, 2013). To date, research investigating the role of self-efficacy in exercise injury rehabilitation is limited.

Identity

As with competitive athletes, many exercisers also perceive "being an exerciser" as part of their self-identity (Strachan, Flora, Brawley, & Spink, 2011; Whaley & Ebbeck, 2002; Yin & Boyd, 2000). When exercisers are injured, they are unable to take part in activities they are typically involved in, and as such, part of their self-identity is challenged (Strachan et al., 2011). Strachan et al. (2011) also found that people who have a strong exercise identity are more likely to have a negative affective response when they are injured and are unable to exercise. As with self-efficacy, research investigating the role of self-identity in sport injury rehabilitation is sparse.

Coping Skills

Coping skills are skills an individual may possess to help them deal with stressful situations. There are a number of coping strategies that have been identified, but typically and broadly speaking these can be categorized into three main categories: (1) appraisal-focused coping, in which an individual modifies their thoughts about the stressful situation; (2) emotion-focused coping, where an individual modifies their own emotional response to the stressor; and (3) problem-focused coping, where an individual will make behavioral modifications with the attempt to minimize or eliminate the stressor (Weiten & Lloyd, 2008). When injured, an exerciser may use all or some of these coping strategies, and depending on the existing coping skill set prior to injury, their appraisal of the injury will vary from individual to individual (Wiese-Bjornstal et al., 1998). Research has suggested that using problem-focused strategies to cope with injuries is the most beneficial (Johnston & Carroll, 2000); however, according to sport medicine professionals working with injured athletes, both emotion-focused and problem-focused coping are important for successful recovery (Arvinen-Barrow et al., 2007; Clement et al., 2013). Research in sporting context has indicated that athletes who are able to maintain a positive and proactive attitude toward their injury and rehabilitation (i.e., use positive emotion-focused coping) and who comply and adhere to their rehabilitation program (i.e., use positive problem-focused coping) are more likely to cope successfully with their injuries (Arvinen-Barrow et al., 2007; Clement et al., 2013). It is likely that similar patterns may be evident among exercise populations as well, but further research is needed.

Mood States

Mood states are emotional states that typically will have either positive or negative valence. Research has demonstrated that exercise has a positive effect on individuals' overall mood (Berger et al., 2007; Gauvin, Rejeski, & Reboussin, 2000) and, more specifically, helps reduce negative mood states, including depression and anxiety (Berger et al., 2007; International Society of Sport Psychology, 1992). In a similar way, research has indicated that some of the main motivations for exercising include to improve mood (i.e., reduce stress, anxiety, or depression) or simply because it is fun (Berger et al., 2007; Wilson, Mack, & Grattan, 2008). However, when injured, individuals will be restricted from taking part in the activity they enjoy doing and possibly use as a way of relieving stress and anxiety, increase positive mood, and enhance their overall well-being. As such, not being able to exercise can alter their typical mood states, which in turn can also potentially affect their reactions to injury (Wiese-Bjornstal et al., 1998). To what extent this cognitive-affective-behavioral cycle is supported in exercise injury context, is still unclear and warrants further research.

Socioeconomic Status

One of the demographic factors that may have a significant impact on individuals' reactions to injury is socioeconomical status. Financial status may determine a person's access to appropriate healthcare and the speed at which it is available (Taylor et al., 2003). In a similar way, if the injury has a hindering effect on the individual's ability to work, particularly in the long term, this can have a substantial impact on their financial situation (Gabbe et al., 2014), which in turn can affect their reactions to the injury, rehabilitation, and their willingness and need to return back to full fitness and eventually back to exercise.

Physical Health

Research has also indicated that an individual's overall health (Hargreaves & Waumsley, 2013) and quality of life (Huffman et al., 2008) can be affected by injury. When injured in an exercise context, it is typical that injury will result in at least temporary, if not more permanent, cessation of exercise (Hootman, 2009), which in itself can have an impact on physical health in a number of different ways, including loss of flexibility, strength, stamina, and cardiovascular fitness; increased body weight; and feeling "run down" both physically and mentally.

Social Support Provision

The provision of social support is probably one of the most significant situational factors influencing an individual's psychological response to injury (Rees, 2007). In the sporting context, if athletes feel they are supported by those close to them (e.g., primary treatment provider, coach, or family members), they are likely to view their situation as more positive when compared to athletes who do not feel adequately supported (Arvinen-Barrow, Massey, & Hemmings, 2014; Clement, Arvinen-Barrow, & Fetty, 2015; Mitchell, 2011; Mitchell, Evans, Rees, & Hardy, 2013). Similar to athletes with injuries, individuals with exercise injuries can also benefit from different types of social support (e.g., emotional, informational, motivational, and tangible; Arvinen-Barrow & Pack, 2013). When dealing with exercise injuries, it is important to ensure that the individuals do not feel like they are becoming socially isolated (Podlog & Eklund, 2007), given that injury is likely to restrict their exercise participation. Furthermore, the possibility exists that they may also experience a "void" in their life due to lack of exercise as part of their daily routine. Social support provided at the right time by the right individuals can possibly help mitigate these effects. It is also important to remember that social support does not always have a positive effect on the individual. Specifically, too much or the wrong kind of social support can diminish individuals' levels of independence and have a hindering effect on rehabilitation and recovery (Arvinen-Barrow & Pack, 2013; Uchino, 2009).

Accessibility to Rehabilitation

Another important factor influencing individuals' reactions to exercise injury is their possible access to rehabilitation. High-level athletes with injuries typically have access to a sport medicine team; however, such access is rare at lower levels of sport participation (Ray & Wiese-Bjornstal, 1999) and even less so among those with exercise injuries. As such, when injured, exercisers typically make their own assessments about severity, their need to seek treatment, and who to seek treatment from (Taylor et al., 2003). This said, in the absence of proper injury treatment and/or lack of access to immediate acute care, the risk of future injury is increased (Hargreaves & Waumsley, 2013).

Impact of Injury on the Dynamic Core: Effects on Cognitive Appraisals and Emotional and Behavioral Responses

All of the above factors have also been found to influence individuals' reactions to injury. When injured, an individual may appraise the injury and the situation of being injured in number of ways. For example, injury may be appraised as a hindrance to or a suspension from an individual's ability to achieve their set goals (Hargreaves & Waumsley, 2013) or as a sense of loss (Heil, 1994), particularly when a person's identity is highly rooted in being an exerciser (Whaley & Ebbeck, 2002; Yin & Boyd, 2000). How an individual will appraise the perceived rate of recovery is also significantly affected by personal and situational factors, and, indeed, appraisals that relate to their need/want to get back to exercise will also influence such appraisals (Wiese-Bjornstal et al., 1998). Moreover, an individual will make appraisals on their perceived ability to recover and return to activity, some of which are largely based on their self-efficacy (e.g., Shaw & Huang, 2005).

Some of the most prominent emotional responses to exercise injuries include a number of distressed emotional states. For example, not being able to make progress toward set goals can disrupt individuals' feelings of control and as such hinder their self-regulatory behavior (Berger, Pargman, & Weinberg, 2006). Typical emotional responses to injuries include negative mood, frustration, depression, stress, and anxiety (Arvinen-Barrow et al., 2007; Arvinen-Barrow, Massey, et al., 2014; Clement et al., 2013; Johnston & Carroll, 2000). The changes in mood and emotional states are generally caused by individuals' inability to be active and the actual disruption caused to daily routines. Moreover, fear of re-injury or re-injury anxiety may present itself during the injury rehabilitation process, particularly when the cognitive appraisal is negative and the individual's perceptions of personal control and ability are low (Taylor et al., 2003; Taylor & Taylor, 1997; Walker, Thatcher, Lavallee, & Golby, 2005). Experiencing fear of injury and/or re-injury anxiety are typical responses among sport participants (Finch et al., 2001; Walker & Thatcher, 2011), but may also be prevalent among exercise participants, particularly when individuals are either experiencing strong pain or are anticipating further pain (Sullivan et al., 2002).

There are a number of behavioral responses that can occur as a result of injury. Disuse of available social support or malingering during rehabilitation can be a sign of poor adjustment to the injury (Berger et al., 2007). Also, poor or lack of adherence to rehabilitation appears to be one of the most common negative behavioral responses to injuries (Arvinen-Barrow et al., 2007; Clement et al., 2013; Granquist & Brewer, 2013). In fact, it has been suggested that only 30–40 percent of injured exercisers perform rehabilitation exercises (Hootman et al., 2002), and that those who do not cope successfully with their injuries tend to be non-compliant or non-adherent with their rehabilitation (Arvinen-Barrow et al., 2007; Clement et al., 2013). It has also been found that those who are regular exercisers, despite negative appraisals and emotional responses to injuries, will adhere to treatment because of the value and positive benefits they experience from being active (Levy, Polman, Nicholls, & Marchant, 2009).

As stated above, research into different psychological responses to exercise injuries is sparse (Hargreaves & Waumsley, 2013). When injured, an individual is automatically faced with a situation that affects their thoughts, emotions, and behaviors. Typically an injured person will experience worrying and negative thoughts (Arvinen-Barrow, Massey, et al., 2014), at least during the early stages of rehabilitation. It is likely that exercise injuries will have negative consequences, given that the typical emotional responses are changes in overall mood, as well as feelings of frustration, stress, and anxiety (Arvinen-Barrow, Massey, et al., 2014; Clement et al., 2013; Tracey, 2003). It is also likely that those who are regularly active will take the steps necessary to return to their pre-injury activity levels and fitness. It is important to recognize the potential "warning signs" in psychological responses among individuals who are not regular or habitual exercisers to ensure that their cognitive appraisals and emotional and behavioral responses to the injury do not impede their return to activity after rehabilitation. When it comes to exercise injury rehabilitation, it is particularly important to understand that when injured, the individual will have to cope with the injury and its consequences. At the same time, they are also required to engage in activities and behaviors that not only are atypical, but new, unknown, and perhaps slightly intimidating at times. It is therefore imperative to understand how willing an individual is to accept the impending change, what barriers may be hindering the process of change, and how to best assist the individual in making a smooth transition.

The Transtheoretical Model of Behavior Change

As with understanding individuals' reactions to injury, using a theoretical framework to estimate their readiness to accept the injury, engage in subsequent rehabilitation, and return to exercise after injury rehabilitation can also be of help.

According to the literature, assessing readiness for change has proven to be effective in a variety of settings (Bucksch, Finne, & Kolip, 2008; Ergul & Temel, 2009; Young et al., 2008). Therefore, one can argue that similar benefits can be derived if this concept is applied to exercise injury. Existing literature proposes that an individual's readiness for change can best be assessed by using the transtheoretical model (TTM) of behavior change (Prochaska & DiClemente, 1983), which provides a framework for investigating how people adapt to new behaviors. These new behaviors in the exercise injury context would be adapting to being injured, completing a rehabilitation program, and preparing to become active again after injury rehabilitation. When initially developed by Prochaska and DiClemente (1983), the TTM included two components: the stages of change and the processes of change. Following empirical testing, two further components were added: the decisional balance (Janis & Mann, 1977) and self-efficacy (Bandura, 1977), both of which play an integral role in explaining how the stages and processes of behavior change work and interact.

The stages of change reflect the varying degrees of readiness experienced by individuals as they initiate new behaviors. According to Prochaska and DiClemente (1983), when entering a new situation requiring a behavior change, an individual would move through five different stages: precontemplation, contemplation, preparation, action, and maintenance. The precontemplation stage refers to when an individual has no intention to change their current behaviors. Contemplation stage is when the person is thinking about changing their behavior, but has not made any tangible changes yet. A person is said to move to the preparation stage when they are making small changes in order to prepare for upcoming change. The action stage occurs when an individual actively starts engaging in the new behavior. Once the new behavior has been consistent for a minimum of six months, an individual is said to have reached the maintenance stage, in which the person regularly continues to engage in the new behavior without great risk of relapsing.

Coupled with the stages of change are the processes of change, which refer to the various techniques and strategies that could be utilized by individuals as they progress through the stages of change (Prochaska & DiClemente, 1983). These 10 processes (consciousness raising, dramatic relief, environmental reevaluation, social liberation, self-reevaluation, counter-conditioning, helping relationships, reinforcement management, stimulus control, and self-liberation) are divided into experiential and behavioral processes. Experiential processes focus on the individual's awareness of the impending behavior change and their thoughts and feelings experienced while initiating this change. Behavioral processes refer to the overt activities that an individual will engage in during the course of behavior modification.

The decisional balance process, an analysis of pros and cons of the situation, allows individuals to make an assessment regarding the perceived benefits versus the drawbacks associated with engaging in the behavior change (Janis & Mann, 1977). Self-efficacy underpins the entire behavior change process as an individual's belief in their ability to successfully engage in the proposed behavior change often determines whether or not the new behavior becomes habitual.

Applying the TTM to individuals with exercise injuries can help determine whether or not the person is ready to accept the injury, enter in a subsequent rehabilitation program, and return back to activity after rehabilitation. By using the different components of the TTM, practitioners can gain a better understanding of the individual's readiness for change by identifying their stage of change, what processes underline their susceptibility for change, how they balance the benefits versus drawbacks of the change, and how their own perceptions about their ability to succeed in the change will affect this process. For example, if an individual is classified as (1) being in an advanced stage of change, (2) using more behavioral than experiential processes of change, (3) perceiving more pros than cons related to the required change, and (4) having high self-efficacy related to their ability to make the change, then they can be deemed psychologically ready for the change to occur. Conversely, based on the model, an individual can be classified as psychologically unprepared for the upcoming change if they report (1) being in the early stages of change, (2) using more experiential than behavioral processes of change, (3) perceiving more drawbacks than benefits with respect to engaging in the rehabilitation program, and (4) having low levels of self-efficacy. By using the TTM, practitioners working with injured exercise participants can get a fairly quick gauge of where an individual is with respect to initiating and completing their rehabilitation program. If an individual is identified as psychologically unprepared for rehabilitation, they could be referred to an exercise or counseling psychology professional who could assist the individual in becoming psychologically more prepared to begin and engage in the injury rehabilitation process.

While the practical utility of assessing readiness for change has been demonstrated in a variety of settings (Bucksch et al., 2008; Ergul & Temel, 2009; Young et al., 2008), its applicability to injury rehabilitation has been limited (Clement, 2008). Few studies have applied the TTM within the context of injury rehabilitation. More specifically Wong (1988) and Udry, Shelbourne, and Gray (2003) have applied select components of the model, while Clement's study (2008) appears to be the only attempt to apply the model as whole to sport injury rehabilitation.

According to the literature, Wong (1988) pioneered the initial application of readiness for change within the sport injury context. Using a sample of injured athletes ($N = 96$) and sports medicine providers ($N = 12$), Wong administered the Processes of Change Questionnaire— Injury Rehabilitation (POCQ-IR; Wong, 1998) to determine which processes of change the sports medicine providers perceived that injured athletes use and which processes of change athletes actually reported using. Results revealed that injured athletes reported using all 10 processes of change as they progressed through the stages of change from precontemplation to maintenance. Sports medicine providers also indicated that they believed that athletes also utilized all 10 processes of change. Moreover, it was revealed that the general utilization of behavioral processes was found to be statistically higher than the use of experiential processes across the stages of change.

Udry et al. (2003) expanded on the initial work of Wong by investigating the usefulness of evaluating the psychological readiness of patients prior to anterior cruciate ligament (ACL) surgery. Using a sample of pre-surgery subjects ($N = 121$), they assessed processes of change (POCQ-IR; Wong, 1988), self-efficacy (Self-Efficacy-Injury Rehabilitation; SE-IR, Wong, 1988) and a 15-item decisional balance measure (Marcus, Rakowski, & Rossi, 1992). Results revealed that participants who were deemed psychologically ready for surgery and rehabilitation exhibited high levels of self-efficacy, perceived more benefits than drawbacks with regards to undergoing surgery, and used more behavioral as opposed to experiential processes of change. These results appeared to be consistent with the findings of Wong (1988), although it must be mentioned that the participants in the current study were assessed prior to beginning their rehabilitation while Wong's (1988) sample was already in the midst of their rehabilitation programs.

More recently Clement (2008), using a sample of injured athletes ($N = 70$) provided additional validation for the applicability of the entire TTM to injury rehabilitation. Clement (2008) determined the sample's psychological readiness by measuring their stages of changes (via a modified version of the Stages of Exercise Scale [SOES; Cardinal, 1995]), processes of change (POCQ-IR; Wong, 1998), self-efficacy (subscale of the Sports Injury Rehabilitation Beliefs Survey [SIRBS; Taylor & May, 1993]), and a 16-item decisional balance measure for physical activity (Marcus & Owen, 1992). Results indicated that individuals who rated themselves as advanced in their stages of change reported an increase in their self-efficacy, perceived more benefits than drawbacks with regards to participating in injury rehabilitation, and increased their use of behavioral processes of change as they moved though the various stages of change during the course of their injury rehabilitation. These results appeared to mirror the earlier results obtained by Wong (1988), Prochaska and DiClemente (1983), and Marcus and Owen (1992). Based on these findings, Clement concluded that the TTM appears to be valid framework to use for determining an individual's readiness for commencing an injury rehabilitation program.

EVIDENCE-BASED APPLICATIONS

Research within the area of exercise adoption has shown that individuals who present in the early stages of behavior change can benefit immensely from the application of cognitive processes and strategies (Marcus et al., 1992). In a similar way, existing literature has highlighted that use of cognitive-behavioral interventions such as goal setting and self-talk during injury rehabilitation can be beneficial (Arvinen-Barrow & Walker, 2013; Beneka et al., 2007; Ievleva & Orlick, 1991). As a result, there are a number of strategies that exercise, counseling, and rehabilitation professionals can use to help injured exercise participants prepare for their impending rehabilitation as well as their return to post-injury activities (see Arvinen-Barrow & Walker, 2013 for a review). Specifically, these professionals can help injured individuals better prepare by educating them about the psychological aspects of the injury, the rehabilitation process, and the benefits of adherence to rehabilitation, as well as informing the individual of the potential negative consequences of not participating in rehabilitation (Hamson-Utley, Arvinen-Barrow, & Granquist, 2014; Marcus et al., 1992). Furthermore, exercise, counseling, and rehabilitation professionals may also implement psychological interventions such as imagery to help injured individuals increase their confidence and motivation for participation in injury rehabilitation. With injured individuals who are in the later stages of behavior change, using systematic goal setting and the use of self-monitoring strategies to enable them to chart their own progress (Arvinen-Barrow, 2008) is probably the most effective strategy to help increase overall motivation and adherence to the rehabilitation process. It must be noted that all interventions should only be implemented by appropriately trained professionals.

FUTURE RESEARCH DIRECTIONS AND PRACTICAL IMPLICATIONS

Given that only a limited number of people seek treatment for exercise injuries, researchers and practitioners should be mindful that the impact of exercise injuries can be a difficult area to research. As such, an adequate understanding of exercise injuries and their potential physical and psychological antecedents and consequences should be an integral part of any exercise promotion program, which in itself is an area rarely studied to date.

It is also not surprising that research investigating the impact of injury among exercisers and physically active populations (Hargreaves & Waumsley, 2013) is still in its infancy. One of the key research questions to explore includes a thorough exploration of the different components of the integrated model (Wiese-Bjornstal et al., 1998) to test its applicability in exercise injury context. What pre- and post-injury personal and situational factors typically influence psychological reactions to exercise injury? How do these factors interact to influence psychological reactions to exercise injuries? Additionally, researchers may want to further explore exercisers' psychological reactions prior to and during rehabilitation and return to participation as their reaction may be different from those of the athletic population.

Equally, the role of self-efficacy in exercise injury rehabilitation and recovery warrants further exploration. As per the integrated model (Wiese-Bjornstal et al., 1998), existing research has highlighted that individuals' self-efficacy is usually negatively affected by injuries (Hargreaves & Waumsley, 2013). On the other hand, self-efficacy has also been found to be a key determinant in facilitating individuals' readiness to engage in new rehabilitation behaviors (Udry et al., 2003). Further research should therefore aim to explore what strategies are the most effective in facilitating self-efficacy during injury rehabilitation and return to activity in individuals with exercise injuries, when these strategies should be implemented, and by whom.

Given the importance of self-efficacy as a factor affecting individuals' readiness for change (Prochaska & DiClemente, 1983), the applicability of using the transtheoretical model of behavior change to facilitate rehabilitation adherence and possible change in post-injury exercise behaviors needs to be further explored. How relevant and applicable is the transtheoretical model for exercise injury rehabilitation? Could the transtheoretical model be used as a theoretical foundation by practitioners in developing cognitive and behavioral strategies for injured exercisers with the aim of (1) possibly increasing exercisers' willingness to start and complete an exercise injury program, and (2) facilitating safe return back to participation post injury?

Given the worldwide attempts to promote exercise and physically active lifestyles for diverse populations (Centers for Disease Control and Prevention, 2010, 2014; Edwards & Tsouros, 2006), ensuring injured exercise participants have access to appropriate care after injury is of importance. This is particularly important as through appropriate care, professionals working with the injured individuals can facilitate safe return to activity and therefore help eliminate the risk of re-injury and physical activity cessation. Future research could possibly be aimed at determining what injured exercisers need and wish to know about their injury, prognosis, injury rehabilitation, and so on. This information could potentially be very helpful in influencing not only the psychological and physical recovery outcomes from the injury, but also adherence to injury protocols and return to participation.

Additionally, the roles and responsibilities of those closest to exercisers during exercise injury rehabilitation needs to be investigated. Who should be directly involved in the rehabilitation of an injured exerciser? In what capacity? What impact does the inclusion of significant others have on injured exercisers' ability to return back to activity and remain physically active post injury? The authors believe that family members, friends, gym instructors, personal trainers, and so on may serve a significant role in facilitating safe return to activity. However this has been rarely researched, thus warranting further research.

Another novel area of research that could be beneficial for exercisers with injuries is the use of alternative treatment modalities during rehabilitation. As identified by rehabilitation professionals, creating variety in rehabilitation exercises is one of the most common strategies used during rehabilitation (e.g., Arvinen-Barrow et al., 2007; Clement et al., 2013) to help sustain motivation and increase adherence. It has been suggested that using active video gaming could be beneficial during rehabilitation (Middlemas, Basilicato, Prybicien, Savoia, & Biodoglio, 2009); however, empirical evidence in support appears to be limited (Arvinen-Barrow, Manley, & Maresh, 2014). What is known is that using active video games does appear to have similar functional benefits to traditional exercises, but also appears to have some additional cognitive, emotional, and behavioral benefits, including increased enjoyment, positive mood, intrinsic motivation, and rehabilitation adherence (Arvinen-Barrow, Manley, et al., 2014). Given the potentially wide array of psychological benefits, investigating the usefulness of active video gaming in rehabilitation, particularly in relation to home exercise completion, is an area worth further research.

REFERENCES

American Psychological Association. (2011). *Stress in America: Our health at risk* (p. 78). Washington, DC: The American Psychological Association.

Andersen, M. B., & Williams, J. M. (1988). A model of stress and athletic injury: Prediction and prevention. *Journal of Sport & Exercise Psychology, 10,* 294–306.

Appaneal, R. N., & Habif, S. (2013). Psychological antecedents to sport injury. In M. Arvinen-Barrow & N. Walker (Eds.), *Psychology of sport injury and rehabilitation* (pp. 6–22). Abingdon and New York, NY: Routledge.

Arvinen-Barrow, M. (2008). Back to basics: Using goal setting to enhance rehabilitation. *SportEX Medicine, 37,* 15–19.

Arvinen-Barrow, M., Hemmings, B., Weigand, D. A., Becker, C. A., & Booth, L. (2007). Views of chartered physiotherapists on the psychological content of their practice: A national follow-up survey in the United Kingdom. *Journal of Sport Rehabilitation, 16,* 111–121.

Arvinen-Barrow, M., Manley, A., & Maresh, N. (2014). The potential psychological benefits of Active Video Games in the rehabilitation of musculoskeletal injuries and deficiencies: A narrative review of the literature. *Physical Therapy Reviews, 19*(6), 410–439.

Arvinen-Barrow, M., Massey, W. V., & Hemmings, B. (2014). Role of sport medicine professionals in addressing psychosocial aspects of sport-injury rehabilitation: Professional athletes' views. *Journal of Athletic Training, 49,* 764–772. doi: 10.4085/1062-6050-49.3.44

Arvinen-Barrow, M., & Pack, S. M. (2013). Social support in sport injury rehabilitation. In M. Arvinen-Barrow & N. Walker (Eds.), *Psychology of sport injury and rehabilitation.* Abington and New York, NY: Routledge.

Arvinen-Barrow, M., & Walker, N. (Eds.). (2013). *Psychology of sport injury and rehabilitation.* Abington: Routledge.

Bandura, A. (1977). Self-efficacy: Towards a unifying theory of behavior change. *Psychological Reviews, 84,* 191–215.

Beneka, A., Malliou, P., Bebetsos, E., Gioftsidou, A., Pafis, G., & Godolias, G. (2007). Appropriate counselling techniques for specific components of the rehabilitation plan: A review of the literature. *Physical Training.* Retrieved from http://ejmas.com/pt/ptframe.htm

Berger, B. G., Pargman, D., & Weinberg, R. S. (Eds.). (2006). *Factors influencing exercise-related injury and factors related to rehabilitation adherence* (3rd ed.). Morgantown, WV: Fitness Information Technology.

Berger, B. G., Pargman, D., & Weinberg, R. S. (2007). *Foundations of exercise psychology* (2nd ed.). Morgantown, WV: Fitness Information Technology.

Biddle, S. J. H., & Mutrie, N. (2008) *Psychology of physical activity: Determinants, wellbeing and interventions* (2nd ed.). London: Routledge.

Brewer, B. W. (1994). Review and critique of models of psychological adjustment to athletic injury. *Journal of Applied Sport Psychology, 6,* 87–100. doi: 10.1080/10413209408406467

Brewer, B. W., Andersen, M. B., & Van Raalte, J. L. (2002). Psychological aspects of sport injury rehabilitation: Toward a biopsychological approach. In D. I. Mostofsky & L. D. Zaichkowsky (Eds.), *Medical aspects of sport and exercise* (pp. 41–54). Morgantown, WV: Fitness Information Technology.

Bucksch, J., Finne, E., & Kolip, P. (2008). The transtheoretical model in the context of physical activity in a school-based sample of German adolescents. *European Journal of Sport Sciences, 8,* 403–413. doi: 10.1080/17461390802438748

Burt, C. W., & Overpeck, M. D. (2001). Emergency visits for sports-related injuries. *Annals of Emergency Medicine, 37*(3), 301–308. doi: 10.1067/mem.2001.111707

Cairney, J., Kwan, M., Veldhuizen, S., & Faulkner, G. (2014). Who uses exercise as a coping strategy for stress? Results from a national survey of Canadians. *Journal of Physical Activity & Health, 11*(5), 908–916. doi: 10.1123/jpah.2012-0107

Cardinal, B. J. (1995). The stages of exercise scale and stages of exercise behavior in female adults. *Journal of Sports Medicine and Physical Fitness, 35*, 87–92.

Carlson, S., Hootman, J. M., Powell, K. E., Macera, C. A., Heath, G. W., Gilchrist, J., . . . Kohl, H. W. I. (2006). Self-reported injury and physical activity levels: United States 2000–2002. *Annals of Epidemiology, 16*(9), 712–719. doi: 10.1016/j.annepidem.2006.01.002

Centers for Disease Control and Prevention. (2010). *Promoting physical activity: A guide for community action* (2nd ed.). Champaign, IL: Human Kinetics.

Centers for Disease Control and Prevention. (2014). *State indicator report on physical activity.* Atlanta, GA: U.S. Department of Health and Human Services. Retrieved from www.cdc.gov/physicalactivity/downloads/pa_state_indicator_report_2014.pdf?s_cid=bb-DNPAO-SIRPA 20140–02&utm_source=external&utm_medium=banner&utm_content=DNPAO-SIRPA 20140–02&utm_campaign=glgb.

Clement, D. (2008). The transtheoretical model: An exploratory look at its applicability to injury rehabilitation. *Journal of Sport Rehabilitation, 17*, 269–282.

Clement, D., Arvinen-Barrow, M., & Fetty, T. (2015). Psychosocial responses during different phases of sport injury rehabilitation: A qualitative study. *Journal of Athletic Training, 50*(1), 95–104. doi: 10.4085/1062-6050-49.3.52

Clement, D., Granquist, M. D., & Arvinen-Barrow, M. (2013). Psychosocial aspects of athletic injuries as perceived by athletic trainers *Journal of Athletic Training, 48*(4), 512–521. doi: 10.4085/1062-6050-49.3.52

Colbert, L. H., Hootman, J. M., & Macera, C. A. (2000). Physical activity-related injuries in walkers and runners in the aerobics center longitudinal study. *Clinical Journal of Sport Medicine, 10*, 259–263. doi: 10.1097/00042752-200010000-00006

Conn, J. M., Annest, J. L., & Gilchrist, J. (2003). Sports and recreation related injury episodes in the US population, 1997–99. *Injury Prevention, 9*(2), 117–123. doi: 10.1016/j.jsams.2006.03.004

Edwards, P., & Tsouros, A. (2006). *Promoting physical activity and active living in urban environments: The role of local goverments.* Europe: World Health Organization.

Ergul, S., & Temel, A. (2009). The effects of a nursing smoking cessation intervention on military students in Turkey. *International Nursing Review, 56*, 102–108. doi: 10.1111/j.1466-7657.2008.00695.x

Finch, C. F., Otago, L., White, P., Donaldson, A., & Mahoney, M. (2011). The safety attitudes of people who use multi-purpose recreation facilities as a physical activity setting. *International Journal of Injury, Control and Safety Promotion, 18*(2), 107–112. doi: 10.1080/17457300.2010.510249

Finch, C. F., Owen, N., & Price, R. (2001). Current injury or disability as a barrier to being more physically active. *Medicine & Science in Sports & Exercise, 33*, 778–782. doi: 10.1097/00005768-200105000-00016

Gabbe, B. J., Sleney, J. S., Gosling, C. M., Wilson, K., Sutherland, A., Hart, M., . . . Christie, N. (2014). Financial and employment impacts of serious injury: A qualitative study. *Injury, 45*(9), 1445–1451. doi: 10.1016/j.injury.2014.01.019

Gauvin, L., Rejeski, W. J., & Reboussin, B. A. (2000). Contributions of acute bouts of vigorous physical activity to explaining diurnal variations in feeling states in active, middle-aged women. *Health Psychology, 19*(4), 365–375. doi: 10.1037/0278-6133.19.4.365

Granquist, M. D., & Brewer, B. W. (2013). Psychological aspects of rehabilitation adherence. In M. Arvinen-Barrow & N. Walker (Eds.), *Psychology of Sport Injury and Rehabilitation* (pp. 40–53). Abingdon and New York, NY: Routledge.

Hamson-Utley, J. J., Arvinen-Barrow, M., & Granquist, M. D. (2014). Psychosocial strategies: Effectiveness and application. In M. D. Granquist, J. J. Hamson-Utley, L. Kenow & J. Stiller-Ostrowski (Eds.), *Psychosocial strategies for athletic trainers: An applied and integrated approach* (pp. 231–268). Philadelphia, PA: FA Davis Publishers.

Hargreaves, E. A., & Waumsley, J. A. (2013). Psychology of physical activity-related injuries. In M. Arvinen-Barrow & N. Walker (Eds.), *Psychology of sport injury and rehabilitation* (pp. 185–198). Abington and New York, NY: Routledge.

Heaney, C. (2006). Physiotherapists' perceptions of sport psychology intervention in professional soccer. *International Journal of Sport and Exercise Psychology, 4*, 67–80. doi: 10.1080/1612197x. 2006.9671785

Heil, J. (1994). Understanding the psychology of sport injury: A grief process model. *Temple Psychiatric Review, 3*(3), 4, 10.

Hemmings, B., & Povey, L. (2002). Views of chartered physiotherapists on the psychological content of their practice: A preliminary study in the United Kingdom. *British Journal of Sports Medicine, 36*(1), 61–64. doi: 10.1136/bjsm.36.1.61

Hootman, J. M. (2009). 2008 Physical activity guidelines for Americans: An opportunity for athletic trainers. *Journal of Athletic Training, 44*(1), 5–6. doi: 10.4085/1062-6050-44.1.5

Hootman, J. M., Macera, C. A., Ainsworth, B. E., Addy, C. L., Martin, M., & Blair, S. N. (2002). Epidemiology of musculoskeletal injuries among sedentary and physically active individuals. *Medicine and Science in Sports and Exercise, 34*(5), 838–844. doi: 10.1097/00005768-200205000-00017

Hootman, J. M., Macera, C. A., Ainsworth, B. E., Martin, M., Addy, C. L., & Blair, S. N. (2001). Association among physical activity level, cardiorespiratory fitness, and risk of musculoskeletal injury. *American Journal of Epidemiology, 154*(3), 251–258. doi: 10.1093/aje/154.3.251

Huffman, G. R., Park, J., Roser-Jones, C., Sennett, B. J., Yagnik, G., & Webner, D. (2008). Normative SF-36 values in competing NCAA intercollegiate athletes differ from values in the general population. *Journal of Bone & Joint Surgery - American, 90*(3), 471–476. doi: 10.2106/JBJS.G.00325

Ievleva, L., & Orlick, T. (1991). Mental links to enhanced healing: An exploratory study. *The Sport Psychologist, 5*, 25–40.

International Society of Sport Psychology. (1992). Physical activity and psychological benefits: A position statement from the International Society of Sport Psychology. *Journal of Applied Sport Psychology, 4*, 94–98. doi: 10.1080/10413209208406452

Janis, J., & Mann, L. (1977). *Decision making: A psychological analysis of conflict, choice and commitment.* New York, NY: Free Press.

Janney, C. A., & Jakicic, J. M. (2010). The influence of exercise and BMI on injuries and illnesses in overweight and obese individuals: A randomized control trial. *International Journal of Behavioral Nutrition and Physical Activity, 7*(1). 10.1186/1479-5868-7-1

Johnston, L. H., & Carroll, D. (2000). The psychological impact of injury: Effects of prior sport and exercise involvement. *British Journal of Sports Medicine, 34*, 436–439. doi: 10.1136/bjsm.34.6.436

Levy, A. R., Polman, R. C. J., Nicholls, A. R., & Marchant, D. C. (2009). Sport injury rehabilitation adherence: Perspectives of recreational athletes. *International Journal of Sport & Exercise Psychology, 7*(2), 212–219. doi: 10.1080/1612197X.2009.9671901

Lox, C. L., Martin Ginis, K. A., & Petruzzello, S. J. (2006). *The psychology of exercise.* Scottsdale, AZ: Holcomb Hathaway Publishers.

Macera, C., & Wooten, W. (1994). Epidemiology of sports and recreation injuries among adolescents. *Pediatric Exercise Science, 6*, 424–433.

Marcus, B., & Owen, N. (1992). Motivational readiness, self-efficacy, and decision making. *Journal of Applied Social Psychology, 22*, 3–16. doi: 10.1111/j.1559-1816.1992.tb01518

Marcus, B., Rakowski, W., & Rossi, J. (1992). Assessing motivational readiness and decision making for exercise. *Health Psychology, 11*, 257–261. doi: 10.1037/0278-6133.11.4.257

Middlemas, D. A., Basilicato, J., Prybicien, M., Savoia, J., & Biodoglio, J. (2009). Incorporating Gaming Technology into Athletic Injury Rehabilitation. *Athletic Training & Sports Health Care: The Journal for the Practicing Clinician, 1*(2), 79–84.

Mitchell, I. D. (2011). Social support and psychological responses in sport-injury rehabilitation. *Sport and Exercise Psychology Review, 7*(2), 30–44.

Mitchell, I. D., Evans, L., Rees, T., & Hardy, L. (2013). Stressors, social support, and tests of the buffering hypothesis: Effects on psychological responses of injured athletes. *British Journal of Health Psychology*, 1–23.

Molina-Garcia, J., Castillo, I., & Queralt, A. (2011). Leisure-time physical activity and psychological well-being in university students. *Psychological Reports, 109*(2), 453–460. doi: 10.2466/06.10.13. pr0.109.5.453-460

Nicholl, J. P., Coleman, P., & Williams, B. T. (1995). The epidemiology of sports and exercise related injury in the United Kingdom. *British Journal of Sports Medicine, 29*, 232–238. doi: 10.1136/bjsm.29.4.232

Podlog, L., & Eklund, R. C. (2007). The psychosocial aspects of a return to sport following serious injury: a review of the literature from a self-determination perspective. *Psychology of Sport and Exercise, 8*(4), 535–566.

Prochaska, J. O., & DiClemente, C. C. (1983). Stages and processes of self-change of smoking: Toward an integrative model of change. *Journal of Consulting and Clinical Psychology, 51*(3), 390–395. doi: 10.1037//0022-006x.51.3.390

Ray, R., & Wiese-Bjornstal, D. M. (Eds.). (1999). *Counseling in sports medicine.* Champaign, IL: Human Kinetics.

Rees, T. (2007). Influence of social support on athletes. In S. Jowett & D. Lavallee (Eds.), *Social psychology in sport* (pp. 223–232). Champaign, IL: Human Kinetics.

Shaw, W., & Huang, Y.-H. (2005). Concerns and expectations about returning to work with low back pain: Identifying themes from focus groups and semi-structured interviews. *Disability and Rehabilitation, 27*(21), 1269–1281. doi: 10.1080/09638280500076269

Strachan, S. M., Flora, P. K., Brawley, L. R., & Spink, K. S. (2011). Varying the cause of a challenge to exercise identity behavior: Reactions of individuals of differing identity strength. *Journal of Health Psychology, 16*, 572–583. doi: 10.1177/1359105310383602

Sullivan, M. J. L., Rodgers, W. M., Wilson, P. M., Bell, G. J., Murray, T. C., & Fraser, S. N. (2002). An experimental investigation of the relation between catastrophizing and activity intolerance. *Pain, 100*, 47–53. doi: 10.1016/s0304-3959(02)00206-3

Taylor, A. H., & May, S. (1993). *Development of a survey to assess athletes' sports injury rehabilitation beliefs [Abstract].* Paper presented at the Annual European Society for Health Psychology Conference, Brussels.

Taylor, J., Stone, K. R., Mullin, M., J., Ellenbecker, T., & Walgenbach, A. (2003). *Comprehensive sports injury management: From examination of injury to return to sport* (2nd ed.). Austin, TX: Pro-Ed.

Taylor, J., & Taylor, S. (1997). *Psychological approaches to sports injury rehabilitation.* Gaithersburg, MD: Aspen.

Tracey, J. (2003). The emotional response to the injury and rehabilitation process. *Journal of Applied Sport Psychology, 15*(4), 279–293. doi: 10.1080/714044197

Uchino, B. N. (2009). Understanding the links between social support and physical health: A life-span perspective with emphasis on the separability of perceived and received support *Perspectives Psychological Science, 4*(3), 236–255. doi: 10.1111/j.1745-6924.2009.01122.x

Udry, E., Shelbourne, K. D., & Gray, T. (2003). Psychological readiness for anterior cruciate ligament surgery: Describing and comparing the adolescent and adult experiences. *Journal of Athletic Training, 38*(2), 167.

Uitenbroek, D. G. (1996). Sports, exercise, and other causes of injuries: Results of a population survey. *Research Quarterly for Exercise and Sport, 67*, 380–385. doi: 10.1080/02701367.1996.10607969

Vallerand, R. J. (2004). Intrinsic and extrinsic motivation in sport. In C. Spielberg (Ed.), *Encyclopedia of applied psychology* (Vol. 2, pp. 427–435). San Diego, CA: Academic Press.

Vallerand, R. J., & Losier, G. F. (1999). An integrative analysis of internal and external motivation in sport. *Journal of Applied Sport Psychology, 11*, 142–169.

Walker, N., & Thatcher, J. (2011). The emotional response to athletic injury: Re-injury anxiety. In J. Thatcher, M. V. Jones & D. Lavallee (Eds.), *Coping and Emotion in Sport* (2nd ed., pp. 235–259). New York, NY: Routledge.

Walker, N., Thatcher, J., Lavallee, D., & Golby, J. (2005). The emotional response to athletic injury: Re-Injury Anxiety. In D. Lavallee, J. Thatcher, & M. V. Jones (Eds.), *Coping and Emotion in Sport* (pp. 91–103). New York, NY: Nova Science.

Weinberg, R. S., & Gould, D. (2011). *Foundations of sport and exercise psychology* (5th ed.). Champaign, IL: Human Kinetics.

Weiten, W., & Lloyd, M. A. (2008). *Psychology applied to modern life* (9th ed.). Wadsworth Cengage Learning.

Whaley, D. E., & Ebbeck, V. (2002). Self-schemata and exercise identity in older adults. *Journal of Aging and Physical Activity, 10,* 245–259.

Wiese-Bjornstal, D. M., Smith, A. M., Shaffer, S. M., & Morrey, M. A. (1998). An integrated model of response to sport injury: Psychological and sociological dynamics. *Journal of Applied Sport Psychology, 10,* 46–69.

Wilson, P. M., Mack, D. E., & Grattan, K. P. (2008). Understanding motivation for exercise: A self-determination theory perspective. *Canadian Psychology, 49*(3), 250–256.

Wong, I. (1988). *Injury rehabilitation behavior: An investigation of stages and processes of change in the athletic-therapist relationship.* (Master's degree unpublished Master's thesis), University of Oregon, Eugene, OR, unpublished.

Yin, Z., & Boyd, M. P. (2000). Behavioral and cognitive correlates of exercise self-schemata. *Journal of Psychology, 134,* 269–282.

Young, M., Eun, J., Hee, Y., Mi, S., Ju, Y., & Hee, J. (2008). Application of the transtheoretical model to identify aspects influencing condom use among Korean college students. *Western Journal of Nursing Research, 30,* 991–1004.

27 Social Physique Anxiety and Muscle Dysmorphia

Urska Dobersek and Robert C. Eklund

Social physique anxiety (SPA) and body dysmorphic disorder (BDD) have the body as a common denominator. These constructs both involve concerns with either others' or one's own perceptions about the body or specific physical features. SPA involves concern about the evaluation of others, while BDD involves concern over self-perceptions. This chapter provides definitions and information on diagnostic and statistical elements of SPA, BDD, and muscle dysmorphia (MD), which is a particular type of BDD. Psychological, physiological, and environmental factors implicated in the experience of these constructs are outlined as are potential co-morbidities. Despite the wide range of physical and psychological benefits derived from exercise and physical activity, evidence suggests that these involvements can have negative effects for some individuals with SPA and MD. Consulting, counseling, and pharmacological strategies for addressing SPA and MD are outlined, including commentary on cognitive behavior therapy (CBT), anti-depressants (e.g., selective serotonin reuptake inhibitors), and a combination thereof.

In this chapter we first provide commentary on the theoretical background of the mechanisms that play an essential role in development of SPA and MD among exercisers and physically active individuals. Main topics and associated concepts are introduced in vignettes to illustrate experiences of SPA and MD, and how they relate to exercise and physical activity. We then describe variables that have been linked to SPA and MD, including potential causes, moderators, mediators, and other correlates. Finally, we provide theoretically grounded recommendations for professionals working with physically active individuals who portray symptoms of SPA and/or MD, and we provide suggested readings for further exploration in the area.

ANNA'S EXPERIENCES: SOCIAL PHYSIQUE ANXIETY

Anna, a 25-year-old high school teacher, felt that she was an attractive woman, except perhaps for a few "extra" pounds. She decided that joining the fitness center to more regularly engage in exercise would put her on the path to losing those extra pounds. Anna had second thoughts when it came time to start her membership. She started worrying that everyone in the gym would stare at her heft and that she would make a fool of herself because of her lack of knowledge on how to operate the machines. Even the thought of going to the gym started causing her to break out in a sweat, get flush, and have a racing heart. Sally, Anna's best friend, realized the distress Anna was experiencing and offered to come along to support her during her workouts. Although Anna still felt uneasy and anxious, she was able to get over her fears enough to attend her very first session at the gym. She still, however, felt as though she was "on display" and that everyone was critiquing her size and shape. Even so, her motivation and social support allowed her to make three workouts per week until she had finally lost 10 lbs. Sally recognized

Anna's progress by saying, "You look amazing! I am so proud of you and your accomplishments. You should be very proud of yourself as well." Unfortunately, Sally was not able to accompany Anna to the gym after a few more months due to scheduling conflicts. Because Anna was uncomfortable going to the gym by herself, she gradually slid into a routine of working out at home and walking around her neighborhood with another friend, while going to the gym to a lesser extent. Before too long, Anna stopped attending the gym completely.

Anna's story is not uncommon, and certainly not rare among individuals who are new to exercise and exercise settings. Many people face similar experiences on a daily basis in their efforts to become (more) physically active and adhere to their new exercise regimens. The additional stress of experiencing body-related anxiety, embarrassment, or even shame at the gym further undermines exercise initiation and subsequent adherence.

THEORETICAL AND EMPIRICAL-BASED EVIDENCE FOR SOCIAL PHYSIQUE ANXIETY

Self-Presentational Processes Lead to Development of Social Physique Anxiety

SPA is a *self-presentational* psychosocial variable that is conceptually grounded in concerns about the extent to which others perceive our bodies in the way we prefer to be seen. At times, we may care a great deal about the impressions others form about us, while at other times we may care less. When we care, we are motivated to attempt to shape those impressions in desired directions. When motivated in social interactions, people usually seek to shape the impressions that others form in socially desirable ways. For the most part, these efforts are not inherently deceptive or manipulative but rather a matter of trying to "put one's best foot forward."

To explain self-presentation, Leary and Kowalski (1990) developed a two-component model involving two discrete processes. *Impression motivation* involves the desire to be perceived in certain ways by others. The extent to which individuals are motivated to control how others view them is influenced by situational and dispositional determinants that include the relevance of the impressions to the individual's goals, the value of desired goals to the individual, and the perceived discrepancy between the desired and current images. In our vignette, Anna's desire to be perceived as an attractive young woman could be considered impression motivation. Her interest in taking up exercise was to lose weight. She experienced anxiety both in contemplating the gym and in working out there. Without her friend's social support, she ended up dropping out despite the visible effects highlighted by her friend. Nonetheless, the importance she placed upon losing weight in order to appear attractive kept her trying to be active, albeit in her "home environment."

The second component of Leary and Kowalski's (1990) model has to do with *impression construction*. This component deals with one's behavioral attempts to self-present to others to create the desired impressions. These behaviors are shaped by personal attributes, attitudes, moods, social status, roles, interests, belief system, and physical states, among many others. Self-concept, or "a person's perceptions of him- or herself" (Marsh & Shavelson, 1985, p. 107), is thought to be the primary determinant of impression construction, but self-presentation does not depend only upon how people see themselves. These efforts are also influenced by how the person would like to be perceived (and/or not be perceived), the constraints on the social role the person occupies, and the person's perceptions of the values of the self-presentational target. Moreover, the impressions people try to construct for others are always affected by their beliefs about how they are currently perceived and by how they think others could perceive them in the future as a consequence of their present self-presentational efforts (Leary & Kowalski, 1990).

Evidence indicates that self-presentational concerns are associated with both increased and decreased exercise participation (Leary, 1992). Anna's goal, for example, was to lose weight to appear attractive, so she was motivated to join and attend a fitness club. At the same time, however, her self-presentational concerns about being perceived as overweight, unfit, and incapable of working out properly (attributes she "knew" to be contrary to the values of regular gym members) undermined Anna's interest in exercising at the club. Also, her unfamiliarity with operating the machines in the gym made her experience as an exerciser unpleasant.

When individuals want to make desired impressions on others but are unsure as to whether they will be perceived as intended, it is common to experience a negative affective state termed *social anxiety* (Schlenker & Leary, 1982). According to the fifth edition of the Diagnostic and Statistical Manual (*DSM-V*; American Psychiatric Association, 2013), *social anxiety* is "marked fear or anxiety about one or more social situations in which the individual is exposed to possible scrutiny by others" (p. 203). Socially anxious individuals often have unrealistically high self-standards, which in turn increase doubts that they will be able to perform successful self-presentation or impression management (Schlenker & Leary, 1985). Their cognitive appraisals tend to be focused upon the status of the self in social settings and their efforts to self-present only serve to exacerbate the intensity of their anxieties, perhaps even causing them to cope by avoidance or withdrawal. *Social physique anxiety* is a specific social anxiety having particular relevance to exercise and physical activity settings. It is the anxiety that is experienced when individuals perceive threat as a consequence of the prospect (or actuality) of physique and appearance evaluation. Exercise settings often come laden with evaluation potential about the physique because, after all, the body is central to the enterprise, and an array of others as potential observers inhabit many of the sites where exercise occurs, including other exercisers, the exercise guide (e.g., personal trainer, aerobics instructor), and sometimes onlookers who are simply spectating.

Social Physique Anxiety

SPA is one of the most studied self-presentational constructs in sport and exercise psychology (Martin Ginis, Lindwall, & Prapavessis, 2007). It has most typically been studied from a dispositional perspective (i.e., a trait that is relatively stable across situations). Reasonably consistent relationships have been observed between SPA and psychological variables related to thoughts and feelings about the self. For example, SPA has been inversely associated with physical self-esteem (Hagger & Stevenson, 2010) and self-presentational efficacy, and positively associated with body dissatisfaction (Martin Ginis, Murru, Conlin, & Strong, 2011), drive for thinness (Thompson & Chad, 2002), and muscularity (McCreary & Saucier, 2009). It has also been identified as a risk factor for such psychopathologies as depression (Woodman & Steer, 2011), disordered eating (Fitzsimmons-Craft, Harney, Brownstone, Higgins, & Bardone-Cone, 2012), and exercise dependence (Goodwin, Haycraft, Willis, & Meyer, 2011).

Perhaps unsurprisingly, SPA has been inconsistently and typically weakly linked to exercise behavior when studied as a trait or disposition. Individuals with heightened levels of SPA may, like Anna in our vignette, be motivated to engage in exercise as a consequence of their desire to lose weight, improve their appearance, and so on, but exercise settings can also come laden with evaluative risk that can stimulate exercise avoidance—at least in settings perceived to be threatening. Investigations of state SPA experiences (i.e., the "right now" experience that fluctuates on a moment-to-moment basis) in exercise have been revealing on that account. For example, Focht and Hausenblas (2004) presented evidence that women's state of SPA during exercise varies across settings according to the extent to which threat is perceived in the exercise environment. Interestingly, the environment in their study prompting the greatest perceived evaluative threat and elevations in state SPA involved a university fitness center. On that account, Martin Ginis, McEwan, Josse, and Phillips (2012) more recently investigated hormonal effects of threatened social evaluation (e.g., presence of an evaluative other, a videotaped recording, negative social comparison) of the physique. Results from this study indicated that participants in a "threatening" environment experienced significantly higher perceived self-evaluation and increased cortisol levels compared to individuals in a non-threatening environment.

Motives for Exercise in Relation to Social Physique Anxiety

Individuals engage in exercise for a variety of reasons. Common reasons for exercise include improvement or maintenance of one's health and fitness, enjoyment, socializing with others, or experiencing psychological benefits associated with exercise involvement. For some individuals, being physically active can be anchored in self-presentational motives, such as appearance related weight management, physical attractiveness, and/or increased muscle mass and tone (Culos-Reed, Brawley, Martin, & Leary, 2002).

Even though exercising for self-presentational reasons can encourage individuals to be physically active, they may exercise considerably less than those who exercise for health-related reasons (Culos-Reed et al., 2002). The former is not surprising given the current aesthetic standard for women to be slender and toned and men to be lean and muscular. It is also important to note that persons who exercise primarily to alter their body shape and weight do not necessarily experience positive psychological benefits associated with exercise (Tiggemann & Williamson, 2000). In fact, exercising to improve one's appearance has been positively related with SPA (Crawford & Eklund, 1994). Additionally, research has demonstrated that SPA is positively associated with introjected regulation (i.e., motivation to avoid negative emotions or to support conditional self-worth; Ryan & Deci, 2000) and negatively associated with intrinsic motivation (Thøgersen-Ntoumani & Ntoumanis, 2006).

As illustrated in the vignette about Anna, the desire to improve appearance can motivate individuals to exercise. Self-presentational concerns, however, can also serve as a barrier to exercise participation for those who have reservations about how they will be perceived while exercising in some settings. Evidence provided by Lantz, Hardy, and Ainsworth (1997) indicates that individuals with bodily insecurities can employ a variety of defense mechanisms to manage self-presentational concerns by avoiding threatening environments and social interactions, and by minimizing their body exposure during exercise. For example, individuals who think they are overweight may not wish to be seen in swimming suits or exercise in tight clothing; individuals who believe they lack appropriate muscle mass, strength, or technique may avoid types of exercise (e.g., weight lifting) that could highlight their self-perceived inadequacies.

Self-Presentational Responses on the Exercise Environment

Environmental attributes including the exercise setting itself (Bain, Wilson, & Chaikind, 1989; Van Raalte, Cunningham, Cornelius, & Brewer, 2004), norms on attire, fitness leader characteristics and leadership style (Raedeke, Focht, & Scales, 2007), social composition of participants, and gender makeup of the exercise group (Kruisselbrink, Dodge, Swanburg, & MacLeod, 2004) can potentially influence psychological responses to acute bouts of exercise. Within exercise settings, an array of environmental factors (e.g., mirrors, presence of others, leader characteristics, etc.) can draw attention to one's physique and appearance that may result in perceived evaluative threat and hence less positive psychological responses (Focht &

Hausenblas, 2004). Bain et al. (1989), for example, reported that obese women tended to avoid public places for exercise because of their worries about appearance evaluation and social disapproval. Similarly, Van Raalte et al. (2004) reported that exercisers' SPA levels were lower in the library than in the fitness center and dining hall, perhaps because of differences in the ambient levels of physique evaluation inherent across the settings.

Even though mirrors are common in many exercise settings, findings reported in the extant literature on their effects have been inconsistent. The presence of mirrors can elevate self-awareness and lead to an increased experience of state SPA (Focht & Hausenblas, 2003). Others suggested that the presence or absence of mirrors may be less important in influencing self-presentational concerns than capably participating in an exercise session (Lamarche, Gammage, & Strong, 2009). Nonetheless, Focht and Hausenblas (2006) presented evidence indicating that women with high SPA were more likely to experience negative feeling states when exercising in a public, mirrored environment than when exercising in a public, unmirrored environment, where increased levels of pleasure and positive feeling states were more likely to occur. However, mirrors have sometimes been found to moderately increase exercise-related self-efficacy, perhaps as a consequence of successful participation in the exercise bout (Katula & McAuley, 2001), and other times to have no effect on the feeling states, enjoyment, or task self-efficacy among women with high levels of SPA (Raedeke et al., 2007).

Swimming pools, malls, locker rooms, sport teams, and presence of peers may also act as environmental antecedents of SPA, with appearance-related conversations and peer comparisons playing a particular role in generating physique-related self-presentational concern (Sabiston, Sedgwick, Crocker, Kowalski, & Mack, 2007). Brunet and Sabiston (2011), for example, found that individuals experienced higher SPA when surrounded by their peers than when surrounded by their parents. Perhaps the heightened experience of SPA results from perceived peer pressure to alter their appearance (Mack, Strong, Kowalski, & Crocker, 2007).

With regard to gender, women have reported that they would experience higher levels of SPA when working out in all-male and mixed-sex settings than they would in all-female settings, whereas males reported low levels of SPA regardless of the gender of other exercisers in the settings (Kruisselbrink et al., 2004). Interestingly, the women in the Kruisselbrink et al. (2004) study reported they would shorten their exercise session in all-male settings relative to their intentions in all-female or mixed-sex exercise scenarios. Martin Ginis et al. (2011) provided further support for this notion in reporting that women exercising in a mixed-sex environment scored higher on the state SPA than in a same-sex environment.

Fitness leaders play an important role in shaping exercise environments; their leadership style, sex, and physical characteristics all potentially affect how they are perceived by the exercisers. For example, Martin and Fox (2001) found that a bland leadership style (i.e., avoiding conversations, comments to the group rather than to individuals, no positive reinforcement or encouragement) contributed to heightened social anxiety among exercisers relative to what was experienced by participants in the enriched leadership style condition (i.e., emphasizing pleasant, energetic social interaction; addressing participants' by name; providing positive reinforcement). Even individuals with increased SPA levels, who are more likely to exercise for appearance-related reasons, responded more positively to a leadership style that did not focus on appearance. Raedeke et al. (2007) found that exercisers whose instructor wore gym shorts and a t-shirt and made health-related comments experienced more positive affect and enjoyment compared to exercisers whose instructor wore tight-fitting attire and made appearance-related comments.

In a qualitative study, Lamarche, Kerr, Faulkner, Gammage, and Klentrou (2012) found that perceived comfortable environments were associated with the presence of supportive others (e.g., family, friends); feelings of calmness, self-confidence, and attractiveness; and unawareness of others' evaluations. Uncomfortable environments, on the other hand, were associated with the presence of ideal others, nervousness, embarrassment, body dissatisfaction, and self-presentational concerns.

As the above presented findings exemplify, social environment and presence of others can have different effects on exercisers' mental representations of their physical self. Large discrepancies are noted in the present body of research, including social and contextualized SPA, warranting for future research to examine a myriad of behavioral, affective, and cognitive outcomes.

The Effects of Exercise on Social Physique Anxiety

Aside from evidence indicating that SPA can influence individuals' exercise involvement preferences in and perceptions of exercise environments, engagement in physical activity has been found to affect their experience of SPA. We comment on how individuals with heightened SPA levels deal with experiences of anxiety and the coping strategies used to manage unwanted potential ramifications.

Exercise Interventions

Physical activity intervention studies have been found to attenuate the extent of SPA experienced by participants. Williams and Cash (2001), for example, have presented evidence that even involvement in a relatively short six-week circuit weight training program can result in not only improved body strength, but also decreased SPA, more positive self-appraisals of appearance, greater body-satisfaction, and enhanced physical self-efficacy among college students, compared to relevant control group participants. Similar effects were reported in McAuley, Bane, and Mihalko's (1995) 20-week aerobic exercise program involving formerly sedentary, middle-age participants. Anticipated decreases in body weight and adiposity were observed as well as increases in self-efficacy and decreases in SPA even after controlling for gender and reductions in body fat, weight, and measures of circumference. Similar findings have been reported in other physical activity intervention studies (e.g., McAuley, Marquez, Jerome, Blissmer, & Katula, 2002) with some evidence indicating that the addition of a brief educational session on relevant issues to an exercise intervention can result in even greater decreases in SPA when compared to control and exercise-only groups (Scott, Joyner, Czech, Munkasy, & Todd, 2009).

Some evidence also suggests that perceived changes in body appearance might be more important to exercise-related improvements in psychological well-being than bodily changes that are objectively identifiable (Martin Ginis et al., 2012). For example, Martin Ginis, Eng, Arbour, and Hartman (2005) reported that improvements in body image measures (e.g., SPA, body satisfaction, and drive for muscularity) at the end of a 12-week, 5-day/week strength-training program were not associated with objective physical changes among the men participating in the intervention even though significant associations were observed with subjective perceptions of physical change. Interestingly, changes in body image measures were significantly associated with both objective and subjective measures among the women participating in the study.

Client Coping With Social Physique Anxiety

An array of coping strategies have been identified to manage aversive SPA experiential states. These strategies can include behavioral and cognitive avoidance, appearance management, social support, dieting, physical activity, substance abuse, seeking of sexual attention, reappraisal, acceptance, and humor (Kowalski, Mack, Crocker, Niefer, & Fleming, 2006; Niefer,

McDonough, & Kowalski, 2010; Sabiston et al., 2007). Interestingly, Kowalski et al. (2006) have reported that even though women typically experience higher levels of SPA than men, they typically have better emotion-coping mechanisms for dealing with the affective experience.

Exercise imagery has also been found to be a useful strategy for many individuals coping with the experience of SPA while participating in aerobics exercise classes (Hausenblas, Hall, Rodgers, & Munroe, 1999). Both motivational (e.g., goal attainment, getting in shape) and cognitive (e.g., performance enhancement, rehearsing strategies, and techniques) imagery during exercise have been positively associated with appearance and health outcomes, and emotions and feelings experienced during the exercise (Giacobbi, Hausenblas, Fallon, & Hall, 2003) as well as improvements in exercise technique (Giacobbi et al., 2003; Hausenblas et al., 1999). Additionally, imagery related to appearance and fitness outcomes has been argued to play an important role in exercise adherence (Giacobbi et al., 2003).

MIKE'S EXPERIENCES: MUSCLE DYSMORPHIA

At 11 years of age, Mike saw a movie with Jean-Claude van Damme. Mike's fascination with van Damme's appearance prompted him to start working out—a behavioral engagement that progressed into working out *a lot* with the passage of time. By the time he had graduated high school, he had acquired the reputation of being "the fit muscular guy." When he set his sights on becoming a professional bodybuilder a few years later, Mike started taking steroids to gain even more bulk. From that point on, his life was dominated by training and workout regimens—and of course his preoccupation with weight, size, and muscularity.

A few years later, when preparing to enter his first body building competition, Mike experienced intense feelings of guilt and shame about the insufficiency of his gains in muscle mass and definition. Despite weighing a very lean 240 lbs and having good muscle definition, he was certain that his "small" size would reveal to everyone that his training efforts had been simply inadequate. To feel better, he intensified and prolonged his workouts, and he began to incessantly troll for reassurance on his muscularity from his girlfriend and other close friends. He also spent a lot of time scrutinizing himself in the mirror to identify body areas that were insufficiently massive. In addition to strict training, Mike became preoccupied with his diet. He spent hours planning his caloric intake, preparing his food, and becoming an expert on nutritional supplements, including protein bars, shakes, and other "natural" methods of promoting muscle growth. He would even bring his own food and beverages to social gatherings to avoid consuming anything that would interfere with his diet plan, or alternatively he would decline invitations that he thought would present uncomfortable choices in diet. In fact, sometimes he declined invitations to avoid meeting people socially on those days when he felt particularly puny and thus embarrassed about his body size.

A few weeks before his contest, Mike felt compelled to increase his time in the gym once again as well as the volume of his training. That was typical: he had been ceaselessly moving his goalposts further out because of the need he felt to acquire more and more size and definition. This time, however, he felt a grinding pain in his wrist when completing one of his heavy sets. He nonetheless continued working out and adhering to his training regimen because the competition was looming. His anxieties over the thought of missing training and getting slimmer were greater than the pain experienced in working out with his injured wrist. With his goals having the nature of a mirage, he experienced no sense of accomplishment in his efforts, despite a bodily massiveness that was evident to everyone. His injury exacerbated this problem because his anxieties and insecurities were skyrocketed by the limits that his wrist placed on his efforts to reach the mirage of his unattainable goals. His girlfriend noticed that he even started to avoid undressing in front of her with the lights on. The final week or so before the bodybuilding contest was the worst of all because Mike's priorities shifted completely to his training and dieting at the expense of his family and friends. Even his relationship with his girlfriend became rocky. His sole focus was on the inadequacies of his muscularity, body size, and weight. His distorted body image had taken over his life.

This vignette introduces Mike as an illustration of an individual obsessed with ideas of being too small, too skinny, and lacking in musculature, even while having a body objectively inconsistent with those beliefs. In the vignette, Mike was not satisfied with being known as the "fit muscular guy" because he perceived himself as being too skinny and thin—perhaps even underweight—and certainly as lacking in muscle mass and definition. His hypervigilance in detecting even small deviations from his perceived ideal reached the point where he was able to ignore the fact that his body image is inconsistent with his atypical lean massiveness at 240 pounds of "ripped" muscle definition. This story represents a glimpse of what a person with MD might be experiencing. In the following paragraphs, we discuss a theoretical background of BDD and MD and provide research on MD related to exercise and physical activity. Finally, we elaborate key points that practitioners should keep in mind when working with individuals showing signs of MD.

Theoretical and Empirical-Based Evidence for Muscle Dysmorphia

Muscle Dysmorphia—A Specific Type of Body Dysmorphic Disorder

MD is a particular type of BDD. BDD is characterized with an excessive concern with a negligible physical deformity in one's appearance. BDD, or "dysmorphophobia" as named in the *DSM-III*, was described as an example of atypical somatoform disorder with no specific formal criteria (American Psychiatric Association [APA], 1980). In the revised version of the *DSM-III*, BDD was categorized as a separate disorder in the somatoform section. In the *DSM-IV*, the diagnosis of BDD was substantially altered by the deletion of the criterion that minimized the distinction between delusional and nondelusional BDD (Phillips et al., 2010; Phillips, Hart, Simpson, & Stein, 2013). In the *DSM-V*, BDD is defined as "preoccupation with one or more perceived defects or flaws with physical appearance that are not observable. . . . individual has performed repetitive behaviors . . . in response to the appearance concerns . . . [causing] significant distress or impairment in social occupational and other important areas of functioning . . . concern with body fat or weight" (APA, 2013, p. 243). Appearance concerns might relate to one or many body areas, but most commonly they involve the face, head, skin, hair, and nose (Phillips, 2005; Phillips et al., 2010). Women tend to be concerned with skin, hips, legs, thighs, and breasts/chest, and they perceive themselves as too large or overweight. Men, on the other hand, tend to be concerned with genitals, body build, height, and excessive body hair, and they perceive themselves as not large enough (Perugi et al., 1997; Phillips & Diaz, 1997; Phillips, Menard, & Fay, 2006).

BDD is associated with high levels of anxiety, depressed mood, neuroticism, shame (Buhlmann et al., 2010), social avoidance (Kelly, Walters, & Phillips, 2010), feeling of embarrassment, unwillingness to reveal peculiar behaviors, and low self-esteem (Buhlmann et al., 2010; Phillips et al., 2010). To deal with negative ramifications of BDD and to minimize their effects, individuals engage in an array of behaviors that can include excessive grooming (e.g., makeup, shaving, styling), mirror checking, camouflaging (e.g., clothing or makeup), skin picking, social comparisons, reassurance seeking, dieting, substance use, excessive exercising, and cosmetic surgeries (Phillips et al., 2006; Pope et al., 2005). Studies indicate that patients with BDD respond poorly to surgical treatments because they rarely experience psychological improvements afterward (Sarwer & Spitzer, 2012). In fact, exacerbation of BDD symptoms are not uncommon following the cosmetic treatments (Crerand, Menard, & Phillips, 2010).

Impairments in the frontal-striatal and temporo-parietal-occipital circuits responsible for processing images and emotional information have been identified among BDD patients in neurophysiological and brain-imaging research. This is not entirely surprising given that BDD is associated with executive dysfunction (e.g., difficulties with manipulating, planning, and organizing information), attentional biases (Grocholewski, Kliemb, & Heinrichsa, 2012), and visual processing abnormalities. Individuals with BDD tend to encode details rather than holistic or configural aspects of the input from the environment (Feusner, Hembacher, Moller, & Moody, 2011). BDD patients portray some common characteristics of other disorders, such as obsessive-compulsive disorder (OCD), anxiety, psychosis, and major depressive disorders. Many of these can be co-morbid with BDD, including OCD and substance-related disorders (Phillips et al., 2010), social anxiety, major depressive disorder (Fang & Hofmann, 2010; Pinto & Phillips, 2005), and social phobia (Kelly, Dalrymple, Zimmerman, & Phillips, 2013).

Past and Present—Where Does Muscle Dysmorphia Belong?

Researchers have long debated MD as a classification because it overlaps with the symptomology of other psychopathologies. Chung (2001) argued that due to the historical and clinical aspects, MD should be classified as OCD. Some authors have suggested that MD should fall under an umbrella of eating disorders (Olivardia, Pope, & Hudson, 2000), because of its similarities with anorexia nervosa, including its symptomology and epidemiological and etiological factors (Murray et al., 2012). Others have considered MD as an exercise disorder due to the exorbitant amounts of time spent working out and some of its common symptomology with exercise dependency (Maida & Armstrong, 2005). In this case, it is important to identify individuals' reasons for exercising (e.g., being muscular vs. desire for "runner's high").

According to the *DSM-V*, MD is a specific type of BDD that occurs almost exclusively in males, even though the BDD's clinical characteristics appear to be largely similar across sexes (Phillips et al., 2010). In addition to BDD symptoms, a person with MD is "preoccupied with the idea that his or her body build is too small or insufficiently muscular" (APA, 2013, p. 243). Individuals with BDD can simultaneously show characteristics of MD (Pope, Gruber, Choi, Olivardia, & Phillips, 1997). Pope et al. (1997) found that among 193 participants with BDD, 9.3 percent of them also had apparent MD symptoms. Men with MD are more likely to exhibit compulsive behaviors, report poorer quality of life, make more attempts at suicide (Lecrubier, 2001), and more frequently abuse substances compared to men with BDD (Pope et al., 2005).

Increasing Evidence for Muscle Dysmorphia

Individuals in the bodybuilding culture colloquially labelled the MD syndrome as *bigorexia*, a term that was first found in the *Oxford English Dictionary* in 1990 (Quinion, 1997). It was first scientifically described in 1993 and termed *reversed anorexia nervosa* (Pope, Katz, & Hudson, 1993). Years later, Pope et al. (1997) named it MD, and the term thereafter rapidly spread through the literature. Nowadays, MD has become a well-established diagnostic entity and has received increased attention in clinical settings and evolving scientific research (Bjornsson, Didie, & Phillips, 2010).

A large number of men suffer from MD, striving for a perfect V-shaped torso and a lean, muscular sculpted body that is rather impossible to achieve through natural developmental processes and engagement in healthy behaviors (Bjornsson et al., 2010). Masculinity signifies health, strength, power, sexual virility, and threat (Buss, 1988), all of which, from an evolutionary perspective, are highly valued by potential partners, as these characteristics denote reproductive fitness (Singh, 1993).

The ideal male was epitomized in images of slim and muscular bodies with broad-shoulders and narrow hips in the mid-19th century. In the 1880s, mainstream Western media idealized naked male bodies as having well-developed muscularity, while often eyes and faces were averted or not visible (Grogan, 2008). Nowadays, companies such as Calvin Klein use men with "perfect" physiques to model and promote clothing and underwear as well as products that are unrelated to the body (Pope, Phillips, & Olivardia, 2000).

The appearance of naked men in popular magazines (e.g., *Cosmopolitan*) rose steeply from the 1950s (3%) to the 1990s (35%) (Pope, Olivardia, Borowiecki, & Cohane, 2001). Leit, Pope, and Gray (2001) suggested that the *Playgirl* centerfold men models lost approximately 5.4 kg of fat and gained about 12.3 kg of muscle mass from 1973 to 1997. Leit and colleagues (2001) also showed the direct effect of the media's portrayal of the ideal male body: men exposed to the muscular images demonstrated greater discrepancy between their ideal and actual subjective muscularity. It is not surprising that societal and cultural expectations start early in life. In fact, over the (past 30) years, action toys for children significantly changed in musculature (Pope, Olivardia, Gruber, & Borowiecki, 1999), which may contribute to body image disturbances for both sexes.

Attributing increased prevalence of MD to social reasons (e.g., media, culture) only may be shortsighted as MD shares some underlying biological and genetic predispositions that are similar to OCD (Phillips, McElroy, Hudson, & Pope, 1995). Therefore, it is not surprising that OCD has been identified as a co-morbid disorder of BDD and MD. Additional psychological risk factors for MD include low self-esteem, body dissatisfaction, drive for muscularity, and eating disorders (Grossbard, Atkins, Geisner, & Larimer, 2013). Nevertheless, most of the psychological research in MD is correlational in nature; therefore, we cannot infer causal relationships.

Characteristics and Manifestations of Muscle Dysmorphia

Despite recent evidence on body image and associated pathologies among men, the literature in this area remains scarce. Given the current research, it is evident that MD affects psychological, physical, and social aspects of one's well-being, which can be evident in the potential negative ramifications and characteristics discussed below.

Dissatisfaction with one's body size and musculature is one typical characteristic of MD (Grieve, 2007). Individuals with MD can spend hours and hours thinking, objectifying, and monitoring their bodies (Olivardia, 2001). Interestingly, they may acknowledge that others are muscular, yet perceive themselves as too small regardless of their actual size. Distortion of body image and internalization of body ideal may lead to compulsive exercise and overtraining. As illustrated in Mike's vignette, the drive to attain an ideal musculature can be associated with extreme dieting and use of dangerous anabolic steroids (Pope et al., 1997).

A confluence of psychological and physical preoccupation with one's physique may lead to impairment in social and intimate relationships, poor occupational functioning (Grieve, Truba, & Bowersox, 2009), and poor quality of life (Pope et al., 2005). For example, individuals with MD may shy away from situations that involve bodily exposure and consequently tend to wear baggy clothing—either to look larger or to hide their "tiny, weak" bodies (Dawes & Mankin, 2004). When attending social events, they are more likely to experience intense anxiety and distress (Pope et al., 1997). Additionally, it is not uncommon for individuals with MD to miss out on important events, such as a birth of a child, either because they are preoccupied with thoughts about their physique or because they do not want to skip their workout (Pope et al., 1993). Another common characteristic of MD is to remain housebound for days due to poor body image and body dissatisfaction (Olivardia, 2001), to prevent body exposure, and to minimize levels of anxiety.

Although there are men who experience a high drive for muscularity, such as those with MD (Grossbard et al., 2013), some other men experience a high drive for thinness (Kelley, Neufeld, & Musher-Eizenman, 2010; Krane, Choi, Baird, Aimar, & Kauer, 2004). Men falling into either of these categories have higher rates of body preoccupation and compulsivity, suggesting that these constructs can be mutually inclusive. Men with MD also characteristically perceive a substantial discrepancy between their desired and actual bodies (Pope et al., 2000), accompanied by body and muscularity dissatisfaction (Grossbard et al., 2013; Olivardia, Pope, Borowiecki, & Cohan, 2004), body distortion, and muscle belittlement (Olivardia et al., 2004). Olivardia and his colleagues (2004) have reported, for example, that ideal body selections in a sample of men with MD were an average of 11.4 kg more muscular and 3.6 kg leaner in body fat than what they carried on their actual bodies. Other researchers have observed individuals with MD reporting greater body dissatisfaction focused on the lower torso (e.g., buttocks, hips, thighs, legs) relative to musculature, muscle tone, weight, and size (Choi, Pope, & Olivardia, 2002; Maida & Armstrong, 2005). MD is associated with poorer body image and a tendency for self-objectification (Choi et al., 2002), which is not surprising as individuals suffering from MD are known to spend a vast amount of time scrutinizing their bodies.

Individuals with body or muscle dissatisfaction and body image issues tend to experience low self-esteem, negative affect, disordered eating, increased depressive symptoms, and perceptions of being fat and out of shape (Grieve, 2007; McFarland & Kaminski, 2009). MD is also associated with trait anxiety and SPA, obsessive-compulsive features, anorexic and bulimic behaviors, risk indicators for interpersonal problems (Chandler, Derryberry, Grieve, & Pegg, 2009), perfectionism, and hostility (Maida & Armstrong, 2005). Individuals with MD experience a sense of shame and embarrassment about having this disorder. To minimize the negative consequences, these individuals may engage in risky muscle-enhancing behaviors, including excessive weightlifting and anabolic steroid and dietary supplement use (Pope et al., 1997).

Bodybuilding, Weightlifting, and Exercise

In 2002, Choi et al. wrote a short report on MD titled *Muscle Dysmorphia: A New Syndrome in Weightlifters*. Bodybuilders were familiar with MD and its symptomology well before it appeared in the *DSM*. In fact, many early studies on MD were conducted with bodybuilders and/or weightlifters (Pope et al., 1993). More recently, competing and non-natural bodybuilders have been reported to be more likely to develop MD symptoms than non-competing and natural bodybuilders (Cella, Iannaccone, & Cotrufo, 2012). Moreover, the symptoms experienced by competing and non-natural bodybuilders tend to be more severe (Santarnecchi & Dèttore, 2012). Baghurst and Lirgg (2009), however, observed non-significant differences in MD symptoms between natural and non-natural bodybuilders other than in pharmacological use.

Discrepancies in MD development may depend on individuals' motivation for exercise. For instance, weightlifters have been reported to exhibit MD symptoms to a greater extent when they are more interested in enhanced appearance than in improved performance (Skemp, Mikat, Schenck, & Kramer, 2013). Interestingly, MD can have state-like properties among men who weightlift on a regular basis, as reported by Thomas, Tod, and Lavallee (2011). Specifically, they reported lower scores on MD attributes of drive for size, appearance intolerance, and functional impairment after a training day compared to a rest day.

Androgenic-Anabolic Steroids and Other Pharmacological Substances Use

Androgenic-anabolic steroids (AAS) are synthetic substances that have effects similar to testosterone (Barceloux & Palmer, 2013). AAS promote protein synthesis leading to growth of skeletal muscles and development of male sexual characteristics (van Amsterdam, Opperhuizen, & Hartgens, 2010). In other words, AAS contribute to an increase in fat-free mass and strength, and a decrease in fat mass, which is appealing to individuals who would like to gain muscle mass and be stronger and faster. Long-term use and excessive doses of AAS can produce harmful health effects, including aggressiveness, depression, negative mood symptoms, irritability, acne, and liver cancer, among others (van Amsterdam et al., 2010). An increased prevalence of AAS use is evident (McCabe, Brower, West, Nelson, & Wechsler, 2007) in sport for performance enhancement, but also in other realms for appearance enhancement purposes (Rohman, 2009; Schwartz, Grammas, Sutherland, Siffert, & Bush-King, 2010).

In addition to AAS, the use of other pharmacological substances, such as diuretics and laxatives, tend to be associated with MD (Pope et al., 2005). It is unclear whether the use of these substances is a function of body dissatisfaction or competitive issues, or whether the symptoms of MD are a cause or an effect of the AAS use (Kanayama, Barry, Hudson, & Pope, 2006). To that end, Rohman (2009) has suggested that perhaps a preexisting body image disturbance leads to AAS use in hopes to enhance physique and minimize negative psychological effects.

Recommendations for Sport and Exercise Psychology Practitioners

Even though SPA and MD differ conceptually, they share considerable commonality. The following recommendations are therefore largely applicable to practitioners working with clients who have MD or SPA. Clearly there is at least one important distinction between the constructs that cannot be ignored. Specifically, MD is a psychosomatic disorder categorized as a subtype of BDD in the *DSM-V*. SPA, on the other hand, is a type of anxiety that is not inherently pathological, but rather a natural human experience elicited under certain circumstances.

Motivating and Adhering to Exercise When Experiencing Social Physique Anxiety and Muscle Dysmorphia

Individuals with SPA and/or MD tend to experience (intense) negative emotions. As such, it is important to build rapport and establish trust through active listening and non-verbal gestures (Grieve et al., 2009). Another critical aspect when dealing with individuals suffering from either of these conditions is the understanding of their needs, motives, and deterrents to exercise.

Unlike MD, SPA can either increase or decrease one's motivation and adherence to exercise. In addition to spending less time exercising, individuals with high SPA are more likely to exercise for appearance-related reasons than individuals with low SPA (Frederick & Morrison, 1996). Psychoeducational approaches for the promotion of individualized programs of healthy exercise behavior (i.e., intensity, duration, mode) as well as for the promotion of healthy exercise-related behaviors (i.e., diet, dietary supplementation) among individuals with SPA and/or subclinical levels of MD can be recommended as having potential utility.

Focusing on health-related (as opposed to appearance-related) motives may increase exercise participation and adherence (Walsh, 2012). Additionally, Thøgersen-Ntoumani and Ntoumanis (2006) showed that promoting self-determined motivation may lead to adaptive (e.g., behavioral, cognitive, physical) self-evaluative strategies to foster exercise. Exercise-related changes in physical and psychological parameters tend to occur over time, and anticipated benefits may not occur immediately. Therefore, realistic client expectations on this account should be fostered by practitioners through well-considered goal-setting programs. Identification of the client's presenting stage of change, perhaps in conjunction with motivational interviewing processes, is warranted in program development because that information can allow intervention strategies to be tailored to optimize progression into healthful exercise maintenance (Thøgersen-Ntoumani & Ntoumanis, 2006). As mentioned earlier, psychoeducational processes providing relevant information on exercise and exercise-related behaviors should be embedded in the consultation process to avoid misconceptions about the effects of exercise.

With regard to doses of exercise for the reduction of anxiety levels, exercising three to four times per week has been shown to be the most effective (Wipfli, Rethorst, & Landers, 2008). Some research suggests that exercising as little as 20 minutes in each bout can help decrease anxiety (Petruzzello, Landers, Hatfield, Kubitz, & Salazar, 1991), although Ekkekakis and Petruzzello (1999) subsequently argued that duration of exercise does not mediate anxiolytic effects. Modalities of physical activity and exercise that have been found to be effective in reducing anxiety include walking, running, resistance training, yoga, and tai chi (Merom et al., 2008), although almost certainly client-preferred modalities have more potential on that account than those that are aversive. Although the stable tendency to experience SPA can be positively influenced by long-term exercise participation (McAuley, Bane, Rudolph, & Lox, 1995), that trait tendency is unlikely to be noticeably affected in acute or short-term programs of physical activity. Exercise interventions of 16 weeks or more have been found to result in decreases in trait anxiety (Petruzzello et al., 1991), and the SPA trait, as a specific type of anxiety, would very likely require a similar length intervention for effects to be observed.

The experience of SPA states are subject to environmental influence (Van Raalte et al., 2004). Offering individuals environmental alternatives for exercise engagement, particularly in initial encounters with activities, may prove useful in overcoming evaluative concerns that clients with SPA and subclinical MD may harbor. After a period of successful engagement, progression to environments previously considered threatening by these clients may be viable. Promotion of autonomy-supporting exercise environments (Hagger & Chatzisarantis, 2009) is likely to have beneficial effects on exercise adherence and lead to positive affect in any event (Vazou-Ekkekakis & Ekkekakis, 2009; Walsh, 2012). Indeed, affective states during acute exercise are likely determinants of continued exercise participation (Ekkekakis, Hall, & Petruzzello, 2005). Finally, implementing self-regulatory strategies designed to increase self-esteem levels among clients can be effective mechanisms in exercise promotion (Thøgersen-Ntoumani, Ntoumanis, Cumming, Bartholomew, & Pearce, 2011), as high levels of self-esteem might protect against the development of body-image concerns, symptoms of MD (Grieve, Jackson, Reece, Marklin, & Delaney, 2008), and eating disorders (O'Dea, 2004).

Additional Recommendations for Muscle Dysmorphia

Most recommendations offered in the previous section refer to individuals who experience SPA, but individuals with subclinical MD can benefit from them as well. When consulting with clients exhibiting MD symptoms, additional therapy might be required. Therefore, sport and exercise psychology professionals may require additional training to enhance their ability to recognize potential challenges in the area while also seeking to develop networks of clinically oriented professionals so that ethically appropriate referrals can be made when needed. To reiterate, MD has a variety of co-morbidities, including depressive disorders, disordered eating, and OCD, so practitioners need to be aware and exercise appropriate caution when clients present with symptoms that may suggest MD even at a subclinical level (Olivardia et al., 2004).

Treatments for MD by appropriately trained clinicians involve psychological (e.g., behavioral, cognitive-behavioral, cognitive) and pharmacological therapies. Cognitive behavioral therapy (CBT) has been recommended as having considerable utility and effectiveness

(Williams, Hadjistavropoulos, & Sharpe, 2006), with rational emotive behavioral therapy modalities offering avenues for practitioners to identify distorted patterns of thinking (Dryden & David, 2008). Moreover, cognitive restructuring and reframing negative self-statements and thoughts about one's appearance can usefully challenge patients' assumptions about being too small or weak (Veale, 2004). Concerns about exposing the *defect* to others and avoidance behaviors such as camouflaging present challenges for practitioners, so clinically relevant strategies available in CBT to reduce anxieties that a person with MD experiences during body exposure or missing a workout can have relevance. Response prevention to manage compulsive behaviors (e.g., mirror checking, self-surveillance) and reassurance seeking can be implemented through self-monitoring and understanding the antecedents of the behavior (Coles, Heimberg, Frost, & Steketee, 2005). Behavioral intervention strategies can also be implemented to address with excessive weightlifting, disproportionate time spent at gym, or use of steroids when appropriate. These involve *behavioral shaping* and *reinforcement of successive approximations* of desired behaviors (Grieve et al., 2009; Skinner, 1985). Using mindfulness techniques including the Mindfulness-Acceptance-Commitment approach (Gardner & Moore, 2007) or Acceptance and Commitment Therapy (Hayes & Strosahl, 2004) can be useful for treating individuals with MD. These approaches emphasize awareness and acceptance of the present moment without being judgmental. Veale (2002) suggests mindfulness techniques can help modify one's values and improve the course of treatment.

Finally, pharmacological therapy may also be effective for treating MD symptoms that are similar to those in eating disorders and OCD (Phillips, 2005). Pharmacological approaches to MD typically involve selective serotonin reuptake inhibitors (SSRIs; e.g., fluvoxamine, sertraline, clomipramine, etc.), which are neurotransmitters to facilitate more positive mood states (Barlow & Durand, 2015). Regardless of whether interventions are psychological or pharmacological in nature, professionals should incorporate techniques for relapse prevention. These might include discussions of fears and reflective thinking on the session to monitor progress and gains (Wilhelm, Phillips, Fama, Greenberg, & Steketee, 2011).

RECOMMENDED READINGS

Asmundson, G. J. G., Fetzner, M. G., DeBoer, L. B., Powers, M. B., Otto, M. W., & Smits, J. A. J. (2013). Let's get physical: A contemporary review of the anxiolytic effects of exercise for anxiety and its disorders. *Depression and Anxiety, 30*(4), 362–373. doi: 10.1002/da.22043

Cafri, G., & Thompson, J. K. (2004). Measuring male body image: A review of the current methodology. *Psychology of Men & Masculinity, 5*(1), 18–29. doi: 10.1037/1524-9220.5.1.18

Campbell, A., & Hausenblas, H. A. (2009). Effects of exercise interventions on body image: A meta-analysis. *Journal of Health Psychology, 14*(6), 780–793. doi: 10.1177/1359105309338977

Grieve, F. G., Truba, N., & Bowersox, S. (2009). Etiology, assessment, and treatment of muscle dysmorphia. *Journal of Cognitive Psychotherapy, 23*(4), 306–314. doi: 10.1891/0889-8391.23.4.306

Hausenblas, H. A., Brewer, B. W., & Van Raalte, J. L. (2004). Self-presentation and exercise. *Journal of Applied Sport Psychology, 16*(1), 3–18. doi: 10.1080/104132004902600

Leone, J. E., Sedory, E. J., & Gray, K. A. (2005). Recognition and treatment of muscle dysmorphia and related body image disorders. *Journal of Athletic Training, 40*(4), 352.

Martin Ginis, K. A., & Bassett, R. L. (2011). Exercise and changes in body image. In T. F. Cash & L. Smolak (Eds.), *Body image: A handbook of science, practice, and prevention* (2nd ed., pp. 378–386). New York, NY: Guilford Press.

Martin Ginis, K. A., Bassett, R. L., & Conlin, C. (2012). Body image and exercise. In E. Acevedo (Ed.), *Oxford handbook of exercise psychology* (pp. 55–75). London, UK: Oxford University Press.

Nieuwoudt, J. E., Zhou, S., Coutts, R. A., & Booker, R. (2012). Muscle dysmorphia: Current research and potential classification as a disorder. *Psychology of Sport and Exercise, 13*(5), 569–577. doi: 10.1016/j.psychsport.2012.03.006

O'Dea, J. A. (2004). Evidence for a self-esteem approach in the prevention of body image and eating problems among children and adolescents. *Eating Disorders, 12*(3), 225–239. doi: 10.1080/10640260490481438

Olivardia, R. (2001). Mirror, mirror on the wall, who's the largest of them all? The features and phenomenology of muscle dysmorphia. *Harvard Review of Psychiatry, 9*(5), 254–259. doi: 10.1080/hrp.9.5.254.259

Phillips, K. A. (1996). *The broken mirror: Understanding and treating body dysmorphic disorder*. Oxford, UK: Oxford University Press.

Phillips, K. A. (2011). Body image and body dysmorphic disorder. In T. F. Cash & L. Smolak (Eds.). *Body image: A handbook of theory, research, and clinical practice* (2nd ed., pp. 305–314). New York, NY: Guilford Press.

Pope, Jr., H. G., Phillips, K. A., & Olivardia, R. (2000). *The Adonis Complex: The secret crisis of male body obsession*. New York, NY: The Free Press.

Ragan, J., Greenberg, J. L., Beeger, E., Sedovic, M., & Wilhelm, S. (2010). Body dysmorphic disorder. In S. G. Hofmann & M. A. Reinecke (Eds.), *Cognitive-behavioral therapy with adults: A guide to empirically-informed assessment and intervention* (pp. 149–161). Cambridge: Cambridge University Press.

Thompson, J. K. (2004). The (mis)measurement of body image: Ten strategies to improve assessment for applied and research purposes. *Body Image, 1*(1), 7–14.

Thompson, J. K., & Cafri, G. (2007). *The muscular ideal: Psychological, social, and medical perspectives*. Washington, DC: American Psychological Association.

Tucker, L. A., & Mortell, R. (1993). Comparison of the effects of walking and weight training programs on body image in middle-aged women: An experimental study. *American Journal of Health Promotion 8*(1), 34–42. doi: http://dx.doi.org/10.4278/08901-1718-.1.34

Veale, D. (2004). Advances in a cognitive behavioural model of body dysmorphic disorder. *Body Image, 1*(1), 113–125. doi: 10.1016/s1740-1445(03)00009-3

Walsh, A. (2012). Exercise intensity, affect, and adherence: A guide for the fitness professional. *Journal of Sport Psychology in Action, 3*(3), 193–207. doi: 10.1080/21520704.2012.674629

Williams, J., Hadjistavropoulos, T., & Sharpe, D. (2006). A meta-analysis of psychological and pharmacological treatments for Body Dysmorphic Disorder. *Behaviour Research and Therapy, 44*(1), 99–111. doi: http://dx.doi.org/10.1016/j.brat.2004.12.006

REFERENCES

American Psychiatric Association (1980). *Diagnostic and statistical manual of mental disorders* (3rd ed.). Washington, DC: American Psychiatric Association.

American Psychiatric Association. (2013). *Diagnostic and statistical manual of mental disorders: DSM-5*. Arlington, VA: American Psychiatric Association.

Baghurst, T., & Lirgg, C. (2009). Characteristics of muscle dysmorphia in male football, weight training, and competitive natural and non-natural bodybuilding samples. *Body Image, 6*(3), 221–227. doi: 10.1016/j.bodyim.2009.03.002

Bain, L. L., Wilson, T., & Chaikind, E. (1989). Participant perceptions of exercise programs for overweight women. *Research Quarterly for Exercise and Sport, 60*(2), 134–143. doi: 10.1080/02701367.1989.10607428

Barceloux, D. G., & Palmer, R. B. (2013). Anabolic—Androgenic steroids. *Disease-a-Month, 59*(6), 226–248. doi: 10.1016/j.disamonth.2013.03.010

Barlow, D. H., & Durand, V. M. (2015). Mood disorders and suicide. In D. H. Barlow & V. M. Durand (Eds.), *Abnormal psychology: An integrative approach* (7th ed.), pp. 212–267. Belmont, CA: Wadsworth Cengage Learning.

Bjornsson, A. S., Didie, E. R., & Phillips, K. A. (2010). Body dysmorphic disorder. *Dialogues in Clinical Neuroscience, 12*(2), 221–232. Retrieved from www.ncbi.nlm.nih.gov/pmc/articles/PMC3181960/

Brunet, J., & Sabiston, C. M. (2011). In the company we keep: Social physique anxiety levels differ around parents and peers. *Journal of Health Psychology, 16*(1), 42–49. doi: 10.1177/1359105310367530

Buhlmann, U., Glaesmerb, H., Mewesc, R., Famad, J. M., Wilhelmd, S., Brählerb, E., & Riefc, W. (2010). Updates on the prevalence of body dysmorphic disorder: A population-based survey. *Psychiatry Research, 178*(1), 171–175. doi: 10.1016/j.psychres.2009.05.002

Buss, D. M. (1988). The evolution of human intrasexual competition: Tactics of mate attraction. *Journal of Personality and Social Psychology, 54*(4), 616. Retrieved from www.apa.org/pubs/journals/psp/

Cella, S., Iannaccone, M., & Cotrufo, P. (2012). Muscle dysmorphia: A comparison between competitive bodybuilders and fitness practitioners. *Journal of Nutritional Therapeutics, 1*, 12–18.

Chandler, C. G., Derryberry, W. P., Grieve, F. G., & Pegg, P. O. (2009). Are anxiety and obsessive-compulsive symptoms related to muscle dysmorphia? *International Journal of Men's Health, 8*(2), 143. doi: 10.3149/jmh.0802.143

Choi, P. Y. L., Pope Jr., H. G., & Olivardia, R. (2002). Muscle dysmorphia: A new syndrome in weight-lifters. *British Journal of Sports Medicine, 36*(5), 375–376. doi: 10.1136/bjsm.36.5.375

Chung, B. (2001). Muscle dysmorphia: A critical review of the proposed criteria. *Perspectives in Biology & Medicine, 44*(4), 565–574.

Coles, M. E., Heimberg, R. G., Frost, R. O., & Steketee, G. (2005). Not just right experiences and obsessive—compulsive features: Experimental and self-monitoring perspectives. *Behaviour Research and Therapy, 43*(2), 153–167. doi: http://dx.doi.org/10.1016/j.brat.2004.01.002

Crawford, S., & Eklund, R. C. (1994). Social physique anxiety, reasons for exercise, and attitudes toward exercise settings. *Journal of Sport & Exercise Psychology, 16*, 70–82.

Crerand, C. E., Menard, W., & Phillips, K. A. (2010). Surgical and minimally invasive cosmetic procedures among persons with body dysmorphic disorder. *Annals of Plastic Surgery, 65*(1), 11–16. doi: 10.1097/SAP.0b013e3181bba08f

Culos-Reed, S. N., Brawley, L. R., Martin, K. A., & Leary, M. R. (2002). Self-presentation concerns and health behaviors among cosmetic surgery patients. *Journal of Applied Social Psychology, 32*(3), 560–569. doi: 10.1111/j.1559-1816.2002.tb00230.x

Dawes, J., & Mankin, T. (2004). Muscle dysmorphia. *Strength & Conditioning Journal, 26*(2), 24–25. Retrieved from http://journals.lww.com/nsca-scj/Abstract/2004/04000/Muscle_Dysmorphia.4.aspx

Dryden, W., & David, D. (2008). Rational emotive behavior therapy: Current status. *Journal of Cognitive Psychotherapy, 22*(3), 195–209. doi: 10.1891/0889-8391.22.3.195

Ekkekakis, P., Hall, E. E., & Petruzzello, S. J. (2005). Variation and homogeneity in affective responses to physical activity of varying intensities: An alternative perspective on dose—response based on evolutionary considerations. *Journal of Sports Sciences, 23*(5), 477–500. doi: 10.1080/02640410400021492

Ekkekakis, P., & Petruzzello, S. J. (1999). Acute aerobic exercise and affect: Current status, problems, and prospects regarding dose-response. *Sports Medicine, 28*(5), 337–374.

Fang, A., & Hofmannn, S. G. (2010). Relationship between social anxiety disorder and body dysmorphic disorder. *Clinical Psychology Review, 30*(8), 1040–1048. doi: 10.1016/j.cpr.2010.08.001

Feusner, J. D., Hembacher, E., Moller, H., & Moody, T. D. (2011). Abnormalities of object visual processing in body dysmorphic disorder. *Psychological Medicine, 41*(11), 2385. doi: 10.1017/S0033291711000572

Fitzsimmons-Craft, E. E., Harney, M. B., Brownstone, L. M., Higgins, M. K., & Bardone-Cone, A. M. (2012). Examining social physique anxiety and disordered eating in college women: The roles of social comparison and body surveillance. *Appetite, 59*, 796–805.

Focht, B. C., & Hausenblas, H. A. (2003). State anxiety responses to acute exercise in women with high social physique anxiety. *Journal of Sport & Exercise Psychology, 25*(2), 123–144.

Focht, B. C., & Hausenblas, H. A. (2004). Perceived evaluative threat and state anxiety during exercise in women with high social physique anxiety. *Journal of Applied Sport Psychology, 16*, 361–368.

Focht, B. C., & Hausenblas, H. A. (2006). Exercising in public and private environments: Effects on feeling states in women with social physique anxiety. *Journal of Applied Biobehavioral Research, 11*(3–4), 147–165. doi: 10.1111/j.1751-9861.2007.00002.x

Frederick, C. M., & Morrison, C. S. (1996). Social physique anxiety: Personality constructs, motivations, exercise attitudes, and behaviors. *Perceptual and Motor Skills, 82*(3), 963–972. doi: 10.2466/pms.1996.82.3.963

Gardner, F. L., & Moore, Z. E. (2007). *The psychology of enhancing human performance: The Mindfulness-Acceptance-Commitment (MAC) approach.* New York, NY: Springer Publishing Company.

Giacobbi, P., Hausenblas, H. A., Fallon, E. A., & Hall, C. A. (2003). Even more about exercise imagery: A grounded theory of exercise imagery. *Journal of Applied Sport Psychology, 15*(2), 160–175. doi: 10.1080/10413200305391

Goodwin, H., Haycraft, E., Willis, A. M., & Meyer, C. (2011). Compulsive exercise: The role of personality, psychological morbidity, and disordered eating. *International Journal of Eating Disorders, 44*(7), 655–660. doi: 10.1002/eat.20902

Grieve, F. G. (2007). A conceptual model of factors contributing to the development of muscle dysmorphia. *Eating Disorders, 15*(1), 63–80. doi: 10.1080/10640260601044535

Grieve, F. G., Jackson, L., Reece, T., Marklin, L., & Delaney, A. (2008). Correlates of social physique anxiety in men. *Journal of Sport Behavior, 31*(4), 329–337.

Grieve, F. G., Truba, N., & Bowersox, S. (2009). Etiology, assessment, and treatment of muscle dysmorphia. *Journal of Cognitive Psychotherapy, 23*(4), 306–314. doi: 10.1891/0889-8391.23.4.306

Grocholewski, A., Kliemb, S., & Heinrichsa, N. (2012). Selective attention to imagined facial ugliness is specific to body dysmorphic disorder. *Body Image, 9*(2), 261–269. doi: 10.1016/j.bodyim.2012.01.002

Grogan, S. (2008). *Body image: Understanding body dissatisfaction in men, women, and children* (2nd ed.). New York, NY: Psychology Press.

Grossbard, J. R., Atkins, D. C., Geisner, I. M., & Larimer, M. E. (2013). Does depressed mood moderate the influence of drive for thinness and muscularity on eating disorder symptoms among college men? *Psychology of Men & Masculinity, 14*(3), 281. doi: 10.1037/a0028913

Hagger, M., & Chatzisarantis, N. (2009). Integrating the theory of planned behaviour and self-determination theory in health behaviour: A meta-analysis. *British Journal of Health Psychology, 14*, 277–302.

Hagger, M. S., & Stevenson, A. (2010). Social physique anxiety and physical self-esteem: Gender and age effects. *Psychology & Health, 25*(1), 89–110. doi: 10.1080/08870440903160990

Hausenblas, H. A., Hall, C. R., Rodgers, W. M., & Munroe, K. J. (1999). Exercise imagery: Its nature and measurement. *Journal of Applied Sport Psychology, 11*(2), 171–180.

Hayes, S. C., & Strosahl, K. D. (Eds.). (2004). *A practical guide to Acceptance and Commitment Therapy.* New York, NY: Springer-Verlag.

Kanayama, G., Barry, S., Hudson, J., & Pope, H. (2006). Body image and attitudes toward male roles in anabolic-androgenic steroid users. *The American Journal of Psychiatry, 163*(4), 697–703.

Katula, J. A., & McAuley, E. (2001). The mirror does not lie: Acute exercise and self-efficacy. *International Journal of Behavioral Medicine, 8*(4), 319–326. doi: 10.1207/s15327558ijbm0804_6

Kelley, C. C., Neufeld, J. M., & Musher-Eizenman, D. R. (2010). Drive for thinness and drive for muscularity: Opposite ends of the continuum or separate constructs? *Body Image, 7*(1), 74–77. doi: 10.1016/j.bodyim.2009.09.008

Kelly, M. M., Dalrymple, K., Zimmerman, M., & Phillips, K. A. (2013). A comparison study of body dysmorphic disorder versus social phobia. *Psychiatry Research, 205*(1–2), 109–116. doi: 10.1016/j.psychres.2012.08.009

Kelly, M. M., Walters, C., & Phillips, K. A. (2010). Social anxiety and its relationship to functional impairment in body dysmorphic disorder. *Behavior Therapy, 41*(2), 143–153.

Kowalski, K. C., Mack, D. E., Crocker, P. R. E., Niefer, C. B., & Fleming, T.-L. (2006). Coping with social physique anxiety in adolescence. *Journal of Adolescent Health, 39*(2), 275.e279–275.e216. doi: http://dx.doi.org/10.1016/j.jadohealth.2005.12.015

Krane, V., Choi, P. Y. L., Baird, S. M., Aimar, C. M., & Kauer, K. J. (2004). Living the paradox: Female athletes negotiate femininity and muscularity. *Sex Roles, 50*(5–6), 315. doi: 10.1023/B:SERS.0000018888.48437.4f

Kruisselbrink, L. D., Dodge, A. M., Swanburg, S. L., & MacLeod, A. L. (2004). Influence of same-sex and mixed-sex exercise settings on the social physique anxiety and exercise intentions of males and females. *Journal of Sport & Exercise Psychology, 26*, 616–622.

Lamarche, L., Gammage, K. L., & Strong, H. A. (2009). The effect of mirrored environments on self-presentational efficacy and social anxiety in women in a step aerobics class. *Psychology of Sport and Exercise, 10*(1), 67–71. doi:10.1016/j.psychsport.2008.06.006

Lamarche, L., Kerr, G., Faulkner, G., Gammage, K. L., & Klentrou, P. (2012). A qualitative examination of body image threats using social self-preservation theory. *Body Image, 9*(1), 145–154. doi: 10.1016/j.bodyim.2011.10.004

Lantz, C. D., Hardy, C. J., & Ainsworth, B. E. (1997). Social physique anxiety and perceived exercise behavior. *Journal of Sport Behavior, 20*(1), 83–93.

Leary, M. R. (1992). Self-presentational processes in exercise and sport. *Journal of Sport & Exercise Psychology, 14*, 339–351.

Leary, M. R., & Kowalski, R. M. (1990). Impression management: A literature review and two-component model. *Psychological Bulletin, 107*, 34–47.

Lecrubier, Y. (2001). The influence of comorbidity on the prevalence of suicidal behaviour. *European psychiatry, 16*(7), 395. doi: 10.1016/s0924-9338(01)00596-x

Leit, R. A., Pope Jr., H. G., & Gray, J. J. (2001). Cultural expectations of muscularity in men: The evolution of playgirl centerfolds. *The International Journal of Eating Disorders, 29*(1), 90–93. doi: 10.1002/1098-108x(200101)29:1<90::aid-eat15>3.0.co;2-f

Mack, D. E., Strong, H. A., Kowalski, K. C., & Crocker, P. R. E. (2007). Does friendship matter? An examination of social physique anxiety in adolescence. *Journal of Applied Social Psychology, 37*(6), 1248–1264. doi: 10.1111/j.1559-1816.2007.00211.x

Maida, D., & Armstrong, S. L. (2005). The classification of muscle dysmorphia. *International Journal of Men's Health, 4*(1), 73–91. doi: 10.3149/jmh.0401.73

Marsh, H. W., & Shavelson, R. J. (1985). Self-concept: Its multifaceted, hierarchical structure. *Educational Psychologist, 20*, 107–125.

Martin, K. A., & Fox, L. D. (2001). Group and leadership effects on social anxiety experienced during an exercise class. *Journal of Applied Social Psychology, 31*(5), 1000–1016. doi: 10.1111/j.1559-1816.2001.tb02659.x

Martin Ginis, K. A., Eng, J. J., Arbour, K. P., & Hartman, J. W. (2005). Mind over muscle? Sex differences in the relationship between body image change and subjective and objective physical changes following a 12-week strength-training program. *Body Image, 2*(4), 363–372. doi: 10.1016/j.bodyim.2005.08.003

Martin Ginis, K. A., Lindwall, M., & Prapavessis, H. (2007). Who cares what other people think? Self-presentation in sport and exercise. In G. Tenenbaum & R. Eklund (Eds.), *Handbook of sport psychology* (3rd ed., pp. 136–157). Hoboken, NJ: Wiley.

Martin Ginis, K. A., McEwan, D., Josse, A. R., & Phillips, S. M. (2012). Body image change in obese and overweight women enrolled in a weight-loss intervention: The importance of perceived versus actual physical changes. *Body Image, 9*(3), 311–317. doi: http://dx.doi.org/10.1016/j.bodyim.2012.04.002

Martin Ginis, K. A., Murru, E., Conlin, C., & Strong, H. A. (2011). Construct validation of a state version of the Social Physique Anxiety Scale among young women. *Body Image, 8*(1), 52–57. doi: 10.1016/j.bodyim.2010.10.001

McAuley, E., Bane, S. M., & Mihalko, S. L. (1995). Exercise in middle-aged adults: Self-efficacy and self-presentational outcomes. *Preventive Medicine, 24*(4), 319–328. doi: 10.1006/pmed.1995.1053

McAuley, E., Bane, S. M., Rudolph, D. L., & Lox, C. L. (1995). Physique anxiety and exercise in middle-aged adults. *Journal of Gerontology: B—Psychological Sciences and Social Sciences 50B*(5), 229–235. doi: 10.1093/geronb/50B.5.P229

McAuley, E., Marquez, D. X., Jerome, G. J., Blissmer, B., & Katula, J. (2002). Physical activity and physique anxiety in older adults: Fitness, and efficacy influences. *Aging & Mental Health, 6*(3), 222–230. doi: 10.1080/13607860220142459

McCabe, S. E., Brower, K. J., West, B. T., Nelson, T. F., & Wechsler, H. (2007). Trends in non-medical use of anabolic steroids by U.S. college students: Results from four national surveys. *Drug and Alcohol Dependence, 90*(2–3), 243–251. doi: 10.1016/j.drugalcdep.2007.04.004

McCreary, D. R., & Saucier, D. M. (2009). Drive for muscularity, body comparison, and social physique anxiety in men and women. *Body Image*, 6(1), 24–30. doi: 10.1016/j.bodyim.2008.09.002

McFarland, M. B., & Kaminski, P. L. (2009). Men, muscles, and mood: The relationship between self-concept, dysphoria, and body image disturbances. *Eating behaviors*, 10(1), 68–70. doi:10.1016/j.eatbeh.2008.10.007

Merom, D., Phongsavan, P., Wagner, R., Chey, T., Marnane, C., Steel, Z., . . . Bauman, A. (2008). Promoting walking as an adjunct intervention to group cognitive behavioral therapy for anxiety disorders—A pilot group randomized trial. *Journal of Anxiety Disorders*, 22(6), 959–968. doi: http://dx.doi.org/10.1016/j.janxdis.2007.09.010

Murray, S. B., Rieger, E., Hildebrandt, T., Karlova, L., Russell, J., Boon, E., . . . Touyza, S. W. (2012). A comparison of eating, exercise, shape, and weight related symptomatology in males with muscle dysmorphia and anorexia nervosa. *Body Image*, 9(2), 193–200. doi: 10.1016/j.bodyim.2012.01.008

Niefer, C. B., McDonough, M. H., & Kowalski, K. C. (2010). Coping with social physique anxiety among adolescent female athletes. *International Journal of Sport Psychology*, 41(4), 369.

O'Dea, J. A. (2004). Evidence for a self-esteem approach in the prevention of body image and eating problems among children and adolescents. *Eating Disorders*, 12(3), 225–239. doi: 10.1080/10640260490481438

Olivardia, R. (2001). Mirror, mirror on the wall, who's the largest of them all? The features and phenomenology of muscle dysmorphia. *Harvard Review of Psychiatry*, 9(5), 254–259. doi: 10.1080/hrp.9.5.254.259

Olivardia, R., Pope Jr., H. G., Borowiecki III, J. J., & Cohane, G. H. (2004). Biceps and body image: The relationship between muscularity and self-esteem, depression, and eating disorder symptoms. *Psychology of Men & Masculinity*, 5(2), 112–120. doi: 10.1037/1524-9220.5.2.112

Olivardia, R., Pope, J. H. G., & Hudson, J. I. (2000). Muscle dysmorphia in male weightlifters: A case-control study. *The American Journal of Psychiatry*, 157(8), 1291–1296. doi: 10.1176/appi.ajp.157.8.1291

Perugi, G., Akiskal, H. S., Psych, M. R. C., Giannotti, D., Frare, F., Di Vaio, S., . . . Psych, F. R. C. (1997). Gender-related differences in body dysmorphic disorder (dysmorphophobia). *The Journal of Nervous and Mental Disease*, 185(9), 578–582. doi: 10.1097/00005053-199709000-00007

Petruzzello, S., Landers, D., Hatfield, B., Kubitz, K., & Salazar, W. (1991). A meta-analysis on the anxiety-reducing effects of acute and chronic exercise. *Sports Medicine*, 11(3), 143–182. doi: 10.2165/00007256-199111030-00002

Phillips, K. A. (2005). *The broken mirror: Understanding and treating body dysmorphic disorder*. Oxford, NY: Oxford University Press.

Phillips, K. A., & Diaz, S. (1997). Gender differences in body dysmorphic disorder. *The Journal of Nervous and Mental Disease*, 185(9), 570.

Phillips, K. A., Hart, A. S., Simpson, H. B., & Stein, D. J. (2013). Delusional versus nondelusional body dysmorphic disorder: Recommendations for DSM-5. *CNS Spectrums*, 19(1), 10–20.

Phillips, K. A., McElroy, S. L., Hudson, J. I., & Pope, Jr., H. G. (1995). Body dysmorphic disorder: An obsessive-compulsive spectrum disorder, a form of affective spectrum disorder, or both? *The Journal of Clinical Psychiatry*, 56(suppl 4), 41–51.

Phillips, K. A., Menard, W., & Fay, C. (2006). Gender similarities and differences in 200 individuals with body dysmorphic disorder. *Comprehensive psychiatry*, 47(2), 77–87. doi: 10.1016/j.comppsych.2005.07.002

Phillips, K. A., Wilhelm, S., Koran, L. M., Didie, E. R., Fallon, B. A., Feusner, J., & Stein, D. J. (2010). Body dysmorphic disorder: Some key issues for DSM-V. *Depression and Anxiety*, 27(6), 573–591. doi: 10.1002/da.20709

Pinto, A., & Phillips, K. A. (2005). Social anxiety in body dysmorphic disorder. *Body Image*, 2(4), 401–405. doi: 10.1016/j.bodyim.2005.10.003

Pope, C. G., Pope, Jr., H. G., Menard, W., Faya, C., Olivardia, R., & Phillips, K. A. (2005). Clinical features of muscle dysmorphia among males with body dysmorphic disorder. *Body Image*, 2(4), 395–400. doi: 10.1016/j.bodyim.2005.09.001

Pope Jr., H. G., Gruber, A. J., Choi, P., Olivardia, R., & Phillips, K. A. (1997). Muscle dysmorphia: An underrecognized form of body dysmorphic disorder. *Psychosomatics* 38(6), 548–557. doi: 10.1016/s0033-3182(97)71400-2

Pope, Jr., H. G., Katz, D. L., & Hudson, J. I. (1993). Anorexia nervosa and reverse anorexia among 108 male bodybuilders. *Comprehensive Psychiatry, 34*(6), 406–409.

Pope, Jr., H. G., Olivardia, R., Borowiecki III, J. J., & Cohane, G. H. (2001). The growing commercial value of the male body: A longitudinal survey of advertising in women's magazines. *Psychotherapy and Psychosomatics, 70*, 189–192.

Pope, Jr., H. G., Olivardia, R., Gruber, A., & Borowiecki III, J. J. (1999). Evolving ideals of male body image as seen through action toys. *The International Journal of Eating Disorders, 26*(1), 65–72. doi: 10.1002/(sici)1098-108x(199907)26:1<65::aid-eat8>3.0.co;2-dc

Pope, Jr., H. G., Phillips, K. A., & Olivardia, R. (2000). *The Adonis Complex: The secret crisis of male body obsession*. New York, NY: The Free Press.

Quinion, M. (1997). *Worldwide words: Investigating the English language across the globe*. Retrieved from www.worldwidewords.org/turnsofphrase/tp-mus1.htm

Raedeke, T. D., Focht, B. C., & Scales, D. (2007). Social environmental factors and psychological responses to acute exercise for socially physique anxious females. *Psychology of Sport & Exercise, 8*(4), 463–476.

Rohman, L. (2009). The relationship between anabolic androgenic steroids and muscle dysmorphia: A review. *Eating Disorders, 17*(3), 187–199. doi: 10.1080/10640260902848477

Ryan, R. M., & Deci, E. L. (2000). Self-determination theory and the facilitation of intrinsic motivation, social development, and well-being. *American Psychologist, 55*(1), 68–78.

Sabiston, C. M., Sedgwick, W. A., Crocker, P. R. E., Kowalski, K. C., & Mack, D. E. (2007). Social physique anxiety in adolescence: An exploration of influences, coping strategies, and health behaviors. *Journal of Adolescent Research, 22*(1), 78–101. doi: 10.1177/0743558406294628

Santarnecchi, E., & Dèttore, D. (2012). Muscle dysmorphia in different degrees of bodybuilding activities: Validation of the Italian version of Muscle Dysmorphia Disorder Inventory and Bodybuilder Image Grid. *Body Image, 9*(3), 396–403. doi: 10.1016/j.bodyim.2012.03.006

Sarwer, D. B., & Spitzer, J. C. (2012). Body image dysmorphic disorder in persons who undergo aesthetic medical treatments. *Aesthetic Surgery Journal, 32*(8), 999–1009. doi: 10.1177/1090820x12462715

Schlenker, B. R., & Leary, M. R. (1982). Social anxiety and self-presentation: A conceptualization model. *Psychological Bulletin, 92*(3), 641–669. doi: 10.1037/0033-2909.92.3.641

Schlenker, B. R., & Leary, M. R. (1985). Social anxiety and communication about the self. *Journal of Language and Social Psychology, 4*(3–4), 171–192. doi: 10.1177/0261927X8543002

Schwartz, J. P., Grammas, D. L., Sutherland, R. J., Siffert, K. L., & Bush-King, I. (2010). Masculine gender roles and differentiation: Predictors of body image and self-objectification in men. *Psychology of Men & Masculinity, 11*(3), 208–224. doi: 10.1037/a0018255

Scott, L. A., Joyner, A. B., Czech, D. R., Munkasy, B. A., & Todd, S. (2009). Effects of exercise and a brief education intervention on social physique anxiety in college students. *International Journal of Fitness, 5*(1), 9–17. doi: http://hdl.handle.net/10518/1661

Singh, D. (1993). Adaptive significance of female physical attractiveness: Role to waist-to-hip ratio. *Journal of Personality and Social Psychology, 65*, 293–307.

Skemp, K. M., Mikat, R. P., Schenck, K. P., & Kramer, N. (2013). Muscle dysmorphia risk may be influenced by goals of the weightlifter. *Journal of Strength and Conditioning Research, 1*. doi: 10.1519/JSC.0b013e3182825474

Skinner, B. F. (1985). Reinforcement today. *American Psychologist, 13*(3), 94–99. doi: 10.1037/h0049039

Thøgersen-Ntoumani, C., & Ntoumanis, N. (2006). The role of self-determined motivation in the understanding of exercise-related behaviours, cognitions and physical self-evaluations. *Journal of Sports Sciences, 24*(4), 393–404. doi: 10.1080/02640410500131670

Thøgersen-Ntoumani, C., Ntoumanis, N., Cumming, J., Bartholomew, K. J., & Pearce, G. (2011). Can self-esteem protect against the deleterious consequences of self-objectification for mood and body satisfaction in physically active female university students? *Journal of Sport and Exercise Psychology, 33*, 289–307. Retrieved from http://journals.humankinetics.com/jsep

Thomas, L. S., Tod, D. A., & Lavallee, D. E. (2011). Variability in muscle dysmorphia symptoms: The influence of weight training. *Journal of Strength and Conditioning Research, 25*(3), 846–851.

Thompson, A., & Chad, K. E. (2002). The relationship of social physique anxiety to risk for developing an eating disorder in young females. *Journal of Adolescent Health, 31*(2), 183–189. doi: 10.1016/s1054-139x(01)00397-4

Tiggemann, M., & Williamson, S. (2000). The effect of exercise on body satisfaction and self-esteem as a function of gender and age. *Sex Roles, 43*, 119–127.

van Amsterdam, J., Opperhuizen, A., & Hartgens, F. (2010). Adverse health effects of anabolic—androgenic steroids. *Regulatory Toxicology and Pharmacology, 57*(1), 117–123. doi: http://dx.doi.org/10.1016/j.yrtph.2010.02.001

Van Raalte, J. L., Cunningham, J., Cornelius, A. E., & Brewer, B. W. (2004). Environmental effects on social physique anxiety. *Kinesiologia Slovenica, 10*(1), 86–95.

Vazou-Ekkekakis, S., & Ekkekakis, P. (2009). Affective consequences of imposing the intensity of physical activity: Does loss of perceived autonomy matter? *Hellenic Journal of Psychology, 6*, 125–144.

Veale, D. (2002). Overvalued ideas: A conceptual analysis. *Behaviour Research and Therapy, 40*, 383–400. doi:10.1016/S0005-7967(01)00016-X

Veale, D. (2004). Advances in a cognitive behavioural model of body dysmorphic disorder. *Body Image, 1*(1), 113–125. doi: 10.1016/s1740-1445(03)00009-3

Walsh, A. (2012). Exercise intensity, affect, and adherence: A guide for the fitness professional. *Journal of Sport Psychology in Action, 3*(3), 193–207. doi: 10.1080/21520704.2012.674629

Wilhelm, S., Phillips, K. A., Fama, J. M., Greenberg, J. L., & Steketee, G. (2011). Modular cognitive-behavioral therapy for body dysmorphic disorder. *Behavioral Therapy, 42*(4), 624–633. doi: 10.1016/j.beth.2011.02.002

Williams, J., Hadjistavropoulos, T., & Sharpe, D. (2006). A meta-analysis of psychological and pharmacological treatments for Body Dysmorphic Disorder. *Behaviour Research and Therapy, 44*(1), 99–111. doi: http://dx.doi.org/10.1016/j.brat.2004.12.006

Williams, P. A., & Cash, T. F. (2001). Effects of a circuit weight training program on the body images of college students. *The International Journal of Eating Disorders, 30*(1), 75–82. doi: 10.1002/eat.1056

Wipfli, B. M., Rethorst, C. D., & Landers, D. M. (2008). The anxiolytic effects of exercise: A meta-analysis of randomized trials and dose-response analysis. *Journal of Sport & Exercise Psychology, 30*(4), 392–410.

Woodman, T., & Steer, R. (2011). Body self-discrepancies and women's social physique anxiety: The moderating role of the feared body. *British Journal of Psychology, 102*(2), 147–160. doi: 10.1348/000712610x507821

28 Eating Disorders and Exercise

Christine L. B. Selby

Exercise has been repeatedly shown to be beneficial in myriad ways. Penedo and Dahn (2005) reported that regular physical activity and exercise contributes to "better quality of life and health outcomes" (p. 189). In 2008, the US Department of Health and Human Services issued a report on exercise guidelines and included a section on the countless systems of the body. Specifically, they reported that exercise can reduce the risk of premature death and improve the functioning of the cardorespiratory, metabolic, and musculoskeletal systems of the body. They also noted that the risk for certain types of cancer can be lowered with regular exercise and that those who are consistently physically active are at lower risk for depression, sleep better, and show lower cognitive decline compared to those who are less physically active. Other sources indicate that the benefits of exercise extend to self-esteem (Fox, 2000), anxiety (DeBoer, Powers, Utschig, Otto & Smits, 2012), executive functioning (Guiney & Machado, 2013), and overall quality of life for the severely mentally ill (Alexandratos, Barnett & Thomas, 2012). See also Chapter 4 in this volume for a more in-depth look at how exercise can benefit mind and body.

Given the health-enhancing benefits of exercise and this culture's general sentiment that "more is better," it is easy to assume that the more one engages in exercise, the better off one will be both physically and mentally. Like with many things in life, this is true to a point; however, beyond that point too much exercise can lead to overuse injuries (Grave, 2008; see also Chapter 26 in this volume) and exercise addiction (see Chapter 25 in this volume), and exercise can be used as a part of an eating disorder. This chapter will initially focus on how exercise can be misused in the context of an eating disorder. Then it will also address how exercise may be beneficial in the treatment of an eating disorder. Finally, it will conclude with a section on how to help someone suspected of having an eating disorder. The chapter will initially address what eating disorders are and risk factors for developing eating disorders.

WHAT ARE EATING DISORDERS?

Eating disorders are a class of psychiatric disorders that are considered to have one of the highest mortality rates of any psychiatric illness, primarily accounted for by anorexia nervosa (Neumärker, 2000). Individuals with anorexia nervosa have been found to be at greater risk of death compared to those with bulimia nervosa (BN) and eating disorder not otherwise specified (EDNOS) (Arcelus, Mitchell, Wales, & Nielsen, 2011; Button, Chadalavad, & Palmer, 2010); however, additional research is warranted to identify what may predict mortality in those with a diagnosis of BN or EDNOS. The most common causes of death in anorexia nervosa are starvation and suicide (Neumärker, 2000). In other cases, the cause of death has been associated with suicide and substance intoxication for both anorexia nervosa and bulimia nervosa (Rosling, Sparén, Norring & von Knorring, 2011). In the absence of death, the harm inflicted on the mind and body as a result of an eating disorder can be far reaching and may make it so that the individual is incapable of engaging in life the way they want to (Winkler et al., 2014). Additionally, those who love and care about an individual with an eating disorder can feel the effects of the disorder as well (Hayas et al., 2014). Given the severity of these disorders, it is important for professionals working with individuals of all ages in any capacity to understand what eating disorders are, factors that may put someone at risk of developing an eating disorder, and signs and symptoms of the disorders themselves.

Eating disorders can be classified in four different ways: anorexia nervosa, bulimia nervosa, binge eating disorder, or unspecified feeding or eating disorder (American Psychiatric Association, 2013). Based on the definition of the American Psychiatric Association (2013), anorexia nervosa is primarily characterized by the continual restriction of intake, intense fear of gaining weight, and misperception of one's weight or shape such that the individual frequently believes they weigh more than they do and/or that they are larger than they actually are. Anorexia nervosa can also be further characterized by whether the individual primarily restricts their intake or uses binging and purging to manipulate their weight. This first subtype is known as "restricting type" and usually means that the individual attempts to achieve weight loss predominantly by dieting, fasting, and/or using excessive exercise. The second, "binge-eating/purging type," is characterized by the predominant use of binging and purging (i.e., self-induced vomiting or misusing diuretics, laxatives, or enemas) to manipulate their weight. It is common when thinking of someone with an eating disorder to imagine someone with anorexia nervosa, who typically is emaciated. The reality is, however, that someone with an eating disorder may be underweight, normal weight, overweight, or obese. Individuals diagnosed with bulimia nervosa usually are normal weight or slightly overweight.

The American Psychiatric Association (2013) states that bulimia nervosa is primarily characterized by repeated episodes of binge eating (i.e., eating a large quantity of food in a discrete period of time with an accompanying sense of loss of control), repeated inappropriate behaviors intended to prevent weight gain (e.g., self-induced vomiting, laxative abuse, excessive exercise), and having a sense of self-esteem and self-worth that primarily rely on the perception of their weight and shape. Binge-and-purge episodes are often conducted in secret, and efforts are made to ensure that no one finds out about the condition. These episodes typically do not result in a change in weight; therefore, those who use binging and purging as a weight loss method will not only find that their efforts are unrewarded, but that they will be placing extraordinary strain on their physical systems.

Binge eating disorder became an official diagnosis in its own right with the publication of the *DSM-V* (American Psychiatric Association, 2013). Prior to its publication, the *DSM-IV-TR* (American Psychiatric Association, 2000) included binge eating disorder as a diagnosis of further study. Thus, individuals showing symptoms of binge eating disorder were diagnosed with "eating disorder not otherwise specified" (EDNOS). According to the *DSM-V*, binge eating disorder is primarily characterized by the recurrence of binge eating episodes without the accompanying compensatory behaviors seen with bulimia nervosa. Thus, someone with binge eating disorder usually does not try to "get rid of" what they have eaten. It is also important to note that binge eating disorder can occur in individuals who are normal weight, overweight, or obese; however, not all overweight or obese individuals have binge eating disorder.

Finally, individuals with eating disorder–related symptoms who do not meet the formal criteria for anorexia nervosa, bulimia nervosa, or binge eating disorder may be diagnosed with "other specified feeding or eating disorder." As noted above, prior to the publication of the *DSM-V*, the diagnostic term used was "eating disorder not otherwise specified." The EDNOS category was routinely criticized because it was the most widely used eating disorder diagnosis—around half of all individuals with an eating disorder were diagnosed with

EDNOS (Fairburn et al., 2007; Ricca et al., 2001; Turner & Bryant-Waugh, 2004). The inclusion of the binge eating disorder diagnosis as well as other changes made to the formal diagnostic criteria for anorexia nervosa and bulimia nervosa in the *DSM-V* were intended to improve the accuracy of eating disorder diagnoses, thereby reducing the percentage of individuals who could not be categorized by one of the other three diagnoses. It is important to note that a diagnosis of EDNOS (*DSM-IV-TR*) or other specified feeding or eating disorder (*DSM-V*) does not mean that the individual has a less serious eating disorder. These two diagnoses simply reflect the fact that the symptoms displayed by the individual do not fit neatly into one of the three specified categories, rather than an absence of or reduction in severity of their symptoms.

The diagnosis of an eating disorder should only be made by a licensed mental or medical health provider—ideally by one who has had specific training in the area of eating disorders; however, other professionals or friends and family can learn to recognize signs and symptoms that frequently precede or accompany eating disorders. Common signs and symptoms include preoccupation with weight, food, and nutritional content of food; rigid rules and rituals with food; concern about eating in public (may refuse to do so); extreme concern about weight and shape (may have a distorted/inaccurate view of their body); social withdrawal; hoarding of food; skipping meals; or exercising despite injury or extreme weather or for the purpose of burning off calories (American Psychiatric Association, 2013). This list is not intended to be comprehensive. There are a number of excellent resources available that include more extensive lists. Some of the most varied and user-friendly materials have been assembled by the National Eating Disorders Association (www.nationaleatingdisorders.org). They have developed myriad printable fact sheets on eating disorders in general, how to talk with someone suspected of having an eating disorder, and how to work with insurance companies to ensure proper coverage for treatment. They have also created three comprehensive "toolkits" designed to help laypeople understand and spot eating disorders. The toolkits are for parents, educators, and coaches and athletic trainers. Readers are encouraged to consult these free references for a comprehensive list of signs and symptoms, as well as other information on eating disorders.

WHEN IS EXERCISE "EXCESSIVE?"

Although non-clinical populations have been found to engage in excessive exercise (Taranis, Touyz, & Meyer, 2011), this chapter will focus on excessive exercise in those with eating disorders. Not all individuals with eating disorders engage in excessive exercise; however, this behavior may be a part of the diagnostic picture for someone with an eating disorder. For example, an individual diagnosed with anorexia nervosa or other feeding or eating disorder may use excessive exercise as a means to weight loss. Individuals diagnosed with bulimia nervosa or other feeding or eating disorder may use excessive exercise as a behavior designed to control their weight. Despite the fact that excessive exercise is recognized by the American Psychiatric Association (2013) as a behavior that may be a part of a patient's eating disorder, there does not seem to be agreement among those researching and writing about this construct on how to precisely define it (Johnston, Reilly, & Kremer, 2011). Thus, agreement on the terms and descriptions of when enough is enough with respect to exercise have proved elusive.

The multitude of terms that have been used to describe the misuse of exercise adds to the confusion. The list of terms includes exercise addiction (Aidman & Wollard, 2003; Sachs & Pargman, 1979), activity anorexia (Epling, Pierce, & Stefan, 1983), exercise anorexia (Touyz, Beumont & Heok, 1987), exercise dependence (Adams & Kirkby, 2002; Hausenblas &

Downs, 2002), obligatory exercise (Brehm & Steffen, 1998; Elbourne & Chen, 2007), exercise abuse (Davis, 2000), compulsive exercise (Adkins & Keel, 2005; Grave, Calugi, & Marchesini, 2008), dysfunctional exercise (Calogero & Pedrotty-Stump, 2010), drive exercise (Stiles-Shields, Goldschmidt, Boepple, Glunz, & Le Grange, 2011), and excessive exercise (Davis, Brewer, & Ratusny, 1993; Le Grange, & Eisler, 1993). Meyer and Taranis (2011) point out that while the multitude of terms used are related to one another, they add to the confusion among professionals in figuring out when a patient is using exercise in a pathological way.

Meyer and Taranis (2011) posit that some terms imply a clinical problem (e.g., "abuse") whereas others do not (e.g., "obligatory"). They note that this can be a diagnostic and treatment issue if one uses a term implying pathology (e.g., "exercise abuse") while also noting that there is no accompanying distress or interference in one's life as a result of this "abuse." Similarly, using a term suggesting that pathology is non-existent (e.g., "obligatory exercise") while also describing how an individual's use of exercise is interfering with normal functioning can be confusing to patients and treatment providers. They therefore suggest that what is most important in determining whether or not a patient's exercise is harmful is understanding the *why* behind the exercise. Others seem to agree (Ackard, Brehm, & Steffen, 2002; Adkins & Keel, 2005; Johnston, Reilly, & Kremer, 2011; Steffen & Brehm, 1999). Some researchers have posited that the misuse of exercise should be conceptualized on a continuum (e.g., Elbourne & Chen, 2007) or as being multidimensional (e.g., Ackard et al., 2002). Regardless, what seems to be clear is that a simple dichotomous categorization of excessive exercise (i.e., you're doing it or you're not) is insufficient and inaccurate in representing excessive exercise in individuals with eating disorders.

In reviewing the literature in this area, Adkins and Keel (2005) determined that the definitions for the various terms used to describe problematic exercise can be categorized as either quantitative or qualitative in nature. Quantitative definitions reference how much or how intensely someone is engaged in exercise; they suggest the term "excessive" best reflects this end of the continuum. Qualitative definitions reflect the underlying or psychological processes motivating the exercise behavior; the term "compulsive" seems to best reflect this end. Quantitative definitions are inherently problematic because what may be too much for one person may be just fine for another. As a result, those who have empirically examined excessive exercise have disagreed on a definition that can be accurately and universally applied to an exercising population (Meyer & Taranis, 2011). Adkins and Keel (2005) concluded that a compulsive or qualitative characterization of exercise is more useful and accurate than the quantitative or excessive characterization of exercise. In their study of male and female undergraduate students, they determined that a compulsion to exercise, particularly in those who were exercising to affect their appearance, was a better predictor of maladaptive eating behaviors than excessive exercise.

More recently, Johnston, Reilly, and Kremer (2011) provided evidence for a "continuum approach to the understanding of excessive exercise" (p. 237). In their qualitative analysis of a community-based sample of women ranging in age from 16 to 77 years old, they found that participants used a variety of terms to describe their exercise experiences (e.g., exercise addiction, normal exercise, exercise buzz). When defining problematic forms of exercise, such as exercise addiction or excessive exercise, participants provided descriptions that emphasized elements of their behavior that extended beyond the frequency and/or intensity of their exercise. Participants reportedly "acknowledged the relevance of psychological factors such as effort, investment and commitment" (p. 244).

In their comparison of individuals with or without the diagnosis of an eating disorder, Boyd, Abraham, and Luscombe (2007) determined that it was important to examine individuals' thoughts and feelings with respect to exercise, rather than how much or how often they engaged in exercise. Boyd et al. (2007) found that despite similar quantities of exercise between the two groups, what differentiated those with an eating disorder from those without were factors regarding whether or not they would be agitated if their exercise was interrupted; others thought they exercised a lot, felt bad if they were not able to exercise as planned, and felt that they may have or have had a problem with exercise. Those with an eating disorder were more likely to answer "yes" to these items than those without an eating disorder.

Mond and colleagues conducted community-based studies (2004, 2006) and a primary care practice–based study (2008) in which they sought to examine the relationships between exercise, eating disorder–related behavior, and quality of life. In their community-based studies, they found that two factors related to the use of exercise were significantly linked to eating disorders: using exercise to influence body shape or weight and feeling guilty due to delaying exercise. Not only was there a connection between these factors and eating pathology, they were also predictive of a reduction in quality of life. The results of their more recent study (2008) were similar to those of their earlier community-based studies despite differences in the demographics of the samples, recruitment of participants, and relatively smaller sample size. In 2006 Mond et al. concluded that a definition of excessive exercise should include the desire to use exercise to manipulate body weight or shape and feelings of guilt when exercise is delayed. Their 2008 study lends additional support to this conclusion.

Calogero and Pedrotty-Stump (2010) suggested the term "dysfunctional exercise (DEX)" in order to adequately capture the disparate terms and definitions proffered by researchers, practitioners, and patients themselves. They proposed that dysfunctional exercise is not an either-or discrete entity; rather it is a continuous concept that ranges from mindlessness to mindfulness. They suggested that mindless exercise includes "orientation to past and/or future, focus on external outcomes, injuries and depletes the body, disrupts mind-body connection, exacerbates mental and physical strain, and brings pain, dreaded" (p. 435). Exercise that encompasses mindfulness, by contrast, includes "orientation to the present moment, attention to internal processes (breathing), rejuvenates the body, enhances mind-body connection, alleviates mental and physical strain, and provides pleasure, joy, fun" (p. 435). They concluded in a manner similar to others that whatever motivates the individual to exercise and whatever beliefs are held about exercise should be the focus of research and clinical attention.

It seems clear from the careful exploration of what constitutes excessive exercise in those with an eating disorder that simply asking a patient how much, how often, and how intensely they exercise will not likely capture exercise behavior that is harmful. A universal qualitative definition of either healthy exercise or harmful exercise has not been developed. Answering questions such as why someone exercises, what it means to them, and what it means if they are unable to exercise can help to determine if exercise occupies a healthy or unhealthy place in someone's life.

HOW DOES EXERCISE AFFECT INDIVIDUALS WITH EATING DISORDERS?

Prior to delving into the relationship between exercise and eating pathology, it is important to note the possibility of differences that may exist between exercisers and athletes. There is some debate as to whether or not athletes are at greater risk for eating disorders than non-athletes (Thompson & Sherman, 2010). Evidence consistently suggests that many athletes face sport-related pressures to modify their weight, shape, and size, which can contribute to an eating disorder culture (Reel, SooHoo, Petrie, Greenleaf, & Carter, 2010). Moreover, some athletes are likely to be more susceptible to developing an eating disorder than their non-athlete peers (Sundgot-Borgen & Torstveit, 2004). By contrast, Madison and

Ruma (2003), in their comparison of athletes and exercisers, found that while the relationship between exercise and eating pathology is positively correlated, that relationship did not hold for athletes. The authors suggested that their findings support the opinion previously reported by Sherman and Thompson (2001), who concluded that exercise can serve a different purpose for athletes than it does for non-athletes. Regardless of whether athletes are at greater risk for developing eating disorders or if participating in sport is a protective factor helping to prevent the development of an eating disorder, the fact that athletes are repeatedly identified as being a population unique from non-athletes makes it important to take this distinction into consideration. Thus, this chapter has maintained a focus on research examining exercise and exercisers and not sport and athletics. For a comprehensive look at eating disorders in sport, see Thompson and Sherman (2010).

The use of exercise as a way to control one's weight is included as a part of the description of both anorexia nervosa and bulimia nervosa (American Psychiatric Association, 2013) and as such may also be a part of the symptom constellation of those diagnosed with other specified eating or feeding disorder. Individuals engaged in behaviors characteristic of anorexia nervosa may use exercise as a weight loss technique, whereas those with behaviors more characteristic of bulimia nervosa may use exercise as a method to prevent weight gain. Independent researchers have identified the maladaptive use of exercise as a significant element of both anorexia nervosa (Beaumont, Arthur, Russell, & Touyz, 1994; Penas-Lledo, Vaz Leal, & Waller, 2002; Thien, Thomas, Markin, & Birmingham, 2000) and bulimia nervosa (Davis et al., 1997; Hechler, Beumont, Marks, & Touyz, 2005; Penas-Lledo, Vaz Leal, & Waller, 2002;). Shroff et al. (2006) reported that up to 55 percent of individuals with anorexia nervosa, 24 percent of individuals with bulimia nervosa, and just over 20 percent of those with EDNOS were likely engaged in excessive exercise. They also found that that those diagnosed with the purging subtype of anorexia nervosa may be the group most likely to engage in excessive exercise.

Others have suggested one's level of commitment to excessive exercise may be predictive of eating pathology (Aruguete, Edman & Yates, 2012; McLaren, Gauvin & White, 2001) and specifically contribute to the cause of eating disorders (Davis et al., 1997). Moreover, excessive exercise seems to be resistant to change (Davis et al., 1997), making this behavior difficult to treat and therefore likely one of the last symptoms of the disorder to dissipate (Crisp, Hsu, Harding, & Hartshorn, 1980; Davis, Kennedy, Ravelski, & Dionne, 1994). Individuals with eating disorders who also engage in excessive exercise are more likely to remain in inpatient treatment longer than those who do not exercise excessively (Solenberger, 2001) and may experience shorter times to relapse when recovering from an eating disorder (Strober, Freeman & Morrell, 1997). Thus, excessive exercise can play a significant role in the development, maintenance, and treatment of eating disorders.

An additional concept that has bearing here is the Female Athlete Triad (Triad) (Nattiv, Agostini, Drinkwater, & Yeager, 1994). As the name suggests, this phenomenon describes what may happen to female athletes; however, the idea behind the interconnectedness of three prongs of the Triad can also be applied to females who over-exercise. Those who are highly active require sufficient intake of food to ensure that their bodies continue to function normally and that they can perform under the strain of exercise. The Triad represents a reciprocal relationship between low energy intake (i.e., not eating enough), menstrual irregularities, and loss of bone mineral density (Hoch et al., 2009; Nattiv et al., 2007). Not eating enough can lead to irregular menstruation or cessation of menstruation, which can further lead to a loss of bone mineral density (i.e., osteopenia or osteoporosis). It is possible, however, that some females who exercise may unintentionally underconsume, not realizing their bodies require more fuel to function adequately and to maintain good skeletal health. Although the motivation for undereating matters in the diagnosis and subsequent treatment of an eating disorder, any female exerciser who shows signs of any of the three elements of the Triad, regardless of their intent, should be evaluated for the other two elements.

Although excessive exercise seems to be relatively common among those with eating disorders and it can create significant problems in the treatment of and recovery from eating disorders, not all who are diagnosed with an eating disorder will engage in excessive exercise. It is important, therefore, to determine what may put some individuals at greater risk of overdoing exercise in the context of an eating disorder. Although the construct of excessive exercise has received comparatively little attention when considering other factors connected to eating disorders (Meyer, Taranis, & Touyz, 2008), those who have conducted research in this area have illuminated several features that seem to be linked with excessive exercise and eating disorder behavior. One hypothesis about excessive exercise is that it may be used by those with an eating disorder to manage negative feelings (Boyd, Abraham, & Luscombe, 2007; Bratland-Sanda et al., 2011; De Young & Anderson, 2010; Vansteelandt, Rijmen, Pieters, Probst, & Vanderlinden, 2007). De Young and Anderson (2010) examined this possible link. They examined how often individuals with eating disorders were likely to engage in exercise for the purpose of managing negative affect. They found that nearly 60 percent of their sample of male and female undergraduate students reported exercising due to experiencing negative emotions, a finding consistent with previous research (Boyd, Abraham, & Luscombe, 2007; Vansteelandt, Rijmen, Pieters, Probst, & Vanderlinden, 2007). In aggregate, this group was also more likely than the comparison group to endorse thoughts and behaviors consistent with eating disorder pathology (e.g., concerns about weight and shape, eating restraint), evaluate their bodies more negatively, report lower self-esteem, and engage in exercise for "obligatory" or "compulsive" reasons. Similarly, Bratland-Sanda et al. (2011) found that exercising for the purpose of regulating negative affect and "vigorous" exercise were significantly related to exercise dependence in both eating disorder patients and the non-clinical control group. De Young and Anderson (2010) noted that some in the group labeled "negative affect exercisers" exercised in response to negative emotions, which may be an effective coping strategy and constitute a healthy response to an unpleasant state. For others, however, they acknowledged that exercise for this purpose may be an adjunct to other unhealthy behaviors (e.g., binge eating, purging) exhibited as a result of negative affect. They cautioned practitioners to be sure to take care in their evaluation of exercise behaviors. What may be a healthy coping strategy for some may be an indicator of significant distress or pathology for others.

Mond and Calogero (2009) sought to differentiate female eating disorder patients from healthy women with respect to their exercise behaviors. They determined that healthy women were more likely to report that they enjoyed exercise, in comparison to those with an eating disorder. More importantly, however, Mond and Calogero (2009) found that what consistently differentiated healthy women from those with an eating disorder were feelings of guilt when exercise was missed and exercising for the purpose of manipulating one's appearance in the latter group. They further noted that those diagnosed with the purging subtype of anorexia nervosa and those diagnosed with bulimia nervosa were more likely to exhibit these behaviors than those diagnosed with the restricting subtype of anorexia nervosa.

More recently Naylor, Mountford, and Brown (2011) also attempted to reveal differences between those with an eating disorder and those without. They were interested in understanding participants' beliefs about exercise (e.g., exercise is based on rules and used to avoid exercise withdrawal symptoms; exercise is used to manipulate weight/shape; exercise is used to improve mood; exercise is not enjoyable), behaviors that may be linked to obsessive-compulsive disorder (OCD), and level of distress experienced with respect to OCD-related behaviors. Their findings indicated that the clinical group (i.e., those with an eating disorder) scored significantly higher than the non-clinical group (i.e., those without an eating disorder) on nearly all measures. The clinical group demonstrated that when they reflected a stronger need to exercise (i.e., compulsive exercise), they also had higher levels of OCD and eating disorder–related behaviors, whereas the non-clinical group did not show this trend. Overall, Naylor et al. concluded that the presence of both obsessive beliefs and beliefs about exercise that are compulsive in nature may maintain exercise behavior in those with eating disorders. These findings are consistent with those found in a clinical sample by Shroff et al. (2006), who reported that those who engaged in excessive exercise were more likely to also display higher levels of obsessions and compulsions. Shroff et al. (2006) also reported a significant connection between excessive exercise and "perfectionism," which was also revealed by Goodwin, Haycraft, Willis, and Meyer (2011).

In addition to the presence of behaviors related to obsessive-compulsiveness, Goodwin et al. (2011a) found that the drive for thinness and perfectionism were also linked to compulsive exercise. They studied these constructs and their potential for predicting "compulsive exercise" among a community-based sample of adolescents (i.e., males and females ages 12–14). In addition to measuring beliefs related to compulsive exercise and level of perfectionism, they also asked participants about attitudes related to eating disorders, depression- and anxiety-related symptoms, and anxiety specifically related to physique/body perception in the presence of others. The authors found that for both sexes, drive for thinness was the strongest predictor of compulsive exercise, followed by perfectionism and obsessive-compulsiveness. Collectively these factors accounted for a sizable 39 percent of the variance in compulsive exercise in boys and 34 percent of the variance in girls. Although Goodwin et al. (2011b) did not find a connection between compulsive exercise and depression, anxiety, or social physique anxiety, which is in contrast to previous findings (Penas-Lledo, Vaz Leal, & Waller, 2002), the authors noted that this inconsistency may reflect the nature of the samples used. Penas-Lledo et al. (2002) studied a clinical sample, whereas Goodwin et al. (2011b) recruited participants from the community. Thus, it stands to reason that a clinical sample may reveal a stronger presence of these behaviors and therefore a stronger and more significant relationship between variables when psychopathology is experienced by those being measured.

McLaren, Gauvin, and White (2001) sampled university students who completed measures of perfectionism, dietary restraint, and commitment to exercise. Both perfectionism and commitment to exercise predicted dietary restraint—this is a central diagnostic indicator of anorexia nervosa and possible compensatory behavior in bulimia nervosa. With respect to exercise specifically, further analyses revealed that an individual's approach to exercise rather than the exercise itself was more important in terms of dietary restraint. That is, the act of engaging in exercise did not necessarily contribute to the presence of dietary restraint; however, the reasons for exercising were likely to do so. Cook and Hausenblas (2008, 2011) reached similar conclusions when they determined that dependence on exercise and not the act of exercising as such mediated the relationship between exercise and eating disorder behaviors. These results are further corroborated by the results of a more recent study conducted with a non-clinical population (Vinkers, Evers, Adriaanse, & de Ridder, 2012).

Vinkers, Evers, Adriaanse, and de Ridder (2012) examined body esteem (i.e., how one feels about one's body) and eating disorder behaviors in female members of a fitness club. They found that what motivated the women to exercise affected the connection between low body esteem and eating disorder behaviors. Specifically, Vinkers et al. (2012) reported that when women exercised for the purpose of changing their appearance, they were more likely to experience lower body esteem and an increase in eating disorder behaviors, compared to those who exercised for the purpose of improving their health. Indeed, exercising for the purpose of improving one's appearance has been previously linked to an increase in eating pathology (Mond, Hay, Rodgers, & Owen, 2006) and to lower body esteem (Strelan, Mehaffey, & Tiggemann, 2003).

Meyer, Taranis, Goodwin, and Haycraft (2011) proposed a model of various factors that contribute to the maintenance of "compulsive exercise" in the context of eating disorders. They discussed the evidence for the connection between compulsive exercise and eating disorder behaviors, affect regulation and compulsive exercise, and compulsivity, perfectionism, and rigidity as maintenance factors for compulsive exercise. Based on their review of the literature, they concluded that those who engage in "compulsive exercise" have a concern with weight and shape and that excessive exercise will continue in order to avoid feelings of guilt and/or negative emotions when they cannot exercise and to avoid their fears of what may happen if they have to stop exercising (e.g., weight gain). As such, Meyer et al. (2011) suggested that definitions of compulsive exercise should reference to these ideas.

The studies discussed above targeted adult populations. Stiles-Shields, Goldschmidt, Boepple, Glunz, and Le Grange (2011) noted that studies examining factors associated with excessive or "driven" exercise among children and adolescents were scarce. Therefore, they recruited male and female participants ranging in age from 7 to 18 who completed measures of eating disorder behaviors and a measure of depression. The researchers indicated that their results were consistent with those found among adults: driven exercise was linked to greater degrees of eating pathology and higher levels of depression. This was particularly true for those who reported both driven exercise and self-induced vomiting.

As noted above, excessive exercise among those with an eating disorder has been linked to longer inpatient stays, shorter time between remission, and greater likelihood of relapse. Therefore, identifying additional factors that may help detect individuals who are engaged in or who will engage in excessive exercise is important. Moreover, Meyer, Taranis, Goodwin, and Haycraft (2011) indicated that individuals who use exercise in response to negative affect have traits reflecting perfectionism, exhibit obsessive and compulsive behaviors, are highly driven to engage in exercise, and report negative affect if they cannot exercise are likely to have higher degrees of eating pathology, which may reflect the presence of an eating disorder. As such, they noted that when any of these factors are present, a thorough assessment of exercise behaviors and accompanying thoughts and behaviors is warranted. It may be tempting to overlook exercise behaviors that may be excessive because as a culture we generally think that exercise is good for you and that if you are misusing exercise or if you are "addicted" to it, it is not as bad as other addictions (Cox & Orford, 2004; Johnston, Reilly & Kremer, 2011). The case has been made, however, that excessive exercise is consistently connected with a variety of factors linked to eating pathology and contributes to an overall reduction in quality of life (Mond, Hay, Rodgers, Owen, & Beumont, 2004). Therefore, excessive exercise ought to be a target of eating disorder treatment programs (Bratland-Sanda et al., 2010a, b).

HOW IS EXERCISE ADDRESSED IN THE TREATMENT OF EATING DISORDERS?

This section will focus on what is known about how eating disorder treatment programs manage exercise in patients with eating disorders. The question is, in part, whether treatment programs identify exercise as a behavior to be assessed and monitored, and when excessive exercise is present, whether they consider it to be a harmful factor in the context of an eating disorder. An additional and somewhat controversial question is whether or not exercise itself should be incorporated into the treatment of eating disorders. Some have cautioned that excessive exercise may be a causal factor in the development of anorexia nervosa and therefore might contribute to poorer outcomes (Davis, Kennedy, Ravelski, & Dionne, 1994; McLaren, Gauvin, & White, 2001; Seigel & Hetta, 2001), whereas others have reported that exercise can be successfully incorporated into the treatment of the disorder (e.g., Thien, Thomas, Markin, & Birmingham, 2000; Tokumura, Tanaka, Nanri, & Watanabe, 2005). In order to determine whether physical activity in the context of the treatment of eating disorders can be beneficial, it is important for researchers to systematically and repeatedly examine this issue. Unfortunately, very little has been done in this area of inquiry, and guidelines with respect to how to address exercise and/or incorporate it as an intervention in the treatment of those with eating disorders are not currently available (Zunker, Mitchell, & Wonderlich, 2011). Those studies that do exist primarily examine exercise in the treatment of anorexia nervosa. This may be because individuals diagnosed with anorexia nervosa have been found to be more physically active in comparison with individuals diagnosed with bulimia nervosa (Davis et al., 1997; Sundgot-Borgen, Bahr, Falch, & Schneider, 1998).

Calogero and Pedrotty-Stump (2010) offer several reasons for this apparent hole in the literature. They noted that a pervasive fear among treatment providers that engaging in exercise during the treatment will hinder weight gain may be a significant factor in the absence of dealing with exercise in treatment protocols. They further suggest that this may be due to overlooking the possibility that individuals with eating disorders may engage in exercise for reasons other than weight loss. Indeed, as was reported above, one additional reason for the use of exercise among those with eating disorders is an attempt to manage negative affect (De Young & Anderson, 2010). Calogero and Pedrotty-Stump (2010) also suggested that there seems to be a pervasive assumption that patients will no longer engage in dysfunctional exercise as a byproduct of treatment itself, without paying particular attention to the behavior during treatment. Moreover, they noted that what distinguishes healthy from unhealthy exercise is unclear. This is likely due to the myriad ways unhealthy exercise is defined, but also due to the known health benefits of exercise. The studies that have been completed in the area of including exercise in the treatment of individuals with eating disorders, however, provide some support for systematically including exercise as a part of treatment programs.

A study conducted over 40 years ago provided initial indication that engaging in physical activity may not interfere with the treatment of anorexia nervosa (specifically weight gain) (Blinder, Freeman, & Stunkard, 1970). Blinder et al. (1970) used access to physical activity as a reinforcer for weight gain in three adolescent/young adult females. As long as patients' respective weights increased by a specified amount each day they were allowed to engage in unstructured physical activity. The authors reported that this behavioral technique was effective in motivating patients to gain weight while in treatment. This study did not, however, examine a formal or structured exercise intervention. Over two decades later, Beaumont and colleagues (1994, 1997) more formally examined the pros and cons of including exercise in a treatment program and described the rationale behind why they elected to include a supervised exercise program in their treatment setting.

Beaumont, Arthur, Russell, and Touyz (1994), summarizing the literature published at that time, described how they saw "overactivity" in their treatment setting and proposed a supervised exercise program that addresses overactivity as a part of treatment. They noted that despite the potential for problems when patients with eating disorders engage in high levels of physical activity, there was the possibility that patients could benefit both physically and psychologically by engaging in supervised physical activity. Their own rationale for using exercise as a part of treatment was guided by a set of three "policy statements." The first is that the elimination of physical activity is ineffective and impractical. They suggested that it required too many resources to effectively enforce and can lead to unnecessary power struggles. An additional policy was that it is important to challenge patients' inaccurate beliefs about exercise and to provide education about using exercise in a healthy way. Finally, they stated that by providing an opportunity for patients to engage in healthy exercise, they would be helping patients return to their "normal life." Moreover, they posited if patients had a healthy exercise model to which to refer, the patients will be better equipped to resist pressures to engage in unhealthy exercise they may encounter in their daily lives. Beumont et al. (1994) sought to strike a balance between supervision and patient responsibility. They provided a summary of the exercise program used in their treatment setting but had not formally examined the effectiveness of the program. They did, however, report that patients anecdotally reported enjoyment in taking part in the exercise program along with experiencing a decrease in anxiety and elevation in overall mood. The exercise program also reportedly helped relieve discomfort after eating.

Touyz, Lennerts, Arthur, and Beumont (1993) empirically examined the effect of the program later summarized by Beaumont et al. (1994) specifically to determine what effect it would have on weight gain in patients with anorexia nervosa.[1] Thirty-nine inpatients diagnosed with anorexia nervosa were divided into an exercise group and a control group. The exercise group engaged in a structured anaerobic exercise program. Their results indicated that weight gain between the two groups was not different from one another. They suggested that this provided further support for including both physical activity and exercising counseling in treatment programs.

Thien, Thomas, Markin, and Birmingham (2000) conducted a three-month study with individuals (15 females and 1 male; only 12 completed the study) diagnosed with anorexia nervosa. The participants were randomly divided into two groups: exercise and control. Thien et al. (2000) reported that both BMI and body fat increased in both groups and that the exercise group showed an increase in overall quality of life, whereas the control showed a decline. The authors posited that their failure to find statistical significance was likely due to the small sample size and a relatively large proportion of dropouts (20% of the original sample).

In 2002, Szabo and Green examined the use of resistance training (i.e., weights and elastic bands) as a part of the treatment for individuals with anorexia nervosa. The study enrolled 21 participants, including patients with anorexia nervosa and a control group composed of healthy exercisers. The researchers reported that the patients with anorexia nervosa exhibited a significant increase in body fat and weight and a decrease in eating disorder–related behaviors in comparison to the control group. Overall they concluded that exercise participation did not interfere with weight gain.

Tokumura, Tanaka, Nanri, and Watanabe (2005) reached a similar conclusion. Tokumura et al. (2005) included a prescribed exercise program for adolescent girls hospitalized for anorexia nervosa. They determined that their exercise program (participants used a stationary bike for 30 minutes, 5 times per week) was beneficial for those who participated. They reported that participants showed an improved capacity for exercise as measured by endurance time, oxygen uptake at each participant's specific anaerobic threshold, and peak oxygen uptake. Moreover, they found that the prescribed exercise program did not interfere with the participants' ability to gain weight nor with the resumption of menses. In fact, the increase in BMI for the exercise group changed significantly, while the BMI increase in the control group did not. They also found that those who participated in the exercise program showed a reduction in emotional stress and reported that they enjoyed the exercise program. Although the sample size of this study was quite small (17 total participants, 9 of whom were in the prescribed exercise group) the findings suggest that patients with anorexia nervosa can benefit physically and psychologically from an exercise program that is a part of their treatment while in hospital. These findings confirm those of Touyz, Lennerts, Arthur, and Beumont (1993), whose two-decade-old study examined whether including anaerobic exercise during the refeeding process of patients with anorexia nervosa would hinder weight gain. Their comparison of a group of patients participating in a structured exercise program with a control group yielded no significant difference between them with respect to weight gain.

The studies briefly summarized above constitute the bulk of the published investigations of the effects of exercise in the treatment of individuals with anorexia nervosa. Studies examining exercise in the treatment of bulimia nervosa are even more sparse. Sundgot-Borgen,

Rosenvinge, Bahr, and Schneider (2002) conducted one of two studies that included patients with bulimia nervosa. Their study compared physical exercise to cognitive behavioral therapy in female outpatients. Participants participated in exercise, cognitive behavioral therapy, or nutritional counseling, or they were placed on a waiting list. The exercise group participated in a combination of aerobic and anaerobic activities in both a supervised and unsupervised capacity. Six- and 18-month follow-ups indicated that those who participated in the exercise group showed a significant decrease in drive for thinness and symptoms of bulimia nervosa. They also reported that at the 18-month follow-up these patients were engaging in regular exercise without co-existing self-induced vomiting.

The second study that included patients diagnosed with bulimia nervosa also included patients diagnosed with anorexia nervosa or eating disorder not otherwise specified (Calogero & Pedrotty, 2004). They studied 254 women in residential treatment for an eating disorder. Half of the women participated in exercise groups, and the other half did not participate in exercise. The researchers found that those diagnosed with anorexia nervosa who participated in the exercise program exhibited more weight gain than those with the same diagnosis who did not participate in the exercise program. Moreover, in aggregate the women who participated in the exercise program showed a greater reduction in dysfunctional beliefs with respect to exercise than those who did not participate in the exercise program. They concluded that their findings provided not only support for the inclusion of a structured exercise program in the treatment of individuals with eating disorders, but that the findings also challenge the conventional belief that exercise will prohibit weight gain.

Taking a different approach to examining the use of exercise in treatment programs, Bratland-Sanda and colleagues (2009) looked at similarities and differences among an international sampling of eating disorder treatment facilities in terms of the role of physical activity in treatment. They collected data from 100 percent of treatment facilities in Norway and the United Kingdom, 80 percent of facilities in Denmark, and 77 percent of the facilities in Sweden. The researchers were interested in determining whether physical activity was assessed at all by treatment facilities and if so the degree which they had policies and staff in place to manage physical activity in an eating disorder population.

Most of the facilities that participated agreed that excessive physical activity is a harmful symptom of eating disorders. All treatment facilities participating in the study reported some type of assessment with respect to physical activity, with discrepancies in terms of what was assessed (e.g., body composition, frequency, type) and the method used to assess (e.g., self-report, observation). All of the facilities, however, agreed that they had guidelines to address excessive physical activity, and the use of physical activity in treatment was reported by most (82%) of the facilities. Due to the range of methods used to determine the level of physical activity, including notoriously unreliable methods of data collection (e.g., self-report), the authors noted it is important for facilities to employ a professional with advanced training in physical activity/exercise (just over 25% of the facilities employed someone with such a background).

Bratland-Sanda et al. (2009) concluded that while most of those studied agreed that physical activity can be both a harmful and helpful agent in eating disorders, the researchers expressed concern that there was not (nor is there now) a universal set of guidelines with respect to how to determine when physical activity is harmful. Indeed, Hechler, Beumont, Marks, and Touyz (2005) found that their sample of treatment facilities agreed that physical activity is a central factor in eating disorders; however, careful assessment and established guidelines were generally not used as a part of treatment. They too recommended that existing treatment guidelines for eating disorders need to be revised to include the assessment and management of physical activity. Moreover, as stated above in the section on "Exercise and the Eating Disorders," Madison and Ruma (2003) and Sherman and Thompson (2001) caution that if the exerciser in question is an athlete, it will be important to consider that they may use exercise differently than non-athletes. Madison and Ruma (2003) specifically noted that since there is a tendency for exercise to be limited among those being treated for eating disorders, athletes may need to be assessed differently. This seems to reflect the general consensus of those describing the nature of how we define excessive exercise: it is not the frequency or intensity of the exercise that matters, but the reasons for or the meaning attributed to the exercise that is critical in determining whether the exercise is harmful.

Another perspective on the use of exercise is offered by an individual diagnosed with anorexia nervosa: "Prior to becoming involved in triathlon, I had simply lived from one day to the next with limited goals, no real friends, and the constant feeling that I had nothing to look forward to. My life was defined by the illness of anorexia" (Axelsen, 2009, p. 343). In her autoethnography, Axelsen described what it was like for her to live chained to her eating disorder and how becoming involved in triathlons helped her to live a life more satisfying and enjoyable. She clarifies that her involvement in sport did not cure her, as she continues to struggle with remnants of the disorder; however, she was able to reorient her view of herself to extend away from and beyond anorexia. It is common for those suffering from an eating disorder to fully identify their sense of self in the context of the disorder: "I am an anorexic." Indeed, family and friends often have difficulty seeing their loved one as someone without the disorder. Axelson illustrated how initially her involvement in triathlons was a way to justify the amount of exercise she was doing, and how it progressed to becoming something she wanted to actually excel at. She also noted how her social life, which prior to triathlons consisted of herself and her eating disorder, which she called "Anna," expanded to largely replace "Anna" and include others who had a passion for sport and who made sure their bodies were properly fueled, trained, and rested to perform at their best. Axelson explained the importance of triathlons and how they helped her in her recovery process by interpreting her experience through various social-psychological theories. In aggregate, these theories suggest that she was able to redefine who she was because of her involvement with others who became important to her and who were positive reflections of who she was and who she could become.

In conclusion, the existing literature in the area of incorporating exercise in the treatment of eating disorders is severely limited. The studies that have been conducted have many differences, making it difficult to draw definitive conclusions. The small sample sizes of the studies warn against developing strong conclusions beyond the specific context of the studies themselves. What these studies suggest is that many treatment providers and facilities seem aware that the use of exercise among those with an eating disorder is a behavior that must be addressed. There is not, however, consensus with respect to how exercise should be assessed and/or included in treatment. The studies concur that exercise can be included successfully and that it will not necessarily interfere with treatment, in particular with weight gain for patients who are underweight. In addition to the formal examinations of this issue, Axelson's experience suggests that using sport helped to broaden her sense of who she was. It is not a stretch to suggest that the same could happen for those who engage in healthy exercise and can consider themselves "exerciser"—a moniker than has the potential to replace "anorexic" or "bulimic."

HOW CAN I HELP SOMEONE WHO MAY HAVE AN EATING DISORDER?

The most important step along the way to helping someone with an eating disorder is to learn the signs and symptoms of eating disorders and not to ignore them when they seem to be present. It may be easy to explain away not eating enough under the guise of "trying to become healthy" and excessive exercise as "getting into shape." However, as has been described above, engaging in excessive exercise can lead to the physiological effects of the Female Athlete Triad and can affect the course of treatment when the individual has an eating disorder.

A quick, five-question screening instrument was developed to help practitioners efficiently identify individuals who may be at risk for an eating disorder. Early detection and early intervention give individuals a greater chance of a full recovery from any eating disorder in a relatively short period of time. Brief screening tools like the SCOFF (Morgan, Reid, & Lacey, 1999) can assist in that effort. This tool is not a diagnostic tool in the sense that it will determine whether an individual has an eating disorder, but it can provide evidence that the individual may be at risk and should be evaluated by a licensed professional who specializes in eating disorders. The SCOFF acronym represents a key element in each of the five questions:

Do you make yourself **S**ick because you feel uncomfortably full?
Do you worry you have lost **C**ontrol over how much you eat?
Have you recently lost more than **O**ne stone [14 lbs] in a three-month period?
Do you believe yourself to be **F**at when others say you are too thin?
Would you say that **F**ood dominates your life (p. 1467)?

The authors, based in the United Kingdom, indicated that each "yes" response equals 1 point, and a score of 2 or more points indicates a greater likelihood of an eating disorder, suggesting the need for a formal evaluation. Since its original publication, the SCOFF has been translated into several languages and has been determined to be an effective screening tool (Hill, Reid, Morgan, & Lacey, 2010). Hill et al. (2010) also found that while administering the SCOFF verbally is effective, providing a written copy of the SCOFF for individuals to complete may help to overcome the embarrassment and secrecy that often accompany eating disorders and that may prevent disclosure. Although both the development of the tool and its subsequent validation were conducted with females and might suggest a limitation of the tool, the symptoms for eating disorders are not different for females and males. Therefore, males who endorse two or more of the SCOFF items would be at risk similarly to females.

In the absence of being able to conduct a formal or informal screening, it is possible to take notice of behaviors that suggest someone may have or may be at risk for developing an eating disorder. In their guidelines for coaches, Selby and Reel (2011) outlined several factors coaches can look for. These same ideas apply to any individual regardless of their participation in sport or other form of physical activity. The signs and symptoms they described were changes in mood, personality, or other behaviors; emphasis on body image; focus on food and eating that is different from others; extremes in eating; strong need to feel in control; and additional stressors. The first factor, changes in mood, personality, or other behaviors can be considered a sign that something is not right for the individual. This can be considered a "non-specific" symptom in the sense that this is not unique to eating disorders. So, even if the individual shows no signs of eating concerns, it is a good idea to encourage the individual to talk with someone because there is a good chance that a noticeable change in how the person is acting may reflect a serious problem that requires treatment.

The next three items, emphasis on body image, focus on food and eating that is different from others, and extremes in eating, are more reflective of a possible eating disorder specifically. These three may be somewhat difficult to detect because many people are concerned about how they look (i.e., body image), may talk about food quite a bit, and may undereat at times or overeat at others. What tends to make these factors potential problems is the degree to which they affect the individual. That is, does their life seem to revolve around body and food concerns? Again this may be difficult to determine, given the focus our culture seems to have on weight and food. It is generally a good idea to encourage the individual to seek help or an evaluation if you suspect that these may be a problem even if you are not sure—that is what the professionals are for. As is the case for the first factor, it is possible that these factors may not reflect an eating disorder but may still reflect a problem requiring professional attention (e.g., eating disturbances can be seen in clinical depression); therefore it is always a good idea to encourage a professional evaluation.

Finally, the strong need to be in control and other stressors can reflect a variety of concerns as well but are frequently present in individuals with eating disorders. The need to be in control will be evident in how the individual handles things that do not go as planned. If they struggle with changes in plans or plans that go awry such that they become irritable and/or begin to avoid making plans unless they have "complete control" over what occurs, they are likely someone who has a strong need to be in control. When this occurs in individuals with eating disorders, their sense of control is often expressed through food (e.g., what they eat, where they eat, how food is prepared). Additional stressors refer to any other event or experience the individual may be going through in addition to everyday stressors. The addition of stressors (e.g., death of a loved one, divorce/marriage, or change in job) tends to exacerbate the expression of other symptoms. For example, they may seem even more rigid in their food choices, they may express more intense concerns about their body shape and weight, and they may withdraw from social interactions more severely.

Selby and Reel (2011) do not address overexercising specifically as a symptom of eating disorders due to the fact that the population of focus was individuals who are already engaged in a high degree of physical activity. However, as has been previously noted, it is possible for athletes to overdo it when it comes to physical activity/workouts. For a complete discussion of how eating disorders affect athletes, see Thompson and Sherman (2010).

With respect to identifying excessive exercise among non-athletes, there is currently not a clear-cut definition or universal tool used by practitioners or researchers. In the section above entitled When Is Exercise "Excessive," the point was made that despite the lack of agreement among professionals and researchers with respect to what to call exercising too much or specifically how to define it, there seems to be a convergence of opinion that it is not necessarily how frequently, how long, or how intensely the individual engages in exercise, but the reasons behind their exercise behavior that matter. Several researchers suggested that the qualitative aspects of exercise behavior (i.e., why do they exercise) are more important than the quantitative elements. Thus, when trying to determine when an individual may be overexercising, it will be important to talk with them about what it is like for them to exercise, what it is like for them when they cannot exercise, and what exercise does for them (e.g., helps to manage stress, helps to take their mind off their eating disorder).

In his book on helping men with eating disorders and compulsive exercising, Morgan (2008, p. 72) proposed a brief checklist to help exercisers determine whether they are using exercise in an unhealthy way. These same questions can be used by practitioners to help determine if their client is misusing exercise. He suggested that answering "yes" to two or more of the following questions might indicate that there is a problem:

Do you get distressed or feel guilty if you miss a training session?
Do you make yourself exercise despite illness or injury?
Do you put training sessions in front of family or friends?
Do you exercise as a pay-off for overeating?
Do you worry about weight gain on rest days?

The above items have not been studied to determine how reliably they predict excessive exercise; however, like the SCOFF (which has been validated), these five questions may provide a preliminary indication that an individual may not be using exercise in a healthy way.

Alternatively, the Compulsive Exercise Test (CET) (Taranis, Touyz, & Meyer, 2011) was formally developed and studied to determine whether it could adequately identify individuals who misuse exercise. The CET is a questionnaire with 24 Likert-scaled items. The 24 items were found to group together such that they reflect five difference factors related to "compulsive exercise." These factors include avoidance and rule-driven behavior (e.g., "If I miss an exercise session, I will try and make up for it when I next exercise"), exercise use for weight control (e.g., "If I feel I have eaten too much, I will do more exercise"), improvement in mood as a result of exercise (e.g., "I feel happier and/or more positive after I exercise"), lack of enjoyment of exercise (e.g., "I do not enjoy exercising"), and being rigid in the use of exercise (e.g., "I follow a set routine for my exercise sessions").

In their evaluation of the usefulness of the CET, Goodwin, Haycraft, Taranis, and Meyer (2011) verified the validity and reliability of the CET and noted that responses to the CET were not robustly related to the *frequency* of exercise. These findings converge with the original evaluation of the instrument and suggest that the CET taps into the qualitative aspects of excessive exercise that other researchers (see section above entitled When Is Exercise "Excessive?") have suggested is more important than the quantitative aspects of excessive exercise in the context of an eating disorder. As with all of the information contained in this section, scores on the CET do not necessarily reflect the presence or absence of an eating disorder. Only a licensed medical health or mental health professional can make that determination.

In 2006 the American Psychiatric Association (APA) approved and published the *Practice Guideline for the Treatment of Patients with Eating Disorders, Third Edition* (Guideline), which provides a 128-page description of treatment recommendations, a review of the evidence, and needs for future research. In 2012 the APA published *Guideline Watch (August 2012)*, in which they reviewed the evidence published since the 2006 Guideline. It concluded that the 2006 publication is "substantially correct and current in its recommendations" (p. 1). It reported one exception to the Guideline that involved the use of a medication for binge-eating disorder; since medications are not a focus of this chapter, it will not be discussed here.

With respect to exercise, the Guideline states that exercise should be a part of the initial assessment of a patient who may have an eating disorder, including how the patient's family perceives exercise (e.g,. does the family encourage/discourage exercise, is exercise used as a punishment). Regardless of what the family's attitude is toward exercise (or any other factor affecting the patient), it is important to discuss these issues in a way that does not blame family members, parents in particular, for the presence of any symptoms. Eating disorders are highly complex. Despite the effect that the family environment may have on the development or maintenance of an eating disorder, there is no evidence that families cause eating disorders.

The Guideline also recommends that physical activity should be considered in the context of food intake and overall energy expenditure. That is, if the patient is not eating enough given their daily needs for maintaining normal bodily functions and their level of additional activity, then it is recommended that physical activity be limited. In some cases physical activity should be prohibited until the patient is able to gain sufficient weight to be considered medically stable. When the patient is eating enough and is determined to be medically healthy, the Guideline states that "the focus of an exercise program should be on the patient's gaining physical fitness as opposed to expending calories" (p. 15). Furthermore, the Guideline notes that exercise should ideally not be a solitary activity and that it should be enjoyable to the patient rather than something that they *must* do.

Regardless of a patient's specific weight, if the patient is cleared for exercise, in addition to enjoyment, the focus on health and fitness rather than on weight will help the patient to develop life-long habits that will improve and sustain overall health. If the patient has used exercise primarily as a tool for manipulating their body shape and weight, it may be difficult for them to believe that exercising without watching the number on the scale can be beneficial. It is difficult to change this type of thinking, especially when we, as a culture, are exposed to numerous messages encouraging us to be sure that our bodies "look right," and if they don't, to do whatever we have to in order to make our bodies acceptable. If friends and family members share this way of thinking, making a shift from diet-oriented thinking and behaviors to those that are health oriented can be a particularly difficult struggle. The Guideline does recommend using exercise in the context of weight loss for treating binge eating disorder. There is ongoing controversy in the field with respect to the focus on weight in overweight or obese patients when many believe the focus should remain on fitness and health, as it is for the other eating disorders. The most prominent proponent of this approach is the Heath at Every Size (HAES) perspective (e.g., Bacon, 2010), which states that people of all shapes and sizes can be either healthy or unhealthy. Simply taking note of how large or small someone seems or what number is reflected on the scale does not reveal their health status.

Consistent with study results reported by researchers, the Guideline notes that "extreme" exercise may be a risk factor in the development of bulimia nervosa and in particular anorexia nervosa. The Guideline also notes that excessive or compulsive exercise will likely be one of the last behaviors to subside. As a friend, family member, treatment provider, or other professional, it may be frustrating to see patients continue behaviors known to be unhealthy for them and not begin behaviors known to be health promoting. It is not uncommon for treatment providers or other professionals to experience what is known as "countertransference" in their work with patients with eating disorders. Countertransference refers to the reactions that a provider has toward their patients. These reactions reflect thoughts and feelings that are not related to the patient themself and are an issue for the psychotherapist to identify and resolve. The Guideline specifically mentions the likelihood of countertransference in work with patients with eating disorders, stating that "[c]linicians need to attend to their countertransference reactions to patients with a chronic eating disorder" (p. 17). It is reasonable to assume that providers will more than likely have countertransference reactions to patients with eating disorders. Therefore, it is imperative for providers to be sensitive to the thoughts and feelings they have about their patients before, during, and after treatment. Countertransference reactions do not preclude the provider from being able to work with the patient, but may require supervision and/or psychotherapy.

Working with individuals with eating disorders is challenging work. These disorders are complex in nature, and the factors that maintain the disorders are varied. The misuse of exercise or "excessive exercise" can be a symptom of an eating disorder and may very well inhibit the patient's treatment and recovery process. It is therefore important that those who intend to interact with these individuals, whether in a treatment or supportive capacity, be highly educated about the disorders as well as about how to interact with these individuals in ways that maximize the possibility of recovery.

NOTE

1 The dates of these two articles are correct despite the fact that it appears as if the study conducted by Touyz et al. (1993) occurred prior to the development of the program itself (Beumont et al., 1994). The dates appear to be an artifact of when the respective journals were able to publish each article.

REFERENCES

Ackard, D. M., Brehm, B. J., & Steffen, J. J. (2002). Exercise and eating disorders in college-aged women: Profiling excessive exercisers. *Eating Disorders, 10*, 31–47.

Adams, J., & Kirkby, R. J. (2002). Excessive exercise as an addiction: A review. *Addiction Research and Theory, 10*, 415–437.

Adkins, E. C., & Keel, P. K. (2005). Does "excessive" or "compulsive" best describe exercise as a symptom of bulimia nervosa? *International Journal of Eating Disorders, 38,* 24–29.

Aidman, E. V., & Wollard, S. (2003). The influence of self-reported exercise addiction on acute emotional and physiological responses to brief exercise deprivation. *Psychology of Sport and Exercise, 4,* 225–236.

Alexandratos, K., Barnett, F., & Thomas, Y. (2012). The impact of exercise on the mental health and quality of life of people with severe mental illness. *The British Journal of Occupational Therapy, 75,* 48–60.

American Psychiatric Association. (2000). Eating Disorders. In American Psychiatric Association (Ed.), *Diagnostic and statistical manual of mental disorders* (4th ed., text revision. pp. 583–595). Washington, DC: American Psychiatric Publishing.

American Psychiatric Association. (2006). *Practice guideline for the treatment of patients with eating disorders* (3rd ed.). Washington, DC: American Psychiatric Association.

American Psychiatric Association. (2012). *Guideline watch (August 2012): Practice guideline for the treatment of patients with eating disorders* (3rd ed.). Washington, DC: American Psychiatric Association.

American Psychiatric Association. (2013). Feeding and eating disorders. In American Psychiatric Association (Ed.), *Diagnostic and statistical manual of mental disorders* (5th ed., pp. 329–354). Washington, DC: American Psychiatric Publishing.

Arcelus, J., Mitchell, A. J., Wales, J., & Nielsen, S. (2011). Mortality rates in patients with anorexia nervosa and other eating disorders. *Archives of General Psychiatry, 68,* 724–731.

Aruguete, M. S., Edman, J. L., & Yates, A. (2012). The relationship between anger and other correlates of eating disorders in women. *North American Journal of Psychology, 14,* 139–148.

Axelsen, M. (2009). The power of leisure: "I was an anorexic; I'm now a healthy triathlete." *Leisure Sciences, 31,* 330–346.

Bacon, L. (2010). *Health at every size: The surprising truth about your weight.* Dallas: BenBella Books.

Beaumont, P. J. V., Arthur, B., Russell, J. D., & Touyz, S. W. (1994). Excessive physical activity in dieting disorder patients: Proposals for a supervised exercise program. *International Journal of Eating Disorders, 15,* 21–36.

Beaumont, P. J. V., Beumont, C. C., Touyz, S. W., & Williams, H. (1997). Nutritional counseling and supervised exercise. In D. M. Garner & P. E. Garfinkel (Eds.), *Handbook of treatment for eating disorders* (2nd ed., pp. 178–187). New York, NY: Guilford Press.

Blinder, B. J., Freeman, D. M., & Stunkard, A. J. (1970). Behavior therapy of anorexia nervosa: Effectiveness of activity as a reinforcer of weight gain. *American Journal of Psychiatry, 126,* 1093–1098.

Boyd, C., Abraham, S., & Luscombe, G. (2007). Exercise behaviours and feelings in eating disorder and non-eating disorder groups. *European Eating Disorders Review, 15,* 112–118.

Bratland-Sanda, S., Martinsen, E. W., Rosenvinge, J. H., Rø, O., Hoffart, A., & Sundgot-Borgen, J. (2011). Exercise dependence score in patients with longstanding eating disorders and controls: The importance of affect regulation and physical activity intensity. *European Eating Disorders Review, 19,* 249–255.

Bratland-Sanda, S., Rosenvinge, J. H., Vrabel, K. A. R., Norring, C., Sundgot-Borgen, J., Rø, O., & Martinsen, E. W. (2009). Physical activity in treatment units for eating disorders: Clinical practice and attitudes. *Eating and Weight Disorders, 14,* e106–e112.

Bratland-Sanda, S., Sundgot-Borgen, J., Rø, O., Rosenvinge, J. H., Hoffart, A., & Martinsen, E. W. (2010a). "I'm not physically active—I only go for walks": Physical activity in patients with longstanding eating disorders. *International Journal of Eating Disorders, 43,* 88–92.

Bratland-Sanda, S., Sundgot-Borgen, J., Rø, O., Rosenvinge, J. H., Hoffart, A., & Martinsen, E. W. (2010b). Physical activity and exercise dependence during inpatient treatment of longstanding eating disorders: An exploratory study of excessive and non-exercisers. *International Journal of Eating Disorders, 43,* 266–273.

Brehm, B. J., & Steffen, J. J. (1998). Relation between obligatory exercise and eating disorders. *American Journal of Health Behavior, 22,* 108–119.

Button, E. J., Chadalavad, B., & Palmer, R. L. (2010). Mortality and predictors of death in a cohort of patients presenting to an eating disorder service. *International Journal of Eating Disorders, 43,* 387–392.

Calogero, R. M., & Pedrotty, K. N. (2004). The practice and process of healthy exercise: An investigation of the treatment of exercise abuse in women with eating disorders. *Eating Disorders, 12,* 273–291.

Calogero, R. M., & Pedrotty-Stump, K. N. (2010). Incorporating exercise into eating disorder treatment and recovery: Cultivating a mindful approach. In M. Maine, B. H. McGilley, & D. W. Bunnell (Eds.), *Treatment of eating disorders: Bridging the research-practice gap* (pp. 425–441). New York, NY: Academic Press.

Cook, B. J., & Hausenblas, H. A. (2008). The role of exercise dependence for the relationship between exercise behavior and eating pathology. *Journal of Health Psychology, 13,* 495–502.

Cook, B. J., & Hausenblad, H. A. (2011). Eating disorder-specific health-related quality of life and exercise in college females. *Quality of Life Research, 20,* 1385–1390.

Cox, R., & Orford, J. (2004). A qualitative study of the meaning of exercise for people who could be labeled as 'addicted' to exercise—can 'addiction' be applied to high frequency exercising? *Addiction Research and Theory, 12,* 167–188.

Crisp, A. H., Hsu, L. K. G., Harding, B., & Hartshorn, J. (1980). Clinical features of anorexia nervosa: A study of a consecutive series of 102 female patients. *Journal of Psychosomatic Research, 24,* 179–191.

Davis, C. (2000). Exercise abuse. *International Journal of Sport Psychology, 31,* 278–289.

Davis, C., Brewer, H., & Ratusny, D. (1993). Behavioral frequency and psychological commitment: Necessary concepts in the study of excessive exercising. *Journal of Behavioral Medicine, 16,* 611–628.

Davis, C., Katzman, D. K., Kaptein, S., Kirsch, C., Brewer, H., Kalmbach, K., . . . Kaplan, A. S. (1997). The prevalence of high-level exercise in the eating disorders: Etiological implications. *Comprehensive Psychiatry, 38,* 321–326.

Davis, C., Kennedy, S. H., Ravelski, E., & Dionne, M. (1994). The role of physical activity in the development and maintenance of eating disorders. *Psychological Medicine, 24,* 957–967.

DeBoer, L. B., Powers, M. B., Utschig, A. C., Otto, M. W., & Smits, J. A. (2012). Exploring exercise as an avenue for the treatment of anxiety disorders. *Expert Review of Neurotherapeutics, 12,* 1011–1022.

De Young, K. P., & Anderson, D. A. (2010). Prevalance and correlates of exercise motivated by negative affect. *International Journal of Eating Disorders, 43,* 50–58.

Elbourne, K. E., & Chen, J. (2007). The continuum model of obligatory exercise: A preliminary investigation. *Journal of Psychosomatic Research, 62,* 73–80.

Epling, W. F., Pierce, W. D., & Stefan, L. (1983). A theory of activity-based anorexia. *International Journal of Eating Disorders, 3,* 27–46.

Fairburn, C. G., Cooper, Z., Bohn, K., O'Connor, M., Doll, H. A., & Palmer, R. I. (2007). The severity and status of eating disorders NOS: Implications for DSM-V. *Behavior Research Theory, 45,* 1705–1715.

Fox, K. R. (2000). Self-esteem, self-perceptions and exercise. *International Journal of Sport Psychology, 31,* 228–240.

Goodwin, H., Haycraft, E., Taranis, L., & Meyer, C. (2011). Psychometric evaluation of the compulsive exercise test (CET) in an adolescent population: Links with eating psychopathology. *European Eating Disorders Review, 19,* 269–279.

Goodwin, H., Haycraft, E., Willis, A., & Meyer, C. (2011). Compulsive exercise: The role of personality, psychological morbidity, and disordered eating. *International Journal of Eating Disorders, 44,* 655–660.

Grave, R. D. (2008). Excessive and compulsive exercises in eating disorders: Prevalence, associated features, and management. *Directions in Psychiatry, 28,* 273–282.

Grave, R. D., Calugi, S., & Marchesini, G. (2008). Compulsive exercise to control shape or weight in eating disorders: Prevalence, associated features, and treatment outcome. *Comprehensive Psychiatry, 49,* 346–352.

Guiney, H., & Machado, L. (2013). Benefits of regular aerobic exercise for executive functioning in healthy populations. *Psychonomic Bulletin & Review, 20,* 73–86.

Hausenblas, H. A., & Downs, D. S. (2002). How much is too much? The development and validation of the exercise dependence scale. *Psychology & Health, 17,* 387–404.

Hayas, C. L., Padiera, J. Á., Bilbao, A., Martin, J., Munoz, P., & Quintana, J. M. (2014). Eating disorders: Predictors of changes in the quality of life of caregivers. *Psychiatry Research, 215*, 718–726.

Hechler, T., Beumont, P., Marks, P., & Touyz, S. (2005). How do clinical specialists understand the role of physical activity in eating disorders? *European Eating Disorders Review, 13*, 125–132.

Hill, L. S., Reid, F., Morgan, J. F., & Lacey, J. H. (2010). SCOFF, the development of an eating disorder screening questionnaire. *International Journal of Eating Disorders, 43*, 344–351.

Hoch, A. Z., Pajewski, N. M., Moraski, L., Carrera, G. F., Wilson, C. R., Hoffman, R. G., . . . Gutterman, D. D. (2009). Prevalence of the female athlete triad in high school athletes and sedentary students. *Journal of Clinical Sports Medicine, 19*, 421–428.

Johnston, O., Reilly, J., & Kremer, J. (2011). Excessive exercise: From quantitative categorization to a qualitative continuum approach. *European Eating Disorders Review, 19*, 237–248.

Le Grange, D., & Eisler, I. (1993). The link between anorexia nervosa and excessive exercise: A review. *European Eating Disorders Review, 1*, 100–119.

Madison, J. K., & Ruma, S. L. (2003). Exercise and athletic involvement as moderators of severity in adolescents with eating disorders. *Journal of Applied Sport Psychology, 15*, 213–222.

McLaren, L., Gauvin, L., & White, D. (2001). The role of perfectionism and excessive commitment to exercise in explaining dietary restraint: Replication and extension. *International Journal of Eating Disorders, 29*, 307–313.

Meyer, C., & Taranis, L. (2011). Exercise in the eating disorders: Terms and definitions. *European Eating Disorders Review, 19*, 169–173.

Meyer, C., Taranis, L., Goodwin, H., & Haycraft, E. (2011). Compulsive exercise and eating disorders. *European Eating Disorders Review, 19*, 174–189.

Meyer, C., Taranis, L., & Touyz, S. (2008). Excessive exercise in the eating disorders: A need for less activity from patients and more from researchers . . . *European Eating Disorders Review, 16*, 81–83.

Mond, J. M., & Calogero, R. M. (2009). Excessive exercise in eating disorder patients and in healthy women. *Australian and New Zealand Journal of Psychiatry, 43*, 227–234.

Mond, J. M., Hay, P. J., Rodgers, B., & Owen, C. (2006). An update on the definition of "excessive exercise" in eating disorder research. *International Journal of Eating Disorders, 39*, 147–153.

Mond, J. M., Hay, P. J., Rodgers, B., Owen, C., & Beumont, P. J. (2004). Relationships between exercise behavior, eating disordered behavior and quality of life in a community sample of women: When is exercise excessive? *European Eating Disorders Review, 12*, 265–272.

Mond, J. M., Meyers, T. C., Crosby, R., Hay, P., & Mitchell, J. (2008). 'Excessive exercise' and eating-disordered behavior in young adult women: Further evidence from a primary care sample. *European Eating Disorders Review, 16*, 215–221.

Morgan, J. F. (2008). *The invisible man: A self-help guide for men with eating disorders, compulsive exercising and bigorexia*. New York, NY: Routledge.

Morgan, J. F., Reid, F., & Lacey, J. H. (1999). The SCOFF questionnaire: Assessment of a new screening tool for eating disorders. *British Medical Journal, 319*, 1167–1168.

Nattiv, A., Agostini, R., Drinkwater, B., & Yeager, K. K. (1994). The female athlete triad. The inner-relatedness of disordered eating, amenorrhea, and osteoporosis. *Clinical Journal of Sport Medicine, 13*, 405–418.

Nattiv, A., Loucks, A. B., Manore, M. M., Sanborn, C. F., Sundgot-Borgen, J., Warren, M. P., & American College of Sports Medicine. (2007). American College of Sports Medicine position stand: The female athlete triad. *Medicine and Science in Sport and Exercise, 39*, 1867–1882.

Naylor, H., Mountford, V., & Brown, G. (2011). Beliefs about excessive exercise in eating disorders: The role of obsessions and compulsions. *European Eating Disorders Review, 19*, 226–236.

Neumärker, K. J. (2000). Mortality rates and causes of death. *European Eating Disorders Review, 8*, 181–187.

Penas-Lledo, E., Vaz Leal, F. J., & Waller, G. (2002). Excessive exercise in anorexia nervosa and bulimia nervosa: Relation to eating characteristics and general psychopathology. *International Journal of Eating Disorders, 31*, 370–375.

Penedo, F. J., & Dahn, J. R. (2005). Exercise and well-being: A review of mental and physical health benefits associated with physical activity. *Current Opinion in Psychiatry, 18*, 189–193.

Reel, J. J., SooHoo, S., Petrie, T. A., Greenleaf, C., & Carter, J. E. (2010). Slimming down for sport: Developing a weight pressures in sport measure for female athletes. *Journal of Clinical Sport Psychology, 4*, 99–111.

Ricca, V., Mannucci, E., Mezzani, B., DiBernardo, M., Zucchi, T., Paionni, A., . . . Faravelli, C. (2001). Psychopathological and clinical features of outpatients with eating disorders not otherwise specified. *Eating and Weight Disorders, 6*, 157–165.

Rosling, A. M., Sparén, P., Norring, C., & von Knorring, A. (2011). Mortality of eating disorders: A follow-up study of treatment in a specialist unit 1974–2000. *International Journal of Eating Disorders, 44*, 304–310.

Sachs, M. L., & Pargman, D. (1979). Running addiction: A depth interview examination. *Journal of Sport Behavior, 2*, 143–155.

Seigel, K., & Hetta, J. (2001). Exercise and eating disorder symptoms among young females. *Eating and Weight Disorders, 6*, 32–39.

Selby, C. L. B., & Reel, J. J. (2011). A coach's guide to identifying and helping athletes with eating disorders. *Journal of Sport Psychology in Action, 2*, 100–112.

Sherman, R. T., & Thompson, R. A. (2001). Athletes and disordered eating: Four major issues for the professional psychologist. *Professional Psychology: Research & Practice, 32*, 1.

Shroff, H., Reba, L., Thornton, L. M., Tozzi, F., Klump, K., Berrettini, W. H., . . . Bulik, C. M. (2006). Features associated with excessive exercise in women with eating disorders. *International Journal of Eating Disorders, 39*, 454–461.

Solenberger, S. (2001). Exercise and eating disorders: A 3-year inpatient hospital record analysis. *Eating Behaviors, 2*, 151–168.

Steffen, J. J., & Brehm, B. J. (1999). The dimensions of obligatory exercise. *Eating Disorders, 7*, 219–226.

Stiles-Shields, E. C., Goldschmidt, A. B., Boepple, L., Glunz, C., & Le Grange, D. (2011). Driven exercise among treatment-seeking youth with eating disorders. *Eating Behaviors, 12*, 328–331.

Strelan, P., Mehaffey, S. J., & Tiggemann, M. (2003). Self-objectification and esteem in young women: The mediating role of reasons for exercise. *Sex Roles, 48*, 89–95.

Strober, M., Freeman, R., & Morrell, W. (1997). The long-term course of severe anorexia nervosa in adolescents: Survival analysis of recovery, relapse, and outcome predictors over 10–15 years in a prospective study. *International Journal of Eating Disorders, 22*, 339–360.

Sundgot-Borgen, J., Bahr, R., Falch, J. A., & Schneider, L. S. (1998). Normal bone mass in bulimic women. *Journal of Clinical Endocrinology and Metabolism, 83*, 3144–3149.

Sundgot-Borgen, J., Rosenvinge, J. H., Bahr, R., & Schneider, L. S. (2002). The effect of exercise, cognitive therapy, and nutritional counseling in treating bulimia nervosa. *Medicine & Science in Sports & Exercise, 34*, 190–195.

Sundgot-Borgen, J., & Torstveit, M. K. (2004). Prevalence of eating disorders in elite athletes is higher than in the general population. *Clinical Journal of Sport Medicine, 14*, 25–32.

Szabo. C. P., & Green, K. (2002). Hospitalized anorexics and resistance training: Impact on body composition and psychological well-being. A preliminary study. *Eating and Weight Disorders, 7*, 293–297.

Taranis, L., Touyz, S., & Meyer, C. (2011). Disordered eating and exercise: Development and preliminary validation of the compulsive exercise test (CET). *European Eating Disorders Review, 19*, 256–268.

Thien, V., Thomas, A., Markin, D., & Birmingham, C. L. (2000). Pilot study of a graded exercise program for the treatment of anorexia nervosa. *International Journal of Eating Disorders, 28*, 101–106.

Thompson, R. A., & Sherman, R. T. (2010). *Eating Disorders in Sport.* New York, NY: Routledge.

Tokumura, M., Tanaka, T., Nanri, S., & Watanabe, H. (2005). Prescribed exercise training for convalescent children and adolescents with anorexia nervosa: Reduced heart rate response to exercise in an important parameter for the early recurrence diagnosis of anorexia nervosa. In P. I. Swain (Ed.), *Adolescent eating disorders* (pp. 69–83). Hauppauge, NY: Nova Science Publishers.

Touyz, S. W., Beumont, P. J. V., & Heok, S. (1987). Exercise anorexia: A new dimension in anorexia nervosa? In P. J. V. Beumont, G. D. Burrows, & R. C. Caspar (Eds.), *Handbook of eating disorders, Part 1: Anorexia and bulimia nervosa* (pp. 143–157). Amsterdam: Elsevier.

Touyz, S. W., Lennerts, W., Arthur, B., & Beumont, P. J. V. (1993). Anaerobic exercise as an adjunct to refeeding patients with anorexia nervosa: Does it compromise weight gain? *European Eating Disorders Review, 1*, 177–182.

Turner, H., & Bryant-Waugh, R. (2004). Eating disorder not otherwise specified (EDNOS): Profiles of clients presenting at a community eating disorder service. *European Eating Disorder Review, 12*, 18–26.

United States Department of Health and Human Services. (2008). *2008 Physical activity guidelines for Americans*. Retrieved from www.health.gov/paguidelines/pdf/paguide.pdf

Vansteelandt, K., Rijmen, F., Pieters, G., Probst, M., & Vanderlinden, J. (2007). Drive for thinness, affect regulation and physical activity in eating disorders: A daily life study. *Behaviour Research and Therapy, 45*, 1717–1734.

Vinkers, C., Evers, C., Adriaanse, M., & de Ridder, D. (2012). Body esteem and eating disorder symptomotology: The mediating role of appearance-motivated exercise in a non-clinical adult female sample. *Eating Behaviors, 13*, 214–218.

Winkler, L. A., Christiansen, E., Lichtenstein, M. B., Hansen, N. B., Blienberg, N., & Støving, R. K. (2014). Quality of life in eating disorders: A meta-analysis. *Psychiatry Research, 219*, 1–9.

Zunker, C., Mitchell, J. E., & Wonderlich, S. A. (2011). Exercise interventions for women with anorexia nervosa: A review of the literature. *International Journal of Eating Disorders 44*, 579–584.

29 Mindfulness

Amy Baltzell and Trevor Cote

INTRODUCTION

This chapter will introduce the concept of mindfulness, highlight how mindfulness has been an integral component of some exercise (e.g., yoga), and discuss how mindfulness-based approaches can further be used to enhance exercise engagement and adherence. Within the field of exercise psychology, there is a strong interest in understanding what contributes to enhancing self-regulation with the end goal of engaging consistently in healthy physical activity. Until recently, mindfulness-based interventions and approaches primarily have focused on addressing physical or psychological suffering and have not focused on exercise. Mindfulness approaches have demonstrated efficacy for clinical issues, particularly stress reduction for those with physical diseases (e.g., Bohlmeijer, Prenger, Taal, & Cuijpers, 2010) and reduction of psychological disorders, such as anxiety and depression (e.g., see Keng, Smoski, & Robins, 2011).

The focus on bringing mindfulness-based practices to those deemed healthy (i.e., not suffering from psychological or physical disorders) is a relatively new phenomenon in current research (Chiesa & Seretti, 2009; Shangraw & Akhtar, 2016). Ironically, Buddhist philosophy has long contended that mindfulness meditation should be practiced to achieve enduring happiness (Ekman, Davidson, Ricard, & Wallace, 2005). Empirically we know that mindfulness practices can lead to a plethora of wellness-related benefits including self-regulation (Evans, Baer, & Segerstrom, 2009), enhanced attentional functions and cognitive flexibility (Moore & Malinowski, 2009), and enhanced adaptive response to stress (e.g., Kabat-Zinn, Massion, & Kristeller, 1992). Also, we know that absence of a mental disorder is not equated with well-being, and human beings can still languish in the absence of mental disorders (Keyes, 2002). Languishing is defined as the absence of mental health (i.e., low in social, psychological, and emotional well-being) and not being mentally ill (Keyes, 2002). In contrast, those who are also not suffering from a mental disorder and are experiencing high levels of emotional, psychological, and social well-being are deemed as flourishing (Keyes, 2002). This chapter will consider the use of mindfulness-based strategies for the non-clinical exercise population to help enhance well-being via exercise participation and exercise adherence.

There is initial support that relatively higher levels of mindfulness are related to greater adoption and adherence to physical activity (Ulmer, Stetson, & Salmon, 2010). Expanding to sport, mindfulness-based interventions contribute to quality of sport experience in recreational athletes via higher levels of flow (Kaufman, Glass, & Arnkoff, 2009) and sport performance of competitive athletes (Gardner & Moore, 2004; John, Verma, & Khanna, 2011). This chapter offers an overview of what mindfulness is and how mindfulness changes one's present moment experience, a consideration of mindfulness research and mindfulness-based programs within sport and exercise psychology, and practical applications of mindfulness training with the end goal of increasing exercise participation.

WHAT IS MINDFULNESS?

There have been two distinct yet overlapping ways that mindfulness has been considered in the literature. The two views include the Buddhist approach and, more recently, Ellen Langer's conception of mindfulness. We will first consider the Buddhist approach, as represented by Jon Kabat-Zinn's work, followed by a discussion of Langerian mindfulness as they each apply to exercise.

Buddhist Mindfulness

Within the Buddhist approach, mindfulness is defined as "the state of being attentive to and aware of what is taking place in the present" (Brown & Ryan, 2003, p. 822) and "attention to experience without attachment to one's experience" (Compton & Hoffman, 2013, p. 92). How can we apply mindfulness to exercise? We can use curiosity and acceptance, for example, to notice avoidant thoughts and desires to shun exercise. Once mindful of such thoughts and desires, we then have more choice about going to the gym or not, without being unduly controlled by such aversive, involuntary thoughts or feelings. In contrast, when we get stuck in mindlessness, instead of being at choice, we can get lost in rumination (e.g, about how unpleasant the workout might be) and get absorbed in the past (e.g., how hard it was to warm up last time out) or future. With such a mindlessness approach, we unfortunately behave or respond automatically, without awareness of our thoughts, reactions, and ultimately our behaviors (which may be avoidance of exercise, the one thing that may be most important to our overall physical well-being).

Jon Kabat-Zinn (1990, 1994) is the leader in bringing Buddhist-inspired mindfulness practices to the West, with initial focus on chronic pain patients. He also was the first to bring mindfulness meditation to sport (Kabat-Zinn, Beall, & Rippe, 1985), though for the past 2,500 years Buddhists have implemented mindfulness meditation practices (Compton & Hoffman, 2013). Kabat-Zinn defines mindfulness as "paying attention in a particular way: on purpose, in the present moment, and non-judgmentally" (Kabat-Zinn, 1994, p. 4). Higher levels of mindfulness represent both higher levels of awareness and acceptance of in-the-moment reality (Kabat-Zinn, 1994). An essential aspect of mindfulness is the concept of acceptance, which can be conceptualized as "taking a stance of non-judgmental awareness and actively embracing the experience of thoughts, feelings and bodily sensations as they occur" (Hayes, Strosahl, Bunting, Twohig, & Wilson, 2004, p. 7). This approach and related strategies to enhance mindfulness lead to an enhanced ability to accept, or tolerate, what has occurred and what is occurring moment-to-moment. Mindfulness meditation is based on the premise that when we try to ignore or repress unpleasant or unwanted thoughts and emotions, sensations tend to increase in intensity (Compton & Hoffman, 2013). To cultivate mindfulness, compassion, and wisdom, within the Buddhist approach, mindfulness meditation is encouraged.

Kabat-Zinn's mindfulness-based program, Mindfulness Based Stress Reduction (MBSR), is implemented worldwide and has been used as the go-to intervention for mindfulness efficacy research (Baer, 2003; Keng et al., 2011). There is a plethora of research on the benefits of such mindfulness-based strategies to serve as antidotes for "psychological distress—rumination, anxiety, worry, fear, anger, and so on—many of which involve the maladaptive tendencies to avoid, suppress, or over-engage with one's distressing thoughts and emotions" (Keng et al., 2011, p. 1042). In addition, several studies using MBSR as the mindfulness intervention have indicated that such practices reflect neuroplasticity. In other words, extended meditation training leads to structural changes of the brain (e.g., Davidson et al., 2003). For example, Hölzel and colleagues (2011) reported an increase in meditators' left hippocampus gray matter concentration (which is critically involved in learning and memory and helps regulate emotion) after participating in an eight-week MBSR program. Mindfulness-based interventions range from formal practice of mindfulness (i.e., sitting meditation) to practicing mindfulness while engaged in day-to-day life activities (e.g., how one engages with self and environment when going for a walk or a run).

Langerian Mindfulness

Ellen Langer, a thought leader in the field of mindfulness, offers a different emphasis on what mindfulness means. Langer emphasizes a flexible, open awareness and attention, which is externally focused on objects, others, and what is occurring in one's immediate external environment (Langer, 2000). Langer and colleagues (Langer, Cohen, & Djikic, 2012) define mindfulness as "a process of actively making new distinctions about objects in one's awareness, a process that cultivates sensitivity to subtle variations in context and perspective about the observed subject, rather than relying on entrenched categorizations from the past" (p. 1115). Langer's understanding of mindfulness is "achieved without meditation," and mindfulness is "the simple act of drawing novel distinctions. It leads us to greater sensitivity to context and perspective, and ultimately to greater control over our lives" (Langer, 1990, p. 220).

Langer's emphasis on novelty in the present, when put into practice, has been demonstrated to enhance the quality of human experience. For example, Langer and colleagues' (2009) study prompted orchestra performers to purposefully "offer subtle new nuances" (p. 126) when performing. The same performers were used as their own control group and asked to re-create their best performance while playing the same musical piece. Langer and colleagues (2009) found that when prompted to be more mindful (i.e., the intervention), the quality of the musical performance was enhanced, based on musician and audience analysis. In addition, the musicians reported enjoying performing more when compared to the control performance.

It is most likely that practicing mindfulness by paying attention to novel stimuli would be most helpful in well-learned tasks within the exercise realm as well, such as going for one's 100th five-mile run of the year or attending yoga class consistently for the seventh consecutive month. Paying attention to novelty can make an ordinary experience more compelling. For example, going for a run down the same road each day can begin to feel monotonous. However, looking up into the sky and noticing the sun and a half moon in the morning sky could be awe inspiring. If we are not aware of what is different, we might miss the novelty in the sky. Another more common experience could be becoming aware of a particular sensation, such as the sensation of wind against one's skin, as one goes for a run. Both examples represent enhanced Langerian mindfulness and, concurrently, increased enjoyment and/or engagement in the run.

Kabat-Zinn's and Langer's conceptualizations of mindfulness share some features: both represent *present moment awareness, acceptance* of what is occurring, and mental flexibility to allow oneself to be aware of what *actually* is occurring in contrast to seeing only what one has a habit of perceiving. Both approaches note that often people do not attend to the present moment and tend to *think and act automatically* (Kabat-Zinn, 1994). Essentially, being mindful includes exercising awareness and cognitive flexibility. For example, for some exercisers running is conceptualized as painful. However, it is possible that a neutral or joyful experience could occur. Instead of always thinking, "I hate running," it is possible that with practicing flexibility in one's awareness that the actual experience of running could have a chance of being experienced differently. For example, the runner does not need to be stuck experiencing running in terms of how *it always has been* or expectation of how *it always will be.* Kabat-Zinn's understanding of mindfulness emphasizes *acceptance* of all experience, whereas Langer emphasizes a more active, intentional effort at noticing external *novelty*. In truth, being mindful includes considering all internal and external information that is occurring—with a fresh, open-hearted, and open-minded interest. When exercising mindfulness with either emphasis, the individual can choose to respond to situations differently from habitual reactions. Both the Buddhist emphasis on non-judgment and Langer's emphasis on novelty are relevant and conceptually helpful in creating practical strategies to increase and maintain healthy physical activity.

HOW DOES MINDFULNESS ENHANCE EXERCISE ENGAGEMENT/ ADHERENCE?: A CONCEPTUAL DISCUSSION

Though the challenges of helping others (or oneself) engage consistently with physical activity may be far reaching, two areas that may limit engagement in physical activity that mindfulness can directly address include a changed relationship to negative thoughts (Frewen, Evans, Maraj, Dozois, & Partridge, 2008; Kabat-Zinn, 1994) and an enhanced interest in the activity at hand (e.g., Langer et al., 2009). Both acceptance of what is occurring, including unwanted thoughts/feelings, and enhanced interest could contribute to the individual being more likely to choose to engage in physical activity. Essentially, the individual who embodies the mindful approach becomes less captive to involuntary thoughts (and feelings) and more empowered to make choices based on authentic values and goals (Gardner & Moore, 2007). To this end, Kabat-Zinn et al. (1992) stated, "the insight that one is not one's thoughts means that one has a potential range of responses to a given thought if one is able to identify it as such. This increased range of options is associated with a feeling of control" (p. 942). When mindful, one is armed with a broader range of choices and action, which creates an enhanced sense of self-control. Even if thoughts flood one's mind, such as "I don't feel like it" or "I'll never be good enough," the individual does not have to be victimized by such involuntary thoughts and can, for example, choose to tolerate the thoughts and still bike down to their yoga class.

Individuals who practice mindfulness strategies learn to *change their relationship* to negative thoughts and emotions such that they become more likely to let go of negative thoughts and, eventually, experience a reduced frequency of negative thoughts (Frewen et al., 2008). Within the exercise context, such a changed relationship to negative thoughts could help reduce blocks to both the initiation of and engagement in physical activity. Clearly exercise resistant negative thinking can serve as an a-motivator for exercise engagement. Thoughts like "I just don't feel like it," "I'm not getting any faster," or "I'd rather turn over and sleep in" can involuntarily flood the mind. Such uninvited thoughts often stop people from getting up and out to activities that they ultimately enjoy and/or value.

Sometimes a cognitive-behavioral intervention can solve such a challenge with a-motivation. A possible solution to related negative thoughts could be to come up with a word or phrase (e.g., "I want to get more fit" and "I value my time to work out") that could inspire the individual to make constructive behavioral changes (Zinsser, Bunker, & Williams, 2010). However, counter-arguments can be ineffective. In fact, some theorists suggest that efforts to suppress negative thoughts can backfire and the negative thoughts can be strengthened (Hayes, 2004; Wegner & Zanakos, 1994), which is also consistent with part of the premise for mindfulness meditation practices (Compton & Hoffman, 2013). Thus, with traditional mental skills intervention, there can remain a flood of resistant thoughts and feelings toward exercise that may be strengthened with the effort to ignore or change them.

With a mindful approach, it is possible to notice such involuntary thoughts in one's mind, accept them, and then focus back to the task of exercising without strengthening the flame of negativity. However, it is important to note that when being mindful, the negative thoughts can also trigger aversive emotions that must be tolerated. Mindfulness includes aversive emotions that often accompany negative thoughts. Over time, with mindfulness practice, such involuntary thoughts can become less frequent (Frewen et al., 2008) and thus not as likely to block the individual from their commitment and engagement in exercise.

Enhanced mindfulness can increase *interest* in participation in physical activity through practicing being open to observing novelty in one's environment (e.g., Langer et al., 2009). Part of the challenge to exercise maintenance can be boredom when going regularly to the gym for a weight workout, spin class, or yoga class. Making the routine interesting may be key for exercisers to be willing to put forth ongoing physical effort or maintain requisite attitudes that are congruent with ongoing exercise even when they do not feel like it. Based on Langer's conceptualization of mindfulness, enhancing interest comes through finding novelty in the mundane or habituated. When engaged in what is occurring, novel options can open up, such as changing workout partners, intensity, or duration of a given activity (e.g., time in pool or speed). Such efforts to vary one's experience of a particular activity are, not surprisingly, also congruent with boosting one's level of chronic happiness (Lyubomirsky, Sheldon, & Schkade, 2005).

Leaders in mindfulness research have concluded that mindfulness practices enhance self-regulation (Hölzel et al., 2011). Self-regulation is a corner stone to consistent exercise and thus is an important end goal for those interested in helping the self and others engage in healthy, consistent exercise. Self-regulation, through cultivating mindfulness, occurs due to the increase in ability to change one's relationship to one's emotions, improve thought patterns, and reduce overall negative mindsets (Siegel, 2007).

What are the mechanisms of such change? How does the practice of mindfulness engagement lead to reported changes, such as less reactivity to stress, reduction of negative thoughts, and reduction in intensity of negative thoughts? In a recent theoretical review, Hölzel et al. (2011) offered four pathways by which the practice of mindfulness ultimately affects the ability to self-regulate. These pathways are attention regulation, body awareness, emotion regulation, "including reappraisal and exposure, extinction, and reconsolidation," and change in perspective on the self (p. 537). In the exercise realm, these pathways facilitate the positive change experienced by those who practice both formal and informal mindfulness strategies.

How does each mechanism of change relate to the exercise realm? The first, *attention regulation*, would help the exerciser place their attention where they choose moment to moment—such as the movements in an exercise class—and strengthen their ability to bring their attention back to class when their minds wander (from, for example, plans for dinner or a fight with a boyfriend.) The second, *body awareness*, is noticing things like breathing, emotions, or other bodily sensations that previously had gone unnoticed. Such awareness could help the exerciser slow down when the exercise is too intense or notice emotions that are evoked by a given exercise class (e.g., joy). The third, *emotion regulation: exposure, extinction, and reconsolidation*, may be the most powerful mechanism of change for the exercise realm. In this mechanism, the exerciser is practicing allowing oneself to experience (positively or negatively) one's environment (internal or external) and "refrain from internal reactivity" (Holzel et al., 2011, p. 539). Essentially the exerciser could learn to experience and tolerate aversive emotion and not be as reactive as it pertains to the exercise realm (e.g., slowing down a running pace versus stopping the run all together). This means that the exerciser could, for example, allow the feelings of not feeling good enough pass through them like a rain cloud passing through the sky. The exerciser would not buy the story but notice the feeling and return back to the exercise routine. Finally, in the fourth mechanism of change, *change in perspective on self*, the exerciser would be able to detach from their judgments or aversive feelings. Put simply, they learn to realize that everything is temporary, including difficult physical sensations, emotions, thoughts, or external challenges.

MINDFULNESS RESEARCH IN FLOW, EXERCISE, AND COMPETITIVE SPORT

Though there is great interest in the concept and application of mindfulness (e.g., Keng, Smoski, & Robins, 2011), research is just beginning to focus on mindfulness within the realms of exercise adherence, recreation, and sport. This section examines how mindfulness-based strategies engender positive health-related and performance outcomes in the various domains, from competitive sport participation to yoga practice. The efficacy of mindfulness approaches and interventions are considered regarding overall well-being and relationship to exercise adherence.

Sport and Mindfulness

Jon Kabat-Zinn was the first on record to use mindfulness training for the physically healthy within sport (Kabat-Zinn, Beall, & Rippe, 1985). His MBSR program was the first mindfulness intervention offered in the Western medical community and has been studied extensively (for a meta-analysis, see Bohlmeijer et al., 2010). In Kabat-Zinn et al.'s (1985) study, rowers preparing for collegiate racing and the Olympics both independently practiced mindfulness meditation using guided mindfulness tapes. Group meditation training sessions were also provided. Kabat-Zinn et al. (1985) found that the U.S. Olympic team rowers who medaled reported the usefulness of mindfulness meditation in helping them optimize performance when racing. The athletes also reported that the intervention enhanced concentration, improved relaxation, improved rowing efficiency, and reduced the effects of negative thoughts and physical pain.

Since this seminal study, there has been growing interest in understanding the role that mindfulness plays in recreational and competitive sport. Kabat-Zin's MBSR program has inspired, or has been the foundation for, most mindfulness-based programs in the physical activity realm. One strand of research has focused on the relationship between mindfulness and flow. Flow can be defined as engaging in activities that are intrinsically motivating, fully focusing on moment-to-moment experience with the challenge at hand meeting one's skill (Csikszentmihalyi, 1996). Csikszentmihalyi refers to flow as an autotelic experience, meaning the experience of engaging in an activity that is intrinsically rewarding, one we choose to do for its own sake (Jackson & Csikszentmihalyi, 1999).

A number of studies within competitive sport have indicated a positive relationship between the occurrence of mindfulness and flow. Bernier, Thienot, Codron, and Fournier (2009) conducted interviews with 10 French national training center swimmers regarding their optimal swimming experience. In addition to the eight qualities that have been identified to align with flow (Jackson & Csikszentmihalyi, 1999), mindfulness emerged as a ninth dimension, an awareness and acceptance of somatic experience prior to performing. This finding aligns with Kee and Wang (2008), who reported a positive relationship between dispositional mindfulness and flow in college athletes. Kaufman et al.'s (2009) study focused on competitive recreational athletes and also reported strong correlations between mindfulness and most dimensions of flow.

This positive relationship between mindfulness and flow suggests that enhancing mindfulness within the exercise realm would lead to increased experience of enjoyment when focused on the activity at hand and thus enhance engagement and participation in physical activity. It makes sense. If we are more aware of what is occurring and at once enjoy the task at hand, we are more likely to want to return to the given activity of choice.

There have been only a few intervention studies designed to enhance mindfulness of sport participants using mindfulness meditation as the intervention. Solberg, Halvorsen, Sundgot-Borgen, Ingjer, and Holen (1995) reported improvement in competitive shooters' performance one season following their meditation-based intervention. John et al. (2011) conducted an experimental meditation study with 96 Indian elite shooters. The experimental group (*n* = 48) significantly increased shooting performance and decreased pre-competitive stress. Aherne, Moran, and Lonsdale (2011) conducted an experimental mindfulness-based intervention with elite athletes in which the intervention group experienced significantly more flow post-intervention. In an experimental study, Stankovic and Baltzell (in preparation) reported increased winning of games and matches of tennis players for those who listened to a mindfulness meditation CD compared to the control group; higher levels of mindfulness were related to winning more matches and games. These results are consistent with Langer's (2000; Langer, Chanowitz, & Blank, 1985) concept of mindfulness. As reflected in her study with elite orchestra musicians, when one is mindful, it would be expected that performance would also be enhanced (Langer, Russel, & Eisenkraft, 2009).

Mindfulness-Based Programs in Sport

Emerging in the research are new ways to cultivate mindfulness for exercise and competitive sport. One approach that integrates teaching mindfulness is the Mindfulness-Acceptance-Commitment (MAC) approach (Gardner, 2016; Gardner & Moore, 2004, 2006, 2007, 2012). The MAC approach was designed and developed specifically for sport performers to develop mindfulness and self-regulated attention skills. The MAC approach includes a seven-module intervention for individual performers. The protocol incorporates education (e.g., about self-regulation) and practices of acceptance, commitment to values, and mindfulness exercises. For example, one mindfulness-based exercise is entitled a "Brief Centering Exercise" (Gardner & Moore, 2007, p. 75). Though not named a mindfulness meditation, it includes all basic elements of a formal mindfulness meditation practice (see Siegel, 2011). The protocol is thorough and time intensive (see Gardner & Moore, 2007 for a detailed explanation of the MAC approach). Enhanced performance has been reported after implementing the MAC protocol with small samples of athletes, including an adolescent springboard diver (Schwanhausser, 2009), a female power lifter (Gardner & Moore, 2004), and golfers (Bernier et al., 2009).

Though the competitive sport environment includes some different demands than the physical activity and exercise realm, Gardner and Moore's (2007) theoretical explanation of the factors that can impede participation in such realms is particularly helpful in understanding how mindlessness can impede engagement or maintenance of a consistent exercise plan. Essentially, internally self-focused, negative assessment of the individual's abilities and lack of belief in their ability to be successful in the physical activity environment can thwart engagement. If the individual has a negative "inflexible rule system," such as thoughts about what he can or cannot do, perceived deficits, self-doubts, efforts to control thoughts and emotions, and negative expectations about possible failure (Gardner & Moore, 2007, p. 8–9), then exercise engagement can be adversely affected.

Gardner and Moore (2007) contend that such inflexible negative ways of thinking about one's abilities or potential create an avoidant coping style and the individual will be more likely to disengage from the activity at hand. As presented by other researchers and theorists, mindfulness practices can break such a pattern. With open-hearted acceptance of what is occurring when faced with aversive experience, such as self-doubt and fear, the exerciser can disengage from the negative thinking (change their relationship to it) and be freed up to make choices to engage in their desired activity and not controlled by uninvited negative self-evaluations and expectations.

Keith Kaufman and colleagues (2009) created Mindful Sport Performance Enhancement (MSPE), which is another mindfulness-based intervention for athletes. This is the only mindfulness program that has been targeted specifically at recreational athletes. This mindfulness meditation training program is composed of a 2.5-hour session each week over the four-week program and was modeled closely after MBSR. Each session includes mindfulness-based activities, including the use of body scan, diaphragmatic breathing, sitting mindfulness meditation, walking meditation, and yoga. Participants are also encouraged to engage in formal mindfulness practice up to six times per week, in 30–45 minute bouts, between weekly group sessions (the outline of MSPE can be found in the appendix of Kaufman et al., 2009).

Kaufman et al. (2009) reported, based on the sample of 32 recreational athlete (11 archers and 21 golfers), an increase in state flow and mindfulness over the four-week session. In a separate study, De Petrillo et al. (2009) implemented MSPE intervention with 25 recreational long-distance runners. Mindfulness increased and sport-related worries decreased for the runners. Thompson et al. (2011) conducted a follow-up study with the long distance runners, and 50 percent of the athletes had significantly higher mindfulness scores. Moreover, in Thompson et al.'s (2011) follow-up study, the runners' mile times were significantly faster than at pre-test assessment, though clearly such increases cannot be directly attributed to MSPE. MSPE is a promising approach for using mindfulness intervention strategies for exercisers and recreational athletes. The MSPE intervention consistently increased flow across experience.

Mindfulness Meditation Training in Sport (MMTS) is a third mindfulness meditation intervention that has been reported. Baltzell, Caraballo, Chipman, and Hayden (2014) created a 12-session, 30-minute mindfulness-based intervention. The intervention was designed to meet the need of collegiate athletes who have limited time per day to devote to sport-related activities. The primary goal of MMTS was to train participants to increase their levels of mindfulness and to practice acceptance and non-judgment of thoughts, feelings, and sensations. There are four main areas to the training: (1) mindfulness meditation, (2) breathing exercises, (3) wishing caring thoughts toward teammates, and (4) practicing acceptance of negative mind-states (participants were asked to visualize an event that involved an aversive feeling, re-experience the emotions, notice the feeling in their bodies, and "label" that state of mind). MMTS increased mindfulness of the Division I women's soccer players (Baltzell & LoVerme-Akhtar, 2014), particularly regarding a changed relationship to aversive emotions on the field (Baltzell, Caraballo, Chipman, & Hayden, 2014). Their coaches also noticed the athletes' abilty to respond more adaptively to negative emotion on the field (Baltzell, Chipman, Hayden, & Bowman, 2015).

Mindfulness and Exercise

Ulmer et al.'s (2010) study is the first to consider the potential benefits of mindfulness as it pertains specifically to exercise participation. Ulmer and colleagues (2010) reported that relatively higher levels of mindfulness of YMCA exercisers ($N = 266$) were related to more consistent exercise initiation and maintenance. The research suggests that the YMCA exercisers with higher scores of mindfulness were empowered to exercise more consistently because they were able to more readily stay in the present moment, accept their negative thoughts, and respond to such thoughts and external experiences in a relatively non-judgmental manner. By avoiding habitual reactions to cognitive, behavioral, or emotional threats induced by the challenge of exercise, the participants responded with a more accepting approach that harnessed an openness to maintain the participation in physical activity. Additionally, consistent exercisers also scored lower in the suppression scale, which underlines the impact of accepting unwanted thoughts rather than to try and ignore or repress them.

Tsafou, Ridder, van Ee, and Lacroix's (2015) study provides additional support for the relationship between mindfulness and exercise adherence. Tsafou et al. (2015) also found that the higher the levels of mindfulness while engaging in exercise, the more likely the exerciser is to experience enjoyment and satisfaction. These researchers surveyed 398 Dutch participants on their levels of mindfulness, exercise routine, satisfaction with physical activity, and levels of mindfulness while exercising. Specifically, they found that those who exercised mindfully experienced greater feelings of satisfaction from the workout. The participants who scored higher on the mindfulness in physical activity scale reported that during the workouts, they were aware and absorbed in their body's internal and external interaction with the physical movements. In other words, being mindful while engaging in physical activity creates an opportunity to be more aware of the positive emotions induced by the physical experience of exercising, and in turn the positive emotions (satisfaction) fuel exercise adherence. Tsafou et al.'s (2015) results suggest that an increase in satisfaction from the experience of exercising mindfully could explain the observed increase in physical activity. Mindfulness while exercising may strengthen the motivation to engage in and maintain an exercise routine.

Tsafou and colleagues (2015) acknowledge the benefit of accepting negative thoughts that sometimes emerge while exercising, as presented by Ulmer et al. (2010). It is not enough simply to be aware of what is occurring (including thoughts, feelings, sounds, and physical sensations); it is also essential to be able to accept what is occurring. This does not mean that the individual likes what is occurring (e.g., being bombarded by negative thoughts or aversive emotions regarding exercise), but they are also able to accept such thoughts. As previously noted, acceptance can simply mean tolerating and not buying into the thoughts, but instead allowing thoughts to appear and then dissipate without necessarily believing or acting on the given aversive thought or emotion. Tsafou et al. (2015) propose, however, that exercisers are better off more closely attending to the awareness of positive physical sensations in their bodies to increase satisfaction and ultimately adherence. Together, Ulmer et al.'s and Tsafou et al.'s studies provide hope: evidence is beginning to emerge suggesting that mindfulness may be a key factor in promoting exercise engagement and adherence.

Yoga

When examining exercise activities and their relatedness to mindfulness, one must look no farther than the movement-based practices of yoga. In fact, in Kabat-Zinn's original design of MBSR, Hatha yoga was defined as one of its three key elements, along with sitting meditation and body scanning (Kabat-Zinn, 2011). The idea was constructed with the aim to improve his medical patients' response to muscle atrophy, which was typical among individuals with a chronic illness, but carried along with it the opportunity to practice mindfulness while engaging in physical activity (Kabat-Zinn, 1990). In essence, theoretically mindfulness is embedded in yoga.

Yoga is an ancient Indian mind-body practice (Salmon, Lush, Jablonski, & Sephton, 2009), but it has received minimal attention from the research community to explore its efficacy regarding healing and well-being benefits. In recent decades, empirical studies have indicated a myriad of benefits of yoga in eliciting balance and physical, mental, emotional, and spiritual well-being (Oken et al., 2006; Pilkington, Kirkwood, Rampes, & Richardson, 2005; Ross & Thomas, 2010). But can engagement in yoga-based exercises increase the level of mindfulness? The following section will explore several different components of the mindfulness-yoga relationship.

Hatha yoga, the primary health and wellness yoga training program practiced and researched in Western culture, is centered around breath regulation, physical movement (gentle transitions to different *asanas* [sequence of poses]), and focused attention (Salmon, Lush, Jablonski, & Sephton, 2009). According to Brisbon and Lowery (2011), there is initial evidence to believe that consistent practice in Hatha yoga could positively affect the capacity to be mindful. When examining mindfulness and stress levels in novice and advanced Hatha yoga practioners, the advanced Hatha yoga trainers had significantly higher levels of mindfulness and lower stress levels (Brisbon & Lowery, 2011). These findings are consistent with previous physiological literature, which discovered that advanced female yoga participants across sessions (at rest and active) had lower levels of interleukin-6 (the body's pro-inflammatory response to stress) compared to novice participants (Kiecolt-Glaser et al., 2010). Experienced yoga participants may not only receive the benefits associated with physical activity but also the health and wellness benefits of mindfulness.

Yoga positively affects health across types or styles of yoga. For example, Bikram participants in an eight-week training program showed improvements in levels of mindfulness and perceived stress levels compared to the control group (Hewett, Ransdell, Gao, Petlichkoff, & Lucas, 2011). Bikram yoga follows Hatha yoga principles but adds a more strenuous experience to the practice where muscle strength, endurance, and flexibility are additional possible outcomes (Hart & Tracey, 2008). It encompasses practicing 26 *asana* positions along with two breathing exercises in a hot-temperature room (106 F degrees) for 90 minutes. As a form of exercise, it seems most yoga participants, regardless of the physical exertion, may cultivate mindfulness and apply it to their everyday lives, including reactions to perceived negative thoughts during physical activity. Practicing yoga can increase one's ability to live mindfully.

Yoga has also been found to be an applicable tool in the face of adversity or pain. Curtis, Osadchuk, and Katz (2011) measured how mindfulness, pain, anxiety, and depression were affected by an eight-week Hatha yoga intervention on a population of 19 women battling with fibromyalgia. Evidence from the post-intervention scores showed that the yoga intervention made a positive impact on the women's experience of chronic pain and pain acceptance, a reduction in pain catastrophizing, and an increase in mindfulness. It is suggested that the yoga practice, which emphasized attending, breath awareness, and being non-judgmental to internal and external factors, can teach one how to accept and tolerate pain rather than engage in avoidance coping strategies (Shangraw & Akhtar, 2016). While not comparing fibromyalgia to discomfort during exercise, one struggling with exercise adherence could use yoga as a platform to learn how to accept distress and reduce catastrophizing thoughts to continue on rather than avoiding the pain and disengaging (see Ulmer et al., 2010).

In a non-clinical athletic environment, similar results were found in transferring skills learned from formal yoga and applying them to an area of interest. A 10-week yoga intervention of 21 elite youth swimmers produced promising results for the use of yoga in sport. Briegel-Jones et al. (2013) conducted a mixed-method design that revealed perceived improvements in mindfulness and dispositional flow in the intervention group. Though there was minimal significance from the quantitative data, the qualitative report indicated that the athletes experienced greater quality of awareness of their thoughts, feelings, and behaviors, which included cognitive reframing, concentration, and decrease of negative thoughts. Additionally, the athletes were able to transfer several of the yoga-based principles (i.e., breathing and poses) into their pre-performance routines. The research has demonstrated that yoga participants can apply learned principles from yoga to increase engagement, adherence, and satisfaction in other exercise activities. The foundation of the deliberate movement-based exercise is embedded with mindfulness techniques, including centering, breath awareness, breath regulation, reduction in response to external stimulus, and being fully present to whatever arises (Salmon et al., 2009).

Martial Arts

Martial arts–designed activities, with an expansive range of self-defense and fighting techniques and which like yoga has roots in mind-body awareness, are also closely linked to and associated with improved levels of mindfulness. Wall (2005) piloted a study that examined whether the combination of MBSR with Tai Chi would have a positive effect on adolescent students' socioemotional behavior. A five-week program was implemented and found that the students reported experiencing greater levels of relaxation, calmness, quality of sleep, self-care, well-being, and self-awareness. Caldwell, Harrison, Adams, Quin, and Greeson (2010) found that when 166 college students enrolled in and completed a pilates, Gyrokeninesis, or Taiji quan course, the overall mindfulness scores increased by the end of the class. Data were collected at three different points during the 15-week course (pre, middle, and post), measuring mindfulness, mood, perceived stress, self-efficacy, and sleep quality. Caldwell and colleagues (2010) were able to establish that an increase in mindfulness was related to significant changes in mood and perceived stress and as a result aided in the improvement of quality of sleep. Exercises that have firm principles of breath focus and regulation (i.e., yoga and martial arts) seem to have a positive link to mindfulness. No matter the movement, the intention of non-judgmental acceptance of what arises and being attuned to the body, internally and externally, consistently has been demonstrated to elicit positive benefits.

PRACTICAL APPLICATION

Thus far we have considered how mindfulness can be cultivated in physical activity (i.e., yoga and the martial arts) and ways to cultivate mindfulness in sport via formal mindfulness meditation and mindfulness-based sport interventions. Together such interventions offer an educational component and implement formal mindfulness practice, mindfulness-breathing, and/or recommend daily practice. Each of these strategies could be used independently with the end goal of offering mindfulness-based strategies for exercise engagement and adherence. The next section will provide suggestions for beginning formal mindfulness meditation practice and suggestions for enhancing mindfulness while preparing for or during exercise. At this point, integrating all of the following into exercise settings must be considered with theory, research, and best practices in the field of exercise psychology. We do not yet have empirical research to specifically guide the type and duration of any mindfulness-based intervention in the exercise setting, with the exception of a few initial studies (e.g., Kaufman et al., 2009).

Formal Mindfulness Meditation Practice

There is growing interest in the concept of mindfulness and application of mindfulness practices. One time-tested way to enhance mindfulness is through practicing formal mindfulness meditation. There are myriad options to learn the how-to of formal mindfulness meditation practice. The research indicating the benefits from Buddhist mindfulness meditation generally includes daily, relatively long bouts of formal mindfulness practice. However, current research indicates that even with brief, initial exposure to such practices, benefits can be reaped, specifically with enhancing self-control (Friese, Messner, & Schaffner, 2012), which suggests that even brief mindfulness practice may offer valuable benefits to the exerciser.

To begin a personal, formal practice, it can be of help to find a group, program, or meditation center to join. Finding educational resources to support a practice is essential. There are many excellent mindfulness meditation trade books that offer clear recommended steps for practice as well as insight into overcoming obstacles (e.g., Salzberg, 2011; Siegel, 2011). The biggest challenge to beginning a mindfulness meditation practice is simply sitting down for the first time. Starting a formal practice involves choosing a time where you can have a quiet experience free from external distractions (though eventually you can practice with

noisy distractions; it just becomes part of your practice). Here are a few things to consider if you choose to begin a practice (Brooks & Summers, 2009):
Commit to practicing most days.

- Start with five minutes a day of practice, five to seven days per week. You can build up to 10, 20, or 45 minutes per day.
- Settle into practicing at the same time every day. Many people like to practice in the morning, but you may prefer another time of day.
- Start with a few moments of paying attention to your breath and then open your attention to sounds, physical sensations, feelings, or thoughts.
- Remember that there is no "right" thing to focus on. It is best to allow your attention to move to where it is drawn.
- Practice accepting whatever is arising. It does not mean you like it or want it, but it is simply a reflection of what is occurring in your mind. It just is. For the formal practice, the intention is to accept. However, you may experience insights that you may want to act on once you complete your formal meditation practice.
- When your mind wanders and you become aware of it, the awareness of wandering in that moment is a good thing. It is a moment of bringing back awareness in the exact moment. At this point you have total freedom to choose to get back to being present. Gently guide yourself to your awareness of what is happening.

There is a myth that meditating feels good and is relaxing. This is not generally true for mindfulness meditation practice, particularly when one starts to practice. Becoming aware of emotions and thoughts that had previously been mindlessly ignored can initially be psychologically difficult to tolerate. Formal mindfulness practice generally creates the opportunity to observe thoughts, feelings, and sensations that have been blocked out of awareness due to fear, irritation, or boredom. However, with consistent practice the benefits of being able to direct one's attention on purpose and to tolerate (and not be lead by) old ways of experiencing or viewing the world can be quite liberating (Hanson & Mendius, 2009). For example, the cyclist can feel unmotivated and have a stream of excuses running through his head and he can notice these thoughts and feelings, experience the related discomfort, and still make the choice to lace up his shoes, put on his helmet, and start to ride.

Informal Mindfulness Meditation Practice: Noticing Novelty

Within the exercise realm, mindfulness practices may support the exerciser in choosing their behavior based on commitment and values versus fear, lack of self-efficacy, lethargy, or other a-motivating psychological states. In this way, being more mindful could help the exerciser tolerate aversive mind states and still engage in valued activities (Gardner & Moore, 2007). The other possible benefit of enhancing mindfulness is to strengthen the habit of noticing novelty in the exercise realm. With the noticing of novelty, interest and enjoyment can be enhanced. Some experts in mindfulness do not recommend a formal meditation practice (e.g., Ellen Langer, 2000). Whether implementing a formal practice or not, there is constantly an opportunity to practice mindfulness in the exercise realm—whether before, during, or after exercise. The following are practical recommendations that can immediately be integrated into daily exercise:

- **Intentionally noticing aspects of *the activity* that are inherently enjoyable.** Notice specific aspects of the activity that create positive emotion. Sometimes increasing enjoyment of particular exercise activities can consist simply of noticing experiences that have previously been mindlessly experienced (Seligman, Rashid, & Parks, 2006). For example one could intentionally notice and appreciate the good feeling as your body moves through space as you bike, walk, or run.

- **Intentionally noticing what is enjoyable in** *the environment*. In some instances, the exercise activity itself may not be enjoyable, but it is possible to purposefully notice and appreciate other aspects of the environment (e.g., music, sounds, sights, positive emotions) that are compelling.

- **Acknowledging but not being led by old thoughts and feelings that get in the way of exercise.** Learning to acknowledge thoughts and feelings that historically have blocked exercise is a powerful first step in implementing mindfulness. Next, the practice of accepting (tolerating) such feelings paired with still choosing to work out is a difficult yet ultimately freeing practice. Such an approach will eventually reduce the experience and power of uninvited negative feelings and thoughts over time. When we purposefully notice what may be different this particular day on the tennis court, we immediately are no longer caught up in old thoughts and feelings.

- **Noticing what works best.** When the exerciser purposefully notices what approach to exercise is the best match for her, this allows the exerciser to make choices that will increase the chances of experiencing positive workout bouts. Choices could include things like what exercise or workout is optimal (for that day), whether to work out alone or with others, and the duration and intensity of exercise that is valued and sustainable.

- **Bringing awareness to the possibility of overexercising.** The body offers signals when the effort and duration of exercise is approaching potential physical harm. Purposefully bringing attention to physical symptoms during and after exercise can help with the threat of overexercising and long-term injury. When we notice what may be different on a given day, we do not force ourselves to do it just the way we always do, ignoring exhaustion and pain.

- **Clarifying the purpose of exercising, whether one feels like it or not.** Practicing mindfulness includes the possibility of no longer being dominated by uninvited a-motivated thoughts and feelings. We do not need to be a victim of our habits of thinking and feeling. We can choose each moment what we would like to be or become. Hence, as discussed, it is possible to not give into such thoughts and often associated negative emotions. A strong anchor for being able to tolerate such thoughts and feelings is to first be clear on what one is committed to for exercise. It is helpful to consider one's values, what matters to the exerciser, whether they feel like exercising in the moment or not. Clarifying values can lead to the choice of getting up to go for the run or make the exercise class regardless of aversive thoughts and feelings (Gardner & Moore, 2007). Learning to accept some flow of negative thoughts and still make the healthy exercise choices is an essential contribution of mindfulness to exercise engagement.

- **Noticing novelty.** Ellen Langer's concept of mindfulness, with a direct emphasis on noticing what is new or fresh, can help the exerciser to become or remain interested in their exercise world, in general. Instead of habitual, robotic ways of experiencing one's environment, the exerciser can intentionally notice what is novel in their exercise experiences.

- **Practicing Yoga.** Having trouble adhering to formal mindfulness meditation but still looking for a new way into the field? You may want to start practicing yoga. Research has shown that the mere engagement in regular, consistent practice of yoga results in higher levels of mindfulness, which is in addition to the benefits of physical activity. There are many different approaches and kinds of yoga being practiced in Western culture. The key is to find what approach aligns with your values, intention, and ability. Looking for a physically demanding workout? Join a Bikram training program. If your interest is in gentle physical movements, seek out Hatha yoga studios. The essential thing to remember is, whether you're male, female, flexible, inflexible, there is a yoga practice for everyone.

CONCLUSION

Based on the review of research in general psychology, sport, and recreational sport, higher levels of mindfulness positively contribute to exercise engagement and enjoyment. To summarize, initial research in sport indicates that mindfulness is related to flow (e.g., Kaufman et al., 2009), meaning that when people are more mindful, they tend to be engaged in chosen activities for intrinsically motivated reasons. These findings suggest that more mindful exercisers would be expected to want to initiate and engage in physical activity. In addition, mindfulness meditation is related to improved sport performance (e.g., John, Verma, & Khanna, 2011); if sport performance improves, we would also expect that experience of physical activity would improve with such practice. We also know that types of physical activity (i.e., yoga and martial arts) that are embedded with mindfulness training do indeed cultivate mindfulness. Ulmer et al.'s (2010) and Tsafou et al.'s (2015) studies specifically focused on enhancing exercise engagement and enjoyment via the cultivation of mindfulness, and provided direct initial evidence that mindfulness is a key factor in promoting exercise engagement, adherence, and enjoyment.

We do know that when mindfulness is practiced in vivo by attending to novel stimuli, as indicated by Ellen Langer, the individual becomes more interested. That which was mundane can be brought back to life; the individual is empowered to experience their moment-to-moment environment differently. They are able to notice new internal responses, attitudes, and choices toward that which had previously become rote. Thus the exerciser can become more enlivened by exercise routines that had become habituated and uninspiring.

Enhancing mindfulness, within the Buddhist influenced understanding of mindfulness, is also expected to reduce the impact of aversive feelings such as fear and aversion (e.g., not being good enough, thin enough, fast enough) that can get in the way of exercise engagement and retention. Though the exerciser may not be able to stop a flood of such involuntary thoughts, by practicing mindfulness, the individual can learn to accept such thoughts and not "buy" them. Though the thoughts and related emotions may be present, the individual retains a choice in how to respond (instead of react) to such occurrences. Thus the exerciser can make choices based on what they value versus what they feel in the moment. No longer do good bouts of training have to rely upon how the individual is *feeling* before their workout. The exerciser can be less influenced and distracted by thoughts that do not support exercise goals. Instead key elements such as quality, intensity, and duration of exercise can become contingent on personal values.

Contrary to popular understanding, bringing mindfulness to any aspect of your life at first can be difficult. We tend to either become consumed by negative thoughts via rumination or try to suppress or change thoughts and feelings (Hanson & Mendius, 2009). When we can strike a balance of acknowledging and accepting our thoughts simply as thoughts, not necessarily truths, we are free to choose how to think and act—and this experience at first can be unsettling. Yet, we have a choice of how we react to unpleasant thoughts and sensations. Kabat-Zinn et al. (1992) offer an inspiring way to think about our harsh internal voice: "The insight that one is not one's thoughts means that one has a potential range of responses to a given thought if one is able to identify it as such" (p. 942). We can choose how we respond to our own uninvited thoughts.

Any of the recommendations on enhancing mindfulness have the potential for great benefit, yet also require personally valued effort. Put simply, effort is required to enhance well-being as it pertains to changing attitudes and behaviors or committing to physical activities that the participant personally values (Lyubomirsky, Sheldon, & Schkade, 2005). A range of mindfulness strategies when consistently implemented are expected to do just that—enhance exercise engagement and adherence via enhanced self-regulation, tolerance of aversive thoughts and feelings, clarification of values, and intentional notice of what is novel and compelling.

REFERENCES

Aherne, C., Moran, A. P., & Lonsdale, C. (2011). The effect of mindfulness training on athletes' flow: An initial investigation. *The Sport Psychologist, 25,* 177–189.

Baer, R. A. (2003). Mindfulness training as a clinical intervention: A conceptual and empirical review. *Clinical Psychology: Science and Practice, 10*(2), 125–143. doi: 10.1093/clipsy/bpg015

Baltzell, A. L., Caraballo, N., Chipman, K., and Hayden, L. (2014). A qualitative study of the Mindfulness Meditation Training for Sport (MMTS): Division I Female Soccer Players' experience. *Journal of Clinical Sport Psychology, 8,* 221–244.

Baltzell, A. L., Chipman, K., Hayden, L., & Bowman, C. (2015, Fall). A qualitative study of the mindfulness meditation training program (MMTS): Division I coach participant experience. *Journal of Multidisciplinary Research, 7*(3), 5–20.

Baltzell, A. L., & LoVerme-Ahktar, V. (2014). Mindfulness Meditation Training for Sport (MMTS) intervention: Impact of MMTS with division I female athletes has been successfully submitted online and is presently being given full consideration for publication in *Journal of Happiness and Well-Being, 2*(2), 160–173.

Bernier, M., Thienot, E., Codron, R., & Fournier, J. (2009). Mindfulness and acceptance approaches in sport performance. *Journal of Clinical Sport Psychology, 4,* 320–333.

Bohlmeijer, E., Prenger, R., Taal, E., & Cuijpers, P. (2010). The effects of mindfulness-based stress reduction therapy on mental health of adults with a chronic medical disease: A meta-analysis. *Journal of Psychosomatic Research, 68*(6), 539–544.

Briegel-Jones, R. M., Knowles, Z., Eubank, M. R., Giannoulatos, K., & Elliot, D. (2013). A preliminary investigation into the effect of yoga practice on mindfulness and flow in elite youth swimmers. *Sport Psychologist, 27*(4), 349–359.

Brisbon, N. M., & Lowery, G. A. (2011). Mindfulness and levels of stress: A comparison of beginner and advanced hatha yoga practitioners. *Journal of Religion and Health, 50*(4), 931–941. doi: 10.1007/s109430-099-3053-

Brooks, M., & Summers, J. (2009). *The Buddhas playbook: Strategies for enlightened living.* South Bend, IN: Better World Books.

Brown, K. W., & Ryan, R. M. (2003). The benefits of being present: Mindfulness and its role in psychological well-being. *Journal of Personality and Social Psychology, 84*(4), 822–848. doi: 10.1037/0022-3514.84.4.822

Caldwell, K., Harrison, M., Adams, M., Quin, R. H., & Greeson, J. (2010). Developing mindfulness in college students through movement-based courses: Effects on self-regulatory self-efficacy, mood, stress, and sleep quality. *Journal of American College Health, 58*(5), 433–442. doi: 10.1080/07448480903540481

Chiesa, A., & Serretti, A. (2009). Mindfulness-based stress reduction for stress management in healthy people: a review and meta-analysis. *The Journal of Alternative and Complementary Medicine, 15*(5), 593–600.

Compton, W. C., & Hoffman, E. (2013). *Positive psychology: The science of happiness and flourishing* (2nd ed.). Belmont, CA: Wadsworth.

Csikszentmihalyi, M. (1996). *Finding flow: The psychology of engagement with everyday life* New York, NY: Basic Books.

Curtis, K., Osadchuk, A., & Katz, J. (2011). An eight-week yoga intervention is associated with improvements in pain, psychological functioning and mindfulness, and changes in cortisol levels in women with fibromyalgia. *Journal of Pain Research, 4,* 189–201. doi: 10.2147/JPR.S22761

Davidson, R. J., Kabat-Zinn, J., Schumacher, J., Rosenkranz, M., Muller, D., Santorelli, S. F., . . . Sheridan, J. F. (2003). Alterations in brain and immune function produced by mindfulness meditation. *Psychosomatic Medicine, 65,* 564–570. doi: 10.1097/01.PSY.0000077505.6757.E3

De Petrillo, L., Kaufman, K., Glass, C., & Arnkoff, D. (2009). Mindfulness for long-distance runners: An open trial using mindful sport performance enhancement (MSPE). *Journal of Clinical Sport Psychology, 4*, 357–376.

Ekman, P., Davidson, R. J., Ricard, M., & Wallace, A. (2005). Buddhist and psychological perspectives on emotions and well-being. *Current Directions in Psychological Science, 14*, 59–63.

Evans, D., Baer, R., & Segerstrom, S. (2009). The effect of mindfulness and self-consciousness on persistence. Personality and individual differences, *47*(4), 379–282.

Frewen, P. A., Evans, E., Maraj, N., Dozois, D. J. A., & Partridge, K. (2008). Letting go: Mindfulness and negative automatic thinking. *Cognitive Therapy & Research, 32*, 758–774. doi: 10.1007/s106080-079-1421-

Friese, M., Messner, C., & Schaffner, Y. (2012). Mindfulness meditation counteracts self-control depletion. *Consciousness and Cognition, 21*, 1016–1022.

Gardner, F. L. (2016). Scientific advancements of mindfulness- and acceptance-based models in sport psychology: A decade in time, a seismic shift in philosophy and practice. In A. L. Baltzell (Ed.), *Mindfulness and performance: Current Perspectives in Social and Behavioral Sciences* (pp. 127–152). New York, NY: Cambridge University Press.

Gardner, F. L., & Moore, Z. E. (2004). A Mindfulness-Acceptance-Commitment (MAC) based approach to performance enhancement: Theoretical considerations. *Behavior Therapy, 35*, 707–723. doi: 10.1016/S0005-7894(04)80016-9

Gardner, F. L., & Moore, Z. E. (2006). *Clinical sport psychology.* Champaign, IL: Human Kinetics.

Gardner, F. L., & Moore, Z. E. (2007). *The psychology of enhancing human performance: The Mindfulness-Acceptance-Commitment (MAC) approach.* New York, NY: Springer.

Gardner, F. L., & Moore, Z. E. (2012). Mindfulness and acceptance models in sport psychology: A decade of basic and applied scientific advancements. *Canadian Psychology, 53*(4), 309–318. doi: 10.1037/a0030220

Hanson, R., & Mendius, R. (2009). *Buddha's brain: The practical neuroscience of happiness, love, and wisdom.* Oakland, CA: New Harbinger.

Hart, C. E., & Tracy, B. L. (2008). Yoga as steadiness training: Effects on motor variability in young adults. *Journal of Strength Conditioning Research, 22*(5), 1659–1669. doi: 10.1519/JSC.0b013e31818200dd

Hayes, S. C. (2004). Acceptance and commitment therapy, relational frame theory, and the third wave of behavioral and cognitive therapies. *Behavior Therapies, 35*, 639–665. doi:10.1016/S0005-7894(04)80013-3

Hewett, Z., Ransdell, L., Gao, Y., Petlichkoff, L., & Lucas, S. (2011). An examination of the effectiveness of an 8-week Bikram yoga program on mindfulness, perceived stress and physical fitness. *Journal of Exercise Science and Fitness, 9*(2), 87–92.

Hölzel, B., Lazar, S., Gard, T., Schuman-Olivier, Z., Vago, D., & Ott, U. (2011). How does mindfulness meditation work? Proposing mechanisms of action from a conceptual and neural perspective. *Perspectives on Psychological Science, 6*, 537–559. doi: 10.1177/1745691611419671

Jackson, S., & Csikszentmihalyi, M. (1999). *Flow in Sports: The keys to optimal experiences and performances.* Champaign, IL: Human Kinetics.

John, S., Verma, S., & Khanna, G. (2011). The effect of mindfulness meditation on HPA-Axis in pre-competition stress in sports performance of elite shooters. *National Journal of Integrated Research in Medicine, 2*(3), 15–21.

Kabat-Zinn, J. (1990). *Full catastrophe living: How to cope with stress, pain and illness using mindfulness meditation.* New York, NY: NY: Bantam Dell.

Kabat-Zinn, J. (1994). *Wherever you go there you are: Mindfulness meditation in everyday life.* New York, NY: Hyperion.

Kabat-Zinn, J. (2011). Some reflections on the origins of MBSR, skillful means, and the trouble with maps. *Contemporary Buddhism, 12*(1), 281–306. doi:10.1080/14639947.2011.564844

Kabat-Zinn, J., Beall, B., & Rippe, J. (1985, June). *A systematic mental training program based on mindfulness meditation to optimize performance in collegiate and Olympic rowers.* Poster presented at the World Congress in Sport Psychology, Copenhagen, Denmark.

Kabat-Zinn, J., Massion, A. O., & Kristeller, J. (1992). Effectiveness of a meditation-based stress reduction program in the treatment of anxiety disorders. *American Journal of Psychiatry, 149*(2), 936–943.

Kaufman, K., Glass, C., & Arnkoff, D. (2009). Evaluation of Mindful Sport Performance Enhancement (MSPE): A new approach to promote flow in athletes. *Journal of Clinical Sport Psychology, 4*, 334–356.

Kee, Y. H., & Wang, C. K. J. (2008). Relationship between mindfulness, flow dispositions and mental skill adoptions: A cluster analytic approach. *Psychology of Sport and Exercise, 9*, 393–411. doi: 10.1016/j.psychsport.2007.07.001

Keng, S. L., Smoski, M. J., & Robins, C. J. (2011). Effects of mindfulness on psychological health: A review of empirical studies. *Clinical Psychology Review, 31*, 1041–1056. doi: 10.1016/j. cpr.2011.04.006

Keyes, C. L. M. (2002). The mental health continuum: From languishing to flourishing in life. *Journal of Health and Social Behavior, 2*(43), 207–222.

Kiecolt-Glaser, J. K., Christian, L., Preston, H., Houts, C. R., Malarkey, W. B., Emery, C. F., & Glaser, R. (2010). Stress, inflammation, and yoga practice. *Psychosomatic Medicine, 72*(2), 113. doi: 10.1097/PSY.0b013e3181cb9377

Langer, E. (2000). Mindful learning. *Current Directions in Psychological Science, 9*(6), 220–223.

Langer, E., Chanowitz, B., & Blank, A. (1985). Mindlessness-mindfulness in perspective: A reply to Valerie Folks. *Journal of Personality and Social Psychology, 48*(3), 605–607.

Langer, E., Cohen, M., & Djikic, M. (2012). Mindfulness as a psychological attractor: The effect on children. *Journal of Applied Social Psychology, 2*(5), 1114–1122.

Langer, E., Russel, T., & Eisenkraft, N. (2009). Orchestral performance and the footprint of mindfulness, *Psychology of Music, 37*(2), 125–136.

Langer, R. (1990). New methods of drug delivery. *Science, 249*, 1527–1533.

Lyubomirsky, S., Sheldon, K., & Schkade, D. (2005). Pursuing happiness: The architecture of sustainable change. *Review of General Psychology, 9*(2), 111–131.

Moore, A., & Malinowski, P. (2009). Meditation, mindfulness and cognitive flexibility. *Consciousness and Cognition, 18*, 176–186.

Oken, B. S., Zajdel, D., Kishiyama, S., Flegal, K., Dehen, C., Haas, M., . . . Leyva, J. (2006). Randomized, controlled, six-month trial of yoga in healthy seniors: Effects on cognition and quality of life. *Alternative Therapies in Health and Medicine, 12*(1), 40–47.

Pilkington, K., Kirkwood, G., Rampes, H., & Richardson, J. (2005). Yoga for depression: The research evidence. *Journal of Affective Disorders, 89*(1), 13–24. doi:10.1016/j.jad.2005.08.013

Ross, A., & Thomas, S. (2010). The health benefits of yoga and exercise: A review of comparison. *Journal of Alternative and Complementary Medicine, 16*(1), 3–12. doi: 10.1089/acm.2009.0044

Salmon, P., Lush, E., Jablonski, M., & Sephton, S. E. (2009). Yoga and mindfulness: Clinical aspects of an ancient mind/body practice. *Cognitive and Behavioral Practice, 16*(1), 59–72. doi: 10.1016/j. cbpra.2008.07.002

Salzberg, S. (2011). *Real happiness: The power of meditation.* New York, NY: Workman Publishing.

Schwanhausser, L. (2009). Application of the Mindfulness-Acceptance-Commitment (MAC) protocol with an adolescent springboard diver. *Journal of Clinical Sport Psychology, 4*, 377–395.

Seligman, M., Rashid, T., & Parks, A. (2006). Positive psychotherapy. *American Psychologist, 61*(8), 774–788.

Shangraw, R., & Akhtar, V. L. (2016). Mindfulness and exercise. In A. L. Baltzell (Ed.), *Mindfulness and performance: Current perspectives in social and behavioral sciences* (pp. 300–320). New York, NY: Cambridge University Press.

Siegel, D. (2007). *The mindful brain: Reflection and attunement in the cultivation of well being.* New York, NY: W.W. Norton & Company.

Siegel, R. (2011). *The mindfulness solution. Everyday practices for everyday problems.* New York, NY: Guilford Press.

Solberg, E., Halvorsen, R., Sundgot-Borgen, J., Ingjer, F., & Holen, A. (1995). Meditation: A modulator of the immune response to physical stress? A brief report. *British Journal of Sports Medicine, 29*(4), 255–257.

Stankovic, D., & Baltzell, A. L. (in preparation). Mindfulness meditation in sport: Improved sport performance of masters tennis players.

Thompson, R., Kaufman, K., De Petrillo, L., Glass, C., & Arnkoff, D. (2011). One year follow-up of Mindful Sport Performance Enhancement (MSPE) with archers, golfers, and runners. *Journal of Clinical Sport Psychology, 5*, 99–116.

Tsafou, K-E., Ridder, D., van Ee, R., & Lacroix, J. (2015). Mindfulness and satisfaction in physical activity: A cross-sectional study in the Dutch population. *Journal of Health Psychology, 21*, 1817–1827.

Ulmer, C., Stetson, B., & Salmon, G. (2010). Mindfulness and acceptance are associated with exercise maintenance in YMCA exercisers. *Behaviour Research and Therapy, 48*, 805–809. doi:10.1016/j.brat.2010.04.009

Wall, R. B. (2005). Tai chi and mindfulness-based stress reduction in a Boston public middle school. *Journal of Pediatric Health Care, 19*(4), 230–237. doi: 10.1016/j.pedhc.2005.02.006

Wegner, D. M., & Zanakos, S. (1994). Chronic thought suppression. *Journal of Personality, 62*, 615–640.

Zinsser, N., Bunker, L., & Williams, J. (2010). Cognitive techniques for building confidence and enhancing performance. In J. Williams (Ed.), *Applied sport psychology: Personal growth to peak performance* (6th ed., pp. 305–335). Mountain View, CA: Mayfield Publishing.

30 Positive Psychology

Gloria H. M. Park and Ashley Anderson Corn

INTRODUCTION

What is a life well-lived? And how do we get there? How do we promote human flourishing and well-being? These are the types of questions explored by positive psychology researchers and practitioners when conducting inquiry into the conditions and processes that enable flourishing in individuals, groups, and institutions. For optimal human functioning, it is crucial to build strength at both the physiological and psychological levels. A healthy mind creates a healthy body, and a healthy body can have a reciprocal effect on aiding happiness and well-being (Hefferon, 2013). The physical and psychological health benefits of physical activity are well documented, and growing connections between physical activity and well-being continue to be established (Acevedo, 2012; Penedo & Dahn, 2005). Despite compelling evidence supporting the link between exercise and well-being, health professionals continue to be challenged by how to move people from contemplation to health behavior transformation. In this chapter, we will introduce you to the basic tenets of positive psychology and explore how positive psychology interventions may also help individuals adopt regular physical activity and adhere to exercise programs. We argue that goal setting is one of the most effective and empirically supported methods for enhancing motivation and adherence to exercise and physical activity, and that several theoretical concepts from positive psychology can enhance our understanding of the nuances of the goal-setting process. In addition to the well-established approaches practitioners are already using to guide clients toward health goals, we will introduce several validated positive interventions that may also provide a new perspective to augment current practices. We will also make suggestions for positive interventions that may make goal setting even more effective, and we will foster discussion about future directions and implications of bridging the two fields in the spirit of enabling well-being and flourishing, both physically and psychologically.

FROM HAPPINESS TO WELL-BEING

The modern-day adaptation of positive psychology grew from a call put forth by past president of the American Psychological Association Martin E.P. Seligman in 1999. Seligman urged social scientists to begin broadening psychology's paradigm beyond curing pathology, mediating deficits, and simply treating disorder and illness (Gable & Haidt, 2005). In the near decade and half following Seligman's address, the study of positive psychology has advanced theory on what is right and good in the human condition, and explored salient approaches to building psychological wellness. It seeks to balance the scale to make goodness, human strength, meaningful relationships, enabling communities, success, meaning, and all that goes right in life equally important areas to explore and illuminate as illness, suffering, and all that is wrong about humanity.

At its outset, Seligman and Csikszentmihalyi (2000) defined positive psychology as the "science of positive subjective experience, positive individual traits, and positive institutions" (2000, p. 7). Much of the initial research was focused on how to increase happiness (as measured by life satisfaction), and, without intent, positive psychology became associated with images of smiling and cheer (Seligman, 2011). It was defined as a "happiology" in the scientific community as well as in public perception. Despite the initially narrow focus, some of the key findings from over 15 years of research highlighted why studying happiness had value in its own right (see Jacobs, Bao, & Lyubomirsky, 2013). Researchers learned that happiness is not merely the byproduct of attaining success, accumulating material or financial assets, or obtaining ideal life circumstances. Happiness has value and practical utility; it is associated with many physical, psychological, social, and cognitive benefits through life. Happiness is associated with, and can *precede*, success in various domains in life, such as marriage, relationships, and work (Lyubomirsky, King, & Diener, 2005; Oishi, Diener, & Lucas, 2007). Happiness and optimism were also associated with better health (Friedman & Kern, 2014), more robust social networks, stronger interpersonal relationships, and greater longevity (Diener & Chan, 2011).

Seligman (2011) recently acknowledged shortcomings in his introductory theory of positive psychology, inadequacies that were often the focus of critics of the field: well-being cannot be reduced to affective contentment and cheer nor measured simply by life satisfaction. The role of current mood states on assessments of well-being need to be disentangled, and the concept of well-being itself needed clarification in terms of what it encompassed and measured. Although research into the domains of well-being have expanded over the past decade, well-being as a multidimensional and complex construct has become increasingly murky. There remains little consensus among theorists on what constitutes well-being (see Jayawickreme, Forgeard, & Seligman, 2012 for a full discussion). Well-being Theory (Seligman, 2011) includes several facets or dimensions, which can be encapsulated in the acronym PERMA: Positive emotions, Engagement, Relationships, Meaning, and Achievement (for a comprehensive discussion of Well-being Theory, see Forgeard, Jayawickreme, Kern, & Seligman, 2011).

POSITIVE PSYCHOLOGY EMBODIED

The authors of this chapter envision a holistic view of well-being, one that is incomplete without a discussion of the role of the human body, the true "engine" of well-being. Human beings are embodied. Without vitality, physical health, and absence from pain and illness, the pursuit of a comprehensive state of well-being is incomplete to the extent that the mind and body are inextricably connected. Although positive psychology aims to study all the factors that promote well-being and optimal human functioning, until recently there has been little focus on the impact of the physical self and good health in positive psychology literature. Exercise and future-mindedness are key components to maximize chances of a long and healthy life (Seligman, 2011), and the field of positive psychology should pay closer attention to the benefits that regular exercise has for well-being. Physical activity is a primary pathway to physical health and should be leveraged as a mechanism that will help individuals and communities thrive and flourish (Mutrie & Faulkner, 2004). Hefferon and Mutrie (2012) argued that physical activity can be considered a "stellar" positive intervention in that exercise can be linked to both hedonic and eudemonic aspects of well-being.

In this section we will briefly discuss some of the current findings related to habitual physical activity and its effects on physical and psychological well-being. It is well known that regular physical activity greatly affects physiological functioning and greatly decreases the risk of developing many adverse health conditions, including coronary heart disease, sleep disorders, osteoporosis, hypertension, obesity, type-2 diabetes, breast and colon cancers, and even premature death (Biddle & Mutrie, 2001; Department of Health, 2004; Lee et al., 2012). In addition to the physical health benefits, there is now a strong body of research supporting the relationship between physical activity and overall psychological well-being (see Acevedo, 2012; Biddle & Mutrie, 2001).

There is evidence to support that regular physical activity can enhance self-esteem and promote physical self-worth, often considered two of the most important indicators of psychological well-being (Fox, 2000). Spence, McGannon, and Poon (2005) conducted a meta-analysis of 113 studies on the effects of exercise on global self-esteem and found that exercise participation leads to small but significant increases in global self-esteem. Physical activity is theorized to increase physical self-worth and self-esteem due to enabling the mastery of new tasks, providing a greater sense of personal control, and allowing for time away from the stressful aspects of one's life (Fox, 2000).

Additionally, physical activity makes people feel better. Regular participation in physical activity is consistently associated with both short- and long-term increases in positive mood and psychological well-being (Biddle & Mutrie, 2001; Dua & Hargreaves, 1992; Maxwell & Lynn, 2015; Penedo & Dahn, 2005 Reed & Buck, 2009;). Some of the strongest evidence supporting the positive correlation between psychological functioning and physical activity comes from the study of depression. A physically active lifestyle is associated with lower levels of depression, and an inactive lifestyle significantly increases the likelihood of developing depression in children and adolescents (Brown, Pearson, Braithwaite, Brown, & Biddle, 2013). Meta-analytic studies revealed that physical activity interventions reduced depression in mentally ill populations (Rosenbaum, Tiedemann, Sherrington, Curtis, & Ward, 2014) and reduced depression (Conn, 2010) and anxiety symptoms (Rebar et al., 2015) in non-clinical populations. Acute bouts of exercise are also associated with a small reduction in state anxiety (Ensari, Greenlee, Motl, & Petruzzello, 2015).

Current research has sought to explain the effects of physical activity on sleep and cognitive functioning. Some of the evidence associated with sleep suggests that individuals who exercise regularly are able to fall asleep quicker and sleep longer and deeper than individuals who do not exercise (Kredlow, Capozzoli, Hearon, Calkins, & Otto, 2015). Though there have been varied results reported on the effects of physical activity and academic improvement in youth, a recent meta-analysis of the literature showed that physical activity has a significantly positive impact on children's cognitive outcomes and academic achievement (Ahn & Fedewa, 2011). In addition, Boutcher (2000) found that cognitive performance in older age is associated with physical fitness, physical activity, and sports participation. Another study by Laurin, Verreault, Lindsay, MacPherson, and Rockwood (2001) demonstrated that regular high levels of physical activity halved the risk for cognitive impairment, Alzheimer's disease, and dementia.

How does exercise produce psychological changes? Some of the theorized mechanisms responsible for how positive psychological changes occur through physical activity include thermogenic changes and shifts in endorphins, serotonin, and neurotransmitters in the body. These changes affect subjective well-being, mood or affect, stress, and self-esteem, which are all important factors in optimal human functioning and overall well-being (Hefferon & Mutrie, 2012). We know that exercise has a somatopsychic effect on mental health and well-being by acting as a buffer against depression and anxiety and as a protective factor in the decline of cognitive function and ability, and plays a large role in acquisition of self-efficacy and competency beliefs (Hefferon, 2013). Despite research supporting the benefits of regular physical activity, and the evidence-based guidelines developed around the amount of physical activity needed to gain health benefits, more than half of the U.S. population does not adhere to the recommended amount of physical activity necessary to reap the benefits (Haskell et al., 2007).

BRIDGING POSITIVE AND EXERCISE PSYCHOLOGY THROUGH GOAL-SETTING

Health promotion and disease prevention practitioners have long used the tenets of goal-setting theory to help aid in the adoption and maintenance of healthy behaviors. Goal-setting theory is based on the idea that "conscious goals affect action" (Locke & Latham, 2002, p. 705), and researchers have devoted much of their attention to examining how goals affect motivation and performance, and how they can facilitate behavior change (see Weinberg, 2014). Goals are effective in shifting behavior because they create challenges and, in turn, feelings of accomplishment when goals are met. Goals have the potential to add meaning to otherwise meaningless activities and can make completing tasks more fun (Latham, 2003). Over 400 studies have shed light on how the practice of effective goal setting can enhance task performance, bolster motivation and feelings of accomplishment, and marshal attention and focus (Locke & Latham, 2006).

Locke and Latham (2002) suggest goals positively affect performance by affecting the goal setter directly and indirectly. First and foremost, goals direct attention to where it is necessary. Second, people are often energized by their goals. Third, goal setters persist in the pursuit of a goal longer than they would other pursuits without a specific goal. Fourth, having goals leads goal setters to use their own knowledge and skills more completely and in new, strategic ways.

Positive psychology theories and interventions can also help advance the way we think about goal-setting theory and change the landscape of the possible methods and strategies available to enhance exercise motivation and adherence. Positive interventions are, in theory, different from typical psychological interventions because they move the focus away from curing illness and pathology or diminishing deficits. These interventions focus instead on building individual strengths and competencies to promote mental health and well-being. It is difficult to truly define what a positive intervention precisely is and is not (Parks & Biswas-Diener, 2013). Broadly speaking, Parks and Biswas-Diener (2013) conceptualize positive interventions as those having a focus on positive topics, interventions that operate by a positive mechanism or that target a positive outcome variable, and interventions that are designed to promote wellness rather than to fix weakness.

Using goal-setting theory as the foundation, positive psychology approaches can help enhance the process in several ways. First, by helping people connect with what they deeply value and bringing the most profound sense of meaning and purpose to their lives during the goal-setting process, practitioners can enhance goal commitment. Second, by building resilience through cognitive-behavioral approaches, fostering a growth mindset, and teaching skills of flexible and accurate thinking, positive psychology interventions can augment cognitive processing of goals and interpretations of setbacks and failures to create more productive styles of thinking. Finally, positive psychology theory can also inform how individuals can shift the way they measure goal progress and achievement, and provide alternative ways of conceptualizing goal success. In the next few sections, we will explore how positive psychology interventions and practice can enhance goal achievement by enhancing goal commitment through self-regulation, managing setbacks through developing a resilient mindset, and maintaining motivation through celebrating successes.

Enhancing Goal Commitment Through Self-Regulation

Goal setting appears to be intuitive, but effective goal setting is nuanced and complicated. It begins with goal commitment and how to set goals in a way that enhances one's long-term commitment to the goal and the goal-directed behaviors. We know from traditional goal-setting theory that goal commitment moderates goals and subsequent behavior, and, without a strong sense of objective commitment, there is a greater chance of low task performance and goal failure (Klein, Wesson, Hollenbeck, Wright, & DeShon, 2001). One well-known, traditionally used strategy to enhance goal commitment is to make superordinate goals concrete and actionable through SMART goals—specific, measurable, attainable, relevant, and time bound—which far exceed the ability to produce high levels of performance and motivation when compared to more generalized goals (Latham, 2003). Goal setting is a complex, social-psychological, and self-regulatory process that can greatly affect health behavior (Mann, Ridder, & Fujita, 2013) and is a promising intervention strategy for changing dietary and physical activity behavior in adults (Shilts, Horowitz, & Townsend, 2004). For a full discussion on psychological skills for health behavior change, see Chapter 8 by Tashman et al. in this book.

How do people decide what goals to set for themselves and which of those are most worth pursuing? The use of effective prospection and planning is one strategy for addressing challenges that affect goal striving (Mann et al., 2013). Seligman, Railton, Baumeister, and Sripada (2013) have recently proposed that counter to the belief that has dominated much of psychology in the past, human beings are not simply driven by their pasts and that "past history, present circumstance, and inner states drive behavior" (p. 119). The process of constructing and evaluating an array of new possibilities and the subsequent selection of action in light of values and goals is called prospection. The theorists argue that "intelligent action is guided by assessment of future possibilities rather than driven by the past" and that "a major function of human consciousness is to permit better prospection of the future" (Seligman et al., 2013, p. 129).

Establishing goals through the lens of prospection can offer an alternative way of thinking about the goals we set out for ourselves. One intervention that may be helpful in enhancing goal commitment is the Best Possible Future Self intervention, which is a validated positive psychology tool that may improve goal adherence through imagery and expressive writing about one's goals and through articulating a vision of their "best possible self" (King, 2008; Lyubomirsky, 2007). Through deeply envisioning what their best selves look like in the future, individuals are able to clarify their values, solidify their approach, and establish the steps necessary to live life congruent with their highest aspirations. King (2008) found that the articulation of best possible self and daily striving toward goals that are aligned with a greater life goal was significantly correlated with well-being. The Best Possible Future Self intervention could provide an excellent platform for practitioners to help clients establish their ultimate exercise goal and their approach for obtaining that goal. For example, one might start by having clients visualize and write about their best possible selves in terms of accomplishing their exercise goal. Having their clients be specific about what it will mean to them and how they will feel, think, and look after their goal is achieved could provide valuable insight to what they want to accomplish and ignite their motivation for pursuing the goal.

Additionally, a strategy called mental contrasting could be used to prospect and plan for barriers in the goal-striving process. Mental contrasting is the process of alternating between visualizing and indulging in what it might look like to attain a goal, and then dwelling on the obstacles that may stand in the way en route to goal achievement. Studies have found that setting proper expectations about the difficulty and potential obstacles one is likely to face in pursuit of a goal increases planning, persistence, and goal-directed behavior (Oettingen &

Stephens, 2009). One caveat to using mental contrasting is that it is only effective with individuals who truly believe they have the ability to reach their goal. If the individual does not really believe that they will be successful, mental contrasting could have a negative effect on the process (Oettingen & Stephens, 2009).

Once the goal has been set, motivation is an essential component in the goal-setting and attaining process, and therefore it is a preeminent concern for practitioners, trainers, and coaches in the sport and exercise field. Self-determination theory illuminates some of the psychological processes that influence exercise participation and adherence. Self-determination theory proposes that humans seek to fulfill three innate psychological needs: relatedness, competence, and autonomy (Ryan & Deci, 2000). Relatedness is the need to feel a deep sense of belonging and connection to others. Competence is the need to feel that one has the skills and abilities required to accomplish goals and ends. Autonomy is the need for free will and having the choice to select experiences. According to Ryan and Deci (2000), the fulfillment of these needs is essential for optimal functioning and personal well-being, as well as kindling intrinsic and internal motivation. Intrinsic and internal motivation is supported when someone feels autonomous and able to engage in an activity out of their own volition, thereby facilitating enjoyment and engagement in the pursuit of an activity, persistence in the face of difficulty, and creativity and enhanced performance (Halvorson, 2010). In addition, multiple studies within the exercise domain support the premise that autonomy-supportive environments produce motivation and cultivate success (Edmunds, Ntoumanis, & Duda, 2006; Wilson & Rodgers, 2004).

Ryan and Deci (2000) believe that the environment either promotes intrinsic motivation or stifles it. Therefore, practitioners and trainers should strive to increase more internal sources of motivation and well-being in their clients by creating a supportive environment. First, this can be done by assisting their client in setting the right goals. Research shows goals that satisfy the need for relatedness, competence, or autonomy are the most fulfilling goals and lead to the most satisfaction (Halvorson, 2010). Connecting goals to deeper values is one way that this can be accomplished. For example, helping reformulate the initial goal of losing weight to look better or adhere to social pressure by connecting the goal to one or more of the basic needs, such as "improving relationship with my spouse" (relatedness) or "having energy I need to accomplish what I want in my career" (competence), will make the goal more meaningful and help to create intrinsic motivation. Second, practitioners can create environments that foster the development of basic needs by connecting these to personal goals. Clients can be encouraged to build on their sense of relatedness by taking group classes or using family members and friends as support through the goal process. Assessing the clients' starting point and gradually building on previously developed skills to move toward more difficult goals can help foster a sense of competence. Lastly, providing an array of options and allowing the client to have some say in developing the exercise routine may help enhance feelings of autonomy.

Another way we see positive psychology concepts enhancing goal commitment is by further connecting goals to an individual's values and providing a deeper sense of meaning and purpose. Goal-systems theory dictates that goal conflict can be reduced by linking health goals to personal goals and making health goals the means to multiple ends (Mann et al., 2013). Along this vein, connecting physical activity goals with gains in the various facets of PERMA (positive emotions, engagement, relationships, meaning, achievement) may also increase goal coherence, reduce goal conflict, and create a cohesive method of connecting the singular goal of increased exercise with the much larger, complex goal of well-being. Health goals are often perceived as conflicting with other goals. When goals can be set to support the development of basic needs and coincide rather than compete with goals in other domains, goal conflict can be reduced and goal adoption may be enhanced (Riediger & Freund, 2004).

Setting the goal and gaining goal commitment are the first steps toward goal attainment, but typically there are numerous obstacles one must navigate through to take action and put effort toward a goal. Often individuals have grand intentions of reaching goals, but they will fail to do so because of missed opportunities to attend to the goals or failure to self-regulate. Executing the behaviors that enable a person to effectively strive toward and stay on track with established goals requires self-regulation, particularly when it comes to adopting health-related goals. Avoiding temptations and goal distractions and regulating impulses that inhibit goal attainment depletes self-regulation, which is a limited resource (Baumeister, Bratslavsky, Muraven, & Tice, 1998). Like a muscle, goal commitment must be trained and exercised in order to avoid depletion. To that end, studies have shown that adherence to a physical activity program could enhance self-regulation across a range of unrelated domains (Baumeister, Gailliot, DeWall, & Oaten, 2006). Physical exercise, then, both requires and restores self-regulation.

Social scientists as far back as William James (1899) have argued that one of the most effective ways to improve well-being is by developing good habits through committing oneself completely to a goal, taking immediate action, and being willing to experience suffering and self-denial along the way. However, new research suggests that self-control is not limited to simply exercising effortful inhibition of maladaptive impulses or suppressing unwanted impulses related to a goal (Galla & Duckworth, 2015). The formation of habits, or "automatic response tendencies that are triggered by contextual cues" and "formed via the gradual development of mental associations between a frequently repeated behavior and recurring situational cues," are critical to goal adherence (Galla & Duckworth, 2015, p. 2). Facilitating automated behaviors and crafting good habits is another way to preserve conscious attention, maintain self-regulatory resources, and prevent ego-depletion. Habitual responses can become solidified with sustained practice through forging connections between contextual and situational cues and the desired behaviors, until eventually environmental triggers lead to automated behaviors (see Galla & Duckworth, 2015 for a full discussion).

Sustained effort at the outset of a goal fosters the automation of good habits, thereby reserving physical and psychic energy. One method to reduce the burden on conscious attention is by utilizing environmental cues and priming strategies. For example, Gollwitzer (1993) proposed a strategy called implementation intentions, which promotes the initiation of goal-directed behaviors when opportunities arise. Implementation intentions are phrased in the format of "I intend to do x when situation y is encountered," thus linking the anticipated future situation to the goal-directed behavior (Gollwitzer, 1993). For example, an implementation intention could look like "Every Monday, Wednesday, and Friday, I will wake up at 6:00 to run 30 minutes before work." When the alarm goes off at 6:00 AM on Monday, it acts as a cue to take action toward the goal. A meta-analysis on 94 studies measured the effects of implementation intentions and found that they promoted the initiation of goal striving and had a strong positive effect on goal attainment (Gollwitzer & Sheeran, 2006).

MANAGING SETBACKS THROUGH DEVELOPING A RESILIENT MINDSET

Goal pursuit is fraught with stress and adversity. As expectations are often met with setbacks, how individuals process, reflect on, and learn from goal setbacks and failures are critical determinants of success. According to Reivich and Shatté (2002), resilience is broadly defined as the ability to bounce back or recover quickly from stress or adversity and appears to comprise a subset of ordinary competencies that enable a person to endure through challenges to reach goals and find constructive ways to respond to challenges. Within any theory of behavior change, and particularly related to exercise and physical fitness goals, there is a high probability that a person will encounter goal failure, especially in the early stages of change. As such, developing a resilient mindset—one that is strengths-focused and oriented toward growth, optimism, and hope—can better equip individuals with the ability to carry forward once a challenge has been met.

To begin, in the goal-setting process, it is common practice to evaluate the barriers and the available resources that may hinder or facilitate goal attainment. It is easy to identify environmental and circumstantial barriers (e.g., lack of time) and exogenous resources (e.g., support network) that one can leverage during goal striving. It is less intuitive for individuals to identify the strengths within themselves that can enable better goal choice and provide them with endogenous resources they can leverage when met with challenges and setbacks. Peterson and Seligman (2004) endeavored to create consensual definitions and a common language around understanding individual strengths of character, codifying the behaviors and attitudes that reflect a person's "signs of nature" or core being. The Values in Action Survey of Character (VIA-IS) is a 240-item, validated questionnaire that produces rankings for an individual's 24 character strengths across six broad classes of virtues: wisdom and knowledge, courage, humanity, justice, temperance, and transcendence (Peterson & Seligman, 2004). The survey can be taken online at no cost at www.viacharacter.org. The results of an individual's survey can then be used as a platform for discussing how strengths can be effectively leveraged in the goal process.

There is compelling evidence to support that greater understanding and employment of character strengths enable well-being. Strengths of bravery, humor, kindness, spirituality, and appreciation of beauty have been associated with successful recovery from physical illness, psychological disorder, and the deleterious effects of trauma (Peterson, Park, & Seligman, 2006). A recent study on character strengths and physical well-being found that all of the character strengths except for spirituality and modesty were positively related to health-related behaviors, such as feeling healthy and leading a healthy way of life (Proyer, Gander, Wellenzohn, & Ruch., 2013). In addition, Proyer et al. (2013) found that self-regulation, curiosity, zest, leadership, and hope were positively related to overall fitness. Although the research on character strengths and physical well-being is still in its infancy, the results portray the positive role that character strengths play in promoting health-related behaviors. Finding novel ways to use one's signature strengths can increase happiness and decrease depression (Gander, Proyer, Rusch, & Wyss, 2012; Mongrain & Anselmo-Matthews, 2012). When work, relationships, and environments support the use of signature strengths on a daily basis, individuals feel more satisfied, energized, and engaged with their lives.

Finding ways to deliberately utilize strengths in conjunction with the pursuit of fitness goals can help to bolster motivation, adherence, and enjoyment along the way. With this premise in mind, Hefferon and Mutrie (2012) proposed that trainers build an exercise program around their clients' top character strengths. For example, fun exercise classes like Zumba may be appealing to those with the stop strength of humor and playfulness, while raising money for a favorite charity through participating in a race may excite someone with a top strength of kindness and generosity. In addition, knowing their clients' strengths could assist trainers in indentifying the most effective delivery method for the fitness program. For example, a fitness plan for someone with caution and prudence as their top strengths would probably need to look different than a fitness plan for someone whose signature strengths are bravery or zest. Daily pursuit of activities congruent with one's signature strengths is robustly correlated with well-being (Peterson & Seligman, 2004). Therefore, it seems reasonable to believe that building a fitness plan around someone's strengths and providing clients with the opportunity to put their strengths to use in the exercise environment will enhance engagement and energy in the processes, help navigate challenges, and build confidence toward goals.

Another key aspect of developing a resilient mindset is optimism, here defined as an attributional style (or explanatory style). Distinct from dispositional optimism, explanatory style describes the way in which an individual interprets events and outcomes that he or she experiences in life, and attempts to make causal inferences about why that event occurred (Weiner, 1985). A person with a pessimistic attributional style explains negative outcomes or failures as one's own fault (internal), as unchanging (stable), and as occurring at all times across all situations (global) (Schulman, Seligman, & Amsterdam, 1987). In contrast, a person with an optimistic attributional style explains negative outcomes as due to environmental factors (external), as variable (unstable), and as occurring as an isolated incident in a specific situation (specific) (Peterson & Seligman, 1984).

The depressive or persistently pessimistic attributional style can lead to a form of helplessness referred to as "learned helplessness," which is characterized by the belief that an individual has no control over negative outcomes (Seligman, Abramson, Semmel, & von Baeyer, 1979) and is strongly related to the development of clinical depression (Metalsky & Joiner, 1992). When coupled with prolonged exposure to uncontrollable aversive events, it results in motivational, cognitive, and behavioral deficits. Optimistic attributional style, on the other hand, has been shown to have positive effects on health behavior, immune function, and recovery from illness (Seligman, 1998). Attributions in general are theorized to influence how people set proximal goals and how those intentions drive future behavior (Shields, Brawley, & Lindover, 2006).

In the realm of physical activity, much of the research on attributional style has been related to sport performance. For example, optimistic attributional style has been associated with improved performance after failure (Martin-Krumm, Sarrazin, Peterson, & Famose, 2003; Seligman, Nolen-Hoeksema, Thornton, & Thornton, 1990) and was found to reduce the effects of a low perceived ability on task value in physical education classes (Martin-Krumm, Sarrazin, & Peterson, 2005). Further, individuals who view themselves as having reached their physical activity goals (measured by attendance at exercise class or change outcomes) tend to attribute their success to more internal, controllable, and stable causes (Shields et al., 2006). One possible moderator between attributions and health behavior is self-efficacy, or a person's perceived beliefs about their abilities to produce a certain level of performance (Bandura, 1994). It appears that one's coping strategies may directly affect one's ability to manage the demands to meet a desired goals, and an individual's perceived self-efficacy is believed to influence the choice of tasks, level of task performance, amount of effort put into performing the task, and perseverance in the task performance (Bandura, 1994). Self-efficacy and the management of attributions becomes a critical part of maintaining motivation to help keep people on track with their physical activity goals.

Attribution retraining programs have been explored as a potential way to boost physical activity levels with the intent of helping individuals make accurate attributions about their levels of physical activity and aiding them in evaluating inaccurate assumptions about why they are not meeting their goals. For example, Sarkisian, Prohaska, Davis, and Weiner (2007) (as a part of an attribution retraining program with sedentary older adults) helped participants disassociate the belief that a sedentary lifestyle is often attributed to old age. By enabling the participants to make more accurate attributions about the causes of their inactivity, the intervention helped increase activity levels (Sarkisian et al., 2007). Thus, thinking more flexibly and accurately, and realistically, about goals can help individuals make more productive attributions toward reaching goals, even in the face of perceived setbacks and failure.

Finally, the prospect of developing a resilient mindset does not have to be a singular endeavor. The most resilient people rely on both resources within themselves and on perspectives outside of themselves to be able to stay on track with goals.

Feedback (whether provided through self-monitoring or from external sources) on progress toward goals is a critical piece of the goal-setting process (Ashfrod & De Stobbeleir, 2013). Often, feedback is focused on addressing failures and shortcomings, with the hope that this information will shape changes and revisions to future efforts. Although corrective feedback is important for successful goal striving, encouragement and praise can provide motivational boosts throughout the process of goal striving. However, as with effective criticism, research has shown that not all praise is created equal (Dweck, 2007). Exercise practitioners, such as coaches and personal trainers, can foster a growth mindset—the belief that one's abilities can be strengthened and developed through hard work and dedication—by enhancing the kind of feedback they provide to clients.

Dweck (2006) argues that praise that is focused on effort rather than ability, is sincere rather than disingenuous, and is specific rather than general appears to contribute to enhanced performance and promote a sense of control and accountability in the final outcome. Dweck's research shed light on how ability-focused praise could potentially lead to underperformance. In the academic sphere, students praised for being smart often chose easier tasks to try when given a choice in order to avoid making mistakes and looking stupid (Dweck, 2006). Since beliefs about physical ability, self-efficacy, and self-esteem can be linked to exercise behavior and participation, it would be useful for practitioners to understand how certain types of praise can be more useful than others to an individual. Through setting mastery goals and providing feedback focused on successful skill acquisition and incremental improvements in ability (vs. outcome attainment), practitioners can reduce all-or-nothing thinking often associated with failure to adopt physical activity goals.

CELEBRATING SUCCESSES

For many individuals, the types of goals they set at the outset of a physical activity program concern weight and/or body fat loss, achieving a particular body shape, or gains in physical strength and cardiorespiratory fitness levels. Success or failure then is measured based on how much or how little headway one makes toward these very specific outcomes. It is often the case that practitioners (e.g., personal trainers) will also use similar metrics as a yardstick of progress. But not all people are primarily motivated to exercise to bring about physical and aesthetic changes. Some may be more inspired to have more vigor and energy to do the things they are most passionate about, make stronger social connections, or enhance psychological well-being. However, often these perceptually secondary goals are not monitored and tracked with as much rigor and regularity as the physiological changes experienced. Here, we explore alternative methods to monitor positive changes in well-being and psychological states enhanced by the adoption of physical activity programs.

As previously discussed, both chronic and acute exercise can lead to positive shifts in mood and reductions in depressive and anxiety symptoms. One of the greatest contributions of positive psychology research comes from studying the benefits of positive emotion. Positive emotions have the capacity to broaden the scope of attention; raise awareness of the surrounding environment and increase openness to stimuli; build durable intellectual (problem solving, learning), physical (coordination, cardiovascular health), social (bonding, interpersonal relationships), and psychological (resilience, goal orientation) resources; and serve as effective antidotes to physiological activation and cardiovascular reactivity that result from experiencing negative emotions (Fredrickson, 2009). Fredrickson and colleagues found that positive emotions are effective antidotes to the damaging physiological effects of negative emotions (Fredrickson, 2000), increase cognitive flexibility (Fredrickson, 2009), and build durable psychological resources that enable well-being (Fredrickson & Joiner, 2002). In addition to affecting psychological factors, positive emotions reduce blood pressure, basal metabolism, heart rate, respiratory rate, and muscle tension (Fredrickson, Cohn, Coffey, Pek, & Finkel, 2008).

Tracking shifts in positive emotions or depressive symptoms can provide an alternative measure of exercise adoption success and perhaps also create a virtuous cycle. Emotional experiences induced by physical activity can also serve as a mechanism to build psychosocial resources, whereas sedentary behavior is inversely linked to positive affectivity and psychosocial resources (Hogan, Catalino, Mata, & Fredrickson, 2015). One study found that higher levels of positive affect were associated with higher levels of habitual physical activity (Pasco et al., 2011). Much in the way many track physiological shifts and consequences of exercise programs, changes in mood and experienced affect, along with the practical outcomes of those changes, should be monitored as a measure of change and progress. For example, one could track shifts in positive emotions and mood that result from participating in physical activity and exercise. Practitioners could create opportunities and tools that would help deepen clients' understanding of the mental health benefits of exercise and expand the traditional perspective on the changes that the adoption of regular exercise can bring to overall health and wellness.

The psychological literature also supports that it is human nature to focus more on the negative than on the positive; the negative, whether it is our own self-perceptions, events in our lives, or the information we see in the world, has a greater valance than the positive (see Baumeister, Bratslavsky, Finkenauer, & Vohs, 2001). Translated to health behaviors, it is easy to see how the focus on the negative can affect the motivation we are able to maintain on the path toward adopting healthier lifestyles. If the bad is stronger than good, then we are likely to spend more time mulling over how we fell short of a goal, how we missed a workout, or how we did not live up to our own expectations than we are on processing what went well. There are several interventions from positive psychology research designed specifically for helping to savor and offset the negativity bias. One such intervention is through the cultivation of gratitude (Emmons, 2004; Wood, Froh, & Geraghty, 2010). Gratitude journal interventions involve creating a daily habit of recording a good thing or what went well in one's life and a reflection on why that good thing happened (Emmons & Stern, 2013). Gratitude has been shown to bring healing effects both personally and interpersonally, as well as have a strong connection to mental health, well-being, and the ability to cope with everyday stress (Emmons & Stern, 2013). For those pursuing exercise goals, gratitude can be cultivated through the use of an adapted journal, instructing users to notice and record at least one thing that went well during a physical activity session and naming the effort or behavior-focused strategy or skill that led to the successful outcome. The gratitude journal also becomes a valuable tool to use to look back on experienced successes, particularly during times when motivation is flagging.

FUTURE DIRECTIONS

This chapter begins to explore but a few of the possible ways that positive psychology and applied exercise psychology can complement and augment each other, both in theory and in practice. There is a clear need for the interventions reviewed in this chapter to be tested specifically within the exercise psychology domain, and while many of these interventions have been empirically tested in other domains, whether they would effectively translate remains to be researched. Collaboration between researchers and practitioners in both of these fields would enable greater understanding of how to bridge positive and exercise psychology to enhance well-being, and to also understand the limitations that each pose in practical applications.

The field of positive psychology can learn how to leverage physical activity as an effective intervention for creating a good life, and the field of exercise psychology can explore ways to augment current coaching, training, and consulting practices by using positive psychology concepts and interventions to aid people in health goal striving and achievement. We hope that one of the possible outcomes of such collaboration would be in the development of assessments and tools that would expand the way we conceptualize success related to the adoption and maintenance of physical activity programs. At the intersection of positive psychology and applied exercise psychology exists the possibility for new and novel ways to enhance holistic well-being, one that accounts for both psychological and physiological facets, and enables flourishing and a life well lived.

REFERENCES

Acevedo, E. O. (2012). Exercise psychology: Understanding the mental health benefits of physical activity and the public health challenges of inactivity. *The Oxford handbook of exercise psychology* (pp. 3–8). New York, NY: Oxford University Press.

Ahn, S., & Fedewa, A. L. (2011). The effects of physical activity and physical fitness on children's achievement and cognitive outcomes: A meta-analysis. *Research Quarterly for Exercise and Sport, 82*(3), 521.

Ashfrod, S. J., & De Stobbeleir, K. E. M. (2013). Feedback, goal setting, and task performance revisited. In E. A. Locke & G. P. Latham (Eds.) *New developments in goal setting and task performance.* (pp. 51–64). New York, NY: Routledge/Taylor & Francis Group.

Bandura, A. (1994). *Regulative function of perceived self-efficacy.* Hillsdale, NJ: Lawrence Erlbaum Associates.

Baumeister, R. F., Bratslavsky, E., Finkenauer, C., & Vohs, K. D. (2001). Bad is stronger than good. *Review of General Psychology, 5*(4), 323–370.

Baumeister, R. F., Bratslavsky, E., Muraven, M., & Tice, D. M. (1998). Ego depletion: Is the active self a limited resource? *Journal of Personality and Social Psychology, 74*(5), 1252–1265.

Baumeister, R. F., Gailliot, M., DeWall, C. N., & Oaten, M. (2006). Self-regulation and personality: How interventions increase regulatory success, and how depletion moderates the effects of traits on behavior. *Journal of Personality, 74*(6), 1773–1801.

Biddle, S. J. H., & Mutrie, N. (2001). *Psychology of physical activity determinants, wellbeing and interventions.* London: Routledge.

Boutcher, S. H. (2000). The effects of exercise on self-perception and self-esteem. In S. H. Boutcher (Ed.), *Physical activity and psychological well-being* (pp. 118–129). New York, NY: Routledge.

Brown, H. E., Pearson, N., Braithwaite, R. E., Brown, W. J., & Biddle, S. J. H. (2013). Physical activity interventions and depression in children and adolescents: A systematic review and meta-analysis. *Sports Medicine, 43*(3), 195–206.

Conn, V. S. (2010). Anxiety outcomes after physical activity interventions: Meta-analysis findings. *Nursing Research, 59*(3), 224.

Department of Health. (2004). *At least five a week. Evidence on the impact of physical activity and its relationship to health.* A report from the Chief Medical Officer (No. 2389). London: British Nutrition Foundation.

Diener, E., & Chan, M. Y. (2011). Happy people live longer: Subjective well-being contributes to health and longevity. *Applied Psychology: Health and Well-being, 3*(1), 1–43.

Dua, J., & Hargreaves, L. (1992). Effect of aerobic exercise on negative affect, positive affect, stress, and depression. *Perceptual and Motor Skills, 75*(2), 355–361.

Dweck, C. S. (2006). *Mindset: The new psychology of success* Random House: New York, NY.

Dweck, C. S. (2007). The perils and promise of praise. *Educational Leadership: Early Intervention at Every Age, 65*(2), 34–39.

Edmunds, J., Ntoumanis, N., & Duda, J. L. (2006). A test of self-determination theory in the exercise domain. *Journal of Applied Social Psychology 36*(9): 2240–2265.

Emmons, R. A. (2004). *The psychology of gratitude: An introduction.* New York, NY: Oxford University Press.

Emmons, R. A., & Stern, R. (2013). Gratitude as a psychotherapeutic intervention. *Journal of Clinical Psychology, 69*(8), 846–855.

Ensari, I., Greenlee, T. A., Motl, R. W., & Petruzzello, S. J. (2015). Meta-analysis of acute exercise effects on state anxiety: An update of randomized controlled trials over the past 25 years. *Depression and Anxiety, 32*(8), 624–634.

Forgeard, M. J. C., Jayawickreme, E., Kern, M., & Seligman, M. E. P. (2011). Doing the right thing: Measuring wellbeing for public policy. *International Journal of Wellbeing, 1*(1), 79–106.

Fox, K. R. (2000). The effects of exercise on self-perception and self-esteem. In S. H. Boutcher (Ed.), *Physical activity and psychological well-Being* (pp. 88–117). New York, NY: Routledge.

Fredrickson, B. L. (2000). Cultivating positive emotions to optimize health and well-being. *Prevention & Treatment, 3*(1), 1a.

Fredrickson, B. L. (2009). *Positivity.* New York, NY: Crown.

Fredrickson, B. L., Cohn, M. A., Coffey, K. A., Pek, J., & Finkel, S. M. (2008). Open hearts build lives: Positive emotions, induced through loving-kindness meditation, build consequential personal resources. *Journal of Personality and Social Psychology, 95*, 1045–1062.

Fredrickson, B. L., & Joiner, T. (2002). Positive emotions trigger upward spirals toward emotional well-being. *Psychological Science, 13*(2), 172–175.

Friedman, H. S., & Kern, M. L. (2014). Personality, well-being, and health. *Annual Review of Psychology, 65*, 719–742.

Gable, S. L., & Haidt, J. (2005). What (and why) is positive psychology? *Review of General Psychology, 9*(2), 103.

Galla, B. M., & Duckworth, A. L. (2015). More than resisting temptation: Beneficial habits mediate the relationship between self-control and positive life outcomes. *Journal of Personality and Social Psychology, 109*(3), 508–525.

Gander, F., Proyer, R. T., Ruch, W., & Wyss, T. (2012). The good character at work: An initial study on the contribution of character strengths in identifying healthy and unhealthy work-related behavior and experience patterns. *International Archives of Occupational and Environmental Health, 85*(8), 895–904.

Gollwitzer, P. M. (1993). Goal achievement: The role of intentions. In W. Stroebe & M. Hewstone (Eds.) *European review of social psychology* (Vol 4, p. 141–185). Chichester, UK: Wiley.

Gollwitzer, P. M., & Sheeran, P. (2006). Implementation intentions and goal achievement: A meta-analysis of effects and processes. *Advances in experimental social psychology* (Vol 38, pp. 69–119). San Diego, CA: Elsevier Academic Press.

Haskell, W. L., Lee, I. M., Pate, R. R., Powell, K. E., Blair, S. N., Franklin, B. A., Macera, C. A., Heath, G. W., Thompson, P. D., & Bauman, A. (2007). Physical activity and public health: Updated recommendation for adults from the American college of sport medicine and the American heart association. *Medicine & Science in Sport & Exercise, 39*(8), 1423–1434.

Halvorson, H. G. (2010). *Succeed: How we can reach our goals.* New York, NY: PLUME.

Hefferon, K. (2013). *Positive psychology and the body: The somatopsychic side to flourishing: The somatopsychic side to flourishing.* New York, NY: McGraw-Hill International.

Hefferon, K., & Mutrie, N. (2012). Physical activity as a "stellar" positive psychology intervention. In E. O. Acevedo (Ed.), *The Oxford handbook of exercise psychology* (pp. 117–128). New York, NY: Oxford University Press.

Hogan, C. L., Catalino, L. I., Mata, J., & Fredrickson, B. L. (2015). Beyond emotional benefits: Physical activity and sedentary behaviour affect psychosocial resources through emotions. *Psychology & Health, 30*(3), 354–369.

Jacobs Bao, K., & Lyubomirsky, S. (2013). The rewards of happiness. In S. A. David, I. Boniwell, & A. Conley Ayers (Eds.), *The Oxford handbook of happiness* (pp. 119–133). New York, NY: Oxford University Press.

James, W. (1899). *The will to believe and other essays in popular philosophy.* New York, NY: Longman Green.

Jayawickreme, E., Forgeard, M. J. C., & Seligman, M. E. P. (2012). The engine of well-being. *Review of General Psychology, 16*(4), 327–342.

King, L. A. (2008). *Personal goals and life dreams: Positive psychology and motivation in daily life.* New York, NY: Guilford Press.

Klein, H. J., Wesson, M. J., Hollenbeck, J. R., Wright, P. M., & DeShon, R. P. (2001). The assessment of goal commitment: A measurement model meta-analysis. *Organizational Behavior and Human Decision Processes, 85*(1), 32–55.

Kredlow, M. A., Capozzoli, M. C., Hearon, B. A., Calkins, A. W., & Otto, M. W. (2015). The effects of physical activity on sleep: A meta-analytic review. *Journal of Behavioral Medicine, 38*(3), 427–449.

Latham, G. (2003). Goal-setting: A five-step approach to behavior change. *Organizational Dynamics, 32*(3), 309–318.

Laurin, D., Verreault, R., Lindsay, J., MacPherson, K., & Rockwood, K. (2001). Physical activity and risk of cognitive impairment and dementia in elderly persons. *Archives of Neurology, 58*(3), 498–504.

Lee, I. M., Shiromo, E. J., Lobelo, F., Puska, P., Blair, S. N., & Katzmarzyk, P. T. (2012). Effects of physical inactivity on major non-communicable diseases worldwide: An analysis of burden of disease and life expectancy. *Lancet, 380*(9838), 219–229.

Locke, E., & Latham, G. (2002). Building a practically useful theory of goal-setting and task motivation. *American Psychologist, 57*(9), 705–717.

Locke, E., & Latham, G. (2006). New directions in goal-setting theory. *Current Directions in Psychological Science, 15*(5), 265–268.

Lyubomirsky, S. (2007). *The how of happiness: A scientific approach to getting the life you want.* New York, NY: Penguin Press.

Lyubomirsky, S., King, L., & Diener, E. (2005). The benefits of frequent positive affect: Does happiness lead to success? *Psychological Bulletin, 131*(6), 803–855.

Mann, T., de Ridder, D., & Fujita, K. (2013). Self-regulation of health behavior: Social psychological approaches to goal setting and goal striving. *Health Psychology, 32*(5), 487–498.

Martin-Krumm, C., Sarrazin, P. G., & Peterson, C. (2005). The moderating effects of explanatory style in physical education performance: A prospective study. *Personality and Individual Differences, 38*(7), 1645–1656.

Martin-Krumm, C., Sarrazin, P. G., Peterson, C., & Famose, J. (2003). Explanatory style and resilience after sports failure. *Personality and Individual Differences, 35*(7), 1685–1695.

Maxwell, R., & Lynn, S. J. (2015). Exercise: A path to physical and psychological well-being. *Health, happiness, and well-being: Better living through psychological science* (pp. 223–248). Thousand Oaks, CA: Sage.

Metalsky, G. I., & Joiner, T. E., Jr. (1992). Vulnerability to depressive symptomatology: A prospective test of the diathesis-stress and causal meditation components of the hopelessness theory of depression. *Journal of Personality and Social Psychology, 63*(4), 667.

Mongrain, M., & Anselmo-Matthews, T. (2012). Do positive psychology exercises work? A replication of Seligman et al. *Journal of Clinical Psychology, 68*(4), 382–389.

Mutrie, N., & Faulkner, G. (2004). *Physical activity: Positive psychology in motion.* In P. A. Linley & S. Joseph (Eds.), *Positive psychology in practice* (pp. 146–164). Hoboken, NJ: Wiley.

Oettingen, G., & Stephens, E. J. (2009). Fantasies and motivationally intelligent goal setting. In G. B. Moskowitz & H. Grant (Eds.), *The psychology of goals* (pp. 153–178). New York, NY: Guilford Press.

Oishi, S., Diener, E., & Lucas, R. E. (2007). The optimum level of well-being: Can people be too happy? *Perspectives on Psychological Science, 2*(4), 346–360.

Parks, A. C., & Biswas-Diener, R. (2013). Positive interventions: Past, present, and future. In T. B. Kashdan & J. Ciarrochi (Eds.) *Mindfulness, acceptance, and positive psychology: The seven foundations of well-being* (pp. 140–165). Oakland, CA: Context Press/New Harbinger Publications.

Pasco, J. A., Jacka, F. N., Williams, L. J., Brennan, S. L., Leslie, E., & Berk, M. (2011). Don't worry, be active: Positive affect and habitual physical activity. *Australian and New Zealand Journal of Psychiatry, 45*(12), 1047–1052.

Penedo, F. J., & Dahn, J. R. (2005). Exercise and well-being: A review of mental and physical health benefits associated with physical activity. *Current Opinion in Psychiatry, 18*(2), 189–193.

Peterson, C., Park, N., & Seligman, M. E. P. (2006). Greater strengths of character and recovery from illness. *The Journal of Positive Psychology, 1*(1), 17–26.

Peterson, C., & Seligman, M. E. P. (1984). Causal explanations as a risk factor for depression: Theory and evidence. *Psychological Review, 91*(3), 347.

Peterson, C., & Seligman, M. E. P. (2004). *Character strengths and virtues: A handbook and classification*. New York, NY: Oxford University Press.

Proyer, R. T., Gander, F., Wellenzohn, S., & Ruch, W. (2013). What good are character strengths beyond subjective well-being? The contribution of the good character on self-reported health-oriented behavior, physical fitness, and the subjective health status. *The Journal of Positive Psychology, 8*(3), 222–223.

Rebar, A. L., Stanton, R., Geard, D., Short, C., Duncan, M. J., & Vandelanotte, C. (2015). A meta-analysis of the effect of physical activity on depression and anxiety in non-clinical adult populations. *Health Psychology Review, 9*(3), 366–378.

Reed, J., & Buck, S. (2009). The effect of regular aerobic exercise on positive-activated affect: A meta-analysis. *Psychology of Sport and Exercise, 10*(6), 581–594.

Reivich, K., & Shatté, A. (2002). *The resilience factor: 7 essential skills for overcoming life's inevitable obstacles*. New York, NY: Broadway Books.

Riediger, M., & Freund, A. M. (2004). Interference and facilitation among personal goals: Differential associations with subjective well-being and persistent goal pursuit. *Personality and Social Psychology Bulletin, 30*(12), 1511–1523.

Rosenbaum, S., Tiedemann, A., Sherrington, C., Curtis, J., & Ward, P. B. (2014). Physical activity interventions for people with mental illness: A systematic review and meta-analysis. *Journal of Clinical Psychiatry, 75*(9), 964–974.

Ryan, R., & Deci, E. (2000). Self-determination theory and the facilitation of intrinsic motivation, social development, and well-being. *American Psychologist, 55*, 68–78.

Sarkisian, C. A., Prohaska, T. R., Davis, C., & Weiner, B. (2007). Pilot test of an attribution retraining intervention to raise walking levels in sedentary older adults. *Journal of the American Geriatrics Society, 55*(11), 1842–1846.

Schulman, P., Seligman, M. E., & Amsterdam, D. (1987). The attributional style questionnaire is not transparent. *Behaviour Research and Therapy, 25*(5), 391–395.

Seligman, M. E. P. (1998). *Learned optimism*. New York, NY: Pocket Books.

Seligman, M. E. P. (2011). *Flourish: A visionary new understanding of happiness and well-being*. New York, NY: Free Press.

Seligman, M. E. P., Abramson, L. Y., Semmel, A., & Baeyer, C. V. (1979). Depressive attributional style. *Journal of Abnormal Psychology, 88*(3), 242.

Seligman, M. E. P., & Csikszentmihalyi, M. (2000). Positive psychology: An introduction. *American Psychologist, 55*(1), 5–14.

Seligman, M. E. P., Nolen-Hoeksema, S., Thornton, N., & Thornton, K. M. (1990). Explanatory style as a mechanism of disappointing athletic performance. *Psychological Science, 1*(2), 143–146.

Seligman, M. E. P., Railton, P., Baumeister, R. F., & Sripada, C. (2013). Navigating into the future or driven by the past. *Perspectives on Psychological Science, 8*(2), 119–141.

Shields, C. A., Brawley, L. R., & Lindover, T. I. (2006). Self-efficacy as a mediator of the relationship between causal attributions and exercise behavior. *Journal of Applied Social Psychology, 36*(11), 2785–2802.

Shilts, M. K., Horowitz, M., & Townsend, M. S. (2004). An innovative approach to goal setting for adolescents: Guided goal setting. *Journal of Nutrition Education and Behavior, 36*(3), 155–156.

Spence, J. C., McGannon, K. R., & Poon, P. (2005). The effect of exercise on global self-esteem: A quantitative review. *Journal of Sport and Exercise Psychology, 27*, 311–334.

Weinberg, R. S. (2014). Goal setting in sport and exercise: Research to practice. In J. L. Van Raalte & B. W. Brewer (Eds.), *Exploring sport and exercise psychology* (3rd ed., pp. 33–54). Washington, DC: American Psychological Association.

Weiner, B. (1985). An attributional theory of achievement motivation and emotion. *Psychological Review, 92*(4), 548–573.

Wilson, P. M., & Rodgers, W. M. (2004). The relationship between perceived autonomy support, exercise regulations and behavioral intentions in women. *Psychology of Sport and Exercise, 5*, 229–242.

Wood, A. M., Froh, J. J., & Geraghty, A. W. A. (2010). Gratitude and well-being: A review and theoretical integration. *Clinical Psychology Review, 30*(7), 890–905.

31 Persons With Medical Conditions

Kate L. Nolt

Most people are aware that regular exercise, essential nutrients from whole food, and lots of water are needed in order to live a higher quality of life (Sloan, Sawada, Martin, & Haaland, 2015, p. 7). Living a healthy lifestyle, however, takes time and a concerted effort on a daily basis. Today, many people are challenged to make the time for a healthy life, due to various reasons. Among those reasons offered are work and family demands, money, and motivation. Consequently, many of the individuals who become clients of an exercise psychologist will present symptoms of an encroaching illness or will already be diagnosed with a disease that may or may not be manageable through exercise and healthy diet alone.

While there may be many other medical conditions that could be encountered, this chapter will address those that are most likely to be presented. Under no circumstances is this to be considered an all-inclusive approach to these conditions. Exercise psychologists should work closely with a client's physician to ensure that risks to the client and practitioner are reduced. What follows are general guidelines to use when working with a client who may present with any medical condition. The intake portion of this chapter is recommended as a business process for any client regardless of exercise and health status, and is suggested as a method to improve quality of service and client satisfaction (Czuchry, Yassin & Norris, 2000, p. 83).

INTAKE

Prior to beginning an initial client session, it is highly recommended that all clients complete a health history form. This type of form would include questions regarding current medical conditions, symptoms a client is experiencing, medications they may be taking regularly, as well as a family health history. While some clients may be asymptomatic (without symptoms) of any disease, they may very well be at *risk* for disease due to a family history of hereditary diseases such as coronary heart disease, high cholesterol, diabetes, and high blood pressure, which are common conditions that can be hereditary. Collecting family health history is a good tool for identifying these risks and helpful in promoting healthy behaviors (Chen, Goodson, Jung, Popoola, Kwok, & Muenzenberger, 2015, p. 632). Figure 31.1 illustrates a sample Health History Intake Form that can be adapted to practice.

The information collected on this form can also help initiate conversation about overall health, wellness, and the role exercise has played in a client's life. Much information regarding exercise and lifestyle, both past and present, can be gleaned from the information presented on the form. The use of the form can also foster a full-disclosure conversation, which will cultivate a safe working environment and a suitable therapeutic rapport between the client and the practitioner.

ASSESSING THE HEALTH HISTORY

Once the health history is complete, the practitioner should review this information thoroughly with the client. This will allow for time to ask the client more about condition(s) and may in fact be the catalyst to a broader conversation about why a client believes they may need the services of an exercise psychologist. For example, upon review of the information, the practitioner may discover that a new client is taking a medication with which the practitioner is unfamiliar. It is incumbent upon the practitioner to explore with the client what condition he or she believes they are taking the medication for and to ask questions regarding what the client may know about possible side effects, as well as any restrictions to exercise that may be inherent in the use of the specific medication. Further, it would be prudent to explore the medical condition and the symptoms the client presents that led a physician to prescribe the medication. A basic internet search on a reliable website, such as www.mayoclinic.com or www.WebMD.com, with easily understood information regarding diseases, signs and symptoms, and possible treatments, can help inform a practitioner. An advanced level of research may need to be conducted, but may not be necessary initially.

Once a review has been completed, a practitioner should investigate chronic conditions and diseases with which they are unfamiliar, so that the services that are subsequently provided take potential risk factors into consideration. Also, implementation of possible protective factors, which will mitigate negative outcomes such as injury, is advised. Protective factors would include, but are not limited to, liability insurance and practicing ethically and within a certain clearly defined scope of practice. This type of approach to medical conditions protects not only the practitioner, but the client as well. If the practitioner omits these steps and a client is hurt as a result, then this could potentially become an ethical, and legal, issue for the practice. A practitioner should ensure that they obtain the correct liability insurance to protect their business from this type of claim. More importantly, however, the practitioner should make it a business process to do due diligence when it comes to exploring presented medical conditions by a client. Unless the exercise psychologist also holds a medical degree that will support his or her approach to a health history, the above approach to a client's health is advised.

MEDICAL CONDITIONS

This part of the chapter begins the introduction of several common medical conditions that a client may present, and while a new client may not present any of these at the onset of receiving services, any of these conditions can develop over time. These conditions are in no particular order, and the information provided is basic in nature but comprehensive enough to allow for initiating a dialogue about personal medical and behavioral practices and beliefs of a client.

STRESS

Stress itself is not a medical condition. However, stress is one of the dominating factors that can promote the development of what are known as *lifestyle diseases* (Seaward, 2002, p. 3). These diseases, according to Seaward (2002), are such that the pathology "develops over a period of several years, and perhaps decades" (p. 3). Unlike infectious diseases, which are treatable with medication, lifestyle diseases are preventable and correctable by making behavioral changes in the habits that caused the disease. Coronary heart disease, which

Health History   Rev. 11.13

Please complete the following form and return it to the provider so that a complete profile can be established prior to beginning your personalized program. Please write legibly and feel free to ask any questions that arise. If extra writing space is needed, please use the back or attach another sheet. Thank you!

Client Name: _____ Date: _____
Height:_____ Weight:_____ Sex: Male Female (circle one) DOB:_____
Physician's Name _____
Physician's Phone Number: _____
Person to contact in case of emergency
Name:_____ Relationship:_____ Phone #:_____

Are you taking any medications or drugs? __ Yes   __ No If so, please list them on the back or on another sheet including how often and the dosage amount if known.

Describe your exercise program now.

Do you (or any member of your family) now have or have had in the past:
Please expand on any Yes answers on the back. (If for a family member, please indicate the relationship to you (e.g., Aunt on Mother's side has high blood pressure)

		Yes	No
1	History of heart problems, chest pain, or stroke	_____	_____
2	Increased blood pressure	_____	_____
3	Any chronic illness or condition	_____	_____
4	Difficulty with physical exercise	_____	_____
5	Advice from physician not to exercise	_____	_____
6	Recent surgery (last 12 months)	_____	_____
7	Pregnancy (now or within last 3 months)	_____	_____
8	History of breathing or lung problems	_____	_____
9	Muscle, joint, or back disorder, or any previous injury still affecting you	_____	_____
10	Diabetes or thyroid condition	_____	_____
11	Cigarette smoking habit	_____	_____
12	Obesity (more than 20 percent over ideal body weight)	_____	_____
13	Increased blood cholesterol	_____	_____
14	History of heart problems in the immediate family	_____	_____
15	Hernia, or any condition that may be aggravated by lifting weights	_____	_____

Comments/Notes:
Adapted from American Council on Exercise, 1996.

Figure 31.1 Sample Health History Intake Form

continues to be a leading cause of death in the United States, is an example of a lifestyle disease.

Hans Selye (1907–1982) is widely known as the "Father of Stress." Selye's work centered on establishing a link between physiological responses to chronic stress and disease (Seaward, 2002, p 4). Specifically, Selye explored whether the body produced a single "nonspecific" reaction to damage of any kind. Initially, he labeled such a physical reaction as an "alarm reaction," which eventually became known as a "stress response." He suggested that the process of this alarm reaction or stress response on the body occurred in these stages (Seaward, 2002, p. 5):

1. Alarm Stage (eventually called fight or flight response by others): Stimuli, such as financial problems, death of a loved one, the smell of fire, a threat to bodily harm, or a car accident, for example, would initiate this stage. The alarm reaction would cause physical changes in the body, such as the release of damaging hormones, increased heart rate, a decrease in disease-fighting white blood cells, bleeding ulcers, constant headaches, and sleep deprivation.
2. Decoding of the Stimulus: The brain will begin to decode a situation as threat or non-threat. If the situation is non-threatening, then the stress response ends. If, however, the threat is real, then the brain will activate the endocrine system and the nervous system to prepare to defend or escape the situation. The body would eventually enter a stage of adaptation, whereby it attempts to adapt to these physiologic changes (coping with the perceived stress).
3. Resistance Stage: Eventually, the body would enter into the resistance stage, wherein it would try to fight off the physiologic response in order to maintain a balanced state, or homeostasis. However, the body may still be in a state of heightened arousal, causing one or more of the body's systems to be in a state of hyperactivity, known as exhaustion stage. The body still remains in a heightened state until the threat is over.
4. Returning to homeostasis (balance): The body will return to a balanced state of calm once the threat is gone.
    Selye referred to this whole process as General Adaptation Syndrome (GAS). Stressors, anything that promotes stress, can be many things, and each person will react to these stressors, real or imagined, very differently (Seaward, 2002, p. 13). Examples of major life stressors might be death of a loved one, divorce, financial loss, or a change of job, among others.

Any of the above-mentioned stress responses could present themselves as a medical condition that a client may mention upon intake. This may lead an exercise psychologist to ask questions related to that client's stressors and to how exercise may help improve the body's response to stress. It is important to mention that there are several theoretical models that attempt to explain stress. However, an explanation of each theory would be outside the scope of this chapter. Nevertheless, each theory states that in order to understand and intercept stress and its relationship to disease, the approach to healing must be a mind-body-spiritual one that emulates the wellness model of treating stress and trauma, rather than the medical model, which includes the use of drugs to treat symptoms (Carrola & Corbin-Burdick, 2015).

Overweight and Obesity

According to the Centers for Disease Control and Prevention (CDC, 2016), nearly 36.5 percent of adults in the United States are obese. According to the World Health Organization

(WHO, 2016), in 2014 more than 1.9 billion adults were overweight, and more than half a billion were obese. Each year at least 2.8 million people die as a result of being overweight or obese (7). While various population groups have higher or lower percentages of obesity, this condition is at pandemic proportions and has many associated medical conditions that can affect an individual's ability to exercise safely.

Signs and Symptoms

According to the Harvard School of Public Health (2017), at its most basic, the word obesity is a way to describe one possessing too much body fat. The word overweight essentially means the same. Yet, the difference between the two will depend on the ratio of body fat to muscle mass that can be measured on the individual. A higher ratio of fat to muscle indicates a person is obese. When a client presents to an exercise psychologist for help, it will be obvious, in most cases, whether they are overweight or obese. What is not so obvious, and varies per individual, are the myriad psychosocial issues and co-morbidities that are associated with being overweight and obese.

Overweight clients may not yet be diagnosed with any of the associated chronic medical conditions. These conditions include various forms of arthritis, type-2 diabetes, and metabolic syndrome. A client may reveal other physical signs that their health status is affected by their weight, such as high blood pressure, high cholesterol, fatigue, and general malaise (reported as "just not feeling well"). Working with an exercise psychologist, clients can unlearn some unhealthy behaviors. For example, not exercising regularly or at all, which contributes to their condition, should be replaced with movement and exercise within their activities of daily living.

Treatment

A well-planned, healthy weight loss and weight management program incorporating exercises that are low to moderate in intensity and impact, such as walking, recumbent bicycling, and/ or swimming, is a likely initial treatment for the obese client. This plan should be an integrative, holistic approach that is implemented in small steps and in conjunction with the client's physicians, where appropriate. Unfortunately, many physicians do not have the time required to discuss the details of such a plan with their patient.

The immediate treatment would be to identify those health behaviors that contribute to the weight issue and work to alter those behaviors while incorporating movement the client may enjoy. In many cases, only the client's physician should recommend the level of exercise that would be appropriate for a client's weight and physical condition. The American College of Sports Medicine (ACSM) recommendations are for adults to engage in 150 minutes of moderate-intensity exercise over the course of a week. This recommendation guideline may or may not be appropriate for the client who presents with overweight or obesity. This recommendation will depend heavily on the client's presented health history, current medications, and physician's orders (Garber, Blissmer, Deschenes, Franklin, Lamonte, Lee, Nieman, & Swain, 2011). Obtaining a completed Par-Q+ form (see Figure 31.2) and/or eParMed-X+ form, both of which assess a client's readiness to exercise depending on health status, is advised. The Par Q form is a short form wherein if the client answers yes to one (1) of the first few questions, then the additional questions would need to be answered to establish the existence of chronic medical conditions and the need to consult and collaborate with the client's medical professionals (Bredin, Gledhill, Jamnik, & Warburton, 2013, p. 274).

Establishing a network of other professionals who can collaborate with an exercise psychologist to assist a client in weight loss and weight maintenance is advised. Developing relationships with nutritionists, personal or athletic trainers, qualified fitness professionals and organizations, and certified health education specialists can provide a network of resources to a client for success in weight loss endeavors. Further, a client may present with a history of having explored many commercial programs (e.g., Jenny Craig, Weight Watchers, or Nutri-system), which have subsequently failed to be effective. An exercise psychologist may explore these previous attempts and incorporate them into a new plan, while taking into consideration any psychosocial and physical limitations that may be present. Conferring with the client's physician, with the client's permission, ensures a comprehensive, integrative approach, and in turn fosters a safer environment between the practitioner and the client. Please note that in order to discuss a client's condition with their physician, a medical release form that is in accordance with the HIPAA privacy rule is required. A sample form is provided in this chapter as Figure 31.2 and can be adapted to practice as needed or downloaded for free from www. athenaeum.edu/pdf/free-hipaa-release-form.pdf.

PHYSICAL ACTIVITY READINESS QUESTIONNAIRE (PAR-Q) AND YOU

Regular physical activity is fun and healthy, and increasingly more people are starting to become more active every day. Being more active is very safe for most people. However, some people should check with their doctor before they start becoming much more physically active. If you are between the ages of 15 and 69, the PAR-Q will tell you if you should check with your doctor before you start. If you are over 69 years of age and you are not used to being very active, check with your doctor.

Common sense is your best guide when you answer these questions. Please read the questions carefully and answer each one honestly: Check YES or NO:

Informed use of the PAR-Q: Reprinted from ACSM's Health/Fitness Facility Standards and Guidelines, 1997 by American College of Sports Medicine

Delay becoming much more active:

- If you are not feeling well because of a temporary illness such as a cold or a fever—wait until you feel better; or
- If you are or may be pregnant—talk to your doctor before you start becoming more active.

Please note: If your health changes so that you then answer YES to any of the above questions, tell your fitness or health professional. Ask whether you should change your physical activity plan.

If you answered: If you answered NO honestly to all PAR-Q questions, you can be reasonably sure that you can:

- Start becoming much more physically active—begin slowly and build up gradually. This is the safest and easiest way to go.

Figure 31.2 Sample Par Q Form

- Take part in a fitness appraisal—this is an excellent way to determine your basic fitness so that you can plan the best way for you to live actively.

YES   NO

☐   ☐   1. Has your doctor ever said that you have a heart condition and that you should only do physical activity recommended by a doctor?

☐   ☐   2. Do you feel pain in your chest when you do physical activity?

☐   ☐   3. In the past month, have you had chest pain when you were not doing physical activity?

☐   ☐   4. Do you lose your balance because of dizziness, or do you ever lose consciousness?

☐   ☐   5. Do you have a bone or joint problem that could be made worse by a change in your physical activity?

☐   ☐   6. Is your doctor currently prescribing drugs (for example, water pills) for your blood pressure or heart condition?

☐   ☐   7. Do you know of any other reason why you should not do physical activity?

Talk to your doctor by phone or in person BEFORE you start becoming much more physically active or BEFORE you have a fitness appraisal. Tell your doctor about the PAR-Q and to which questions you answered YES.

- You may be able to do any activity you want—as long as you start slowly and build up gradually. Or, you may need to restrict your activities to those which are safe for you. Talk with your doctor about the kinds of activities you wish to participate in and follow his/her advice.
- Find out which community programs can be helpful in supporting you in engaging in the physical activities in which you are interested.

Figure 31.2 (Continued)

Diabetes

According to Kapur, Schmidt, and Barcelo (2015), diabetes mellitus (DM) is a global epidemic that is rapidly increasing (p. 1). The researchers further state that an estimated 415 million people are living with DM worldwide, and another 318 million people have impaired glucose tolerance, which is an indicator for DM. According to WHO (2016), healthy diet, regular physical activity, maintaining a normal body weight, and avoiding tobacco use can delay the onset of type-2 diabetes.

Diabetes is a condition where the release of insulin, a hormone released by the pancreas that helps to regulate the metabolism of carbohydrates, is compromised, thereby causing glucose to accumulate in the body—a condition known as *hyperglycemia* (elevated blood sugar). There are three types of diabetes. Type-1 diabetes, formerly known as juvenile diabetes, is the most serious form of diabetes. This is an insulin-dependent form of diabetes, meaning that a person with type-1 diabetes must depend on insulin injections or oral medications since their bodies cannot produce insulin on its own. This form of diabetes typically occurs in childhood or adolescence. Type-2 diabetes is a condition normally linked to being overweight or obese. This is a non-insulin-dependent form of diabetes, meaning the body

Authorization for Use or Disclosure of Protected Health Information (Required by the Health Insurance Portability and Accountability Act, 45 C.F.R. (Parts 160 and 164)

1. Authorization

I authorize _____ (healthcare provider) to use and disclose the protected health information described below to _____ (individual seeking the information).

2. Effective Period

This authorization for release of information covers the period of healthcare from: a. ☐ _____ to _____.   **OR**
b. ☐ all past, present, and future periods.

3. Extent of Authorization

a. ☐ I authorize the release of my complete health record (including records relating to mental healthcare, communicable diseases, HIV or AIDS, and treatment of alcohol or drug abuse).

OR

b. ☐ I authorize the release of my complete health record with the exception of the following information:
☐ Mental health records
☐ Communicable diseases (including HIV and AIDS)
☐ Alcohol/drug abuse treatment
☐ Other (please specify): _____

4. This medical information may be used by the person I authorize to receive this information for medical treatment or consultation, billing or claims payment, or other purposes as I may direct.
5. This authorization shall be in force and effect until _____ (date or event), at which time this authorization expires.
6. I understand that I have the right to revoke this authorization, in writing, at any time. I understand that a revocation is not effective to the extent that any person or entity has already acted in reliance on my authorization or if my authorization was obtained as a condition of obtaining insurance coverage and the insurer has a legal right to contest a claim.
7. I understand that my treatment, payment, enrollment, or eligibility for benefits will not be conditioned on whether I sign this authorization.
8. I understand that information used or disclosed pursuant to this authorization may be disclosed by the recipient and may no longer be protected by federal or state law.

Signature of patient or personal representative _____

Printed name of patient or personal representative and his or her relationship to patient

_____

Date:

Figure 31.3 Sample HIPAA Medical Release Form

can still produce its own insulin. Due to increasing body fat to muscle ratios, however, it does so at a slower rate than optimal. Normally, this disease occurs after the age of 40; however, the incidence rate, or new cases, in younger ages have increased dramatically due to the prevalence of obesity in general. When lifestyle and behavior changes are made, clients presenting with this form of diabetes may avoid having to self-inject insulin or take oral medications. Finally, gestational diabetes occurs in pregnant women and usually disappears after childbirth (WHO, 2016).

Diabetes is a serious disease, and can result in life-altering difficulties, from needing to self-inject insulin several times a day to loss of limbs due to diabetic neuropathy, a form of paralysis, or even to diabetic coma. If a client indicates on a health history form that diabetes runs in the family, or if the client indicates that they have been diagnosed with diabetes, specific questions regarding insulin control should be asked. Depending on the severity of the disease and how it is controlled, the client's physician should make recommendations for participation in exercise.

Signs and Symptoms

Generally, the signs and symptoms of diabetes will include elevated blood sugar levels (as measured in a blood test), high glucose levels in urine, excessive thirst, frequent urination, hunger, tendency to tire easily, and wounds that heal slowly (Donatelle, 2007). Symptoms may also include tiredness and tingling in extremities, which will be relevant when discussing ability, attitude, and beliefs with respect to exercise as this could be a reason why a client does not exercise or rarely exercises.

Treatment

Treatment may include daily self-injected insulin, oral medications, dietary changes, increase in physical activity, or any combination of these. Medications listed on the health history form that may indicate a diagnosis of diabetes include Byetta, Symlin, Januvia, Metformin, Glucophage, Riomet, Amaryl, Glynase, and Glucotrol. This is not a complete list of the medications prescribed, but is a partial list of the most recognized medications.

Arthritis

According to the Summary of Health Statistics for U.S. Adults: National Health Interview, 2012 (CDC, 2014, p. 5), 21 percent of adults have been told they have some form of arthritis, and 26 percent have chronic joint symptoms. Arthritis refers to inflammation (swelling) and stiffness that occurs in the joints. The most common forms of arthritis are osteoarthritis and rheumatoid arthritis. Osteoarthritis (OA) is the main cause of joint pain in older people, and it has been linked to anxiety and depression (Richardson, Grime, & Ong, 2013). This is a degenerative condition wherein joint cartilage, which protects surfaces of bones in the joints, is deteriorating. As the cartilage deteriorates, the bony surfaces will touch and erode over time (Dirckx, 1997). Joint pain and stiffness are likely to result in a decrease in motivation to exercise or participate in activities of daily living that may require a lot of movement. In fact, a lack of movement of the affected joints can cause an increase in joint stiffness and pain. This can lead to less social engagement and may place sufferers at a risk for mental distress (Richardson et al., 2013). Regular exercisers and athletes who possess repetitive use injury or other activity-related injury can also suffer from the pain and stiffness of OA at the site of their injury.

The Mayo Clinic (2014b) defines rheumatoid arthritis (RA) as an autoimmune disease, where the body's immune system attacks its own body tissues, mistaking it for an infectious agent to be destroyed. While OA is primarily found in the elderly population, RA can be found in people of all ages. The causes of RA are unknown. RA can be characterized by "flares" and "remissions," and it can affect other areas of the body in addition to the joints, such as glands and organs (www.Medicinenet.com, 2014).

Signs and Symptoms

The common signs and symptoms of OA and RA are the chronic presence of joint pain and stiffness. As indicated above, RA can affect not only the bone joints, but also organs. Some additional signs and symptoms of RA include fever; redness, swelling, and tenderness around the affected area; and fatigue. RA also causes permanent joint destruction and deformity, thereby also causing functional disability.

Treatment

There is no known cure for RA or OA. The goal of treatment, generally, is to reduce the joint inflammation and pain. For RA, the additional goal would be to reduce the rate of joint destruction and deformity. Medications are used to treat both OA and RA. The medications to treat OA can be obtained over the counter, such as Aleve and ibuprofen. Some other medications to treat OA can only be obtained through prescription from a physician, such as Meloxicam, Naprosyn, and Feldene. Aspirin and steroids can be used for both RA and OA to reduce inflammation and swelling. RA medications have a second line of defense after the steroids, which are slow-acting medications, such as Trexall and Rheumatrex. Regardless of the medications indicated on the health history intake from a client, an exercise psychologist should collaborate with the client's physician to create a plan that will include safe movement, while delving into the client's motivation and adherence to exercise and activities of daily living.

According to the ACSM exercise guidelines for arthritis sufferers, some suggested exercises include non-impact exercises such as yoga, pilates, swimming, or cycling. Because RA involves the immune system, more rest days may be needed if there is a flare up. Further, the ACSM guidelines suggest that regular exercise is beneficial to arthritis sufferers in the following ways: "decreased joint pain and stiffness, improved or maintained joint motion, decreased risk of cardiovascular disease (higher in those with rheumatoid arthritis), improved ability to do activities such as getting in and out of a car or going up and down stairs, decreased disease activity" (Millar, 2012, para. 3).

Coronary Heart Disease

The CDC advances the following facts about heart disease in the U.S.:

> Heart disease is the leading cause of death for both men and women. More than half of the deaths due to heart disease in 2009 were men. About 610,000 Americans die from heart disease each year—that's 1 in every 4 deaths. Coronary heart disease is the most common type of heart disease, killing more than 370,000 people annually. In the United States, someone has a heart attack every 43 seconds. Each minute, someone in the United States dies from a heart disease-related event. Heart disease is the leading cause of death for people of most racial/ethnic groups in the United States, including

African Americans, Hispanics, and whites. For Asian Americans or Pacific Islanders and American Indians or Alaska Natives, heart disease is second only to cancer.

(CDC, 2015)

Coronary heart disease (CHD) and cardiovascular disease (CVD) are different diseases that are sometimes considered interchangeable. CHD refers to a buildup of plaque in the arteries of the heart, which limits blood flow, thus increasing the risk of a heart attack (CDC, 2015). CVD includes CHD, but also includes other diseases of the heart. According to the Mayo Clinic (2014a),

the term 'heart disease' is often used interchangeably with the term 'cardiovascular disease.' Cardiovascular disease generally refers to conditions that involve narrowed or blocked blood vessels that can lead to a heart attack, chest pain, or stroke. Other heart conditions, such as those that affect the heart's muscle, valves, or rhythm, also are considered forms of heart disease.

(Mayo Clinic, 2014b)

Signs and Symptoms

Symptoms may include chest pain, known as angina; shortness of breath; numbness; and tingling or pain in the legs, arms, jaw, neck, and or back. Some risk factors include elevated blood pressure (significantly over normal reading of 120/80), increased heart rate, and increased release of the stress hormone cortisol. Cortisol, which cannot be measured by an exercise psychologist, can lead to an increase in cholesterol, which then interferes with the efficient operation of the heart muscle (American Heart Association, 2016). Some of these signs and symptoms could be a result of other non-heart-related conditions; however, when taken in combination with a client's health history, they could be indicative of CVD. Relevant terms to look for on the intake form that may indicate this condition would be *atherogenesis, atherosclerosis*, and *arteriosclerosis*.

Treatment

Medications, dietary changes, and surgical intervention are sometimes required. Minimally, a client should indicate that they are under the monitoring and care of a cardiologist.

Recommended Exercise Modifications

Depending on the severity of disease, low-to-moderate intensity cardio exercises, stretching and breathing exercises as a coping strategy, and imagery and other stress-reducing alternative approaches should be altered in accordance with the client's physician. If a client presents with this condition in their own or family history, then a medical release to exercise from the client's physician should be obtained.

Psychosocial Issues

As indicated at various times throughout this chapter, medical conditions can be accompanied by other issues, such as depression; low self-esteem and social competence; family, social, and economic changes; anxiety; and heightened stress response, as well as a general sense of lack of motivation for daily living, let alone exercising on a regular basis (Stoeckel & Weissbrod, 2015). Exercise psychologists, who are not licensed clinical counselors or psychologists, can assist clients struggling to cope with a chronic illness, but on a limited basis.

There are many available resources for exercise psychologists to learn more about these issues in an effort to increase the likelihood of success with clients. The American Psychological Association (2015) has the Health & Emotional Wellness resource online, for example, as do many of the other online references from this chapter. As indicated previously, exercise psychologists should be aware of the psychosocial issues that can accompany chronic illnesses and assist clients in building a support network which can provide resources when needed.

CONCLUSION

An exercise psychologist may encounter many medical conditions in their practice. Some of the medical conditions mentioned within this chapter may present complications that are not mentioned herein; thus it is highly recommended that a practitioner exercise due diligence, collecting as much information as possible about a client's health and medical history. This information can serve to inform the exercise psychologist about what may be causing a lack of motivation to exercise, challenges of adhering to exercise, or both. Conversely, a client may present with no signs or symptoms of a medical condition, but may have a family history of certain diseases, which may also play a role in the course of discussions between the client and exercise psychologist.

The best, most effective way to work with clients with medical conditions is to establish a working relationship with not only the client's medical doctor, but *all* other health professionals that the client deems as important to their quality of life. In many cases, the psychosocial issues presented may correlate with a medical condition. Thus, exercise psychologists would benefit from considering this information for a holistic approach to resolve a client's exercise issues.

REFERENCES

American Council on Exercise (1996). Cotton, R. T. (Ed.). Personal trainer manual (2nd ed.). San Diego: American Council on Exercise.

American Heart Association (2016). *Understand your risks to prevent a heart attack – Major risk factors you can modify, treat or control.* Retrieved from http://www.heart.org/HEARTORG/Conditions/ HeartAttack/UnderstandYourRiskstoPreventaHeartAttack/Understand-Your-Risks-to-Prevent-a-Heart-Attack_UCM_002040_Article.jsp#.WV3GBhAiBTZ

American Psychological Association (2015). *Health and emotional wellness resource.* Retrieved from http://www.apa.org/helpcenter/wellness/index.aspx

Bredin, S., Gledhill, N., Jamnik, V., & Warburton, D. (2013). New risk stratification and physical activity clearance strategy for physicians and patients alike. *Canadian Family Physician, 59,* 273–277.

Carrola, P., & Corbin-Burdick, M. (2015). Counseling military veterans: Advocating for culturally competent and holistic interventions. *Journal of Mental Health Counseling, 37*(1), 1–14.

Centers for Disease Control (2014). Prevalence of arthritis in the United States. Retrieved from https://www.cdc.gov/arthritis/data_statistics/arthritis-related-stats.htm

Centers for Disease Control (2015). *Coronary heart disease.* Retrieved from https://www.cdc.gov/heartdisease/coronary_ad.htm

Centers for Disease Control (2016). *Adult obesity facts.* Retrieved from https://www.cdc.gov/obesity/data/adult.html

Chen, L., Goodson, P., Jung, E., Popoola, O., Kwok, O., & Muenzenberger, A. (2015). A survey of Texas health educators' family health history-based practice. *American Journal of Health Behavior, 39*(5), 632–639. doi:10.5993/ajhb.39.5.5

Czuchry, A., Yassin, M., & Norris, J. (2000). An open system approach to process reengineering in a healthcare operational environment. *Health Marketing Quarterly, 17*(3), 77–88.

Dirckx, J. H. (1997). *Disorders of joints: Arthritis. Human diseases.* Modesto, CA. Health Professions Institute.

Donatelle, R. J. (2007). Infectious and non-infectious conditions; risk and responsibilities. In *Health: The basics* (7th ed., pp. 405–406). San Francisco, CA. Pearson Education, Inc.

Garber, C. E., Blissmer, B., Deschenes, M. R., Franklin, B. A., Lamonte, M. J., Lee, I. M., . . . Swain, D. P. (2011). Quantity and quality of exercise for developing and maintaining cardiorespiratory, musculoskeletal, and neuromotor fitness in apparently healthy adults: guidance for prescribing exercise. *Medicine & Science in Sports & Exercise, 43*(7), 1334–1359

Harvard School of Public Health Obesity Prevention (2017). *Obesity definition - What does it actually mean to be overweight or obese?* Retrieved from https://www.hsph.harvard.edu/obesity-prevention-source/obesity-definition/

Kapur, A., Schmidt, M., & Barcelo, A. (2015). Diabetes in socioeconomically vulnerable populations. *International Journal of Endocrinology.* Article ID 247636, 1–2 http://dx.doi.org/10.1155/2015/247636

Mayo Clinic (2014a). *Heart disease – Definition.* Retrieved from http://www.mayoclinic.org/diseases-conditions/heart-disease/basics/definition/con-20034056

Mayo Clinic (2014b). *Rheumatoid arthritis – Overview.* Retrieved from http://www.mayoclinic.org/diseases-conditions/rheumatoid-arthritis/home/ovc-20197388

Millar, A. (2012). *Exercise and arthritis.* Retrieved from http://www.acsm.org/public-information/articles/2016/10/07/exercise-and-arthritis

Richardson, J. C., Grime, J. C., & Ong, B. N. (2013). 'Keeping going': Chronic joint pain in older people who describe their health as good. *Ageing and Society, 34*(8), 1380–1396. doi: 10.1017/S0144686X13000226, Published online: 11 April 2013.

Seaward, B. L. (2002). *Managing stress* (3rd ed., p. 13). Sudbury, MA: Jones and Bartlett Publishers.

Sloan, R. A., Sawada, S. S., Martin, C. K., & Haaland, B. (2015). Combined association of fitness and central adiposity with health-related quality of life in healthy men: a cross-sectional study. *Health and Quality of Life Outcomes, 13*(1), 188. doi. 10.1186/s129550-150-3853-

Stoeckel, M., & Weissbrod, C. (2015). Growing up with an ill parent: An examination of family characteristics and parental illness features. *Families, Systems, & Health. American Psychological Association, 33*(4), 356–362. 1091-7527/15. http://dx.doi.org/10.1037/fsh0000140

32 Professional and Ethical Issues in Applied Exercise Psychology

Vanessa R. Shannon and Sam J. Zizzi

With the prevalence of obesity and chronic disease on the rise worldwide, the field of applied exercise psychology is expanding considerably. This said, it is estimated that more than 90 percent of graduate programs in exercise and sport psychology have a heavy emphasis on sport rather than exercise. While exercise psychology within our field has certainly grown in the past decade, further expansion is required to meet demands of a growing market of unhealthy clients. Considering that the exercise psychology professional can help individuals set goals, identify barriers, and maintain an active lifestyle through the instruction of and subsequent use of mental skills, it is imperative to discuss professional and ethical issues related to this field. The first part of this chapter encompasses the training of exercise psychology professionals. The second part of this chapter addresses the ethical issues surrounding content knowledge, training, and practical experiences related to applied exercise psychology. The ultimate goal of the chapter is to present a framework for practitioners who want to ensure they are professionally trained and ethically sound in the practice of applied exercise psychology.

WHAT IS EXERCISE PSYCHOLOGY?

Much like sport psychology, the definition of exercise psychology depends on an individual's training. For example, if an individual is trained primarily in mental health counseling, then applied exercise psychology involves integrating physical activity into therapeutic modalities in order to reduce negative and promote positive emotional states. On the other hand, if an individual is trained in exercise science and performance psychology, then applied exercise psychology is "the application of psychosocial principles to the promotion and maintenance of leisure physical activity" (Lox, Martin Ginis, & Petruzzello, 2014, p. 5). The authors of this chapter are both educational exercise psychologists who are trained in sport and exercise science–based graduate programs that practice exercise psychology with a performance psychology and behavioral medicine perspective. As such, this chapter will focus on the latter definition of applied exercise psychology.

The Need for Exercise Psychology

Obesity and Physical Inactivity Epidemic

Over the past 30 years, worldwide obesity has nearly doubled. The World Health Organization (WHO) reports that in 2008, more than 1 out of every 10 adults, age 20 and older, were obese and more than 1 out of every 3 adults were overweight throughout the world. Many cases of obesity are caused by a simple energy imbalance (i.e. more calories consumed than expended); however, obesity is a very complex disease influenced by a variety of factors, including an individual's genetics, metabolic parameters, environmental and behavioral variables, and social influences (Brownell & Horgan, 2004). Furthermore, the consequences of obesity are many. Obesity is a significant contributor to the global burden of chronic disease and disability (Kumanyika, Jeffery, Morabia, Ritenbaugh, & Antipatis, 2002). The obesity epidemic is not restricted to individualized countries. In fact, recent reports suggest that the prevalence of obesity in developing countries is comparable to the prevalence of underweight and malnutrition (WHO, 2003). The occurrence of obesity in developing countries may be due to diminished physical activity, urbanization, and/or the shift in dietary consumption that coincides with economic growth in developing countries (Misra & Khurana, 2008). The WHO reports that overweight and obesity are the fifth leading risks for death throughout the world, with over 2.5 million adults dying each year. Furthermore, the burden of 23 percent of coronary artery disease, 44 percent of diabetes, and up to 41 percent of certain cancers is associated with overweight and obesity (WHO, 2013).

The obesity epidemic alone is a global public health issue; however, when coupled with the physical inactivity epidemic, it becomes a global crisis. Experts suggest that those individuals who are "fit and fat" are in better health than those individuals who are "skinny and not fit," suggesting that obesity alone is not as detrimental to health as the combination of obesity and physical inactivity (Gaesser, 2002). New research suggests that physical inactivity is a greater threat to individuals than being overweight or obese, with over three million deaths annually attributed to the lack of appropriate levels of physical activity. Despite the known benefits of regular physical activity, approximately 50–80 percent of adults do not meet the recommended level of 150 minutes of moderate activity each week to gain health benefits (Centers for Disease Control and Prevention, 2013). The wide disparity in estimates reflects measurement issues with self-reported (surveys) versus objective physical activity (accelerometers).

As for the problem of physical inactivity, the problem does not seem to be a lack of desire to be physically active, as many individuals initiate physical activity programs each year. The true challenge seems to be in the ability to maintain physical activity when challenges and barriers are presented. The solution would be to consider the factors that influence that individual's ability to maintain a healthy weight and an active lifestyle while subsequently providing that individual with a weight loss/management and physical activity program that would best suit their abilities. However, knowledge is not always power. Even with the appropriate program, a previously health-unconscious individual may fall victim to the many barriers that deter the ability to maintain a healthy lifestyle. Additionally, with the proliferation of wellness information on the internet in recent years, clients often struggle to differentiate between useful, accurate information and marketing noise.

At this stage, including an applied exercise psychology professional could effectively assist the individual in setting attainable goals, identifying and avoiding potential pitfalls, and adopting and adhering to new behaviors. There is a great deal of evidence to support the use of behavioral approaches in the treatment of obesity and physical inactivity (Ellis, 1994; Jones & Wadden, 2006; Wadden, Webb, Moran, & Bailer, 2012); however, if applied exercise psychology professionals hope to contribute to reversing the physical activity and obesity epidemics, it is imperative these professionals have the necessary training.

The State of Exercise Psychology

Training in Applied Exercise Psychology

Over the past 20 years, the number of sport and exercise psychology graduate programs has grown. However, when examining the curriculum of these programs more closely, it is clear that sport is still the emphasis. So where do individuals interested in practicing applied exercise psychology attend graduate school? One option would be to seek a degree in public health; many institutions throughout the world have programs designed to train public health professionals. In general, these programs deliver courses directed at epidemiology, biostatistics, and health services with the intention of training public health practitioners. However, not all public health practitioners work in the areas of obesity and physical activity; therefore, the coursework offered in a public health degree program may not be specific to exercise. The other option would be to seek a degree in sport and exercise psychology within a program that allows students to craft their own curriculum, while emphasizing research in exercise psychology.

To increase the number of qualified exercise psychology professionals, it is imperative that graduate programs increase the number of courses and experiences offered related to the field. If programs are incapable of offering more exercise psychology related courses due to lack of resources, then program coordinators should identify courses outside of the program that may be accessible and of use to these students. For example, a health psychology course offered in a psychology department or a social and behavioral theory course offered in public health are good options. If a sport and exercise psychology (SEP) program has access to a public health unit, then the program coordinator may consider discussing a list of cross-listed courses or a dual-degree option with that unit. For example, SEP doctoral students at West Virginia University are able to integrate coursework from counseling and public health into the PhD plan of studies. Additionally, there is an option at George Washington University and the University of Texas to obtain training in physical activity and public health, while subsequently pursuing a master's degree in sport and exercise psychology.

Grants and Contracts

Many of the individuals practicing exercise psychology may also be members of faculty at universities; as such, a thorough understanding of how to secure grants and contracts may be integral to performance and productivity. Furthermore, even those individuals working exclusively in the applied sector would benefit from knowledge regarding grants and contracts. Many funding agencies, both public and private, offer funding for programming related to obesity and physical inactivity. As a result, an exercise psychology professional with a firm knowledge base regarding grants and contracts may be able to incorporate external funding into their practice.

Professional Membership, Development, and Certification

Individuals interested in pursuing a career in applied exercise psychology should be encouraged to identify appropriate professional development opportunities and professional organization memberships. As for professional organization memberships, the International Society for Physical Activity and Health (ISPAH) is an organization with a mission of "advancing the science and practice of physical activity and health"; the Society hosts the International Congress on Physical Activity and Public Health every other year. Two additional examples of professional organizations that may be appropriate would be the International Society for Behavioral Nutrition and Physical Activity (ISBNPA) or the Society for Behavioral Medicine (SBM), both of which host an annual meeting. Furthermore, many organizations in sport and exercise psychology and public health have special interest groups directed toward physical activity and exercise (e.g., Association for Applied Sport Psychology, American Public Health Association).

Many professional organizations offer a limited number of professional development opportunities at annual and regional conferences; in addition, individuals interested in pursuing a career in applied exercise psychology should identify alternative professional development experiences. For example, the Centers for Disease Control and Prevention, in conjunction with the University of South Carolina prevention research center, offers two physical activity and public health (PAPH) courses, an eight-day post-graduate course on research directions and strategies, and a six-day practitioner's course on community interventions.

Currently, certification through the Association for Applied Sport Psychology (AASP) is directed at those individuals interested in practicing applied sport psychology. Although graduate exercise psychology courses would count toward the required courses necessary to becoming an AASP Certified Consultant, the emphasis of the required coursework is on sport. Individuals interested in pursuing AASP certification and a career in applied exercise psychology should be encouraged to complete a mentored experience in the field of exercise psychology (e.g., worksite wellness program, weight management program). The American College of Sports Medicine (ACSM) and the NSPAPPH offers a Physical Activity in Public Health Specialist (PAPHS) certification. This certification is directed at professionals with a bachelor's degree in a health-related field with a minimum of 1,200 hours of applied experience working in the promotion of physical activity or healthy lifestyle management, while also requiring applicants to satisfactorily pass an exam.

Ethical Issues Related to the Practice of Applied Exercise Psychology

When practicing applied exercise psychology, professionals should consider appropriate ethical guidelines. Both AASP and the American Psychological Association (APA) have codes of ethical principles and standards. Both the AASP and APA codes address competence, integrity, responsibility, respect of rights and dignity, dual or multiple relationships, beneficence, and nonmaleficence.

General Competency

At the very least, those individuals working in applied exercise psychology should have an understanding of physical activity epidemiology and behavior change models and theories (e.g., Prochaska & DiClemente, 1983; Ryan & Deci, 2000). Physical inactivity is often coupled with overweight or obesity, which makes initiating and maintaining a physical activity journey far more complicated. Individuals with obesity typically have other co-morbid conditions that may impede their ability to become physically active. For example, a 2010 meta-analysis confirmed a bidirectional relationship between obesity and depression, where depression was found to be predictive of obesity and obesity was found to increase the risk of depression (Luppino et al., 2010). Although being physically active would help manage the symptoms of depression, an individual dealing with depression may have unique barriers to physical activity. As such, it would be useful for an individual working in applied exercise psychology to have basic knowledge of depression and other psychological conditions so that he or she could refer any client to the appropriate mental health professional.

For an applied exercise psychology professional to be adequately prepared, he or she should have extensive practical experience during graduate training. Graduate programs in sport and exercise psychology should identify internship and mentored experiences for those students interested in applied exercise psychology. If no related experiences are available, supervisors should help graduate trainees to develop these types of experiences. By making relationships with other academic departments and communities, the graduate program may be able to co-facilitate a multifaceted behavior change intervention. For example, faculty at Humber College in Ontario, Canada, launched the Humber Centre for Healthy Living, a project in the School of Hospitality, Recreation, and Tourism, which combines the efforts of faculty in Food and Nutrition Management with Fitness and Health Promotion to provide a service-oriented training experience for students. These types of practical experiences are time consuming for faculty on the front end, but the pay-off for students is invaluable.

Blurred Lines and Dual Roles

It is important for an applied exercise psychologist working from an exercise science/performance psychology perspective to know their limitations and be able to refer individuals to the appropriate mental health professional. Since an individual seeking assistance from an exercise psychologist will likely see that professional as a part of their social support system, the individual may bring up their struggles with mental health issues. In order to avoid feelings of abandonment on the part of the client, it is important for an applied exercise psychologist to clearly outline their role to the client and let the client know that they may be referred to another professional should mental health–related issues arise.

Another ethical issue in applied exercise psychology is the emergence of multiple roles with a client. Many applied exercise psychology professionals, with graduate training in the exercise and sport sciences, will have an understanding of exercise prescription and behavioral nutrition. However, within the context of an applied exercise psychology consultation, the exercise psychologist should leave exercise and nutritional advice to the exercise and nutrition professionals. If an applied exercise psychology professional is working in a partnership with an exercise facility or a corporation, they may have already established exercise and nutrition referrals. However, those working in private practice should establish connections with appropriate referral sources. An individual's ability to change behavior and establish lasting healthy lifestyle habits will be significantly greater if the professionals helping them utilize an open, unrestricted communication style. The most effective model would be to build an applied exercise psychology practice around an integrated team of health professionals. An applied exercise psychology professional might consider a practice where an individual could be assessed by a medical professional working from an "exercise is medicine" perspective (Sallis, 2009). After the assessment, the individual would consult with an exercise professional and a behavioral nutritionist or dietician to establish physical activity and weight-related goals. The exercise professional would provide an exercise prescription or program and the nutritionist or dietician would provide a meal plan. All of this information would be shared between the team of professionals so that each professional could reinforce or prescribe around a similar outcome. The final component would be the applied exercise psychologist who, using the guidelines given by the medical, exercise, and behavioral nutrition professionals, would help the individual identify strategies for success (e.g., process goals, create a relapse prevention plan). These strategies would be guided by the applied exercise psychologist professional's theoretical framework (e.g., stages of change, social ecological model, self-determination theory).

Legal Issues Related to the Security and Privacy of Health Information

A US-based federal law, HIPAA (i.e., Health Insurance Portability and Accountability Act), requires that medical providers secure medical information and seek approval from patients before sharing information with third parties. In the sport world, athletic trainers and sports medicine providers would be familiar with these practices, but the legal issues surface less often in sport consultations that are focused on team or individual performance. However, given the multitude of health concerns that a client may present in an exercise psychology setting, an aspiring provider of services in this area is suggested to familiarize themselves with the rules, as these issues are not ethical suggestions, but rather legal issues that can be strictly enforced (Richards, 2009). Thus, the professional must have a heightened sense of how and where session records are kept, and knowledge of the means in which this information is shared with the treatment team.

Considerations for SEP Graduate Students Pursuing a Career in Applied Exercise Psychology

1. *How would you describe your credentials, your competencies, and the services you would be able to deliver to clients at the center?* Those individuals pursuing a career in applied exercise psychology are encouraged to think diligently about their credentials and competencies and, in turn, what services they would be qualified and prepared to offer to clients. For example, not all professionals are qualified to help corporations develop worksite wellness programs; individuals interested in this area of exercise psychology should have coursework and practical experiences directly related to corporate wellness (e.g., I/O psychology, group-level interventions). Supervisors should help graduate trainees shape themselves with regard to competencies and potential services provided. Supervisors should assist in identifying the appropriate coursework for supervisees dependent on the supervisee's specific career goals within applied exercise psychology.

2. *How would you evaluate your value (i.e., how much are the services that you are able to provide clients worth, per hour)?* Value of services is an interesting topic of conversation in the sport and exercise psychology world. Some professionals are more than willing to share opinions regarding value of services, while others are less forthright. Individuals interested in a career in applied exercise psychology should seek advice regarding prices and business planning from successful applied exercise psychology professionals. In addition, if an individual is interested in starting a stand-alone, private practice in applied exercise psychology, the individual should consider taking graduate business courses that would complement their exercise psychology training. Graduate supervisors should be willing to discuss value with supervisees; if the supervisor is not currently practicing applied exercise psychology, they may be able to connect the supervisee with a professional in the field who is practicing.

3. *How would you describe yourself during an interview for an applied exercise psychology job, and what title would you suggest for yourself?* The question of title is another question that remains a debate among sport and exercise psychology professionals. Individuals seeking to practice applied exercise psychology should first consider the legal ramifications of their title. For example, in some states in the United States, the terms "psychologist" and "psychology" are protected by law and reserved only for those individuals who are licensed psychologists within that state. Graduate students interested in a career in applied exercise psychology should take time to consider their title and the implications of that title carefully. Supervisors should provide graduate trainees with guidance regarding titles; specifically, supervisors should discuss a variety of potential titles, as well as the implications of each title with supervisees.

CASE STUDY

Victoria is a 58-year-old retired attorney. She is 5'9" and weighs 225 lbs. She has been diagnosed with emphysema, and her physician has prescribed exercise as a treatment. She also suffers from chronic pain related to back and neck injuries. Although she was active into her 40s, she has been sedentary for the past 15 years. She is highly involved in charity and philanthropic organizations. In addition, her son, daughter-in-law, and two grandsons live with Victoria and her husband. She serves as one of the primary caretakers of her grandsons (ages 2 and 4) for several days of the week. After reading her health history (conducted by the exercise physiologist), it is clear she is suffering from some mild depression and sleep issues, and the combination of caretaking and poor health is causing significant stress. Victoria is meeting with you because you are working part-time at a local fitness center as their adherence consultant. All new members get two to three meetings with you as part of their initial fee. When you set up your first meeting, you were able to speak with her for a few minutes and build rapport. She mentioned that before joining the gym, she has been using workout videos at home (one cardio, one yoga) for 20–30 minutes, a few times a week, for the last month, but that she "just needs some extra motivation and accountability." Her grandchildren are wearing her out! A self-described perfectionist, she also mentioned that she would like to lose some weight, gain strength, and look better, but that feeling and sleeping better are what she wants right now. Based on her previous experience, she is familiar with most of the equipment in the gym and thinks exercise is "awesome and going to really help her quickly get back to her former health." After the first week, she is not enjoying the exercises prescribed by the personal trainer, and she has asked you to help her clarify her goals related to exercise and identify exercises that she would better enjoy. Additionally, she has enjoyed your conversations and finds you inspiring and has asked if you might be willing to accompany her to some of the classes at the gym and serve as her "workout buddy." Given the circumstances of the case, what ethical dilemmas are you facing as an applied exercise psychology professional? In addition, how would you navigate or handle the potential issues presented?

REFERENCES

Brownell, K. D., & Horgan, K. B. (2004). *Food fight: The inside story of the food industry, America's obesity crisis, and what we can do about it.* New York, NY: McGraw-Hill.

Centers for Disease Control and Prevention (CDC). (2013). *Behavioral risk factor surveillance system survey data.* Atlanta, GA: U.S. Department of Health and Human Services, Centers for Disease Control and Prevention.

Ellis, A. (1994). The sport of avoiding sports and exercise: A rational emotive behavioral perspective. *The Sport Psychologist, 8*(3), 248–261.

Gaesser, G. (2002). *Big fat lies: The truth about your weight and your health.* Carlsbad, CA: Gurze Books.

Jones, L. R., & Wadden, T. A. (2006). State of science: Behavioural treatment of obesity. *Asia Pacific Journal of Clinical Nutrition, 15*(1), 30–38.

Kumanyika, S., Jeffery, R. W., Morabia, A., Ritenbaugh, C., & Antipatis, V. J. (2002). Obesity prevention: The case for action. *International Journal of Obesity, 26,* 425–436.

Lox, C. L., Martin Ginis, K. A., & Petruzzello, S. J. (2014). *The psychology of exercise: Integrating theory and practice* (4th ed.). Scottsdale, AZ: Holcomb Hathaway Publishers.

Luppino, F. S., de Wit, L. M., Bouvy, P. F., Stijnen, T., Cuijpers, P., Penninx, B. W. J. H., & Zitman, F. G. (2010). Overweight, obesity, and depression: A systematic review and meta-analysis of longitudinal studies. *Archives of General Psychiatry, 67*(3), 220–229.

Misra, A., & Khurana, L. (2008). Obesity and the metabolic syndrome in developing countries. *Journal of Clinical Endocrinology Metabolism, 93*(11, Suppl. 1), S9–30.

Prochaska, J., & DiClemente, C. (1983). Stages and processes of self-change in smoking: Toward an integrative model of change. *Journal of Consulting and Clinical Psychology, 5,* 390–395.

Richards, M. M. (2009). Electronic medical records: Confidentiality issues in the time of HIPAA. *Professional Psychology: Research and Practice, 40*(6), 550–556.

Ryan, R. M., & Deci, E. L. (2000). Self-determination theory and the facilitation of intrinsic motivation, social development, and well-being. *The American Psychologist, 55(1),* 68–78.

Sallis, R. (2009). Exercise is medicine and physicians need to prescribe it! *British Journal of Sports Medicine, 43*(1), 3–4.

Wadden, T. A., Webb, V. L., Moran, C. H., & Bailer, B. A. (2012). Lifestyle modification for obesity: New developments in diet, physical activity, and behavior therapy. *Circulation, 125,* 1157–1170.

World Health Organization. (2003). *Controlling the global obesity epidemic (website).* Retrieved from www.who.int/nutrition/topics/obesity/en/

World Health Organization. (2013). *Global health observatory (GHO) data (website).* Retrieved from www.who.int/gho/ncd/risk_factors/obesity_text/en/

Index